EIGHT AMERICAN AUTHORS

REVISED EDITION

EIGHT AMERICAN AUTHORS

A review of research and criticism

edited by James Woodress

REVISED EDITION

Essays by Jay B. Hubbell, Floyd Stovall, Walter Blair,
Lewis Leary, Nathalia Wright, Roger Asselineau,
Harry Hayden Clark, and Robert L. Gale

*Sponsored by the American Literature Section of
the Modern Language Association*

The Norton Library

W · W · NORTON & COMPANY · INC ·

NEW YORK

W. W. Norton & Company, Inc. also publishes *The Norton Anthology of English Literature,* edited by M. H. Abrams et al; *The Norton Anthology of Poetry,* edited by Arthur M. Eastman et al; *World Masterpieces,* edited by Maynard Mack et al; *The Norton Reader,* edited by Arthur M. Eastman et al; *The Norton Facsimile of the First Folio of Shakespeare,* prepared by Charlton Hinman; and the Norton Critical Editions.

To the Memory of
Stanley Williams
contributor to the original edition of this work
and
Harry Hayden Clark
scholar, teacher, and contributor
to the present volume
clara et venerabilia nomina

CONTENTS

PREFACE

This volume first appeared in 1956 under the editorship of Floyd Stovall, who also wrote the chapter on Emerson. The other contributors then were Jay B. Hubbell on Poe, Walter Blair on Hawthorne, Lewis Leary on Thoreau, Stanley Williams on Melville, Willard Thorp on Whitman, Harry Hayden Clark on Twain, and Robert Spiller on James. Since 1956 Professor Williams has died and several other contributors have retired. All of the original contributors still living were invited to update their essays, and five out of the seven did so: Hubbell, Blair, Leary, Clark, and Stovall.

The original plan of the volume was to have the essays written by scholars who were knowledgeable in American literature but not specialists in the author surveyed. The aim, which was to obtain a certain objectivity and detachment, was admirably achieved by this method. Since 1956, however, the explosion of scholarship has made it impossible for one scholar to review all the scholarship concerning any author he has not been working with rather closely and continuously. The total number of items on American literature listed in the annual MLA bibliography in 1955 came to less than 900, while the total for 1969 was 2,266. If the overall proliferation has been two and one-half times, the increase in scholarship devoted to the authors treated here has been even more spectacular. Henry James, for instance, was the subject of 27 articles and studies in 1955 but 92 in 1969, an increase of 3.4 times; Melville went from 15 to 85 for an increase of 5.67 times. Thus for this revised edition of *Eight American Authors* I have invited specialists, Nathalia Wright on Melville, Roger Asselineau on Whitman, and Robert Gale on James, to join the original list of contributors.

This quantitative analysis, however, is not so interesting as a qualitative assessment. A comparison of the 1956 volume with the present revision shows clearly the trends in scholarship in the past decade and a half. Though there are exceptions (such as Leon Edel's huge biographical study of James), by 1956 most of the biographical record of the authors surveyed here had been completed, and the intervening years have been used to pile higher the critical exegesis, which already was considerable. Much of the criticism of the last 15 years, fortunately, adds greatly to our insight and understanding, though the winnowing provided in this survey is absolutely essential. This volume demonstrates the truth of Emerson's belief that each age must write its own books.

Two other trends also are unmistakable in the recent past. We finally have gotten to work, under the aegis of the MLA's Center for Editions of American Authors, to produce accurate texts for the first time in our literary history, and while the process will take another decade to complete, it now is well launched. We also have experienced in the last decade and a half a large expansion of world-wide interest in American literature. This volume records many studies of American authors written abroad, i.e., in languages other than English—far more than the 1956 edition surveys—and it indicates clearly that the attention our literature gets is no longer confined mainly to France and Germany (where interest began early), but our writers now are being intensively studied in Italy, Scandinavia, Eastern Europe, Israel, India, Japan, and on around the globe.

The plan of this edition has been to *consider* all the scholarship on the authors reviewed, but it has been utterly impossible within the space of one compact book to *discuss* all the biblio-biographical material and critical exegesis. Therefore the contributors have had to be selective. While few book-length studies have been omitted from the following pages, hundreds of articles or chapters from books have not been discussed at all. If the reader fails to find reviewed any particular essay, he should conclude that the reviewer silently relegated it to the category of material for which there was no space. The contributors and the editor do not claim infallibility, but we believe that the bibliographical essays included here are reasonably complete and up to date. The cut-off date for scholarship reviewed—with a very few exceptions— was the calendar year 1969.

No effort has been made to impose rigorous uniformity on the individual chapters of this work. The contributors have organized as they saw fit, and the table of contents reflects the variations. The same general framework, however, is used throughout in the major categories, as the essays treat bibliography, editions, biography, and criticism in that order. Some contributors, however, have called attention to standard bibliographical sources like the bibliographical section of *LHUS*, Lewis Leary's *Articles on American Literature, 1900—1950*, and *AAL, 1950—1967*, my own compilation, *Dissertations in American Literature, 1891—1966* (1968); but most have not. The student of

American literature will need to consult these references and also the following: Jacob Blanck's *BAL* (still to be completed), *Dissertation Abstracts*, Clarence Gohdes' *Bibliographical Guide to the Study of the Literature of the U.S.A.* (3rd ed., 1970) and *Literature and Theater of the States and Regions of the U.S.A.* (1967); the Library of Congress' *Guide to the Study of the United States of America* (1960), bibliographies in *LAP*, all the standard catalogues of the Library of Congress and the British Museum, Lyle Wright's several volumes of bibliography of American fiction, the *Dictionary of American Biography*, and the *Oxford Companion to American Literature*.

To use this volume effectively, one will sometimes have to go to standard indexes like the *Reader's Guide to Periodical Literature*, the *Humanities and Social Science Index*, and the annual indexes to the various periodicals. To save space and to allow in this work the inclusion of the maximum number of bibliographical citations, we have given the barest possible reference. A citation such as (*AL* 56) means that the article discussed appeared in *American Literature* in 1956. The journal *AL* (as do most academic journals) publishes an annual index, and it takes only a few seconds to locate an article if one knows the author and year. A journal like *Publisher's Weekly*, which has no index of its own, is indexed in the *Reader's Guide*. General magazines like *Harper's* or *Atlantic* publish their own indexes and are also included in library indexing services. All the abbreviations or acronyms used in this work, *AL*, *NEQ*, *JEGP*, etc., will be found listed in the "Key to Abbreviations" in the front matter. Other abbreviations used internally within specific essays are explained when first used. That is, Emerson is referred to throughout the Emerson essay as E or RWE, and *The Scarlet Letter* and *The Marble Faun* are referred to as *SL* and *MF* in the Hawthorne essay.

The editor is grateful to all the busy scholars who were willing to contribute to this volume. On their part it was a disinterested and unselfish act for the advancement of scholarship and for the assistance of students and teachers. Specific help by other scholars on specific chapters for this edition has been acknowledged by footnote where appropriate. Scholars who read the MS of the original edition of this book and to whom thanks are still due are in alphabetical order: Raymond Adams, Oscar Cargill, Charles T. Davis, Leon Edel, Walter Harding, Harrison Hayford, Sherman Paul, Henry Pochmann, Lyon Richardson, Arlin Turner. Also assisting were the late T. O. Mabbott, Randall Stewart, and Stephen Whicher. For general assistance in preparing the MS for publication, thanks go to JoAnn Cedarleaf and Judy Kalivas, in particular, Betty Kimura, Evelyn Kasmire, and Jean Walraven, all of whom typed and proofread. Michele Bannon prepared the "Key to Abbreviations" and Jan Dooley the index. The entire project has been carried out under the sponsorship of the American Literature Section of the Modern Language Association and with the aid of funds from the Research Committee of the University of California at Davis.

James Woodress

Davis, California
January, 1971

KEY TO ABBREVIATIONS

AAL Lewis Leary, *Articles on American Literature, 1900–1950* (1954), and *Articles on American Literature, 1950–1967* (1970)
A&S Arts and Sciences
ABC American Book Collector
AH American Heritage
AHQ Arkansas Historical Quarterly
AHR American Historical Review
AI American Imago
AION-SG Annali Istituto Universitario Orientale, Napoli, Sezione Germanica
AJP American Journal of Psychology
AL American Literature
ALS American Literary Scholarship: An Annual (1965–   )
AM American Mercury
AmR F. O. Matthiessen, *American Renaissance* (1941)
AN&Q American Notes and Queries
APK Aufsätze zur Portugiesischen Kulturgeschichte
AQ American Quarterly
AR Antioch Review
ArlQ Arlington Quarterly
ArQ Arizona Quarterly
AS American Speech
ASch American Scholar
Atl Atlantic Monthly
ATQ American Transcendental Quarterly
AUP Annales de l'Université de Paris
AWS American Writers Series
BAASB British Association for American Studies Bulletin
BAL Jacob Blanck, *Bibliography of American Literature* (1955–   )
BB Bulletin of Bibliography

BBr Books at Brown
BNYPL Bulletin of the New York Public Library
BPLQ Boston Public Library Quarterly
BQR British Quarterly Review
BSUF Ball State University Forum
BuR Bucknell Review
BUSE Boston University Studies in English
BYUS Brigham Young University Studies
CalR Calcutta Review
CambJ Cambridge Journal
C&P Character and Personality
CaW Catholic World
CCC College Communication and Composition
CE College English
CEA CEA Critic
CEAAN Center for Editions of American Authors Newsletter
CEJ California English Journal
CentR The Centennial Review
CHA Cuadernos Hispanoamericanos
CHAL Cambridge History of American Literature (1918)
ChEx Christian Examiner
ChiR Chicago Review
Chris Sci Mon Christian Science Monitor
CJ Classical Journal
CLAJ College Language Association Journal
CLC Columbia Library Columns
CLQ Colby Library Quarterly
CLS Comparative Literature Studies
CM Cornhill Magazine
ColQ Colorado Quarterly

Com *Commentary*
CompD *Comparative Drama*
ConnR *Connecticut Review*
CQ *The Cambridge Quarterly*
CR *Classical Review*
CraneR *The Crane Review*
Crit *Critique: Studies in Modern Fiction*
CritQ *Critical Quarterly*
CW *Classical Weekly*
CWH *Civil War History*
DA *Dissertation Abstracts*
DAL James Woodress, *Dissertations in American Literature, 1891–1966* (1968)
DLT *Doshisha Literature* (Japan)
DM *Dublin Magazine*
DR *Dalhousie Review*
DUM *Dublin University Magazine*
EA *Etudes Anglaises*
EAL (EALN) *Early American Literature* (formerly *Early American Literature Newsletter*
E&S *Essays and Studies by Members of the English Association*
EIC *Essays in Criticism*
EIE *English Institute Essays*
8AmA *Eight American Authors*
EIHC *Essex Institute Historical Collections*
EJ *English Journal*
ELH *Journal of English Literary History*
ELN *English Language Notes*
Eng Rec *English Record*
Eng Rev *English Review*
ES *English Studies*
ESA *English Studies in Africa* (Johannesburg)
ESBAL *Essays and Studies in British and American Literature*
ESELL *Essays and Studies in English Language and Literature* (Tohoku Gakuin University Review, Sendai, Japan)
ESQ *Emerson Society Quarterly*
ESRS *Emporia State Research Studies*
ETC *ETC: A Review of General Semantics*
EUQ *Emory University Quarterly*

EWR *East-West Review* (Doshisha University, Japan)
Expl *Explicator*
FAGAAS *Frankfurter Arbeiten aus dem Gebiete der Anglistik und der America-Studien*
FHQ *Florida Historical Quarterly*
FMod *Filologia Moderna* (Madrid)
FN *Fitzgerald Newsletter*
FNE Van Wyck Brooks, *The Flowering of New England* (1936)
ForumH *Forum* (Houston)
FR *French Review*
FRLS *Fukuoka Review of Literature and Science*
FurmS *Furman Studies*
4Q *Four Quarters*
GaR *Georgia Review*
GR *Germanic Review*
GRM *Germanisch-romanische Monatsschrift*
GSE *Gothenburg Studies in English*
H & H *Hound and Horn*
HarM *Harvard Magazine*
HarR *Harvard Review*
HCE *Hawthorne Centenary Essays*
HLB *Harvard Library Bulletin*
HLQ *Huntington Library Quarterly*
HM *Harper's Monthly*
HudR *Hudson Review*
HULN *Harvard University Library Notes*
HW *Harper's Weekly*
IEY *Iowa English Yearbook*
IUB *Indiana University Bookman*
JA *Jahrbuch für Amerikastudien*
JAAC *Journal of Aesthetics and Art Criticism*
JAF *Journal of American Folklore*
JAmS *Journal of American Studies*
JAS *Journal of the Acoustical Society*
JASA *Journal of the American Statistical Association*
JCMVASA *Journal of Central Mississippi Valley American Studies Association* (see *MASJ*)
JEGP *Journal of English and Germanic Philology*

JGE Journal of General Education

JHI Journal of the History of Ideas

JISHS Journal of the Illinois State Historical Society

JNH Journal of Negro History

JNYES Journal of the New York Entomological Society

JQ Journalism Quarterly

JRUL Journal of the Rutgers University Library

KAL Kyushu American Literature (Fukuoka, Japan)

KBAA Kieler Beiträge zur Anglistik und Amerikanistik

KFLQ Kentucky Foreign Language Quarterly

KFR Kentucky Folklore Record

KJ Kipling Journal

KM Kansas Magazine

KN Kwartalnik Neofilologiczny

KR Kenyon Review

L&P Literature and Psychology

Lang&S Language and Style

LanM Les Langues Modernes

LAP A. H. Quinn. et al., Literature of the American People (1951)

LCrit Literary Criterion (University of Mysore, India)

LCUT Library Chronicle of the University of Texas

LetM Lettres Modernes

LH Lincoln Herald

LHB Lock Haven Bulletin (Lock Haven, Pennsylvania)

LHJ Ladies Home Journal

LHR Lock Haven Review

LHUS R. E. Spiller, et al. Literary History of the United States (1948)

LitR Literary Review

LonM London Magazine

MAQR Michigan Alumnus Quarterly Review

MarkR Markham Review

MASJ Midcontinent American Studies Journal (formerly JCMVASA)

MCAT V. L. Parrington, Main Currents in American Thought (1927)

MD Modern Drama

MFS Modern Fiction Studies

MH Minnesota History

MHM Maryland Historical Magazine

MHR Missouri Historical Review

MHSB Missouri Historical Society Bulletin

MinnR Minnesota Review

MissQ Mississippi Quarterly

ML Modern Languages (London)

MLN Modern Language Notes

MLQ Modern Language Quarterly

MLR Modern Language Review

ModA Modern Age (Chicago)

MP Modern Philology

MQ Midwest Quarterly (Pittsburg, Kansas)

MQR Massachusetts Quarterly Review

MR Massachusetts Review (University of Massachusetts)

MSE Massachusetts Studies in English

MSSP Melville Society Special Publications

MTJ (MTQ) Mark Twain Journal (formerly Mark Twain Quarterly)

MVHR Mississippi Valley Historical Review

N&Q Notes and Queries

NAR North American Review

Nat Rev National Review

NCF Nineteenth Century Fiction

NEQ New England Quarterly

NewS New Statesman

NHB Negro History Bulletin

NLR New Left Review

NM Neuphilologische Mitteilungen

NMQ New Mexico Quarterly

NR New Republic

NRF Nouvelle Revue Française

NS Die Neueren Sprachen

NSN New Statesman and Nation

NY New Yorker

NYFQ New York Folklore Quarterly

NYH New York History

NYHSQ New York Historical Society Quarterly

NYHTB New York Herald-Tribune Book Section

NYT New York Times

NYTBR *New York Times Book Review*

OSAHQ *Ohio State Archeological and Historical Quarterly*

OSE *Osmania Studies in English*

PAAS *Proceedings American Antiquarian Society*

PBSA *Papers of the Bibliographical Society of America*

PBSUV *Papers of the Bibliographical Society of the University of Virginia*

PLL (PELL) *Papers on Language and Literature (formerly Papers on English Literature and Language)*

PMASAL *Papers of the Michigan Academy of Science, Arts, and Letters*

PMHB *Pennsylvania Magazine of History and Biography*

PMLA *Publications of the Modern Language Association of America*

PN *Poe Newsletter (now Poe Studies)*

PNJHS *Proceedings of the New Jersey Historical Society*

PP *Philologica Pragensia*

PQ *Philological Quarterly*

PR *Partisan Review*

PrS *Prairie Schooner*

PS *Pacific Spectator*

PSA *Papeles de Son Armadans (Mallorca)*

PULC *Princeton University Library Chronicle*

PW *Publishers' Weekly*

QH *Quaker History: Bulletin of the Friends Historical Association*

QJS *Quarterly Journal of Speech*

QQ *Queen's Quarterly*

QRL *Quarterly Review of Literature*

QR *Quarterly Review*

RAA *Revue Anglo-Américaine*

RCam *Revista Camoniana*

RDM *Revue des Deux Mondes*

RdP *Revue de Paris*

REL *Review of English Literature (Leeds)*

Ren *Renaissance*

RES *Review of English Studies*

RG *The Rising Generation (Tokyo)*

RI *Revista Iberoamericana*

RLC *Revue de Littérature Comparée*

RLM *La Revue des Lettres Modernes*

RLMC *Rivista di Letterature Moderne e Comparate (Firenze)*

RLV *Revue des Langues Vivantes (Bruxelles)*

RMS *Renaissance and Modern Studies (University of Nottingham)*

RNC *Revista Nacional de Cultura*

RomN *Romance Notes (University of North Carolina)*

RR *Romanic Review*

RS (RSSCW) *Research Studies (Washington State University) (formerly Research Studies of State College of Washington)*

SA *Studi Americani*

SAB *South Atlantic Bulletin*

SAL *John Macy, Spirit of American Literature (1913)*

SAQ *South Atlantic Quarterly*

SatR (SatRL) *Saturday Review (formerly Saturday Review of Literature)*

SB *Studies in Bibliography*

SCB *South Central Bulletin*

ScH *Scripta Hierosolymitana*

SchM *Schweizer Monatshefte*

SciM *Scientific Monthly*

SCQ *Southern California Quarterly*

SCR *South Carolina Review*

SDR *South Dakota Review*

SEER *Slavic and East European Review*

SEL *Studies in English Literature 1500–1900*

SELit *Studies in English Literature (Japan)*

SFQ *Southern Folklore Quarterly*

SG *Studium Generale*

ShawR *Shaw Review*

SHEN *Shenandoah*

ShN *Shakespeare Newsletter*

SHR *Southern Humanities Review*

SIR *Studies in Romanticism*

SLitI *Studies in the Literary Imagination*

SLJ *Southern Literary Journal*

SLM *Southern Literary Messenger*

SLNewsletter *Sinclair Lewis Newsletter*

SLT Svensk Litteraturtidskrift

SN Studia Neophilologica

SNNTS Studies in the Novel (North Texas State University)

SoQ The Southern Quarterly (University of Southern Mississippi)

SoR Southern Review (Louisiana State University)

SoRA Southern Review: An Australian Journal of Literary Studies (University of Adelaide)

SP Studies in Philology

SQ Shakespeare Quarterly

SR Sewanee Review

SRAZ Studia Romanica et Anglica Zagrabiensia

SS Scandinavian Studies

SSF Studies in Short Fiction

SSJ Southern Speech Journal

SUB Stetson University Bulletin

SUS Susquehanna University Studies (Selinsgrove, Pennsylvania)

SWR Southwest Review

Sym Symposium

TArts Theatre Arts

TBM Temple Bar Magazine

TCJ Teachers College Journal

TCL Twentieth Century Literature

Thoth (Department of English, Syracuse University

TLS Times Literary Supplement

TQ Texas Quarterly (University of Texas)

TR Texas Review

TriQ Tri-Quarterly (Evanston, Illinois)

TSB Thoreau Society Bulletin

TSBK Thoreau Society Booklet

TSE Tulane Studies in English

TSL Tennessee Studies in Literature

TSLL Texas Studies in Literature and Language

TuK Text und Kritik

TWA Transactions of the Wisconsin Academy of Sciences, Arts, and Letters

UCSLL University of Colorado Studies in Language and Literature

UESALL University of Uppsala Essays and Studies in American Language and Literature

UIHS University of Iowa Humanistic Studies

ULR University of Leeds Review

UMPAW University of Minnesota Pamphlets on American Writers

UMS University of Missouri Studies

UMSE University of Mississippi Studies in English

UR (UKCR) University Review (formerly *University of Kansas City Review*

URLB University of Rochester Library Bulletin

UTLC University of Texas Library Chronicle

UTQ University of Toronto Quarterly

UTSE University of Texas Studies in English

VMHB Virginia Magazine of History and Biography

VN Victorian Newsletter

VQR Virginia Quarterly Review

VS Victorian Studies

WAL Western American Literature

WascanaR Wascana Review

WBEP Wiener Beitrage zur Englischen Philologie

WF Western Folklore

WHR Western Humanities Review

WSL Wisconsin Studies in Literature (Wisconsin State University, Oshkosh)

WMQ William and Mary Quarterly

WR Western Review

WUS Washington University Studies

WWR (WWN) Walt Whitman Review (formerly *Walt Whitman Newsletter*)

YR Yale Review

YULG Yale University Library Gazette

EIGHT AMERICAN AUTHORS

EDGAR ALLAN POE

Jay B. Hubbell

I. BIBLIOGRAPHY

Although the present state of Poe (hereafter P, EP, or EAP) bibliography must be described as poor, it represents a definite improvement over what its state was in 1956 when *8AmA* was first published. In 1956 only Vol. I of Jacob Blanck's admirable *BAL* had appeared. Vol. VI, which will include Melville, is not expected to be in the printer's hands before the spring of 1971. So we shall have to wait many months for the section on P. When that section does appear, scholars will have an excellent bibliography of P's books and appearances in books, but a definitive P bibliography must include much that will not be in *BAL*.

Meanwhile the student must fall back on two antiquated bibliographies which were prepared rather for collectors than students: J. W. Robertson, *A Bibliography of the Writings of EAP* (2 vols., 1934) and C. F. Heartman and J. R. Canny, *A Bibliography of First Printings of the Writings of EAP* (1940; rev. ed., 1943). The latter represents a revision of Heartman and Kenneth Rede, *A Census of First Editions and Source Materials by EAP in American Collections* (2 vols., 1932). The many shortcomings of both bibliographies were pointed out by D. A. Randall (*PW* 34, 40). Of the published descriptions of various collections of Poeana two of the best are Randall's account of the J. K. Lilly collection in *IUB* (50) and W. B. Todd's "The Early Issues of P's [1845] Tales" (*LCUT* 61).

As G. T. Tanselle noted in an informative article, "The State of P Bibliography" (*PN* 69), "the present state of the secondary bibliography is more encouraging than that of the primary." That is particularly true for the student who wishes to keep abreast of current materials. The 1956 edition of *8AmA* included no books or articles published after December 1954. For Norton's 1963 reprint J. C. Mathews compiled a checklist, covering the years 1955–1962, which is still useful. Beginning with 1963 we have the invaluable annual, *ALS*, founded by James Woodress and now (beginning with the 1968 volume) edited by J. A. Robbins, who in the first five volumes had reviewed the new materials on P. In the 1968 volume P. F. Quinn took over this assignment. The *ALS* has its basis in the *MLA International Bibliography*, which now includes important materials in foreign languages. In addition to these the student has in *AL* both reviews of books and "Articles on American Literature Appearing in Current periodicals." R. P. Benton's admirable "EAP: Current Bibliography," which appeared in *ESQ* in 1965 and 1967 and was transferred to *PN* in January 1969, lists with comments not only articles and books but also reviews of books.

For earlier critical materials there is Lewis Leary's *AAL* (1954), of which a new edition covering the years 1951–1967 appeared in 1970. The critical materials in *CHAL* and *LHUS* are not yet superseded by later bibliographies, but they will be when J. L. Dameron and I. B. Cauthen bring out their *Complete Bibliography of P Criticism, 1827–1967*. The *CBPC* will include the material in Cauthen's University of Virginia master's thesis, "A Descriptive Bibliography of Criticism of EAP, 1827–1941" (1942). In 1966 Dameron published *EAP: A Checklist of Criticism, 1942–1960*. Thirty foreign scholars from eighteen countries have been asked to submit entries for the *CBPC*.

Numerous dissertations on P are listed in Woodress's *DAL* (1968). New dissertation topics are listed in "Research in Progress" in *AL*. G. R. Thompson is preparing for publication a descriptive bibliography of M.A. and Ph.D. theses on P which will provide for every thesis not abstracted in *DA* both an abstract and a brief critique.

The Letters of EAP, edited by J. W. Ostrom (1948), was reprinted in 1966 with a supplementary chapter containing newly discovered letters. For a letter not in Ostrom, see "New Letter of EAP" (*ESQ* 68). For an account of the problems involved in editing the *Letters*, see Ostrom's pamphlet, *The Letters of P: Quest and Answer* (1967). A new edition of the *Letters* should include letters addressed to P or written about him by Lowell, Hawthorne, Cooke, Thomas, Mrs. Browning, and others. For a checklist of P MSS in academic, historical, and public libraries in the United States, see *American Literary Manuscripts* (1960). One wonders what unknown MSS are in the hands of private collectors. Students of P, more interested in his tales and critical writings, have made too little use of the admirable *Concordance of the Poetical Works of EAP* (1941), compiled by Bradford Booth and C. E. Jones. Other useful aids are J. L. Dameron and L. C. Stagg, *An Index to P's Critical Vocabulary* (1966); L. A. Lawson, "P and the Grotesque: A Bibliography, 1695–1965" (*PN* 68); and B. R. Pollin, *Dictionary of Names and Titles in P's Collected Works* (1968) in the Virginia Edition (1902).

Of the various checklists the best is the Merrill *Checklist of EAP* (1969), compiled by J. A. Robbins. For a classified and annotated list of articles dealing with the more important poems and tales, see Robert Gale's *Barron's Simplified Approach to EAP* (1969). There is a more detailed "Bibliography of P Criticism" in Louis Broussard's *The Measure of P* (1969), pp. 105–65, which "presumes to include all the books written about P, in whole or in part, since his death in 1849, and all the periodical essays published since 1925." R. P. Benton describes *The Measure of P* as "A book characterized by curious omissions [including] the important estimates of Davidson, Patrick Quinn, and Wilbur, and other recent work. . . . The essays are followed by an attempt at a complete bibliography of P criticism since 1925 in which, however, the work of Wilbur and many others is not listed" (*PN*, 70).

II. EDITIONS

By the standards of the time R. W. Griswold was a competent editor, but *The Works of the Late EAP* (4 vols., 1850–56) omitted many reviews and was marred by typographical errors. Somewhat more inclusive was Ingram's *The Works of EAP* (4 vols., Edinburgh, 1874–75). The best of the nineteenth-century editions, though it was far from complete, was *The Works of EAP*, edited by E. C. Stedman and G. E. Woodberry (10 vols., 1894–95). Like earlier editors, Stedman and Woodberry reprinted the tales from Griswold's imperfect text.

The most useful of all editions is the Virginia Edition, edited by J. A. Harrison, *The Complete Works of EAP* (17 vols., 1902), which is available in an AMS reprint. It includes Harrison's two-volume *Life and Letters* and what was meant to be a complete bibliography of P's writings. Harrison did not reprint all the reviews, and he left out several installments of the "Marginalia." On the other hand, he included certain materials that P did not write; among them, reviews of Bryant's *Poems*, Manzoni's *I promessi sposi*, and Paulding's *Slavery in the U. S.*, which was written by Beverley Tucker.

An excellent edition, although far from complete, is the Borzoi P, *The Complete Poems and Stories of EAP with Selections from His Critical Writings*, edited by A. H. Quinn, (2 vols., 1946), who wrote the biographical introduction and the explanatory notes, and E. H. O'Neill, who established the text and supplied the brief bibliographical notes. The selections from P's nonfiction prose, which in the Virginia Edition fill nine volumes, occupy only about 200 pages in the Borzoi P.

As long ago as 1924 T. O. Mabbott wrote to Killis Campbell that he hoped eventually to bring out a complete edition of P's writings, but the first volume of the *Collected Writings of EAP* was not published until 1969, the year after Mabbott's death. Meanwhile he had published a great number of articles and notes chiefly of a factual nature embodying findings which would find a place in the Harvard Edition. He edited *Selected Poems of EAP* (1928) and *Selected Poetry and Prose of EAP* (1951) and supplied the editorial apparatus for three P volumes published by the Facsimile Text Society. He gave material assistance to many who were interested in P. The essay on P published in the 1956 edition of *8AmA* is substantially better for the assistance he gave me. Before his death he had completed the editing of the *Poems* and had advanced considerably in preparing the tales and critical writings for the printer. In his Preface he wrote: "The bulk of P's writings here to be presented has been increased about twenty per cent."

P's poems are available in scholarly editions far superior to anything we have for either the tales or the critical writings. Campbell's *The Poems of EAP* (1917) contains an admirable introduction, copious and illuminating notes, and textual variants carefully collated. An excellent later edition, *The Poems of EAP* (1965), was published by the University Press of Virginia and edited by Floyd Stovall, who dedicated it to the memory of his former teacher, Campbell. The book contains an excellent introduction, variant readings, and textual (but not explanatory) notes.

Mabbott's edition of the *Poems* seemed to P. F. Quinn to deserve the term "definitive." "The background, publishing history, and sources of each poem are given. . . . In addition there are discussions of why 111 poems that have been ascribed to P should be consigned to outer darkness," (*SLJ* 69). J. A. Robbins wrote: "This is not the ultimate, the perfect edition of the poems, but it is of great importance and will continue to be for a long time" (*AL* 70). He noted that Mabbott had "poured a heavy stream of research and personal judgment into the commentary," but too much of it seemed to the reviewer "idiosyncratic, garrulous, and antiquarian."

Two excellent collections of P's short stories, both published in 1927, were edited by Campbell and J. S. Wilson. There are three separate volumes of P's critical writings, edited by F. C. Prescott (1909), J. B. Moore (1926), and R. L. Hough (1965). There are numerous books that include selections from the poems, the tales, and sometimes the criticism. Two of the best are E. H. Davidson's *Selected Writings of EAP* (1956) and E. W. Carlson's *An Introduction to P: A Thematic Reader* (1966). There are many other volumes of selections in hard covers and in paperbacks, and not all of them are to be found in even large university libraries. Many of them contain introductions by competent scholars and perceptive critics; and the student will miss something if he fails to read introductory essays written by Roger Asselineau, Margaret Alterton and Hardin Craig, W. H. Auden, Campbell, Carlson, David Galloway, Davidson, Mabbott, Dwight MacDonald, Roy Male, Allen Tate, Richard Wilbur, J. S. Wilson, and others.

Among new materials that have been discovered since the Virginia Edition appeared in 1902 are P's *Doings of Gotham*, edited by Mabbott and J. E. Spannuth (1929), reprinted from the 1844 Columbia, Pennsylvania, *Spy*; C. S. Brigham, "EAP's Contribution to *Alexander's Weekly Messenger*" (PAAS 42); and D. R. Hutcherson, "The *Philadelphia Saturday Museum* Text of P's Poems" (*AL* 33). Poe's unfinished tale, "The Light-House," was first printed in Mabbott's *Selected Poetry and Prose* (1951). Some uncollected installments of "Marginalia" are reprinted in E. H. O'Neill, "The P-Griswold-Harrison Texts of the 'Marginalia' " (*AL 43*). See also Lewis Leary, "Miss Octavia's Autograph Album and EAP" (*CLC* 68) for a poem that P may have written. In "P as the Probable Author of 'Harper's Ferry' " (*AL* 68), B. R. Pollin made an excellent case for an unsigned article in the February 1848 issue of *Graham's Magazine*.

When Campbell wrote "The P Canon" (*The Mind of P*, 1933), he was doubtful of the authenticity of two early poems that most scholars now regard as genuine. See I. B. Cauthen, Jr., "P's 'Alone': Its Background, Source, and Manuscript" (*SB* 50) and J. B. Hubbell, " 'O Tempora! O Mores!': A Juvenile Poem by EAP" (*UCSLL* 45). Stovall is not fully convinced that P wrote the latter poem. Mabbott, who regarded the poem as authentic, discovered that Robert Pitts, who is ridiculed in the poem, was an employee of Ellis & Allan. Mabbott was certain that P did not write "The Musiad." Stovall, though he did not include this satire in his edition of the *Poems* (1965), discussed it at length in *EP the Poet* (1969) and suggested that it is likely that P had a hand in it.

Of the various facsimile editions of *Tamerlane* the best was edited by Mabbott in 1941 for the Facsimile Text Society, which also published *Al Aaraaf* (1935) and *The Raven and Other Poems* (1942), both with introductions by Mabbott, and the 1831 *Poems* (1936) with a bibliographical note by Campbell. Two recent facsimiles are the 1843 *Prose Romances*, edited by George Hatvary and Mabbott (1968) and the two 1845 volumes published by Wiley & Putnam, *Tales* and *The Raven and Other Poems*, edited by Hubbell (1969). P's five earliest stories were reprinted in facsimile from the *Philadelphia Saturday Courier* with an Introduction by J. G. Varner in 1933.

III. BIOGRAPHY

Of all major American writers P is the most misunderstood, and the misunderstanding extends to both the man and his writings. The legendary P is still too frequently mistaken for the man who wrote "The Raven" and "Ligeia." His critics, like those of Whitman, have always been too ready to read into his writings their own facile interpretations of his character and personality; and the man they have seen is generally, in the words of J. S. Wilson, "a creature fashioned out of hearsay and cheap journalism and fabricated likenesses by painters and penmen" (*AL* 68).

For nearly every major British and American author of the nineteenth century there is an official biography prepared by a relative or friend who felt it his duty to present his subject in a favorable light. Christopher Wordsworth suppressed the story of his uncle's love affair with Annette Vallon, and Samuel Longfellow presented his brother Henry in such a fashion that the poet strikes the modern reader as a prig. But when P died in Baltimore on 7 October 1849, there was at hand no friendly biographer to gloss over his failings and emphasize his better traits. There was no compact circle of disciples comparable to those who jealously guarded Whitman's reputation. There was, it is true, what appeared to be an official memoir, but it was written by R. W. Griswold, who at that time was certainly no friend of P. Two days after the poet's death Griswold published in the New York *Tribune*, under the pseudonym "Ludwig," an obituary article in which he asserted that P had "few or no friends"; that he was cynical, envious and arrogant; and that he had "no moral susceptibility" and "little or nothing of the true point of honor." In the memoir, which first appeared in September 1850, in the third volume of P's *Works*, Griswold replied to those friends who had protested against the "Ludwig" article; and to justify himself he printed what purported to be his correspondence with P. Although Griswold was long suspected of making changes in these letters, the extent of his forgeries was not fully revealed until 1941, when A. H. Quinn published his life of P. As Griswold painted him, P was the one black sheep in the American literary flock, and very black indeed he seemed when placed beside the great New Englanders.

The conception of P as a man of unprincipled character was formed and perpetuated by his literary enemies, the men who never forgave him for his criticism of them in his book reviews and "The Literati of New York City." As long as they lived, L. G. Clark, T. D. English, C. F. Briggs, and Hiram Fuller continued to defend Griswold's memoir as an accurate portrait; and they repeatedly suggested that Griswold had mercifully refrained from printing the most damning facts in his possession. English published his "Reminiscences" in the *Independent* as late as 1896, and the Griswold tradition colored the *Recollections* of R. H. Stoddard, published in 1903, well over half a century after P's death. The conception of P which comes from his enemies colored not only many later biographical sketches but also a large number of the critical estimates published in England and the United States.

Yet while the widespread popular conception of P the man owes much to Griswold and other literary enemies, it is based also in part on the fallacious notion that in his criminal and insane narrators P was indirectly revealing his own character. Some of the factual errors in the memoir came directly from P's own memoranda. It should be remembered also that J. R. Thompson, J. M. Daniel, and J. E. Cooke, who knew P only in the last two years of his life, regarded the memoir as a fairly accurate account. There were undoubtedly two sides to P's character. He was not an easy person to get on with. His fondness for rebuking literary pretenders and for charging better writers with plagiarism did not endear him to those whose books he reviewed. And it was apparently impossible for those whom he had abused while intoxicated ever to think of him as the courteous and considerate gentleman portrayed for us in the reminiscences of his friends.

These friends—N. P. Willis, C. C. Burr, G. R. Graham, L. A. Wilmer, Mrs. Osgood, and others—protested against the injustice which Griswold had done to P. None of them, however, produced a biography which might have superseded Griswold's memoir; and for a quarter of a century it had no rival. After Griswold's death, Sarah Helen Whitman, the Providence poet who had been at one time engaged to P, published an able defense, *EP and His Critics* (1860, 1949, 1968). See also Caroline Ticknor, *P's Helen* (1916); S. T. Williams, "New Letters about P" (*YR* 25); and J. A. Robbins, "EP and His Friends: A Sampler of Letters Written to Sarah Helen Whitman" (*IUB* 60).

The first real biographer of P was an Englishman, J. H. Ingram, who in 1874–75 published a four-volume edition of P's writings, which included a 90-page biographical sketch. In 1880 he brought out a two-volume biography. He had obtained valuable information from the poet's friends, especially Mrs. Whitman and Mrs. Annie Richmond. Ingram, however, was reluctant to admit any shortcomings in his hero. (See J. C. Miller, *John Henry Ingram's P Collection at the University of Virginia*, 1960.)

G. E. Woodberry's *EAP* (1885, 1968), in the American Men of Letters series, is a better biography than any of its predecessors. A New Englander and a friend of Lowell, he shared in some degree the unfavorable view of P held by most New England writers. In 1909, the year of the P Centenary, he brought out a two-volume edition (repr., 1965) which contained many letters. P's expanding fame and new materials which had come to light since 1885 led Woodberry to take a somewhat more favorable view of both the man and his writings. J. A. Harrison's *Life and Letters of EAP* (2 vols., 1902) is not as good a biography as Woodberry's, but it gives a more sympathetic account of the man. Hervey Allen's *Israfel: The Life and Times of EAP* (1926, 1934, 1956; reviewed by J. S. Wilson in *VQR* 27 and Campbell in *Al* 35) was among the first to make use of the correspondence between P and John Allan preserved in the Valentine Museum in Richmond. M. E. Phillips' huge two-volume *EAP: The Man* (1926) is not conspicuous for insight, and it is inadequately indexed, but it contains some materials that the scholar cannot afford to overlook.

The best factual account we have is A. H. Quinn's *EAP: A Critical Biography* (1941), which unfortunately is out of print. The author of *American Fiction* (1936) understood P's literary background better than any of his predecessors. He unearthed some new biographical materials—the marriage record of P's parents, for instance; and he revealed for the first time the extent of Griswold's forgeries, which had served temporarily to alienate so friendly a critic as E. A. Duyckinck. Yet "Fine as it is in so many ways, Arthur H. Quinn's biography fails to capture some of P's more elusive qualities and is weak in its critical judgments" (J. A. Robbins, *PN* 68). We have for P nothing comparable to Jay Leyda's *Melville Log*, but the Harvard Edition of the *Poems* (1969) contains Mabbott's "Annals" (pp. 529–72), an elaborate chronological table of great value to any future biographer. No scholar has as yet undertaken the laborious task of preparing a biography on the scale of Leon Edel's *Henry James*.

Haldeen Braddy, who reviewed Vincent Buranelli's *P: A Biography* (1961), found it "the finest brief treatment available" (*AL* 62). Only a minority of American critics, however, would agree with Buranelli's final estimate: "He has a strong claim to the titles of our best poet, our best short story writer, and our best critic." Edward Wagenknecht's *EAP: The Man Behind the Legend* (1963) is not a formal biography but a scholarly and fully-documented study of P's character and personality. In the words of Floyd Stovall, "it is sensible and readable, and it cuts a clear path through a wilderness of error." The reviewer praised Wagenknecht for "his success in avoiding, in his own interpretation, the pitfalls of psychoanalysis, the careless misuse of imaginative works as biographical documents, and other 'modern' methods of insinuating ideas without indisputable factual evidence" (*AL* 64).

Legend has distorted much of what has been written about P ever since his death in 1849. (See, for example, A. L. Cooke, "The Popular Conception of EAP from 1850 to 1890," *UTSE* 42). The P literary legend is explored in F. B. Dameron, "P in Drama, Fiction, and Poetry" (*BB* 54) and in J. E. Reilly's dissertation, "P in Imaginative Literature: A Study of American Drama, Fiction, and Poetry Devoted to EAP or his Works" (*DA* 65). Sam Moskowitz's *The Man Who Called Himself P* (1969) is an anthology of fiction and poetry written about P, but it includes none of the notable poetic tributes to P written by J. H. Boner, Vachel Lindsay, DuBose Heyward, J. G. Fletcher, Hart Crane, or Mallarmé.

P has long been a favorite subject for speculation and investigation with critics who thought they had found in psychoanalysis a method that would explain the mysteries of artistic creation. Typical examples are *EAP: A Psychological Study*, by J. W. Robertson, M.D. (1922), and D. M. Rein's *EAP: The Inner Pattern* (1960), neither of which seemed of much value to those qualified to judge. Lorine Pruette's "A Psycho-Analytical Study of EAP" (*AJP* 29) was reprinted in *The Literary Imagination: Psychoanalysis and the Genius of the Writer*, edited by H. M. Ruitenbeck (1963). This essay is characterized by R. P. Benton as "A study which is based on such errors of fact, such illogical interpretations of data, and such blind ignoring of alternative possibilities as to be misleading in the extreme" (*PN* 69). More useful studies are Mario Praz's "P and Psychoanalysis" (*SR* 60) and V. W. Grant's *Great Abnormals: The Pathological Genius of Kafka, Van Gogh, Strindberg, and P* (1968). J. W. Krutch's *EAP: A Study in Genius* (1926) is a brilliant interpretation based upon the belief—repudiated by Quinn—that P was sexually impotent. Krutch later expressed doubts as to the validity of his thesis.

The most influential of Freudian studies is Marie Bonaparte's *EP: Etude psychoanalytique* (Paris, 1933). John Rodker's English translation appeared in London in 1949 as *The Life and Works of EAP: A Psycho-Analytic Interpretation*. The thesis of the book is that P's writings are deeply colored by "intense emotional fixations and painful infantile experiences." Marie Bonaparte should have heeded the caution that her master, Sigmund Freud, expressed in his Foreword to her book: "Investigations such as this do not aim to explain creative genius, but they do reveal the factors which awaken it and the sort of subject matter it is destined to choose." The book contains some shrewd criticism of P's fiction, as P. F. Quinn has pointed out in *The French Face of EP* (1957). The excesses of the psychoanalysts moved Allen Tate to write in "The Angelic Imagination": "To these ingenious persons, P's works have almost no intrinsic meaning; taken together they make up a *dossier* for the analyst to peruse before Mr. P steps into his office for an analysis."

In *The Histrionic Mr. P* (1949) N. B. Fagin rode very hard his thesis that the poet was an actor *manqué* who carried his histrionic talents into the writing of poems and tales. P, he suggested, did not live his tales; he merely acted them; hence their air of unreality. P's characters are not people but "masks." A more accurate appraisal of P's personality and character is J. S. Wilson's "The Personality of P" (*VMHB* 59). Killis Campbell made no use of Freudian methods, but in *The Mind of P* (1933) he included a useful essay, "Self-Revelation in P's Poems and Tales." P's interest in phrenology is discussed in Edward Hungerford's "P and Phrenology" (*AL* 30), which makes no mention of the letter to F. W. Thomas, 22 October 1841, first printed in *AL* (34), in which P wrote, "Speaking of heads—my own *has been examined* by several phrenologists—all of whom spoke of me in a species of extravaganza which I should be ashamed to repeat." The phrenologists' continuing interest in P is discussed in M. B. Stern's "P: 'The Mental Temperament' for Phrenologists" (*AL* 68). Two studies of a long-neglected subject, both in *SSJ* (63), are J. W. Gray, "The Public Reading of EAP" and Kathleen Edgerton, "The Lecturing of EAP."

For the New York period in P's life there are some important books and articles; among them, John Stafford, *The Literary Criticism of "Young America"* (1952); Claude Richard, "P and Young America" (*SB* 68); M. B. Stern, "The House of the Expanding Doors: Ann Lynch's Soirees, 1846" (*NYH* 42); and J. B. Reece's Duke University dissertation, "P and the New York Literati" (1954). See also Reece's "A Reexamination of a P Date: Mrs. Ellet's Letters" (*AL* 70).

The scope of *The Raven and the Whale* (1956) by the late Perry Miller is suggested by its subtitle: *The War of Words and Wits in the Era of P and Melville*. In what Willard Thorp calls "the longest and most acrimonious of our literary wars" Melville was generally a spectator, but P was often an active participant and frequently the victim of unrestrained abuse by his literary enemies. Thorp points out that "scarcely a review was written in these fifteen years without partisan bias and that failure to review was often a partisan act as well" (*AL* 57). S. P. Moss's *P's Literary Battles: The Critic in the Context of His Literary Milieu* (1963) also deals in large part with the acrimonious literary wars of New York. As Floyd Stovall summarized the book, "it is the story of an uncompromising champion of literary values who loved truth, not wisely but too well, and whose bitter exposure of the faults and follies of

America's numerous third-rate 'patriotic' writers and the organized cliques that supported them precipitated such a storm of fear and hate that he was virtually annihilated by its violence" (*AL* 63).

H. E. Spivey's "P and Lewis Gaylord Clark" (*PMLA* 39) gives a more favorable view of the *Knickerbocker's* editor than one finds in *P's Literary Battles* or Moss's "P and his Nemesis: Lewis Gaylord Clark" (*AL* 56). See also Moss's "P, Hiram Fuller, and the Duyckinck Circle" (*ABC* 67). For the tangled relations between P and T. D. English, see L. B. Hurley, "A New Note in the War of the Literati" (*AL* 36); F. B. Dedmond, "The War of the Literati: Documents of the Legal Phase" (*N&Q* 53) and "P's Libel Suit against T. D. English" (*BPLQ* 53). For further information, see three articles in *PULC* (44) by Willard Thorp, T. O. Mabbott, and W. H. Gravely, Jr.

For the Richmond period the student should consult R. D. Jacobs, "P among the Virginians" (*VMHB* 59) and his "P in Richmond: The Double Image" in *Southern Writers: Appraisals in Our Time*, edited by R. C. Simonini (1964); and Agnes Bondurant, *P's Richmond* (1942), a Duke University master's thesis which occasioned the essay "Mr. Ritchie's Richmond" in J. B. Cabell's *Let Me Lie* (1947); and Clifford Dowdey, "P's Last Visit to Richmond" (*AH* 56). For the Baltimore period, see M. G. Evans, "P in Amity Street" (*MHM* 41) and J. C. French, "P's Literary Baltimore" (*MHM* 37). For the Philadelphia period not much is available outside of the biographies of Woodberry, Allen, and Quinn.

P, who in June 1844 referred to himself as "so far essentially a Magazinist," was not only a literary artist but a professional writer. And as the late William Charvat wrote in *The Profession of Authorship in America, 1800–1870* (1968), "The problem of the professional writer is not identical with that of the literary artist, but when a literary artist is also a professional writer, he cannot solve the problems of the one function without reference to the other." In his chapter on "P: Journalism and the Theory of Poetry" Charvat pointed out that "P's professional fate to a certain extent was determined by the position he took in the squeeze between the book and magazine economies in the 1840's, when publishers' rivalry in the reprinting of foreign works was at its height" (p. 26).

The subject of Michael Allen's monograph, *P and the British Magazine Tradition* (1969), is not new, but in the words of J. B. Reece, "Mr. Allen has written a work of carefully disciplined, significant scholarship which affords many fresh insights into the situation that confronted P as a practicing journalist and his response to it" (*AL* 70). As M. C. Peterson noted in his review, "the *Blackwood's* influence accounts for some of the characteristics of P's writing customarily considered the products of his own idiosyncracies" (*PN* 69). P was strongly influenced by four conventions which *Blackwood's* had used with success: "(1) the creation of a literary personality . . . , (2) the 'self-consciously learned pose,' . . . (3) the exploitation of the hoax, (4) the burlesque and the horror tale as major fictional modes." "What the book contributes," as P. F. Quinn has well said, "is a very detailed documentation that enables us to see for the first time how pervasively influenced P was by the conventions of British journalism and how he made use of those conventions not in a simply imitative way, but in Mr. Allen's phrase, 'with an intensity all his own' " (*SLJ* 69).

Among earlier studies which still have value are F. L. Mott's *History of American Magazines* (I, 1930, 1938; consult Index); J. C. French, "P and the *Baltimore Saturday Visiter*" (*MLN* 18); P. H. Boynton, "P and Journalism" (*EJ* 32); D. K. Jackson, *P and The SLM* (1934); A. W. Green, "The Weekly Magazines and P" (*English Studies in Honor of J. S. Wilson*, 1951); and J. L. Dameron, "P and *Blackwood's* on the Art of Reviewing" (*ESQ* 63). (R. D. Jacobs's *P: Journalist & Critic* [1969] is discussed below under "Criticism.")

Among the more useful studies of P's relations with his literary contemporaries are Joy Bayless, *Rufus Wilmot Griswold* (1943), which seemed to Mabbott not altogether just to P (*SAQ* 44); R. B. Davis, "P and William Wirt" (*AL* 44); J. B. Hubbell, "Charles Chauncey Burr: Friend of P" (*PMLA* 54); Elizabeth Binns, "Daniel Bryan: P's Poet of the Good Old Goldsmith School" (*WMQ* 43); Charles Bohner, "The P-Kennedy Friendship" (*PMHB* 58); Joseph Jackson, "George Lippard: Misunderstood Man of Letters" (*PMHB* 35); Gerald Grubb, "The Personal and Literary Relationship of Dickens and P" (*NCF* 50); and A. B. Nisbet, "New Light on the Dickens-P Relationship" (*NCF* 51).

For P's relations with Chivers, see S. F. Damon, *Thomas Holley Chivers: Friend of P* (1930) and C. H. Watts II, *Thomas Holly Chivers: His Literary Career and His Poetry* (1956). R. B. Davis's *Chivers' Life of P* (1952) is based upon manuscripts in the Huntington Library. P's Southern background and his relations with other Southern writers are discussed in Hubbell's *The South in American Literature* (1954) and his "EAP and the South" in *South and Southwest* (1965), a revised version of "P and the Southern Literary Tradition" (*TSLL* 60). J. D. Allen, whose *Philip Pendleton Cooke* appeared in 1942, published in 1969 a volume of selections from Cooke (reviewed by D. K. Jackson in *SLJ* 70).

IV. CRITICISM

1. General Estimates

"Recognition came early from those close to him," wrote Mabbott, and he added: "There has never been even a temporary decline of his popularity among general readers. Among critics there was disagreement from the start" (*Poems*, 1969, p. xxiii). The estimates of the earlier critics were deeply colored by what they thought they knew about P's character. Those who accepted Griswold's memoir as authoritative conceded his technical competence, but they condemned or ignored his critical writings and maintained that his poems and tales were largely vitiated by a lack of moral purpose. More than any other American writer except perhaps Whitman, P has been a controversial figure in English and American literary criticism.

Throughout the nineteenth century P's standing was lower in New England than anywhere else in his own country. The poet himself was, of course, partly responsible for this situation. He had attacked the New England writers for their provincialism and condemned their fondness for moralizing. He had ridiculed Boston as the "Frogpond" and charged Longfellow, Lowell, and Hawthorne (though he often praised them) with plagiarism. Soon after Bryant's death J. G. Holland, a native of Massachusetts, wrote in *Scribner's* (1878): "Of one thing we may be reasonably sure, viz., that when the genuine geniuses of this period shall be appreciated at their full value . . . their countrymen will have ceased discussing P and Thoreau and Walt Whitman." At the close of the century Howells summed up the New England attitude:

The great New Englanders would none of him. Emerson called him "the jingle-man"; Lowell thought him "three-fourths [two-fifths] sheer fudge"; Longfellow's generous voice was silenced by P's atrocious misbehavior to him, and we can only infer his slight esteem for his work; in a later generation Mr. [Henry] James speaks of P's "very valueless verses." Yet it is perversely possible that his name will lead all the rest when our immortals are duly marshalled for the long descent of time ("A Hundred Years of American Verse," *NAR* 01).

While P was scandalizing the New England literati in the "Longfellow War," he failed to foresee that the Boston-Cambridge-Concord view of the function of literature would dominate American literary criticism throughout the later nineteenth century. On 27 May 1893 the New York *Critic* announced the results of a poll which it had taken of its readers to select "The Best Ten American Books." Emerson's *Essays* and Hawthorne's *The Scarlet Letter* were

at the top of the list with around 500 votes apiece; and the poems of Longfellow, Lowell, Holmes, and Whittier were all among the first ten; but nothing
by P got as much as 20 votes. Edmund Gosse wrote from England to protest
against the exclusion of P, "the most perfect, the most original, and the most
exquisite of the American poets." The exclusion of P seemed to him "extraordinary and sinister."

The praise heaped upon P in the Centenary year made it evident that in
the eyes of Europeans he was one of America's major writers. In 1910 he
was finally admitted to the Hall of Fame for Great Americans. Yet there was
still wide disagreement among critics as to his place in our literature. Campbell
in 1917 attributed much of this disagreement to "the world-wide difference
among critics as to the province and aims of poetry, the traditional clash between those who insist upon the inculcation of moral ideas as the chief business
of poetry and those who adhere to the doctrine of art for art's sake."

Hardly more than half a dozen of the critical essays on P written in America before 1900 are intrinsically worth reading today. Two of the best, however,
appeared during his lifetime: Lowell's "EAP" (*Graham's Mag* 1845), which
is concerned primarily with the poems, and P. P. Cooke's "EAP" (*SLM* 1848),
which emphasized the tales. Lowell's essay was reprinted by Griswold in a
revised version which qualified the high praise that Lowell had bestowed in
1845. Of the later nineteenth-century essays one of the best is that of E. C.
Stedman (*Scribner's* 1880; *Poets of America*, 1885).

Of the British essays on P perhaps the best—though it suffers from inadequate biographical information—is that of the Scottish critic, J. M. Robertson, in his *New Essays towards a Critical Method* (1889). James Hannay's
introduction to *P's Poetical Works* (1853) contains an excellent discussion of
P's poetry as well as incidental high praise for Melville's *Moby-Dick*. George
Saintsbury, who early and late praised P, in his old age published an excellent
essay in the *Dial* (27), which was reprinted in his *Prefaces and Essays* (1933).

For the P Centenary G. B. Shaw in the London *Nation* (09) described P
as "this finest of fine artists, this born aristocrat of letters":

He was the greatest journalistic critic of his time, placing good European work at
sight when the European critics were waiting for somebody to tell them what to say.
His poetry is so exquisitely refined that posterity will refuse to believe that it belongs
to the same civilization as the glory of Julia Ward Howe's lilies or the honest doggerel of Whittier.

Of American essays occasioned by the P Centenary one of the best is that of
W. P. Trent in his *Longfellow and Other Essays* (1910). The ablest and the
least sympathetic is that in W. C. Brownell's *American Prose Masters* (1909,

1923), which concludes that "whatever his merits as a literary artist," P's writings lack "substance" and hence as literature are "essentially valueless."

The severest judgment passed upon P since the Centenary is found in Yvor Winters' "EAP: A Crisis in the History of American Obscurantism" (*AL* 37; *Maule's Curse*, 1938). Winters practically charged that there was a conspiracy among scholars to maintain P's traditional standing as a major American writer. His own opinion was that P is "a bad writer accidentally and temporarily popular," "an explicit obscurantist," and a critic of poetry who did not understand the fundamental principles of versification and whose poems are "an art to delight the soul of a servant girl."

Few of our earlier literary historians, most of whom were New England professors of English, revealed any real understanding of P; and they had difficulty in fitting him into the American literary tradition as they conceived it. J. G. Huneker, writing in the *Musical Courier* (1901), maintained that P was "the victim of Yankee college professors who found him lacking the patriotism of Whittier, the humor of O. W. Holmes, the sanity of Lowell, and the human qualities of Longfellow" (see A. T. Schwab, "James Huneker's Criticism of American Literature" in *AL* 57). The chapter on P in Barrett Wendell's *Literary History of America* (1900) is unsympathetic and suffers from various misconceptions of P's life, character, and background. The Centenary address which Wendell delivered at the University of Virginia reveals for the first time in Wendell's writings a comprehension of P's importance. (See my *South in American Literature*, 1954). P was treated with sympathy and understanding in *American Literature* (1889) by C. F. Richardson, who edited the Knickerbocker Edition of P's *Works* (1902), and in W. P. Trent's *History of American Literature* (1903). In *SAL* (1913) John Macy included an impressionistic and sympathetic essay.

Still worth reading are Campbell's chapter in Vol. II (1918) of *CHAL*, his Introduction to the *Poems* (1917), and *The Mind of P and Other Essays* (1933). Before publishing his life of P in 1941, A. H. Quinn had discussed the tales in his *American Fiction* (1936). The best summary of what Quinn had to say about P's writings is found in *LAP* (1951) in a chapter entitled "Beauty and the Supernatural." In his chapter on P in *LHUS* (1948, *SR* 46) F. O. Matthiessen made use of the same methods he had applied with notable results to P's great contemporaries in *AmR* (1941), but he did not bring to P the full knowledge and sympathetic understanding that he had brought to them.

V. W. Brooks in *The World of Washington Irving* (1944) carefully placed P in his Southern and Northern backgrounds, but he could not fit him into the American literary tradition. H. S. Canby wrote in *Classic Americans*

(1931): "P the writer is nearest to our norm. . . . as a man of letters, [he] was the true professional." In *MCAT* (1927) V. L. Parrington concluded his brief discussion of P, "The problem of P, fascinating as it is, lies quite outside the main currents of American thought, and it may be left with the psychologist and the belletrist with whom it belongs." In *Ideas in America* (1944) H. M. Jones protested:

Now P was not, as Parrington seemed to think, merely an "aesthete and a craftsman" who "made a stir in the world." He was not merely a disappointed artist or merely a disgruntled and deracinated Southerner. . . . to think of P in terms of a damaged and therefore ineffectual angel, a misunderstood genius, a Satanic being, a problem for the psychologist and the belletrist only, is to give up literary history as an instrument for cultural analysis (p. 41).

Not one of the major American writers of the later nineteenth century—Henry James, Walt Whitman, Mark Twain, Howells, or Emily Dickinson—can be numbered among P's admirers. James wrote in an essay on Baudelaire in *French Poets and Novelists* (1878):

An enthusiasm for P is the mark of a decidedly primitive stage of reflection. Baudelaire thought him a profound philosopher, the neglect of whose golden utterances stamped his native land with infamy. Nevertheless, P was much the greater charlatan of the two, as well as the greater genius.

In the same essay James referred to P's "very valueless verses"; later he changed the phrase to "very superficial verses." When Andrew Lang took him to task for his failure to appreciate P's poems, James said, "I suppose I made a mistake."

In November 1875 when a monument was at last placed over P's grave in Baltimore, Whitman was the only major American writer to attend the ceremonies. In his brief essay, "EP's Significance" (1880) he wrote:

Almost without the first sign of moral principle, or of the concrete or its heroisms, or of the simpler affections of the heart, P's verses illustrate an intense facility for technical and abstract beauty, with the rhyming art to excess, an incorrigible propensity toward nocturnal themes, a demonic undertone behind every page—and, by final judgment, probably among the electric lights of imaginative literature, brilliant and dazzling, but with no heat.

In *Studies in Classic American Literature* (1923) D. H. Lawrence included an influential essay on P (quite different from an earlier version in *Eng Rev* 19) which W. H. Auden has described as "conspicuous for its insights." Lawrence was among the first to see in psychoanalysis a key to the understanding of P, who, he thought, was "absolutely concerned with the disintegration-processes of his own psyche." "He was an adventurer into vaults and cellars and horrible underground passages of the human soul. He sounded the horror and warning of his own doom." In *The Forlorn Demon* (1953) Allen Tate, taking his cue from Lawrence, suggested that "P is the transitional figure in modern literature because he discovered our great subject, the disintegration of the personality, but kept it in a language that had developed in a tradition of unity and order."

Our twentieth-century poets and novelists often disagree with one another as to P's place in our literature, but they do not ignore him. J. B. Cabell, whose grandfather witnessed P's boyhood swimming exploit in the James River, expressed the opinion in *Ladies and Gentlemen* (1934) that of our earlier literature about all that has any importance is "A sufficing amount of P, and a tiny fraction of Mark Twain." Very different is the estimate expressed a year later in *Green Hills of Africa* by Ernest Hemingway, who apparently cared little for any of our major writers except Mark Twain: "P is a skillful writer. It is skillful, marvellously constructed, and it is dead." In their youth many of our poets have been fascinated by the music of P's poems; but most of them, I suspect, like Sidney Lanier and Robert Frost, have been more deeply influenced by other poets. Not so, however, with Vachel Lindsay, whose "The Wizard in the Street" is one of the better poetic tributes to P. In the Autobiographical Foreword to his *Collected Poems* (1923) Lindsay wrote that in the histories of American literature which he read in the Springfield High School, "There was nothing to be found but the full-page portraits of a famous mutual-admiration society. I knew exactly P's opinion of these whiskered worthies." For W. C. Williams, who in his *In the American Grain* (1925) included a highly eulogistic essay, P was "in no sense the bizarre, isolate writer, the curious literary figure. On the contrary, in him American literature is anchored, in him alone, on solid ground." P's criticism was, he said, a movement, first and last to clear the GROUND." "On him," wrote Williams, "is FOUNDED A LITERATURE. . . ." Hart Crane, after reading Williams' essay, wrote, "I was so interested to note that he puts P and his 'character' in the same position as I had *symbolized* in 'The Tunnel' section of *The Bridge* (*Letters*, 1952).

T. S. Eliot's sometimes contradictory comments on an author that he never really liked are discussed by H. H. Kühnelt (*NS* 56) and B. R. McElderry, Jr. (*PN* 68). Eliot, however, did finally come to see P's work as "a mass of unique shape and impressive size." In reviewing Allen's *Israfel* he pronounced P "a critic of the first rank," but he added, "In the end, P remains inscrutable" (*Nation & Athenaeum* 27). In *From P to Valéry* (1945) he wrote: "P indeed is a stumbling block for the judicial critic. If we examine his work in detail, we seem to find in it nothing but slipshod writing, puerile thinking unsupported by wide reading or profound scholarship, haphazard experiments in various types of writing, chiefly under pressure of financial need, without perfection in any detail." P's intellect seemed to Eliot that of "a highly gifted young person before puberty." In his St. Louis address, "American Literature and the American Language," Eliot said in 1953: "The landmarks I have chosen for the identification of American literature are not found in New England. . . . The three authors of my choice are P, Whitman, and Mark Twain."

Eliot's friend Ezra Pound wrote, "P is a good enough poet, and after Whitman the best America has produced (probably)," but, he added, "He is a dam bad model. . . . A dam'd bad rhetorician half the time." Eliot, Pound, and their followers among the New Critics had no enthusiasm for P or for the English poets that he admired: Milton, Tennyson, Shelley, Keats, and Coleridge. Of the Fugitive-Agrarian poet-critics, only Allen Tate has shown much interest in P. In their *Literary Criticism: A Short History* (1957) W. K. Wimsatt and Cleanth Brooks treated P's critical writings as of little importance. Perhaps P. F. Quinn was right when he wrote, "The conventional yardsticks prove to be never quite accurate in taking P's measure" (*SLJ* 69). And yet while P is undoubtedly one of our major writers, he is, as Quinn has said elsewhere, "one whose credentials are always being challenged" (*ALS* for 1968).

In 1949 at the request of UNESCO the American Literature Section of the MLA sponsored a poll of 27 specialists in an effort to identify the 20 best American books. Hawthorne led with 164 points; P was second with 163. Until 1950, when Auden included both *Eureka* and *Pym* in a book of selections, American scholars paid scant attention to works which had long seemed important to French critics. In more recent times American scholars have thrown new light upon the poems and tales by studying what P called the "undercurrent of meaning." They have discovered that in P's mind the relation of truth and morality to beauty and art were far more complex than was generally inferred from his brief treatment of "the heresy of the didactic" in "The Poetic Principle." We are now—in academic circles at least—in the midst of a P Revival.

Impressive evidence of this continuing interest in P's work is found in *New Approaches to P: A Symposium* (1970), edited by R. P. Benton, which also appeared as a Supplement to the Fall 1970 number of *ESQ*. The symposium appeared too late to permit discussion in the proper places of these essays. Among the stories discussed, however, are "Ligeia," "William Wilson," "Metzengerstein," and *Pym*. Three of the fourteen essays deal with the poems, especially "To Helen" and "For Annie." The quality of the essays is high, and the editor is right in thanking his contributors for their "memorable cooperation." He concludes his brief introduction: "What will the '70's reveal? I hope a fuller understanding of P's art and greatness, which, though defying complete assessment, still can challenge perceptive readers. . . ."

2. Cosmopolitan Fame

In the 1920's and 1930's when the Young Intellectuals were attacking the traditional American literary canon and down-grading the old New England poets, P managed to hold on to his position as a major American writer. In those years many of our writers lived for a time in France, and some of them were impressed by the French conception of P. See Jean Simon, "French Studies in American Literature and Civilization" (AL 34).

In the early 1920's American critics were increasingly conscious of the disturbing fact that in Europe and Latin America P was regarded as one of the major writers of the nineteenth century. P, wrote Edmund Wilson, "has figured in Europe for the last three-quarters of a century as a writer of the first importance, [while] we in America are still preoccupied with . . . his bad reputation as a citizen" (NR 26). In 1948 Mattheissen wrote, "Like Henry James and T. S. Eliot, [P] took his place, almost from the start, in international culture as an original creative force in contrast to the more superficial international vogue of Cooper and Irving" (LHUS, p. 342). In the words of C. B. Green, P "appears to be free of the limitations of a particular place and a specific time." It is possible to consider his merits as a writer "without stressing the fact that he belongs either to the South or to the nineteenth century" (SCR 70).

An examination of the text and bibliography in Haldeen Braddy, *Glorious Incense: The Fulfillment of EAP* (1953, 1968), will suggest the vast extent of P's worldwide reputation. See also J. C. French, editor, *P in Foreign Lands and Tongues* (1941) and W. T. Bandy, *The Influence and Reputation of EAP in Europe* (1951). In his "EAP: Current Bibliography" (PN 69) R. P. Benton notes that *The National Union Catalog*, published by the Library of Congress, lists 60 editions of P's works, coming from 13 different countries, published between January 1966 and July 1968. In *EAP: A Checklist of Criticism, 1942–1960* (1966) J. L. Dameron lists 595 titles in English and 328 in foreign languages.

P's vogue in English, which was influenced by the Griswold memoir, is discussed in D. R. Hutcherson, "P's Reputation in England and America, 1850–1909" (AL 42); Clarence Gohdes, *American Literature in Nineteenth-*

Century England (1944); and in H. H. Kühnelt, *Die Bedeutung von EAP für die englische Literatur* (Innsbruck, 1949; reviewed by Mabbott in *AL* 51).

In France P has had a wide and continuing influence ever since Charles Baudelaire discovered him in 1846 or 1847 and became his chief champion. His three essays on P (1852, 1856, 1857) are available in English in *Baudelaire on P* (1952), translated by Lois and F. B. Hyslop, Jr. For Baudelaire, who knew very little about the man, P was in effect a displaced European artist victimized by a Philistine American society. For further information see Marcel Françon, "P et Baudelaire" (*PMLA* 45); W. T. Bandy, "Baudelaire et EP" (*RLC* 67) and "Baudelaire and P" (*TQ* 58). Baudelaire translated the tales and *Eureka*, and Mallarmé rendered the poems into rhythmical prose; and in their versions the poems and tales were widely read not only in France but also in Italy, Spain, and Portugal and throughout Latin America.

The number of important French writers who have praised P is very large, and it includes Théophile Gautier, Rimbaud, Villier de l'Isle-Adam, Maupassant, Sardou, Jules Verne, Maeterlinck, the Goncourt brothers, and many more. P's poems inspired musical compositions by Debussy and other French composers. (See M. G. Evans, *Music and EP*, 1939.)

P is the only American writer of the nineteenth century who made a substantial contribution to European literary theory. "Here is the literature of the twentieth century," wrote the Goncourt brothers in 1876. In *From P to Valéry* (1948) T. S. Eliot commented on the French poetic tradition which starts with Baudelaire, runs through Mallarmé, and "culminates in Valéry" and added, "I venture to say that without this French tradition the work of three poets in other languages . . . I refer to W. B. Yeats, Ranier Maria Rilke, and, I if I may, to myself—would hardly be conceivable." And this French tradition, he concluded, "owed a good deal" to P.

The Symbolists found in P support for their theory of *la poésie pure*. Their influence is very evident in George Moore's English *Anthology of Pure Poetry* (1924), which includes six of P's poems, more than he chose from any other poet except Shakespeare.

An early appraisal is C. H. Page's Centenary article, "P in France" (*Nation* 09). In 1912 G. D. Morris published *Fenimore Cooper et EP d'après la critique française du dix-neuvième siècle*. These, however, were superseded by C. P. Cambiaire, *The Influence of EAP in France* (1927). Better than Cambiaire's study in some respects are three books by Léon Lemonnier: *EP et la critique française de 1845 à 1875* (1928), *Les Traducteurs d'EP en France* (1928), and *EP et les poètes français* (1932). See also Lemonnier's articles in *AAL*; Valéry's "Situation de Baudelaire" in his *Variété* II (1930); Louis Seylaz, *EP et les premiers symbolistes français* (Lausanne, 1923); and C.-E. Engel, "L'Etat des travaux sur P en France" (*MP* 32).

French critics and scholars are still interested in P, and American students cannot afford to neglect significant studies done by such accomplished scholars as Claude Richard and Roger Asselineau. Nevertheless the American student should heed Richard's warning in "P Studies in Europe: France" (*PN* 69) that "the bane of French studies" of P is the twofold influence of the Baudelairean tradition and the psychoanalytical concern which derives from Marie Bonaparte. In an important essay, "EP et la tradition 'gothique'" (*Caliban* 68) Maurice Lévy maintains that P's insights are closer to those of Jung and Bachelard than to those of Freud and Marie Bonaparte.

The best introduction to P's reputation and influence in France is P. F. Quinn's *The French Face of EP* (1957). As Quinn phrased it in his closing sentence, "an examination of the French response to P necessarily implies a reappraisal of his work and of his place in American literature." There is, he maintained, much more in P's work than can be got by asking to what extent his tales exemplify the aesthetic principles that he outlined.

It is rather [Quinn concluded] the other component of his mind—at the opposite pole from the analytic—which gave him a power the extent of which he scarcely knew himself, to bring up to the surface of consciousness the kind of submerged emotional life that the intelligence prefers to ignore. It is this element in the work of P that Baudelaire pointed to when he spoke of P's profundities, and it is this element that the critiques of Marie Bonaparte and Gaston Bachelard explore.

Quinn's fine study, however, has its limitations. Apart from *Pym* and the tales, he is no great admirer of P. The poems, which Mallarmé praised so highly, and *Eureka*, which seemed to Valéry a great book, he treats as failures. The poems he calls *"tours de force."*

Poe's vogue in Spain, Portugal, Italy, and Latin America had its beginning with writers who discovered him in Baudelaire's translation of the tales. There is an informative section on P in J. D. Ferguson's *American Literature in Spain* (1916). Both Spain and Spanish America are covered in J. E. Englekirk's *EAP in Hispanic Literature* (1934). See also his " 'The Raven' in Spanish America" (*Spanish Review* 34) and "Bibliography of Mexican Versions and Criticism of P" (*PMLA* 37). Another important work is R. H. Valle's "Fichas para la bibliografía de P en Hispanoamerica" (*RI* 50). In "P in Spanish America: A Bibliographical Supplement" (*PN* 69) H. C. Woodbridge added some 80 new items not listed by Englekirk or Valle. See also Armando Rojas, "EAP en la America Hispana" (*RNC* 60) and Muna Lee, "Brother of P" (*SWR* 26), which traces the influence of P on the Colombian poet Asunción Silva.

Ada Giacarri in 1959 published two articles in *SA*: "La Fortuna di EAP in Italia" and "Poe nella critica italiana." Federico Olivero's *EP* (Turin, 2nd ed., 1939) was translated into English by Dante Milani.

Various German and Austrian scholars have discussed P's reputation and influence in their countries. Some of the better studies are P. Wächtler, *EAP und die deutsche Romantik* (Leipzig, 1911); Fitz Hippe, *EAPs Lyrik in Deutschland* (Münster, 1913); and Kuno Schumann, *Die Erzählende Prosa EAPs: Ein Beitrag zu einer Gattungsgeschichte der "Short Story"* (FAGAAS 58). See also Manfred Durzak, "Die Kunsttheoretische Ausgangsposition Stefan Georges: Zur Wirking EAPs" (*Arcadia* 69). In addition to *Die Bedeutung von EAP für die englische Literatur* (1949), the able Austrian scholar H. H. Kühnelt has published four articles: "Deutsche Erzähler in Gefolge von EAP" (*RLMC* 51); "EAP und die phantasische Erzählung in österreichishen Schriftum von 1900–1920" (*Enzinger-Festschrift*, Innsbruck, 1952); "Die Aufnahme und Verbreitung von EAPs Werken in Deutschen" (*Walter Fischer Festschrift*, Heidelberg, 1959); and "EAP und Alfred Kubin: Zwei kunstlerische Gestalter des Grauens" (WBEP 1957).

There are 81 items that concern P in *Russian Studies of American Literature* (1969), a bibliography compiled by V. A. Libman, translated by R. V. Allen, and edited by Clarence Gohdes. In date they range from 1852 to 1963. See also Vladimir Astrov, "Dostoievsky on EAP" (*AL* 42) and Avraham Yarmolinsky, "The Russian View of American Literature" (*Bookman* 16). For P's reputation in Sweden, Hungary, and Yugoslavia, see Erik Vandelfelt, "Fröding och P: Nägra anteckningar" (*SLT* 66); Gyorgy Radó, "The Works of EAP in Hungary" (*Babel* 66); and Sonja Basić, "EAP in Croatian and Serbian Literature," *SRAZ* 66).

3. Literary Theory

Of earlier critical studies the two best are Margaret Alterton's *Origins of P's Critical Theory* (1925) and Norman Foerster's *American Criticism: Studies in Literary Theory from P to the Present* (1928). Alterton stressed the essential unity underlying everything that P wrote. A more concise expression of her view is found in the AWS *EAP* (1935). Foerster's own view of the function of literature is different from P's, but no other critic has more thoroughly and systematically studied the critical materials in the Virginia Edition of P's *Works*. See also Foerster's "Quantity and Quality in the Aesthetic of P" (*SP* 23). E. H. Davidson's *P: A Critical Study* (1957) has been described by R. D. Jacobs as a "brilliant study [which] placed P within the context of romantic aesthetics and focused upon his poems and his tales to reveal a unitary prin-

ciple informing all of P's creative work from his youthful poems to his cosmogony, *Eureka*" (*P: Journalist and Critic*, 1969 [hereafter *P:J&C*], p. viii).
Geoffrey Rans, who opened his *EAP* (1965) with a discussion of *Eureka* and
the critical writings, stressed the "interpenetration of P's sense of universal
harmony and symmetry with his aesthetic" (p. 37). E. W. Parks's *EAP as
Literary Critic* (1964) is thus characterized by J. A. Robbins:

Parks has usefully noted the critical works that P knew, the authors and literary forms
he admired or disliked, his contribution to our thinking on the purposes and means
of fiction and poetry, shifts in his critical thinking, and finally aspects of his strength
and weakness. For all his limitations, P sought a broader, less provincial criticism, set
an example of close textual analysis, tried to fashion a more flexible theory of metrics,
and believed that meaning should be woven artfully into the very texture of literature. And, Parks contends, much of what he did in his own writing and much of what
he advocated in his criticism can be related to his evolving aesthetics for a magazine
literature (*ALS* for 1964).

R. D. Jacobs found it so "difficult to separate P the journalist from P the
artist" that in his *P:J&C* (1969) he felt compelled to examine every aspect of
P's work as author, editor, and reviewer. P, he maintains, was "an eclectic
[who] sought to have the best of both worlds, that of the soaring imagination
and that of a practical methodology based upon 'mental science.'" P, he
concluded, "never developed an aesthetic system that could withstand intensive scrutiny. . . ." P. F. Quinn, who found Jacobs's discussion of *Eureka* and
the colloquies "superb," summed up his impressions of the book:

As a journalist-critic, a book reviewer and literary hatchet-man, P made no major
contribution to the development of aesthetic theory. . . . it was in and through his
work as a reviewer . . . that P's thought developed beyond the confines of both journalism and criticism into an imaginative theory of nature, man, and God, into a
cosmic myth (*SLJ* 69).

"On the subject of P's journalistic career," wrote Floyd Stovall, "the book is
both new and thorough, and is likely to be the definitive study for years to
come. Unfortunately," he added, "to achieve this thoroughness and to be
comprehensive, he had to sacrifice the advantages of conciseness; the book is
large, sometimes repetitive, and difficult to follow. It is not suitably arranged
to be used as a reference work" (*GaR* 70). Many of the best passages in the
book are comments on individual poems and tales. Jacobs's treatment of P's
indebtedness to such late eighteenth-century writers as Hugh Blair and Archibald Alison seemed to the reviewer "relatively new and welcome." Unlike
some latter-day critics, Jacobs does not see P as an artist alienated from the
society in which he lived.

[P] saw more clearly than most the alienation of the artist that would occur if he neglected his public function in the interest of self-expression, if he engaged in technical frolics that would appeal only to the aesthete, or if he plunged into obscurities that only the philosophically apt could comprehend. P would have approved of *Finnegans Wake* or Pound's *Cantos* no more than he approved of *Paradise Lost* (p. 450).

Other studies that have value are G. E. De Mille, *Literary Criticism in America* (1931); Marvin Laser, "The Growth and Structure of P's Concept of Beauty" (*ELH* 48); A. J. Lubell, "P and A. W. Schlegel" (*JEGP* 63); George Kelly, "P's Theory of Beauty" (*AL* 56); R. P. Benton, "The Works of N. P. Willis as a Catalyst of P's Criticism" (*AL* 67); J. L. Dameron and L. C. Stagg, *An Index to P's Critical Vocabulary* (1966, also *ESQ* 67); J. L. Dameron and E. H. Marks, "P as Literary Theorist: A Reappraisal" (*AL* 61); and J. J. Moldenhauer, "Murder as a Fine Art: Basic Connections between P's Aesthetics, Psychology, and Moral Vision" (*PMLA* 68); J. L. Dameron, "P at Mid-Century: Anglo-American Criticism, 1928—1960" (*BSUF* 67); and "The Critical Estimate of P" in Louis Broussard, *The Measure of P* (1969). There are two excellent collections of essays: E. W. Carlson's *The Recognition of EAP: Selected Criticism since 1829* (1966) and Robert Regan's *P: A Collection of Critical Essays* (1967), which consists chiefly of modern essays on P's fiction.

Like T. S. Eliot, Edmund Wilson pronounced P a critic of the first order ("P as a Literary Critic," *Nation* 42). Griswold had considered him "little better than a carping grammarian." George Snell in "First of the New Critics" (*QRL* 45) advanced the view that "Textual criticism, as we know it today, was born" with P; and, without noting significant differences, he pointed out similarities in critical method between the New Critics and P. The classical background of P's criticism is treated in J. P. Pritchard, *Return to the Fountains* (1942), which is chiefly concerned with Aristotle's "Poetics" and Horace's "Ars Poetica." In his *Criticism in America* (1956) Pritchard again emphasized the classical element in P, who had in fact little knowledge of, or interest in, literary history.

4. Poetry

Academic interest in P is now concentrated upon his tales and critical writings; but for three-quarters of a century after his death he was regarded as primarily a poet. And so he has been seen by Campbell, Mabbott, and Stovall, who wrote in *EP the Poet* (1969), "He was, in his own estimate of himself, and in fact, essentially a poet, and remained so to the end of his life, not only in his poetry, but also in the best of his fiction and his essays on the nature and function of poetry" (p. 282). The view of P's poetry found in H. H. Waggoner's *American Poets* (1968) is so unfavorable that as P. F. Quinn sums it up, "In essence he agrees with Henry James, who found admiration for P the sign of 'a very primitive stage of reflection' " (*ALS* for 1968).

With P poetry was a kind of music, and verse was not the "dying technique" that Edmund Wilson saw in modern poetry. Poe would have agreed with Robert Frost that to abandon meter is like playing tennis without the net. In P's best poems—to borrow some phrases from Pound's "How to Read" —the words "are charged over and above their plain meaning, with some musical property, which directs the bearing or trend of that meaning. . . . it is poetry on the borders of music and music is perhaps the bridge between consciousness and the unthinking sentient and even insentient universe." Some critics have complained of a lack of significant purpose or content in P's poems. Not so Geoffrey Rans, who wrote, "The poet aims, then, for a moment, to free man from the shackles of time, and reinstate him in the eternity he has lost, to present man with a vision of unity in his world of chaos (*EAP*, p. 280).

The best general study of P's versification is in G. W. Allen's *American Prosody* (1935), but see also three articles in *AL*: W. L. Werner, "P's Theories and Practice in Poetic Technique" (30); R. C. Pettigrew, "P's Rime" (32); and Anthony Caputi, "The Refrain in P's Poetry" (53). See also C. S. Lenhart, *Musical Influences on American Poetry* (1956). Two essays by American poets are Horace Gregory, "On EP: A Belated Epitaph" in *The Shield of Achilles* (1944), and Allen Tate, "The Poetry of EAP" (*SR* 69).

Of the various discussions of that difficult early poem, "Al Aaraaf," the best is probably that of Floyd Stovall in *EP the Poet* (1969). "Eldorado," one of P's last poems, is briefly discussed in four articles, all in *MLN*, by O. S. Coad (44), T. O. Mabbott (45), W. S. Sanderlin, Jr. (56), and E. W. Carlson (61).

There has been much speculation about the meaning of "Ulalume." In 1922 F. L. Pattee wrote in *Sidelights on American Literature*: " 'Ulalume' is the epitome of P's last years. It is the picture of a soul hovering between hope and inevitable despair, a soul longing passionately for a sympathy which it can never have. . . ." W. H. Auden saw the poem as "an interesting experiment in diction but only an experiment, for the poem is about something which never quite gets said because the sense is sacrificed to the vowel sounds." Woodberry, however, considered "Ulalume" one of P's finest poems, and so did Hardin Craig, who wrote in the AWS *EAP*, "The age in which 'Ulalume' appeared was incompetent to cope with it. . . ." Mallarmé regarded "Ulalume" as "perhaps the most original and the most strangely suggestive of all P's poems." Cleanth Brooks and R. P. Warren, who discussed the poem in *Understanding Poetry* (1950), are not among P's admirers.

"Ulalume" still intrigues the critics. Important articles that have appeared since 1954 are E. W. Carlson, "Symbol and Sense in P's 'Ulalume' " (*AL* 63); J. E. Miller, Jr., " 'Ulalume' Resurrected" (*PQ* 55); and Mother Mary Eleanor, "The Debate of the Body and the Soul" (*Renascence* 60), which places the poem in the tradition. In 1847 a school girl listened to P's explanation of "the ideas intended to be embodied" in "Ulalume," but unfortunately for us she did not take the trouble to record them in her "Recollections of EAP" (*Home Jour* 1860; see C. D. Laverty, "P in 1847," *AL* 48).

Critics disagree as to which are P's best poems. Campbell in 1917 rated "Israfel" (Stedman's favorite), "The City in the Sea," and "The Sleeper" as "certainly as richly poetic as anything that P wrote." Auden did not include "The Sleeper" (which P thought superior to "The Raven") among the 11 poems he reprinted in 1950. He did, however, include "To One in Paradise," which W. C. Williams in 1925 thought the best of the poems. Auden omitted that general favorite, the first "To Helen," which he thought could have been written by Landor, and commented, "P's best poems are not his most typical or original." Auden also omitted "For Annie," which had seemed to Saintsbury (*Dial* 27) one of P's three best poems, the other two being "Ulalume" and "Annabel Lee." "But in its own kind," he said, "I know nothing that can beat, if indeed I know anything that can equal, *Annabel Lee*." For Allen Tate P's best poems are "The City in the Sea," "The Sleeper," "To Helen," and "The Raven" (*SR* 69).

5. Fiction

In his 1959 Library of Congress lecture, "The House of P," Richard Wilbur said: "P is a great artist, and I would rest my case for him on his prose allegories of psychic conflict. In them, P broke wholly new ground, and they remain the best things of their kind in our literature." And yet while most contemporary critics would agree that the tales are P's best claim to a place among our major writers, his fiction is not available in any edition worthy of comparison with those that Campbell, Stovall, and Mabbott have provided for the poems. There is no critical study of P's fiction that can be compared to several studies of his critical writings.

Until long after the P Centenary the critical attitude toward the tales was influenced by Brander Matthew's "The Philosophy of the Short-Story." Matthews had elaborated "the doctrine of the single effect" to which P had devoted a paragraph in his review of *Twice-Told Tales*. Matthews's conception of the short story was influenced also by the practice of Maupassant and other French masters, and it fitted in with the critical standards of editors of quality magazines like *Harper's* and the *Century*. Matthews disregarded the satirical tales and the colloquies.

Earlier critics neglected to study what P called the "undercurrent of meaning" which now often seems as important as the more obvious "single effect." What our generation sees in the tales is well described by Roy Male (*American Literary Masters*, 1965): "P's themes and fictional situations speak directly to us in our oft-analyzed Age of Anxiety: the threatened disintegration of the self, the encounter with Nothingness, the faceless Man of the Crowd, the dread of being buried alive in underground shelters." In "P's Gothic Waste Land" (*SR* 62) S. L. Mooney developed the thesis that out of "plot-ruses and character-disguises, secret crimes and immolations, pseudo-science and reincarnation theories, P fashioned ironic images of man in a nineteenth-century age of anxiety which derive from Gothicism and forecast the twentieth century waste land as a theme for literature."

New light has been thrown upon some of the tales by scholars who have studied them with a meticulous attention to detail. One of the most significant of such studies is "The Question of P's Narrators" (*CE* 63), in which J. W. Gargano demonstrated that P's narrators are not to be identified with the author; they differ from one another in traits and attitudes, and they characterize themselves by their speech.

The numerous revisions that P made in his poems have been carefully studied, but until recently not much attention has been paid to the changes he made in his tales. A good example is G. R. Thompson, " 'The Oval Portrait': A Reconsideration of P's Revisions" (*ELN* 68). In "P's 'Metzengerstein': Not a Hoax" (*AL* 71) B. F. Fisher finds no evidence of a satirical intention in the earliest version of the tale. In "P Recognizes 'Ligeia' as His Masterpiece" Ruth Hudson noted that in revising the tale P transferred from "The Assignation," "Bon-Bon," "Bernice," and other stories "favorite details and images" to enrich the story which he had written at "the peak of his creative vigor as a talewriter" (*English Studies in Honor of J. C. Wilson*, 1951).

In the space allotted to me I can discuss only a few significant examples of the various interpretations of the poems and tales. I begin with "Ligeia," which P considered his best story. In his Centenary article G. B. Shaw wrote: "The story of the Lady Ligeia is not merely one of the wonders of literature. It is unparalleled and unapproached. There is really nothing to be said about it: we others simply take off our hats and let Mr. P go first." In *A Manual of the Art of Fiction* (1918) Clayton Hamilton included a useful classroom analysis of "Ligeia" modeled upon "The Philosophy of Composition." In "P and Phrenology" (AL 30) Edward Hungerford showed that P had used the terminology of a popular pseudo-science to point up Ligeia's will to live and her gift for languages. In "The Interpretation of 'Ligeia' " (CE 44; *Sex, Symbolism, and Psychology*, 1948) R. P. Basler maintained that the tale is not to be interpreted as a story of the supernatural but as a study of "the *idée fixe* of obsession in an extreme form of monomania." After Ligeia dies the narrator's obsession becomes "an intense megalomania motivated by his will to restore her to life" in the body of the second wife (whom he has murdered) "through a process of metempsychosis." In "A Misreading of P's 'Ligeia' " (PMLA 61) James Schroeter maintained that Basler had given an inaccurate account of what actually happens in the story. (See Basler's rebuttal and Schroeter's reply in PMLA 62). Jacobs, who accepts Basler's interpretation, comments, ". . . Mr. Basler's reading of the tale is close to P's concept of the proper use of terror in fiction, whereas Richard Wilbur's recent symbolic interpretation is not" (P: J&C, p. 213 n.). Stovall, however, feels that Jacobs' interpretation "does little credit to P's ingenuity or his artistic intelligence" (GaR 70). Jacobs sees P's tales as " 'Arabesque,' heavily pictorial, with characters who represent ideas, not human beings. . . . His women are . . . art objects" (p. 451).

The ablest of our critics and scholars disagree as to what actually happens in "The Fall of the House of Usher" as well as in "Ligeia." This is especially disconcerting in the case of an author who wrote in "Marginalia," "For my own part, I have never had a thought which I could not set down in words, with even more distinctness than that with which I conceived it. . . ." Are these great stories to be classed as "psychal" fancies, "the shadows of shadows," "to which *as yet*," wrote P, "I have found it absolutely impossible to adapt language?" For D. H. Lawrence "All this underground vault business only symbolizes that which takes place *beneath* the consciousness." Richard Wilbur suggested that the story of Roderick Usher is to be understood "as a dream of the narrator's." Jacobs sees "Usher" as "a tableau, the illustration of an idea, in which the symbolic significance of scene is just as important as the sequence of events" (P: J&C, p. 165).

In *Supernatural Horror in Literature* (1945) H. P. Lovecraft noted that "Usher" "hints shudderingly of obscure life in inorganic things, and displays an abnormally linked trinity of entities as the end of a long and isolated family history—a brother, his twin sister, and their incredibly ancient house all sharing a single soul and meeting one common dissolution at the same moment" (p. 58). In *Understanding Fiction* (1943) Brooks and Warren maintained that

"The horror is relatively meaningless—it is generated for its own sake; and one is inclined to feel that P's own interest in the story was a morbid interest." In "A Reinterpretation of 'Usher' " (*CL* 52) Leo Spitzer attacked the Brooks-Warren interpretation and suggested that the tale is a study of the psychological consequences of fear. The vampire motif, which Lawrence had hinted at, was developed by L. H. Kendall, Jr., in "The Vampire Motif in 'Usher' " (*CE* 65) and by J. O. Bailey in "What Happens in 'Usher' " (*AL* 64). E. W. Carlson, who has compiled a case study of the tale, maintains that to think of "Usher" and "Ligeia" only in terms of "black magic" and "female vampirism" is "to miss their real import."

Until recent years not much attention was paid to P's humorous tales. They were discussed, however, in W. F. Taylor's "Israfel in Motley" (*SR* 34) and in Constance Rourke's *American Humor* (1931). See also S. L. Mooney, "The Comic in P's Fiction" (*AL* 62); Terence Martin, "The Imagination at Play: EAP" (*KR* 66); and the Introduction to *Histoires grotesques et sérieuses* (1966), edited by Roger Asselineau. In his Introduction to *Tales of EAP* (1927) and in "The Devil Was in It" (*AM* 31) J. S. Wilson discussed the early tales and pointed out that Woodberry and other critics had failed to see that some of these tales were "satirical burlesques of the familiar styles and themes of his day." See also Mabbott, "On P's 'Tales of the Folio Club' " (*SR* 28) and Hubbell, "The Apprenticeship of EAP" (*SLJ* 69). Later studies of the humorous tales have thrown new light upon the objects of P's satire. See, for example, G. E. Gerber, "P's Odd Angel" (*NCF* 68); B. R. Pollin, "P's 'Diddling': The Source of Title and Tale" (*SLJ* 69); and three articles in *PN* (69) by E. R. Kanjo, Eliot Glassheim, and Claude Richard.

P's only book-length story, *The Narrative of Arthur Gordon Pym* (1838), was not a commercial success, and P once referred to it as a "very silly book." Few English or American critics had any praise for it before Malcolm Cowley called the conclusion the finest single passage in P's prose writings ("Aidgarpo," *NR* 45). And yet Henry James, who branded P's poems as "very valueless verses," had written in *The Golden Bowl* (1904) that "the story of the shipwrecked Gordon Pym" was "a wonderful tale . . . a tale to show . . . what imagination Americans *could* have. . . ."

In America contemporary interest in *Pym* dates from 1950 when Auden reprinted it in full in *EAP: Selected Prose and Poetry*. It is, he maintained:

one of the finest adventure stories ever written, [and it] is an object lesson in the art. Every kind of adventure occurs—adventures of natural origin like shipwreck; adventures like mutiny, caused by familiar human beings, or, like the adventures on the island, by strange natives; and, finally, supernatural nightmare events—yet each leads credibly into the next.

Two years later P. F. Quinn published in *KR* his impressive article "P's Imaginary Voyage" (also in *The French Face of EP*, 1957), in which, taking his cue from Gaston Bachelard, he interpreted what he regarded as the "undercurrent of meaning" in the story, which, he said, "is so strangely marked by conflicts of a very evident sort—between man and man, and between man and nature—is also charged by an incessant struggle between reality and appearance. Pym is caught up in a life in which nothing is stable, in which nothing is ever really known" (p. 181). Wagenknecht, however, has expressed a doubt as to the ability of *Pym* to "bear all the significance" the critics "would read into it" (*EAP: The Man Behind the Legend*, p. 248). In their "Chartless Voyage: The Many Narratives of *Pym*" (*TSLL* 66) J. V. Ridgely and I. S. Haverstick maintained that P planned the story as a hoax; that "the book has only a spurious unity"; and that "the story lacks a controlling theme and has no uncontrovertible serious meaning."

In addition to the various sailors' and travelers' narratives that P made use of (see Robbins' *Checklist*), P also used Jane Porter's novel, *Sir Edward Seaward's Narrative of His Shipwreck*, as Randel Helms pointed out in "Another Source for *Pym*" (*AL* 70). Just how much do the many sources that P used really mean? Certainly P. F. Quinn was right in saying, "It is as true of P as of any writer worth reading that his work cannot be reduced to the materials he started from and the hints he used."

6. The Colloquies; *Eureka*

Before 1952 when Allen Tate published "The Angelic Imagination: P as God" (*KR* 52), not much attention had been paid to the colloquies. Of "The Colloquy of Monos and Una" he remarked: "P's critics . . . have not read it. When they refer to it, it is to inform us that P was a reactionary Southerner who disliked democracy and industrialism." These cosmic fantasies are poetic dialogues in the tradition that goes back to Plato. When "Monos and Una" was printed in 1841, the Millerites were predicting the imminent end of the world. Poe, however, was less interested in eschatology than in expressing his ideas of God, nature, and man and his convictions about the corrupt state of American society. Although the colloquies do deal with death and destruction, they lend themselves to another interpretation, as E. W. Carlson has shown in "P's Vision of Man" (paper read at MLA in Dec. 69). He finds in *Eureka* and the colloquies a central unifying theme which "is not simply death and destruction but rather the spiritual rebirth and rediscovery of the lost psychal power essential to every man and artist seeking the fullest self-realization."

In 1950 when Auden reprinted *Eureka*, he was impressed by P's "very daring and original notion to take the oldest of the poetic themes . . . the story of how things came to exist as they are . . . [and to attempt] in English in the nineteenth century what Hesiod and Lucretius had done in Greek and Latin centuries before." Auden noted also that *Eureka* "combines nearly all of P's characteristic obsessions . . . in [a] poem of which the prose is as lucid, as untheatrical, as the best of his critical prose." Twenty-nine years earlier, in a foreword to Baudelaire's translation of *Eureka*, Valéry had praised it as "an abstract poem, one of the rare modern examples of a total explanation of the material and spiritual universe, a *cosmogony*."

There are troublesome ambiguities in *Eureka* of the kind that foreign critics like Baudelaire and Valéry were likely to overlook. In the words of S. L. Mooney, "Behind all of P's doors lurks the ghost of the hoaxer, secretly working toward the construction of fantastic ironies to plague the literalist" (*MLN* 61). In the first of several articles, "Ham, Bacon, Ram, and Other 'Savans' in *Eureka* . . ." (*PN* 69), H. R. Holman has shown that the satiric passages bulk much larger than is generally thought. She finds P mocking "the sagacity of the greatest and most justly reverenced of men"—some two dozen of them. "The common denominator of the group," she suggests, is that "they are pretenders to learning, either encyclopedists and universalists or, by contrast, fools." They are in general the kind of people P had ridiculed earlier: scientists, economists, Transcendentalists, Emerson, Carlyle, the Mills, father and son, etc. P, like Mark Twain, found it difficult to resist the temptation to mingle burlesque with serious writing. Holman concedes that much of P's satire may be regarded as "window-dressing . . . piling up names like shoddy goods half-displayed in a thieves' market to gull the unwary." Perhaps it is still possible to agree with Tate that *Eureka* contains "great passages of expository prose . . . unsurpassed in their kind in the nineteenth century."

V. CONCLUSION

In "The State of P Studies" (*PN* 68) J. A. Robbins expressed sharp disagreement with the view found in E. H. Davidson's *P* (1957) that P was "the most thoroughly and intelligently investigated writer in American literature."

Oh, there is [Robbins conceded] no shortage of books and articles on P. They flow in a steady stream year after year—journalistic and rehashed biographies, more often than not; source studies (useful but not definitely illuminating) and critical hunches (some useless, some interesting, a few significant). On rare occasions a truly significant article or book appears, but the total effect is pathetic.

P's peers, the other major writers included in *8AmA* (1956), had all, Robbins suggested, fared better than P. Even more than Melville or Whitman, P continues to attract amateur critics with fixed ideas and dubious theories which lead them to disregard known facts and are of little value to anyone who would understand the mind of a writer so complex as P's.

A history of P scholarship and criticism would reveal much prejudice and ill will among those who wrote about his life and writings. Griswold, English, and Clark hated and libeled him; Mrs. Whitman and Ingram detested Griswold; and Woodberry thought that Ingram was not to be trusted. In the early 1930's the late Lewis Chase, whose literary passions were Chivers and P, said to me, "The last time I saw Mary Phillips she said: 'I am sharpening my claws for Hervey Allen!' "

Today we have perhaps no living P scholar so able or so fully committed as Campbell or Mabbott; but there are some 20 or more men and women who are making substantial contributions to P scholarship. They appear willing to cooperate in order to provide the basic materials that biographers and critics must have. These scholars are fortunate that since April 1968 they have had in *PN* an organ which provides reviews of books, checklists, notes, queries, and helpful suggestions.

In "Scholarly Strategy: The P Case" (*AQ* 65) Stuart Levine emphasized the feebleness and scattered nature of our published research. It was high time, he felt, that in the humanities scholars were emulating the scientists, who systematically build upon the published findings of other scientists. In the first number of *PN* the editor commended Levine's suggestion and indicated that while he would not "try to act as a final arbiter on the proper 'cumulative' value of any particular P study," *PN* would not hesitate to suggest "the direction in which major efforts might go and to support such efforts . . . ."

Cooperative effort among scholars can give us better texts and better editions; it can correct factual errors; and it can perhaps keep some able scholars from spending their time on subjects that have little importance. A group of competent scholars can produce an invaluable bibliography or something approximating a definitive edition of an author's writings; but is it possible for more than two competent and congenial scholars to produce a first-rate critical study or a great biography? In the past such books have been almost invariably the work of individual, devoted scholars willing year after year to give their days and nights to the study of the life and writings of an author whom they admired and loved. Still one must remember that Campbell, Quinn, and Mabbott never hesitated to acknowledge their great indebtedness to all those who had contributed anything important to the understanding of the man and his writings.

The young scholar who feels that only trivial or unattractive subjects remain to be investigated needs to be reassured. There are important topics that have not been adequately studied, and there are obsolescent studies which need to be done over in the light of new materials and changed critical points of view. Anyone who hopes to contribute something substantial to P scholarship will need to employ both new and traditional methods of research and criticism.

We need better to understand P's critical vocabulary; his conception of genius, originality, and plagiarism; the reasons for the revisions he made in the tales; and his policies as editor of four different magazines in three different cities. A glance at the checklists will show that in recent years scholars have paid little attention to such poems as "Annabel Lee" and "The Conqueror Worm" and have had little to say about "Eleanora," "The Man of the Crowd," and the colloquies. We need to pay more attention to P's uncollected reviews and to "Marginalia," which Matthiessen described as "that magnificently fertile series of suggestions on literary method." There is need for further research into P's reputation and influence both in the United States and the many other countries where his name is known. In particular, we know too little about his influence upon American writers from the time of Fitz-James O'Brien to that of Conrad Aiken. There is need also for a detailed study of P criticism abroad and at home, especially since 1909.

It would be useful to have in hand a new volume of critical essays written by academic critics, who do not figure prominently in recent collections. I would like to see brought together in one volume the many poems written about P from the time of Stoddard's "Miserrimus" to that of Vachel Lindsay's "The Wizard in the Street" and Hart Crane's "The Bridge." Since we do not know just what effect the various misconceptions of the poet had upon his biographers and critics, it would be useful to have for P a book comparable to R. P. Basler's *The Lincoln Legend*. I should like to see for P such a compilation as Simon Nowell-Smith's *The Legend of the Master*. Such a book would contain descriptions of P written by friends and enemies, and it should show us what sort of lecturer he was and tell us how he read his poems. We need to have in one volume the various portraits and daguerreotypes done by those who saw the man and also some of the portraits done since his death. The book should be done with the meticulous attention to details that one finds in J. D. Ferguson's "Charles Hine and His Portrait of P" (*AL* 32). Elsewhere (*SLJ* 69)

I have suggested the need for a study of the part that the dual personality or the divided self plays in the poems and tales. What did P know about the "doctrine of Identity as urged by Schelling" to which he referred in "Morella"? Was P aware that there was something of the divided self in his own personality?

We need to know more about P's relations with other writers, women as well as men, the obscure as well as those whose names are in every history of American literature. *The Raven and the Whale* gave us an illuminating picture of P's New York, but there is no comparable book for Philadelphia, Baltimore, or Richmond. Some scholar with a talent for portraiture should bring to life attractive personalities like J. P. Kennedy, J. B. Latrobe, and William Wirt and thus help us to see more clearly the obscure Baltimore background from which P emerged in 1833. For the Philadelphia period we need to understand better P's relations with Burton, Graham, Godey, Griswold, and Thomas. These figures are all too dimly seen in the standard biographies. We know too little about P's Richmond associates in the *SLM* period: White, Heath, Minor, Tucker, and P. P. Cooke; and we need to know more about J. R. Thompson, J. M. Daniel, and J. E. Cooke, who knew him only in the late 1840's. Some of the men whom I have named have a literary importance in their own right, notably Kennedy and the Cooke brothers. D. K. Jackson, Agnes Bondurant, and R. D. Jacobs have contributed to our knowledge of P's Virginia background, but there are still little-used materials such as the Galt Papers in the Duke University Library. One would like to know more about P's teachers and school friends, especially J. T. L. Preston and Robert Stanard. Preston wrote to Ingram that his mother (a Randolph) had read P's boyish verses and encouraged him to continue to write; yet she is a blank in the standard biographies. Frances Valentine Allan and her sister Nancy have been sentimentalized out of all resemblance to the women to whom the poet owed most in his formative years. And just what kind of man was John Allan, and why is it that P's letters were always addressed not to Mrs. Allan but to "Pa"?

Not many of the topics that I have suggested constitute suitable subjects for doctoral dissertations—upon which our scholarship depends rather heavily —but they will, I hope, attract competent scholars, young and old, who have a keen sense of critical values. For P's life and writings offer to the investigator the abiding satisfaction which comes from the study of a fascinating personality and a major American writer.

RALPH WALDO EMERSON[1]

Floyd Stovall

I. BIBLIOGRAPHY

Bibliographies of Emerson (hereafter E or RWE), though not all that one might wish, are adequate and generally accessible. G. W. Cooke's *Bibliography of RWE* (1908, 1966) is an indispensable guide to editions and to biographical and critical works, including a number of contemporary reviews of E's books, up to the date of its original publication. Jacob Blanck's *BAL*, Vol. III (1959), should be consulted as the latest authority. The section on E is in three parts: I, original publications; II, reprinted material including collections and separate publications issued under the author's name; III, books by authors other than E which contain material reprinted from his earlier books. H. R. Steeves compiled the bibliography in *CHAL* (1917), which is selective but is intended to include all publications of importance that appeared during the years intervening since Cooke. The American Art Association catalogue of the *Stephen H. Wakeman Collection of Books of Nineteenth Century American Writers* (1924) contains much useful and interesting bibliographical information, though the book titles listed can doubtless be more conveniently seen elsewhere.

A supplemental bibliography prepared by R. A. Booth and Roland Stromberg (*BB* 48) is intended specifically to fill the gap between Cooke and 1920, the first year covered by Lewis Leary's volume, *AAL* (1947). A new edition, corrected and greatly expanded, was published in 1954 covering 1900–1950, and a further edition covering 1951–67 appeared in 1970. J. R. Bryer and R. A. Rees compiled *A Checklist of E Criticism, 1951–1961* (*ESQ* 64), which contains 420 items, annotated and indexed; also, K. W. Cameron published a supplementary list as "Current Bibliography" in *ESQ* through 1968. *AL*

1. Professor Stovall and the editor wish to acknowledge gratefully the help of Professor Elinore Partridge of the University of Wisconsin at Milwaukee, who read, corrected, and suggested additions for this essay. Her own contribution to Emerson scholarship, which is not reviewed in this chapter, is "Emerson: A Stylistic Analysis of His Prose" (1970), a dissertation written at the University of California at Davis.

contains quarterly and *PMLA* annual bibliographies. Selective bibliographies by T. H. Johnson in *LHUS* (1948, 1964) and F. I. Carpenter in his *E Handbook* (1953) are excellent. For dissertations see James Woodress's *DAL* (1968) and the lists of "Research in Progress" published quarterly in *AL*.

In *E's Reviewers and Commentators: Nineteenth-Century Periodical Criticism* (1968), W. J. Sowder provides a biographical and bibliographical analysis of nineteenth-century British periodical criticism.

An extensive manuscript collection owned by the RWE Memorial Association, including the unpublished journals, a large number of letters to E, lectures, sermons, and a typed volume of notations found in the books of E's library, is deposited in the Houghton Library of Harvard University. Some of these materials are now being published (see II below). Persons wishing to examine these manuscripts should write in advance for permission to Mr. William H. Bond, Houghton Library, Harvard University.

II. EDITIONS

E has been fortunate in his editors, and his works have now for most of this century been available in the excellent Centenary Edition in 12 volumes (1903–04), edited by his son, Edward Waldo Emerson. It has extensive notes and a useful index. It is based upon the 12-volume Riverside Edition, edited by J. E. Cabot (1884), which in turn was based on collected editions of 1869, 1876, and 1881, which had the benefit of E's personal supervision. Both Cabot, E's literary executor, and Edward Waldo Emerson, though not literary scholars in the present limited sense of the term, were well fitted for the work they accomplished. However, these "complete" editions have since been supplemented by several volumes, and others are to come. In 1912 C. C. Biglow edited *The Uncollected Writings: Essays, Addresses, Poems, Reviews, and Letters by RWE*, which contains 54 items altogether, mostly short. In 1938 A. C. McGiffert in *Young E Speaks* edited 25 of E's sermons, chosen from approximately 170 manuscript sermons available. His introduction and notes throw much light on the intellectual development of E during the critical years from 1826 to 1836. A list of all sermons is appended.

Three of E's college compositions not in his collected works have been made available. In 1896 E. E. Hale edited two essays, "The Character of Socrates" and "The Present State of Ethical Philosophy," written respectively in 1820 and 1821 in competition for the Bowdoin Prize. In 1954 K. W. Cameron edited E's college poem "Indian Superstition," with an introductory essay and notes on "E's Orientalism at Harvard." This was reprinted in *ESQ* (63).

Some of E's lectures are printed in the Centenary Edition, and many others are summarized in an appendix of Cabot's *Memoir*. Still others are listed by Cabot for which no manuscript copies were available. Some of these were reported, with summaries, in contemporary newspapers, and have been found and reprinted. Jeanne Kronman edited "Three Unpublished Lectures of RWE" (*NEQ* 46), and Clarence Gohdes edited a volume made up of newspaper reports of *Uncollected Lectures* in 1933. Of these lectures, Gohdes states that the newspaper accounts are full in two of the seven reported lectures and contain material not available elsewhere. Two volumes of E's *Early Lectures*, edited by S. E. Whicher, R. E. Spiller, and W. E. Williams, have been published; Vol. I, covering the years 1833–36, in 1959, and Vol. II, 1836–38, in 1964. A third volume is projected including lectures through 1847. Each volume contains an introduction, variant readings, notes, bibliography, and index. William Charvat's "A Chronological List of E's American Lecture Engagements" (*BNYPL* 60–61; repr. as pamphlet, 1961) lists approximately 1,500 lectures. K. W. Cameron has published *A Commentary on E's Early Lectures (1833–1836)* with an index-concordance (1961). Those interested in E's sermons may wish to consult Cameron's "History and Biography in E's Unpublished Sermons" (*PAAS* 56) and his *Index-Concordance to E's Sermons* (1963).

E's basic writings have been printed several times in cheap editions, and there have been numerous volumes of selections. K. W. Cameron's facsimile edition of *Nature* (1940) has interesting notes on the text, and there are other facsimile and critical editions of this essay, edited by Warner Berthoff (1968) and M. M. Sealts and A. R. Ferguson (1969). C. D. Mead has edited E's "*The American Scholar*" (1970), which includes the text of the essay as well as essays in criticism. F. I. Carpenter's *E* (AWS, 1934) is still of interest to scholars. The *Essays* have been frequently reprinted, and since 1892 the poems have been available at modest prices in the one-volume Household Edition.

G. S. Hubbell's convenient and dependable concordance of the poems (1932, 1967) is based on the text of Vol. IX of the Centenary Edition.

Ten volumes of selected material from the manuscript journals, edited by E. W. Emerson and W. E. Forbes, were published in 1909–14 in a format uniform with the Centenary Edition of the *Works*. The editors state that they have omitted much that had been incorporated by E in his essays and other materials of little significance, but that they have included "the greater part of the contents" of the journals. Now, however, a new and complete unexpurgated edition, projected in 16 volumes, of *The Journals and Miscellaneous*

Notebooks is being published, edited with authority and modern techniques by W. H. Gilman, A. R. Ferguson, and others. So far eight volumes of this edition have been published. For those who do not require the full text of the published journals, Bliss Perry's *The Heart of E's Journals* (1926) may be consulted. The original of one of E's "lost" journals, printed in the new edition of the journals from a transcript, has recently been found. See John Broderick's "E and Moorfield Storey: A Lost Journal Found" (*AL* 66).

E's correspondence has received a good deal of attention and is now available in great quantity, though not yet in completeness. R. L. Rusk's edition of the *Letters of RWE* in six large volumes (1939) contains all the letters known to him at the time which were available for publication, with the exception of about 200 previously published, and has a calendar of other letters both published and unpublished. The text is a literal printing from the original manuscripts or reproductions of them, without corrections. The editor's introduction is a biographical and critical essay based on information available in the letters. His notes are a mine of useful information and his index is a model. The letters not here published are listed among the printed letters in their chronological order, where they are described, and, if they have been published elsewhere, bibliographical reference is made to that fact.

Among the collections of E letters needed to supplement Rusk's edition, *The Correspondence of Thomas Carlyle and RWE, 1834–1842* is the most important. It was edited by C. E. Norton and published in two volumes in 1883. In 1888 a revised edition was issued containing 13 additional letters. A new edition in one volume (1964), edited by Joseph Slater, restores the passages omitted in the Norton editions and provides a bibliography and index that are very helpful. Slater's extensive introductory essays are both informative and critically illuminating. Less important, but very useful, is *A Correspondence between John Sterling and RWE*, edited by E. W. Emerson (1897), with a brief account of the circumstances leading up to the correspondence. Of special interest as illustrations of the character of E's friendship with younger men are *Letters from RWE to a Friend, 1838–1853*, edited by C. E. Norton (1899). The friend was Samuel Gray Ward. In this connection should be mentioned also *Correspondence between RWE and Herman Grimm*, edited by F. W. Holls, originally published in 1903 in the *Atl* and reprinted in book form the same year; and the *E-Clough Letters*, edited by H. F. Lowry and R. L. Rusk (1934). *Records of a Lifelong Friendship, 1807–1882*, edited by H. H. Furness (1910), contains the correspondence of E and W. H. Furness. "The E-Thoreau Correspondence," edited by F. B. Sanborn

(*Atl* 1892), includes interesting letters written while E was editor of the *Dial* and others written while he was in Europe in 1847–48.

Since the publication of Rusk's edition, numerous letters have been published in *AL*, *ESQ*, *HLB*, and other periodicals. E. M. Tilton is editing an edition in three or four volumes of the "Additional Letters of E," perhaps 1800, together with a checklist of all known and probable letters, with annotations. The date of publication is uncertain, perhaps 1973.

"E's Translation of Dante's *Vita Nuova*," edited by J. C. Mathews, with annotations, was originally published in *HLB* 57. It was reprinted in book form in 1960 and again in 1966.

A new edition of *The Works of RWE* is being prepared under the aegis of the Center for Editions of American Authors, in ten to 12 volumes. A. R. Ferguson is general editor. Vol. I is scheduled for publication in 1971, but the entire edition will not be ready for several years. C. F. Strauch's edition of the poems, on which he has been working for some time, will be made part of the new edition of the *Works*.

III. BIOGRAPHY

There was little biographical writing on E until after his death in 1882. It is true that G. W. Cooke's *RWE: His Life, Writings, and Philosophy* (1881) has about 200 pages of biography, but it is based exclusively on published materials and is intended, as the author states, merely as a background of biographical facts for the discussion of E's ideas. The first book-length biography was that of O. W. Holmes (1885, 1968); it is valuable to the modern reader chiefly as it reflects the friendly but somewhat skeptical Bostonian attitude toward E at the time of his death. It also has interesting information about E's immediate family, most of whom were known to Holmes.

The best early biography, and still an indispensable primary source, is *A Memoir of RWE* (2 vols., 1887), by E's literary executor and authorized biographer, J. E. Cabot. Though a personal friend of E, Cabot wrote an unbiased and thoroughly dependable biography, consisting largely of extracts from the journals and letters then in manuscript, together with many personal reminiscences of Cabot and other contemporaries. The appendices contain a list of E's contributions to the *Dial*, valuable letters, and a chronological list of E's lectures and addresses, with summaries of many not available in substance in E's published works.

Others who knew E personally contributed, during the 1880's and later, many reminiscences and impressions which have supplemented Cabot's *Memoir*. M. D. Conway's *E at Home and Abroad* (1882, 1968) is a treasury of delightful anecdotes, some from books, some from letters, and some from conversations with E and others, including, no doubt, a deal of gossip and rumor. Alexander Ireland's *In Memoriam: RWE* (1882) records his recollections of E's visits to England in 1833, 1847–48, and 1872–73, with extracts from unpublished letters. In the same year this book was largely augmented with an extended biographical introduction, and it was republished as *RWE: His Life, Genius, and Writings*. J. B. Thayer's *A Western Journey with E* (1884) describes a trip by rail which E made, in a party of 12 persons, to California in 1871. D. G. Haskins' *RWE: His Maternal Ancestors* (1886) is worth mentioning for its firsthand reminiscences of E's mother and father during their first married years and the childhood of E. More important is E. W. Emerson's *E in Concord* (1889), an intimate, firsthand account of E's private life by his son, who supplements his recollections with extracts from the journals. Much of this material is incorporated in later biographies. Three books afford valuable insight into E's remarkable influence on younger men. John Albee's *Remembrances of E* (1901) relates to the 1850's; C. J. Woodbury's *Talks with E* (1890) covers the 1860's; and F. B. Sanborn's *The Personality of E* (1903), the most important of the three, gives the author's impressions on visiting E when he was a college student, and again later when he was the teacher of E's children, and reports many of E's conversations with him and other persons through many years.

There was no further full-length biographical study of E based on original sources for half a century, though there were some good biographical studies based on these earlier sources. Richard Garnett's *Life* (1888) was based chiefly on Cabot but contains some appreciative criticism; and G. E. Woodberry's *RWE* (1907, 1968) was based on Cabot's *Memoir* and such additional records as those named above. Yet Woodberry's is, for the general reader, a very satisfactory biography. It is scholarly and yet very readable; it is not wholly sympathetic, yet it is fair; and his last chapter is a fine characterization. Of later biographies, D. J. Snider's (1921) attempts to co-ordinate E's life with his intellectual development according to a logical scheme; Phillips Russell's (1929) gives a readable account of the facts of E's life but hardly justifies its subtitle, "The Wisest American," since it does not enter deeply into a discussion of his ideas; and V. W. Brooks's (1932) has the charm of E's own style, in addition to the considerable gifts of the biographer, for it is largely presented in the language of the journals. Its impressionistic manner holds the reader's interest and gives him the sense of reality, with many side glances at personalities, places, and moods of the time. One misses specific dates and the orderly progression of events. André Bruel's *E et Thoreau* (Paris, 1929) deals justly with the growing coolness between E and Thoreau during the 1850's, following their earlier intimacy, and Townsend Scudder's *Lonely Wayfaring Man* (1936) is an entertaining account of E's visits to England and his relations with Carlyle based on a fresh examination of the original sources. H. H. Hoeltje tells the story of the friendship of E and Alcott in *Sheltering Tree* (1943, 1965), often in the language of the diaries and other original sources. *RWE* by O. W. Firkins (1915, 1965) and *E Today* by Bliss Perry (1931, 1969) have some biographical materials, but they are primarily works of criticism and will be discussed in that category. Biographies written by foreigners are not likely to provide the American student with values which he cannot more readily come at in English, but he may find different points of view. One of the best books on E by a foreigner, though it is not primarily biographical, is Marie Dugard's *RWE: sa vie et son oeuvre* (Paris, 1907; rev. ed., 1913), a thorough and scholarly book. The author understands E, but her lack of sympathy with Transcendentalism inhibits her from doing what she often insists the critic must, viz., see E whole. Régis Michaud's *La vie inspirée d'E* (Paris, 1930; trans. and pub. in America also in 1930 as *E: the Enraptured Yankee*) is very readable but popular rather than scholarly in treatment.

The definitive biography is *The Life of RWE* (1949), by R. L. Rusk, the only detailed and thorough factual biography since Cabot's, and as such it will remain for many years an indispensable tool for all students of E. Rusk has made use of all published materials, including Cabot's biography, but he has also made a minute examination and analysis of the original manuscripts, particularly the manuscript journals, many of which are still unpublished. Although the book is mainly a factual account, as a good biography must be, there is enough of interpretative criticism to reveal E as a developing mind as well as an actual person in the midst of events. Considering the great condensation of materials, the biography is remarkably clear and readable. The work is thoroughly documented, and yet the reader who does not care for bibliographical details may read ahead without impediment of reference numbers or footnotes. It must be admitted that one who attempts to follow the author through his source materials will find the notes and bibliographical apparatus at first puzzling, but it can be done without vast trouble. Critics have found objections to the book: that E's personality is obscured by the multitude of facts; that it does not add as much as one might expect to an understanding of the structure of E's thought; that it is not brilliant or profound. Yet they have agreed that it is a complete and living portrait, that it is readable, and that it introduces us for the first time to the real and great E. It is an authoritative work, designed for the student, and more likely to be consulted for information than read for pleasure, though it is by no means barren of promise for the casual reader who comes to it conditioned by an interest in the subject.

Recent contributions to E biography have not been numerous. P. F. Jamieson's "E in the Adirondacks" (NYH 58) is an interesting narrative, especially if read in connection with E's poem "The Adirondacks." Josephine Miles's RWE (UMPAW, 1964) is an attempt to put E in a capsule and comes near succeeding. Two other small books recently published throw light on E's personal life. One First Love: The Letters of Ellen Louise Tucker to RWE, edited with an introduction by E. W. Gregg (1962), the granddaughter of E's daughter Edith, is a fitting memorial to the sweet sad story of Ellen Tucker E. There are 48 letters that survive. None of E's letters to her has survived. H. F. Pommer's E's First Marriage (1967) is the fullest account available of the life of Ellen Tucker and reveals in E a tenderness not often apparent to his friends of later years. K. W. Cameron's E, Thoreau, and Concord in Early Newspapers (1958) provides a source for biographical material in reprints of articles in contemporary newspapers.

IV. CRITICISM

It was through his character and personality that E made the strongest impression upon his own generation, but he survives into our own time primarily as a thinker and an artist, although his rank in both categories has been disputed. Much criticism is therefore to be found in the biographies, particularly in Cooke, Firkins, Woodberry, Dugard, and Rusk. Of works exclusively of criticism, there are, in general, three types: 1. the book-length study of varied aspects of E's works, 2. the general critical essay, and, 3. specialized studies, whether books or essays. It seems most convenient to organize the criticism under the following heads: 1. General Estimates, 2. Sources, 3. Philosophy, 4. Science, 5. Practical Affairs, 6. Aesthetics, and 7. Reputation and Influence. Since many of the books and essays discuss several aspects of E's work, it will be necessary sometimes to mention a critical work and discuss it in part under two or more of these heads.

1. General Estimates

For contemporary opinion of E there is no better resource than K. W. Cameron's *E Among His Contemporaries* (1967). This huge volume reproduces a large number of reviews of E's books, essays on his work, reminiscences, and tributes from friends and others dating from the 1840's to the end of the nineteenth century. It is literally a library of E criticism, and an excellent index increases its usefulness. Margaret Fuller wrote an appreciative review of E's essays for the *Tribune* (7 Dec. 1844; repr. by Mason Wade in *The Writings of Margaret Fuller*, 1941); but the most important early essay on E was written by Theodore Parker (*MQR* 1850; repr. in his *Works*, 1907), who calls him the most American of American writers, though he is also the most cosmopolitan. Thus the clear-eyed Unitarian minister sees at once what generations of critics, in America as well as in Europe, have not clearly seen; namely, that an American writer need be none the less American for belonging in the European tradition. E, he thinks, exaggerates the value of intuition and is defective in the power to organize his thought; yet he would rank him higher than any other writer since Milton. Less perceptive, Lowell ("E the Lecturer" in *My Study Windows*, 1871) remembers his personal charm and inspirational power over youthful minds, but is somewhat condescending in reference to E's lack of substance. A. B. Alcott in an essay written in 1865 and published as *RWE: An Estimate of His Character and Genius in Prose and Verse* (1882, 1968) sees that E is a realist as well as an idealist (as Lowell had seen too in *A Fable for Critics*, 1848), and that he is also at once a poet and moralist in the same class with Plutarch, Epictetus, Montaigne, Bacon. His only "subtraction" is that E is too impersonal. Another contemporary and friend of E, Henry James, Sr. (*Literary Remains*, 1885, and *Atl* 04), attributes E's authority to his character more than to his ideas; he brought his hearer, or reader, face to face with the infinite in humanity. Like many later critics, James could account for E's concept of evil only by supposing that he had no personal experience of it and therefore no conscience. Henry James, Jr., who reviewed the Carlyle-E *Correspondence* (*Century*, 1883) and Cabot's *Memoir* (*Macmillan's Mag* 1887; repr. in *Partial Portraits*, 1888), agreed in part with his father's opinion; he said that so far as evil was concerned E's eyes were "thickly bandaged," but that he had a faculty, never surpassed, for speaking to the soul in a voice of authority. Yet it seems obvious that Henry James, Jr., could find little in E to interest him and that, until after 1887, he never attempted seriously to understand him. Holmes and Woodberry, though sympathetic, did make an effort to understand E, yet both placed the value of his character above that of his ideas. Holmes thought he was very near an embodiment of his own ideal of humanity. Woodberry agreed and added that E embodied also the American spirit in his works and was himself "a shining example of it." This personal force Bliss Perry defined as the "emanation of spiritual energy." Yet he recognized the dynamic quality in E by calling him "the herald and attendant of change, the son and father of Revolution," and he rated him as "the only great mind that America has produced in literature." E. C. Stedman (*Poets of America*, 1885) has a balanced criticism of E, but he was among those who viewed E's writing in verse and prose as a means to an end, and that end not art but the "enfranchisement and stimulation of his people and his time."

British opinion of E in the nineteenth century was appreciative but always sharply critical. Carlyle's attachment was to E the man more than to E the Transcendental philosopher. Richard Garnett, his biographer and most appreciative British critic, thought that the "diffused beauty" in which his works lie "bathed" is ample recompense for his defects as an artist, and he saw that E was at one with the moral consciousness of the American nation. More objective appraisals were made by Matthew Arnold, Leslie Stephen, and John Morley, all eminently qualified to judge the worth of a man of letters. Arnold's essay in *Discourses in America* (1885) has been widely quoted, agreed with, and disagreed with. Arnold declared that E does not rank with the great men of letters (Plato, Bacon, Pascal, Swift, Voltaire) because his style does not have the "requisite wholeness of good tissue." He is not a great philosophical writer (like Aristotle, Spinoza, Kant) because he cannot build a philosophical system; his ideas have no evolution. He gives E high praise nevertheless. He is "the friend and aider of those who would live in the spirit," and his essays are the most important work done in prose in the nineteenth century. Leslie Stephen in *Studies of a Biographer*, Vol. IV (1902), while he condemns E's thought as too vague to have meaning or else meaning something which is "palpably absurd," yet assures us that E is worth reading because he is inspirational and because his optimism teaches us how to maintain a cheerful temper and make the best of things. John Morley's "E" in *Critical Miscellanies*, Vol. I (1904) finds fault with E's inconsecutive thought, his faulty diction and grammar, and his inability to appreciate the darker side of life. Yet he declares that he is among the most persuasive and inspiring of those who awaken us from the "deadening slumbers of convention and conformity" and lifts us up from "low thoughts and sullen moods of helplessness and impiety." Morley believes, and J. M. Robertson agrees ("E" in *Modern Humanists*, 1895), that

E's reaction against what is superficial in Locke and Hume blinded him to much besides that is sound and valuable. Robertson points out that E denied inspiration to analytic processes of thought and thus made the way easy for the bigot and the crank as well as for the seer. Yet he inclines to agree with Arnold that E wrote the most important prose of the nineteenth century, and he rates the poetry higher than Arnold.

But E has had strong defenders both as an artist and as a philosopher. J. J. Chapman ("E Sixty Years After," in *E and Other Essays*, 1898, 1909), after describing E's literary effects, says, "If the man who can do these things be not an artist, then must we have a new vocabulary and rename the professions." Yet he says the poetry is too intellectual and the prose is more effective because it is more emotional. Santayana in *Interpretations of Poetry and Religion* (1900) begins by saying that E is "not primarily a philosopher, but a puritan mystic with a poetic fancy," yet in the end he concludes, "If not a star of the first magnitude, he is certainly a fixed star in the firmament of philosophy." No other American, he thinks, has earned a place there. Though he denies the originality of E's thoughts, he praises the originality and beauty of their expression. William James, in an address at Concord on the centenary of E's birth (published the same year in a volume containing fifteen centenary addresses), declared that the matter and manner of E's expression are inseparable, and that if he must be defined in a word we must call him Artist; "He was an artist whose medium was verbal and who wrought in spiritual material." James says that the "headspring" of all his writing is that "the commonest person's act, if genuinely actuated, can lay hold of eternity"; and that for this truth, posterity will call him a prophet. Hugo Munsterberg, on the same occasion, declared that it was E's influence that brought him from his native Germany to America. The highest tribute by a philosopher to the philosophy of E was paid by John Dewey at an E memorial meeting in Chicago in 1903 (*Characters and Events*, 1929). Dewey charges that the critic who complains of E's lack of method simply "writes down his own incapacity to follow a logic that is finely wrought," and he affirms that he knows no writer "whose movement of thought is more compact and unified." In fact, Dewey calls E more than a philosopher, saying that he is "a maker rather than a reflector," a perceiver more than a reasoner. Yet he agrees in effect with William James that E is essentially an artist, though none the less a genuine philosopher; in fact, he calls him the Philosopher of Democracy. E, says Dewey, is "the one citizen of the New World fit to have his name uttered in the same breath with that of Plato." His final word is that the heart of E's philosophy is "the identity of Being, unqualified and immutable, with Character." A few years later another philosopher of a very different school, Josiah Royce, said in *William James and Other Essays on the Philosophy of Life* (1911) that there were then only three representative American philosophers, and they were Jonathan Edwards, E, and William James.

The critic W. C. Brownell, in his judicial appraisal of E in *American Prose Masters* (1909, 1963), says that he "has limitations but no infirmities." He proceeds to place him in the company of Plato and Pascal, of Shakespeare and Goethe. More specifically, he says that E's nature was "flooded with light, but it lacked heat"; and that his philosophy had elevation but not depth. Such antitheses sometimes lead Brownell to inconsistency and distortion, as when he says that E is not essentially religious because he is concerned with the mind yet calls him less the descendant of Erasmus than of Luther. He concludes with many others that E serves best as a stimulus, not a literal guide, for which he is too extreme a nonconformist. Yet in saying that E is the enemy of "culture" he is surely going too far. He adopts the view that the poems lack art and sentiment and are inferior to the essays. In general it may be said that his total estimate, which is very high, contradicts his detailed criticism, which finds many faults. John Macy says in *SAL* (1913) that E "gathers the wisdom of twenty sages into one discourse," but fails in his attempt to be a poet. P. E. More writes in *CHAL* (1917) that "Emersonianism may be defined as romanticism rooted in Puritan divinity." He repeats the complaint, originating with Lowell, that whereas E is the inspirer of youth, older men turn from him. In *MCAT* (1927, 1954) Parrington agrees that he was largely the product of the Romantic movement, yet he too recognizes the Puritan influence—"Roger Williams and Jonathan Edwards come to more perfect fruition." He classifies E as a Jeffersonian in politics. S. P. Sherman (*Americans*, 1922) sees E as a humanist bent upon liberating all the "properly human powers," and he extenuates E's apparent defects (lack of design, incoherence, etc.) as due to the excess of his virtues. The idea that E is one of the Romantics is pursued by Charles Cestre (*RAA* 29). It is a mistake, he thinks, to call E a pure intellectual; he was rather a mystic. Although H. W. Garrod (*Poetry and the Criticism of Life*, 1931) finds fault with Arnold for not exploring the hiding places of E's power, he agrees with him that E is a poet only in epigrams and that only his ardor saves him from triviality. But he agrees with William James that in his prose E is a verbal artist. Where Arnold found a disconnectedness in his sentences, Garrod finds a "diffused eloquence." In contrast with Parrington, H. S. Canby says in *Classic Americans* (1931) that when we think now of democracy, it is in terms of E, not Jefferson, of potentiality, not right. Though E valued the great inventors (like Goethe, Shakespeare, Sophocles), he himself,

Canby thinks, lacked invention, and this was his great weakness. In English belles-lettres, he concludes, E must take his place with Pope, not with Milton or Shakespeare.

But the twentieth century has witnessed another type of criticism, a wholesale condemnation and repudiation, which is unlike anything said of E since the first alarmed protests of the 1830's and 1840's. There have been chiefly two grounds for such repudiation. The first is his alleged shallow optimism, and the second is his alleged heretical and anarchic doctrine of self-reliance. J. T. Adams, in "E Re-Read" (*Atl* 30), revived the old complaint that E is not to be taken as a serious thinker. He has tried to reread E at 50 but finds it almost impossible, although he was stirred by him at 16. He is "amazed" at the "shallowness" of the essays. He cites E's estimates of Swedenborg and Alcott for the purpose of ridiculing his critical judgment. E's fatal weakness, according to Adams, is that he "makes life too easy by his insistence on intuition and spontaneity." The judgment of F. O. Matthiessen (*AmR*, 1941), though less severe, is that E, like his poet Saadi, is limited by the very virtues imputed to him—his cheerfulness and his resources against pain and failure—as if pessimism and skepticism might be proofs of spiritual strength.

In two esays, "E" and "The Puritan Heresy" (*H&H* 32), H. B. Parkes rejects E on the basis of a formal analysis of his thought. He returns to the argument of Orestes Brownson almost a century before that Transcendentalism is the logical end of all Protestantism and is the supreme heresy; it is "Edwardian Calvinism modified by European romanticism, French and German." It is marked by a refusal to accept authority, a tendency to obey impulse as the voice of God, a worship of enthusiasm, a belief in perfectibility in this world. He finds the source of E's error not in his mind so much as in his character; he was without a sense of evil, as Henry James, Sr., had said, and was hence led into the delusion that the soul is of the substance of God and untouched by original sin. Parkes reverted to the subject of E in *The Pragmatic Test* (1941) and *The American Experience* (1947) with somewhat milder judgments, but retracted nothing. Yvor Winters attacked E on the same logical and theological grounds. In *Maule's Curse* (1938) Winters states that E's central doctrine is the submission to emotion, which destroys all values and renders man an automaton. He concludes that E is "a fraud and a sentimentalist," and devalues him by comparing him unfavorably with Jones Very. Later, in an essay ostensibly concerned with Hart Crane (*In Defense of Reason*, 1947), Winters returns to the attack on E, asserting that his whole philosophy is based on the theory of natural goodness and reliance on irresponsible impulse.

F. I. Carpenter (*E Handbook*, 1953) shows on what grounds Parkes and

Winters may be answered, and with regard to the often-remarked dichotomies of E's philosophy (nature and the soul, law and impulse, etc.) Robert Spiller believes (*LHUS*, 1949) that E sets up a provisional dualism in order to explore the ultimate unity; the dualism is of method only. In this view, E's philosophy can be called anarchic only by ignoring his ideal of unity, his faith in the power of the Over-Soul to make itself felt in the individual. The extent of E's later compromise and withdrawal from an extreme optimism and self-confidence is explored and stated by S. E. Whicher in "E's Tragic Sense" (*ASch* 53). His conclusion that E was an extremist, that "he had to have entire assurance or he had none at all," is itself perhaps an extreme view, but the essay is valuable as a correction of the common misconception of E as a man of easy faith. The evidence of E's awareness of actuality and the means by which he reconciled the real with the ideal are shown by Sherman Paul in *E's Angle of Vision: Man and Nature in American Experience*, (1952). F. I. Carpenter, among others, has pointed out E's tendency towards pragmatism in the reconciliation of his apparent dualism in experience (Introduction to *E*, AWS, 1934). The prevailing pessimism of the last five decades in America has made E appear to many to be a naïve idealist merely. Others have attempted to show that E was aware of evil (see C. E. Jorgenson's "E's Paradise under the Shadow of Swords," *PQ* 32), and that his philosophy of power is not a denial of evil but an affirmation of the ability of man to cope with evil by building up his potential spiritual resources. It is recognized that the inspirational value of E cannot be saved in an age of skepticism without first restoring confidence in his common sense.

The general estimates of E and interest in his work have risen considerably during the last ten to 15 years, especially among academic critics, as the numerous articles in *ESQ* (founded in 1955) amply illustrate. But the movement goes beyond the E Society. A useful collection of critical and biographical essays is found in Carl Bode's edition of *RWE* (1969) for American Profiles. Newton Arvin in "The House of Pain" (*HudR* 59; repr. by Milton Konvitz and Stephen Whicher in *E: A Collection of Critical Essays*, 1962) affirms that E's "celebrated optimism" was not the product of good fortune or a native happy temperament, but "was an achievement both of intellectual and emotional discipline." R. L. Cook in "E and Frost: A Parallel of Seers" (*NEQ* 58) has shown that Frost has many qualities in common with E; and Frost himself (*Daedalus* 59; repr. in Konvitz and Whicher), while admitting that he thought E too Platonic about evil, named him along with Washington, Jefferson, and Lincoln as one of the four greatest Americans. In a stirring defense of E's value in an "existential age," Alexander Cowie called him "Still a Good Light to Guide By" (*NYTBR* 63; repr. *ESQ* 64). All admirers of E will be pleased to read in H. H. Waggoner's *American Poets from the Puritans to the Present* (1968) the opinion that E is central in American literary history. There are still some who do not accept this upward valuation. For example, Joel Porte in *E and Thoreau: Transcendentalists in Conflict* (1966) says that E was unable to feel grief, duplicity was his besetting sin, and he was driven to accept the Ideal theory because he found sense experience distasteful.

2. Sources

The main sources of E's thought are not difficult to discover and have often been pointed out, though there has been much disagreement on their relative importance. In broad terms they may be stated as follows: 1. New England Puritanism and related English thought of the seventeenth century; 2. Platonism especially in the form of Neoplatonism, and related ideas from Swedenborgianism; 3. European Romanticism as derived through the English Romantic poets and German Romantic philosophers, especially as the latter were interpreted by Coleridge; and 4. Orientalism, particularly the Hinduism of the sacred writings of ancient India. All of these were mentioned by Cooke in the critical biography of 1881. Stedman pointed out (*Poets of America*, 1885) that E "refined and digested what was good in all philosophies," and that his earliest and chiefest models were Plato and Plotinus. Stedman also cited E's debt to the English poetry of the seventeenth century and to the Persian Saadi and Hafiz. P. E. More (*CHAL*) expressed the view of many others in saying that he owed much to his New England background, to German thought through Coleridge and Carlyle, and to Greek philosophers and the poets and preachers of the English seventeenth century as they were interpreted in the light of the Romantic movement. Parrington associated E with the French Romantic school and with Jefferson. Spiller (*LHUS*) expresses a view now widely held in saying that E was essentially romantic by disposition, akin to Goethe and Coleridge, and that he was strongly influenced by Neoplatonism, German idealism, and Oriental mysticism, but that he never departed from the Christian tradition.

Comparatively little has been written specifically on the survival of early New England thought in E's mind because it was derived not so much from discoverable sources in his reading as from early religious teaching and his theological studies at Harvard. The most detailed study of this aspect of E's thought is to be found in Perry Miller's article "Edwards to E" (*NEQ* 40), in which he traces the pantheism and mysticism of E back through Edwards to an inherent tendency in orthodox Calvinism. One should consult in this connection also "E and Quakerism," by F. B. Tolles (*AL* 38), and Yukio Irie's *E and Quakerism* (Tokyo, 1967). His Puritanism and his Quaker tendencies had their roots in the English seventeenth century. For light on this relationship, see J. R. Roberts, "E's Debt to the Seventeenth Century" (*AL* 49). Roberts believes that the vitality and spirit of the English seventeenth century armed him against rationalism and expanded his idealism to the point where it broke through the limits of Unitarian dogma. This reading antedated E's reading of Coleridge and Carlyle. Another step towards these nineteenth-century contemporaries was by way of the Scottish philosophers, whom he read as college assignments and independently, and from whom he learned the distinction between the "moral sense" and the "affections." This is discussed by M. R. Davis in "E's 'Reason' and the Scottish Philosophers" (*NEQ* 44). The influence of the seventeenth century on E's poetry is discussed incidentally in several general criticisms, and more particularly by N. A. Brittin in "E and the Metaphysical Poets" (*AL* 36). Brittin shows that E was fond of all the metaphysical poets, but especially of George Herbert, to whom he says E shows a strong kinship. The next strongest influence he finds was that of Marvell. The American seventeenth century had no significant poetry (Taylor then being unknown) and E found the eighteenth-century literary fashions, whether in England or America, unattractive.

Strong as was the hold upon E of New England Puritanism, Platonism was the dominant influence upon his philosophy. The first book-length study of E's sources was J. S. Harrison's *The Teachers of E* (1910, 1966), which attempts "to show the essentially Platonic quality of E's thought," though it also deals less extensively with other sources. Harrison says E derived his Platonism chiefly from Thomas Taylor's translations of Plato and from the Neoplatonists, from Ralph Cudworth's *True Intellectual System of the Universe* (1820), from De Gerando's *Histoire comparée des systèmes de philosophie* (Paris, 1822–23), and from Coleridge, whose *Aids to Reflection* and *Friend* he read as early as 1829. A good account of Taylor's importance in the study of Plato by E and his contemporaries is given by G. M. Harper in his essay "Thomas Taylor in America" in the volume which he edited in collaboration with Kathleen Raine, *Thomas Taylor the Platonist* (1969). Taylor's identification of Platonism with Neoplatonism was, Harrison thinks, at first accepted by E, and not greatly questioned later when he had read Plato in the more accurate Bohn translation (1848). He says E's theory of opposites reconciled in the One, originally derived from the Neoplatonic interpretation of Pythagoreanism, was later confirmed by his reading of Victor Cousin. He derived most of the ideas in *Nature*, Harrison thinks, from Plato and the Neoplatonists and also the later idea that intellect has power to amend fate. His theory that art is the universal mind working through plastic nature was suggested by Cudworth, who quotes Plotinus. (In this connection see Vivian Hopkins, "E and Cudworth: Plastic Nature and Transcendental Art," *AL* 51, who develops this thesis in some detail.) Harrison wrote his book without the benefit of E's published journals, and while it is the basic work on E's Platonism, it must be supplemented by later studies. F. I. Carpenter thinks (*E and Asia*, 1930, 1968) that Harrison ascribed too great an importance to the influence of Platonism, pointing out that E had not read Taylor's translations when he wrote *Nature*, though he had read many excerpts from Platonists in Cudworth's volumes. It is Carpenter's opinion that Neoplatonic books formed an important but small fraction of his reading. S. G. Brown, however, agrees with Harrison that the essence of E's thinking is Platonic, though the taste of the time required him to disguise it in the cloak of German idealism and Oriental mysticism ("E's Platonism," *NEQ* 45). Many of the Neoplatonic ideas to be found in E may also be found in the writings of the Swedenborgians. Clarence Hotson has made an intensive study of E in relation to Swedenborg and the Swedenborgians (see "E and the Swedenborgians," *SP* 30; "Sampson Reed, a Teacher of E," *NEQ* 29; also numerous articles listed in *AAL*, 1954). Hotson thinks E became interested in Swedenborgian ideas through reading Sampson Reed's *Observations on the Growth of the Mind* (1826) and his later articles (1828 ff.) in the *New Jerusalem Magazine*, citing many passages from the *Journals* as evidence. He emphasizes especially the importance of Swedenborg's doctrine of correspondence in determining the thinking of E. Sherman Paul (*E's Angle of Vision*, 1952) thinks E had been working towards this idea before he knew Swedenborg's doctrine and that Channing had given him help in that direction. For evidence that E was influenced appreciably by other Greek writers, particularly by Aristotle's *Poetics* see J. P. Pritchard, *Return to the Fountains* (1942).

Though E, as noted by Stedman, drew from all philosophies, and though his own thinking was in the Platonic tradition, he was in fact, as P. E. More declared, a product of the Romantic movement as it manifested itself in New England in the early nineteenth century. Perry Miller's *The Transcendentalists* (1950) will prove useful in this connection, especially as background material for the early essays of E. H. C. Goddard (*Studies in New England Transcendentalism*, 1908) and H. D. Gray (*E*, 1917) agree that Schelling was a more stimulating if less continuous influence than the Platonists. Coleridge was E's most important helper in the formulation of his idealistic philosophy, and through him chiefly he knew the German idealists, particularly Schelling. Carlyle was his next best source of German thought. F. B. Wahr says in *E and Goethe* (1915) that E was comparatively ignorant of German ideas until he read Coleridge in 1829–30. Later he read all Goethe's works in German, which he learned for the purpose, but Wahr believes he read merely for corroboration, maintaining his independence of thought. In a later study, "E and the Germans" (*Monatshefte* 41), Wahr says that E was more or less familiar with the works, in translation chiefly, of Schiller, Herder, Lessing, Schlegel, and others, and with German idealistic philosophy from Kant to Hegel, but that the foundation of his thought was already laid in Plato and the Neoplatonists. René Wellek's "E and German Philosophy" (*NEQ* 43) is a careful study of the subject. Wellek says that aside from his secondhand knowledge through Coleridge, Carlyle, Cousin, and De Staël, E knew the Germans at first hand, including Böhme (though "E was no mystic") and Kant in the early years and Hegel later. He was chiefly interested in Kant's moral philosophy, Wellek thinks, and could not have penetrated very deeply into Kant's *Critique of Pure Reason* (though he owned a copy of the translation of 1838), since he misunderstands Kant after the fashion of Coleridge and Carlyle. He knew Leibniz, Fichte, and Schleiermacher but slightly; Schelling he knew much better, but chiefly through Coleridge. In this connection see also F. T. Thompson's two essays in *SP*, "E's Indebtedness to Coleridge" (26) and "E and Carlyle" (27). Thompson says E spent the autumn and winter following his European tour in "mastering Coleridge's interpretation of Kant's philosophy." He states that Coleridge was the means by which he bridged the gap between Platonism and Romanticism, and that this was done by 1834.

An article of some interest is J. O. McCormick's "E's theory of Human Greatness" (*NEQ* 53), where it is asserted that Coleridge gave sharpness and clarity to E's idealism, provided him with a method, and clarified for him the organic theory of art and the doctrine of correspondence between mind and nature. McCormick emphasizes the importance of Cousin in introducing E to the Hegelian philosophy and particularly to the idea of the great man as representative. E. R. Marks in "Victor Cousin and E" in *Transcendentalism and Its Legacy*, edited by Myron Simon and T. H. Parsons (1966), says that Cousin taught E "his Hegel and much of his Fichte."

Every scholar working on E's sources must be grateful for the enterprise of K. W. Cameron, both for promoting the *ESQ* and for his own indefatigable research in the background of E's thinking. Beginning with *RWE's Reading* (1941; repr. in *ESQ* 62), he continued with *E the Essayist* (2 vols, 1945), which contains numerous excerpts from the books read by E with parallel passages from *Nature* and the *Journals*. While not minimizing the influence of Plato, Cameron affirms that "Coleridge is pre-eminent among the teachers of E." He also devotes much space to Swedenborg and the Boston Swedenborgians as important influences on E at the time he was developing some of the ideas presented in *Nature* in 1836. More recently he has supplemented these works with *E's Workshop* (2 vols., 1964), *The Transcendentalists and Minerva* (2 vols., 1958), and other valuable contributions.

J. W. Beach (*Concept of Nature in Nineteenth-Century English Poetry,* 1936) thinks that E's philosophy is mostly a "loose and popular rendering of Schelling," who is "no better than a Kant run wild." He thinks that E's Schelling came through Coleridge and that E missed some of the metaphysical implications of Coleridge's statement. This is much the position that H. D. Gray (*E*, 1917) had taken in his study. For other studies of E and the Germans, see S. M. Vogel, *German Literary Influences on the American Transcendentalists* (1955), and H. A. Pochmann, *German Culture in America 1600–1900: Philosophical and Literary Influences* (1957). Vogel's book includes a useful commentary on E's reading of German literary writers, especially Goethe, and their influence on him. German philosophers, he thought, had little interest for E. Pochmann's study is broader and more searching. It undertakes a detailed history of E's intellectual development from Platonic dualism before 1830, through Kantian Transcendentalism by way chiefly of Coleridge and Carlyle during the 1830's, and through a mystical intuitionalism influenced by the Neoplatonists during the 1840's, to an eclectic philosophy in which the idealism of Schelling and Hegel combined with Darwinian evolutionary theory to form E's nearest approach to a system of thought that fully satisfied him.

E's Orientalism was well known to his contemporaries even as early as 1845, as evidenced by an anonymous article on "Mr. E and Transcendentalism" (*Amer Whig Rev,* Mar.). It was the subject of a lecture at the Concord School of Philosophy by the Hegelian, W. T. Harris, which F. B. Sanborn published in *The Genius and Character of E* (1885), and it was recognized by G. W. Cooke and other early critics. Yet no thorough study was made until the end of the third decade of this century, when F. I. Carpenter published his *E and Asia* (1930). Two years later A. E. Christy's *The Orient in American Transcendentalism* appeared. In 1928 George Williamson in "E the Oriental" (*Univ Calif Chron*) had said there are four Es: the Yankee, the Romantic, the Platonist, and the Oriental; and by an analysis of "Brahma" and comment on the essays, particularly "Experience," "Fate," and "Illusions," he had decided that E was more Oriental than Platonic. Carpenter shows how E was introduced to Orientalism through his reading among the Neoplatonists between 1830 and 1837. He had also been introduced to Kalidasa and some of the Persian poets through Goethe. By 1845 he had become "an Orientalist in earnest." The essence of Orientalism for E, Carpenter says, was Hindu philosophy, which is most fully represented in E's writings in the poems "Brahma" and "Hamatreya," and in the essay "Illusions," which Carpenter analyzes in detail. The influence of Persian, Arabian, and Chinese literature is also discussed. Carpenter concludes that he was drawn to Hafiz and Saadi for their "joyful humanity and love of nature," and that he was repelled by the formalism of Chinese literature. Christy begins by reminding the reader that E, like Thoreau, was interested, not in metaphysics, but only in the literature of the Hindus. Though Neoplatonism and Western mysticism generally prepared the way for Oriental mysticism, E, Christy points out, never accepted the fatalism of the latter. He says E's Over-Soul is the Hindu Brahma, his doctrine of Illusion is like the Hindu concept of Maya, and his theory of Compensation is comparable to the Hindu Karma, except that E did not subscribe to the doctrine of Transmigration. Christy attributes E's optimism, in part at least, and his belief in evil as negative, to the influence of Hinduism. Christy says it was the urbane E that was attracted to Confucius, but he was held by the corroboration he received of his belief in the goodness of man. Leyla Goren in another study of this subject, *Elements of Brahmanism in the Transcendentalism of E* (1959), argues that the symbolism and imagery of the Hindus appealed to E more strongly than did that of the early Greek philosophers. Both Vedic scripture and Neoplatonism operate in E and reinforce each other. The Persian contribution is only in the realm of poetry, and E profited in his own verse by the example of the pithy, epigrammatic wisdom of the Persian poets. For a discussion of E's poetry in relation to Persian models, see two articles by J. D. Yohannan (*AL* 43), "E's Translations of Persian Poetry from German Sources" and "The Influence of Persian Poetry upon E's Work." For E's early attitude towards Orientalism, see K. W. Cameron's introductory essay and notes to his edition (1954) of E's college poem, "Indian Superstition," in which he appears unsympathetic and not well informed.

There were, of course, numerous other sources not included in any of the groups discussed above. Obviously, the Bible was one, as indicated in H. R. Zink's *E's Use of the Bible* (1935). Paul Sakmann in *E's Geisteswelt nach den Werken und Tagebüchern* (Stuttgart, 1927) has linked Rousseau with Goethe and Swedenborg as one of the antecedents of his nature-philosophy. For E's interest in Dante see J. C. Mathews, "E's Knowledge of Dante" (*UTSE* 42) and for Milton, R. C. Pettigrew, "E and Milton" (*AL* 31). Many have commented on E and Montaigne including D. L. Maulsby in *The Contribution of E in Literature* (1911), W. L. Ustick in "E's Debt to Montaigne" (*WUS* 22), and, most completely, C. L. Young in *E's Montaigne* (1941). Young says E read

Montaigne chiefly as a tonic and cared more for him as a moralist than as a skeptic.

Like Montaigne, Emerson was a close reader of Plutarch. E. G. Berry demonstrates (*E's Plutarch*, 1961) that E was a lifelong student of both the *Lives* and the *Morals*, more especially the latter, and that he was much influenced by them. He points out that Plutarch's blend of Platonism and Stoicicism was very close to the philosophy which E formulated, largely from other sources. He cites examples of E's use of themes from Plutarch and his habit of collecting brilliant and provocative passages to illuminate his intellect and stimulate his imagination. He calls E "the last great devotee of Plutarch," as Montaigne was perhaps the first among modern men. Bacon was another of E's favorites. V. C. Hopkins shows in "E and Bacon" (*AL* 58) that "E saw and appreciated the drift of Bacon's empirical science, took from it what he needed and went his own way." A good way to realize the extent of E's reading is to look through Walter Harding's *E's Library* (1967), based on a catalogue preserved by the Concord Antiquarian Society.

3. Philosophy

Something has been said already, under the heading "General Estimates," on the question whether E may or may not be called a philosopher, and we have seen that the most distinguished American philosophers have been willing to acknowledge him as one of themselves. The historians of American philosophy have usually treated his philosophical ideas with respect. Woodbridge Riley (*American Thought from Puritanism to Pragmatism and Beyond*, 1915, rev., 1941) discusses the sources of Transcendentalism and analyzes E's *Nature* in detail but does not deal effectively with the later essays. (On Transcendentalism the student will find O. B. Frothingham's *Transcendentalism in New England*, 1876, still useful.) H. G. Townsend (*Philosophical Ideas in the United States*, 1936) finds fault with E because his thought is not stated in a logical and systematic fashion, but in the main his discussion is just and useful, especially in his sound view of E's treatment of evil and in his statement that there was in E a latent pragmatism. P. R. Anderson and M. H. Fisch (*Philosophy in America*, 1939) find a causal relationship between Transcendentalism and the maturing of democratic thought. They designate the essay "Experience" as E's masterpiece and take note, as most significant in his work, of the "gradual shift from the neoplatonic doctrine of emanation and return, to the scientific theory of evolution," culminating about 1849. H. W. Schneider (*History of American Philosophy*, 1946) deals inadequately and somewhat condescendingly with E as a philosopher. A very different note is sounded by H. B. Van Wesep in *Seven Sages: the Story of American Philosophy* (1960). Van Wesep calls E a "Gentle Iconoclast," and though he adds little to our knowledge of E, he assigns to him a key position in the development of what he conceives to be "the American philosophy." His seven sages are Franklin, E, James, Dewey, Santayana, Peirce, and Whitehead, all of whom believe "there is something in the universe answering the human thirst for righteousness and beauty."

Of books that attempt a full statement of E's philosophical ideas, the first was G. W. Cooke's biography, and it is remarkably sound considering the fact that it was based solely on the works published before 1881. He says E's "intuition" is the same as Schelling's "intellectual intuition" and Coleridge's "reason." His "moral sentiment" is much the same as the "inner light" of the Quakers, the "ecstasy" of Plotinus, and the "divine illumination" of Swedenborg. Like Kant, he does not distinguish between morality and religion. "Fate" is the term, says Cooke, which E uses to indicate the limits of intuition, spontaneity, and freedom; yet freedom is itself, for man, a necessity.

Marie Dugard's long book on the life and work of E (1907, 1913), already mentioned as biography, should not be ignored by any student who would make a serious study of his ideas. The author summarizes E's thought and provides ample extracts. She concludes that E was a monist, that he rejected the past as a dead letter, and that he believed truth cannot be reached through the rational faculties but only by intuition. Human problems have no solution but in idealism, since the individual is but a momentary fixation in which certain powers and functions of the Spirit become active and are then released. Evil exists, but only conditionally; and in all its variety of forms, nature only repeats two laws: the law of compensation and the law of universal amelioration. Dugard has some acute criticism of E's ideas. She says that he fails to reconcile the many antinomies he recognizes, that his complacent optimism is useless and unintelligible to those who are discouraged and defeated in life, and that if truth comes only in a series of moods, it is lost in the flux and is not dependable. In spite of these defects, she concludes, E "was very great and he did a good work."

Firkins's biography (1915) has a long and stimulating chapter on E's philosophy. Firkins says that E was "perfectly capable of using the syllogism" if he chose. He was impatient, not incapable, of logic. The moment of experience contains all, annihilates time and space, cancels the authority of custom, and solves the problem of immortality. The perceived object expands to the dimensions of the cosmos and the perceiver to the stature of God when the perceiver has that self-reliance which is reliance on God. E was not an idealist in the sense of a disbeliever in the actuality of matter, but he was an idealist in the sense of one who "maintains the absolute dependence of sense impressions on character and intelligence." Firkins thinks E's theory of evil is a logical outcome of his faith in benevolence and in the perfection of the cosmos as a moral mechanism analogous to its perfection as a physical mechanism. But Firkins does not believe that the moral world has the precision of physical laws. His interpretation of E's philosophy was based on a sympathetic, though critical, study of his work.

The earlist and one of the best books devoted exclusively to a study of E's philosophy is H. D. Gray's *E: A Statement of New England Transcendentalism as Expressed in the Philosophy of Its Chief Exponent* (1917, 1958). Gray says that E was primarily a poet and that he approached philosophy with a religious attitude, but he denies the popular notion that his want of logic and system was congenital, saying it was rather the result of a perpetual openness of mind to receive new truth and a distrust of formalism. E believed, according to Gray, that the laws of nature are the laws of the mind and that the evolution of nature back to spirit produces in progress the individual human minds. To state the laws of nature is to summarize E's philosophy, and he names these as the law of permanence, the law of correspondence (of nature with spirit), universality, progress, and the moral law, which underlies the rest. Intellect is primary, nature secondary; intellect takes body in nature, for nature "will not remain orbed in thought, but rushes into persons." When persons break the laws, they lose their hold on reality. Gray raises the question: how does that which is "never a cause but a perpetual effect" produce those persons "who have this fatal ability to lose hold on the central reality"? He answers by saying that the confusion in E's mind arose from "his endeavor to equate an inherited idealism, to which his adherence was largely emotional, with a theory of evolution which more and more forced itself upon him in his attempt to take account of an individual whose impulses proceed from within himself." In 1836 E conceived of God as pure spirit and the world as an illusion which God uses for the education of individuals. Then he came under the influence of Lamarck. Gray objects to E's statement that man seeks to abstract himself from effects and dwell with causes—to ascend into the region of law, where all men belong. He says man cannot "belong" in one kind of existence and "be" in another. To E's statement that man is related by his form to the world about him and by his soul to the universal, Gray objects that this "leaves an impossible dualism in the nature of man." What E wanted, Gray continues, was "thoughts which are more than thoughts,—which in being 'plastic forces' are not thoughts at all." Hence he was driven from the theory of emanation to the theory of evolution, but continued to cling to idealism out of a fear, half realized, that his thinking would end in materialism. It becomes his task, then, to find a common ground for spirit and nature, and for this he turns to Schelling's theory of the identity of subject and object in a substance older than either mind or matter. This Reality is difficult to name, and when E calls it Spirit or Nature, he is speaking symbolically. In his effort to define this ineffable One he "rises out of the realm of Philosophy altogether and dwells in the pure region of Religion." Gray thinks E came finally to believe that this underlying Reality rises in the lower animals to the point of instinct and arrives at consciousness in man. Whether there is a self-consciousness in the Totality, as well as in man, E seems to question, though he is not clear on such matters. Gray thinks E remained a pantheist to the end, that his philosophy had no room for a theistic conception of God. He says E's concept of immortality in the moment, by abolishing time, has no meaning and he doubts whether he ever gave up completely the idea of individual survival.

It was ten years before another important study of E's philosophy was published, and this was the German Paul Sakmann's *RWE's Geisteswelt* (1927). Sakmann's is one of the more important studies by foreign critics. He says E's thought on the sovereignty of virtue is in harmony with the virtuous idealists of all times from the Sermon on the Mount and from Plato to Kant. He finds the parallelism with Kant particularly close. E agreed with Hegel's saying that all things move towards the right, and it disturbed him as little as it did Hegel that so much time is required to achieve justice. With the sovereign romantic "I" and with the godless superman of Nietzsche, the Emersonian soul had hardly anything in common other than the denial of happiness in slavery. Nature was throughout affirmative and had nothing of the negation of one weary of society, of world-sickness, wherewith Rousseau, Schopenhauer, and Nietzsche confined it. As to immortality, Sakmann says E felt, as did many enlightened spirits from Spinoza to Schleiermacher, that we can know nothing of it except that it is to be, in the midst of the finite, one with the Infinite, to exist eternally in each moment. In his mystical philosophy of nature he was in line with Rousseau, Goethe, and Swedenborg as against the theories of Newton, Voltaire, and the materialists. Sakmann concludes that E appeals, as America does, especially to youth and to those who have faith.

F. O. Matthiessen says (*AmR*, 1941) that E wanted, like Plato, to bridge the gap between reason and the understanding, the one and the many, but never could, and now, paradoxically, "The Over-Soul" proves unreadable, whereas on the level of the understanding he "has left us the best intellectual history that we have of his age." Matthiessen also asserts that although E claimed to be a "seeker," all his mature work "proceeded from *a priori* deductive assertion."

During the last two decades several important books on E's philosophy have appeared, demonstrating the fact that E's ideas are still dynamic and susceptible of new and broader interpretations than those to which we have been long accustomed. The first of these books was Sherman Paul's *E's Angle of Vision* (1952). Paul says E begins with the dualism of mind and matter, and seeks by means of the theory of correspondence to bridge the gap and pass from the eighteenth-century concept of the universe as mechanism to the concept of the universe as organism. The act of intuitive perception is the means by which the gap is bridged, unifying the finite (outer) and the infinite (inner) worlds in the experience of the self. Kant, though retaining the dichotomy of noumena and phenomena, indicated the way to unity by asserting that the moral self in its acts of will transcends the limits of the knowing self and takes its inspiration from noumenal sources. With the help of Fichte, Schelling, and Coleridge, E came to see how the two worlds are united in perception as the expressive unfolding of the self. For though knowledge begins with reception, the mystical union of finite and infinite, it ends in action. The mind is the lens converging the rays of the spirit on the daily affairs of men. The faculties of the mind are seeds planted in man in anticipation of the nutrition they find ready for them in a universe designed to call them forth, and self-culture begins with the calling out (the education) of these faculties. Modern science is a manifestation of the polarity of the mind as it represents the human concern with commodity and limit. But it is balanced by the "organic vitality" of the mind's other pole of intuitive perception by means of which man overcomes this limitation in moments of insight. From his position at the center of the universe, man looks through nature in such moments and perceives an arc of the spheric unity of the soul. This is his "angle of vision," by means of which the expansive, creative faculty of the Reason is able to complete the circle. The condition of this experience is the correspondence of nature and spirit and the mind's mediative relationship to both. Since the expressive aspect of perception is inseparable from the receptive aspect, self-culture becomes a duty and results in the development of character. In this process, limitations become benefits, the self becomes knowable by being objectified, and man attains sphericity by taking the world into himself. Paul says that E's theory of correspondence owed much to the "sympathetic" character given to it by Cudworth and even more to his reading of the Swedenborgian books and articles of his early years, particularly those of Sampson Reed and J. J. Garth Wilkinson (the friend of Henry James, Sr.).

The second of these books is S. E. Whicher's *Freedom and Fate: An Inner Life of RWE* (1953). Part I discusses E's loss of faith in historical Christianity and his discovery of a new ground of faith about 1831–32 in the recognition of man's potential greatness by the power of God working through him. Part II shows how E's faith in the greatness of man was later impaired and "driven underground" by a clearer understanding of the facts of experience. A new skepticism seized him, such as he expresses through the mouth of Montaigne in the essay on him in *Representative Men*. The skeptic's position (recognizing fate and illusion) is based on life not as it ought to be but as it is. Yet though in the essay "Experience" he openly and honestly deals with the facts of experience, he does not consciously yield to skepticism, but he saves his faith only by transferring it from the "impotent self" to the "All-disposing fate," from "the God within" to "the God of the universe." From teaching men their power to rise above fate, he turns to teaching them "how to make the best of it," chiefly through the means of Vocation and Intellect; that is, "obedience to his genius" and "the habit of the observer." (See also H. N. Smith's "E's Problem of Vocation: A note on 'The American Scholar,' " *NEQ* 39.) Whereas before he had believed that "every man was equal in his potentiality," now he recognized the idiosyncrasy of individuals, each of whom must obey his peculiar bias. Hence the wise man, instead of being a rebel withdrawing from society, must be one who participates in society by following his vocation—doing his own work. His best method of overcoming the limitations of freedom through doing his own work and of freedom through observing is to resolve both Doer and Knower in the Sayer, which is accomplished in the essay "The Poet." Eventually the acceptance of the theory of evolution completed the process by which his concept of man as the God-possessed creator of nature became the concept of man as the latest product of nature. *The Conduct of Life*, according to Whicher, states E's latest attitude: that we are subject to necessity, yet must act as if we were free. Fate and freedom are still reconciled in his thought, but freedom is not, as in its Transcendental phase, the release of greatness, but the natural and relative power of choice. This, Whicher says, is the position of the humanist.

Five books on E published in the 1960's are interesting in different ways, and all merit some discussion. P. L. Nicoloff's *E on Race and History: An Examination of "English Traits"* (1961) is more than a study of one book; it develops a critical interpretation of all of E's thought and does much to correct the opinion of some contemporary critics that E is a mere fossil of immature romantic idealism. After some biographical details as background, Nicoloff discusses E's cyclic theory of history and race and its philosophical and scientific sources. He presents a detailed analysis, chapter by chapter, relating E's views in this book to his earlier and later views and to kindred but different views expressed by such philosophers of history as Spengler and Toynbee. "More and more," he comments, "E was inclined to explain the human past, present, and future in terms of some long-range destiny implicit in racial seed and the fated cycle of circumstance." He warns, however, that it would be "a serious misreading of E's character and purpose" to suppose his "fatalism" was intended to encourage the subordination of the individual to the state or to advocate the use of fascist and communist methods of social organization.

Another book that is more comprehensive than its title would suggest is Jonathan Bishop's *E on the Soul* (1964). It is arranged in three parts. In Part I Bishop defines E's conception of the Soul as a conjunction of the organic faculty, the intellect, and the moral sentiment. His comments on the ways in which the soul functions through these faculties are often illuminating. In Part II, which is perhaps the most original and useful, he explains how, in terms of literary style, the organic faculty expresses itself through rhythm, the intellect through metaphor, and the moral sentiment through tone. In Part III, following the pattern best exemplified in Whicher's *Freedom and Fate*, he undertakes to show how E's conception of the Soul, like his beliefs, changed as he grew older. Nature, which had been subjective, became objective and identified with Fate. This, he seems to say, restricts the Soul, although E insisted in the essay "Fate" that the Soul is not subject to Fate. E, Bishop thinks, moved from radical to conservative, from Romantic to Victorian, and from prophet of the Soul to preacher about the Soul.

The fullest and probably the best study of E ever made by a European, Maurice Gonnaud's *Individu et société dan l'oeuvre de RWE* (1964), subtitled *Essai de biographie spirituelle*, is divided into four parts corresponding to the four principal phases of E's changing conception of himself as an individual and his relationship to society, religious, political, and moral. The first phase is concerned chiefly with the problem of vocation, in which E attempts unsuccessfully to conform his beliefs to the doctrines and conventions of the Unitarian Church. It ends with his resignation from his pastorate. The second phase traces his early career as a lecturer, emphasizes his increasingly radical individualism, and ends with his two lectures, "The American Scholar" and the "Divinity School Address," and shows E beginning to lose some of his confidence in intuition as a guide to conduct and to make concessions more willingly to the requirements of society. As the problem of slavery became more acute, he found his social consciousness driving him more and more to oppose it. His experience as a lecturer in England in 1847–48 helped to move him away from his conception of ideal democracy toward that of natural aristocracy. The fourth phase, in which slavery and the Civil War played a great part, led to his final acceptance of the practical necessity and rightness of the individual's fulfilling, even at the sacrifice of much individual freedom, his duties as a citizen. The author follows in general the thesis of Whicher's *Freedom and Fate*, but he has enriched and fortified his study with full documentation, utilizing not only all of E's published works, but much that still remains in manuscript in the Houghton Library.

In *Three Children of the Universe: E's View of Shakespeare, Bacon, and Milton* (1966) W. M. Wynkoop begins with E's famous trinity of the Knower (the lover of truth), the Doer (the lover of goodness or justice), and the Sayer (the lover of beauty) and undertakes to demonstrate how, for him, these three representative men of the English Renaissance, Shakespeare, Bacon, and Milton, illustrate three stages of growth corresponding to the divine cycle of the Father, the Spirit, and the Son, or the historical cycle of the Age of Innocence, the Fall, and the Redemption. He thinks Milton was E's ideal poet and gives more weight, apparently, to his 1835 lecture on Milton, in which the emphasis is on Milton's ability to inspire, than to later essays. His argument is somewhat abstruse though interesting, but it is not always convincing.

In *City of the West: E, America, and Urban Metaphor* (1967) M. H. Cowan uses the City of the West as a metaphor for E's ideal of American civilization that should combine the values implied in the earlier metaphors of the City of God and the City of Man, with the values of Nature represented by the Organic Metaphor; in other words, a civilization that would reconcile the polarities of real and ideal, material and spiritual, the individual and society, freedom and law.

It is not possible here to discuss all the shorter studies that deal in one way or another with E's philosophy, but a number of them deserve to be mentioned briefly. C. E. Jorgenson's "E's Paradise under the Shadow of Swords" (*PQ* 32) is devoted to an exposition of E's view of evil as privative only and of fate as immutable limitation only when unpenetrated by thought. The degree of E's skepticism has been the subject of some recent essays. C. F. Strauch in "The Importance of E's Skeptical Mood" (*HLB* 57), after discussing E's unpublished poem "The Skeptic," develops the thesis that between 1838 and 1845 he passed through a period of struggle against tendencies toward skepticism to a firm balance between skepticism and faith. In "Intellect and Moral Sentiment in E's Opinions of 'The Meanest Kinds' of Men" (*AL* 58) A. J. Kloeckner notes that although E regularly used the term moral sentiment to denote an intuitive relationship to the moral laws, he frequently, especially in later years, asserted that the intellect is more important in the daily practice of virtue, and he was constitutionally disposed to limit effective intelligence to the gifted few—a disposition against which he struggled valiantly. In the 1840's, according to J. A. Ward ("E and 'The Educated Will,'" *ELH* 67), E turned from faith as a synthesis of reason and the individual will "educated" by nature to the validation of faith through empirical observation of the outer world. In his essay "Conservative and Mediatory Emphases in E's Thought," originally published in *Transcendentalism and Its Legacy*, a group of essays edited by Myron Simon and T. H. Parsons (1966), H. H. Clark, in his usual thorough and systematic way, shows that E had a balanced view of such matters as worldly prudence, sin and evil, social reform, tradition, and individualism, and that his characteristic attitude was mediation between extremes.

Several writers recently have examined E's philosophy anew in the light of Christian doctrine and other religions. R. C. Pollock's "A Re-Appraisal of E" (*Thought* 57; repr. in H. C. Gardiner's *American Classics Reconsidered*, 1958) is a rather extended study of E's philosophy in the light of the Christian tradition. He says E found Plato's dialectical procedure congenial because his own mind was "spontaneously dialectical," though he tried to recapture "the single vision." He thinks that if he "had had a better acquaintance with the Classical-Christian tradition he would have been entranced by its marvelous fusion of elements dear to him." He says neohumanist critics have had a bad effect on readers of E by closing their eyes to elements of mysticism in his thought. On the other hand, Randall Stewart (*American Literature and Christian Doctrine*, 1958) calls E "radically anti-Christian." Paul Lauter says that E's religious ideas, when examined in the light of Paul Tillich's theology, are seen to be "not vague, soft, and platitudinous, as many have felt, but vital and strikingly pertinent to our anxious culture today" ("E Through Tillich," *ESQ* 63). Harold Fromm in "E and Kierkegaard: the Problem of Historical Christianity" (*MR* 68) finds E and Kierkegaard similar in their conception of spirit as inwardness, in their dialectical method, in their objection to historical Christianity, and other ways of thinking and feeling. H. M. Campbell points out numerous parallels in the philosophy of E and A. N. Whitehead, especially in their attitudes toward historical Christianity ("E and Whitehead," *PMLA*

60). Robert Detweiler compares E's vision of Transcendentalism to Zen Buddhism and finds a parallel between the relation of E's views to Unitarianism and the relation of Zen to traditional Buddhism ("E and Zen," *AQ* 62).

E's theory of compensation still puzzles or intrigues some critics. A well-balanced study of it is made by H. F. Pommer in "The Contents and Basis of E's Belief in Compensation" (*PMLA* 62). Pommer quotes numerous passages in which E defines his belief in the theory, and he concludes that it is based largely on his temperament and personal experience. The philosophical basis of his belief is that since it is better in the view of the mind than any other, it must be true. R. F. Lee argues in "E's 'Compensation' as Argument and as Art" (*NEQ* 64) that he does not succeed because he had two purposes working against each other: his desire to show the presence of God in the law of compensation and his desire to kindle a sense of the creative or beneficent spirit as an end in itself. One is intellectual, the other existential. In combining the two and subordinating the higher motivation to the "law" he disappoints his reader.

Other essays of interest are A. M. Cory's "Humor in E's Journals" (*UTSE* 55), where more than 200 citations are made to show that E "had a definite appreciation of humor" and S. W. Liebman's "E's Transformation in the 1820's" (*AL* 68), which undertakes to show from the journals that E's change from Unitarianism to Transcendentalism was gradual and not the result of any crisis in his personal or intellectual experience. In "E and the Doctrine of Sympathy" (*SIR* 67), C. F. Strauch studies a number of early poems that show affinities between man and nature at every level of the Platonic scale. "Woodnotes" is central to the theme. "The Sphinx," however, depicts disjunction, man's falling away from cosmic harmony. Ray Benoit in "E on Plato: The Fire's Center" (*AL* 63) says that E's apparent inconsistency in being, as it has been claimed, both a pragmatist and an idealist, is reconciled in Plato's theory that matter and spirit are aspects of a ground of being higher than both.

Ever since Lowell wrote in *A Fable For Critics* that E had a "Greek head on right Yankee shoulders," readers have found in him something of a realist and pragmatist. Among those who have made a special study of the pragmatic aspects of E's philosophy, F. I. Carpenter is preeminent. His essay, "Points of Comparison between E and William James" (*NEQ* 29), was the earliest, and his later "William James and E" (*AL* 39) is the fullest treatment available on the subject. He also discusses E's pragmatism in the introduction to his *E* (AWS, 1934), and in his *E Handbook* (1953) he summarizes his own ideas on the subject as well as other works, including the German scholar Eduard Baumgarten's *Der Pragmatismus: die geistigen Grundlagen des amerikanischen*

Gemeinwesen (Frankfurt, 1938). E. C. Lindeman in "E's Pragmatic Mood" (*ASch* 46–47) says E's "allegiance to the experimental approach to life . . . guarantees his permanent place in American life and thought." In *Puritans and Pragmatists: Eight Eminent American Thinkers* (1968) Paul Conklin includes E as an important transitional thinker between the Puritans and the Pragmatists.

4. Science

E's identification in the popular mind with idealism and romanticism has made it difficult for critics to estimate properly his lifelong interest in science. Yet this interest has not gone unnoticed. John Burroughs wrote in 1889 ("Science and the Poets," *Works*, 1924): "In chemistry, in botany, in physiology, in geology, in mechanics, he found keys to unlock his enigmas. . . . There is hardly a fundamental principle of science that he has not turned to ideal uses." It is precisely because he turned science to ideal uses (Burroughs says he "fertilized it with his own spirit") that critics have often thought he rejected it or ignored it. Richard Garnett (*Life of RWE*, 1888) said that "science has found no such literary interpreter as E," and he quoted Tyndall as saying, "By E scientific conceptions are continually transmuted into the finer forms and warmer hues of an ideal world." Norman Foerster expressed the view of most critics in "E as a Poet of Nature" (*PMLA* 22) when he said that E is essentially an idealist though he was deeply interested in the science of nature. Paul shows in the last chapter of *E's Angle of Vision* how E used science in his "astronomy of ideas."

The first and only detailed study of E's reading in the scientific literature of his time is H. H. Clark's "E and Science" (*PQ* 31). Clark says E became acquainted with Newton's *Principia* at the age of 20, and that it was the reading of works on astronomy by Mary Somerville, F. W. Herschel, Laplace, and others in the summer of 1832 that precipitated his resignation from the pulpit of the Second Church. Helping him to an acceptance of the theory of evolution were the evolutionary philosophers Leibniz, Kant, Goethe, and Coleridge, and the evolutionary scientists Linnaeus, Buffon, Cuvier, John Hunter, Erasmus Darwin, Saint-Hilaire, Lamarck, Lyell, Robert Chambers, and later, Asa Gray and Charles Darwin. German Transcendentalism and science, Clark believes, "were not mutually exclusive in their influence." He finds evidence of scientific reading in *Nature*, "The American Scholar," and "The Divinity School Address." His study does not go beyond 1838. The most thorough study of E's reception of the theory of evolution, first from the philosophers and later from the scientists, is J. W. Beach's "E and Evolution" (*UTQ* 34). Beach repeated and expanded the materials of this essay to give them a setting in philosophy in his book *The Concept of Nature in Nineteenth-Century English Poetry* (1936). Beach says that E's scientific opinions "were not shaped primarily by the great scientific writers, Buffon, Lamarck, Saint-Hilaire, and Darwin, but by a succession of second-rate, popular, and more or less dubious authorities, and the first of these was Coleridge." He says E's early concept of evolution was really not evolution at all but the "graduated scale of being" theory, which was held by many philosophers in the eighteenth century, and which E took from Coleridge, who took it from Schelling. This was a "mere logical, or conceptual, unfolding, or disinvolvement, of the lower category of being from the higher, or *vice versa*," and not a chronological evolutionary sequence of events. E's transition from belief in this scale-of-being theory to a belief in scientific evolution was very gradual, and he was not himself wholly aware of the process. The change, Beach says, began after the writing of *Nature*, had made considerable progress by 1841, and had so far advanced by 1844 that the reading of Robert Chambers's *Vestiges of Creation* gave him no shock. Beach thinks E had fully accepted the scientific theory of evolution by 1854, that his Transcendentalism enabled him to accept it "without a qualm," and that the more he learned of natural history the more certain he was that "it is all a projection of the mind, an expression of the inherent moral purpose of the universe which is found in the human spirit." He thinks it never occurred to E that ethical concepts may also be a product of evolution, for his remained arbitrary, traditional, and vague, whereas those of naturalism are relative and precise. It is evident that Beach is unsympathetic with idealism and Transcendentalism, and that he is thoroughly in sympathy with scientific naturalism.

A much more sympathetic study of the subject is that of F. W. Conner in his book *Cosmic Optimism* (1949), though his conclusions are not materially at variance with those of Beach. Connor agrees that E's evolution was not that of the scientist, that he never mentioned natural selection, and that he was not interested in the immediate cause of the transformations of organic nature. He saw no gulf between the ultimate cause of things and the things themselves; hence for him there was no question whether living forms were attributable to a natural or transcendental purposive cause, there being for him no such distinction. Whether species developed through the survival of chance variations or the inheritance of acquired characteristics, E saw "only the phenomenal manifestation of a Creative Mind." Such a view of the cosmos made possible an optimistic view of life.

There has been comparatively little scholarly interest in E's scientific views in recent years. In 1955 C. F. Strauch published an article on "The Sources of E's 'Song of Nature' " (*HLB*), an unpublished poem, the general theme of which is that of ameliorating evolution through preservation and destruction. The poem reveals E's acceptance of the laws of science, but a distaste for the unimaginative method of science. Perhaps more important is Strauch's "E's Sacred Science" (*PMLA* 58). E's "sacred science"—a term borrowed from Iamblichus—was the imaginative process by which he was able to reconcile such polarities as emanation and evolution, skepticism and faith, amelioration and fate, and come at last to believe in the "Beautiful Necessity" that embraces and reconciles freedom and law. In this connection H. M. Jones's *Belief and Disbelief in American Literature* (1967) is interesting. Jones says E never resolved the question of how man can be subjected to evolutionary development and also participate in an absolute spiritual order. But P. L. Nicoloff in *E on Race and History* (1961) thinks E resolved the question by regarding the organic process of evolution as a release of hitherto "arrested" development in a purposive creation.

5. Public Affairs

Many have recognized that E had a good deal of "Yankee" common sense to balance his idealism, and we have seen to what extent he is thought to have been a precursor of the pragmatic philosophers and how he kept abreast of the scientific thought of his day. Indeed, E is a notable example of the obvious fact that a thinker may be an idealist and a realist without inconsistency. John Morley said some 67 years ago (*Crit Misc* 04), "It is only the great idealists, like E, who take care not to miss the real." It was also Morley who said that E "values mundane circumspection as highly as Franklin." It is well known that he took an active interest in the civic affairs of the town of Concord (see H. H. Hoeltje, "E, Citizen of Concord," *AL* 40), and his very opposition to some of the prevalent attitudes of his time is proof that he was keenly aware of their existence. (See P. H. Boynton, "E in His Period," *Ethics* 29, and Mildred Silver, "E and the Idea of Progress," *AL* 40). He belonged to the "Party of the Future," as H. N. Smith has said ("E's Problem of Vocation," *AL* 39) and he chose the part of student rather than active reformer; yet he had no objection to reform except as it hardened into institutional patterns or organized movements.

One of the earliest and fullest studies of this phase of E is Raymer McQuiston's *The Relation of RWE to Public Affairs* (1923), which deals with E's political, economic, and social ideas and his attitude towards slavery and the Civil War. McQuiston says E preferred democracy, though he recognized its weaknesses, particularly the crudeness of its leaders of the Jacksonian period. At first he was a Whig, but he eventually lost confidence in Whig leadership (Webster, especially, about 1850), and allied himself with the Republican Party in the late 1850's. Emerson opposed the tariff, but had no other strong economic views. In his individualism he tended to undervalue society and theoretically refused to recognize social classes, though he was aware of their existence and the practical need of them. He spoke in favor of equal political and educational rights for women. He disliked the early anti-slavery agitators but was driven into their camp by his dislike of the Fugitive Slave Law. He thought Lincoln too conservative in the Civil War, and after the war he favored the radical reconstructionist policies of Sumner and Stevens. This proves that E's reasoned theories could be broken down by the passions evoked by public events.

Of specialized studies, the student should read A. I. Ladu's "E: Whig or Democrat" (*NEQ* 40). Ladu says E thought the Democrats had the more laudable objectives but the Whigs had the better men. His chief objection to the Democratic Party was that it failed to base political action on morality or to promote individual culture. He objected to the Whigs because they seemed to treat property as an end in itself and not a means to cultural ends. Perry Miller in "Emersonian Genius and the American Democracy" (*NEQ* 53; repr. in *E: A Collection of Critical Essays*, 1962) shows how E struggled to reconcile democratic philosophy with his Boston distaste for crudeness in men like Jackson and Lincoln, and is able to do so by his theory of genius. "The genius is great not because he surpasses but because he represents his constituency."

During the 1830's and 1840's E took relatively little interest in national affairs, and he certainly had no sympathy for the theory of "manifest destiny" that attracted Whitman at the time of the War with Mexico. But in a sense E was a literary nationalist, as we are often reminded by his address on "The American Scholar." In this connection one may consult Chapter Five of B. T. Spencer's *The Quest for Nationality* (1957), where there is a discriminating assessment of the contribution of E, and of Transcendentalism in general, to the development of literary nationalism. Until the middle of the century his own work was not widely known outside of New England. J. B. Hubbell has shown in his chapter on E and the South in *The South in American Literature* (1954, enlarged and repr. in *South and Southwest*, 1965) that he was not well known in the South, and his work was not readily available there until after 1865. When he was a young man, he was interested in the South and usually felt kindly toward its people, but the passions of the abolition movement and the Civil War produced a radical change in his feelings.

On E and the abolitionist movement, M. M. Moody's "The Evolution of E as an Abolitionist" (*AL* 45) should be consulted. She indicates the progressive steps from 1837 to 1862 by which E moved from an attitude of "detached

criticism" to "unqualified demand for emancipation." (See also Rudolf Schottlaender, "E as Abolitionist," *NEQ* 33.) E, according to W. A. Huggard, saw
in the Civil War not only the liberation of the Negro but "a hope for the liberation of American culture" ("E and the Problem of War and Peace," *UIHS*
38; also "E's Philosophy of War and Peace," *PQ* 43). It has generally been
supposed that the "Ode Inscribed to W. H. Channing" was a kind of apology
for E's lack of enthusiasm for abolition, but C. F. Strauch argues in "The
Background and Meaning of the 'Ode Inscribed to W. H. Channing'" (*ESQ*
66) that the poem expresses also E's dissatisfaction with Webster's public stand
on slavery.

As to economics, E had no theory, says A. C. Kern in "E and Economics"
(*NEQ* 40), but he was in effect a *laissez-faire* expansionist who was saved from
materialism by his demand that wealth and material growth shall be not ends
in themselves but means to the enlargement of man's spiritual and moral
world. J. C. Gerber in "E and the Political Economists" (*NEQ* 49) is more
specific, agreeing that E was for *laissez-faire* and free trade, much after the
school of Adam Smith, though he favored an agricultural economy rather
than Smith's balance of agriculture and industry. (See also D. C. Stenerson,
"E and the Agrarian Tradition," *JHI* 53.) Of the developments out of Adam
Smith—utilitarianism, pessimism, and optimism—he approved only the third.
He disliked utilitarianism, though he seems not to have known Bentham or
Mill (see R. T. Harris, "Nature: E and Mill," *WHR* 51–52). He agreed with
the American school of Raymond, Everett, and Carey only in part, they being
too close to the Hamiltonian view for E's taste. Gerber says E's ideal economic
system probably would "combine socialistic ends with capitalistic means."
With this latter estimate J. T. Flanagan ("E and Communism," *NEQ* 37) seems
to agree, saying that E was sympathetic with the aims of the Brook Farm and
Fruitlands experiments, but against their methods. His individualism predis-
posed him to distrust any reform that did not begin with the inner life of the
individual. While recognizing that E's admiration for men of power unwit-
tingly gave comfort to ruthless manipulators of wealth in the Gilded Age,
Daniel Aaron sees him chiefly as a "transcendental democrat," who encouraged men rather to "cultivate their inward greatness," and as a founder of the
progressive tradition in America (*Men of Good Hope*, 1951).

Doubtless E's lecture tours over the country, particularly in the West,
affected his attitude towards democracy and public affairs in general. Ernest
Marchand, in "E and the Frontier" (*AL* 31), takes the view that native culture
exercised a more powerful influence over E's thinking than foreign philosophy,
and he tends to minimize the influence of Puritan New England in order to

emphasize that of the Western frontier. (See also Lucy Hazard, *The Frontier in American Literature*, 1927, and for a view at variance with Marchand's, Ladu's article mentioned above.) It may be that E taught more than he learned in the West; for as Willard Thorp has pointed out in "E on Tour" (*QJS* 30), he made his strenuous lecture tours less for the fees he earned than to fulfill a need to teach and improve the American mind where he could. Several articles, giving details of E's lecture tours, have been published by H. H. Hoeltje (three), Louise Hastings, R. B. Nye, E. B. Scott, C. E. Shorer, and others.

E's interest in educational theory probably grew out of this need to teach. His turn from the ministry to the public lyceum was the first proof of this need. H. D. Gray said that the one reform to which he could devote himself with consistency was in the field of education, where he might hope to provide a better means for the development of the powers of the individual. R. M. Gay says in *E: A Study of the Poet as Seer* (1928) that E's pedagogy rested on the belief that "education consists in invigorating the imagination," and that his own purpose was not to inculcate ideas but to "increase sensibility." H. C. Carpenter's "E, Eliot, and the Elective System" (*NEQ* 51) reviews and marshals the evidence, including Eliot's own statements, that E was an important influence in shaping the educational theory of Charles W. Eliot. The subject is discussed briefly in F. I. Carpenter's *E Handbook*.

6. Aesthetics

E made no attempt to develop a theory of art, and most of what he has said on the subject is casual and fragmentary. Several attempts, however, have been made to formulate what appear to have been his aesthetic principles. H. D. Gray's book has a chapter on the subject. Gray thought it surprising that "E should have so little of value to offer us by way of an esthetic theory"; yet he accounts for the fact perhaps by suggesting that the doctrine of intuition and E's Puritan ancestry "predetermined all he had to say regarding the meaning of beauty and the utility of art." E believed, according to Gray, that beauty is that which inheres in the object to be imitated, and art is the expression which genius is able to give it. While beauty is perceived by the Reason, art must be wrought under the guidance of the Understanding. The office of art is "to educate the perception of beauty," and the principles of art to be deduced from the nature of beauty. Whatever is adequate to its purpose must be beautiful, E thought, and he saw no antagonism between sensuous charm and moral beauty. It is this, Gray says, that prevents E's aesthetics from being more than "a mere offshoot from his ethics."

The next treatment of this subject is E. G. Sutcliffe's *E's Theories of Literary*

Expression (1923), the aim of which is to show, by means of related quotations from E, the connection between his philosophy of style and his philosophy in general. Sutcliffe says the reason for E's lack of unity is in his theory, which is dualistic, as Gray has said. E was not willing to deal with "the high inspirations of the Reason" according to the methods of the Understanding. He found some comfort in the belief that the whole is mirrored in each part, so that a faithful adherence to his inspired moments will give him the image of eternity. An art so produced must depend largely upon symbols adequate to express the correspondence between mind and nature. Hence the best style must be both simple and symbolic.

Norman Foerster, in "E on the Organic Principle in Art" (*PMLA* 26), speaks of "qualitative and quantitative beauty," the one derived through intuition and the other through the externalization of this intuition. This is much the same as the distinction made by Gray and Sutcliffe in terms of the Reason and the Understanding. A work of art is supreme when it is a synthesis of these two, and such a synthesis E found in the work of Michelangelo. (For the influence of Michelangelo on E, especially in "The Problem," see F. B. Newman's "E and Buonarroti," *NEQ* 52.) E's distinction between genius and talent, Foerster says, is the same. Genius alone, E conceived, is organic. Foerster has a more thorough analysis of E's theory of art in *American Criticism* (1928). Here he says E's greatest debt is to Plato and the Platonists, though he probably came to his organic theory immediately through Coleridge and Schlegel. He emphasizes the classical quality of E's taste, perhaps too much, and says E belittled all the Romantics except Wordsworth. He agrees more or less with Gray that for E the highest type of imagination is ethical (or humanistic), and virtue, in the end, becomes superior to beauty. E's ideal is the poet-priest, and he proposes a union of art and religion. In this connection see N. F. Adkins, "E and the Bardic Tradition" (*PMLA* 48).

Others who have written about the importance of the organic metaphor in E's aesthetic theory are R. P. Adams "The Basic Contradiction in E" (*ESQ* 69), in which he sees E struggling to resist the static conclusion of organicism yet to retain the organic method. P. W. Brown in "E's Philosophy of Aesthetics" (*JAAC* 57) indicates the influence upon E of the Swedenborgian doctrine of correspondence and the idea that a work of art should arise from and be a reflection of a mind in active creative operation.

Among others who have written on the subject, Régis Michaud has collected in *L'Esthétique d'E* (Paris, 1927) a large number of statements from E's works illustrating his aesthetic ideas. Art for E, he says, consists in the individualization of the universal, the reduction of the many to the one; it is not an end in itself but is instrumental to the individual's appropriation of the universe. In *AmR* Matthiessen shows from the *Journals* that E does not always belittle talent and that he realized that genius is ineffectual without the talent by which it is channeled into understandable form. With this compare the interpretation of Jean Gorely in "E's Theory of Poetry" (*Poetry Rev* 31) that, in the order of genius, thought precedes form, comes from within, and is not subject to the will, though it is conditioned by the artist's physical and mental health and the conventions of his time.

The most extensive study of E's aesthetics is in V. C. Hopkins's *Spires of Form: A Study of E's Aesthetic Theory* (1951). E's theory, as explained by Hopkins, has three phases: first, the creative process, which itself has the three phases of inspiration, imagination, and expression; second, the completed work of art, which in its organic form is derived from nature, but in its spiritual form (objectified in the art form) is derived from the Divine Spirit; and third, the reception of the work of art by an observer, whose imagination is awakened by sense impression, memory, and the subconscious, and who finally, in the climax of recreative escape, shares with the creator the sense of freedom from time and space. (See Hopkins's earlier article, "The Influence of Goethe in E's Aesthetic Theory," *PQ* 48, in which she points out various aspects of E's aesthetic theory which were indebted to Goethe, without minimizing numerous differences.)

Very acute, though less comprehensive, is Charles Feidelson's chapter "Toward Melville: Some Versions of E" in his *Symbolism and American Literature* (1953). Though he prefers Melville's tragic view of the world to E's brighter outlook, he thinks their methods are reciprocal and that "if we feel Melville as one of ours, we must take E into the bargain, whether we like it or not." For E, says Feidelson, "poetic vision 'is the perception of the symbolic character of things,' and poetic structure, the form of this vision," and yet it did not occur to him, as it did to Melville, "to exploit the most exciting quality of modern symbolism—the tension between opposite meanings in paradox and the tension between logical paradox and its literary resolution—even though this quality was implicit in his own approach." E's great failing, he thinks, "was too simple a confidence in the power of poetic harmony." It seems to me that in emphasizing E's predisposition to find "poetic harmony" Feidelson underestimates E's consciousness of the reality of the terms of the paradox. René Wellek in Vol. III of his *History of Modern Criticism* (1965) is interesting in this connection. Wellek says E's reading of Goethe corrected the fervent symbolism he derived from the Neoplatonists, yet he calls E "the outstanding representative of romantic symbolism in the English-speaking world."

C. R. Metzger's *E and Greenough: Transcendental Pioneers of an American Esthetic* (1954) is a comparative study of the organic theory of art as expressed by E and Horatio Greenough, the sculptor. It contains some interesting suggestions on the relation of E's "protestant esthetic" with his "protestant theology," both reaching through nature toward God. Metzger's work enlarges and develops the study of E's and Greenough's statements of the organic principle in art made by Matthiessen in *AmR*. Another work discussing E as a proponent of the organic aesthetic and an important influence upon Greenough is T. M. Brown's, "Greenough, Paine, E's essay and the Organic Aesthetic," (*JAAC* 56). In *E as Mythmaker* (1954) J. R. Reaver discusses E's use of the imagination for the purpose of drawing his deepest meanings from the soul through the subconscious mind into the intellectual world of conscious mind. He thinks E is less a mystic than a psychological interpreter and that his method has much in common with the method of present-day psychologists. One of E's achievements, according to Reaver, is the resolution of ethics in aesthetics.

On E's aesthetic practice, a good deal of criticism has been published. From the beginning critics have disagreed, more or less, on the question of the structure of his poems and prose works and on the merits of his style. W. T. Harris said ("RWE," *Atl* 1882) that E's poems often lack logical unity but have organic unity. Some of his essays, and Harris names particularly the essay "Experience," have "a true genetic development," whereas others do not, and he specifies "The Over-Soul." Charles Malloy, in a series of articles in *The Coming Age* (1899–1900) and also in *The Arena* (1904), found a clue to E's structure in the *Bhagavad Gita*, and this clue was the Platonic concept of Identity. Firkins has a good deal to say on this subject, and in general he agrees with Harris. He finds the essays structurally sound. "An essay is a structure, a contrivance," says Firkins "not an efflux; but in its highest evolution, it mimics the efflux. . . ." Some of the poems are also structurally sound (he cites "Days"), but most of the philosophical poems, though they contain fine lines, lack organization. Matthiessen attributes E's alleged incoherence to lack of "tension between form and liberation" due to his having escaped completely from the practical restrictions of his age. In his poetry, except where he achieved the condensation of "Days," he was, says Matthiessen, likely to exemplify the "Heraclitean doctrine of the Flowing." E's formlessness was, he thinks a consequence of his practice of the organic theory of art.

Walter Blair and Clarence Faust in "E's Literary Method" (*MP* 44) describe a method, suggested to them by E's discussion in *Representative Men*, of Plato's "twice bisected line." This is the key to the two worlds of the mind and the senses by which E related a given subject both to that which was above it and to that which was below it in the scale of being and so achieved a balanced judgment. They successfully apply the method, by way of illustration, to several essays and poems. Sherman Paul says in *E's Angle of Vision* that E also employed this method in the organization of some of his books. In the *Essays, First Series*, for example, "History" is balanced by "Self-Reliance," and in *The Conduct of Life* the first three essays are preparatory to and balanced by the last three. R. P. Adams continues the theme in "E and the Organic Metaphor" (*PMLA* 54), but he thinks the "twice bisected line" is too rigid an analogy, and that E explains his own method, if not Plato's, better when he says in "Plato: New Readings" that Plato "represents the privilege of the intellect, the power, namely, of carrying up every fact to successive platforms and so disclosing in every fact a germ of expansion." Such expansion, Adams says, is organic; and he thinks it is closer to the Romantic than to the Platonic conception of organicism. C. F. Strauch, "E's Use of the Organic Method" (*ESQ* 69), speaks of a "mythic center" in some of the essays and of the importance of understanding the accommodation which E must make between "the Platonic archetypal cosmos and the concept of growth in the plant analogy."

R. F. Lee finds some parallels between E and Kierkegaard. In "E through Kierkegaard: Toward a Definition of E's Theory of Communication" (*ELH* 57) he says E's purpose was not merely to tell people something but to do something to them—to arouse religious faith, "a *condition* that one knows *only by being in it*." Similarly, for Kierkegaard truth is "a quality of the whole person . . . truth is a becoming, an *inwardness*," and cannot be imposed by logical system. He says the theory of indirection was conscious in Kierkegaard but instinctive practice in E. Yet the two were poles apart in their views of Christianity: Kierkegaard would have seemed to E such a man as Swedenborg, limited by "theologic cramp." In "Truth and Nature: E's Use of Two Complex Words" (*ELH* 60) Paul Lauter picks up some of the ideas in Lee's essay and redirects them: "One determines 'truth' by the act of living it." Lauter thinks E depended for communication primarily on imagery, the ambiguous potential of language, the tensions of paradox, and the impact of sheer expression. R. L. Francis discerns in *Nature* a dialectical and forward movement of which "Prospects" is the synthesis. In "The Architectonics of E's *Nature*" (*AQ* 67) he says the eight chapters constitute four pairs of contrasting movements corresponding more or less to the understanding and the reason; for example "Commodity" is paired with "Beauty," "Language" with "Discipline," and so on. Lawrence Buell in "Transcendentalist Catalogue Rhetoric: Vision versus Form" (*AL* 68) discusses the catalogues of Whitman's verse and E's prose as a type of

Transcendental rhetoric based on the sense of the universe's spiritual unity in diversity.

Several recent essays and one book have dealt with specific aspects of E's poetry and his concept of the poet. In France Michel Gresset in a perceptive study, "Le 'Dieu Libérateur' ou le poète selon E" (LanM 66), sees in E's creative life a drama which prefigures in part the modern writer's problem of facing a psychological barrier between the self and an unfriendly creation. In "Archangel in the Pleached Garden: E's Poetry" (ELH 66) R. L. Francis says E's problem as a poet was to solve the paradox, "how to find a language that would be appropriate both to the ideational realm and to the phenomenal realm, or, how to reconcile the lyrical form and the philosophic." Two articles compare E's poetic theory with Poe's. D. D. Anderson in "A Comparison of the Poetic Theories of E and Poe" (Personalist 60) stresses the differences. If he had examined more than "The Poet" and two essays by Poe, he would have found many similarities that he does not mention. J. E. Mulqueen's "The Poetics of E and Poe" (ESQ 69) is more extensive and much sounder. But more should be done on this interesting topic. Edith Mettke, Der Dichter RWE: Mystiches Denken und poetisher Ausdruck (Heidelberg, 1963), tries to relate the form of E's mystic perception of unity in variety to the form and theme of selected poems, paying special attention to E's imagery and symbolism which become, when successful, realizations in language of his experience of unity.

On the subject of E's rhetoric two recent essays may be of interest: M. W. Edrich's "The Rhetoric of Apostasy" (TSLL 67), which attributes the vehement reaction to the "Divinity School Address" not to E's doctrinal heresies but to his rhetorical excesses; and S. W. Liebman's "The Development of E's Theory of Rhetoric" (AL 69), which traces E's rhetoric from the late eighteenth-century principles of Hugh Blair, learned at Harvard, to the colorful, indirect, and individual rhetoric of his essays, showing that Renaissance and seventeenth-century writers as well as Romantic symbolism and American colloquialism influenced the changes. In " 'The Lyceum Is My Pulpit': Homiletics in E's Early Lectures" (AL 63) A. M. Baumgartner shows the influence of E's homiletical training upon his early lectures. V. L. O. Chittick in "E's 'Frolic Health' " (NEQ 57) says he loved the language of his countrymen whether of East or West and was more of a humorist than is popularly supposed. Some excellent studies have been made of particular poems. R. H. Pearce in his stimulating book, The Continuity of American Poetry (1961), says that in scenic poems like "The Snow-Storm" and "Seashore" E imputes his own sensibility to the world in order to understand it as somehow akin to him. For this reason such poems are subjective. "Woodnotes" he calls "dialectic" because it tends to break into two parts, one a rendering of the scene and the other an explicit interpretation of that rendering. C. F. Strauch calls 1834 "The Year of E's Poetic Maturity" (*PQ* 55) because by then he had "learned to transmute the essence of ideas into imagery, color, sound, and motion." Among interpretations of individual poems T. R. Whitaker's "The Riddle of E's 'Sphinx' " (*AL* 55) and B. J. Paris's "E's 'Bacchus' " (*MLQ* 62) are particularly good. Studies of E as a practical critic may be found in G. E. DeMille, *Literary Criticism in America* (1931), who agrees with Foerster that there is a "strong vein of classicism" in E's literary taste; J. T. Flanagan, who writes of "E as a Critic of Fiction" (*PQ* 36); and R. P. Falk, "E and Shakespeare" (*PMLA* 41), who says that E's derogatory comment on Shakespeare as "master of the revels" has been ridiculously overstressed. Paul Lauter's "E's Revisions of *Essays* (First Series)" (*AL* 61) shows that E eliminated unnecessary words, improved the style in clarity and force, and changed the sense slightly in the direction of greater conservatism.

7. *Reputation and Influence*

The extensive critical literature discussed in this essay is proof enough that E's reputation has been great both in this country and abroad. Of his younger contemporaries, Theodore Parker and Thoreau felt his influence before 1850 (see E. D. Mead, *The Influence of E*, 1903, and André Bruel, *E et Thoreau*, 1929). With regard to Thoreau and the coolness that comes between him and E after 1850, see also Charles Cestre, "Thoreau et E" (*RAA* 30), and J. B. Moore, "Thoreau Rejects E" (*AL* 32). The relationship of E and Whitman is more complex. It seems certain that he was Whitman's most important teacher and that Whitman read him thoroughly and heard him lecture during the late 1840's and early 1850's, though objective evidence is slight. After 1860 Whitman, like Thoreau after 1850, stood more firmly on his own feet and was inclined to minimize his debt to E. Whitman's criticism of E in *Specimen Days* (1882) points up the wide differences between them as well as their agreement on basic issues. Helpful studies of this relationship are J. B. Moore, "The Master of Whitman" (*SP* 26), Clarence Gohdes, "Whitman and E" (*SR* 26), and Carlos Baker, "The Road to Concord: Another Milestone in the Whitman-E Friendship" (*PULC* 46). The progress of the E-Whitman relationship is fully documented in *The Shock of Recognition* (1943), edited by Edmund Wilson. The latest extended study of the E-Thoreau relationship is Joel Porte's *E and Thoreau: Transcendentalists in Conflict* (1966). Porte claims that for Thoreau experience was all and for E the moral law was all. He thinks E got his belief in the moral law and his conception of the moral sense from eighteenth-century writers at a very early age and never changed.

Others of more or less importance whom E influenced were the mystic Jones Very (see Carlos Baker, "E and Jones Very," (*NEQ* 34), Margaret Fuller (see H. R. Warfel, "Margaret Fuller and REW," *PMLA* 35), Christopher Cranch (see H. C. Carpenter, "E and Christopher Pearse Cranch, *NEQ* 64), and Herman Melville, though it must be said that on Melville opinion is divided. William Braswell studied Melville's annotations in his E books and discussed his findings in "Melville as a Critic of E" (*AL* 37). See also E. S. Oliver, "Melville's Picture of E and Thoreau in *The Confidence Man*" (*CE* 46). For E's relationship to Hawthorne, see B. B. Cohen's "E's 'The Young American' and Hawthorne's 'The Intelligence Office'" (*AL* 54).

G. W. Cooke, writing in 1881, said, "This period from 1860 to 1870 is that in which E secures the widest hearing, has the strongest personal influence in molding the thought of his time, and when his character shines out in the most emphatic manner." Emily Dickinson, about this time, was much under E's influence (see G. F. Whicher, *This Was a Poet*, 1938, 1952, 1957), and in one way or another William James certainly drew largely upon E, as F. I. Carpenter has shown. In an anniversary speech (*NR* 43), Irwin Edman placed James in the tradition of E, Thoreau, and Whitman. Henry James, Jr., had ambivalent feelings toward E, but Earl Rovit in "James and E: The Lesson of the Master" (*ASch* 64) records a change in James between 1887 and 1907 parallel to his personal and artistic development and leading to a fuller understanding and acceptance of E. An interesting analysis of the opinions of the three Jameses on E may be found in W. T. Stafford's "E and the James Family" (*AL* 53). As for Chapman, S. G. Brown has said ("John Jay Chapman and the Emersonian Gospel," *NEQ* 52) that he understood and believed in E's teachings better than any other man. "He points to E," says Brown, "and E points to the inherent strength and benign power of the human spirit," which America now so badly needs to believe in. Among twentieth-century poets who have been influenced by E, besides Robinson and Frost, are Wallace Stevens (see, for example, Harold Bloom, "The Central Man: E, Whitman, Wallace Stevens," *MR* 66, and more particularly, for differences, Richard Eberhart's "E and Wallace Stevens," *LitR* 63); and Hart Crane (see "The Significance of *The Bridge*" in Yvor Winters's *In Defense of Reason*, 1947). Additional evidence may be found in Carpenter's *E Handbook*, R. H. Pearce's *The Continuity of American Poetry*, and in most other literary histories. In "Robert Henri and the E-Whitman Tradition" (*PMLA* 56) J. J. Kwiat discusses the extraordinary influence of E and Whitman on Henri (1865–1929), a leading spokesman of the continuing tendency toward an organic theory of art, and through him on many others; in the process, he provides a useful review of E's aesthetic principles. For the impact of E on a musical composer, see Charles Ives, *Essays before a Sonata and Other Writings* (1964).

E was well received on his lecture tours in Great Britain in 1847–48 and 1872–73, an account of which is given by Alexander Ireland in his biography of E (1882). The tour of 1847–48 is outlined and discussed in detail by Townsend Scudder in "E's British Lecture Tour, 1847–48" (*AL* 35), in "E in London and the London Lectures" (*AL* 36), and in "E in Dundee" (*Asch* 35). For Scudder's story of E's friendship with Carlyle, Clough, and other Englishmen, see his book, *The Lonely Wayfaring Man* (1936). The attitude of Carlyle may be studied in the correspondence of Carlyle and E and in the various biographies, particularly Rusk's. Interesting sidelights may be gained from numerous comparisons of the writers, among which may be mentioned that of Lowell in *A Fable for Critics* (1848), that of Henry James, Jr., in his review of the *Correspondence* in the *Century* (1883), that of E. P. Whipple in *American Literature and Other Papers* (1887), and that of E. D. Mead in *The Influence of E* (1903). See also Clarence Gohdes, *American Literature in Nineteenth-Century England* (1944). The most complete study of the reception of E in England is W. J. Sowder's *E's Impact on the British Isles and Canada* (1966). Sowder traces, chiefly through periodicals, the British and Canadian reception of E's essays and poems from about 1840 to 1870, with a brief summary of later views. For E's recognition in Australia and New Zealand see Joseph Jones, "E and Whitman 'Down Under': Their Reception in Australia and New Zealand" (*ESQ* 66). Jones says E's strongest influence there was exterted indirectly through Whitman.

The best survey of the reception of E in France is Hans Keller, *E in Frankreich; Wirkungen und Parallelen* (Giessen, 1932). Among the first in France to write of E were Philarète Chasles in the *RDM* (1844), and Edgar Quinet, who hailed E in 1845 as the most idealistic writer of the time. These were followed by Marie de Flavigny, Comtesse d'Agoult (pseud., Daniel Stern) in 1846, and Emile Montégut in 1847. E continued to be heard of occasionally during the next twenty years, and in 1871 he was welcomed on his European tour as a master by Renan and Taine. By 1898 he was beginning to be studied seriously by moralists and philosophers. The most important critical result of this growing interest was Marie Dugard's biography in 1907, which was crowned by the Academy. Later studies of importance were Régis Michaud's critical study *Autour d'E* (Paris, 1924), which has an essay on E and Nietzsche, another on E and Achille Murat (see also H. L. Richmond's "RWE in Florida," *FHQ* 39, on E's relations with Achille Murat), and another on E's reading of the work of G. L. L. Oegger; and also Michaud's *L'Esthétique d'E* and his *La vie inspirée d'E* (Paris, 1930), translated the same year as *E: the Enraptured Yankee*, discussed earlier. Evidence of a continuing interest in E may be found in Charles Cestre's "La pédagogie d'E" (*AUP* 29), Maurice Chazin's "E's Disciple in Belgium: Marie Mali" (*RR* 33), and three articles by the same author on Edgar Quinet, one in *PMLA* (33) and two in *RLC* (35). B. D. Howard's "The First French Estimate of E" (*NEQ* 37) is a study of "Daniel Stern." Margaret Gilman says in "Baudelaire and E" (*RR* 43) that E was the only American writer except Poe who "won more than a passing mention" from Baudelaire, and she says his *Journaux intimes* have "an unmistakeable Emersonian tang." A strong indication of interest in E in the 1960's is a book already discussed, Maurice Gonnaud's *Individu et Société dans l'oeuvre de RWE*.

For detailed information of E's fortune in Italy, there is "La fortuna di RWE in Italia" (*SA* 66) by M. T. DeMajo, covering the period 1847–1963. When E died he was almost unknown in Italy, but during the next several decades all his principal works were translated into Italian and a number of critical studies appeared in Italy. Interest lapsed during the war years 1939–45, but afterward revived and has become quite lively, including more interest in E's poetry than ever before. In "Lombardo on E and American Art" J. C. Mathews translates a section of Agostino Lombardo's *La ricerca del Vero* (Rome, 1961), in which Lombardo notes that E is important not only as an intermediary between European culture and America, but also as an active force in the development of a native American culture.

A very good survey of E's reception in Germany is Julius Simon's *RWE in Deutschland* (Berlin, 1937). German interest in E began about 1855 with Herman Grimm as the earliest important reader of E in Germany. Grimm tried to interest others in E but with little success. Simon says the period during which Germans interested themselves most in E was between 1894 and 1907. After the first World War there was another upsurge of interest in E culminating in the excellent studies by Paul Sakmann and Eduard Baumgarten (1927 and 1938) already discussed. Baumgarten, it appears, emphasized the American characteristics of E's thought, whereas others, including H. S. Chamberlain (1935) and Simon himself, attempted to relate it to the current of thought then prevailing among the followers of Hitler. Hedi Hildebrand's *Die amerikanische Stellung zur Geschichte und zu Europa in Es Gedankensystem* (Bonn, 1936) is oriented somewhat as Baumgarten's work. All inevitably discuss E's ideas in comparison with those of Nietzsche. More recently Baumgarten has published "Mitteilungen und Bemerkunger über den Einfluss Es auf Nietzsche" (*JA* 56), a close comparison of Nietzsche's work with specific essays of E based partly on Nietzsche's marginal notes in his copy of the essays. In 1958 Stanley Hubbard published a full-scale study of *Nietzsche und E* in Basel. This is one of the best recent books on the subject. His method is to emphasize parallels in the lives of E and Nietzsche and to compare their ideas. He reprints selections from the essays together with Nietzsche's comments on them, arranging the selections according to thematic ideas common to both. In "RWE in Modern Germany" (*ESQ* 65) Martin Christadler gives an excellent summary of a large number of important books and articles published in Germany. Some of E's ideas were distorted and made to support the mystic element in National Socialism in the 1930's. In recent years E has been better understood in Germany. Two other studies of E and Nietzsche are Rudolf Schottlaender's "Two Dionysians: E and Nietzsche" (*SAQ* 40) and Hermann Hummel's "E and Nietzsche" (*NEQ* 46). Hummel conveniently reviews previous writings on E and Nietzsche, and though like Baumgarten he finds considerable influence on Nietzsche, he condemns those who have tried to derive from E's works a justification of the racial theories current during Hitler's regime.

It hardly seems worth while to indicate specifically the evidence of E's influence in other countries. The Soviet Russian point of view is presented in S. L. Jackson's translation, "A Soviet View of E" (*NEQ* 46), drawn from a Russian statement of American philosophy. The reader should refer to *Russian Studies of American Literature*, a bibliography compiled by V. A. Libman, translated by R. V. Allen, and edited for publication in America by Clarence Gohdes (1969). A brief survey of E's reception in a few other countries, such as Japan, India, and Sweden, is given by F. I. Carpenter in his *E Handbook*. Bunsho Jugaker's "A Bibliography of RWE in Japan from 1878 to 1935," originally published in a limited edition in Kyoto in 1947, has been reprinted in *ESQ* (67). This is a checklist of 228 items, annotated.

The attempt to saddle E with the responsibility for the "rugged individualism" and materialism of the American Gilded Age and for the philosophy of force in Nazi Germany of the present century has been no less misleading than the opposite effort to identify him with the sentimental optimism that was widespread in his own time. As Rusk and others have seen, E has been a harmonizer of discordant values and has yet something to teach mankind. (See especially R. L. Rusk "E and the Stream of Experience," *CE* 53.) Firkins wrote in 1930 ("Has E a Future?" *MLN*), "E means for us pre-eminently an enlargement of the possibilities of man's experience; the inextinguishable thirst of the race for what is larger and deeper in the psychic life cannot finally ignore him." Recent opinion, after all deductions have been made, supports this view. Stephen Whicher concludes his study by saying that "to reject E utterly is to reject mankind." C. F. Strauch (*Personalist* 52) believes that E's moral idealism, resulting from his struggle to maintain his poise in the midst of the conflicting elements of life, puts him in the stream of the most enduring intellectual and imaginative tradition of the Western World. S. G. Brown says (*Ethics* 54) that his value today is perhaps as great as it was to his contemporaries. H. M. Jones, speaking at the sesquicentennial of E's birth, asserts that E is badly needed today for the very thing which causes him to be neglected: his faith in the individual man and his courage to face the principal evil of our time, cowardice and conformity. There is, then, evidence of renewed, if more critical, appreciation of E in America and in other countries. More recently Richard Poirier in *A World Elsewhere: The Place of Style in American Literature* (1966) considers E essential and central to understanding those American writers who attempted to free themselves from the influence of existing forms and institutions and create a "new" world through their style.

NATHANIEL HAWTHORNE

Walter Blair

I. BIBLIOGRAPHY

E. M. O'Connor's 1882 *Analytical Index to the Works of Nathaniel Haw-thorne* (hereafter NH, H), still useful, was reissued in 1967 with Introduction by C. E. F. Clark. But three 1905 bibliographies have been supplanted by those listed by Clark, bibliographies in studies by Martin and Turner cited be-low, and the following: R. L. Gale, *Plots and Characters in the Fiction and Sketches of NH* (1968), with chronologies, synopses, and character identifica-tions; S. L. Gross and A. J. Levy, "Some Remarks on the Extant Manuscripts of H's Short Stories" (*SB* 61); Fredson Bowers, "H's Text" (*H Centenary Es-says*, hereafter *HCE*), edited by R. H. Pearce (1964); N. F. Adkins, "Notes on the H Canon" (*PBSA* 66); Robert Phillips *et al.*, "NH: Criticism of the Four Major Romances . . ." (*Thoth* 62); Buford Jones, *Checklist of H. Criticism, 1951–1966* (1968), with *précis*; augmented by K. W. Cameron, *H Index to Themes, Motifs, Topics, Archetypes, Sources, and Key Words . . . in Recent Criticism* (1968); and Arlin Turner, "Recent Scholarship on H and Melville," in *The Teacher and American Literature*, edited by Lewis Leary (1965). At press time, C. E. F. Clark was preparing useful items for publication in the early 1970's—*The Literary Manuscripts of NH* and a bibliography listing ephemera, contributions to periodicals and newspapers, books by H, studies of him, portraits and other Hawthorneana. Clark was to edit the *NH Journal*, scheduled to start publication in 1971. Buford Jones also was preparing an an-notated and fully indexed bibliography of H criticism—books, reviews, bibli-ographies, critical introductions to editions, studies, doctoral dissertations, ma-jor foreign discussions.

Bertha Faust, *H's Contemporaneous Reputation . . . in America and Eng-land, 1828–1864* (1939, 1968), has been supplemented by *H Among His Con-temporaries*, edited by K. W. Cameron (1968), a huge compilation of anec-dotes, table talk, and critical discussions; and by two critical surveys: *H: A Collection of Critical Essays*, edited by A. N. Kaul (1966), and *The Recogni-*

tion of NH: Selected Criticism since 1828, edited by B. B. Cohen (1969). With similar concerns, E. H. Cady, " 'The Wizard Hand': H, 1864–1900," and S. L. Gross and Randall Stewart, "The H Revival" (*HCE*), are perceptive. A model compilation on a single work is *Twentieth-Century Interpretations of "The Scarlet Letter,"* edited by J. C. Gerber (1968).

H's reputation in Europe also was studied recently. Roger Asselineau, "H Abroad" (*HCE*), glances at England, France, and Germany. More comprehensive studies for single nations are Camilla Zauli-Naldi, "La Fortuna di H in Italia" (*SA* 60); E. F. Timpe, "H in Germany" (*Sym* 65); and J. E. Rocks, "H and France" (*TSE* 69).

Such guides to a proliferating literature make unnecessary an exhaustive survey in the present essay—a happy circumstance since, as they prove, to attempt such an examination in the space available would be downright foolhardy. Instead, not even attempting to defend omissions, I shall deal only with writings which I find indispensable, interesting, or innovative, trusting more extensive surveys to alleviate injustices that result from prejudice or sheer ignorance.[1]

So voluminous is the literature that a suggestion that four-fifths of the books and articles about H now in the works be strangled and eaten seems no more than a modest proposal. One perforce agrees with Philip Young's lighthearted but informed "H and 100 Years: A Report from the Academy" (*KR* 65) that H has been over–"explicated, allegorized, source-hunted, theologized, annotated, romanticized, de-romanticized, decoded, psychoanalyzed, and mythologized."

II. EDITIONS

Whether H also—as Young claims—has been over-edited, time must decide. To the Riverside edition of *The Complete Works of NH*, edited by G. P. Lathrop (12 vols., 1883), *Doctor Grimshawe's Secret*, edited by Julian Hawthorne, was added as Vol. 13. This edition and the two 1900 editions (the Autograph and the Old Manse—each 22 volumes) are now standard. To these should be added the *American Notebooks* (1932) and the *English Notebooks* (1941), with deletions from MSS restored by Randall Stewart, and a more faithful printing of *Doctor Grimshawe's Secret*, edited by E. H. Davidson (1954). These in time will be supplanted by the Centenary edition (William

---

1. More of each would have been apparent in this essay had I failed to take advantage of valuable suggestions made by John Gerber and Marjorie Elder, and of very thorough critical readings of the entire article by Arlin Turner and Buford Jones. Of course, as usual, I was able to make all my errors without assistance from anybody.

Charvat, R. H. Pearce, C. M. Simpson, general editors; Fredson Bowers, J. J. Bruccoli, textual editors). H's five novels appeared in four volumes of this edition between 1962 and 1968, each—since the emphasis is on the text—with prodigious bibliographical supplements; and other volumes are forthcoming. Though Centenary editors may regard them with scorn, heretics concerning some dogmas of the New Bibliographers may prefer less formidable editions of two novels: In his Riverside edition of *The House of the Seven Gables* (1964) H. H. Waggoner collated the MS and the first printing and (as R. H. Fogle says) "has done his full duty by his text, explained his rationale with great lucidity and literary balance, and has been able to apply first-class critical intelligence, an intimate knowledge of H as a whole, and a long commitment . . . as a scholar and a teacher." Some also will cherish the Chandler Publishing Company's facsimile of *The Scarlet Letter*, first edition, edited by Waggoner and George Monteiro (1968).[2]

Uncollected works include *H's First Diary*, edited by S. T. Pickard (1897); "H's 'Spectator,' " edited by E. L. Chandler (*NEQ* 31); D. C. Gallup, "On H's Authorship of 'The Battle-Omen' " (*NEQ* 36); *H as Editor: Selections from His Writings for the American Magazine of Useful and Entertaining Knowledge*, edited by Arlin Turner (1941); Randall Stewart, "H's Contributions to *The Salem-Advertiser*" (*AL* 34), and "Two Uncollected Reviews by H" (*NEQ* 36); and *Poems*, edited by Richard Peck (1967). H's authorship of the "First Diary" and "The Battle-Omen" is not established. (See Pickard, "Is H's 'First Diary' a Forgery?" *Dial* 02, and Gallup, *op. cit.*) A complete collection of H's letters has long been promised and awaited. Manuscript collections are in the Boston Public Library, Essex Institute Manning Collection, Huntington Library, Houghton Library, National Archives in Washington, D. C., Duyckinck and Berg Collections of the New York Public Library, and the Pierpont Morgan Library.

Letters are quoted in biographies by Lathrop, Julian Hawthorne, and Bridge (listed hereafter) and in Samuel Longfellow, *Life of Henry Wadsworth Longfellow* (2 vols., 1887), and *Final Memorials of Henry Wadsworth Longfellow* (1887). Collections include Manning Hawthorne, "H's Early Years" (*EIHC* 38), "NH Prepares for College" (*NEQ* 38), and "N and Elizabeth H, Editors" (*Colophon* 39); Randall Stewart, "H and Politics: Unpublished Letters to William B. Pike" (*NEQ* 32); E. C. Sampson, "Three Unpublished Letters by H to Epes Sargent [1842–47]" (*AL* 62); *Love Letters of NH, 1839–41*

---

2. Hereafter H's major novels will be abbreviated as follows: *The Scarlet Letter*—*SL*; *The House of the Seven Gables*—*H7G*; *The Blithedale Romance*—*BR*; *The Marble Faun*—*MF*.

and 1841–63 (2 vols., 1907); Manning Hawthorne, "H and Utopian Socialism" (*NEQ* 39); *Letters of H to William D. Ticknor, 1851–64* (2 vols., 1910); Caroline Ticknor, *H and His Publisher* (1913, 1969); N. L. Eagle, "An Unpublished H Letter [1851]" (*AL* 51); Harold Blodgett, "H as Poetry Critic: Six Unpublished Letters to Lewis Mansfield" (*AL* 40); R. H. Lathrop, "The Hawthornes in Lenox: Told in Letters by N and Mrs. H" (*Century* 1894); R. M. Aderman, "Newly Located H Letters [1885]" (*EIHC* 52); J. C. Austin, *Fields of "The Atlantic Monthly"* (1953); Randall Stewart, "The Hawthornes at the Wayside, 1860–1864" and "H's Last Illness and Death" (*More Books* 44).

J. D. Hart, "H's Italian Diary" (*AL* 63) describes the newly discovered diary kept in Italy, the basis of the Italian Notebooks—an important document in the Rare Book Room, University of California, Berkeley.

III. BIOGRAPHY

Supplementing H's letters and journals, books, articles, and letters by relatives, friends, and acquaintances comprise primary sources: G. W. Curtis (Brook Farmer, Concord neighbor), *Homes of American Authors* (1853) and "H and Brook Farm," *From the Easy Chair* (3rd Ser. 1894); S. G. Goodrich (publisher), *Recollections of a Lifetime* (1856); Elizabeth Peabody (sister-in-law who did much to encourage the long-prevalent conception of H's early years), "The Genius of H" (*Atl* 1868) and "The Two H's" (*Western* 1875); Sophia Hawthorne (wife), editor, *Notes on England and Italy* (1869); J. T. Fields (publisher), *Yesterdays with Authors* (1872), repr. as *H* (1876); Julian (son), "The Salem of H" and "Scenes of H's Romances" (*Century* 1884); *NH and His Wife* (2 vols., 1884, 1968); and *H and His Circle* (1890, 1968)—invaluable though often inaccurate; M. D. Conway (acquaintance), *Life of NH* (1890, 1968); Horatio Bridge (friend from college days), *Personal Recollections of NH* (1893); Rose H. Lathrop (daughter), "My Father's Literary Methods" (*Ladies Home Jour* 1894) and *Memories of H* (1894); G. B. Loring (Salem postmaster acquaintance), "H" in *Papyrus Leaves*, edited by W. F. Gill (1898); Annie (Mrs. J. T.) Fields, *H* (1889); R. H. Stoddard (acquaintance), *Recollections* (1903); F. B. Sanborn (Concord schoolmaster), *H and His Friends* (1908).

Since secondary biographical writings are interpretative, users do well to consider which facts they exclude and include, ways they weight facts and emphases in discussions of writings in relation to theses being developed. To the very present two views—an earlier traditional one and a newer interpretation—are distinguishable.

Letters and contemporaneous accounts provided the basis for the first picturing—a H withdrawn from society and the world, aloof from their problems but driven to brood over them and to treat them fancifully. Henry James, *H* (1879, 1968) struck the keynote: H's career "had few perceptible points of contact with what is called the world, with public events, with the manners of the time, even with the life of his neighbors," and H's "mind in so far as it was a repository of opinions and articles of faith . . . had no development"; H was an unworldly artist with a provincial New England Puritanical background. This interpretation in James's avowed "critical essay" P. E. More repeated with slight variations in "The Solitude of NH," *Shelburne Essays* (1st ser., 1904), and G. E. Woodberry, *NH* (1902, 1967), offered arguments for the characteristic claim that H had the temperament "of the solitary brooder upon life" whose tenuous relationship with the world was a "race quality"—an "inheritance from Puritanism"—a child of New England who "took practically no interest in life except . . . in its normal moral aspects." Woodberry nevertheless saw H as well-adjusted in two ways, in his political affiliations and in his family life. With slight changes this picture was reproduced in literary histories and biographical studies into the 1920's and beyond. Herbert Gorman, *H: A Study in Solitude* (1927), stressed the concept indicated by the sub-title and Lloyd Morris, *The Rebellious Puritan* (1927), documented more thoroughly H's tendency toward withdrawal.

Gorman and Morris both, however, partly anticipated later picturings by representing H as somewhat more closely related to his intellectual milieu than Woodberry had seen him. Newton Arvin, *H* (1929), showed other deviations as he used contemporaneous psychological techniques to relate H's preoccupation with guilt to his reclusiveness: "The essential sin, he would seem to say, lies in whatever shuts up the spirit in a dungeon . . . beyond the reach of common sympathies. . . . All that isolates, damns; all that associates, saves . . . thus fearfully . . . did he represent . . . the pitfalls he had peculiarly to avoid." The theme Arvin saw as coming not from H's Puritan inheritance but from his own tragic struggle. Thus Arvin differed in his conception of precisely how H's isolation shaped the fiction.

The later interpretation was based in part, as it had to be, upon primary sources used through 1929. But later students questioned hitherto accepted "facts," e.g., the tradition that the love of solitude of H's mother lasted for decades and infected her son. Later students used some documents—notebooks, to cite an important example—in more authentic versions. And they utilized materials previously only partly studied or unknown. The later picture showed H as less isolated, less abnormal, and conversely better adjusted and more in tune with his fellows and the day's leading issues.

Special studies filled in this outline; e.g., J. B. Osborne, "NH as American Consul" (*Bookman* 03), held that H's official letters to the State Department proved him a hard-working, efficient, and practical consul. G. E. Jepson, "H in the Boston Custom House" (*Bookman* 04), revised earlier accounts, as did W. S. Nevins, "NH's Removal from the Salem Custom House" (*EIHC* 17). N. F. Doubleday, "H's Satirical Allegory" (*CE* 42), related satires to current events; Arlin Turner, "H and Reform" (*NEQ* 42), studied H's social attitudes. L. S. Hall, *H: Critic of Society* (1944), surveyed relevant documents and concluded that H was knowledgeable and committed. Two later studies have added details: B. B. Cohen, "Edward Everett and H's Removal from the Custom House" (*AL* 55), and K. W. Cameron, "New Light on H's Removal from the Customs House" (*ESQ* 61).

Manning Hawthorne, H's great-grandson, used unexplored family MSS to fill in the story of H's earlier years: "H and 'The Man of God' " (*Colophon* 37); "H's Early Years" (*EIHC* 38); "NH Prepares for College" (*NEQ* 38); "Maria Louisa Hawthorne" (*EIHC* 39); "N and Elizabeth Hawthorne, Editors" (*Colophon* 39); "Parental and Family Influences on H" (*EIHC* 40); "NH at Bowdoin" (*NEQ* 40); "The Friendship between H and Longfellow" (*EJ* 39); "Aunt Ebe: Some Letters of Elizabeth K. Hawthorne" (*NEQ* 47); "A Glimpse of H's Boyhood" (*EIHC* 47). Similar were N. F. Adkins, "The Early Projected Works of NH" (*PBSA* 45), and N. H. Pearson's unpublished monograph, "The College Years of NH" (Yale 32). Pearson has published several studies which, with the aid of neglected documents, supplement the above: "H and the Mannings" (EIHC 58); Elizabeth Peabody of H" (*EIHC* 58); "H's Duel" (*EIHC* 58); "A 'Good Thing' for H" [throwing added light on the Boston Custom House appointment] (*EIHC* 64); "The Pyncheons and Judge Pyncheon" (*EIHC* 64); and *H's Two "Engagements"* (1963). Two recent studies cast doubt on Julian H's reliability—Maurice Bassan, "Julian H Edits Aunt Ebe" (*EIHC* 64), and George Monteiro, "Maule's Curse and Julian H" (*N&Q* 67).

Randall Stewart was more responsible than any other scholar for presenting and documenting the second concept of H. Convinced while editing the restored notebooks that overnice wifely tinkering had helped create an inaccurate image, he re-examined the re-evaluated primary sources, unearthed valuable documents, and between 1929 and 1946 published eleven important biographical articles arguing for changes in traditional concepts. He summarized and climaxed his years of work in *NH: A Biography* (1948). The book was not overcrowded with factual information or heavily annotated since he rightly assumed that his introductions and notes to the *Notebooks* (1932, 1941), his articles (listed in his bibliography), and those of other scholars provided documentation. Stewart portrayed a more worldly, more sociable, more "normal" figure than earlier biographers—a philosophically sophisticated author who "touched his times at point after point with admonitory finger"—a thinker with a positive message: "essentially the recognition of man's fallibility, the restoration of sympathy, the sharing of the common lot. H's 'moral' comprehends the Christian doctrine of charity, the psychological doctrine of participation, the social doctrine of the democratic way."

During the years when Stewart's studies were appearing, book-length biographies displayed both the old and the new H. Edward Mather [Jackson] in *NH: A Modest Man* (1940), with the extraordinary aim of showing its subject as "a man rather than . . . an author," accepted the older view of H as a diffident recluse whose solitary ways colored his work and shaped his life. Paradoxically, however, Mather's book is chiefly valuable for the light that it casts upon H's relationships with his contemporaries and "his violent opinions concerning the English." Robert Cantwell in *NH: The American Years* (1948), proclaiming eagerness to correct the "narrow and lopsided portrait" with its emphasis upon H's "brooding seclusion," tried to restore the real H by giving a "fuller treatment of people whose lives were linked with his" and by dealing at length with "the depth and nature of his political work." His discussion of H's family and of even casual associates, overfull and often irrelevant, has encyclopedic value. Discussing H and politics, Cantwell develops a startling thesis—that H was detached from Salem life during the twelve years after Bowdoin, not because of his temperament or artistic concerns, but because he was a secret agent of the United States Treasury Department—a hypothesis backed by little evidence.

Two later books also place H in relation to his family: L. H. Tharp, *The Peabody Sisters of Salem* (1950) and Vernon Loggins, *The Hawthornes: The Story of Seven Generations . . .* (1951), ending with the death of Julian's widow in 1949. These may well be checked against "Mrs. H to Mrs. Fields," edited by Ellen Oldham (*BPLQ* 57), a hitherto unpublished article pieced together by Annie Fields on the basis of letters from the author's wife written between 1859 and 1865.

Identical with the major aim of these books—to place H's works in biographical and historical contexts—was the aim of three noteworthy studies of the early 1960's. In *NH: Man and Writer* (1961), "a study of H's character and personality, based on his writings, his letters and journals, and on all that has been written about him," Edward Wagenknecht joins Stewart in picturing H as better balanced and more a man of his time than initial biographers had believed. In a "psychograph" arranged topically rather than chronologically, illuminating chapters explore the life, learning, and attitudes of the author to render him "understandable as a human being." In his unduly modest *NH: An Introduction and Interpretation* (1961), Arlin Turner utilizes many external records, H's own assertions about himself and his writings "to learn what made its way into [H's] mind and also what was his attitude toward it." His claim is that H's tendencies toward skepticism, his satire, and his irony "fit together in the pattern of his mind" and shape his views and his literary achievements. H. H. Hoeltje in *Inward Sky: The Mind and Heart of NH* (1962) is eager, as Turner is, to understand his subject from his subject's own point of view—to see him fully, that is, in his daily life as a man closely related to the nineteenth-century world. This biographer's habit of quoting H constantly, often without using quotation marks, betokens (as H might put it) a deeply sympathetic attitude and a consequent refusal to stand aside and view his subject through twentieth-century eyes. A labor of love mellowed over many years, this is a book which even scholars disagreeing with its chief findings are compelled to admire.

For various reasons, many scholars will disagree. In the turbulent 1960's when denigration became *de rigueur* among intellectuals, so venerated a figure as H inevitably became a target. Not surprisingly, Great Britain's Martin Green, who seems to have embarked upon a career as a debunker, includes in *Re-appraisals* (1965) a two-year-old essay, "The H Myth," which charges that the author is a stupid, uncultivated man and a negligible author. More surprisingly, a good half of the essays in *HCE*, of all places, downgrade H. Even so, when Irving Howe reviews the collection (*AL* 65), he doubts that H deserves even this tribute. For how much of H, he asks, "apart from one superb novel and seven or eight first-rate stories . . . is truly alive and not merely propped up by academic piety?" Nor is Howe alone in assuming that the answer must be, "Very little." A very certain condescension towards H (and those who have praised him) also is present in two essays by a second British critic: David Howard, "*BR* and a Sense of Revolution," in *Tradition and Tolerance* (1967) and "The Fortunate Fall and M's *MF*" in *Romantic Mythologies*, edited by Ian Fletcher (1967). Howard, like Green, finds H dim-witted and—more lamentably—incapable of facing up to the need for social change. Proof that old England had no patent on such doubts was furnished by Alfred Kazin in "H: The artist of New England" (*Atl* 66), which held that regardless of his artistry H did not "influence our living and thinking now" since "if literature embodies the consciousness of a generation, H is no part of our generation."

Pro- or anti-H, many who judge him today do so in modern terms, making use of current psychology, mythology, or methods of the New Critics. Though writers using one or more of these approaches may illuminate the author's biography, since they are chiefly interested in the content and form of his works, they may be discussed under the headings "Studies of Ideas" and "Criticism."

IV. STUDIES OF IDEAS

As interest grew in H's involvement, disputes arose concerning his position on various issues. Austin Warren summarized in his *NH: Representative Selections* (AWS, 1934): "Critics of ability and acumen urge contradictory interpretations [picturing H as] the defender of Puritanism; its opponent and satirist; a Transcendentalist; the adversary of the movement; a believer; a skeptic; a democrat; an aristocrat; a moralist of New England rigor and even prudery; a prophet (albeit perhaps unaware) of the Freudian gospel; a romantic, imbued with belief in the essential rightness of human instincts and faith in the masses; a Christian and realist with suspicion of reform and no credence of 'progress.'"

Since such disagreements still exist, it is impossible to cite a definitive treatment of most areas of H's thought. Leading biographers already cited necessarily concern themselves with H's ideas and contribute in some ways to an understanding of them. In the 1930's and 1940's, however, three pioneered in making surveys which have continued to have value—Warren, F. O. Matthiessen, and Stewart. Others then and later wrote specialized studies of particular facets of H's mind which are outstanding.

Warren's Introduction to *Representative Selections* attempts "to trace the development of H's religious, ethical, political, social, and literary ideas" under appropriate headings. The author's summaries of his own and other studies of H's mind are all well documented, though later scholars have cast a great deal of doubt on the claim that H "was nearly impervious to . . . intellectual movements." H is one of five authors considered by Matthiessen in *AmR* (1941), and since Matthiessen is concerned with his authors' interrelationships and the movement of American literature, he thoroughly considers H in relation to his milieu and notices any parallels between his thought and that of his contemporaries. He is eager, moreover, to describe writings as works of art, and to do this he tries to discover "conceptions held by five . . . major writers concerning the functions and nature of literature, and the degree to which their practice bore out their theories," evaluating any "fusions of form and content." His consideration of form leads to a study of other ideas and attitudes, since (like Croce) he thinks of form as "nothing else than the entire resolution of the intellectual, sentimental and emotional material into the concrete reality of the poetic image and word." So in dealing with H he includes discussions of his ideas about religion, philosophy, politics, society, and art, and relates them to unusually fine analyses of individual narratives. Stewart's introductory chapters, "The Development of Character Types . . ." and "Recurrent Themes . . . ," in his edition of *American Notebooks*, discuss the author's chief ideas as they are embodied in writings. And the final chapter of Stewart's fine biography, "The Collected Works," is a concise but brilliant essay based upon thorough knowledge which considers the works taken together as "in the highest sense a criticism of life" and precisely defines this criticism.

Studies more specialized in their approach fall under three headings: Religious and Philosophical Concepts, Social and Political Ideas, and Literary Theories.

1. Religious and Philosophical Concepts

Lathrop and Julian Hawthorne note that though H was reared a Unitarian, as an adult he did not join or attend a church. The generally accepted implication is that he was not a practicing Unitarian, and few see him showing Unitarian bias. Discussions of his belief largely concern his attitudes towards Puritanism, Catholicism, and contemporary nonsectarian attitudes.

Those holding that H was basically a Puritan differ in defining his Puritanism. Emile Montégut, "Un Romancier pessimiste en Amérique" (*RDM* 1860), holds that H, emphasizing one Puritan doctrine but scanting another, stressed the depravity of man but did not see it as "a prelude to recommending the grace of God." W. C. Brownell, *American Prose Masters* (1909), thinks him so much a Puritan that he usually succeeded only when developing Puritan themes. In other ways, too, Brownell feels that innate Puritanism shaped H's words, e.g., *SL* was "the Puritan *Faust*." As indicated, Woodberry in his biography—and also in "The Literary Age of Boston" (*HM* 03)—expresses the opinion of many earlier writers: He sees H as less a conscious Puritan than one who absorbed the moral atmosphere and emphasis of Puritanism as his inheritance and part of his temperament. One result was deep concern with moral matters; another a relentless attitude toward his characters and emphasis upon dark aspects of life; another a democratic attitude which made him "see all men as in the light of the judgment day."

Similarly, writers held that Puritanism, instead of leading H to adopt specific dogmas, caused him to arrive at related attitudes such as excessive fatalism (Arvin) or skepticism (Morris and others). H. W. Schneider in his brilliant *The Puritan Mind* (1930) characterized H as one who "did not need to believe in Puritanism" since "he understood it." "He," continues Schneider, "saw the empirical truth behind the Calvinistic symbols [and] recovered . . . the spirit of piety, humility, and tragedy in the face of the inscrutable ways of God." And Matthiessen enlarged upon this conception.

Numerous related studies discriminate between different aspects of "Puritanism" and consider where H stood or how he shifted positions. F. I. Carpenter, "Puritans Preferred Blondes" (*NEQ* 36), sees H for a time wavering between the ideal of personal freedom and the religious sense of sin, but in time denying "the progressive ideal of self-reliant experience" and returning to "the old morality of purity." Barriss Mills, "H and Puritanism" (*NEQ* 48), finds H approving of certain Puritan attitudes such as "toughmindedness" and sharing beliefs in such matters as innate depravity, the futility of external reforms, and (with reservations) determinism, but differing in tolerance and other attitudes. Mills's classification of H as anti-intellectual is the most questionable part of a useful article. C. E. Eisinger, "Pearl and the Puritan Heritage" (*CE* 51), finds Pearl "the hypostatization . . . of the Puritan conception of nature and the nature of the state." Joseph Schwartz, "Three Aspects of Puritanism" (*NEQ* 63), after defining H's attitudes towards Puritanism as a theology, a recipe for living and a political concept, decides that it gave H neither "metaphysical roots" nor values. J. E. Miller, Jr., in "H and Melville: No! in Thunder" and "H and Melville: The Unpardonable Sin," *Quests Surd and Absurd* (1967) sorts out H's agreements and disagreements with particular Puritan doctrines on the basis of discerning readings of the writings. And Larzer Ziff utilizes his uniquely profound knowledge of seventeenth-century Puritan doctrines in "The Artist and Puritanism" (*HCE*) to link concepts of predestination and original sin with H's preference for psychological drama and to relate the Puritan scorn for *belles lettres* and for violations of privacy to H's attitude towards art. A result, Ziff plausibly argues, was H's creation of such recurrent types as the restrained "moral male" and the antinomian dark lady.

As early as 1885, A. F. Hewitt published "H's Attitude Toward Catholicism" (*CaW*) holding that H's contacts with Catholicism in Europe brightened his religious belief and made his religious views "more vivid and elevated," with Catholic art and "the pervading atmosphere of faith, in Italy and Rome" playing important roles. H, however, showed "no sign of . . . having attained a perception of the . . . evidence that the Catholic Church is the only church of Christ and way of salvation." Gilbert Voight, "H and the Roman Catholic Church" (*NEQ* 46), traces H's movement from initial hostility to a more judicious view between Kenyon's disapproval and his daughter Rose's acceptance. More recently two authors with Catholic interests wrote books which thoroughly explore the topic of these earlier studies. The Rev. L. J. Fick, *The Light*

Beyond: A Study of H's Theology (1955), relates the author's observations of the Catholic Church, especially in Italy, to his views concerning Providence, the nature and effects of evil, the unpardonable sin, and sin's nature, remission and consequences. He finds that H's personal theology came close to orthodox Arminian beliefs founded in part on revelation, in part on reason. H. G. Fairbanks in *The Lasting Loneliness of NH* (1965) is interested in the modern sense of man's alienation from a vision that "links God, Nature, and Man organically," H's life and work as a "classic American embodiment" of this predicament, and H's continuing quest for such a vision. The author sees H as one who, becoming dissatisfied with both Calvinism and Unitarianism, came to think as a Catholic (*anima naturaliter catholica*) concerning the "four major dislocations" of the period.

H's associations with New England Transcendentalists naturally led students to investigate the extent to which their beliefs affected him. Bliss Perry, *Park Street Papers* (1908), sees H as in fact a Transcendentalist. F. P. Stearns in *The Life and Genius of NH* (1906), John Erskine in his chapter on H in *CHAL* (1918), Matthiessen in *AmR*, cited above, and Floyd Stovall in *American Idealism* (1943) all see him accepting at least some Transcendental tenets. Several articles concern H's interrelationships with one or more Transcendental neighbors. B. B. Cohen, "Emerson's 'The Young American' and H's 'The Intelligence Office' " (*AL* 54), sees more mutual influence, especially between 1842 and 1844, than predecessors noticed, and perhaps overstates his claims. R. E. Hull, "H's Effort to Help Thoreau" (*ESQ* 63), and Buford Jones, " 'The Hall of Fantasy' and the Early H-Thoreau Relationship" (*PMLA* 68), call attention to an interrelationship which has been underestimated except by Frank Davidson in his consideration of Thoreau's contribution to *Mosses* (*NEQ* 47). H. H. Waggoner, " 'Grace' in the Thought of Emerson, Thoreau, and H" (*ESQ* 69), interestingly relates the ideas of the three concerning an important concept. J. K. Folsom in his extraordinary book, *Man's Accidents and God's Purposes: Multiplicity in H's Fiction* (1963), holds that far from being a Transcendentalist H is a "heretical" Platonist whose central emphasis is not upon God and Purposes but upon Man and Accidents, not upon Being but upon Becoming, not upon the One but upon the Many—that "H's world," in short, "is not amenable to order." The study provides an illustration of the way a dubious interpretation can be supported by misreadings.

Several useful or challenging studies concentrate on H's attitudes concerning specific nineteenth-century philosophical or psychological concepts. In *H's Ambivalence Toward Puritanism* (1965) J. G. Taylor ponders the clashes between the author's admiration for his Puritan ancestors and the nineteenth-century views of man which he encountered. In like fashion J. T. Frederick in a chapter on H in *The Darkened Sky: Nineteenth-Century Novelists and Religion* (1969) thoroughly canvasses H's involvement in Christian and anti-Christian contests throughout his lifetime; the section combines meticulous scholarship with sympathetic understanding. P. L. Thorslev, Jr., "H's Determinism: An Analysis" (*NCF* 64), makes use of philosophic distinctions to notice that in his best writings H postulated that free will is self-determined and that when fatalistic explanations of moral decisions are offered, scientific explanations ironically undercut them.

Borrowing a phrase from Matthiessen for his starting-point, D. A. Ringe, "H's Psychology of the Head and Heart" (*PMLA* 50), defines H's attitude toward Sin and the Fall of Man by examining H's characters in terms of a prevalent psychology. His well-documented suggestion is that while one solution lay in a balance between head and heart (Holgrave), another solution was superior (Hester): "If man is to develop the noblest qualities of mind and heart and so achieve true and profound insight into the problem of human existence, he must sin, incur the perilous state of isolation and sacrifice whatever happiness can be achieved in a troubled world." Ringe sees the story of Kenyon and Hilda in *MF* presenting the first solution, that of Donatello and Miriam the second. C. E. Eisinger, "H as Champion of the Middle Way" (*NEQ* 54), sees "a champion of a norm" in H's sympathetic portrayal of balanced characters and his less sympathetic picturing of abnormally isolated or ambitious ones. Readings of some stories—though not Eisinger's general theses—are questioned in S. R. Price, "The Heart, the Head, and 'Rappaccini's Daughter'" (*NEQ* 54). F. H. Link, *Die Erzählkunst NHs* (1962), despite its title, is chiefly concerned with H's moral meanings, e.g., the discovery of Hilda and Kenyon that when a way is found to allow the "head" to develop without destroying the "heart," sin is avoided. Nina Baym, "The Head, the Heart, and the Unpardonable Sin" (*NEQ* 67), continues the dialogue by arguing against the belief that sinners in H "can be arranged in a hierarchy depending on the preponderance of head or heart." Not the intellect, she holds, but "selfish passions produce sin." H's fiction focuses on the heart, "seen in its capacities for both good and evil." The arguments and citations are convincing. R. R. Male, *H's Tragic Vision* (1957), though it makes important contributions to the analysis and criticism of H's writings, probably is chiefly valuable for its examination of "part of the climate of opinion in H's time in connection with a detailed study of his work," in other words, as part of the history of ideas, particularly of Romanticism.

2. Social and Political Ideas

Lathrop and Julian Hawthorne saw a H of a split personality: a man of affairs practical and efficient, but an artist withdrawn from contemporary problems. Following these biographers, students believed that the aloofness was not confined to H's art, and several defended his detachment, e.g., James and Woodberry. But beginning with Brownell in 1909, some held that his ignorance about society and politics weakened his work. Gorman, Morris, and V. L. Parrington in 1927—the last in *MCAT*—so condemned him. Shortly afterward Marxist historians scolded him—V. F. Calverton, *The Liberation of American Literature* (1932), and Granville Hicks, *The Great Tradition* (1933).

Long before, however, as has been indicated, some scholars had begun to furnish details for a portrait showing H to be aware of society and politics, e.g., Randall Stewart, "H and Politics: Unpublished Letters to William B. Pike" (*NEQ* 32), offered proof that H had not been passive in politics. It was the first of several articles and grist for Stewart's biography, which in 1948 would give many instances of H's involvement. Manning Hawthorne's "H and Utopian Socialism" (*NEQ* 39) unearthed comments in two letters to David Mack relevant to the Brook Farm experiment. N. F. Doubleday published three relevant articles: "H's Hester and Feminism" (*PMLA* 39), "H's Criticism of New England Life" (*CE* 41), and "H's Satirical Allegory" (*CE* 42). Arlin Turner's "H and Reform" (*NEQ* 42) refuted claims about the author's indifference, and two years later L. S. Hall's *H: Critic of Society*, examining a great deal of evidence, much of it new, found that H, keenly aware of contemporaneous problems, studied them and took his stand. The year 1948 was climactic in this development since it brought both Stewart's and Cantwell's books. The latter in fact went somewhat too far in its representation of H's political activity as "active" and "vigorous," and even, when he became a secret agent, characterized by "considerable excitement and hazard." Other studies dealt with H's alleged conservatism: Russell Kirk, "The Moral Conservatism of H" (*Contemp Rev* 52); Darrel Abel, "H's Skepticism about Social Reform" (*UKCR* 53); Morton Cronin, "H on Romantic Love and the Status of Women" (*PMLA* 54); H. W. Schneider, "The Democracy of H" (*EUQ* 66); G. D. Josipovici, "H's Modernity" (*CritQ* 66); Allen Flint, "H and the Slavery Crisis" (*NEQ* 68); and David Singer, "H and the 'Wild Irish'" (*NEQ* 69).

Three books which might have been considered under the heading "Religious and Philosophical Ideas," or possibly as critical works, will be mentioned next because they relate H's thinking to broad concepts of American history prevalent during the decades before the Civil War. Essentially alike in their method, they have been praised for providing historiography of a new kind in narratives which interrelate "dialogues" and "myths." R. W. B. Lewis in the first of these, *The American Adam* (1955), suggests a rationale: The annals of the thought and the writings of a culture he analogizes to a dialogue (Lionel Trilling in 1940 had called it "a dialectic"), with authors expressing beliefs (Matthiessen in 1941 had called them "recurrent themes") in two ways —in (1) "the orderly language of rational thought" and (2) "a recurring pattern of images" and "a certain story," a native mythology. Lewis therefore charts ideas that some authors express in factual prose between 1820 and 1860 and that others dramatize in "the special and identifying myth of our culture" —the Biblical myth of Adam. Writers formed three groups: the party of Hope or Innocence, the party of Memory or Calvinistic Tradition, and the party of Irony which synthesizes the truths seen by both the other parties and which in time converts Adam, in the earlier fiction "a figure of heroic innocence and vast potentiality," into "the hero of a new kind of tragedy." Lewis places H in the party of Irony since his best works combine the insights of both other parties and his *MF* "sought to summarize the whole of [his] experience of America." Leo Marx locates *The Machine in the Garden* (1964) in "the region of culture where literature, general ideas, and certain products of the collective imagination—we may call them 'cultural symbols'—meet." For Marx, the clash or dialogue is between ideal innocence and nature (called "the Pastoral Ideal" in a subtitle) and what the subtitle calls "Technology" and its consequences; the two forces are imaged respectively in metaphors of the Garden and the Machine. H, so the passages about him hold, represents these in his *Notebooks*, "The Celestial Railroad," and "Ethan Brand." In the last of these, says Marx, "Ethan Brand is destroyed by the fires of change associated with factories," and the story "conveys H's inchoate sense of the doom awaiting the self-contained village culture." Edwin Fussell in *Frontier: American Literature and the American West* (1965) summarizes opposites and their metaphorical embodiments discussed in the books just mentioned and similar books. As John Stafford notices in his review (*NCF* 65), Fussell "puts before us most of the pervasive . . . antitheses that . . . preoccupied the nineteenth century: the factual world and the imaginative world, the East and the West, the settlement and the wilderness, white civilization and Indian liberty, and other such literary and philosophical opposites as realism and imagination, humanity and isolation, Christianity and savagery, sanity and insanity, waking and sleeping, and even life and death." Fussell finds H referring many times to the frontier concept as it is here defined. More surprisingly, he finds that "H was at heart a Western writer," whose imaginative works are permeated with images representing that concept. "Young Goodman Brown" for Fussell adumbrates the American advance to the Pacific and "penetrates into the dark forest of the unmapped future which is also the buried past." In *SL* Pearl becomes "the Spirit of the West," Hester a frontierswoman; and in other novels H reacts to the disappearance of the frontier.

These studies and some like ones which I plan, somewhat arbitrarily, to discuss as critical works, raise such questions as these: Are the concepts, the beliefs, the dialogues considered pervasive and important? Does the author define them vaguely or inconsistently? Does he ignore exceptions—ideas and metaphors, rhetoricians and imaginative writers—that fail to fit into his scheme? And as he turns specifically to an individual writer such as H, does he (it may well be unconsciously) ignore important deviations—does he mis- or over-read—to relate that writer to the interpretation that is being urged? Useful though many of their insights are, Lewis, Marx, and Fussell, I believe, at times fail to meet some of these tests. Hence what they say about H and his works must constantly be read with caution.

A spate of articles concern H's attitudes towards American history as they are revealed in specific works. G. G. Jordan, "H's 'Bell': Historical Evolution through Symbol" (*NCF* 64), holds that in an article "Bells" (1836) and an 1837 story, "A Bell's Biography," H symbolically represented the evolution of European history in the American wilderness and expressed a philosophy of history akin to that of contemporaneous German interpreters of Biblical history—a philosophy also related to the symbolism of some of H's greatest stories. Viola Sachs, "The Myth of America in H's *H7G* and *BR*" (*KN* 68), interestingly defines the myth and discusses its relevance to two books. Julian Smith, "H's 'Legends of the Province House' " (*NCF* 69), finds "a subtle moral balance between the rebellious colonists and the loyalists" which shows that H was "highly ambivalent towards and sometimes critical of the American Revolution." More ambitious than any of these is Johannes Kjørven, "H and the Significance of History" (Sigmund Skard and Henry Wasser, eds., *Americana-Norwegica*, Oslo, 1966), which interrelates the author's sense of the past and his deep interest in the operation of moral laws and analyzes historical themes in several stories and novels.

3. Literary Theories

Detailed studies of H's literary theories as they affected his work began when Austin Warren in 1934 surveyed H's comments on his artistry. Arlin Turner, "H as Self-Critic" (*SAQ* 38), scanning many passages, argued that H made "as accurate a judgement of his own writings as could be passed by any unbiased critic now" since he chided himself for qualities that critics often disliked—love of allegory, meager detail, and too continuously dark an outlook. But Turner notes that despite such awareness, H did not change his ways, probably because he realized that his sensibilities and beliefs forced him to write as he did.

Turner mentions H's use of understatement in his self-abasement, and as students increasingly sympathized with H's aims and methods, they attended more to his ironic tone and saw that much self-criticism actually constituted a justification; Matthiessen, for instance, often is favorable where previous critics were censurious.

When Matthiessen finds sources of H's critical beliefs among his Transcendental neighbors, he shows an interest shared by others. N. F. Doubleday, "H and Literary Nationalism" (*AL* 41), relates him to a larger group, those who urged authors to attempt what Scott had achieved in Scotland. Maurice Charney, "H and the Gothic Style" (*NEQ* 61), cites passages in the notebooks that show H expressing a preference for Gothic artistic aims and achievements. J. C. Stubbs in "H's *SL*: The Theory of Romance and the Use of the New England Situation" (*PMLA* 68) decides that H's literary theory is "an intelligent reappraisal of the typical concerns of the romancer" and he "should be seen as a master of an established genre."

Several studies concern the development of H's theories about writing. N. F. Adkins, "The Early Projected Works of NH" (*PBSA* 45), calls attention to H's plans from the start of his career onward to write more coherent works than those published before 1850, evinced by his comments upon abandoned collections. R. H. Fossum, "Time and the Artist in 'Legends of the Province House' " (*NCF* 67), remarks that "nowhere in the H canon is the narrative action so consistently an analogue of the artistic process by which it is created, and nowhere is the purpose of the fiction clearer" than in this group. H. H. Clark, "H's Literary and Aesthetic Doctrines as Embodied in his Tales" (*TWA* 61), provides a "genetic or chronological approach" to H's literary theories as they are expressed in a score of tales about artists and writers. Robert Shulman, "H's Quiet Conflict" (*PQ* 68), develops the thesis that "H's way of following his calling made for a life-long and gradually devitalizing conflict between the demands of his vocation as Romantic artist and the imperatives of a Protestant ethic he shared with his businesslike contemporaries." R. H. Pearce, "H and the Twilight of Romance" (*YR* 48), claims a change took place in H's critical theory when he wrote *MF*, replacing an earlier belief—that the aim of romance is conveying moral truth—with a concept placing more emphasis upon a suitable atmosphere—on matter rather than means. This—and the shift to an unfamiliar locale—accounts for a falling off. Pearce makes valid points about the importance of H's experience to his success, though a careful reading of the author's earlier prefaces seems to indicate that H's belief was that both means and matter ("fashion and material") are equally important in his concept of romance before 1859, and it may be argued that the Preface to his final completed novel differs less in theory than Pearce claims.

Most students, though, believing H's shifts in theoretical beliefs less important than constants, therefore treat constants. Meaty and useful is Charles Foster's pioneering "H's Literary Theory" (PMLA 42). Foster holds that in H's opinion the chief purpose of literature is conveying spiritual truth. An idealization which nature initiates but which the artist completes by "carrying out the tendencies of nature in an imaginative realm" does not, H believes, alienate art from reality since the idealization is so shaped as to convey a value deeper than reality itself provides. The shaping modifies externals in the service of allegory and symbolism. Foster finally discusses H's belief that the artist needs more than intellect and emotion as attributes; he also needs to be able to respond to inspiration. And the task of H's artist is to live within his age, to comprehend it, and to so work and discipline himself as to realize his capabilities. Foster may overestimate the uniqueness of H's beliefs, but his summary of them is intelligently set forth and well documented. In "H on the Romance: His Prefaces Related and Examined" (MP 55) Jesse Bier carefully scrutinizes forewords to the major romances and finds that (as Foster implies) they show a consistent set of ideas about the nature of romance, the imagination, truth, allegory, and atmosphere. N. F. Doubleday had a brilliant idea for a study, followed it through, and came up with a very illuminating article, "H's Estimate of His Early Works" (AL 66). Studying the choices that H made as he decided over the years which stories he would reprint in collections, Doubleday found very convincing evidence that, unlike many critics today, the author did not admire most those which lacked clarity—that he neither sought nor esteemed ambiguity.

A final group of valuable studies scrutinize H's critical theories in various philosophical contexts. Larzer Ziff, "The Ethical Dimension of 'The Custom House' " (MLN 58), notices that much as H balances the material world and man's moral nature in his ethical scheme, he balances the actual and the ideal in his aesthetic scheme. Concerned with much the same problem, H. H. Waggoner, "Art and Belief" (HCE), stresses relationships between H's firmest beliefs and his use of allegory, and between his blurred beliefs and his use of "the so-called ambiguity device." Darrel Abel, "Giving Lustre to Gray Shadows: H's Potent Art" (*AL* 69), sees H's interrelating of past, present, and future ("he saw the past and future as they met in a timeless present in the heart of man") as akin to his ideas about the operation of the imagination and to his writing practices.

Millicent Bell, *H's View of the Artist* (1962), thorough, often penetrating, consistently well written, usefully surveys H's critical theories in relation to Romanticism. Its chief weakness is insistence that H, in his attempt to reconcile art and morality, was inconsistent, and her crucial reading of "The Artist of the Beautiful" as ironic is particularly vulnerable. L. B. Levy, "H and the Sublime" (*AL* 66) and "Picturesque Style in *H7G*" (*NEQ* 66), places the author in the context of conventions of painting of his day. Darrel Abel, " 'A More Imaginative Pleasure': H on the Play of the Imagination" (*ESQ* 69), canvasses H's beliefs concerning a central doctrine. And R. J. Jacobson, *H's Conception of the Creative Process* (1966), relates his conceptions to a number of those of romantic theorists.

Marjorie Elder, who in *NH Transcendental Symbolist* (1969) briefly criticizes Bell for failing, "despite fine insights . . . to picture H's Artist clearly and completely," attempts to remedy this deficiency. An accurate picturing, she tries to show, is aided by examining H's personal relationships with Transcendentalists and, more important, conspicuous and decisive resemblances between Transcendental aesthetic theories and H's aesthetic intentions. "The Work of Art, for H and for Emerson," she asserts, "is an expression of Unity, Truth, Beauty by Variety; that is, by Symbol . . . . The Artist sees by means of light and reflects his vision in the mirror by means of light." Elder supports this claim and others by pondering H's many relevant utterances rather more exhaustively than predecessors have and by relating the theories to practices in eight often-discussed tales and *SL* and *MF*. Thoroughly documented, sensible and thoughtful but imaginative too, this is a rich study which concludes with some superb critical discussions in the mode of H.

V. CRITICISM

1. Studies of Sources

Critics of H's fiction chiefly ponder two topics, sources and artistry, discussions of the former not always excluding concern with the latter. Students of the sources at times, of course, contribute to an appreciation of H's skill as an author.

Each of three types of sources Stewart discriminates in "Introductory Essays" to *American Notebooks*—notebooks, reading, and H's own fiction—

has been studied. Stewart often, as in his remarks about *SL*, explores sources thoroughly and, by comparing them with the works, illuminates H's artistry. Arlin Turner, "H's Methods of Using His Source Material," *Studies for W. A. Read* (1940), compares journal notes with finished fictions, documenting the claim that H began with a "central theme or basic idea" suggested by personal experiences, reading, or independent speculations. The next task was to find illustrations, with materials often developed as "catalogues" or "processions" and carefully wrought atmospheres that underline meanings. These two scholarly investigations illustrate such studies at their best, proving that alleged sources are indeed sources and showing precisely how and why the artist transmuted materials. A later study looks at several kinds of sources but is somewhat vague about H's literary merits. Eugene Arden, "H's 'Case of Arthur D' " (*AI* 61), finds that knowledge gained from experience, talks with O. W. Holmes, and extensive reading made possible extraordinarily profound psychological insights in H's fiction.

Biographical sources were discussed in a 64-page article, Anton Schönbach, "Beitrage zur Charakteristik NHs" (*Englische Studien* 1884), which uses posthumously published romances to generalize about H's methods, and which relates completed narratives to relevant notebook passages. P. E. Burnham, decades later, turns to early biographical sources of an early work in "H's *Fanshawe* and Bowdoin College" (*EIHC* 44).

Three works most obviously drawing upon H's experiences have been much discussed. Notebook passages recording H's stay in North Adams, germinal to "Ethan Brand," are related to it by Bliss Perry, "H at North Adams," *The Amateur Spirit* (1904), which finds influential not only observed men and events but also H's concept of his own personality. Brother Joseph, F.S.C., in "Art and Event in 'Ethan Brand' " (*NCF* 60) asseverates that H here not only uniquely bases all his details on actuality but also manages to shape them into a harmonious whole. Continuously discussed has been the extent to which actuality entered *BR*. To what degree was Coverdale a self-portrait, Zenobia a portrait of Margaret Fuller? Practically all readers have agreed that Fuller provided many details (an interesting exception: E in an 1880 lecture, "Historic Notes of Life and Letters in New England"). A minority holds that Zenobia was a satirical representation—Margaret's nephew, Frederick Fuller in "H and Margaret Fuller Ossoli" (*Lit World* 1885), and Oscar Cargill in "Nemesis and NH" (*PMLA* 37). Most hold that other objectives than satire were involved in modification of details in Margaret Fuller's character in the romance. Arlin Turner so argues in "Autobiographical Elements in H's *BR*" (*UTSE* 35), as do two replies to Cargill—Austin Warren (*PMLA* 39) and W. P. Randel (*AL* 39).

Lina Bohmer, *Brookfarm und Hs BR* (1936), elaborately analyzes correspondences between book and journal and argues, unconvincingly, that the book should be read more as autobiography than as fiction. J. T. Gordon, "NH and Brook Farm" (*ESQ* 63), provides a recent recapitulation of evidence and conclusions. N. H. Pearson's discussion of the author's European experiences in relation to *MF* in his unpublished edition of the *Italian Notebooks*, as well as passages by Stewart, Davidson, and Matthiessen on H abroad, are used by Christof Wegelin in "Europe in H's Fiction (*ELH* 47). G. J. Scrimgeour, "*MF*: H's Faery Land" (*AL* 64), shows that social and political conditions in Italy during H's years there figure importantly in the book and in fact may help readers in their study of the characterization and the theme. Nathalia Wright, "The Language of Art: H," *American Novelists in Italy* (1965), surveys other impacts of the sojourn. W. B. Miller, "A New Review of the Career of Paul Akers, 1826–1861" (*CLQ* 66), offers convincing arguments for belief that descriptions of Kenyon's sculptures were suggested by Akers' works. Finally, F. E. Kearns, "Margaret Fuller as a Model for Hester Prynne" (*JA* 65), makes a good case of seeing Fuller's prototype in a figure outside of *BR*.

Biographical sources of a different kind were explored beginning in the 1920's when, like other prominent figures, H of course was subjected to psychological and psychoanalytic studies. A. L. Reed, "Self-Portraiture in the Work of NH" (*SP* 26), noticed that he revealed himself as he actually was and as he feared he might be. In 1929, as has been noticed, Newton Arvin in his biography employed psychological procedures: he was one of many who did this. Malcolm Cowley in "Introduction" to *The Portable H* (1948) and J. E. Hart, "*SL*: One Hundred Years After" (*NEQ* 50), opened new vistas as they carried similar inquiries further.

These relatively tentative interpretations were followed by more militant ones. Rudolph Von Abele, *The Death of the Artist: A Study of H's Disintegration* (1955), sees signs of H's forthcoming demise in stories which show a clash between his "pseudoplatonic conception" of art and the loneliness of an artist living in a democracy, as early as 1843 and 1844. And although *SL* uniquely and successfully dramatized the man's inner condition, Von Abele sees his "death" throes beginning as early as 1850. Thereafter H's obsessions with inner sufferings flawed or ruined the rest of his longer works. S. O. Lesser, *Fiction and the Unconscious* (1957), pondering the adventures of Robin in "My Kinsman, Major Molineux," finds a resemblance to the narrator's story in Anderson's "I Want to Know Why": both youthful protagonists are rebelling against adult economic and sexual domination.

This particular Oedipal interpretation triggered an attack which might well be leveled against others which preceded and followed it: R. H. Pearce, "Robin Molineux on the Analyst's Couch" (*Criticism* 59). Subtitled "A Note on the Limits of Psychoanalytic Criticism," it makes this valid claim: "The danger . . . is one of inadequacy and partiality . . . Mr. Lesser's approach takes us deeply into the heart of the tale. But he forgets that the heart has meaning only as it activates and is activated by a body." As Pearce also says: "The one criterion for all criticism, psychoanalytic and otherwise, would be just this: the degree to which the critic has accounted for all that goes on in the tale, all that is there; and then, and only then, the degree to which he has related his total analysis to his sense of the tale's humanistic import."

In a prize-winning paper, "H's Unfinished Works" (*Harvard Med Alum Bul* 62), a professional psychoanalyst, Dr. J. H. Lamont, explores some of the territory explored by Von Abele and Lesser and shows a similar weakness. A cause of H's failure, he holds, was a psychological breakdown, evidenced by the author's identification with his heroes and the use of Oedipal themes of incest and parricide. L. B. Salomon makes a like approach in "H and His Father" (*L&P* 63), noticing the frequency with which H develops the theme of "filial impiety." The subtitle, "A Conjecture," describes his suggestion that some stories "constitute a sort of expiatory ritual." Allan and Barbara Lefcowitz provide a variation in a parade which by now has become rather monotonous with "Some Rents in the Veil: New Light on Priscilla and Zenobia in *BR*" (*NCF* 66). They find that "dangerous psychosexual feelings" account for the ambivalent representations of the two characters and consequent serious weaknesses of the novel. Incidental suggestions are that Old Moodie may helpfully be thought of as a pimp, Priscilla as a whore, and Coverdale as a client.

Although these revelations may startle some readers, not surprisingly they do not unduly distress Frederick Crews, who approvingly cites the article in *The Sins of the Fathers: H's Psychological Themes* (1966)—not surprisingly since Crews himself, delving as deep with a psychoanalytic shovel as any commentator has dug or is likely to dig, mines equally arresting treasures. Crews something of a dogmatist, is contemptuous of most earlier studies of his author, but his general thesis and some specific arguments for it are less novel than he indicates. In his belief H, "a self-examining neurotic," wrote fiction which constantly revealed "with incredible fidelity" obsessions with patricide, masochism, incest, repression, fantasies, and other manifestations of his own "unresolved Oedipal conflict." The book often demonstrates the fatal tendency of psychoanalytic criticism to be reductive which Crews elsewhere hilariously parodies: Since Crews sees H as "everywhere" a psychological writer and *therefore* not a moralist, his readings concentrate on one aspect to the neglect of others. And since Crews's psychology is pretty exclusively Freudian, and moreover unrevised Freudian, as R. R. Male mildly remarks in his perhaps too severe review (*NCF* 66), he is "somewhat over-alert to sexual innuendo." H. H. Waggoner, who calls attention to some highly questionable aspects of the study in *ALS* for 1966, balances his judgment by noticing some solid merits—frequent valuable insights and convincing demonstrations of what Crews calls "H's distinction as a psychologist." By providing such insights, Crews contributes critical evaluations and analyses such as those discussed hereafter, offering evidence (if any is needed) that scholars and critics join artists in frustrating writers of bibliographical essays who attempt to classify them too neatly.

What is perhaps Crews's most valid general thesis—modified in rather useful ways—is supported by J. E. Miller in "H and Melville: No! in Thunder," in *Quests Surd and Absurd* (1967), which concludes that

> ... it would be closer to the truth of their fiction to call H and Melville *psychological* rather than *religious* writers. In their explorations of the incredible complexities of the human mind, they made discoveries which sometimes seemed to confirm such ancient doctrines as original sin—but these confirmations did not lead to the broadside reinstitution and reaffirmation of religious dogma. On the contrary, they inspired further and deeper exploration leading ultimately to the mapping of heretofore uncharted psychological terrain.

A highly suggestive chapter of the same book, which had been published as an article in 1964, "Uncharted Interiors," indicates (tentatively as Miller carefully cautions) how a Jungian approach may revealingly relate H to five of his American Romantic contemporaries.

Discussions of literary sources fall—with overlappings—into three groups: (1) H's reading, (2) sources influencing procedures or materials in a number of works, (3) sources of specific works. The best studies of the first, in the order of their appearance, were Austin Warren, "H's Reading" (*NEQ* 35), and M. L. Kesselring, "H's Reading, 1828–1850" (*BNYPL* 49). The latter, which revises a study published in 1932 (*EIHC*), is the more inclusive.

P. E. More's "The Origins of H and Poe" in *Shelburne Essays* (1904) is one of a group of source studies ranging through several periods: it lists as influences the writings of Mather, Wigglesworth, Edwards, Freneau, and C. B. Brown—a group concerned with "the weirder phenomena of life." E. L. Chandler, *A Study of the Sources of the Tales and Romances . . . before 1853* (1926), is sound in scholarship and makes important contributions. The same may be said for Arlin Turner's inclusive "H's Literary Borrowings" (*PMLA* 36). Jane Lundblad, *NH and European Literary Tradition* (1947), opens with chapters stressing continental influences on H's reading, his life, and his work. Lundblad then discusses three "traditions"—Gothic romance, Mme de Staël, and Balzac. She believes that de Staël shaped depictions of passionate and exotic women and that Balzac influenced H's ideas about art and architecture and perhaps depictions of cold-hearted villains. N. F. Doubleday, "H's Use of Three Gothic Patterns" (CE 46), emphasizes the fact that H's working in the tradition, instead of proving him morbid or uninventive, showed his awareness of current literary vogues and remarkable skill in adapting conventions to his own requirements. The author then considers, with many insights, H's adaptation —with varying success—of mysterious portraits, witchcraft, the Wandering Jew, elixir of life, and allied occult experiments. Richard Chase, *The American Novel and Its Tradition* (1957), finds that "contradictions" rather than "the harmonies of our culture" have caused fictionists to combine the tradition of the romance with the tradition of the novel in a peculiarly American blend. In Chapter IV, "H and the Limits of Romance," Chase looks at *SL* and *BR* and concludes that "although H was a superb writer of Romance and a considerable novelist . . . he was aware that his romances . . . proceeded in part from his final failure to take a place among the great novelists." Although Chase is somewhat thesis-ridden, he manages in this chapter to define interestingly some of H's qualities. The traditions with which Leslie Fiedler is concerned in *Love and Death in the American Novel* (1960, 1967) are those of sentimental and gothic novels, the tragedy of seduction, and the historical romance; and the author manages to see some significant ways in which these shape H's writings. But since his aim is also to "emphasize the neglected contexts of American fiction, largely depth-psychological and anthropological, but sociological . . . as well," he mingles with his valid remarks about H wild and undemonstrable conjectures.

The earliest authors nominated as influential on several works are considered in a chapter of J. P. Pritchard, *Return to the Fountains* (1942), which, discussing H's indebtedness to classical literary critics for his own theories, proves that the influence was minimal. The same way be said about Werner Peterich's study of an influence upon "Rappaccini's Daughter" and "Ethan Brand" in an essay, "H and the 'Gesta Romanorum,' " included in *Kleine Beiträge zur Amerikanischen Literaturgeschichte*, edited by Hans Galinsky and H.-J. Lang (Heidelberg, 1961).

N. F. Doubleday, "H's Inferno" (CE 40), and J. C. Mathews, "H's Knowledge of Dante" (UTSE 40) and "The Interest in Dante Shown by Nineteenth-Century Men of Letters" (SA 65), find evidence of H's acquaintance with the Italian author's writings by 1835 and of a fair amount of indebtedness, most impressively in treatments of sin and pride. Moving to the sixteenth century, Randall Stewart in "H and *The Faerie Queene*" (*PQ* 33) finds significant relationships. So does Buford Jones in "The *Faery Land* of H's Romances" (*ESQ* 67), concentrating on H's increasing and frequent use of Spenser's "fairy land" as a symbol for the immortal world of art and inspiration. Frank Davidson, "H's Hive of Honey: A Few Specific Influences of Shakespeare and Milton" (*MLN* 46), briefly discusses, in addition to the authors of the title, Sir Thomas Browne and the Bible. Millicent Bell, "Melville and H at the Grave of St. John (A Debt to Pierre Bayle)" (*MLN* 52), demonstrates an acquaintance of minor importance. Demonstrably much more important is the author considered in W. S. Johnson, "H and *The Pilgrim's Progress*" (*JEGP* 51); Robert Stanton, "H, Bunyan, and the American Romances" (*PMLA* 56); and a 44-page treatment, "Bunyan and H" in D. E. Smith, *John Bunyan in America* (1966). The last of these usefully discriminates three primary images derived from Bunyan and often used by H—the unsuccessful search for the Celestial City, the disingenuous pilgrim, and the labyrinthine wilderness. Inevitably, scholars have studied the influence of records of Puritanism in seventeenth-century America—G. H. Orians, "New England Witchcraft in Fiction" (*AL* 30) and "H and Puritan Punishments" (*CE* 52); Tremaine McDowell, "NH and the Witches of Colonial Salem" (*N&Q* 34); and the chapter on H in David Levin, *In Defense of Historical Literature* (1967).

That H knew eighteenth-century authors well enough to be influenced in important ways by them is made clear by several scholars. A. L. Cooke, "Some Evidences of H's Indebtedness to Swift" (*UTSE* 38), finds Swift influential on "ideas and literary patterns" in six shorter works. Frank Davidson, "H's Use of a Pattern from the *Rambler*" (*MLN* 48), finds Johnson's catalogue echoed in three short works and other elements influential on "The Intelligence Office" and "A Virtuoso's Collection." Marvin Fisher, "The Pattern of Conservatism in Johnson's *Rasselas* and H's Tales" (*JHI* 58), traces references to Johnson in writings of many sorts and finds that both writers favored "preservation of traditional human values" in religion, reform, psychology, and society. Two books touch upon Tieck as an influence—Percy Matenko, *Ludwig Tieck and America* (1954), and H. A. Pochmann's rather more specific section in *German Culture in America* (1957). J. X. Brennan and S. L. Gross, "The Origin of H's Unpardonable Sin" (*BUSE* 57) find significant—as their readers will—H's reading of Thomas Stackhouse's Biblical commentaries in 1832 and his utilization of them in "The Man of Adamant" five years later. O. B. Wheeler, "H and the Fiction of Sensibility" (*NCF* 64), sees H so refining his handling of four important conventions that in his greatest works they have been completely adapted to the author's purposes. This is the source study at its perceptive and imaginative best.

As early as 1888, T. W. Higginson in "A Precursor of H" (*Independent*) discussed a nineteenth-century author whose influence was almost certainly important—a fact that becomes clear when one examines William Austin's short story "Peter Rugg" (1824) and notices that it introduced the device of providing alternative explanations of happenings between which readers may choose. Douglas Grant, "Sir Walter Scott and NH" (*ULR* 62), presents convincing evidence that Scott's influence was "first and longest." P. M. Ryan, "Young H at the Salem Theatre" (*EIHC* 58), breaks new ground and offers strong proofs that the dramas that H saw "during the theatrically significant decade from 1820 to 1830" shaped later writings, notably H's masterpiece. And Marvin Laser, " 'Head,' 'Heart,' and 'Will' in H's Psychology" (*NCF* 55), credibly pinpoints T. C. Upham's faculty psychology as a decisive influence.

Some of the most interesting source studies in recent years were stimulated by the burgeoning interest in folklore, mythology, legendry, and allied subjects. The thesis of W. B. Stein, *H's Faust: A Study of the Devil Archetype* (1953), is that a "mythic formula based on the devil-archetype"—the Faustian story—"provides H with the medium of inquiry into the riddle of good and evil." The sources, allegedly, were the Mathers, the "Faust Chapbook," Marlowe, and Goethe (Stein's favorite)—but the demonstration of their use is rather weak. However, as Stein holds, Faustian elements may have been drawn from other works; and Gothic romancers were demonstrably influential. The author's effort to "disclose the unbroken continuity of H's art and thought" makes possible his showing several interrelationships and developments. Though some of the philosophical readings are oversystematic or overingenious and need checking (see E. C. Sampson's criticism in *N&Q* 55), the book says important things about H's development. G. C. Erlich, "Deadly Innocence: H's Dark Women" (*NEQ* 68), in much shorter space shows that many of H's "plots are really versions of the Fall, that a large number of his settings are new Edens, and that a conspicuous number of his characters are representative of Satan, Adam and Eve, plus one who is an important onlooker"; and that as "H contemplates the Fall from many angles . . . especially significant [is] the role of woman." Other enrichments of allegory and symbolism are explored by R. W. Browne in "The Oft-Told *Twice-Told Tales*: Their Folklore Motifs" (*SFQ* 58).

In *Form and Fable in American Fiction* (1961) Daniel Hoffman's concern is the reliance of leading fictionists "upon allegory and Gothicism, didactic, religious, and travel writings, and traditions of folklore, popular culture, and mythology." In more than 129 pages devoted to H, Hoffman "concentrates on a close reading of each" of six important works and "assesses whatever contributions the text itself demands" from these antecedents. He finds that "archetypal patterns . . . enacted in both individual and communal experience, provide structures for [H's] explorations of [typically American] themes." Despite too complete agreement with Richard Chase, a few misreadings, and a failure to do quite all that he believes he has done, Hoffman makes valuable contributions. He does so because, refusing to indulge in Jungian speculations, he concerns himself with specific folkloristic materials (which he knows in detail) and H's artistic use of them to unify his narratives.

Using H's comments on myths and mythology in his children's books as a starting point and examining additional fictional works, Hoffman in "Myth, Romance, and the Childhood of Man" (HCE) adds proofs for his claim that, "building verisimilitude upon a structure of myth," H achieved "symbolic architecture" that was "faithful both to the truth of the human heart and the laws of art." In H as Myth-Maker: A Study in Imagination (1969), Hugo Mc-Pherson begins similarly, describes "the shape of H's myth," then discusses at length the "New England myth" of the longer works and H's character types—"the personae of his myth." Like Northrop Frye, to whom he acknowledges indebtedness, as McPherson classifies mythological materials and characters, he constructs a formidable schematization—one so complex, in fact, that many readers may turn from it in despair before winnowing away its pedantries and discovering its occasional but real values.

Inevitably in studies concerning sources of individual works, some of the same begetters, as well as some new ones, appear. The most useful of such studies, ordered alphabetically according to titles of the works discussed, include: B. B. Cohen, "The Sources of 'The Ambitious Guest' " (BPLQ 52); K. W. Cameron, Genesis of H's "The Ambitious Guest" (1955); R. H. Woodward, "Automata in H's 'Artist of the Beautiful' and Taylor's 'Meditation 56' " (ESQ 68); A. S. Reid, "H's Humanism: 'The Birthmark' and Sir Kenelm Digby" (AL 66); Buford Jones, "H's Coverdale [in BR] and Spenser's Allegory of Mutability" (AL 67); J. W. Shroeder, "Miles Coverdale as Actaeon, as Faunus, and as October: With Some Consequences" (PLL 66) and "Miles Coverdale's Calendar; or a Major Literary Source for BR" (EIHC 67); Frank Davidson, "Voltaire and H's 'The Christmas Banquet' " (BPLQ 51); Louise Hastings, "An Origin for 'Dr. Heidegger's Experiment' " (AL 38); J. W. Shroeder, "H's 'Egotism . . .' and Its Source" (AL 59); M. L. Ross, "H's Bosom Serpent and Mather's Magnalia" (ESQ 67); R. D. Arner, "H and Jones Very: Two Dimensions of Satire in 'Egotism . . .' " (NEQ 69); E. J. Gallagher, "History in

'Endicott and the Red Cross' '' (*ESQ* 68); W. B. Stein, "A Possible Source of H's English Romance' '' (*MLN* 52); Ely Stock, "The Biblical Context of 'Ethan Brand' '' (*AL* 65); N. F. Doubleday, "The Theme of H's 'Fancy's Show Box' '' (*AL* 38); G. T. Little, "H's *Fanshawe* and Bowdoin's Past" (*Bowdoin Quill* 04); G. H. Orians, "Scott and H's *Fanshawe*" (*NEQ* 38); J. S. Goldstein, "The Literary Source of H's *Fanshawe*" (*MLN* 45); Alexander Kern, "The Sources of H's 'Feathertop' '' (*PMLA* 31); Millicent Bell, "H's 'Fire Worship': Interpretation and Source" (*AL* 53); R. R. Male, "Criticism of Bell's 'H's "Fire Worship" . . .' (*AL* 53); M. J. Griswold, "American Quaker History in the Works of Whittier, H, and Longfellow ['The Gentle Boy'] (*Americana* 40); G. H. Orians, "The Sources and Themes of H's 'The Gentle Boy' "(*NEQ* 41); W. R. Thompson, "Patterns of Biblical Allusions in H's 'The Gentle Boy' '' (*SCB* 62); G. H. Orians, "The Angel of Hadley in Fiction: A Study of the Source of H's 'The Gray Champion' '' (*AL* 32); W. R. Thompson, "Theme and Method in H's 'The Great Carbuncle' '' (*SCB* 61); K. G. Pfeiffer, "The Prototype of the Poet in 'The Great Stone Face' '' (*RS* 41); C. S. Burhans, "H's Mind and Art in 'The Hollow of the Three Hills' '' (*JEGP* 61); T. M. Griffiths, *Maine Sources in* H7G (1945); H. T. Emry, "Two Houses of Pride: Spenser's and H's [*H7G*]" (*PQ* 54); Norman Farmer, "Maule's Curse and the Rev. Nicholas Noyes: A Note on H's Source [for *H7G*]" (*N&Q* 64); L. B. Levy, "Picturesque Style in *H7G*" (*NEQ* 66); F. N. Cherry, "A Note on the Source of H's 'Lady Eleanore's Mantle' '' (*AL* 35); J. W. Shroeder, "H's 'The Man of Adamant': A Spenserian Source-Study" (*PQ* 62); L. A. Haselmeyer, "H and the Cenci [*MF*]" (*Neophil* 41); Nathalia Wright, "H and the Praslin Murder [in *MF*]" (*NEQ* 42); Sacvan Bercovitch, "Hilda's 'Seven-Branched Allegory': An Echo from Cotton Mather in *MF*" (*EAL* 66); G. H. Orians, "H and 'The Maypole of Merrymount' '' (*MLN* 38); M. L. Allen, "The [Minister's] Black Veil: Three Versions of a Symbol" (*ES* 66); Darrel Abel, "LeSage's Limping Devil and 'Mrs. Bullfrog' '' (*N&Q* 53); M. G. Rose, "Theseus Motif in 'My Kinsman, Major Molineux' [hereafter ''MM'']" (*ESQ* 67); A. T. Broes, "Journey into Moral Darkness: 'MM' as Allegory" (*NCF* 64); A. L. Cooke, "The Shadow of Martinus Scriblerus in H's 'The Prophetic Pictures' '' (*NEQ* 44); Charles Boewe, "Rappaccini's [hereafter R's] Garden" (*AL* 58); Oliver Evans, "The Cavern and the Fountain: Paradox and Double Paradox in 'R's Daughter' '' (*CE* 63); Julian Smith, "Keats and H: A Romantic Bloom in R's Garden" (*ESQ* 66); A. J. Kloeckner, "The Flower and the Fountain: H's Chief Symbols in 'R's Daughter' '' (*AL* 66); N. A. Anderson, " 'R's Daughter': A Keatsian Analogue?" (*PMLA* 68); S. W. Liebman, "H and Milton: The Second Fall in 'R's Daughter' '' (*NEQ* 68); G. H. Orians, "The Sources of 'Roger Malvin's Burial' [hereafter "RMB"]" (*AL* 38); D. S. Lovejoy, "Lovewell's Flight and H's 'RMB' " (*NEQ* 54); W. R. Thompson, "The Biblical Sources of H's 'RMB' " (*PMLA* 62); Ely Stock, "History and the Bible in 'RMB' " (*EIHC* 64); J. T. McCullen, "Ancient Rites for the Dead and 'RMB' " (*SFQ* 66); A. S. Reid, *The Yellow Ruff and "SL": A Source* . . . (1955); *"Sir Robert Overbury's Vision" (1616) by Richard Niccols and Other English Sources of NH's "SL"*, edited by A. S. Reid (1957); R. L. Brant, "H and Marvell [as a source of *SL*]" (*AL* 58); Charles Ryskamp, "The New England Sources of *SL*" (*AL* 59); Charles Boewe and M. G. Murphy, "Hester Prynne in History" (*AL* 60); G. P. Wellborn, "Plant Lore in *SL*" (*SFQ* 63); Peter Schwarz, "Zwei Mögliche 'Faust'—Quellen für H's Roman *SL*" (*JA* 65); E. W. Baughman, "Public Confession and *SL*" (*NEQ* 67); Darrel Abel, "Immortality *vs.* Mortality in *Septimius Felton*: Some Possible Sources" (*AL* 56); John Homan, "H's 'The Wedding Knell' and Cotton Mather" (*ESQ* 66); F. N. Cherry, "The Sources of H's 'Young Goodman Brown' [hereafter "YGB"]" (*AL* 34); J. T. Krumpelmann, "H's 'YGB' and Goethe's 'Faust' " (*NS* 56); E. A. Robinson, "The Vision of GB: A Source and Interpretation" (*AL* 63).

These source studies vary greatly in value. Some make doubtful cases for indebtedness, depending upon far-fetched parallels. An instance is T. M. Griffiths on sources of *H7G*. Griffiths moves from the likelihood that the Pyncheons's legendary holdings are identifiable with the Waldo patent in Maine to the improbable identification of the Knox mansion with the House and the equally dubious identification of characters in fantastic detail with members of the Waldo, Flucker, and Knox families. Most source studies have been sounder in establishing indebtedness; but too few say enough of value about the adaptation of sources. E. L. Chandler, in an early study (see above), despite sound demonstrations of indebtedness, regrettably attempted no specific consideration of H's manipulation of source materials. When the needed additional step was taken by Doubleday in his study of H's transmutation of Gothic materials as indicated above, the value of the article was greatly enhanced.

Some interesting recent studies have added values by carefully considering H's use of establishable sources in such a way as to help to determine his intended meanings. An instance is "Public Confession and *SL*," wherein E. W. Baughman, after surveying Puritan beliefs and practices during the period of the story, concludes that "the dark necessity that follows the first step awry flowers as it does because all of the major characters live outside the prescribed practices of the church" and that when H was ambiguous about a heavenly reunion between Hester and Arthur, he may well have been so because he "knew Puritan doctrine too well to be definite." Other (above listed) studies which similarly illuminate meanings by relating sources to narratives include: Boewe's "R's Garden," Robinson's study of H's use of *Magnalia Christi Americana* in writing "YGB," Stock's analysis of Biblical symbols in "RMB," Broes on borrowings from Dante, Spenser, and Bunyan in "MM," Reid on the use that H made of Sir Kenelm and Lady Digby in "The Birthmark," Shroeder's study of Spenser's poems for the light they throw upon Coverdale as a narrator, and McCullen's discoveries about the bearing of folk traditions upon the signification of "RMB."

2. Evaluations and Analyses

From the start H was often fortunate in his critics. Great contemporaries wrote thoughtfully about him; and later, perceptive readers, not the least of them Henry James, discussed him at length. Criticisms fall under two headings: some deal with a large number of works, others with individual works.

Though Poe died before H's first great novel appeared in 1850, he discussed H's tales on four occasions—in a review of the second edition of *Twice-Told Tales* (*Graham's Mag* 1842); a paragraph in "Marginalia" (*Demo Rev* 1844); another in *The Literati of New York* (*Godey's* 1846); and a review of *Twice-Told Tales* and *Mosses* called "Tale Writing: NH" (*Godey's* 1847). All were laudatory, but the last differed interestingly from the first. The first finds that H's distinctive trait is "invention, creation, imagination, originality—a trait which in the literature of fiction, is worth all the rest," with H showing originality in both "tone" and materials. The last holds that H was not "original"—merely "peculiar," his peculiarity deriving largely from a fondness for allegory evidenced in too many tales. Puzzled about the change, H. M. Belden, "Poe's Criticism of H" (*Anglia* 01), suggested that Poe had decided between 1842 and 1847 that H, having copied Tieck, could not be truly original; Bertha Faust thought that the difference could be accounted for by the different subject matter of Poe's two articles; Stewart felt that Poe changed his mind because he felt that H's art had deteriorated. Another possibility is that Poe's theories about literature had changed—supported by his growing disapproval of H's monotony of tone and allegory and by his introduction in 1847 of talk about originality of effect. Poe strikes a note long to be echoed: allegory is a product of the fancy (rather than the higher imaginative faculty), appealing "to our sense of adaptation, not of matters proper, but of matters improper for the purpose, of the real with the unreal. . . . The deepest emotion aroused within us by the happiest allegory, as allegory, is a very imperfectly satisfied sense of the writer's ingenuity in overcoming a difficulty we should have preferred his not attempting to overcome." Allegory, Poe holds, cannot be made to enforce a truth and if it establishes a fact it does so by overturning a fiction: even the best interferes with the unity of effect for which an artist should strive. Only when the suggested meaning is an unobtrusive undercurrent can it fail to injure "earnestness of verisimilitude" in fiction. Hence Poe advises H to shake off Transcendental influences which had encouraged him to allegorize.

The next great American author to discuss H, Melville, reviewed *Mosses* in *The Literary World* (1850) and the next year commented on *H7G* in a letter to its author. (Both critiques have been frequently reprinted.) Melville was less interested in discussing H's art—he says nothing about allegory—than his personality and his philosophy. He writes metaphorically, praising H for "the sunlight"—his humor and warmth—even more, for "the great power of blackness in him," his sense of the tragic which enabled him to express great truths. Not unresponsive himself to the plea for a national literature, Melville expresses pride that America has produced such a literary genius. Like Poe's discussions, Melville's illuminate both H and his critic.

Another contemporaneous writer, E. P. Whipple, reviewed the longer romances and two collection of tales, concluding with an evaluation of H's whole career: reviews of the first three great novels appeared in *Graham's* (1850–52), of *The Snow Image* (1852), of *Tanglewood Tales* in *The Literary World* (1853), and of *MF* and H's career in *Atl* (1860)—reprinted in Whipple's *Character and Characteristic Men* (1866). The articles have value because Whipple had stature and was H's personal friend and his favorite critic. Whipple emphasizes H's depth of insight into moral laws—the profound philosophy underlying his fiction. He also lauds his originality, observation, and characterization. Also, like H, Whipple is interested in the author's representing various facets of his genius, tempering skepticism and pessimism with sunnier insights.

The 1870's brought four valuable discussions. The biographical part of H. A. Page (pseud. for Alexander Japp), *Memoir of NH* (1872), says nothing new, but a concluding essay is an admirable interpretation and evaluation by an Englishman writing for his countrymen. H's son-in-law, G. P. Lathrop, in *A Study of H* (1876, 1969) was a shade too laudatory and shared contemporaneous prejudices against the allegorical mode. But having derived from Coleridge a distinction between symbolism and allegory, this intelligent and sensitive critic initiated discussions of aspects of H's artistry of particular interest today. Furthermore, his analyses of themes in relation to characters and events are often enlightening. Anthony Trollope's "The Genius of NH" (*NAR* 1879) appeared after the British author had heard that H admired his novels because they were "written on the strength of beef and through the inspiration of ale."

Trollope confesses that he in turn likes H, though the two are very different and despite the fact that he finds a strange mingling in H's books of romance and austerity. Remoteness from reality accounts for a "weird, mysterious, thrilling charm"; the austerity for a pervasive melancholy endurable only because it, too, is illusory. Since Trollope proves to be one who tends to read specific works, nevertheless, as if their virtues and faults derive largely from lifelikeness or lack of it, some of his summaries sound strange. He remarks on the drollery, humor, and satire in even the darkest narratives; on the lack of plot; and on the admirable adaptation of tone when H turns from New England to Italy. He shows in an extreme form the difficulty lovers of realism then had appreciating romances.

More subtly showing the same difficulty, Henry James's H (1879) resembles earlier studies in possibly casting more light upon its author than upon its subject. Despite this, given its point of view, this conscientious study by a great literary theorist is full of insights and understandably influential. James, expatriate and man of the world, underlines H's provincialism and defines faults and merits arising from it. Extraordinary parochialism, he claims, was inevitable for an early nineteenth-century New Englander; it drove a man inward and led, too, often, to the excessive use of symbolism, conceits, and over-elaborated allegory. James, agreeing with Poe, sees allegory as "one of the lighter exercises of the imagination" which often spoils both the form and the development of a theme in a fictional work. On the other hand, James wistfully concedes that H benefits from his close ties. His sense of the past and his temperament so definitely derive from his background that he saturates writings with local flavorings. Indirectly as a rule, since—James repeatedly emphasizes—H is not a realist, he writes fictional works in which at least half the virtue derives from their impregnation with New England air. Moreover, H's past and upbringing made the Puritan conscience his natural heritage. And though (so James believes—surely erroneously) H took little stock in Puritan dogma, this old moral sense, this old awareness of sin and hell, lodged in this man of imagination and fancy, stimulate his fancy to manipulate them, to see and utilize their artistic possibilities for entertainment and irony. A fortunate result is that H at best plumbs deep to write—with artistry—narratives which are moral, whose purpose is moral, and which (though James does not say this) therefore resemble those of James in fundamental aims. The discussion based on these partly sound premises contains brilliant remarks about many novels and tales.

N. Dhaleine, *NH: Sa vie et son oeuvre* (1905), a meaty, generally sound, though hardly inspired, discussion from the French point of view, works acute analyses into a biography and concludes with six chapters on the author's style, intentions, methods, backgrounds, characters, and handling of the problem of evil.

W. C. Brownell's chapter in *American Prose Masters* (1909) caustically attacks H and, though urbane, shows exasperation. H, Brownell holds, wrote one great book, *SL*, otherwise frittering away his talents, employing fancy instead of imagination to mingle bad allegory with worse symbolism. Allegory, he claims, mounts to the level of art only when "its representation is as imaginatively real as its meaning" and H's allegory, the product of unleashed fancy, lacks the substance of reality. And since H is a fatalist in art (as in morality), instead of struggling against vicious habits, he nurtures them. Brownell thus repeats and enlarges upon hostile criticisms typical of his period.

Yvor Winters, "Maule's Curse, or H and the Problem of Allegory," in *Maule's Curse* (1938) and *In Defense of Reason* (1948), condemns H's shorter writings because they lack meaning or reality, or having both seem incapable of justifying H's intensity. Turning to longer works, Winters finds *SL* faultless because it is pure allegory which utilizes fitting material: "By selecting sexual sin as the type of all sin, H was true alike to the exigencies of drama and history. In the setting which he chose, allegory was realism, the idea was life itself; and his prose, always remarkable for its polish and flexibility, and stripped, for once, of all superfluity, was reduced to the living idea. . . ." But having done all that could be done with allegory, H thereafter moved towards the novel, unfortunately doomed to write impure novels in which themes and characters were insignificant and disparate. For Winters, H illustrates the thesis that when nineteenth-century authors swapped their heritage for a mess of European Romanticism, their artistry and the validity of their beliefs deteriorated. Perceptions of Winters, a brilliant though dogmatic critic, have value. But readers who do not share his disdain for Romantic beliefs (including Emersonianism) or his concept of artistry cannot applaud his sternest strictures.

Leland Schubert, *H, the Artist: Fine-Art Devices in Fiction* (1944), deals, he asserts, with form, not content; hence he will discuss H's work as he would that of any artist, "whether a painter, a sculptor, or even musician." To artistic devices such as rhythmic motifs, color, and sound, he finds analogous devices in H's works. He notices, for instance, that a picture is admirable "when there is a kind of balance . . . within the outline," and so on. True, picture parts are spatially arranged, and nothing in fiction exactly corresponds, but vaguely similar are successive pages. Hence, considering *SL*, "in two parts, in three parts or better yet in seven parts," he discerns "a beautifully constructed novel." The parts he determines in various ways—a three-part division based on scaffold scenes, a seven-part one on characters in the center of the stage. Canvas areas are thus equated with chapters, a painting's forms with characters and their deeds. Turning to music, Schubert analogizes "recurring use of melodies and chords" with fiction's "repeated . . . words and phrases, or colors, or masses, or whole images, or even sounds or philosophic concepts." So he studies such reiterations. The present writer made two adverse criticisms of the approach in a review (*MP* 44): he believes that in literary works (1) most of the patterns that Schubert discusses lack significance; (2) the divorcing of form from content makes impossible discovery or demonstration of such significance. He has coped with similar problems in a way he believes more revealing in "Color, Light and Shadow in H's Fiction" (*NEQ* 42). Here he attempts to demonstrate that H used color and chiaroscuro as well as other devices for one or more of three purposes—to indicate character, to stress narrative changes, and to articulate themes. His preference is based upon beliefs that (1) fiction can best be studied in its own peculiar terms, and (2) the study is most valuable when it relates fictional parts or elements to one another or to wholes. The ideas, if not the justification of the method, were rather more novel in 1942 than they have become today.

Mark Van Doren in *H* (1949) attempts to relate alleged warring aspects of the author's nature to his writings. Here was a man of the world, with sound sense—watchful, objective, without illusion, cool, dubious. But here was an unworldly poet, imaginative, mystical, capable of being deeply moved by symbolic objects, with a strong instinct to accept. The former is the man of the fancies and the sketches, the latter the Romantic moralist, and the two never are made thoroughly acquainted. Both contribute failures and successes. The former too often forced his imagination to work on the world about him where it was ineffective. This H crippled the other and was suspicious of his imagination. But the mystical, moral H too often succumbed to Gothicism, melodrama, contrivances, abstractions, sentimentality, and vague or oversimple significations. At his best in allegory—for "without allegory H was nothing"—H wrote great tales and novels. His greatest allegory keeps significations solid and clear, has reality in characterization and motivation; its characters are vehicles for ideas, its thought universal and complex. Van Doren adapts some conventional interpretations to provide a discussion of H's life psychologically more up to date. Similarly, he combines what he believes are sound older judgments with valuations based upon new critical methods. He frankly indicates some dissatisfaction with his findings, perhaps because—despite safeguards his great common sense provides—he shares the fears of some readers that his interpretation is a bit too neat. Yet his discussions in many instances are excellent.

E. H. Davidson, *H's Last Phase* (1949), is the definitive consideration of the four fragments composed during the author's final years. Q. D. Leavis's two-part "H as Poet" (*SR* 51) was intended to correct what she considers two misapprehensions of previous critics—the belief that H was aloof and that he was an allegorist. The author essentially, she holds, was concerned about society and deeply involved in his writings—in fact, was a sociological fictionist. The essential H was not an allegorist but a dramatic writer who conveyed meanings by employing symbolism. For proof, she analyzes tales and romances and finds they criticize society and employ poetic symbols. The discussion is weakened by an extraordinary lack of familiarity with many earlier discussions of H, by its need to exclude much writing to denote what is "essential," and by a failure to consider recurrent symbols. The strength of the study derives from freshness of approach to important problems and its sensitive (though hardly unique) perception of certain symbols.

R. H. Fogle, *H's Fiction: The Light and the Dark* (1953; rev. ed. 1964, the chief change being added essays on "MM" and "Birthmark"), argues that H is a great writer in absolute terms by discussing some tales and the longer romances at length and other writings more briefly. The "light" of the title stands for clarity of design. In a typical work, "YGB," for instance, "the clarity is embodied in the lucid simplicity of the basic action; in the skillfull foreshadowing by which the plot is bound together; in the balance of episode and scene; in the continuous use of contrast;" firm, selective pictorial composition; climactic ordering of incident and tone; detachment, irony; and the purity, grave formality, and rhetorical balance of style. The "dark" stands for H's "tragic complexity," achieved by complicated characterization and motivation and a deliberate ambiguity in the use of allegory, symbolism, and author's commentary—all necessitating "multiple interpretations." H's excellence, Fogle believes, derives from combinations of light and dark thus defined: "His clarity is intermingled with subtlety, his statement interfused with symbolism, his affirmation enriched with ambiguity"—an inevitable expression of H's psychology. Some readers, including the present writer, will hold that some elements of clarity Fogle has described are overschematized, and that some ambiguities he admires are based upon over-ingenious exegesis or upon H's own actual indecisions. (For a detailed discussion of the second point, see Leon Howard's review, *NCF* 53.) Nevertheless, many discussions of imagery, allegory, and symbolism reveal neglected but very important facets of artistry and meaning. Fogle's later *H's Imagery: the "Proper Light and Shadow" in the Major Romances* (1969) returns to the theme of the earlier book, "now specifically in terms of image patterns," with "the dialectic . . . specifically centered only in the central opposition of light and dark images."

H. H. Waggoner in *H: A Critical Study* (1955, 1963) acknowledges indebtedness to Fogle, and Fogle in turn has praised Waggoner (*AL* 64). Not surprisingly, Waggoner is ingenious in discovering many intricate image patterns in H's writings and discussing them at length; and the analyses, when not overelaborated, have great value. The study has value partly because its author is forthright and lucid in defining his methods, though his book raises questions. H, he suggests, is so puzzling a figure that even after reading—as he must—several biographies, the notebooks, and H's other writings, the student can "finally understand the man, if at all, by a leap of intuitive sympathy." What Waggoner is driven to do, then, is to study sketches and tales to determine H's "special concerns and the shape of his sensibility," thus providing a better preparation for reading the tales and novels "than any study of the externals of his life" would. Therefore biographical insights, which previous scholars based upon facts, this critic bases upon intuitions, while readings, previously thought in danger of distortions unless subjected to factual checks, are thought of as the best means of interpreting and of documenting biographical insights. The method was scrutinized with some expressions of worriment in reviews by Leon Howard (*NCF* 56) and the present writer (*AL* 57) and a note, L. B. Levy, "H's 'Middle Ground' " (*SSF* 64). The rather extensive revision (1963) demonstrates Waggoner's ability, an admirable and unusual one, to change his estimates of some other critics and even some of his own readings. The latter change, however, may be a bit alarming to readers who are led to wonder whether this critic's comprehensions of H's biography, sensibilities, and achievements may be subject to future more drastic revisions.

Jean Normand, *NH: Esquisse d'une analyse de la création artistique* (1964) and Terence Martin, *NH* (1966) have a similar aim—to assess H's achievements. The former is a complex 397-page enterprise which utilizes modern psychology, philosophy, formidable explication, and comparisons based upon wide reading, to reveal H as a writer relevant to our own period. (Its publication is an English translation by Derek Coltman was scheduled for 1970.) And despite its relatively modern guise (it is about half as long as Normand's study), Martin's book analyzes six important tales and four major romances in relation to H's life, attitudes, and intentions with great intelligence and excellent taste.

Several surveys of two or more of H's writings, although only portions of books or articles, provide valuable insights. Listed chronologically, these include: D. H. Lawrence, "H and *SL*" and "H's *BR*," *Studies in Classic American Literature* (1923, 1964); H. S. Canby, "H and Melville," *Classic Americans* (1931); S. T. Williams, "NH," *LHUS* (1948); Austin Warren, "NH," *Rage for Order* (1948); Alexander Cowie, "NH," *The Rise of the American Novel*

(1948); Charles Feidelson, "H," *Symbolism and American Literature* (1953); Norris Yates, "Ritual and Reality: Mask and Dance Motifs in H's Fiction" (*PQ* 55); E. H. Davidson, "H and the Pathetic Fallacy" (*JEGP* 55); R. P. Adams, "H: The Old Manse Period" (*TSE* 58); Harry Levin, "H" in *The Power of Blackness* (1958); M. L. Allen, "H's Art in His Short Stories" (*SA* 61); J. F. Adams, "H's Symbolic Gardens" (*TSLL* 63); W. L. Vance, "The Comic Element in H's Sketches" (*SIR* 64); J. A. Zaitchik, "H as Truth-Teller: An Analysis of Moralistic Techniques in the Tales and Sketches" (*DA* 65); Sister M. E. Joseph, "Substance as Suggestion: Ambiguity in H" (*Renascence* 65); J. C. Pattison, "Point of View in H" (*PMLA* 67); J. J. Murphy, "The Function of Sin in H's Novels" (*ESQ* 68); Agostino Lombardo, "I racconti di H," in *Il simbolismo nella letteratura nord-americana: atti dell symposium tenuto a Firenze . . .* (1965); Jean Normand, "Thoreau et H à Concord—les ironies de la solitude" (*Europe* 67); Robert Dusenbery, "H's Merry Company: The Anatomy of Laughter in the Tales and Short Stories" (*PMLA* 67); R. H. Fogle, "Weird Mockery: An Element of H's Style" (*Style* 68); M. S. Mattfield, "H's Juvenile Classics" (*Discourse* 69); Darrel Abel, "Black Glove and Pink Ribbon: H's Metonymic Symbols" (*NEQ* 69).

Some of these merit special comment. Highly impressionistic, deliberately provocative, Lawrence's essays stressing H's alleged hidden diabolism and sexuality have been germinal to a number of other startling and demonstrative (if undemonstrable) interpretations. Feidelson finds as a common denominator in Whitman, Melville, Poe, Emerson, H, and the writers of today the concept of symbolism, but he claims that H, a symbolist "in spite of himself," makes his romances "a kind of exposition of the nature of symbolic perception." To justify an approach which he himself labels "experimental," "synthetic," and "speculative," he uses readings which are perceptive but at times questionable. Yates, Levin, and both Adamses call attention to recurrent motifs and their significations and admirably document their findings. Sister Joseph and Zaitchik offer new arguments in the debate about H's moralizing versus his psychologizing. And Allen, Vance, Pattison, Lombardo, Dusenbery, and Fogle examine aspects of H's technique.

We come now to an all but overwhelming flood of critical studies concentrating on single works or on interrelated collections made or contemplated by H. Though approaches and concerns vary greatly, most use modern critical procedures to discuss matter or manner or both. The values vary; but my attempt will be to consider the best of such discussions (excepting those incorporated in books on H) which appeared down to the end of 1969. The order is alphabetical according to the title of the work considered.

S. P. Moss, "The Mountain God of H's 'The Ambitious Guest' " (*ESQ* 67), attempts with considerable success to account for some heretofore puzzling details in the narrative which H published in 1835: Moss argues well for interpreting it as a parable concerning Providence and man's faith in it. L. H. Moore, "H's Ideal Artist as Presumptuous Intellectual" (*SSF* 65), weighs evidence for and against readings of "The Artist of the Beautiful" as satire. Cleanth Brooks and R. P. Warren consider "The Birthmark" in *Understanding Fiction* (1943), stressing the relationship between the theme and the parable as a whole. In "H's 'The Birthmark': Science as Religion" (*SAQ* 49) R. B. Heilman accepts their findings, then examines the enrichment of the meaning by the recurrent use of religious metaphors.

Frank Davidson, "Toward a Reevaluation of *BR*" (*NEQ* 52), urges a reformulation of the theme, claiming that the novel "records the tragedy attendant on ambiguities which rise from man's false assumption that his convictions about life . . . are absolute realities" and that the story and repeated symbols develop this theme well. J. F. Ragan finds that "The Irony in H's *BR*" (*NEQ* 62) operates in three ways. Kelley Griffith, "Form in *BR*" (*AL* 68), holds, without quite proving his point, that the book falls into two distinct parts, with chapter 16 as the dividing line, and the second half a dream-voyage that allies it with Kafka and Joyce. Nina Baym, "*BR*: A Radical Reading" (*JEGP* 68), makes good points as she attacks numerous previous critics but is less convincing as she proposes a radically new interpretation. R. R. Male in an excellent critique of recent studies of this novel in *ALS* for 1968 observes that her thesis "often makes *BR* sound as if it were written by Joan Baez." His argument that what he calls "Moodie's movable patch" has peregrinated in ways that need attention and that hence "we are still in trouble with *BR*" is well taken.

L. B. Levy discusses a little noticed short piece in "H's 'The Canal Boat': An Experiment in Landscape" (*AQ* 64). In "Endicott's Breastplate: Symbolism and Typology in 'Endicott and the Red Cross' " (*SSF* 67) Sacvan Bercovitch cites the tale as "an important early demonstration of [H's] symbolic method."

C. A. Reilly, "On the Dog's Chasing His Own Tail in 'Ethan Brand' " (*PMLA* 53), finds a surprising number of alterations between the North Adams notebook entry and the tale and demonstrates their relevance to the theme—an enlightening, though blessedly compressed, critical analysis. Carl Bode, "H's *Fanshawe*: The Promising of Greatness" (*NEQ* 50), stresses the superior characterization and the devotion to character and theme at the expense of plot as predictions of future achievements. R. E. Gross, "H's First Novel: The Future of a Style" (*PMLA* 63), sees other prefigurations of H's later work in this early narrative.

"The Gentle Boy" [hereafter "GB"] is related to *Pierre* by Louise Dauner in "The 'Case' of Tobias Pearson: H and the Ambiguities" (*AL* 50). S. L. Gross, "H's Revision of 'GB' " (*AL* 54), finds in the changes valuable clues to the author's way of working and to his final meaning. A. M. Donohue, " 'The Fruit of that Forbidden Tree': A Reading of 'GB'," *A Casebook on the H Question* (1963), notices how the division of the story, the ambiguity and irony, and such typical ingredients as isolation, guilt, the universalized past, the quest for home and father, and initiation into evil all help develop H's theme.

Harold Orel's "The Double Symbol" (*AL* 51) led a procession of articles on *H7G*. Darrel Abel in "H's House of Tradition" (*SAQ* 53) sees the book as a five-movement "allegory of love versus self-love, of human tradition versus personal ambition and family pride, of imagination versus preoccupation with present fact." Clark Griffith, "Substance and Shadow: Language and Meaning in *H7G*" (*MP* 54), examines recurrent symbols connoting substance and shadow, relating these plausibly to a central meaning. R. C. Carpenter, "H's Scarlet Bean Flowers" (*UR* 63), studies Holgrave's flowers as a symbol reiterating motifs and preparing for the book's conclusion. Two psychological interpretations joined the parade—Donald Junkins's Jungian 'H's *H7G*: A Prototype of the Human Mind" (*L&P* 67) and C. H. Carlson's "Wit and Irony in H's *H7G*," *A Handful of Spice* (1968), a Freudian analysis. And F. J. Battaglia, "*H7G*: New Light on Old Problems" (*PMLA* 67), truly and effectively reassesses the book to defend against earlier attacks the plotting, the characterization, and the ending.

R. H. Fossum considers the legends as units and as parts of a unified whole in "Time and the Artist in 'Legends of the Province House' " (*NCF* 68). L. B. Levy, in "The Temple and the Tomb: H's 'The Lily's Quest' " (*SSF* 66), properly worries about engaging in "too rigorous a reading" of this previously neglected sketch, then argues more ingeniously than convincingly for it as "a paradoxically joyful Hymn to Death."

Especially in recent years, *MF* has vied with *SL* for attention in analytical articles concentrating on a single work. Perhaps this is not surprising since even in H's day this book evidently invited analysis. J. R. Lowell's review (*Atl* 1860) discussed the book quite perceptively as embodying "the most august truths of psychology, . . . the most pregnant facts of modern history, and . . . a profound parable of the Christian Idea." M. T. Gale, "*MF*; An Allegory, with a Key to its Interpretation" (*New Englander* 1861), found the characters representative of various faculties as mid-century psychology defined them, and stated the objections that some Calvinists made to H's views. Elizabeth P. Peabody in 1868 in the *Atl* discussed the book from the Transcendental point of view and discovered "an interpretation of Christianity more vital than has yet been symbolized by any ritual, or systematized by any ecclesiasticism."

Much more recently, Dorothy Waples, "Suggestions for Interpreting *MF*" (*AL* 41), although disavowing psychoanalysis, believes five Freudian concepts helpful to understanding the book and so argues in an article which now seems delightfully restrained. Darrel Abel, "Masque of Love and Death" (*UTQ* 53), finds that the characters represent degrees of experience and approaches to living and that H tried to make the book his best consideration of favorite problems—the personal ego in relation to the cosmic tragedy and the moral vision of life. M. E. Brown, "The Structure of *MF*" (*AL* 56), makes the valid point that in tracing the story of each of four characters, the book develops "a single idea, the transformation from innocence to experience." C. R. Smith, "The Structural Principle of *MF*" (*Thoth* 62), sees the narrative structured around the murder and the transformations that it brought in each main character. G. A. Barnett, "H's Italian Towers" (*SIR* 64), relates an important symbol to the depictions of the same characters and the development of the theme of the fall, and S. P. Moss, "The Problem of Theme in *MF*" (*NCF* 64), and P. G. Beidler, "Theme and the Fortunate Fall in *MF*" (*ESQ* 67), also address themselves to the task of settling the apparently endless argument about the position the romance takes concerning the paradox of the Fortunate Fall. S. W. Liebman, "The Design of *MF*" (*NEQ* 67), argues that what actually "sets the pace for the novel as a whole" is not one of the motifs heretofore championed but the reiterated image of the sarcophagus. The debate continued in D. J. Schneider, "The Allegory and Symbolism of H's *MF*" (*SNNTS* 69).

T. F. Walsh, "H's Satire in 'Old Esther Dudley'" (*ESQ* 61), attempts to locate the object of the satire in John Hancock's attitude. M. E. Dichmann, "H's 'Prophetic Pictures'" (*AL* 51), was a rather early contribution to a continuing dialogue about H's ambivalent attitude concerning the artist, on the one hand godlike in his vision, on the other in danger of committing the greatest sin— the violation of the human heart. The author also finds that the tale is concerned with the responsibility of the artist to society, again anticipating future interests. The most damaging evidence against her interpretation is found in H's own words at the end of the story, which seem to summarize a less complex "deep moral." R. P. Adams, "H's *Provincial Tales*" (*NEQ* 57), has value as an analysis of recurrent patterns of characterization, symbols, and themes in this abandoned collection.

Brief analyses of one tale often discussed, "Rappaccini's Daughter" [hereafter "RD"], are found in R. B. West and Robert Stallman, editors, *The Art of Fiction* (1949), and F. L. Gwynn, "H's 'RD' " (*NCF* 52). The former discusses the tale as a symbolic narrative dealing with innocence and evil; the latter as dealing with H's dualism of Head versus Heart. The contrast between the interpretations, although the terms seem different, is not irreconcilable. Oliver Evans, "Allegory and Incest in 'RD' " (*NCF* 64), notices repetitions of the incest motif and their value in a story representing a great nineteenth-century dilemma, the conflict between moral idealism and scientific materialism. S. P. Moss offers "A Reading of 'RD' " (*SSF* 65) based upon the doubt that critics ever will be able to find a single theme that can be properly formulated in a sentence: he suggests therefore that "the best way [is] to formulate the theme . . . by a series of related propositions which have the virtue of reflecting the complexity of the entire allegory." A criticism of the article by Fogle is a telling one: "It remains a question . . . whether the method conveys an adequate sense of the story's artistic unity, or, if one likes, its lack of it" (*ALS* 65).

Two articles on "RMB" have merit—V. O. Birdsall, "H's Oak Tree Image" (*NCF* 60), and R. E. Whelan, " 'RMB': The Burial of Reuben Bourne's Cowardice" (*RS* 69).

SL has been analyzed in so many articles that only a fraction can be discussed. Early articles that still are useful include Françoise Dony, "Romanticisme et puritanisme chez H, à propos de la 'Lettre Pourpre' " (*EA* 40), and F. I. Carpenter, "Scarlet A Minus" (*CE* 44). Two discussions which are comprehensive and illuminating, interestingly, were worked out jointly, in part, by their two authors: J. C. Gerber, "Form and Content in *SL*" (*NEQ* 44)—republished, somewhat revised, as "Introduction" to the Modern Library College edition (1950), and Gordon Roper, "Introduction" to "*SL*" *and Selected Prose Works by NH* (1949). Roper's, the more detailed essay, considers H's creative experience preparatory to the writing of his masterpiece—his methods and his adaptation of popular fiction and allegory to his purposes, then turns to the book and discusses it in relationship to H's theory of Romance, as a work developing a theme, and as a form (the parts and devices in relation to the work as a whole). Two articles comment on the Gerber-Roper reading: Darrel Abel, "H's Dimmesdale: Fugitive from Wrath" (*NCF* 56), and G. T. Tanselle, "A Note on the Structure of *SL*" (*NCF* 62). Abel wrote about the book on two other occasions—in "H's Hester" (*CE* 52) and "The Devil in Boston" (*PQ* 53). C. C. Walcutt, "*SL* and Its Modern Critics" (*NCF* 53), classifies readings of the book as orthodox Puritan, Romantic, Transcendental, and relativist, then gives thought to reasons for the variations: the nature of the symbolism, H's sympathy for erring characters, a tendency of readers to identify with the characters, and H's contradictory attitudes. While the classification in some instances is open to question, the over-all distinctions are useful, and reasons offered for divergences are generally sound. Quite possibly, though, Walcutt was too polite to mention a larger reason for disagreements—the shaping of some readings by the readers' preconceptions of what they will find.

During the years since Walcutt's survey appeared, critics have tended to urge concentration on a certain aspect or a certain character as a means of understanding SL. Feidelson, in a more detailed and less slanted analysis than that in *Symbolism and American Literature*, "SL" in HCE focuses upon the historical setting in relation to characters, action, and meaning. W. H. Nolte, "H's Dimmesdale: A Small Man Gone Wrong" (NEQ 65), rejects readings that make the minister the crucial character and returns to Carpenter's 1944 view that Hester towers above him. R. E. Whelan in "Hester Prynne's Little Pearl: Sacred and Profane Love" (AL 68) argues that since "Pearl's sole reality is that of an allegorical mirror," a careful study of her story and its significance clarifies the ending and the theme. Several quite noteworthy articles find it very revealing to relate "The Custom House" to the novel as a whole. Ziff's article of 1958 has been mentioned: it glances at the problem. S. S. Baskett, "The (Complete) SL" (CE 61), sees the prefatory section sharing with the narrative ironic contrasts and attitudes toward alienation. Allen Austin, "Distortion in 'The (Complete) SL'" (CE 61), attacks some aspects of Baskett's argument, and in a reply Baskett claims that he has been misread. W. R. Moses, "A Further Note on 'The Custom House'"(CE 62), suggests an extension of Baskett's claims. Meanwhile, E. H. Rovit, "Ambiguity in H's SL" (Archiv 61), had pointed out the value of the prefatory section in interpretation. Marshal Van Deusen, "Narrative Tone in 'The Custom-House' and SL" (NCF 66), finds other aspects unifying the two portions of the book. D. E. McCall, "The Design of H's 'Custom-House'" (NCF 67), sees the preface moving from the public world of Salem to the imaginative realm of the romance.

L. B. Levy, "The Mermaid and the Mirror: H's 'The Village Uncle'" (NCF 64), throws light not only upon the sketch but also upon H's attitude towards the artist. Andrew Schiller, "The Moment and the Endless Voyage: A Study of H's 'Wakefield'" (Diameter 51), is good in its perception that though Wakefield resembles Chillingworth, Kenyon, and Holgrave, he differs from them in significant ways.

Four articles on the much-discussed "YGB" merit attention. D. M. McKeithan, "H's 'YGB': An Interpretation" (MLN 52), stresses Brown's unreliability as a witness of the events in the story. T. F. Walsh, "The Bedeviling of YGB"

(*MLQ* 58), has valuable comments on the symbolism of the story and on Brown's own responsibility for his plight. David Levin, "Shadows of Doubt: Specter Evidence in H's 'YGB' " (*AL* 62), holds that the young man is misled by the devil's impersonations of the innocent folk that he believes he encounters. P. J. Hurley, "YGB's 'Heart of Darkness' " (*AL* 66), attacks Levin from a position much closer to McKeithan's and Walsh's than to those of other critics.

3. Discussions of Hawthorne's Influence

The question of H's influence has been a matter of increasing interest, especially during recent years. There are brief dicta on H's influence on the short story in F. L. Pattee, *Devolpment of the American Short Story* (1923); Malcolm Cowley, "One Hundred Years Ago: H Set a Great New Pattern" (*NYHTB* 6 Aug. 50); Herschel Brickell, "What Happened to the Short Story" (*Atl* 51); and Danforth Ross, *The American Short Story* (1961). None of these, however, is as precise or as well documented as one would like it to be. Martin in his book *NH* (1965) has a final chapter, "A Significant Legacy," which surveys various influences, in particular those on James and Faulkner.

The influence on James and that on Melville has been remarked in several studies. Biographers of both Melville and H naturally have given the matter attention. Randall Stewart discusses personal and literary influences in "Melville and H" (*SAQ* 52). The best overall discussion is Harrison Hayford, "Melville and H: A Biographical and Critical Study," an unpublished Yale doctoral dissertation (1945). Some of Hayford's most important findings are set forth in two articles—"The Significance of Melville's 'Agatha Letters' " (*ELH* 46) and "H, Melville, and the Sea" (*NEQ* 46). Articles by others focus on influences upon specific works. E. G. Lueders considers an important interrelationship in "The Melville-H Relationship in *Pierre* and *BR*" (*WHR* 50). Nathalia Wright suggests H as the source of the fire imagery and the head *vs.* heart theme in Melville's masterpiece in "*Mosses from an Old Manse* and *Moby-Dick*: The Shock of Discovery" (*MLN* 52). L. B. Levy, "H, Melville, and the *Monitor*" (*AL* 65), holds that H's "Chiefly About War Matters" was palpably influential on four of Melville's poems. Gerhard Friedrich indicated his findings in the title of "A Note on Quakerism and *Moby-Dick*: H's 'GB' as a Possible Source" (*QH* 65). In "H and the Idea of 'Bartleby' " (*ESQ* 67), L. B. Levy finds striking evidence that "The Old Apple Dealer" inspired Melville's story.

Matthiessen dealt with H's influence upon James in *AmR* and *Henry James: The Major Phase* (1946). Marius Bewley, "James's Debt to H," in *The Complex Fate* (1952) finds several important parallels. Peter Buitenhuis, "Henry James on H" (*NEQ* 59), traces evaluations in 1872, 1879, 1897, 1904, and 1914, to determine, among other things, his indebtedness. Other studies are of influences upon individual works: J. R. Lucke, "The Inception of 'The Beast in the Jungle' " (*NEQ* 53), holds that the description of Hollingsworth as "a tiger out of a jungle" gave James's story its title, suggested the tiger image in chapter two, and even influenced James's thought. R. F. Gleckner, "James's *Madame de Mauves* and H's *SL*" (*MLN* 58), found many similarities and, in addition, an incorporation of the later author's objections to H's allegory. R. L. Gale makes a good case in "*MF* and *The Sacred Fount*: A Resemblance" (*SA* 62). R. E. Long, "The Society and the Masks: *BR* and The Bostonians" (*NCF* 64), claims that not merely the subject-matter and the characterization in H's story were influential; even the ideas of the earlier authors were. And Richard Poirier, "Visionary to Voyeur: H and James," in *A World Elsewhere* (1966) finds that H's style in his *BR* was germinal to the characterization of Lambert Strether and the narrative method of *The Ambassadors*.

Two recent articles make convincing cases for considering passages in H as sources for poems by Emily Dickinson. S. E. Lind finds that a portion of an essay in which H views a mid-summer scene and has intimations of autumn not only in all likelihood inspired the poem but also casts light upon its meaning: "Emily Dickinson's 'Further in Summer than the Birds' and NH's 'The Old Manse' " (*AL* 67). D. E. McCall, " 'I Felt a Funeral in My Brain' and 'The Hollow of the Three Hills' " (*NEQ* 69), properly asserts that "there are too many close parallels . . . for us reasonably to doubt that Miss Dickinson used the H story for her poem."

H's influence upon two American novelists was considered in two brief but convincing notes—George Perkins, "Howells and H" (*NCF* 60), claims that although Howells met the New England author only once, he was greatly influenced by his fiction; and Richard Bridgman, "As Hester Prynne Lay Dying" (*ELN* 65), claims that nothing but "deliberate planning" could have led to all the resemblances between *SL* and *As I Lay Dying*, but that Faulkner in his book "travesties the constituents" of the earlier novel.

The only studies of H's influences abroad are tentative, and rightly so. R. J. Niess, "H and Zola—An Influence?" (*RLC* 53), suggests that *SL* may have influenced *Thérèse Raquin*. And Vladimir Astrov, "H and Dostoievski as Explorers of the Human Conscience" (*NEQ* 42), is even more tentative, as he argues that the Russian author might have known H's works and that parallels between some of the novels might justify study.

HENRY DAVID THOREAU[1]

Lewis Leary

I. BIBLIOGRAPHY

Thanks to the dedication of students over many years, Thoreau (hereafter T, HT, HDT) is better groomed bibliographically than many of his contemporaries. S. A. Jones's pioneer "Contribution toward a Bibliography of T" (*Unitarian* 1890), reprinted in his *T: A Glimpse* (1890; rev. ed. 1903) and expanded in his *Bibliography of HDT* (1894), was slightly enlarged by J. P. Anderson for the bibliography appended to H. S. Salt's *HDT* (1890). These early listings were superseded by F. H. Allen's *Bibliography of HDT* (1908, 1968), supplemented by J. S. Wade's "A Contribution to a Bibliography from 1909 to 1936" (*JNYES* 39), but especially by William White's "A HDT Bibliography, 1908–1937" (*BB* 38–39), by P. E. Burnham and Carvel Collins's "Contribution to a Bibliography of T, 1938–1945" (*BB* 46–47), and C. A. Hildenbrand's *A Bibliography of Scholarship about HDT: 1940–1967* (1967).

Since 1941 Walter Harding has contributed "Additions to the T Bibliography" to each issue of *TSB*. Helpful selective bibliographies have been prepared by Mark Van Doren in *CHAL*, by B. V. Crawford in *HDT: Representative Selections* (AWS, 1934), and by T. H. Johnson and his associates in *LHUS*. Special bibliographies include Raymond Adams's "The Bibliographical History of T's *A Week*" (*PBSA* 49), Harding's "A Bibliography of T in Poetry, Fiction, and Drama" (*BB* 43), "A Check List of T's Lectures" (*BNYPL* 48), *A Centennial Check-List of the Editions of HDT's "Walden"* (1954), and *T Handbook* (1959). Finding lists include Adams's *The T Library of Raymond Adams* (1936, sup. 1937), V. C. White's "Check List of T Items in the Abernethy Library of Middlebury College" in R. G. Cook's *The Concord Saunterer* (1940), Harding's "The T Collection of the Pierpont Morgan Library of New York City" (*TSB* 47), F. B. Dedmond's "A Check List of Manuscripts Relating to T in the Huntington Library, the Houghton Library of Harvard University, and the Berg Col-

---

1. Both the author and the editor wish to thank Walter Harding for reading this essay in manuscript and for making additions and corrections.

lection of the New York Public Library" (*TSB* 53) and Alexander Kern's note on uncatalogued "T Manuscripts at Harvard" (*TSB* 55), Mrs. H. W. Kent's "A Catalog of the T Collection in the Concord Antiquarian Society" (*TSB* 54), Harding's "The Francis H. Allen Papers" (*TSB* 54, 55), and his description of "Manuscripts in the Clifton Waller Barrett Collection in the University of Virginia Library" (*TSB* 65).

II. EDITIONS

Textually, T has been somewhat more unkempt. The bulk of his writing was issued posthumously. From 1840 through 1860 he contributed some 24 items in prose and verse to the *Dial* and something just over a dozen more to other periodicals. Only two volumes were published during his lifetime: in 1849 *A Week on the Concord and Merrimack Rivers* (hereafter *Wk*) in an edition of 1,000 copies printed at the author's expense, and in 1854 *Walden; or Life in the Woods* (hereafter *Wa*), published by Ticknor and Fields in an edition of 2,000 copies. During his last illness T worked some of his lectures into essays for the *Atl*, where they appeared, after his death, in 1862 and 1863. His literary effects, manuscripts, some letters, and thirty volumes of journals were left to his sister Sophia who, aided by Emerson, Ellery Channing, and other friends, saw to the preparation of five posthumous volumes.

Excursions in Field and Forest in 1863 (hereafter *Exc*), prefaced by a memoir by Emerson, was composed of papers collected by Sophia Thoreau from the *Dial*, the *Boston Miscellany*, the *Democratic Review*, the New York *Tribune*, and the *Atl*. *The Maine Woods* (hereafter *MW*), the first two of the three parts of which had appeared in the *Union Magazine* and the *Atl* during T's lifetime, was edited in 1864 by Sophia Thoreau and Channing. *Cape Cod* in 1865 (hereafter *CC*), also edited by Sophia Thoreau and Channing, was made up in its first four chapters of materials which had appeared in *Putnam's* ten years before. *Letters to Various Persons* in 1865 (hereafter *LVP*) was prepared by Emerson, who selected from and edited the correspondence to present an austere portrait of T. *A Yankee in Canada, with Anti-Slavery Papers* (1866) contained in its first three chapters materials which had appeared in *Putnam's* (1853), but inadvertently contained also an essay on "Prayers" from the *Dial*, which Emerson had written. T's executors did their work devotedly, if not always scrupulously well.

Yet before he had been dead five years, the best of T, with the exception of the journals, was available in print. The journals, however, were zealously guarded. "These papers are very sacred to me," wrote Sophia Thoreau in 1866, "and I feel inclined to defer giving them to the public for the present." Channing and F. B. Sanborn each used them in preparing their biographies of T, but it was not until after Sophia Thoreau's death that H. G. O. Blake excerpted from the journals to produce *Early Spring in Massachusetts* (1881), *Summer* (1884), *Winter* (1888), and *Autumn* (1892).

These posthumous volumes, the materials rearranged and obvious errors corrected, but not apparently compared again with T's manuscripts, form the basis, together with *Wk* and *Wa*, for the ten-volume Riverside edition of *The Writings of HDT, with Bibliographical Introductions and Full Indexes* (1893), edited by H. E. Scudder. A year later Sanborn's *Familiar Letters* was added as an eleventh volume. Then, in 1906, fourteen volumes of the *Journals* (hereafter *Jo*), edited by Bradford Torrey and F. H. Allen (repr. with a foreword by Walter Harding, 1962) supplanted Blake's four volumes of seasonal excerpts to make up the twenty-volume "standard" Walden or Manuscript edition of the *Writings*; but, except for the addition of a few letters and a new distribution of the contents of some of the posthumous volumes, the text for the most part was as casually reproduced as before: R. L. Cook's brief statement of "T's Annotations and Corrections in the First Edition of *Wa*" (*TSB* 53) pointed to textual errors uncorrected even after one hundred years; see also Walter Harding's "The Corruption of *Wa*" (*TSB* 67). Meanwhile Sanborn had edited T's early essay *The Service* (1902) and, from then unpublished journals and manuscripts, *The First and Last Journeys of T* (1905), both in limited editions.

T's poems have fared hardly better. Emerson included nine of them in *LVP*, G. P. Lathrop printed another in *A Masque of Poets* (1878), and Sanborn published more in *Commonwealth* (1863), *Critic* (1881), *Scribner's* (1895), *The Personality of T* (1902), and elsewhere. Fifty poems were brought together in *Poems of Nature* (1895), edited by Sanborn and Salt, and the Walden edition contained "A List of the Poems and Bits of Verse Scattered among T's Prose Writings." Not until 1943 was all available T verse except the poetic translations presented by Carl Bode in *Collected Poems* (enlarged 1964), which first appeared both in a trade and an annotated edition and which F. H. Allen (*AL* 45) reviewed as "an admirable, but not an impeccable piece of work"; see also W. S. Thomas, "T as His Own Editor" (*NEQ* 42).

The letters also, faithfully collected but not always meticulously reproduced by previous editors (see Harding's "Franklin B. Sanborn and T's Letters" (*BPLQ* 51), were edited with greater discrimination by Bode and Harding as *The Correspondence of HDT* (1958); but more letters have come to light; see K. W. Cameron's *Companion to T's Correspondence* (1964) and *Over T's Desk: New Correspondence, 1838–1861* (1965). J. J. Moldenhauer in "T to

Blake: Four Letters Re-edited" (*TSLL* 66) presented a model of textual presentation and annotation for future editors.

More letters and manuscripts have been discovered, most of them examined or presented in *TSB* or *ESQ*. Among the more important are Wendell Glick's "Three New Early Manuscripts by T" (*HLQ* 51), the "lost" journal of 1840–41 edited with extensive commentary by Perry Miller as *Consciousness at Concord* (1958), Lawrence Willson's "T's Canadian Notebook" (*HLQ* 59), Harding's record of "T and the Kalmuks" (*NEQ* 59) and of *T's Minnesota Journey* (1962), and Cameron's *T's Fact Book . . . in the Harvard Library* (1962) and *T's Literary Notebooks in the Library of Congress* (1964). T's translation of *The Transmigration of the Seven Brahmins* was edited by A. E. Christy (1932) and of *Seven Against Thebes* by Leo Kaiser (1960). Among many modern editions of *Wa*, most useful are Larzer Ziff's *Wa: A Writer's Edition* (1961) and Willard Thorp's facsimile *Wa* (1969). Harding's *The Variorum Wa* (1963), though misnamed, contains useful commentary; see also Joseph Jones's *Index to Wa* (1955) and J. S. Sherwin and R. C. Reynolds's *A Word Index to Wa* (1960, 1969).

A complete new Thoreau Edition, under the general editorship of Walter Harding, sponsored by the National Endowment for the Humanities and the Center for Editions of American Authors of MLA, is currently being published by the Princeton University Press.

III. BIOGRAPHY

T's life was not long, he travelled little beyond Concord, and during the years of his maturity he kept a detailed account of what he found important in each day. His biography, then, might be supposed easily written. But T's journal discloses his thoughts and observations; on matters of personal concern he was doggedly reticent. He dramatized his ideas through unusual action, so that he became a symbol of quiet rebellion and self-sufficiency, and the center of a local legend which he did little to discourage. He used the first person perpendicular more than most men, yet he was the least inward-looking of writers; he revealed what he saw, seldom what he felt or exactly what he did. Biographers have therefore been handicapped by a paucity of particulars and have too often been satisfied with presenting him within the limits of the legend or with examining his writings for secret explanations of his activity. Reading between lines of the record T or his friends provided, they have written sympathetic defenses of his way of life or critical examinations of the efficacy or impotence of his ideas.

Because T has meant *Wa*, and *Wa* seems so dramatically to reveal the essence of T, much that preceded or followed the two years on Emerson's few acres has until recently been obscured, by T himself, by his friends, and inevitably by his biographers. Details of what happened before or after his adventure in retirement have been remembered and recorded too often only in relation to that premature climax. Reminiscent friends recalled events of his childhood or youth or of his post-Walden maturity which lead like spokes to a hub in explanation of the experiment beside the pond. Much early biographical information is untrustworthy, distorted, contradictory. "All of the sources," Brooks Atkinson has said, "are poisoned by good intentions."

As a result, T's life story has not been definitively told. He has been much at the mercy of goodhearted friends who speak with more enthusiasm than judgment; he has been too often stretched out of shape as a rallier of causes; his prickly character has attracted partisans, so that he has been libelled by people who do not like him, his way of life, or his ideas, or who do not like his friends or his friends' enthusiasms. Almost everyone who has written about T has attempted to prove something—that he was a hermit or not a hermit, a naturalist or a humanist, a scientist or a poet, a warm man disappointed in love or a cold man for whom love in the ordinary sense had no meaning.

First knowledge of T inevitably derives either directly or indirectly from Emerson's memoir, read as a eulogy at T's funeral, then revised for the *Atl* (1862), and reprinted often since, notably as the introduction to *Exc*. "It was such an address," said Sophia Thoreau, "as no other man could have done." Though some of her friends shared her disappointment at Emerson's emphasis on "stoical" elements of T's character, the essay is remembered as a beautifully poised analysis and even, as J. W. Krutch suggested, the "best thing ever written on T." It shares with Lowell's review of *LVP* the distinction of probably having been quoted or paraphrased by succeeding commentators more often than any other single writing about T.

Bronson Alcott's "The Forester," in the *Atl* one month before T's death, had underlined much the same Spartan and Stoic qualities. Other early essays of biographical interest include Storrow Higginson's "HD.T" (*HarM* 1862), which is both the first posthumous notice of T and also the first of recollections by men who had known T in their youth; G. W. Curtis's urbane reminiscences (*HM* 1862), and Joseph Palmer's brief sketch in the Boston *Advertiser* (1862). T's friends were eager that his life story be truly told, for, said his sister, "the profit of all men." She discussed with Daniel Ricketson who could do it best: Harrison Blake or Theo Brown, she thought, would "be truer to him" than any others; Bronson Alcott "best understood his religious character"; Emerson possessed the "rare wisdom, discrimination, and taste requisite for the purpose"; and Ellery Channing and Ricketson himself could be of assistance. "Henry's character," she explained, "was so comprehensive that I think it would take many minds to portray it" (*Daniel Ricketson and His Friends*, 1902; hereafter *DRF*).

Meanwhile Channing had been at work on reminiscences which appeared in eight installments in the Boston *Commonwealth* (1863–64) and which nine years later were revised and expanded to *T: The Poet Naturalist* (1873), an eccentric but indispensable volume (especially in Sanborn's corrected edition of 1902). Channing alone among the early admirers seems to have recognized that T, a lover of nature and an austere eccentric, was also a literary artist; see F. B. Dedmond, "Channing on T" (*MLN* 52). As biography, his book is sketchy indeed, but as testimony to T's literary inclinations it is, in spite of panegyric and self-glorification, more useful than some of its critics have admitted.

By the time Channing's volume appeared, T's reputation needed defense. John Weiss's article on "T" (*ChEx* 1865) recalled him as strange and withdrawn even in college; Hawthorne's notations on T in *Passages from the American Note-Books* (1868) did little to dispel such opinions; and W. R. Alger in *Solitudes of Nature and Man* (1867) charged that egotism was T's outstanding characteristic. But it was Lowell's review of *LVP* (*NAR* 1865, repr. in *My Study Windows*, 1871) which solidified public notions of T as a strange, perverse eccentric who lacked grace or social sense, an attitude toward T which was pretty much to prevail in the United States through the rest of the nineteenth century.

From England, however, came an ardent defense when, four years after Channing's biography, A. H. Japp, a Scot who scrambled his name to the pseudonym "H. A. Page," published in Boston and London *T: His Life and Aims* (1877–78), praising T, not as a person of "morbid sentiment, weak rebellion, and contempt for society," but as a latter-day St. Francis whose understanding of nature led him surely to an understanding of man. The book, which curiously misdates the last years of T's life, is of less value as biography than as a harbinger of later transatlantic enthusiasm for T's ideas.

Meanwhile T's American friends had not been completely silent. Bronson Alcott remembered him generously in *Concord Days* (1878). The "T Annex" to the Concord *Freeman* (6 May 1880) contained Joseph Hosmer's sympathetic account of a day spent with T at Walden. Most importantly, Sanborn's *HD.T* (1882) appeared as one of the American Men of Letters series. Sanborn, who had known T from 1855 to his death, had been schoolmaster in Concord, and had boarded for a time in the T home, seems never to have been accurate in

any of the numerous volumes he wrote or edited on T. But his carefully collected reminiscences, his use of T's journals, his extended quotations from the
college essays, and his printing of much of the correspondence with Horace
Greeley brought forward for the first time important details of T's activities.

M. D. Conway's graceful recollections in *Emerson at Home and Abroad*
(1882) added to the growing fund of stories about T. He was briefly noticed in
the *BQR* (1874), the London *Spectator* (1883), and *DUM* (1877). Theodore
Watts-Dunton, reviewing Page's *T* in *Athenaeum* (1877), wondered whether
T was not the original of Donatello in *The Marble Faun*. On this side of the
Atlantic, George Stewart read a paper on "T: The Hermit of Walden" before
the Literary and Historical Society of Quebec in 1882; John Burroughs wrote a
discriminating estimate for *Century* (1882); W. G. Barton in 1885 read an essay on "T, Flagg, and Burroughs" before the Essex Institute at Salem; T. W.
Higginson in *Short Studies of American Authors* (1888) defended T against
Lowell's charges of indolence, imitativeness, and pretense; and S. A. Jones
spoke in defense against these charges before the Unity Club of Ann Arbor
in 1889.

In 1890 appeared *The Life of HDT* by H. S. Salt, an English critic who two
years before had included in his *Literary Studies* an appreciative essay on T,
which had first appeared in the *TB* (1886). Here for the first time a disinterested professional was at work. Salt solicited new information from T's friends—
Sanborn, Ricketson, Blake, Edward Hoar, Higginson, and E. W. Emerson; he
corresponded with Burroughs, W. S. Kennedy, and Jones. "My objective," he
wrote Ricketson, "is to give (1) a clear and succinct account of T's life, gathering up and arranging in their due order all the scattered records of him to be
found in the periodicals, as well as the information given by Messrs. Channing,
Sanborn, and Page; (2) a fuller and more serious estimate of T's *doctrines* than
any hitherto published, and a critique of his literary qualities" (*DRF*, 1902; see
also J. T. Flanagan, "Henry Salt and His Life of T," *NEQ* 55). And Salt succeeded in both objectives, so that his book remains the most satisfactory single
account of T's life. Prepared before the journals were made public and before
many important small discoveries by modern students, it yet brings together
as no other biography does those elements which seem to remain essential to
an understanding of T. It was revised and abridged in 1896 for the Great Writers series, and this version was reprinted in 1968.

More facts now began to appear. E. W. Emerson's lecture of 1890, expanded
to *HT as Remembered by a Young Friend* (1917, 1968), was intended to correct
contemporary notions of T as a strange and unsocial fellow. The publication
of Sanborn's *Familiar Letters* (1894), A. W. Hosmer's edition of personal im-

pressions in *Three Letters* (1900), S. A. Jones's collections of early articles and reviews in *Pertaining to T* (1901), Sanborn's *The Personality of T* (1901), E. H. Russell's *A Bit of Unpublished Correspondence between HT and Isaac Hecker* (pub. as pam. and in *Atl* 02), *DRF* (1902) each added something of significant biographical detail.

A. R. Marble's *T: His Home, Friends, and Books* (1902, 1969) was the first full-length biography by an American not a member of the Concord group. It presents a sympathetic portrait, based on materials found in Channing, Sanborn, and Salt, on available T letters and journals, and on interviews with Concord neighbors. M. D. Conway's *Autobiography* (1904) added testimony on T's anti-slavery activities. New family background was provided by E. H. Russell's "T's Maternal Grandfather" (*PAAS* 09). F. L. H. Willis offered evidence of T's attraction for children and his power over birds in *Alcott Memoirs* (1915). Mark Van Doren's *HDT: A Critical Study* (1916), less important as biography than as criticism, came to the conclusion based on study of *Jo* that T's life ended in disappointment and defeat—a view shared by, among others, Gilbert Seldes in *American Writers on American Literature* (1931) and, with some reservations, by Leo Stoller in *After Walden* (1957), but forcefully rebutted by J. L. Shanley in "T: Years of Decay and Disappointment?" (*The T Centennial*, 1964).

The centennial of T's birth saw the appearance of Sanborn's posthumous *The Life of HDT* (1917, 1968), expanded and rewritten from the 1882 American Men of Letters volume, containing "memoirs of his ancestors not before given to the public; and also, in their complete form many essays written in his early youth," mainly college exercises. Every student of T recognizes large debts to Sanborn. "In matters," says B. V. Crawford (*T*, 1934), "of family history, neighborhood associations or gossips of Concord, the anti-slavery agitation in which he was also a leader, his testimony is almost final." Sanborn is often irritating because of the freedom with which he treats his material, rearranging paragraphs, deleting at will, and interpolating words and phrases wherever it seems to him proper. He knew the minutiae of T's life, but lacked understanding like that of Channing of his thought or literary accomplishment. "However much one might be irritated by Sanborn's attitude of ownership of all that pertained to T," said F. H. Allen in *T's Editors* (1950), "one had to admit that he occupied a unique place as the only one among T's biographers who had personal acquaintance with him, and who was at the same time an active and energetic seeker for information about his life and writings, also that he had a keen mind as well as a gift for expression."

Leon Bazalgette's *HT: Sauvage* (Paris, 1924), translated by Van Wyck

Brooks as *HT: Bachelor of Nature* (1924), is a dramatized biography taking literally T's admonition (used as a motto on its title page), "My friend will be bold to conjecture. He will guess bravely at the significance of my words." W. L. Phelps's *HDT* (1924) contributes nothing new to biography but suggests that T "is certain to outlive many of his more showy contemporaries." M. H. Brown's chapter on T in *Memories of Concord* (1926) presents affectionate personal recollections. Brooks Atkinson's *HT: the Cosmic Yankee* (1927) is written with infectious enthusiasm and, with H. S. Canby's chapter on T in *Classic Americans* (1931), is perhaps the most useful brief biographical introduction.

During the 1930's professional students, already at work in critical evaluation, began to uncover new biographical evidence. Raymond Adams's "T's Literary Apprenticeship" (*SP* 32), competently exact, established 1841 as the year when T decided on a literary career; his "T Buried Twice" (*SatR* 33) cleared up a misunderstanding on T's final resting place. J. T. Flanagan wrote of "T in Minnesota' (*Minn Hist* 35). H. H. Hoeltje found new evidence on "T in Concord Town and Church Records" (*NEQ* 39). Fresh evidence was discovered about T's relationships with his contemporaries. Scattered T manuscripts were being gathered in university or public repositories. The time seemed ripe for a fresh, detailed, and objective biography which would bring all these materials together.

Written as if in response to this requirement, H. S. Canby's *T* (1939, 1968) proved, however, to many students to be a disappointing book. It did mark what T. L. Collins called "T's Coming of Age" (*SR* 41), but it was marred by an aloofness from its subject and an inept toying with Freudian psychology. Canby perhaps discovered too many facets in T: (1) "a creative artist and thinker in search of a career," (2) a "Yankee Pan" such as Channing had found him, (3) a poor boy who made good in a familiar American fashion, (4) a Transcendentalist, (5) an individualist independent to excess, and (6) "Next to Poe the most professional of American writers." T was "typically American," and the story of his life "a success story, the history not of an ascetic hermit but of a man of letters of deep and troubled emotions."

Canby's unquestioning acceptance of the accounts of some of T's contemporaries was challenged by Raymond Adams in "T at Harvard" (*NEQ* 40) and "T's Diploma" (*AL* 45), and by F. T. McGill in "T and College Discipline" (*NEQ* 42). Other errors of minor fact were corrected by Max Cosman in "Apropos of John Thoreau" (*AL* 40) and again by Adams, who spoke of "T's Burials" (*AL* 40). In all essential details Adams's review of Canby's *T* (*AL* 40) gives a more satisfactory summary of the achievements and shortcomings of the book than there is space for here.

Most provocative was Canby's treatment of T's love life, a subject which had briefly intrigued previous writers. The tradition of an abortive love affair, known in outline since Sanborn's *T* (1882), had been dismissed by Van Doren as of negligible importance, and by Atkinson as a flimsy "sop to gossip." T's reasons for not marrying had been set forth by Channing in 1867 when he wrote in his journal that "Henry made no account of love at all." It had been hinted at by Robert Louis Stevenson (preface to *Familiar Studies of Men and Books*, 1882), who accused T, though "once fairly and manfully in love," of being "devoid . . . of any quality of flesh and blood." It had been discussed tentatively in psychological terms by A. R. Marble in 1902 and mentioned by E. W. Emerson in 1917. The story of T's refusal by Ellen Sewall, known briefly since Sanborn's *T*, was recounted by T. M. Raysor in "The Love Story of T" (*SP* 26) and explained more fully in Harding's "HT and Ellen Sewall" (*SAQ* 65). But the older notion that T was incapable of love prevailed. Ludwig Lewisohn in *Expression in America* (1932) wrote him off as a "clammy prig . . . hopelessly inhibited, probably to the point of psychological impotence or else physiologically hopelessly undersexed."

Canby attacked the "serious misunderstanding, which makes T a sexless Platonist." He retold the story of Ellen Sewall, drew on correspondence of the Ward family, and discovered significant meanings in the then unpublished journal for 1840–41. He suggested that "T was what the common man would call in love with Emerson's wife," and he speculated on the identity of other women who were or who might have been attracted to T, even wondering whether the "idea that Margaret Fuller . . . proposed" to him was as "ridiculous as it seems": he concluded that Sophia Foord had probably proposed to T and, when spurned, attempted suicide, a guess rejected by Harding in "T's Feminine Foe" (*PMLA* 54). Refining a suggestion found in Van Doren and Bazalgette, Canby explained that when T's true love, first for Ellen Sewall, then for Lidian Emerson, was not returned, he turned to "new obsessions with nature. . . . He found compensation there."

Later explanations of T's sexual troubles, or lack of them, have been more forthright but no less presumptuous. Extending Raymond Gozzi's suggestion in "Tropes and Figures: A Psychological Study of HDT" (*TBS* 57) of "an unconscious homoerotic orientation" in T, Perry Miller in commentary prefaced to *Consciousness at Concord* (1958) marshalled evidence to prove "the androgynous nature of T's monomaniac discussions of friendship." Miller discovered in T a "delirium of self-consciousness" fed by sublimation of sexual love and a subsequent fear of inferiority made more intense by fear of being found out; he accused such pre-Freudian biographers as Emerson, Channing, and

Sanborn of bewilderment or embarrassment when confronted by intimations of sexual strangeness. Less magisterially, W. C. Thompson wondered about "The 'Uniqueness' of T" (*Paunch* 65), and Joel Porte wrote of "T on Love: A Lexicon of Hate" (*UR* 64, 65). Clayton Hoagland's "The Diary of T's 'Gentle Boy'" (*NEQ* 55) reveals little to substantiate charges of sexual aberration. Most students have avoided latter-day psychoanalytical exploration and are neither bewildered nor embarrassed by what T has to reveal.

During the 1940's, writings on T were increased by the establishment in 1941 of *TSB*, the pages of which provide an attractive melange of information and appreciation. Elsewhere Max Cosman wrote of "T and Staten Island" (*S I Hist* 43), Kurt Steele of his pencil manufacturing in "Prophet of the Independent Man" (*Progressive* 45), Frank Buckley of "T and the Irish" (*NEQ* 40), and Raymond Adams of "An Irishman on T" (*NEQ* 50); R. L. Straker found additional information on "T's Journey to Minnesota" (*NEQ* 41), E. G. Berry on "T in Canada" (*DR* 43), and Max Cosman on "A Yankee in Canada" (*Canadian Hist Rev* 44). Francis Henry put together materials on "HDT and Bronson Alcott" (*TCJ* 42), Walter Harding on "T and Horace Greeley" (*TSB* 45), and Ruth Frost on "T's Worcester Friends" (*Nature Outlook* 44–47). T's abolitionist activities were briefly explored by N. A. Ford in "HDT, Abolitionist" (*NEQ* 46), by Harding in "T and the Negro" (*NHB* 46), and by W. P. Glick in "T and the *Herald of Freedom*" (NEQ 49). H. H. Hoeltje wrote of "T as Lecturer" (*NEQ* 49). R. F. Stowell published a *T Gazetteer* (1948, 1969), and R. W. Robbins in *Discovery at Walden* (1947) told of his excavation of the site of T's house beside the pond. J. W. Krutch's American Men of Letters *T* (1948) was a mature and sensible appraisal, unmarred by the condescension or speculation of Canby's book.

The following decade showed no abatement in activity. Masses of detail were being gathered, not only in *TSB*, but after 1955 by K. W. Cameron in in *ESQ*. Cameron also presented material on *Emerson, T, and Concord in Early Newspapers* (1958), *T's Harvard Years* (1964), and *T and His Harvard Classmates* (1965). Christopher McKee told of "A Week on Mt. Washington and in Tuckerman's Ravine" (*Appalachia* 54) and of "T's First Visit to the White Mountains" (*Ibid.* 56). J. O. Eidson suggested in *Charles Stearns Wheeler: Friend of Emerson* (1951; repr. *ESQ* 68) a man who might have inspired T's experiment in retirement, and R. J. Harmon discovered an unnoticed letter from "T to His Publishers" (*AL* 54). J. C. Broderick told of "T, Alcott, and the Poll Tax" (*SP* 56), "T's Proposals for Legislation" (*AQ* 55), "The Thoreau Family and Concord Fires" (*TSB* 55), and "T and My Prisons (*BPLQ* 55). Lawrence Willson wrote of "The Transcendentalist View of the West" (*WHR* 60), R. C.

Albrecht of "T and His Audience" (*AL* 61), Harriet Sweetland of "The Significance of T's Trip to the Upper Mississippi in 1861" (*TWA* 62; see also Harding's *T's Minnesota Journey*, 1962), Charles Boewe of "T's 1854 Lecture in Philadelphia" (*ELN* 64), and W. H. Bonner of "Captain T: Gubernator to a Piece of Wood" (*NEQ* 66.)

Books about T, mostly laudatory, also began to appear in increasing numbers in the 1950's, among them William Condry's brief but sensible *T* (1954), Charles Norman's *To a Different Drum* (1954), L. C. Keyes's *T: Voice in the Edgelands* (1955), H. B. Hough's *T of Walden* (1956), August Derleth's *Concord Rebel* (1962), Joseph Ishill's *T: The Cosmic Yankee* (1962), A. B. Hovey's *The Hidden T* (1962), and N. H. Seefurth's *T: A View from Emeritus* (1968). Milton Meltzer, with Walter Harding, presented in *A T Profile* (1962) an attractive combination of picture and text; see also Meltzer's *T: People, Principles, and Politics* (1963). T was introduced to young readers by Betty Schecter in *The Peaceable Revolution* (1962), J. P. Wood in *A Hound, a Bay Horse, and a Turtle Dove* (1962), and by T. M. Longstreet in *HDT: American Rebel* (1963). The centenary of T's death in 1962 and his election that year to the Hall of Fame of Great Americans brought forth a bust, a commemorative medal, and a stamp, and a number of privately printed small broadsides and pamphlets probably of more interest to the collector than to the scholar.

But during the past thirty years the most consistently active recorder of T's activities has been Walter Harding, founder of the T Society and editor since 1941 of *TSB*. Among his scores of notes and articles there and elsewhere, he has discussed "T on the Lecture Platform" (*NEQ* 51), has spoken of "The Influence of T's Lecturing on His Writing" (*BPLQ* 56), and has written movingly of T's last years in "This Is a Beautiful World" (*AH* 62). His *T Handbook* (1959) is indispensable, especially for its bibliographical notes, as in his *T's Library* (1957), *T: Man of Concord* (1960), and his edition of *Sophia Thoreau's Scrapbook* (1965). These and all his other writings were preludes to *The Days of HT: A Biography* (1965) which, though its usefulness may be diminished by an occasional mixture of fact and local lore, is more complete in detail and more maturely sympathetic than any previous life. Every future biographer will cull from it with care in creating his portrait of the artist as man.

IV. CRITICISM

"The character and works of HDT, who chose to live alone in the world, have roused stabbing assailants like Lowell and Stevenson, or complete panegyrists like Emerson and the biographers, but few critics." When Mark Van

Doren (*HDT: A Critical Study*) made this charge in 1916, T was just coming into his own as, if not a major, at least an important American man of letters. As Randall Stewart noted in "The Growth of T's Reputation" (*CE* 47) T had been singularly neglected at the beginning of the twentieth century: Barrett Wendell had lumped him casually with Bronson Alcott and Ellery Channing as one of the "Lesser Men of Concord" in his *Literary History of America* (1900), and W. C. Brownell had not included him at all in *American Prose Masters* (1909). By 1913, however, John Macy dignified T with a chapter in *SAL*; two years later H. S. Canby published in the *Dial* the first of his several evaluations of "The Modern T"; and soon Norman Foerster was to begin the series of penetrating papers which culminated in his essay on T in *Nature in American Literature* (1913).

Except for these four men, with whom Mark Van Doren takes his place as a fifth, to be joined in the 1940's by F. O. Matthiessen and S. E. Hyman, there have been until recently few serious critics of T as a literary craftsman. He does invite further study and a more effective putting together of biographical detail; but he invites criticism more, an estimate of his worth, not as a prophet crying alone in the Walden wilderness, but as a writer skilled in his trade.

1. The Emersonian Eccentric

The tone of much early criticism of T was set by J. R. Lowell, first in *A Fable for Critics* (1848), a year later in his remarks on *Wk* in the *MQR*, but principally in his review of *LVP* (*NAR* 1865). Whether in *A Fable* T was portrayed as the "brother bard" who treads "in Emerson's track with legs painfully short," as Austin Warren suggested in "Lowell on T" (*SP* 30), or whether he is the disciple who "has picked up all [Emerson's] windfalls before" as Sandborn (*The Personality of T*, 1901), and E. J. Nichols ("Identification of Characters in Lowell's *A Fable for Critics*," *AL* 32) believed, the indictment was the same: "For all practical purposes the damage was done, and T went through life ticketed as Emerson's man—a pale, cold luminary reflecting only the radiant glory of Emerson's genius" (Crawford, *T*, 1934).

After T's death, his friends were quick to counter this among other charges, but with little effect, and the extent of Emerson's influence on T has been argued by students ever since. Page (*T: His Life and Aims*, 1877) made first effective public denial, "T has been too completely . . . treated as a mere disciple of Emerson." Conway, though he admitted that T "looked not the least like his parents, but closely resembled Emerson," stated with force that T, however, "was quite as original" (*Emerson at Home and Abroad*, 1882). John Burroughs, acknowledging T "too directly under [Emerson's] influence," concluded that

"T was just as positive a fact as Emerson. . . . He was no . . . soft-shelled egg to be dented by every straw in the nest" (*Century* 1882). And Emerson's son Edward stated unequivocally, "The charge of imitating Emerson, too often made against T, is idle and untenable" (*Emerson in Concord*, 1889),

Charges of imitation were repeated almost thirty years later by Archibald MacMechan in *CHAL*. But the tide was turning. Norman Foerster in "The Intellectual Heritage of T" (*TR* 16) temporized that "what T received from Emerson he found in the man rather than in his books," and Mark Van Doren was equally moderate in explaining that even if T "were insignificant in that he took all his ideas from Emerson, he would be significant in that he reduced them to their practical and visualized essence." But it was E. W. Emerson who again a year later (*HT as Remembered*, 1917) expressed the view still held, with one shade of emphasis or another, by many present students: that rather than imitating Emerson, T put the older man's ideas into operation. By 1921 even the New York *Times* could identify T as "a literary figure too long overshadowed by St. Ralph, the Optimist."

André Bruel in *Emerson et T* (Paris 1929) capably brought together evidence of relationships between the two, their shared admiration for natural law, their affirmation of human liberty; Charles Cestre discussed "T et Emerson" (*Revue Anglo-Américaine* 30); but the most convincing study is J. B. Moore's "T Rejects Emerson" (*AL* 32) which, through an analysis of the journals of each man, concludes that T was early attracted to and influenced by Emerson, but that by the early 1850's he had grown away from and beyond him. For an extension of Moore's argument, see Leonard Gray's "Emerson and T" (*Unity* 52). More recently Joel Porte in *Emerson and T: Transcendentalists in Conflict* (1966), an attractive but oversimplified explanation of a dialectical relationship, and G. M. Ostrander in "Emerson, T, and John Brown" (*MVHR* 63) indicated political differences.

Lowell's review of *LVP* further saddled T with charges of morbid self-consciousness (charges amplified by Perry Miller in *Consciousness at Concord*, 1958), lack of humor, faulty logic, failure to discriminate between the trifling and the significant, cynicism, and misanthropy. Next to the charge of being Emerson's man, that which followed T most doggedly was the charge of being a cold, misanthropic person; an oddity, a recluse. Emerson himself had established that pattern in his memoir and in selection of materials for *LVP*, in which were omitted, said Sophia Thoreau, "passages betraying natural affection" (*DRF*, 1902).

T's friends contributed almost unanimously to the charge, even when they defended him on other grounds, so that it grew out of proportion to its significance in almost all early estimates of his work. Hawthorne's description of him in 1842 as "ugly as sin" seemed more often remembered than the novelist's subsequent qualification that T's ugliness was honest and agreeable, and became him "much better than beauty" (*American Note-Books*, 1869). Emerson in his journal described him as "stubborn and implacable . . . rarely sweet": he was argumentative to excess. A college friend remembered him as cold, with a moist hand and slack handshake (ChEx 1865). G. W. Curtis (*Commonwealth* 1853) spoke of the "inflexible HT, a scholastic and pastoral Orson, then living among the blackberry bushes of Walden Pond," and (HM 1862) described him as a man who "seemed to think that civilization had gone astray; that much fine wisdom perished with the Indians," that the "Stoics were the true heroes, and the Indian Vedas and Norse Eddas the most interesting religious legends."

Even among eccentrics, he seemed strange. Bronson Alcott described him in his diary (1847) as a "wood nymph," a "sylvan soul," and wrote publicly of him as a "little over-confident" and "stiffly individual" (*Atl* 1862). Ellery Channing in his journal (1853) found him a "spartan" who had "gone over the rough places and thorns in order to crucify and kill out human virtues." To John Burroughs he was "devoid of sympathy, devoid of generosity" (*Indoor Studies*, 1895). O. W. Holmes wittily wrote him off as an oddity who "insisted on nibbling his asparagus at the wrong end" (*Ralph Waldo Emerson*, 1885). The something more than a dozen articles about T in the New York *Tribune* before 1902 almost without exception outlined his eccentricities. Nor did temptation to make a phrase at T's expense elude later writers. V. W. Brooks (*FNE*, 1936) described him as a little man whose "nose and . . . thoughts were the biggest things about him."

But T was not denied recognition as a man of letters by his contemporaries; see J. C. Broderick, "American Reviews of T's Posthumous Books" (*UTSE* 55) and Walter Harding, "A Century of *Wa*" (*ColQ* 54). Though *Godey's Lady's Book* (1849) thought the anonymous *Wk* was certainly by Whittier because it was so charming, "just the book to read in idleness of summer," and though it was slightingly noticed in *Athenaeum*, T's first volume did receive some friendly attention. An unsigned reviewer, probably Horace Greeley, in the New York *Tribune* condemned its "second-hand, imitative, often exaggerated" pantheistic egotism and denounced its attitude toward the Christian Bible as "revolting alike to good sense and good taste," but he liked its literary quality: "Nearly every page is instinct with poetry, except those wherein verse is haltingly attempted."

Lowell's review in the *MQR*, patronizing and often flippant, was on the whole good natured and friendly; see Austin Warren, "Lowell on T" (*SP* 30). It praised T's natural history, his spontaneity, even his humor, and—this in contrast to Lowell's later estimate—his lack of self-consciousness: "Pepys is not more minute and with no uncomfortable sense of a public looking over his shoulder." He admired T's prose for its "antique purity, like wine grown colorless with age," but he found the verse bad indeed. T was at his best, said Lowell, when he remained himself; when he copied Emerson or any other master, then he became obscure, digressive.

Wa was distributed and reviewed more widely; see Harding, "Some Forgotten Reviews of *Wa*" (*TSB* 54). Its reviews, however, were on the whole less favorable. What was said about it created attitudes toward T which his countrymen would maintain for many years. The book was pleasantly noticed in the *NAR* as "more curious than useful," but filled with pithy and piquant suggestions. The New York *Tribune* also found it of "curious interest." C. F. Briggs in *Putnam's* called T "A Yankee Diogenes" who preferred a shanty to a tub and who "lived happily, too, though it don't exactly speak volumes in favor of his system . . . that he only continued his economical mode of life two years. If it was the thing,' why did he not continue it? . . . Mr. T. would have done the world a better service by purchasing a piece of land, and showing how much it might be made to produce instead of squatting on another man's premises."

So the pattern was set. T was an eccentric, anti-social, a hermit, good perhaps as a diarist of wood and stream, but hardly to be taken seriously. Youthful Edwin Morton described *Wa* as charming and its author the "high priest and poet of nature" (*HarM* 1855), but other writers were not so kind. T was compared to P. T. Barnum (*Knickerbocker Mag* 1855) in a gayly irresponsible essay on "Town and Country Humbugs": "One sneers at and ridicules the pursuits of his contemporaries with the same cheerfulness and good will that the other cajoles and fleeces them." An Englishman (*Chambers's Jour* 1857) followed much the same line, though he did admit that "if Barnum's autobiography is the bane, T's woodland experiences may be received as the antidote."

From England, however, came another notice, this by George Eliot (*Westminster Rev* 1856), which found in *Wa* "a bit of true American life (not the go-ahead species, but its opposite pole) animated by that energetic yet calm spirit of innovation . . . which is peculiar to some of the finer American minds." Almost alone among contemporary reviewers of *Wa*, George Eliot took the book and its author seriously, finding in T "deep poetic sensibility" and a "refined as well as a hardy mind": "There is plenty of sturdy sense mingled with his unworldliness."

2. Posthumous American Reputation

After T's death, friends published reminiscent accounts which praised him without stint, but which continued the impression that he was, in spite of and even because of their testimony, a very strange man, the archrepresentative of elements of Transcendentalism which sensible men disdained. As a result, discussion of T in the United States was for a long time concerned with matters other than his accomplishment as a man of letters. The intimate personal details and rhapsodic praise of Ellery Channing's reminiscences, Sanborn's printing of T's verse, the activities of Sophia Thoreau, Emerson, and Channing in seeing the posthumous volumes through the press, the fervent discipleship of men like Ricketson and Blake—these made T seem, as indeed in fact he was, the property of a cult. With missionary zeal, Conway presented him to British readers (*Frazer's Mag* 1866) as a "pious Yogi" who received homage from the little band of men which made Concord in truth an "American Weimar."

Reaction to such unqualified admiration inevitably set in. Austin Warren in "Lowell on T" (*SP* 30) explained how Lowell, the humanist, in his review of *LVP* charged T, the romanticist, "with substituting egotism and individualism for the social sense, nationalism for the study of man, and eccentricity for centrality." Lowell's sharp, brilliant phrases about whimsical and superficial aspects of T have often been better remembered than the critical core from which they radiate, so that his essay seemed to Salt (*HDT*, 1890) "a masterpiece of hostile innuendo," to John Macy (*SAL*, 1913) "the product of a mind from which poetry and youth had evaporated," and to John Burroughs (*The Last Harvest*, 1923) a diatribe of "smug respectability." Almost every commentator on T has pointed his lance briefly toward Lowell, many with aim distorted by anger.

But few defenders of T have penetrated to the essence of Lowell's argument. Some of his charges had already been made in his review of *Wk*: that T managed form badly, had no sense of architectonics and was unable to select the significant from the trivial, that he needed condensation, that he was self-centered, that he was not good at poetry. Now, in reviewing *LVP*, Lowell extended his indictment by finding T representative of a whole modern school of unhealthy sentimentalism about nature, "one more symptom of the general liver complaint" which fails to provide for man as part of nature, an argument that was later intensified by P. E. More, and first effectively answered by Norman Foerster. Finally, Lowell attacked the Romantic concept of individuality as absurd: "A man cannot escape in thought any more than he can in language from the past and the present."

Two years later, a Unitarian abolitionist, the Rev. W. R. Alger, in *The Solitudes of Nature and Man* (1867) repeated Lowell's indictment by attacking T's strain of egotism, his "interior aggrandizement of himself" which made him in every social sense a sterile man. Nature was not enough; man's responsibilities to other men, his unselfish devotion to the welfare of his fellows—these must take precedence if society were to advance. Sometimes criticism hostile to T seems specious, as when J. V. O'Connor suggested (*CaW* 1878) that the "incompleteness of [T's] life cannot be concealed by all the verbiage and praise of his biographers": he "gave up his life to . . . desultory study and admiration of Nature, and got for his worship a bronchial affliction which struck him down in the full vigor of his manhood."

Raymond Adams has called attention to "An Early and Overlooked Defense of T" (*TSB* 50) which spoke out strongly in opposition to Lowell. Eugene Benson in "Literary Frondeurs" (*Galaxy* 1866) described T as "a man of letters without the artistic spirit, but so thoroughly emancipated and so sincere that his writings have the beauty of truth if not the truth of beauty." Benson found T a nonconformist, like Emerson, Poe, and the elder Henry James: "Today, among the rising men we know of none; all are under the rule of conformity, express the average sentiment." It was to the conformity of Boston that "Lowell loaned his wit, his humor, the prestige of his literary reputation, to arraign and pronounce judgment against the most blameless and sincere man of letters who ever in this country resisted the majority."

3. Reputation abroad

As late as 1909 T. W. Higginson in *Carlyle's Laugh and Other Essays* supposed that Lowell's criticism, so effective in making T suspect in this country, had also limited his popularity. abroad. Critical commentary in the British press, however, indicates that this certainly was not the fact, for as J. P. Wood demonstrated in "English and American Criticism of T" (*NEQ* 33), during the late nineteenth century T, and especially T's ideas, received more attention in England than in the United States. While remaining in this country essentially the property of a clique concerned with reminiscence and panegyric, he was listened to in England as a voice which industrial and social reformers heard with respect.

The *BQR* (1873) responded to Channing's biography by finding "seriousness and severity" in T, and such "fiery hatred of wrong" as to provide the "main ingredients of heroism." Here was no American Rousseau who retired to escape men; T went to Walden to discover in himself what could be useful to all men, to prepare himself for a free and vigorous life of action. Four years later, he was introduced to Irish readers in *DUM* (1877) as certainly not "only an odd sort of character who lived alone in a wood." The London *Spectator* (1883) described the two years at Walden as "liberty expressed in the clearest language." Walter Levin in the *Academy* (1884) emphasized the practicalness of T's ideas, and the *Spectator* (1885) suggested that though "he wrote nothing by which he will be long remembered," yet his fight for freedom will live on. Salt in the *TBM* (1886) found him a "prophet of warning and remonstrance," more narrow and more intense than Walt Whitman, but like him the "incarnation of all that is free, healthy, natural."

To Salt and other liberal Englishmen, T seemed "in the truest sense an original thinker." The Christian Socialist, Thomas Hughes, then principal of the Workingman's College in London, praised T's contribution of "something simpler and nobler" than the "trappings and baggage of social life" (*Academy* 1877). The Fabian, Edward Carpenter, protested in *England's Ideal* (1877)—a volume which Salt (*HDT*, 1890) described as "worthy to rank with *Wa* in the literature of 'plain living and high thinking'"—that the real truth about T was "that he was a thorough economist" who in reducing life to its simplest terms established for all men an understanding of the relationship between labor and the rewards of labor. T was to Salt "an idealist who looked through the outer husk of life, and saw the true reality."

Robert Blatchford's popular socialist tract, *Merrie England* (1895), quoted T beside J. S. Mill, Adam Smith, and Henry George, and recommended *Wa* as a text for English workers. H. M. Tomlinson in "Two Englishmen and a Whale" (*HM* 26) recalled that hundreds of Blatchford's disciples carried T's book in their pockets and that literary groups in English industrial areas were often called Walden Societies. "It would scarcely be too much to say," reported Wood in "English and American Criticism of T" (*NEQ* 33), "that the first . . . British Labor government can be traced back to the youthful reformers who were so strongly influenced by T." His chapter on "Economy" in *Wa* became, as G. F. Whicher said in *Walden Revisited* (1945), "a minor gospel to the British Labor Party because of its uncompromising emphasis, not on reform, but on proceeding at once to realize the ultimate values of life and on living only for them."

As the nineteenth century ended, T reached Holland also, where Frederik Van Eeden established not far from Amsterdam a socialist colony devoted to literature and social reform and called it Walden; see Lewis Leary, "*Wa* Goes

Wandering," (*NEQ* 59). It was in 1907 that Mahatma Gandhi first came on the writings of T—see Salt, "Gandhi and T" (*Nation and Athenaeum* 30) and H. S. L. Pollack, "Gandhi and T" (*TSB* 43)—and in South Africa translated portions of "Civil Disobedience" (hereafter "CD"), the principles of which he was later to work into his doctrine of passive resistance; see Mahatma Gandhi, (*Young India* 1923). This influence was most thoroughly examined by George Hendrick, notably in "Influence of T and Emerson on Gandhi's *Satyagraha*" (*Gāndhi Mārg* 59) and "The Influence of T's 'CD' on Gandhi's *Satyagraha*" (*NEQ* 56); but also of interest are Pyarelal Nair, "T, Tolstoy and Gandhiji" (*New Delhi Statesman* 57), G. L. Mehta, "T and Gandhi" (*Congress Rec* 57), and E. N. Rao, "T and Ghandhi" (*Aryan Path* 66).

Even writers like Havelock Ellis, who in his remarks on T in *The New Spirit* (1890) put chief emphasis on his relation to nature, found timely tonic also in his ethical strictures. When Page in *T: His Life and Aims* (1877) hailed the American as a modern St. Francis whose "great aim is to recommend Nature to man," he also insisted that T "went to Nature an individualist, and came back a prophet of society." Theodore Watts-Dunton seconded him strongly in the *Athenaeum* (1877), where he praised T as a "Child of the Open Air" because he loved the wind, because more than St. Francis or Cowper, Burns, Coleridge, or Bisset, he understood that animals were not really dumb, and because he saw through the sophism which lay at the heart of the modern concept of work.

But all Englishmen did not praise T. R. L. Stevenson, as gracefully witty and as patronizing as Lowell, dismissed him (*Cornhill Mag* 1879) as an antisocial ascetic, a "melancholy, lean degeneration of human character," a "skulker" who lacked manliness or grace. Page replied heatedly in the *Spectator*, "I think the most charitable assumption is that Mr. R. L. S.'s studies of T have not been quite so exhaustive as they might have been"; and he presented examples of T's humanity, honor, and friendliness. When Stevenson included his essay on T in *Familiar Studies of Men and Books* (1882), he apologized for the harshness of his first estimate of T the man, but did not rescind his strictures on the cold inhumanity of his ideas.

Watts-Dunton in a second *Athenaeum* article (1892) agreed with Stevenson that T was too self-conscious: ". . . what racoon or chickadee in Walden Wood lived in such a perpetual state of sensitiveness as to himself and his fellows?" For all the lessons T had learned from Wordsworth, without whom there would "not have been any T or Emerson or Walt Whitman," T could not forget himself long enough to know nature. It was an American trait: "Nature worship such as Borrow's or even Wordsworth's is scarcely possible in America. . . .

Will Nature reveal her secrets to a man who can never look at her with the frank eyes of a child, but looks at her with the eyes of the bookishly, self-improving, transcendental species?" When Watts-Dunton wrote some of these attitudes into his introduction to the Oxford World's Classics edition of *Wa* (1906), he was mildly scolded by Arthur Rickett (*The Vagabond in Literature*, 1906), and more severely by Salt (*Fortnightly Rev* 08).

The subsequent amazing spread of T's reputation abroad has been outlined by Harding in "T's Fame Abroad" (*BPLQ* 57) and in his *T Handbook* (1959); see also William Condry, "A Hundred Years of *Wa*" (*DM* 53). *Wa* has been translated into almost every European language, into Chinese, into several of the languages of India, and at least eleven times into Japanese; "CD" has inspired reformers, old and young, across the world. S. J. Kahn and Irving Halperin have both written of "T in Israel" (*TSB* 63, 66), E. F. Tempe of "T in Germany" (*TSB* 65), and J. F. Lacey of "HDT in German Criticism: 1881–1965" (*DA* 68), Robert Francis of "T in Italy" (*MR* 62), and T. N. W. Burts of "T in South Africa" (*MR* 62). Testimony to the extraordinary interest in T in Japan was given by an exhibition of almost a hundred books or articles about T in Japanese or of his writings in that language prepared by Akiko Tokusa at the Pierpont Morgan Library in 1962 for the centennial commemoration of T's death. Until recently, most articles on T in foreign periodicals have been introductory or appreciative, but during the past several years important contributions have appeared in France, Italy, Germany, and especially in Japan; representative are Roger Asselineau's "Un narcisse puritain" (*Europe* 67), Agostino Lombardi's "L'arte di HDT" (*Belfagor* 59), Stefan Andres's "HDT: der Eremit von Walden Pond" (*Perspektiven* 55), and, among many others, Masayoshi Higashiyama's "T: A Japanese View" (*Eng and Amer Lit* 62).

4. Student of Nature

During the last decades of the nineteenth century, little of importance was written on T in the United States, except by John Burroughs, whom his contemporaries thought particularly qualified as a naturalist to interpret—as indeed he effectively did—the writings of T. Sanborn's *T* (1882) was in no substantial sense critical, nor were the brief items about T which Sanborn and others among T's admiring countrymen scattered through the press. W. S. Kennedy's proposal for "A New Estimate of T" (*Penn Mag* 1880) was perhaps typical in presenting T as the "saintliest of men . . . whose only crime was to be too pure . . . and to love too well the meadows, woods, and streams." The appearance between 1881 and 1892 of Harrison Blake's extracts from the journals, and the publication in 1906 of *Jo* in fourteen volumes, however, soon brought forth fresh commentary, particularly in respect to the question, never completely neglected before, of whether and to what extent T was a naturalist or a nature lover or a scientist.

"T by the charm of his writings," said E. W. Emerson in *HT As Remembered* (1917), "led many young people to wood walks and river journeys. . . . A whole literature of this kind has sprung up . . . inspired by him." He became, and was to some extent to remain, the property of another cult, that of the Romantic back-to-nature movement. Thus he was set forth by J. A. Prinzinger as *HD.T: ein amerikanscher Naturschilderer* (1895). "He was the chief of poetic naturalists," agreed Brander Matthews in his *Introduction to the Study of American Literature* (1896). He was a maker of "Literature of Field and Hedgerow," reported the London *Nature Notes* (oo). Salt wrote of the relationship between "T and Jeffries" (*Ibid.*), between "T and Gilbert White" (*New Age* oo), and of "HDT and the Humane Study of Natural History" (*Humane Rev* 03). His "Gospel of the Open Air" was praised by E. G. Ives (Boston *Transcript* 01). Maurice Muet in Paris wrote of him as "Une poète-naturaliste Américain" (*La Revue* oo). Jeanette Perry asked, "Was T a Lover of Nature?" (*Critic* 03), and answered emphatically in the affirmative. H. W. Mabie talked of "T: A Prophet of Nature" (*Outlook* 05) and described him as "A Theocritus of Cape Cod" (*Atl* 12). W. D. Howe expressed a popular attitude (*Reader* 05) when he said: "Nature was to T the solace, the refuge, from the business and worldiness of society. There he found simplicity, variety, harmony, truth, and beauty."

In vain did Sanborn plead (*Outlook* 06) that T's "chief interest "was literature rather than Nature-study, though the world has long otherwise fancied." Even John Macy, who valued T for more significant things, found (*SAL*, 1913) the "growing cult of the open air, the increase in number of amateur prodigals returning to nature, have given a fresh vogue to his sketches." F. E. White brought together "T's Observations on Fogs, Clouds, and Rain" (*Nature Study* 20), and G. A. Parker wrote of "The Moon in T" (*Ibid.* 22). Régis Michaud (*Vie des peuples*, Paris, 1924) found in T's writings new revelations of the wonders of nature. "As Nature's lover," said D. C. Peattie (*NAR* 38), "HDT is the greatest in the English language. And it is as a Nature writer that I hope he will be read forever." In this estimate Peattie was joined by Krutch in "The Wilderness at Our Doorstep" (*NYTBR* 53) which attested that "as a nature writer, T is still the greatest of them all," and by Alec Lucas in "T: Field Naturalist" (*UTQ* 54).

But many students have found him something more than this. As early as 1877 Page had complained that T was "rejected too decisively by the purely scientific men, for whom, nevertheless, he has many hints that are equally original and valuable." John Burroughs did not agree. In "T's Wilderness" (*Critic* 1881) he explained that T "cared little for science," that what he was "finally after in nature was ulterior to science . . . philosophy . . . [or] poetry; it was something vague which he calls 'the higher law,' and which eludes all direct statement." A year later in the *Century* Burroughs authoritatively charged T with "failure to make any new or valuable contribution to natural history." His "ornithology was not sure"; T looked so "intently for the bird behind the bird" that he was even "a long time puzzled to distinguish the fox-colored sparrow from the tree or Canadian sparrow." Burroughs was subsequently to multiply his charges of scientific inaccuracy: T's "night-warbler" was really the oven-bird; he confused the indigo bunting with the black-throated blue warbler; he failed to differentiate between the song of the hermit and the wood thrush; he misunderstood the habits of the woodpecker (*The Last Harvest*, 1922). But as a nature writer, T was supreme. Like Peattie, Krutch, and Bradford Torrey ("T's Demand on Nature," *Friends on the Shelf*, 1906), Burroughs praised his "rare descriptive powers" and proclaimed other nature writers "tame and insipid beside T."

Havelock Ellis, who thought Burrough's essay in the *Century* the most discriminating estimate of T ever made, concurred thoroughly, "It has been claimed for T by some of his admirers, never by himself, that he was a man of science, a naturalist;" he was neither: "his science is that of a fairly intelligent schoolboy—a counting of birds' eggs and a running after squirrels." T was not a naturalist; he was an artist and a moralist (*The New Spirit*, 1890). Salt agreed also. Though "Nature," he said, "was the solid groundwork of [T's] faith, and *out-of-doors* was his ritual, T's methods were not those of the . . . man of science; he held that 'nature must be viewed humanly to be viewed at all' "—an attitude toward T later to be reinforced by Foerster. Salt thought that it was "supernatural rather than natural history that T sudied" (*HDT*, 1890). For rephrasings of Burroughs's essential view, effectively restated in "A Critical Glance into T" (*Atl* 19), see Odell Shepard, "The Paradox of T" (*Scribner's* 20) and, especially, Ethel Seybold, *T: The Quest and the Classics* (1951), who says, "The truth, the quite incredible truth about T . . . is that he spent a quarter of a century in a quest for transcendent reality, in an attempt to discover the secret of the universe."

P. E. More expressed much the same attitude in "A Hermit's Notes on T" (*Atl* 01; repr. *Shelburne Essays*, 1st ser., 1904). To him T was "the greatest by far of our writers on Nature, and the creator of a new sentiment in literature." He was not at his best, however, in merely describing nature: "Much of

his writings, perhaps the greatest part, is mere record of observation and classification, and has not the slightest claim to remembrance." T was "far from
having the truly scientific spirit; the acquisition of knowledge with him was in
the end quite subordinate to his interest in the moral significance of Nature."
His writing was successful only when he infused description with "qualities
of awe and wonder" inherited from colonial times in New England when men
experienced the "strange and often threatening forces of untried wilderness."

More found T's attitude toward nature not at all to resemble Keats's "passion for beauty and voluptuous self-abandonment," Byron's "fiery spirit of
rebellion," or Shelley's "unearthly mysticism"; least of all did T, like Wordsworth, hear "in the voice of Nature any compassionate plea for the weakness
and sorrows of the downtrodden." Nature to him was awful and wonderful;
it was a "discipline of the will as much as a stimulant to the imagination." John
Macy in *SAL* (1913) disagreed: "T misreads Nature as a collection of moral
lessons, but he is not blind to her naked loveliness, and he finds her lessons
not austere, but consoling." But for Macy, T was misunderstood as simply a
mystic Transcendentalist; he was, as people in England had recognized, "an
anarchist of great literary power," whose "poetic notes on the seasons are
recommended," but whose eloquent social philosophy is ignored.

People continued to watch over T's shoulder to see whether his annotations
and descriptions of natural objects were correct. F. H. Eckstrom in "T's *MW*"
(*Atl* 08) found fault with his lists of plants and animals found in Maine;
Frances Allen in *T's Bird Lore* (1925) and R. H. Welker in "Literary Birdman:
HDT" (*Birds & Men*, 1955) thought that, barring a few errors, his observation
was pretty keen. M. E. Sherwood returned to an older attitude in exposing
"Fanny Eckstrom's Bias" (*MR* 62) by arguing that, facts aside, T as "articulate
woodsman . . . created [in *MW*] one of the most coniferous-pungent books in
the English language." But, in spite of all the writing about it, T's scientific,
or even his observational, expertise has not been more expertly established
than by John Burroughs in the 1880's.

Lowell had characterized T's retirement as a search for a physician, Burroughs had suggested in the *Century* that T's search for wildness was a search
for health, and Mark Van Doren (*HDT*, 1916) suggested that T found in nature
a substitute for the kind of friendship he could not find in men. What will be
remembered of T, said Van Doren, is not what he wrote about nature, some of
which is prosy indeed, but what he has to say of people and of human relations,
"talking of friendship and charity and solitude"—these "will be remembered
when T the visitor of wild flowers will beg for notice."

Norman Foerster explained even more emphatically than Burroughs the relation between "T and 'The Wild' " (*Dial* 17). He pointed to T's attraction to the Indian, to all wildness, and he underlined both the insistence of Page and Salt that T had gone to nature better to know men, and the suggestion by Burroughs that T looked through nature for secrets behind those which any observation of a plain naturalist could disclose. But nature, explained Foerster, though excellent for its own purposes, was better when its wildness was somewhat tamed, humanized, as Concord was humanized, to become "more expressive, not only of man, but also to man."

Foerster, like More and Van Doren, with whom in most matters he is substantially in agreement, was one of the first American critics to view T dispassionately, to consider the man entire, and weigh his weaknesses against his strengths. He built carefully on what Burroughs had suggested; he accepted, but judiciously modified, many of the indictments of Lowell and Stevenson, but explained them in terms of T's total personality. To him also, T was at best an "amateur scientist," Rousseauistic rather than Platonic. The "leading error in T's intercourse with nature" seemed to Foerster "the tyranny of observation, and not the abandonment of sentimental mysticism." Full of contradictions, "forever baffling if we insist on resolving into perfect harmony all his ideas, which he never harmonized himself," T nonetheless gave order and direction to his insights and observations by depending on that "most human of human qualities, the inner voice which places us on the pinnacle of humanity."

T's conception of "humanized landscape" was praised by G. P. Morley in "T and the Land" (*Landscape Arch* 34), and Foerster's interpretation of T as a humanist was accepted by such subsequent commentators as Canby (*T*, 1939), Whicher (*Walden Revisited*, 1945), and, with some modification, Krutch (*T*, 1940), and Harding (*The Days of HT*, 1965). The most discriminating explanation of T's humanism, touched on with sympathy in Sherman Paul's *The Shores of America* (1958), is R. L. Cook's *The Concord Saunterer* (1940), revised and expanded as *Passage to Walden* (1949, 1966), which explained how T found in nature correspondences which resulted in rare insights into his own human nature and the nature of man; see also Walter Ong's discriminating "Personalism and the Wilderness" (*KR* 59).

T's increasing concern after 1845 with the collection of fact was noticed as early as 1865 by T. W. Higginson in his review of *CC* in the *Atl.* Bradford Torrey in *Friends on the Shelf* (1906) and, more recently, Raymond Adams in "T and Science" (*SciM* 45) also called attention to T's turning in his later years toward the accumulation of particulars. The apparently unimaginative piling of detail in the journals of the 1850's led Van Doren (*HDT*, 1916) to conclusions concerning T's final discouragement and defeat, and Canby (*T*, 1939) blamed the "bog of classificationist detail into which he sank deeper and deeper" on the seductive influence of Agassiz and his disciples. For T's assistance to Agassiz, see Joseph Wade, "Friendship of two Old-Time Naturalists" (*SciM* 26).

But Thoreau as a scientist has had his champions. Wade wrote of "Some Insects in T's Writing" (*JNYES* 27). C. D. Stewart said "A Word for T" (*Atl* 35) in answer to certain of Burroughs's charges, concluding that T was capable of the most exact scientific observation; W. L. McAtee in "Adaptionist Naivete" (*SciM* 39), however, disagreed. T's influence on the precise study of nature was set forth by A. B. Comstock's "HDT" (*Nature and Sci Ed Rev* 30), his influence on the study of wild life in Helen Cruikshank's *T on Birds* (1964). E. S. Deevey in a "Re-examination of T's *Wa*" (*Quar Rev Biol* 42) challenged Canby's view by contending that, if T did mistake the means of observation for its end, the fault was not with Agassiz but with the formal curriculum at Harvard, together with T's innate distaste for empiricism. Deevey presented T as the "first American limnologist" and, as Adams also suggested in "T and Science," a plant ecologist interested in the relations between organisms and their environments, rather than as a botanist. Aldo Leopold and S. E. Jones in "A Phenological Record for Sauk & Dane Counties, Wisconsin" (*Ecological Rec* 47) named T the "father of phenology in this country" because of his detailed notes on the blooming, pollination, and leafing of plants. Leo Stoller disagreed in a "Note on T's Place in the History of Phenology" (*Isis* 56).

Alec Lucas defended "T, Field Naturalist" (*UTQ* 54), Howard Zahniser wrote authoritatively of him as a conservationist in "T and the Preservation of Wilderness" (*TSB* 57), William Drake wrote of T's search for reality in "Spiritual Ideals and Spiritual Fact" (*TSBK* 63), and Nina Baym presented a measured review of "T's View of Science" (*JHL* 65). But the best words had been earlier said. Paul Oehser had included T among "Pioneers in Conservation" (*Nature Mag* 45) because of the conclusion of the essay "Chesuncook" in *MW*, and this essay of T's, said Kathryn Whitford in "T and the Woodlots of Concord" (*NEQ* 50; see also Philip and Kathryn Whitford, "T: Pioneer Ecologist and Conservationist, *SciM* 51), "is mild indeed by comparison with the wisdom and bitterness of comments found in the last Journal." T's science, Whitford concluded, cannot be judged "without recognition of the fact that he was working alone in this country. To a large extent he had to compile his own textbook in ecology." She claimed for him the true scientist's reverence for factual data, and supposed that, had his career not been cut short, he might have utilized much of the detail with which he filled his notebooks.

Much of this later detail concerned T's interest in the American Indian, pointed out but only briefly explained by Channing, Sanborn, and other early commentators, and later woven, first by Burroughs and then by Foerster, more closely into the whole fabric of T's attitude toward the wildness and complexity of nature. Since then his Indian notes have been studied by J. A. Russell in "T, the Interpreter of the Real Indian" (*QQ* 27), Albert Kaiser in "T's Manuscripts on the Indians" (*JEGP* 28) and *The Indian in American Literature* (1932), and Lawrence Willson in "From T's Indian Manuscripts" (*ESQ* 58) and "T and the Natural Diet" (*SAQ* 58). A valuable brief account is found in R. H. Pearce's *The Savages of America* (1953, rev. 1965), but T's Indian studies require further study from modern students.

5. Intellectual Background

Though Daniel Gregory Mason had written perceptively of "The Idealistic Basis of T's Thought" (*HarM* 1897), it was publication of *Jo* in 1906 that made possible the first objective investigation of T's mind and of the books that fed it. P. E. More wrote of "T and German Romanticism" in reviewing the Walden edition (*Nation* 06; repr. *Shelburne Essays*, 5th ser., 1908), finding T shallow and derivative, with "only a scant handful of ideas"; he was "the shadow of a shadow" who "excelled several of his contemporaries only through greater precision of details." Like other Concord Transcendentalists, T echoed German Romanticism in his sublime egotism, his reaching out to embrace all nature in ecstatic communion, his attempts to find the basis of man's nature through pure emotionalism; but, unlike his New England fellows, he also rose above what More felt was sickliness in the *romantische Schule* through exercise of "one great offset—character," a will toward self-discipline, a "higher self-restraint." For a later, less didactic view, see R. P. Adams, "Romanticism and the American Renaissance" (*AL* 52) and also Perry Miller's forthright "T in the Context of International Romanticism" (*NEQ* 61).

The sources of this difference between T, on the one hand, and Novalis, on the other, were five: (1) the inheritance of Puritan religion which made possible a return to the kind of medievalism found among German Romantics; (2) the British notion of practical individualism found in the philosophy of Adam Smith; (3) the lesson of austerity in Wordsworth's attitude toward nature; (4) a "spirit of fine expectancy" drawn from T's favorite seventeenth-century poets; and (5) the "incalculable force of Emerson's personality." Thus More opened doors which many another later student would enter. He found that T's journal, for all its provincialism and tedium, was a record of "romanticism striving to work itself out in character." T's contemplation of nature in all its aspects, his "sympathetic knowledge of savage life among the Indians, and the tradition of New England's struggle with the wilderness kept him, in a word, from sentimental softening of reality."

Mark Van Doren in *HDT* (1916) found faults in More's emphasis on German sources of T's Transcendentalism. Drawing on testimony in *Jo* and on the testimony of Channing and Sanborn, he explained T as "most durably nourished by three literary springs"; (1) the Oriental scriptures, from which "he took figures and sentences, not ideas"; (2) the Greek classics which furnished "means for artistic discipline"; and (3) the poets of seventeenth-century England to whose style and temper he "owes more than to any other group."

In "The Intellectual Heritage of T" (*TR* 17) Norman Foerster presented an analysis of T's literary background which agreed substantially with Van Doren's. Foerster pointed to what Channing had called T's "very uncompleted reading," his avoidance of fiction, his almost complete ignorance of English letters from Dryden to Matthew Arnold, his failure to read the literature in modern languages at his command. In an examination of quotations from *Wk*, Foerster identified 12 from Latin and Greek authors, 12 from early English, 34 from Elizabethan and seventeenth-century England, 14 from English and American contemporaries. Among the latter, he suggested that T owed more to Wordsworth than had yet been recognized, found (as Van Doren had also) more hints of Carlyle in T's style than in his matter, and concluded that less had been derived from Emerson the writer than from Emerson the man, who drew T not only to the classics and the literature of seventeenth-century England, but also to Goethe and the religious books of the Orient.

Since the mid-1920's there has been a proliferation of brief articles on the literary ancestry of T, for the most part underlining or changing the emphasis of what Channing, Sanborn, Van Doren, and Foerster had already pointed out. J. H. Birss wrote of "T and Thomas Carew" (*N&Q* 33), C. A. Manning of "T and Tolstoy" (*NEQ* 43), Raymond Himelick of "T and Samuel Daniel" (*AL* 52), E. E. Leisy of "T and Ossian" (*NEQ* 45) and "Francis Quarles and HT" (*MLN* 45), and George Anastalpo of "On Civil Disobedience: T and Socrates" (*SWR* 69). J. B. Moore found likenesses between "T and Crèvecoeur" (*PMASAL* 26). A. B. Benson discovered "Scandinavian Influences on the Writings of T" (*SS* 41), Howard Schultz came upon "A Fragment of Jacobean Song in T's *Wa*" (*MLN* 48), and J. C. Matthews explored "T's Reading in Dante" (*Italica* 50). Fred De Armond compared "T and Schopenhauer" (*NEQ* 32), L. M. Kaiser presented "Remarks on T's Translation of *Prometheus*" (*CW* 53), K. W. Cameron on "Ralph Cudworth and T's Translation of an Orphic Hymn (*ESQ* 57), and Edith Peairs considered the influence of *Zadig* in "The Hound, the Bay Horse, and the Turtle Dove: A Study of T and Voltaire" (*PMLA* 37).

"Sources of T's Borrowings in *Wk*" (*AL* 46) were explored by E. E. Leisy; see also J. P. Wood, "Mr. T. Writes a Book," (*New Colophon* 48) and "T's Borrowings in *Wa*" (*N&Q* 43) briefly outlined by Joseph Leach. When William Templeman in "T: Moralist of the Picturesque" (*PMLA* 32) claimed T a disciple of William Gilpin and the vogue which he had created for the wild and rough in nature, J. G. Southworth answered him (*PMLA* 34), not by denying the influence of Gilpin, but by claiming that of Wordsworth to have been more profound. Canby (*T*, 1939) mediated by acknowledging T to have learned something of composition and design from Gilpin, but that he had found him on the whole artificial and unsatisfactory.

T's relations with American writers were noticed by E. J. Dias, "Daniel Ricketson and T" (*NEQ* 53), Walter Harding, "T and Timothy Dwight" (*BPLQ* 58), Frank Davidson, "Melville, T, and the Apple-Tree Table" (*AL* 54), and W. B. Stein, "Melville Roasts T's Cock" (*MLN* 59). Andrew Schiller in "T and Whitman: The Record of a Pilgrimage" (*NEQ* 55) revealed new aspects of relationship, and perhaps influence; see also Viola White, "T's Opinion of Whitman" (*NEQ* 35), but especially the informed conclusions in C. R. Metzger's *T and Whitman: A Study of Their Esthetics* (1961).

Nathalia Wright discovered similarities between "Emily Dickinson's Boanerges and T's Atropos" (*MLN* 57). Richard Bridgman pointed to caustic references to T in *Elsie Venner* in "Holmes, T, and the Ponds" (*TSB* 63); Jean Normand compared two isolatoes in "T et Hawthorne à Concord: Les ironies de la solitude" (*Europe* 67); Frank Davidson wrote of "T's Contributions to Hawthorne's *Mosses*" (*NEQ* 47); and Raymond Adams of "Hawthorne and a Glimpse of Walden" (*EIHC* 58). Francis Henry discussed "T and Bronson Alcott" (*TCJ* 42), and N. C. Carpenter "Louisa May Alcott and T's Flute" (*HLQ* 60). W. J. Griffin in "T's Reaction to Horatio Greenough" (*NEQ* 57) explained T's misreading of Greenough's aesthetic theory; but see also T. M. Brown, "T's Prophetic Architectural Program" (*NEQ* 65). The relationship between Ellery Channing and T was detailed by F. T. McGill, Jr., in *Channing of Concord* (1967). William Wasserstrom compared "Howells' Mansion and T's Cabin" (*CE* 65); D. G. Hoffman found links between "T's 'Old Settler' and Frost's Paul Bunyan" (*JAF* 61); and R. L. Cook spoke with great charm on "A Parallel of Parabolists: T and Frost" (*The T Centennial*, 1964).

T's political ideas were influenced by William Godwin, said V. L. Parrington in *MCAT* (1927); by Johann Ritter von Zimmerman, said Grant Loomis (*NEQ* 37) and Canby. But the sources of T's ideas are difficult thus simply to pin down. Almost every modern commentator has recognized him as an eclectic who took what he needed from many sources, using it as he wished. Raymond Adams in "T's Sources for 'Resistance to Civil Government' " (*SP* 45) found that Emerson's "Politics," the writings of the Garrisonian abolitionists, and William Paley's *Moral and Political Philosophy* all contributed to T's best known political essay—but, said, Adams, "He took from all three and rejected much from all three, and . . . so fashioned the material and individualized it and so intensified it or translated it that it became his own." Differences with Emerson were suggested by G. M. Ostrander in "Emerson, T, and John Brown" (*MVHR* 53).

Leo Stoller's valuable *After Walden* (1957), though found faulty in some minor details, successfully explored "T's Changing Views of Economic Man" to discover a growing recognition "that the success of a single man in his private life was dependent on the success of the community of men in their social life," and that "the achievement of correspondence with a higher law is not a matter solely for the individual but for society as well." Stoller's study was in part anticipated by James Dabbs, "T: the Adventurer as Economist (*YR* 47) and F. B. Dedmond, "Economic Protest in T's Jo" (*SN* 54). It is amply outlined in Stoller's "T's Doctrine of Simplicity" (*NEQ* 56) which explained that in "his youth, T sought the conditions for such a [simple, personality-realizing] life in an individualized distortion of the economic order then being displaced by the industrial revolution. After his experiment at Walden Pond, he moved toward a reconciliation between simplicity and an economy of machines and profit." This is a subject on which more study seems to be needed.

"T's reading, aside from that in natural history, falls into certain clearly marked categories," said Ethel Seybold in *T: The Quest and the Classics* (1951): (1) the Greek and Latin classics, (2) the Oriental scriptures, (3) the English poets, (4) New England history and legend, (5) data on the Indian, and (6) early accounts of travel, adventure, and exploration. Of these, she explained, "he valued the classics most," and she appended to her study a list of Greek and Latin books which T owned or read, and a list of his quotations from the classics. Few have disagreed with this estimate. Channing, Sanborn, and Salt all testified to T's learning in Greek and Latin. Foerster's statement (*TR* 17) that T "without his classical background would simply not have been T," and Brooks's in *FNE* (1936) that T was "the best Greek scholar in Concord" were corroborated forcefully by Clarence Gohdes in "HT, Bachelor of Arts (*CJ* 28), Raymond Adams in "T's Literary Apprenticeship (*SP* 32), and J. P. Pritchard in *Return to the Fountains* (1942).

"Alone among American writers," said Pritchard, "he devoted his attention to the [classical] writers on rural life: Hesiod and Theophrastus, and especially Cato, Varro, and Columella." Though "Greek philosophy held no spell over him," as it did over Emerson, and "though he did not care for Plato" and Aristotle "interested him chiefly as a zoologist," he revered Homer and the Greek tragedians, and Virgil, and the satirist Persius. Seybold, however, went farther, by expanding her study of T's interest in the classics to an investigation which located "in his classical reading the specific foci of his interest and their relationship to experiences of his life and thought," to "his quest for transcendental reality," and his attempt to discover the secret of the universe by following a pattern of Homeric experiment." But for all his interest, he did not translate well: L. M. Kaiser in "Remarks on T's Translation of the *Prometheus*" (*CW* 53) found T's rendering only adequate and in *T's Translation of "The Seven against Thebes"* (1960) agreed with T that this also was very rudely done. T did not do well with other men's phrasings.

Oriental influences on T, noted by almost every commentator, were studied in detail by H. A. Snyder in *T's Philosophy of Life, with Special Consideration of the Influence of Hindoo Philosophy* (1900). His adaptation of Eastern ideas was noted briefly by Frances Fletcher in "HT, Oriental" (*Open Court* 30) and touched upon by F. I. Carpenter in *Emerson and Asia* (1930), but was most authoritatively set forth in A. E. Christy's chapter on "T and Oriental Asceticism" in *The Orient in American Transcendentalism* (1913). Christy took issue with Van Doren's statement that "T took figures and sentences, not ideas from his Oriental reading," but his own conclusions were not finally different; "He used the Hindus to bolster his own thoughts," and when he read Confucius, it was not to "read mystic divinity into the Chinese; he quoted . . . in connection with flora and fauna." Christy also seriously considered whether T really was, as Conway had described him, "like the pious Yogi." He found that T resembled the Oriental mystic in courting solitude for the purpose of spiritual discipline, but, unlike the Yogi, he had no interest in exotic self-torture; he consciously sought none of the Yogi disciplines, for he "had no interest in systems"; he did not share the Oriental attitude toward benevolence; he "probably never accepted . . . the Hindu insistence that the man who has reached a stage of true enlightenment is freed from the consequences of his work." What had seemed to Van Doren the ultimate failure of T's life in his "never succeeding in stepping entirely out of his little private darkness," may however be, Christy suggested, the result of his having accepted the attitude of the Oriental mystic: that one's individuality is ultimately indistinguishable from universal being. If by Occidental standards T was a failure, he was certainly not by standards of the Orient.

To bolster further studies of this influence, W. B. Stein presented a valuable "Bibliography of Hindu and Buddhist Literature Available to T through 1854"

(*ESQ* 67) and a provocative study of *"Wa* and the *Bhagavad Gita"* (*Topic* 63). Sreekrishna Sarma contributed a useful "Short Study of the Oriental Influence on HDT" (*JA* 56), and L. V. Cady listed "T's Quotations from Confucian Books in *Wa"* (*AL* 61). Kurt Leidecker wrote of "That Sad Pagan T" (*Visva-Bharati Quar* 51) and E. S. Oliver "T Finds the Dawn in Asia" (*Korean Survey* 53); see also Frank MacShane, "Walden and Yoga" (*NEQ* 64). Kamla Bhatia's *The Mysticism of T and His Affinity with Indian Thought* (1966) may have found more orientalism in T than he himself would have admitted.

The intellectual climate to which T was exposed during his college years, considered by Sanborn, Canby, and Adams in relation to the books he had read, was further investigated by J. J. Kwiat in "T's Philosophical Apprenticeship" (*NEQ* 45), which suggested that T's reaction against the materialism of Locke and the utilitarianism of Paley was the result of the Scottish common sense philosophy which served him, as it served others of his time, as transition to the idealism of the Germans and of Coleridge.

Further investigation may discover new facets of T's intellectual background. Meanwhile Whicher's *Walden Revisited* (1945) and Krutch's *T* (1947) supplied excellent summaries of what had been done, and K. W. Cameron mined a generous mass of miscellaneous matter in *Emerson the Essayist* (1945), "Emerson, T, and the Society of Natural History" (*AL* 52), "T Discovers Emerson: A College Reading Record" (*BNYPL* 53), "T, *Sic Vita*, and Harvardiana" (*TSB* 54), his helpful collection, *The Transcendentalists and Minerva* (1956), and his numerous notes and further listings in *ESQ*. All these supplement the work done by Foerster, Adams, and Seybold (together also with the pioneer suggestions of Ellery Channing) in making available a more complete and accurate record of T's reading than is found in the appendix to Sanborn's *Life*; each contributes its share to the interesting game of discovering why someone else thought what he did, particularly when it is an artist who is thought to have thought.

6. The Social Philosopher

After John Macy in *SAL* (1913) took his contemporaries to task for overlooking T's "eloquent social philosophy" and Canby called attention to "The Modern T" (*Dial* 15), a gradually increasing number of Americans discovered in T a reliable guide for the solution of problems of their time. "To our amazement," said Brooks Atkinson in "T the Radical" (*Freeman* 20), "we discover this odd fellow . . . a stupendous radical," worthy of place beside Samuel Butler, Anatole France, and Bernard Shaw. C. J. Finger wrote admiringly of *HDT*:

The Man Who Escaped from the Herd (1922); David Boyd wrote of "T, the Rebel Idealist" (*Americana* 36); John Cournos described him as a "Hater of Shams" (*Century* 28); and Parrington (*MCAT*, 1927) rephrased what English commentators had said years before: "The single business of HT . . . was to discover an economy calculated to provide a satisfying life . . . to explore the true meaning of wealth."

During the 1930's commentary of this kind increased. Canby called attention to the timeliness of T's social criticism in "T in the Machine Age" (*YR* 31); Gorham Munson pointed to "A Lesson in T" (*Thinker* 31); E. M. Schuster included him in her study of "Native American Anarchism" (*Smith Coll Stud in Hist* 32); Sinclair Lewis described him as "A One Man Revolution" (*SatR* 37); and Canby in "American Challenge: A Study of *Wa*" (*SatR* 39) called attention to the "significant paralleling of dates between *The Communist Manifesto* of 1848 and *Wa*, ready for publication a year later: "The same diseases of the profit system impressed the American recluse and the German scholar." Max Lerner affirmed "T, No Hermit" (*Ideas Are Weapons*, 1939) and explained his social thought as "tighter than Emerson's," his economics as anticipating Ruskin's, his pragmatic aesthetics as looking toward William Morris's: "It was his tragedy to be forced by the crudities of capitalism into a reclusion . . . that has until recently obscured the real force of his social thought."

In reply to Canby's and Lewis's claim that T lived on while most of his contemporaries were dated, D. C. Peattie asked "Is T a Modern" (*NAR* 38), and replied that he was not, that T represented the end, not the beginning of an era, and that his time was separated from the present by a gap, "one of the greatest in the history of man. . . . It asks too much of him to bridge it." Science and society had outstripped T; his way of life could only be practiced by bachelors. In answer to Peattie and in rebuke to Canby for "virtually ignoring the tremendous weight of T's social criticism and handling the bombshells of his most explosive thoughts as if they were roses," C. C. Walcutt proposed in "T in the Twentieth Century" (*SAQ* 40) "to consider how [T's] thought can be applied —and indeed is being applied—to the most pressing modern problems."

Walter Harding wrote of "The Significance of T's *Wa*" (*Humanist* 45) and of "T, Pioneer of Civil Disobedience" (*Fellowship* 46), H. F. West pointed to "Modern Values in T" (*TSB* 47), and S. E. Hyman emphasized the efficacy of "T in Our Time" (*Atl* 46) as an artist, but also as a political writer, "the most ringing and magnificent polemicist America has ever produced." J. H. Holmes spoke admiringly of "T's 'CD' " (*Christian Century* 49), Wendell Glick explained T's relations with the *Herald of Freedom* (*NEQ* 49), and Henry Miller in a preface to *Life without Principle* (1946) prophesied that the young people of America would be true heirs to T's "homely wisdom," but to "his example even more."

C. C. Hollis wrote perceptively of "T and the State" (*Commonweal* 49), J. M. Dabbs depicted "T, the Adventurer of Economist" (*YR* 47), and F. B. Dedmond called attention to "Economic Protest in T's *Jo*" (*SN* 54). W. S. Thomas presented "Marti and T" (*Dos Pueblos* 49) as "pioneers of personal freedom," C. R. B. Combellack and R. N. Stromberg followed Canby in comparing T with Marx, the first in "Two Critics of Society" (*PS* 49), the second in "T and Marx" (*Social Stud* 49), and R. L. Cook in "T in Perspective" (*UKCR* 47) found him "like Thomas Paine . . . one of the watchdogs of human rights." Townsend Scudder in *LHUS* emphasized his effective "reappraisal of life's values in the modern industrial state" and his "ringing challenge to totalitarianism." Heinz Eulau described him as a "Wayside Challenger" (*AR* 49) who is "as germane today as he ever was in the development of political thought" because of his final "conversion to violence as a legitimate means in social conflict." J. L. Blau wrote of "HDT: Anarchist" in *Men and Movements in American Philosophy* (1952), and Wendell Glick described "CD" as "T's Attack on Relativism" (*WHR* 53).

To L. B. Salomon's "The Practical T" (*CE* 56), W. C. Thompson replied with "The Impractical T" (*CE* 57), and Vincent Buranelli's "The Case against T's Ethics" (*Ethics* 57) was answered by R. L. Ketcham (*Ethics* 59). N. A. Ford wrote on "HDT, Abolitionist" (*NEQ* 46) and Walter Harding on "T and the Negro" (*NHB* 46). Aspects of his social aims were outlined by C. H. Nichols, "T and the Citizen and His Government" (*Phylon* 52), J. C. Broderick, "T's Proposals for Legislation" (*AQ* 55), and Lawrence Bowling, "T's Social Criticism" (*YR* 66). R. S. Forte spoke of "The Political Thought of HDT" (*Ed Leader* 59), and Leo Stoller in "T's Doctrine of Simplicity" (*NEQ* 56) discovered T finally without an economic plan. T's thoughts on freedom, solitude, and justice were underlined in James Daugherty's *HDT: A Man for Our Time* (1966).

The influence of T's social philosophy on present-day leaders in social or civil reform was again testified to by Martin Luther King, Willard Uphaus, and Paul Lauter in "A Centenary Gathering for HDT" (*MR* 62), which also contained W. S. Nelson's "T and the American Non-Violent Resistance" and an anonymous "T and the Danish Resistance." A relation with Marxism was again suggested by Combellack, "Marx und T" (*Amerikanische Rundshau* 49), Samuel Sillen, "T and Today's America" (*Masses and Mainstream* 54), and E. S. Smith, "A T for Today" (*Mainstream* 60). F. B. Dedman wrote of "T and the Ethical Concept of Government" (*Person* 55), Richard Drinno on "T's Politics and the Upright Man" (*Anarchy* 63), J. W. Cook on "Freedom in the Thought of HDT" (*TSB* 68), and Alfred Kazin on "T and American Power" (*Atl* 69). Staughton Lynd in *Intellectual Origins of American Radicalism* (1968) praised T's "anarcho-pacificism" and "revolutionary socialism." "CD" was reprinted as a "peace calendar" illustrated with contemporary photographs of social protest as *Days of Civil Disobedience* (1969), and excerpts from T illustrated with photographs "which do much to emphasize just how contemporary his thoughts were" appeared as *The Wind That Blows Is All That Anybody Knows* (1970) with an introduction by Rod McKuen. *The Night Thoreau Spent in Jail* (1970) by Jerome Lawrence and Robert E. Lee was an effective though not in every respect correct dramatic expression of T's views.

Nor has his usefulness in other fields gone unnoticed. His influence on education was discussed by H. E. Hurd, "HDT: A Pioneer in the Field of Education" (*Education* 29), Raymond Adams, "T: Pioneer in Adult Education" (*Institute Mag* 30), H. H. Hoeltje, "T and the Concord Academy" (*NEQ* 48), and W. C. Thompson, "The Straight-Cut Ditch" (*AQ* 66). His dietary eccentricities were explained by John Davies, "T and the Ethics of Food" (*Vegetarian Messenger* 47), Joseph Jones, "Transcendental Grocery Bills: T's *Wa* and Some Aspects of American Vegetarianism" (*UTSE* 57), K. A. Robinson "T and the Wild Appetite" (*TSBooklet* 57), and Lawrence Willson, "T and the Natural Diet" (*SAQ* 58), who also wrote of "T's Medical Vagaries" (*Jour Hist Med* 60). Lawrence MacDonald presented him, without photographs, as "HDT—Liberal, Unconventional Nudist" (*Sunshine and Health* 43), and C. G. Loomis spoke briefly on "HDT, Folklorist" (*WF* 57).

T has been described as "An Ideal for Freethinkers" (*Truth Seeker* 1893) and as a "Theosophist Unaware" (*Theosophy* 44). His religious attitudes were further examined in H. E. Hurd, "The Religion of HDT" (*Christian Leader* 28), Raymond Adams, "T and Immortality" (*SP* 29), Walter Harding, "T Attends a Quaker Meeting" (*Friends Intelligencer* 44), R. L. Mondale, "HDT and the Naturalizing of Religion" (*Unity* 51), Lawrence Willson, "T and Roman Catholicism" (*Catholic Hist Rev* 56), and Jonathan Bishop, "The Experience of the Sacred in T's *Wk*" (*ELH* 66).

7. The Literary Artist

"No writer more demands," said Channing in 1873, "that his reader should look at his writings as a work of art." But like most nineteenth-century commentators, Channing was satisfied to allow description to do the work of criticism, pointing to T's "piquant humor" and "unstudied felicities." Until recently, almost everything that has been said about T's style has been thus a matter of statement, an acknowledgment of its precision, its raciness, its homely effectiveness. Even Burroughs, most perceptive among nineteenth-century critics, did little beyond speak of its "restrained extravagance" and "compressed exaggeration." From Lowell's description of T's language as of "an antique purity like wine grown colorless with age" (*MQR* 1849) to E. B. White's description of it as "100-proof anchovy" (*NY* 49), phrases have been ingeniously manufactured to picture T's art. To some, he seemed not an artist at all (on this both Stevenson and the English reformers agreed) but an edifying proponent of self-improvement, sometimes because of what he said, sometimes because of the tone in which he said it.

Much of the better recent criticism of T has seen beyond the naturalist or the mystic supernaturalist to the man of letters. Among the first to analyze T's achievement as a literary man was Mark Van Doren (*HDT*, 1916) who praised his "genius for the specific," his sense of the drama of ordinary things, which allowed him to avoid the fatal lure of generalization which trapped Emerson. In his "passion for writing perfectly," his distaste for wooden and lifeless words, his self-consciousness about individuality in style, he was a "nineteenth-century euphuist of the stamp of Flaubert, Stevenson, and Pater; he travailled to catch consciousness itself in the trap of the specific." In this, T was a pioneer, but "isolated in America, his wits straying through the endless and utterly formless reaches of a transcendental journal," he failed to "end his literary career as happily as Flaubert and Stevenson . . . and Pater" because he was fatally committed to sphericity, to what he described as a sense of "eternity and space gambolling through my depths." In his reach for the Transcendental whole, he finally lost disciplined contact with reality.

Norman Foerster in "T as Artist" (*SR* 21) discovered in T's reading of William Gilpin on landscape and John Ruskin on painting an interest in aesthetic principles which was reflected in his literary workmanship. Like Van Doren, Foerster recognized T's unflinching demand for truth in observation and phrase, but he proposed also that T's perfection of the senses, his physical dexterity, familiarity with natural fact, knowledge of literary tradition, his moral energy, insight, and imagination were all "given order and direction" by his essential humanism. Foerster also called attention to T's humor, as many others had before him, such as George Beardsley, "T as Humorist" (*Dial* oo), H. W. Mabie, "T" (*Outlook* o5), and G. T. Coleman, "T and His Critics" (*Dial* o6), and concluded that "much of the charm of T's best pages resides in . . . lurking humor . . . dry wit always ready to kindle."

Brooks Atkinson, however, in "Concerning T's Style" (*Freeman* 20), though he admired much besides *Wa*, especially *Wk*, described T's kind of humor, his "strange propensity for puns and plays on words," as disagreeable: "So reserved and austere a writer had no business to deal with elephantine touch in such bastard humor." Later, J. B. Brawner defended "T as Wit and Humorist" (*SAQ* 45), Tyrus Hillway in "The Personality of T" (*CE* 45) explained that "T's well-nourished sense of humor saved his egotism from becoming boorish," and E. B. White in *The Subtreasury of American Humor* (1941) offered expert testimony that "there is hardly a passage in *Wa* which does not seem humorous to me." E. J. Rose wrote of "The Wit and Wisdom of T's Higher Laws" (*QQ* 63), Alan Holder briefly discussed T in "The Writer as Loon" (*ESQ* 66), and J. G. Taylor produced a joyously appreciative account of *Neighbor T's Critical Humor* (1966).

On the whole, the critical atmosphere of the late 1920's and the 1930's was not hospitable to T as a man of letters. Odell Shephard in "The Paradox of T" (*Scribner's* 20) aroused little resentment when he proclaimed that T never learned to write, only to exclaim. Llewelyn Powys in "T: A Disparagement" (*Bookman* 29) announced him "neither a profound thinker nor a great writer." G. S. Hubbard found him equally inadequate in "*Wa* Re-Visited" (*SR* 29). Ludwig Lewisohn in *Expression in America* (1932) disliked his literary manner as much as he did his personality. The best product of the period, Raymond Adams's "HT's Literary Theory and Criticism" (Univ. of N. Car. diss., 1928), remained unpublished, though much of its detail and many of its conclusions have been utilized by later critics, notably and most effectively by B. V. Crawford in *HDT* (1934).

Though Brooks (*FNE*, 1936) and Canby (*T*, 1939) each had pleasantly judicious things to say about T's style, it was F. O. Matthiessen in *AmR* (1941) who, just one hundred years after T decided to become a man of letters, first approached him seriously and sympathetically as an artist. Matthiessen's section on "*Wa*: Craftmanship *vs.* Technique" has become a classic of literary criticism, setting forth an approach to the study of T which Matthiessen explored briefly in testing to what extent *Wa* meets Coleridge's requirement of shaping, "as it develops, itself from within." His emphasis on T, the artist intent on the exact word and the homely image, owed something to Van Doren and other earlier critics, as did his review of T's literary and intellectual background and his expert exposition of the organic principle, all of which was extended, however, to consider T, not in isolation, but as part of the pattern of his time.

Students responded to Matthiessen's placing of T in a literary tradition which extended, not only to the past and to his New England contemporaries, but which also stretched forward to Robert Frost and Hemingway, D. H. Lawrence, Yeats, and Eliot. His suggestions of relations which T discovered between symbol and myth, his demonstration of T's use of myth as protagonist in the drama of cosmic ritual, led S. E. Hyman in "HT in Our Time" (*Atl* 46) to claim T "not only a writer, but a writer in the great stream of American tradition," one with mythic and moralistic writers like Hawthorne, Melville, Mark Twain, Henry James, Hemingway, and Faulkner, and to find *Wa* "a vast rebirth ritual, the purest and most complete in our literature." The relation with Yeats, briefly mentioned by Matthiessen and by R. L. Cook in *Passage to Walden* (1949), was further discussed by Robert Francis, "Passage to Innisfree" (*Chris Sci Mon* 52), Wendell Glick, "Yeats' Early Reading of *Wa*" (*BPLQ* 53), and J. L. Shanley, "T's Geese and Yeats's Swans" (*AL* 58); Laurence Stapleton, *HDT: A Writer's Journal* (1960) found him closely akin to Gerard Manley Hopkins, and R. P. Predmore found links between "Unamuno and T" (*CLS* 69).

Whicher's examination of *Wk* in *Walden Revisited* (1945), Krutch's chapter on "The Style and the Man" (*T*, 1947), Townsend Scudder's well-rounded appraisal in *LHUS* (1948), Cook's chapter on "The Sinews of Style" in *Passage to Walden* (1949) are all thoughtfully penetrating. T's use of sound, noted by almost every commentator from Emerson and Channing to Matthiessen and Cook (see Cook's chapter on "Correspondence with Nature") is carefully explored by Sherman Paul in "The Wise Silence: Sound as the Agency of Correspondence in T" (*NEQ* 49). Fresh critical attitudes were put forward in Paul's study of T's symbolism in "Resolution at Walden" (*Accent* 53), Charles Feidelson's treatment in *Symbolism and American Literature* (1952), and R. W. B. Lewis's considerations in *The American Adam* (1955). P. W. Brown's "A Metropolite's Notes on T" (*Re-Appraisals*, 1952) insisted that T was first, a Transcendental poet, second, a nature-mystic, but supremely an artist. The pattern of maturely informed criticism established by Raymond Adams in his address before the Grolier Club in March 1954, and printed as "T's Mock Heroics and the American Natural History Writers" (*SP* 55) and by Frank Davidson's explanation of "T's Hound, Bay Horse, and Turtle-Dove" (*NEQ* 54) set a standard toward which later criticism would reach.

T's poetry has not received intensive critical attention. Early commentators almost without exception pronounced it bad. Greeley found it "for the most part sorry prose" (N Y *Trib* 1849), Lowell dismissed it as "worsification" (*MQR* 1949), and T's classmate John Weiss found it crude and slovenly, seldom "touched with the bloom of beauty" (*ChEx* 1865). Again, however, Emerson set the critical pattern when he explained (*Atl* 1862) that T "had the source of poetry in his spiritual perception," but that he "wanted a lyric facility and technical skill." In England, Stevenson passed T's verses by, and Watts-Dunton

(*Athenaeum* 1882) called them "unmitigated doggerel." There were a few defenders, like Page who found in T's verses "rarity and chastity" (*T*, 1877), and Sanborn (Intro. to Channing's *T*, 1902), who described T as having "more completely than any man since Keats the traditional poetic temperament, intensive, passionate, capricious."

Most explicit of the early critics was Joel Benton, who discovered in "The Poetry of T" (*Lippincott's* 1886) all of T's salient traits: his sturdy self-assertion, his love of paradox, his defiance of truth which is anti-proverbial and not apparent, his vision of each in all, his emphasis on the present tense, and his almost Swedenborgian belief in the double meaning of all things. T's poetic endowment was unique and not easily grasped: "He would not court the listless or holiday auditor. You must wrestle with his thought, as he did, to entertain it properly"; he was not a modern, but an Elizabethan, and his poetry "appeals to the inner spirit, like the lines of Wordsworth and Emerson"; but for all this, "poetry was either T's diversion or his reliance when prose failed. He believed that, in the main, prose was the better medium."

Most later critics were less generous, agreeing rather with Emerson or with Salt, who concluded (*HDT*, 1890; see also "T's Poetry," *Art Rev* 1890) that "strictly speaking he can hardly be called a poet at all," for "although he had a large gift of poetic inspiration, he lacked . . . lyrical fire and melodious utterance" (see also the introduction to Salt and Sanborn's edition of *Poems of Nature*, 1895), or with John Macy who in *SAL* (1913) dismissed T as in spirit close to the nature poet of all times, especially to Wordsworth, though in execution "his verses were not good." Foerster in "T as Artist" (*SR* 21) also wrote him off as no poet, because "a man can scarcely be a poet without achieving a certain bulk of successful verse," and the bulk of T's verse, most of it unsuccessful, was small. Brooks in *FNE* (1936) described the poems as homespun, "well-woven, but indifferently cut."

T's theory of poetry was carefully examined by F. W. Lorch in "T and the Organic Principle of Poetry" (*PMLA* 38), which demonstrated that his conception of the organic principle, whether he got it directly from the German Romantics or Carlyle or Coleridge "furnishes a key to a better understanding of his basic attitudes toward life" and illuminates his critical point of view. T never embodied his ideas about poetry in a single essay, but he was, said Lorch, "deeply interested in the theory of poetry." Like Emerson, he found its basis in beauty, truth, and goodness. No foe to the didactic, he demanded of poetry that it be ethical and useful, as well as beautiful. Form was "inseparably linked with idea, or intuition." Character and style, thought and word, substance and expression were but different aspects of the same thing. By means of poetry, man might establish relationship with the Divine, for poetry, said T, "is the mysticism of mankind"; but, because the end of art is spiritual improvement in man, "its finest expression is not poetry but the character of the poet."

The appearance of the *Collected Poems* in 1943 brought from H. W. Wells "An Evaluation of T's Poetry" (*AL* 44), which G. F. Whicher (*Walden Revisited*, 1945) greeted as the "only competent critical study of the complete poems." Wells noted T's search for a poetic style in the Greeks, in Horace, Skelton, Ben Jonson, Herbert, Marvel, Blake, and Wordsworth, but found him neither imitative nor derivative: "His scholarship is merely the outward sign of his universality as a poet. . . . T found all schools of poetry his teachers, none his master." He was in no sense a poet with his face to the past, nor even a "strictly representative figure of either the early or the later phases of romanticism," but was one who, "like Emily Dickinson or Baudelaire, anticipates the bold symbolism, airy impressionism, stringent realism, and restless inconsistencies of modern verse." His "breadth of vision is precisely what our age, tragically seeking a new consolidation of mankind, most of all requires."

More recently, P. O. Williams in "The Concept of Inspiration in T's Poetry" (*PMLA* 64) remarked that in many poems T "laments the loss or absence of inspiration," that "uplifted mental state, so important to the transcendentalist thinker," and came finally to feel that prose was a better vehicle for poetic expression than was verse, because prose was solid and progressive and with foundation: "the poet," T had said in *Wk*, "only makes an irruption. . . . and is off again."

The centennial of the publication of *Wa* brought forth in 1954 several pleasantly appreciative essays, among them those by Raymond Adams in *TSB*, H. S. Canby in *SR*, Robert Frost and Reginald Cook in *Listener*, Joseph Jones in *UTLC*, Lewis Leary in *Nation*, and E. B. White in *YR*. But a new era in T scholarship was ushered in by J. L. Shanley's *The Making of Walden* (1957), a small book of painstaking detail and unassertive competence which effectively demonstrated that textual study can be raised to the level of serviceable criticism. Through examination over many years of successive versions of *Wa* from 1849 to 1854, Shanley was able to reveal T as a craftsman rounding out and filling in an intricately structured book. The artistry of T, earlier suggested by Matthiessen and Hyman, and by R. P. Adams in "Romanticism and the American Renaissance" (*AL* 52), was now fully and firmly set forth. Shanley's brief "The Pleasures of *Wa*" (*TSBK* 60) played counterpoint by presenting T's masterwork as "a delight to read, . . . humorously gay, . . . wise and inspiring," happily fulfilling T's "artistic desires and precepts." Further evidence of T's conscious shaping of his materials was explained by D. G. Rohman, "Second Growth in

Wa" (*PMASAL* 62), and Thomas Woodson, "The Two Beginnings of *Wa"* (*ELH* 68).

At the same time Sherman Paul in *The Shores of America* (1958) explained T's inward exploration as a literary aspirant assured of his destiny, laboring to maintain himself as a pure instrument capable of recognizing and reflecting correspondences between appearance and truth; his attempt as an artist "to expand the principle of perception to structure: to create fables as well as symbols, or to make the structure itself symbolic." A more revitalizing study of T had not appeared for many years. Perry Miller's commentary in *Consciousness at Concord* (1958) spoke of a man, uncertain and evasive, but of a craftsman supremely self-conscious; Laurence Stapleton garnered from *Jo* T's observations on his craft in *HDT: A Writer's Journal* (1960) (see also F. W. Hamilton, *T on the Art of Writing*, 1962); and Paul Schwaber, "T's Development in *Wa"* (*Criticism* 63), spoke of the shaping growth of T's thought. In somewhat different vein, W. B. Stein wrote of "*Wa*: The Wisdom of the Centaur" (*ELH* 58) and "The Motif of the Wise Old Man in *Wa"* (*MLN* 60), and L. A. Pederson discovered "Americanisms in T's *Jo"* (*AL* 65).

Shanley's revelation of the secure and cohesive artistry of *Wa* had been in part anticipated by J. C. Broderick's "Images in *Wa"* (*UTSE* 54) and was reinforced by his "The Movement of T's Prose" (*AL* 60), Lauriat Lane's "On the Organic Structure of *Wa"* (*CE* 60), and R. C. Cook's "T and His Imagery: The Anatomy of an Imagination" (*TSB* 60). Most specifically detailed were three studies by J. J. Moldenhauer, "Images of Circularity in T's Prose" (*TSLL* 59), "The Extra-vagant Maneuver: Paradox in *Wa"* (*Graduate Jour* 64; repr. with some changes as "*Wa*: the Strategy of Paradox," *The T Centennial*, 1964), and "The Rhetorical Function of Proverbs in *Wa"* (*JAF* 67). Meanwhile David Skwire furnished "A Checklist of Wordplays in *Wa"* (*AL* 59), and Carl Strauch spoke of "The Essential Romanticism of *Wa"* (*ESQ* 60).

Also with an eye on T as craftsman, C. F. Hovde examined T's use of his journals in the composition of *Wk* in "Nature into Art" (*AL* 58), explained "The Conception of Character in *Wk"* (*The T Centennial*, 1964) and revealed "Literary Materials in T's *Wk"* (*PMLA* 65); see also J. J. Boies, "Circular Imagery in T's *Wk"* (*CE* 65). Sherman Paul explained "T's 'The Landlord' " (*JEGP* 55), and J. R. Sweeney "The Cosmic Drama in T's 'Spring' " (*ESQ* 61). W. H. Bonner in "Mariners and Terreners" (*AL* 63) revealed T's nautical imagery, F. D. Ross revealed "Rhetorical Procedure in T's 'Battle of the Ants' " (*CCC* 65), and Nina Baym in "From Metaphysics to Metaphor" (*SIR* 66) spoke of water imagery in T and Emerson. R. C. Cosbey watched "T at Work" (*BNYPL* 61) as he wrote "Ktaadn" (see also J. G. Blair and Augustus Trowbridge, "T on

Ktaadn," *AQ* 60); and Lauriat Lane watched him (*BNYPL* 65) working through four versions of "A Walk to Wachusetts"; Leo Marx wrote of "T's *Exc*" (*YR* 62) and of "*Wa* as Transcendental Pastoral" (*ESQ* 60); M. E. Lyon examined "Walden Pond as Symbol" (*PMLA* 67); and V. M. Parsons presented an "essay in appreciation" of "T's *MW*" (*HudR* 67). Also of value is D. M. Green's *The Frail Duration* (1966), a well-tooled "key to symbolic structure in *Wa*."

But J. A. Christie's *T as World Traveller* (1965) most effectively revealed T as both a scholar and an artist, whose readings in travel literature were transformed in his writings both to "subtle nuance" and to "deliberate and manoeuvered exploitation" in the "formal framework of his finished compositions." T. S. Tillinghast's note "On the West of T's Imagination" (*Thoth* 65) quite independently underlined some of Christie's observations. Like Shanley, Christie did not allow his years of dogged research to obscure for him, or for his readers, T's ultimate triumph as craftsman.

C. R. Anderson's *The Magic Circle of Wa* (1968) examined T's masterwork "*as if* it were a poem," to reveal it, not an autobiography, a study of nature or morals, but as a superbly contrived literary achievement. Anderson's reading was perceptive throughout and his insights attractively phrased, but seemed divorced, as perhaps any attempt to rescue the artist from himself must be, from considerations which T would have considered important. As Sherman Paul in a review (*AL* 69) explained, "art was not for T an end in itself . . . but a means of life," so that *Wa*, rightly read, is "an autobiographical work of art, . . . a unique form for true witnessing of the self," not as poetry, but as "the *poetry of T's life.*" T was a man, said Leon Edel in his brief *HD.T* (1970), "whose works were the anchors of his days." Meanwhile Leonard Gilley explained "Transcendentalism in *Wa*" (*PrS* 68) and A. F. McLean "T's True Meridian: Natural Fact and Metaphor" (*AQ* 68). Perhaps recalling Emerson's statement, "We are all a little wild with numberless projects," H. H. Hoeltje spoke of "Misconceptions in Current T Criticism" (*PQ* 68). But wildness in pursuit of T may seem appropriate.

Many of the more stimulating critical essays on T were collected by Walter Harding, *T: A Century of Criticism* (1954), Lauriat Lane, *Approaches to Wa* (1961), Sherman Paul, *T: A Collection of Essays* (1962), Richard Rutland, *Twentieth-Century Interpretations of T* (1968), and Wendell Glick, *The Recognition of HDT* (1969). Papers read at a meeting in New York commemorative of the centenary of T's death were brought together by Harding in *The T Centennial* (1964), and J. G. Taylor collected those read at *The Western T Centenary* (1963). *New Approaches to T* (1969), edited by W. B. Stein, contained essays on T as a craftsman by, among others, D. L. Gerstenberger, J. M. Marshall, J. M. DeFalco, and Frederick Garber, and, especially to be recommended, "Thoughts" by George Hendrick, which question the excellence of Harding's *Variorum* "*CD*" (1967).

But some of the most perceptive fresh commentary appeared in "A Centenary Gathering for HDT" (*MR* 62, expanded to *T in Our Time*, 1962), edited by J. H. Hicks, particularly Theodore Baird's delightful balancing in "Corn Grows in the Night" of reasons why T is to be admired, and why not; and S. E. Hyman's wry comments in "HT Once More" on Stoller's *After Walden* and Paul's *The Shores of America*, on Miller's *Consciousness at Concord* and Harding's *T Handbook*, and his higher praise to Van Doren's *HDT* (1916), and his highest for Matthiessen's *AmR* (1941), "which is *still* our best account of T." One thing seems certain: that a person must write as well as Van Doren or Matthiessen, or Baird or Hyman, to write effectively on a man who writes as well as T.

HERMAN MELVILLE[1]

Nathalia Wright

I. BIBLIOGRAPHY

The first bibliography of the writings of Melville (hereinafter called M or HM), is for the present the most comprehensive one: Part II of Meade Minnigerode's *Some Personal Letters of HM and a Bibliography* (1922), which gives bibliographical descriptions of the first editions (including the reproduction of one title page) and publication information about most of the reprints of his books to that time and lists most of his contributions to periodicals and other publications. It was preceded by and depended upon bibliographies in Weaver's biography (see below), and in Michael Sadleir's *Excursions in Victorian Bibliography* (1922). Sadleir also prepared the descriptive bibliography of the first American and English editions of all the works except the poems, which appears in Vol. 12 of the Constable Edition of M's works (see below). A descriptive bibliography of all the works, prepared by G. T. Tanselle, will be included (as Vol. 16) in the Newberry-Northwestern Edition of M's writings, now in progress (see below). A list of M's publications in foreign languages, "A Preliminary Check-List of the Works of HM in Translation," was compiled by L. R. Phelps (MSSP, No. 2, Pt. 2, Apr. 61; mimeographed).

The most extensive bibliography of works about M, despite its acknowledged irregularities of format, is that compiled by N. E. Jarrand in "M Studies: A Tentative Bibliography" (MSSP, No. 1, Dec. 58; repr. with addenda, Dec. 59; mimeographed); it covers the years 1846–1958. Three more such bibliographies covering shorter periods have also been distributed by the M Society: "Annual M Bibliography 1951" and "M Bibliography 1952–1957," by J. H. Briss, Gordon Roper, and S. C. Sherman (multilithed at the Providence, R. I., Pub. Lib., 1952, 1959); and "A Preliminary Check-List of Foreign Language Materials on the

---

1. This chapter in the original edition of *8AmA* was written by the late Stanley Williams, to whose earlier labors both Nathalia Wright and the present editor wish to acknowledge their great indebtedness. Professor Wright also wishes to thank Hershel Parker for reading parts of this chapter in manuscript.

Life and Works of HM" by L. R. Phelps (MSSP, No. 2, Dec. 60; mimeographed). Three other extensive bibliographies of secondary material are useful: "A Checklist of M Studies" in Stern's *Fine Hammered Steel of HM* (see below); Maurice Beebe, Harrison Hayford, and Gordon Roper's "Criticism of
HM: A Selected Checklist" (*MFS* 62); and J. D. Vann's "A Selected Checklist
of M Criticism, 1958–1968" (*SNNTS* 69). (An extensive secondary bibliography on cards, prepared by Harrison Hayford, is available for examination in
the M Room at the Newberry Library.)

More easily available but highly selective bibliographies of works about M
are in the *LHUS* (1948; sup., 1959), in Thorp's *HM: Representative Selections*
(see below), and in many of the critical books themselves, notably those by
Arvin, Bernstein, Hillway, Humphreys, Mayoux, Miller, Pommer, Rampersad,
Rosenberry, and Stone (see below). Comprehensive bibliographies of criticism
of two of M's works are contained in the Hayford-Sealts edition of *Billy Budd*
(hereafter *BB*) and in the M Annual *Bartleby the Scrivener* (see below). "*Moby-
Dick* [hereafter *MD*] by HM . . . Catalogue of an Exhibition" (*PULC* 52) lists a
variety of critical notices, reprints, translations, and adaptations of that novel,
as well as many items peripherially related to it. "Directory of M Dissertations," compiled by Tyrus Hillway and Hershel Parker and mimeographed in
1962, brings forward Hillway's "Doctoral Dissertations on HM: A Chronological Summary (1933–1952)," mimeographed in 1953; both sponsored and distributed by the M Society. *The Merrill Checklist of HM*, edited by H. P. Vincent (1969), is a selective compilation of books by and about M.

Lists of the chief collections of M's manuscripts and books once owned by
him have been made publicly available. That at Princeton is included in "*MD*
by HM . . . Catalogue of an Exhibition." "HM: A Check List of Books and
Manuscripts in the Collections of the New York Public Library," compiled by
Herbert Cahoon, appeared in the *BNYPL* (51). The collection at Harvard (including the largest number of manuscripts, notably those of *BB*, *Timoleon*,
John Marr and Other Sailors, and the two longer journals) is itemized in the
"Bibliography" of Freeman's edition of *BB* (see below). "General Inventory of
the Collections in the M Room" at the Berkshire Athenaeum, Pittsfield, Mass.,
was mimeographed in 1953, with addenda in 1955.

II. EDITIONS

1. Collections

The Constable Edition (*The Works of HM*, 16 vols., London, 1922–24;
repr., 1963), with no critical editing and an Anglicized text, is for the present

the most nearly complete as well as the first collection of M's writings. It incorporates all but his journals, letters, lectures, and a few short prose pieces and poems.

In the Hendricks House Edition (*Complete Works of HM*, Chicago, New York, 1947–   ) under the general editorship of H. P. Vincent, seven of the projected fourteen volumes have appeared, edited with introductions and explanatory and textual notes: *MD* (Vols. 6, 7, 1949), by H. A. Murray; *The Piazza Tales* (hereafter *PT*) (Vol. 9, 1948), by E. O. Oliver; *The Confidence-Man* (hereafter *CM*) (Vol. 10, 1954), by Elizabeth Foster; *Collected Poems* (Vol. 14, 1947), by Vincent; *Clarel* (1960), by W. S. Bezanson; and *Omoo* (1969), by Harrison Hayford and Walter Blair.

This edition makes an attempt to establish texts by examination of manuscripts, editions, periodical versions, and manuscript revisions as these versions were available. Each volume incorporates emendations in spelling, punctuation, and like matters by the individual editors, lists of which are recorded in the textual notes. The textual policy is inconsistent, however, and the collation incomplete.

The explanatory notes of the volumes in this edition are the fullest that have been made of the works which have appeared. They are correspondingly valuable, particularly for their identification of sources and allusions.

The introductions vary considerably. Those for *PT*, *Collected Poems*, and *MD* are brief, confined to the essential facts of composition, publication, and general reception. Those for *CM* and *Clarel*, approximately 100 pages each, constitute the most comprehensive studies which have been made of those works. In both introductions not only are facts of composition and publication recorded, but the main characters, themes, structure, and style are discussed, and the chief critical interpretations and appraisals summarized. Foster gives special attention to the Moredock story in *CM* (comparing it with its source and calling it the crux of the novel) and to the argument for identifying the philosophy of Winsome and Egbert with that of Emerson. Her interpretation of that enigmatic work is chiefly in moral and religious terms (with the Confidence Man as a diabolic figure), and she sees the conclusion as a prediction of the death of religion and the triumph of uncharitable individualism. Of particular interest in Bezanson's introduction to *Clarel* is the section on the M-Hawthorne relationship as reflected in that of Rolfe, Clarel, and Vine (said to be a portrait of Hawthorne). In the introduction for *Omoo*, about fifty pages, Hayford and Blair trace the combination of M's own experiences with material he obtained from books, identifying sources more fully than has hitherto been done; analyze the character of the narrator and the style; record the facts about composition and publication; list later editions and translations; and summarize the chief critical estimates.

The introduction to *Pierre* (approximately 100 pages) is the longest study which has been made of that novel, though it is not a conventionally literary one, being written by a professional psychiatrist from his specialized point of view. It nevertheless offers the most nearly complete and unified explanation of that problematic work. It is, moreover, an essay bearing monumentally on M's writings as a whole and on his life. The first fourth is devoted to a description of the inward nature of the autobiographical elements in the works before *Pierre*. M should be commemorated, Murray asserts, "as the literary discoverer of . . . the Darkest Africa of the mind, the mythological unconsciousness. As a depth psychologist he belongs with Doestoevsky and Nietzsche, the greatest in the centuries before Freud." *Pierre* he calls not only M's chief work supporting this claim but the key to an understanding of M himself, it being his "spiritual autobiography." The implications in the remainder of the essay are thus far-reaching. There, in an analysis of the novel as divided into three parts, Murray demonstrates that Pierre, essentially, exhibits in his life at Saddle Meadows the Oedipus complex, discovers in Isabel the dark or tragic anima, and at last turns fatally into himself, showing symptoms of a mana personality. Murray also identifies most of the characters as being drawn from M's relatives and friends (of particular interest is the suggestion that Plinlimmon corresponds to Hawthorne), and a number of literary parallels are pointed out. Insofar as he considers the novel in literary terms, Murray rates it very low, objecting chiefly to the style.

Some of these volumes contain other useful extra-textual features: transcriptions of portions of the documents relating to the revolt on the *Lucy Ann* in *Omoo*; an index of sources in *MD*; transcriptions of the four manuscript fragments relating to the text in *CM*; and a map, chronology of the pilgrimage, and critical index of the principal characters in *Clarel*.

The Northwestern-Newberry Edition (*The Writings of HM*, Chicago, 1968–   ), under the general editorship of Harrison Hayford with Hershel Parker and G. T. Tanselle, to be completed in sixteen volumes (including a bibliography), provides for the first time a critical text of the total body of M's writing. Each work is edited either from manuscript or from the edition closest to it, all editions published during M's lifetime being collated. Each volume (except the volumes of the letters and journals) will contain a "Historical Note" (dealing with the sources, composition, publication, and critical history—without advancing any particular critical interpretation—of the work), and a "Textual Record" (consisting of a "Note on the Text," a discussion of adopted readings, lists of emendations and of substantive variants, if any, transcriptions of any manuscript fragments, and discussions of manuscript revisions) by the editors. Three volumes have appeared: *Typee* (1968; Hist. Note by Leon Howard); *Omoo* (1968; Hist. Note by Gordon Roper); *Redburn* (1969; Hist. Note by Hershel Parker). This edition, which is being issued in both hard and paper covers, thus promises to be the most generally useful as well as the authoritative one. It originated under the auspices of the Center for Editions of American Authors of the MLA and bears the seal of the Center's approval.

A virtually complete collection of M's letters has been made and the texts critically edited by M. R. Davis and W. H. Gilman, *The Letters of HM* (1960), with a brief introduction, annotations, a check list of unlocated letters, textual notes, and illustrations, including reproductions of portions of five manuscript letters; of the 271 letters, 42 are here published for the first time. The chief earlier collection is that in Minnigerode's *Some Personal Letters of HM and a Bibliography* (1922), consisting of 20 letters (with excisions) from M to Evart Duyckinck, a memorandum to M's brother Allan, and portions of a few letters to other persons quoted in Weaver's biography; one of the letters to Duyckinck is reproduced. Four other letters written by M are printed for the first time by Hennig Cohen, "New M Letters" (*AL* 67); one by G. T. Tanselle, "M Writes to the New Bedford Lyceum" (*AL* 67); one by K. W. Cameron, "Scattered M Manuscripts" (*ATQ* 69); and one in *The American Writer in England: An Exhibition Arranged in Honor of the Sesquicentennial of the University of Virginia* (1969).

The texts of M's public lectures, reconstructed largely from contemporary newspaper reports by M. M. Sealts, have been published in his *M as Lecturer* (1957). Part I is devoted to a discussion of M as lecturer, and an appendix reproduces his notebook of lecture engagements and memoranda of travel expenses while lecturing in 1857–58.

2. Individual Works

All M's volumes of fiction and two of his four volumes of poetry have been published individually since his death, nearly all the novels many times. Most often reprinted have been *MD*, *Typee*, *Omoo*, and *White-Jacket* (hereafter *WJ*); less often, *Israel Potter* (hereafter *IP*), *Redburn*, *Mardi*, *CM*, and *Pierre*. *PT* has been reprinted three times, *Battle-Pieces* twice, *John Marr and Other Sailors* once. Many of these reprints have introductions—often illuminating ones—by well-known scholars and critics (for example, those of Quentin Anderson, Newton Arvin, W. M. Gibson, Maxwell Geismar, Leon Howard, Alfred Kazin, Viola Meynell, and Sherman Paul for *MD*, Van Wyck Brooks for *Omoo*,

Carl Van Doren and William Plomer for *WJ*, H. B. Franklin for *Mardi*, Lewis Leary for *IP*, and R. W. B. Lewis for *CM*). Otherwise, however, these editions are notable chiefly for their bearing on M's reputation in the present century. The most important ones are described below. Unless otherwise noted, the texts (and those in the volumes of selections described below) are those of the first English edition of *Typee* and the first American editions of the other works (the most nearly authoritative versions published in M's lifetime).

The Signet Edition of *Typee*, edited by Hayford (1964), has a text showing all the changes and expurgations which M made after the first publication; it also has a brief Afterword. The Oxford Edition of *WJ*, edited by A. R. Humphreys (1966), with a text based on the first English edition, contains a brief introduction, explanatory notes, an appendix consisting of nautical terms, and a short bibliography. The Rinehart Edition (1967) of *WJ*, edited by Hennig Cohen (with a text incorporating some variants in the first English edition and with the Preface and a draft of the Preface from that edition) has a thorough introduction covering the factual elements, the literary sources, and the naval abuses under attack; there is also a selected bibliography of criticism.

Three editions of *MD* are notable. That edited by Willard Thorp in 1947 provides a brief general introduction, a modest number of annotations (with special attention to geographical names and technical terms), illustrations relating to whaling, and a map on the end-papers. The Bobbs-Merrill Edition, edited by Charles Feidelson (1964), has an introduction surveying M's career, the backgrounds of the novel, and the chief approaches to a study of it, as well as a bibliographic note on critical works; the annotations are the most generally satisfactory which have been made, and maps and drawings of ships and whales further enhance this edition's usefulness. The Norton Critical Edition, edited by Hayford and Parker (1967), has a text anticipating that of the Newberry-Northwestern Edition and a variety of extra materials: a technical textual essay, a glossary of nautical terms, a description with drawings of whaling and whalecraft, reproductions of contemporary engravings on the subject, book reviews and letters by M pertinent to the composition of the novel, and selections from analogues, sources, and critical comments; the edition is thus the most useful for students.

The first attempt to produce a critical text of *Pierre* and to give that novel serious consideration in the M canon was made by R. S. Forsythe in the edition in Knopf's Americana Deserta series appearing in 1930. It contains a list of emendations and an introduction relating *Pierre* to *Mardi* and *MD*, identifying the chief autobiographical elements and literary sources (notably *Hamlet*), interpreting the theme as the loss of youthful illusion, and calling attention to the varied aspects of the style.

Three editions of *CM* deserve notice. The Rinehart Edition, edited by Hennig Cohen (1964), has an introduction concentrating on the novel's structure, at the same time giving descriptions of the Confidence-Man's guises and of the principal other characters; it is particularly notable for pointing out the significance of the animal imagery. The Bobbs-Merrill Edition, edited by H. B. Franklin (1967), contains an introduction treating the place of the novel among M's works, the setting, general fictional characteristics, the guises of the Confidence Man, and the relationship of the story to Hindu mythology; the text is fully annotated, and there is a chronological outline of M's life, a selected bibliography, and, in an Appendix, a transcription of the related manuscript fragment "The River." The novel has also been edited, in 1968 by J. D. Seelye, in a facsimile of the first edition, with an introduction which surveys the chief critical evaluations and relates the work to M's life and other works, but which is most notable for relating it to contemporary periodical literature; the volume also has a selected bibliography of criticism and illustrations from contemporary caricatures.

Battle-Pieces and Aspects of the War, edited by Sidney Kaplan (1960), is a facsimile of the first edition with a brief introduction and a list of M's revisions in that edition. *The Battle-Pieces of HM*, edited by Hennig Cohen (1963), with illustrations from drawings of Civil War scenes by the English artists A. R. and William Waud, has an introduction summarizing M's use of personal experience, literary works, and contemporary periodical reports in the poems, analyzing their structure and themes, and giving an account of the Wauds.

BB has been printed in three texts. The first was that of Raymond Weaver, the first version of which appeared in Vol. 13 of the Constable Edition and a second (with a brief description of the differences) in his collection *Shorter Novels of HM* (see below). The text of F. B. Freeman in his edition *M's BB* (1948) was the first attempt to present a transcription with all variant readings, but it failed to do so and was followed by several corrected versions by others. Freeman's reading of the manuscript led him, moreover, to the untenable theory that the work was an extension of a shorter one, which he reconstructed and included under the title "Baby Budd, Sailor." He also erred, like others before him, in taking the *Somers* mutiny case to be the point of the work's origin. These arguments aside, his introduction contains valuable treatments of the sources, structure, characters, themes, and language of the novel, and of M's last years. The volume also has a transcription of manuscript fragments related to the manuscript though not the text of *BB* (some of which Freeman erroneously assumed were related to it) and a bibliography consisting chiefly of a list of M's books and manuscripts at Harvard.

The third text is the authoritative one (which will be incorporated in the Northwestern-Newberry Edition), *BB Sailor*, edited from the manuscript by Hayford and Sealts (1962). Besides the reading text, the volume contains an introduction, annotations, an exhaustive bibliography of criticism, textual notes, the genetic text, and plates showing sample manuscript pages. (A paper edition omits the genetic text and plates.) The concise but definitive introduction describes the growth of the manuscript (in three stages: first focussing in prose and verse on Budd, then introducing Claggart and more briefly Vere, finally fully delineating Vere), traces the history of the text, and points out the chief "perspectives" for criticism of the work. W. T. Stafford's *M's BB and the Critics* (1961, 1968) has in the second edition the Hayford-Sealts text, as well as the dramatization of the story by L. O. Coxe and Robert Chapman, and selections from criticism.

M's journals have also been edited from manuscripts. The first journal was edited as *Journal of a Visit to London and the Continent by HM 1849–1850* (1948) by Eleanor Melville Metcalf, with a brief introduction, annotations, and illustrations of three manuscript pages, but no textual notes (the illustrations also include portraits of M, his wife, and their son Malcolm). The second journal was first edited as *Journal Up the Straits October 11, 1856–May 5, 1857* (1935) by Weaver, with annotations and an introduction summarizing M's career to 1856 and giving a brief description of the manuscript, a facsimile of one of the leaves being included. That journal was more critically edited by H. C. Horsford as *Journal of a Visit to Europe and the Levant October 11, 1856–May 6, 1857 by HM* (1955), with an introduction discussing M's journey, the content of the journal and his subsequent use of it in writing and lecturing, a chronology of the journey, explanatory and textual notes, type facsimiles and plates of sample manuscript pages, and maps. The journal which M kept during his voyage to the Pacific in 1860 was first printed as "Journal of M's Voyage in a Clipper Ship" (*NEQ* 29); another transcription of the manuscript appears in Leyda's *Portable M* (see below).

The full text of M's "Fragments From a Writing Desk: No. 2," which appeared in *The Democratic Press and Lansingburgh Advertiser*, 18 May 1835, was first reprinted in Gilman's *M's Early Life and Redburn* (see below), the version in the Constable Edition being incomplete. The most reliable text of the poem "Rammon" is Eleanor Tilton, "M's 'Rammon': A Text and Commentary" (*HLB* 59).

3. Selections

The largest selection of M's fiction which has been made is that in *The Romances of HM* (1931), which contains all the novels except *CM* and *BB*; its brief preface is inconsequential.

Two more widely selective volumes are more useful to M students. Thorp's AWS *HM: Representative Selections* (1938) contains selections from *Typee, Omoo, Mardi, WJ, MD,* and the three volumes of short poems; two book reviews; a hitherto unpublished poem; and 21 letters. It also has a 120-page introduction constituting a thorough introduction to M's life and writing, with special attention to *Mardi, MD,* and *Pierre* as a trilogy, to the poetry, to M's social ideas, and to his reputation; a 30-page annotated bibliography, including early reviews; and notes covering the essential aspects of all the selections.

The Portable M, edited by Jay Leyda (1952), contains the complete texts of *Typee, BB,* "Bartleby," "Hawthorne and his Mosses," the lecture "The South Seas," the 1860 journal, and 35 letters; and selections from *Mardi, MD, IP, PT,* the four volumes of poetry, the other two journals, and marginalia—all arranged chronologically. An attempt is made in all the texts to come as close as possible to M's intention (MS corrections and MSS—notably that of *BB*—being consulted when possible). The volume also contains an introduction, an account of M's life before 1845, and a bibliographic note—all very brief.

Three selections from M's shorter fiction are of importance. *The Apple-Tree Table and Other Sketches* (1922) brought together for the first time nine pieces originally published in magazines, with an introductory note by Henry Chapin. *Shorter Novels of HM*, edited by Weaver (1928), contains "Benito Cereno," "Bartleby," "The Encantadas," and *BB* (in Weaver's second version); the introduction, which has a brief description of the manuscripts preserved by Mrs. M, is largely devoted to a summary of M's life and works, with the same general reading of both as that in Weaver's biography (see below). *The Complete Stories of HM*, edited by Leyda (1949), contains 15 stories, all that M is known to have written; the texts have been prepared by collation of all available versions, the general introduction is often illuminating, and the notes are informative about composition, original publication, and sources. *Selected Writings of HM* (Mod. Lib., 1952) has *Typee, BB,* and the stories in Leyda's texts, but no critical features.

Three selections from M's poems have been made. *Selected Poems of HM*, edited by William Plomer (1943), and *HM Selected Poems*, edited by F. O. Matthiessen (1944), have approximately 25 poems each and negligible introductions. *Selected Poems of HM*, edited by Hennig Cohen (1964), is more sub-

stantial, with 90 poems and extensive selections from *Clarel*, a brief introduction summarizing M's career, and general explanatory comments on the poems.

Four other volumes of selections deserve mention. Rinehart's *Selected
Tales and Poems by HM*, edited by Richard Chase (1950), has ten prose pieces,
including *BB*, and 39 poems; the introduction concentrates on the stories and
offers interpretations in agreement with the psychological-mythical approach
to M made by Chase in his *HM* (see below). *Typee* and *BB* have been brought
together in editions with introductions by M. R. Stern (1958) and by Maxwell
Geismar (1962), making provocative comparisons of these works. *BB and
Other Tales* (1961) (including *PT* and "The *Town-Ho's* Story") has an Afterword by Thorp, commenting incisively on each work.

III. BIOGRAPHY

1. Books

Since M's works are so extensively based on his experience and his experience is so deeply represented by them, the number of works by others
which deal in some way with his biography is large—approximately as many
as a third of all those which have been written. The number of essentially biographical studies, however, is small, approximately half a dozen.

The first book-length biography was *HM: Mariner and Mystic* (1921,
1961) by Weaver, the virtual discoverer of M—his literary remains as well
as his achievement. Still correct in outline, Weaver's account has two major
weaknesses: it draws on M's fiction as fact (especially his young sailors' accounts of their experiences and the description of Pierre's disillusion with
his parents) and dismisses the last 30 years of his life in a single, final chapter
as "The Long Quietus." According to Weaver, M was disillusioned from youth
(being particularly disappointed in his marriage and in his attempt to establish
a friendship with Hawthorne) and a literary failure after *MD*. The volume
also contains illustrations of members of M's family and a bibliography of his
publications, which increases its original value and adds to its permanent
interest.

The next book which may be called a biography was *HM: A Study of His
Life and Vision* (1929) by Lewis Mumford. It is not a conventional study: M's
words are often used without quotation marks (the account of his trip abroad
in 1849 being cast in the form of a soliloquy); much of the fiction is taken as
autobiography (most significantly, the depiction of Pierre as sexually frustrated); the style is emotionally charged. It is, however a landmark in M scholarship, since Mumford was first to recognize the unusual degree to which M's

life and works are one, the depth of his inner or spiritual experience, and the magnitude of his literary achievement. M (with Whitman) was, Mumford declared, "the greatest imaginative writer that America has produced" and in "depth of experience and religious insight" comparable only to Doestoevsky in the nineteenth century. In his analysis of M's works (the first penetrating one which had thus far been made of the complete canon), he opened a new approach to *MD* by pointing out its epic and mythic qualities, rescued *Mardi* and *Clarel* from almost total neglect, but found little of a purely literary nature to praise in *Pierre*, *CM*, and *IP*.

In the revised edition of his study (1962) Mumford deleted the Epilogue (in which he had attempted to account for M's belated critical recognition), substituted a less one-sided account of the M-Hawthorne relationship (originally he had assumed Ethan Brand to be a portrait of M), and toned down a few descriptions (for example, saying that M's parents wore "fashionable false faces" instead of calling them "monsters"). He also substituted another Preface, in which he paid tribute to the chief biographical and critical studies subsequent to his own, but defended his general approach (he had been concerned with biographic data, he said, "only in so far as they threw a light on M's mind") and his critical judgments; he took the occasion, moreover, to deplore the tendency of many M critics (presumably including Chase and Lawrance Thompson) to make strained and eccentric judgments.

The first attempt to separate fact from fiction in M's works—and thus a major contribution to a full biographical account of him—was made by C. R. Anderson in *M in the South Seas* (1939, 1966). Drawing on assorted manuscripts and documents—contemporary journals, log books, crew lists, and the like—as well as on newspapers and other printed accounts, Anderson reconstructed, as far as it seems possible to do so, M's actual experiences from 1841 to 1845. He also identified the chief sources of *Typee*, *Omoo*, and *WJ*, and largely verified M's accounts of the islanders by reference to twentieth-century anthropological studies. The notes are valuable, and a map on the end papers and a bibliography of materials consulted in the study are useful.

Another contribution to M biography is contained in Book I of *M's Early Life and Redburn* (1951) by Gilman. There, in 150 pages, M's years from 1819 to 1841 are chronicled more fully than anywhere else, on the authority of various primary sources. Gilman's most important discovery (*MLN* 46) was the name of the vessel (the *St. Lawrence*) on which M sailed to Liverpool, the crew list, and the date of the voyage, which was 1839, two years later than the date which had long been assigned it, on the assumption that M had been the age of Redburn—17—at the time. One of the appendices of the volume contains letters relative to the Philo Logos society in Albany, to which M belonged in 1838. The notes are chiefly documentary, and end papers provide genealogical charts of the Gansevoort and M families.

In 1951 also appeared the cooperative venture which constitutes the definitive biography of M: *The M Log: A Documentary Life of HM, 1819–1891* (2 vols.), edited by Leyda (new ed., with sup., 1969), and Howard's *HM: A Biography*. The first work consists chiefly of extracts from a multiplicity of documents (letters, journals, marginalia, newspaper notices, ship logs, periodical articles, book reviews, and M's own writing) representing all the facts which an exhaustive search revealed about M's life—all arranged in a day-by-day chronology. Brief biographical sketches of M's chief associates precede the body of the text, an identification of sources and a listing of possible lines of further research follow it; and plates, illustrations, and facsimile reproductions of manuscripts appear throughout. This work is thus literally a mine of information. It may be said to fulfill what Leyda calls his "main aim: to give each reader the opportunity to be his own biographer of HM." As biography itself, however, it lacks both focus (establishing no relationships except immediate temporal ones) and narrative line (having no transitions between entries).

Howard's *HM* was designed to complement Leyda's work as a formal narrative biography, its chief source material and documentation being found in *The M Log*. Howard's aim, he says, was "to place the basic facts of M's life in their proper physical, historical, intellectual, and literary contexts," to understand him "as a human being living in nineteenth-century America." He deals with M's works as activities on which he was engaged at various times rather than as literal autobiography. Admirably balanced and factual, the book is, in itself, the most satisfactory biography which has appeared. Intentionally it sets the outward record straight (most importantly, keeping in place M's uncertain domestic relationships, earlier overemphasized), and avoids sounding very deeply the inner life—for example, M's alternating moods of exhilaration and despair and his tendency to unresolved philosophic speculation.

Another documentary biography of M, using highly selected documents, is *HM: Cycle and Epicycle* (1953) by his granddaughter Eleanor Melville Metcalf. This volume recounts M's life largely by means of extended quotations from family papers (including his own letters and journals), supplemented by Metcalf's recollections of conversations about him among relatives and friends and by family legends and anecdotes. Though not altogether reliable textually or factually, it presents new material and makes persuasively moderate judgments of M's wife (as sympathetic though not deeply understanding) and of M himself in his last years (as unembittered though irascible). Genealogical charts of the M, Gansevoort, and Shaw families appear on the end papers, and illustrations of members of the family and friends are included.

Five more books contain material relevant to M biography. *Family Correspondence of HM 1830–1904 In the Gansevoort-Lansing Collections*, edited by Victor Paltsits (1929), has letters by M since collected, but also many by his wife and a few by his brothers and other relatives. M's family background is further explored in *The Gansevoorts of Albany: Dutch Patricians in the Upper Hudson Valley* (1969) by Alice Kenney. In the chapter "Escape from Tradition" she compares the relationship of M and of his cousin Henry Gansevoort (a lawyer who became a lieutenant in the Union Army and remained in service until his death in 1871) to the Dutch tradition in Albany.

Among the journals kept by those associated with M two have been printed entirely. *Journal of a Cruise to the Pacific Ocean, 1842–1844, in the Frigate United States with Notes on HM*, edited by Anderson (1937), though making no mention of M, records events on a ship on which he sailed for a short time; appendices contain the log of the ship, letters from the records of the Pacific Squadron about the attack on Monterey in 1842, and excerpts from W. H. Myers's "Journal of a Three Years Cruise" from 1841 to 1844 in the sloop of war *Cyane*, then part of the Squadron. *Gansevoort M's 1846 London Journal*, edited by Parker (1966), makes available a document important for its records of the arrangements M's brother Gansevoort made for the English publication of *Typee*.

Finally the fictional *Genoa: A Telling of Wonders* (1965) by M's grandson Paul Metcalf should be mentioned. Ostensibly a story of two brothers, Michael and Carl Mills, it proposes an influence of Columbus on M and describes him and his family, quoting liberally from his works and family letters.

2. Articles

A good deal of biographical information about M has appeared in periodical articles, but since most of it has been incorporated in the chief documented biographical studies of him, those articles have not been noted in the following discussion. Only a few, in fact, have supplemented or corrected those studies.

Hayford's "Melville's Freudian Slip" (*AL* 58) sets matters straight about the fact that the official birth record of M's son Stanwix gives as the name of the mother that of M's mother (and the repeated Freudian interpretation that fact has received) by reporting that the record contains also the wrong day of birth and a misspelling of the child's name and was made several months afterward, almost certainly not by M himself. F. V. Lloyd in "A Further Note on HM, Lecturer" (*MHSB* 64) reports that M was invited to lecture by the Mercantile

Library Association of St. Louis, though whether or not he accepted is unknown. In "A Checklist of Portraits of HM" (*BNYPL* 67) Morris Star surveys
the known paintings, photographs, and prints, characterizing and locating
each. M's granddaughter, Frances Thomas Osborne, records her reminiscences
of him in "HM Through a Child's Eyes (*BNYPL* 65); she was eight when he
died.

Finally, a few articles may be mentioned as fuller treatments of aspects
of M's life which are briefly covered by Howard and Leyda. Chief of them are
William Charvat, "M's Income" (*AL* 43); Hayford and M. R. Davis, "HM as
Office-Seeker" (*MLQ*) 49; Tanselle, "HM's Visit to Galena in 1840" (*JISHS* 60)
and "The Sales of M's Books" (*HLB* 69); and Parker, "Gansevoort M's Role
in the Campaigne of 1844" (*NYHSQ* 65).

IV. CRITICISM

1. Books

Some 63 books of criticism about M have appeared, at the rate of one in
the 1920's, six in the 1930's, nine in the 1940's, 20 in the 1950's and 26 in the
1960's. About a fourth are general surveys of his works with short accounts of
his life. Another fourth survey the works from specialized points of view, with
slight attention to biography. The remaining number treat particular aspects of
M's writing or concentrate on individual works.

Insofar as these studies reflect trends in M scholarship, it has moved in
emphasis from his themes or ideas to his religious or philosophic thought to
his reading to psychological-mythical and cultural-political interpretations of
his work (in the 1940's and 1950's) to his reputation (in the 1960's), with a
few studies of his technique throughout the period. *MD* has been most often
the subject of a single volume; one study has been devoted respectively to
Redburn, Mardi, Clarel, and the factual-ficitional content of *Typee, Omoo*,
and *WJ*.

a. *General Surveys.* The first book to survey M's life and works was John
Freeman's *HM* (1926). Not quite half is devoted to the life (the material condensed from Weaver), the rest to the works, which are summarized and freely
quoted. Like Weaver, Freeman regards as insignificant most of the fiction between *MD* and *BB*, and he virtually dismisses *Clarel*; but his estimate of the
shorter poems and of M's style in general is a sensitive one. An appendix reprints the article on "Mocha Dick" in the Detroit *Free Press* (1892) and refers

to a manuscript journal of J. N. Reynolds (author of the chief account of that whale). There is also a bibliography of M's works.

The next general study of M, with hardly any attention to biography, was K. H. Sundermann's *HM's Gedankengut: Eine kritische Untersuchung seiner weltanschaulichen Grundideen* (Berlin, 1937), the first book about him in a foreign language. Considering M as essentially a thinker, Sundermann discusses his chief ideas in three categories—religious, philosophical, and historical, with numerous subdivisions. A provocative as well as a pioneer study, it is too broad to be exhaustive and too systemized to allow for the nuances and polarities of M's thought. An introduction gives a brief account of his life, and an appendix reprints three of his book reviews. Only published materials were used, Sundermann not having visited the United States.

The fullest consideration which has yet been made of M's life and works together appeared next: *HM: Martin, métaphysicien, et poète* (1939) by Jean Simon (the first book about him in French). Unfortunately, all but 95 copies were destroyed during World War II. Simon examined unpublished materials and talked with M scholars in the United States. His 623-page work is divided into three parts, devoted respectively to the life, works and "originality" of M (the last part subdivided as The Man, The Thinker, and The Artist). It also has extensive primary and secondary bibliographies.

In a category by itself is the next book about M: Jean Giono's *Pour Saluer M* (1941). It is largely a fictionized account of his visit to Europe in 1849–50 but contains sympathetic responses to his work.

A decade later came *M* (1949) by Geoffrey Stone. Roman Catholic in orientation, it attributes both M's personal problems and literary failures to his possession of a Protestant-Romantic attitude, defined as one of rebellion. Slight connection is made with the body of M scholarship and little literary judgment is exercised.

In 1950 and 1951 three notable surveys appeared—in France, the United States, and England respectively. Pierre Frédérix's *HM* (1950) is still the most available comprehensive one in French. Unlike Simon's, it makes no pretense to original research, depends for biography on Weaver and Mumford, and quotes extensively from M's writing. Photographs chiefly of members of M's family and maps of Pacific islands enhance the interest of the volume.

Newton Arvin's *HM* (1950), despite weaknesses, is the most satisfactory general account of M and his works. Like Mumford, Arvin considers M's life and writing inseparably, from a Freudian point of view. Though offering few new judgments (and some old questionable ones, such as the low rating of

"Benito Cereno"), it is a fluently written account, taking cognizance of the chief discoveries in M biography and giving his literary affiliations their due. Its high point is the chapter on *MD*, which analyses structure, style, and four levels of meaning: literal, psychological, moral, and mythic.

Ronald Mason's *The Spirit Above the Dust: A Study of HM* (1951), the second English account, is avowedly a critical estimate rather than a biography, summarizing M's life in two pages in the Introduction. It proposes, moreover, that his prevailing theme is "the search for the rediscovery of that innocence in the human soul of which contact with worldly experience has deprived it." This thesis does not distort Mason's discussion of M's works, however, which is a fresh and illuminating one, stylistically often distinguished. Emphasis is placed on M's evolving use of symbols (with a persuasive account of Hawthorne's influence) and on his national consciousness and place in American literature. The three chapters on *MD* soundly explore its symbolic and mythic content, and the analysis of the intellectual content of *Clarel* justifies the high praise of that poem.

Most of the remaining general surveys are less notable. In 1958 appeared J. J. Mayoux's short *M par lui-même*, translated in 1960 by John Ashbery as *M*. The biographical facts are only the most salient—and only for about the first half of M's life. The discussion of *MD* is not unusual, and little is said of the works after *Pierre*. Mayoux is provocative, however, in noting motifs of clothing, of the narrators' companions, and of cannibalism-death-suicide; giving *Omoo* perhaps its highest assessment; and suggesting the pervasive symbolism of *WJ*. The volume incorporates selections from *Mardi*, *WJ*, *MD*, "The Encantadas," and the complex text of "Bartleby"; is profusely illustrated; and has a selected bibliography.

Four surveys were published in 1962. A. R. Humphreys's *M*, appearing in England, is short, with an introductory chapter on the life, the rest on the fiction, and the 1856–57 journal. No penetrating analysis of the works is undertaken. The primary and secondary bibliographies, however, are commendable. Leon Howard's pamphlet *HM* (UMPAW) is an admirable account in this form.

The other two surveys of 1962 merit more attention. *A Reader's Guide to HM* by J. E. Miller has a minimum of biographical data. It has, moreover, a thesis: that M's works ask what man's response to evil should be and answer in terms of three types of characters: those who refuse to acknowledge its existence and so wear a "mask"; those who accept their share of guilt and so are "maskless"; those who have not decided which attitude to adopt—young "wanderers" or "seekers." The argument is generally persuasive and often entails rewarding comparisons, but the categories are too limited to allow for radical differences between major characters (those with "masks" include Ahab, Billy Budd, and Claggart), and the thesis excludes discussion of half the stories and all the poems except *Clarel*. An annotated secondary bibliography is especially useful.

A fourth study published in 1962 was Warner Berthoff's *The Example of M*, which examines the works of fiction apart from their thematic content. After two chapters outlining M's career as a writer from 1846 to 1856 come chapters on "The Melvillian Setting" (defined as the context of the action and illustrated chiefly by *MD*), "M's Characters" (described as fated but also making choices), "M's Narrators," "M's Story-Telling" (his best mode is said to be the "told story"), "Words, Sentences, Paragraphs, Chapters," " 'Certain Phenomenal men': the Example of *BB*" (called a story of the kinship of two magnanimous natures), and a brief conclusion. Though the chapters do not probe deeply, the division is refreshing and suggestive. The best chapter is that on style.

A more conventional general survey is Tyrus Hillway's *HM* (1963) with, however, a rather loose organization. Chapter one considers M's style, symbols, sources, and humor; chapters two through five recount the story of his life; chapters six through eight are devoted to the works; chapter nine describes the M revival. There are notes and a selected bibliography.

Two brief studies for the beginning student deserve mention. Darrel Abel's *A Simplified Approach to HM* (1963) recounts the chief events of M's life, summarizes and gives sound evaluation of all the works, and provides a short bibliography; in some ways it is the most trustworthy introduction to M. D. E. S. Maxwell's *HM* (1968) has an introductory account of M's life (and a chronological table) followed by extracts from novels and stories; there are short primary and secondary bibliographies.

b. *Surveys from Specialized Points of View*. Some dozen studies survey M's works (with little reference to his life) from specialized points of view. The first study was Stanley Geist's *HM: The Tragic Vision and the Heroic Ideal* (1939, 1966), with the point that M demanded a heroism measured by triumph over the tragic nature of experience. Geist's attention is limited, however, principally to *MD* and *Pierre*.

The first comprehensive thematic study—and one of the most durable—was W. E. Sedgwick's *HM: The Tragedy of Mind* (1945). The thesis is that, in M's view, whereas "a great man combines a great heart with a great mind," the ideal of the head is at odds with the humanitarianism of the heart and impelled eventually to destroy it. Sedgwick is particularly illuminating on *Typee*, whose essential subject he calls "an inward and universal phase of human experience . . . in which life lies along the easy slopes of spontaneous, instinctive being," a phase which it is necessary both to find and to escape; and on *BB*, in which he finds a return to that subject. Gracefully written, it has the tone of belletristic criticism rather than professional scholarship.

The next survey of M's works from a specialized point of view is Chase's *HM: A Critical Study* (1949)—a controversial study but a brilliant and perhaps the most penetrating one which has been made. As Chase reads him, M created a cultural-historical myth, with a hero represented as Prometheus-Oedipus. This myth has two themes: the Fall and the Search for what was thereby lost; and three central characters: Ishmael, the disinherited or victim of the Fall, who searches for a Promethean-Oedipean nature (and is equated with post-Revolutionary America); the true Prometheus; and the false Prometheus, who betrays his humanity through pride or pursuit of an absolute. The Search moves between polarities (symbolized by Light, Space, Mountain, Tower, Fire, Phallus, Life, Dark, and Time, Valley, Cave, Stone, Castration, Death) in two rhythms—withdrawal and return—by which these opposites are reconcilable. Its great incident peril is immobilization at either extreme, by failure to return from an archaic level of existence (like Harry Bolton, Donjalolo, Pip, Bartleby, and Benito Cereno) or by inability to withdraw from a capitalist-military civilization except by suicide (like Taji, Ahab, Pierre, and John Paul Jones). A further peril is the denial of the Fall (represented by Falsgrave, Plinlimmon, Captain Delano, Derwent, the Confidence Man, Benjamin Franklin—and the liberal progressive tradition in America). As for the true Prometheus-Oedipus, only a few examplars emerge: chiefly Marnoo, Bulkington, Jack Chase, and Ethan Allen. Its chief hypothesis aside, Chase's study is particularly valuable for establishing the relationship of M's work to the folk tradition in American literature.

In 1952 appeared two books, in different countries, from the same point of view, namely, that M's works are expressions of religious sentiment. Gabriele Baldini's *Melville o le ambiguità* (the first book-length Italian study), defines his prevailing theme as the relationship between man and God (whether the diety as in *Clarel*, an idealized female as in *Mardi* and *Pierre*, the whale, the negation of Bartleby, or the sacrifice of Billy Budd)—God being an ambiguity, with which M finally achieved a reconciliation, in terms of art if not of religious faith. Part I gives an account of the novels from *Typee* through *WJ*; Part II discusses *MD* and *Pierre*; and Part III covers the remaining works. It is an intelligent and a useful study, partly because of the flexibility of its thesis.

In direct opposition is Lawrance Thompson's *M's Quarrel with God* (1952), perhaps the most controversial study of all, its thesis being that M was a blasphemer who disguised in devout language his hatred of a God whom he regarded as malicious. Important for calling attention to his use of ironic modes and religious doubts (minimized by earlier critics), the argument is totally assertive and subjective. No allowance is made for the ambiguity and paradox in M's depiction of creation, and the overworking of the thesis results in many extravagant interpretations (the *Pequod's* name for example, is said to be a pun on the words "pique God"). Few poems and no stories are examined.

C. L. R. James's *Mariners, Renegades and Castaways: The Story of HM and the World We Live in* (1953) is in effect a survey of M's chief works of fiction. With the thesis that they depict the degeneration of Western Civilization, James devotes the first three chapters (and most of the sixth) to *MD*, picturing Ahab as the head of a totalitarian state (comparable to Hitler and Stalin) and the crew of the *Pequod* as the workers in such a state (Ishmael being a weak intellectual). Chapters four and five discuss most of the other novels. Chapter seven contains an account of the four months which James, a native of Trinidad who had applied for United States citizenship, spent on Ellis Island while his alleged Trotskyite sympathies were investigated; during this period he wrote most of his book. An irregular study, it is highly provocative.

E. H. Rosenberry's *M and the Comic Spirit* (1955) surveys M's fiction from *Typee* through *CM*, predicting that the comedy advances through four phases: "jocular-hedonic," "imaginative-critical," "philosophical-psychological," and "dramatic-structural." In his discussion of the works, Rosenberry takes up chiefly topics, techniques (such as exaggeration, understatement, and puns), characters, and satire. Important as the first venture into a prominent aspect of M's writing, it is too brief to do justice to the subject.

Another study, intended like Thompson's, to be corrective, is M. R. Stern's *The Fine Hammered Steel of HM* (1957), answering critics emphasizing M's tendency to philosophic speculation. M is called a naturalist in that he was committed to the non-absolute, non-abstract, and non-ideal—to "rationalism, empiricism, objectivity, and relativism"—and that in his writing he explored the disastrous results of an idealistic vision or quest. Only *Typee, Mardi, Pierre,* and *BB* are discussed, however. The thesis itself, moreover, does not fully allow for M's numerous dualistic tendencies.

Klaus Lanzinger's *Primitivismus und Naturalismus im Prosaschaffen HMs* (1959) is divided into two parts. Under the heading *primitivismus* (defined as criticism of civilization and exaltation of the noble savage) M's life and writing before and during the composition of *MD* are discussed. In the remaining half of the book his relation to the late nineteenth-century literary movement

Naturalism is analyzed, with reference to his later life (especially his journey to Palestine), and to the nihilism or determinism reflected in *MD, Pierre, Clarel,* and *BB.*

The Long Encounter: Self and Experience in the Writings of HM (1960) by Merlin Bowen proposes that M's prevailing theme is the "pitting . . . of the single individual against the universe." Part I, "The Antagonists," describes the self and the external world as he depicted them. Part II, "The Meeting," identifies three "strategies" of encounter between the two: "The Way of Tragic Heroism" (exemplified by Tahi, Ahab, and Pierre), "Submission: The Way of Weakness" (represented by several minor characters, Benito Cereno, Babbalanja, Falsgrave, Plinlimmon, and Captain Vere); and "Armed Neutrality: The Way of Wisdom" (represented chiefly by Ishmael and Clarel). In its categorizations of characters it may be compared to Miller's study.

John Bernstein's *Pacificism and Rebellion in the Writings of HM* (1964) is a more comprehensive survey but one with a thesis (like Stern's) somewhat limiting. It argues that pacificism or non-violence and rebellion are themes throughout M's writing, for the most part appearing as polarities, the pacificist being typically Christian in outlook and concerned with man's relationship to his fellows, the rebel seeing the universe as chaotic and concerned primarily with man's place in it. Bernstein's assertion that M shifts from sympathy with pacificism in early works to sympathy with rebellion in later ones seems rather perverse, and many of the minor works, as the author acknowledges, do not lend themselves to analysis in terms of the thesis. His reading of the poetry, however, is a notably sensitive one.

Max Frank concentrates on an interesting aspect of M's symbolism in *Die Farb- und Lichtsymbolik im Prosawerk HMs* (1967), providing four tabular analyses. There is no consideration, however, of *IP, CM,* and most of the stories.

Another study, of monograph length, surveys M's fiction from *Typee* through *MD* from a point of view similar to Bernstein's: Nicholas Canaday's *M and Authority* (1968). The conclusion is that M's attitude to authority (of state, church, ship, captain, parent, society, or God) ranged from acceptance to rebellion according as the authority represented or violated moral right.

M's Thematics of Form: The Great Art of Telling the Truth (1968) by E. A. Dryden considers M's fiction only. Assuming that the novel is a metaphysical rather than a literary form, Dryden argues that though M regarded fiction as the "Art of Telling the Truth," he found both human and natural worlds to be voids under masquerades and therefore created a fiction in inverse relation to life. Interesting though intricate as it is, this argument is not always clearly exemplified by references to the works. The treatment of "Benito Cereno" and *BB* is the most successful.

c. *Studies of Special Aspects of Melville's Writing.* About a dozen books are devoted to special aspects of M's writing: his literary technique and tradition, his religious thought and use of mythology, his reading, and his reputation. The first book in this general category is Walter Weber's *HM: eine stilistische Untersuchung* (1937), which divides the material for examination into rhythm, diction, sentence structure, miscellaneous rhetorical devices, and symbols, and presents it largely in tabulated form. Heinz Kosok's *Die Bedeutung der Gothic Novel für das Erzählwerk HMs* (1963) discusses four aspects of the Gothic novel, giving examples of each in M's work: setting (chiefly haunted castles); characters (notably villains, represented by Jackson, Fedallah, and Claggart); action, characterized as being forecast largely by dreams and forebodings; and narrative method, said to be calculated primarily to excite suspense.

After Weber's, the next study of a particular aspect of M's writing was William Braswell's *M's Religious Thought* (1943, 1959). Though only some 125 pages long and sometimes oversimplified—picturing Melville as having been brought up in orthodoxy, becoming a questioner and an accuser of the deity in mid-life, and finally finding religious peace (as evidenced in *Clarel* and *BB*), it is a reliable and useful study. Indeed, it is the only comprehensive one of this important subject.

James Baird's *Ishmael* (1956) is essentially a study of M as a mythmaker. Avowedly a book about the "nature of modern primitivism," it is devoted for most of its 450 pages to a discussion of M as the most important example of that phenomenon. Modern or "existential" primitivism (as opposed to the "Rousseaustic" variety) is defined as "the mode of feeling which exchanges for traditional Christian symbols a new symbolic idiom referring to Oriental cultures of both Oceania and Asia." (The definition and the discussion which follows is indebted notably to the writings of Jung.) After an analysis of primitivism in this sense and an account of the voyages of M and other westerners of the last century and a half to the Pacific, Baird proceeds in Part Three to identify the major symbols (or "avatars") in M's works which belong to the primitivistic system, grouping them under the headings of "Obsession with the Primeval East," "*Puer Aeternus*: Eternal Innocence," "Polynesian Ethos" (Queequeg in particular is discussed), "Whiteness," "Shadows and Erotic Symbols," "Tree and Cross," and "The Dragon Whale." The fourth part of the study, "Images from the Urwelt: The World before Civilization," identifies symbols from the sea and from the forest and animals. The fifth and last part, "Entombment: Christianity Revisited," is devoted to M's images of cities (including Jerusalem) which are chiefly infernal ones. An intellectually sophisticated book, it is a deeply rewarding one.

The Wake of the Gods (1953) by H. B. Franklin is primarily concerned with M's use of existing myths. Concentrating on *Mardi, MD, Pierre,* "Bartleby," "Benito Careno," *CM,* and *BB,* it points out the chief myths alluded to and argues that mythology itself is part of M's subject. The interpretations of *Mardi* as a study of comparative mythology and *MD* as "An Egyptian Myth Incarnate" (that of Osiris hunting Typhon) are generally illuminating, but those of *CM* as an "Eastern Masquerade" (based on certain Hindu Religious practices) and *BB* as a version of the story of the Celtic God Hu, Beli, or Budd are not. An index of non-Judaic-Christian gods, myths, and religions is useful.

The chief study of M's reading—and one of the indispensable works—is Sealts's *M's Reading: A Check-List of Books Owned and Borrowed* (1948–50); sup., 1952, 1966). In addition to the alphabetical list, it contains a short chronological account of this reading, an analytical index, and plates of documents relative to M's book borrowings and purchasings.

Two studies examine M's debt to specific literary works. Nathalia Wright's *M's Use of the Bible* (1949, 1969) discusses this use as manifested in four aspects of his writing: imagery, characters, themes, and style. H. F. Pommer's *Milton and M* (1950) points out influences on M of Milton's minor poems, *Paradise Lost,* and general vocabulary and sentence structure; included in the appendices are lists of words and phrases in M which can be matched in Milton.

M's Orienda (1961) by Dorothee Finkelstein is also in part a study of literary influences. As a whole, it surveys his interest in and literary treatment of the Near East (particularly Egypt, Assyria, Babylonia, Arabia, Turkey, and Palestine), the "old Orienda" of his *Mardi.* Part One discusses his reading and use of books related to this area (chiefly *The Arabian Nights,* Saadi's *Gulistan, The Rubaiyat,* Beckford's *Vathek,* Hope's *Anastasius,* and several travel accounts), and Part Two analyzes the major Near Eastern characters, images, and symbols in his works (the most notable being Fedallah, who is interpreted in terms of the Assassins or hemp-smoking Islamic fanatics). The bibliography is of value for a study of the whole vogue of the Near East in America and England in the late eighteenth and the nineteenth centuries.

M's reputation, with its unusual fluctuations, is the subject of three books. *M's Reviewers British and American 1846–1891* (1961) by H. W. Hetherington summarizes the reviews of each of M's works, identifies a number of the anonymous reviewers, and explains the biases of many of the reviewers. It is unfortunately incomplete and often inaccurate. For a detailed account of its errors, see Parker's strictures (*AL* 70). *M: A Collection of Critical Essays*, edited by Chase (1962), reprints eleven essays on M by twentieth-century critics, with a particularly illuminating introduction by Chase (who also furnishes the essay on *MD*). A more extensive collection is *The Recognition of HM*, edited by Parker (1967), with excerpts from reviews and other appraisals from 1846 to 1967.

d. *Studies of Individual Works.* Two books which are valuable accounts of portions of M's life are equally valuable criticism of individual works: Anderson's *M in the South Seas* (1939, 1966) (bearing on *Typee, Omoo, WJ*, and part of *MD*) and Gilman's *M's Early Life and "Redburn"* (1951). As criticism both establish the difference between biographical fact and fiction in these novels and demonstrate M's tendency to rely on printed works.

The earliest work of M's to receive central and substantial treatment in book form was *Mardi*, in M. R. Davis's *M's Mardi: A Chartless Voyage* (1952, 1967). After a brief account of M's literary career before the publication of that novel, its composition is detailed and its content analyzed. Appendices reprint letters of M to his English publishers, Murray and Bentley, and from his brothers to Murray—all relative to the publication of the book in England. It is an admirably sound and compact treatment of this first major, uneven novel.

MD has been the subject of some eleven books and pamphlets. First to appear was W. S. Gleim's *The Meaning of MD* (1938, 1962), also the first book to be concerned with a single M work. Apparently influenced by Swedenborg's theory of correspondences, Gleim proposes that Moby Dick be considered as Fate: Ahab as a would-be savior; Starbuck, Stubb, and Flask, as Platonism, Epicureanism, and Stoicism; Queequeg, Tashtego, and Daggoo as religion, sin, and ignorance; Ishmael as Spiritual and Rational man.

Charles Olson's *Call Me Ishmael* (1947) is a highly individualistic (typographically as well as stylistically) commentary on *MD*. About a third is devoted to the activity of whaling, described as "industry," "frontier," and "space" (special attention being given the story of the survivors of the whaleship *Essex*, sunk by a whale, who were reduced to cannibalism, including M's notes in his copy of first-mate Owen Chase's account); a third to the influence of Shakespeare on *MD* (M's marginalia are quoted); and the rest to M's journey to Palestine in 1856–57, seen as a tragic complement to his Pacific voyages.

The most comprehensive study is H. P. Vincent's *The Trying-Out of MD* (1949), which discusses the composition, sources, and meaning of the novel, with emphasis on the cetological chapters. Vincent not only analyzes M's use of his five chief authorities for these chapters, but points out their allegorical and expository nature. There are numerous illustrations of whales. Tyrus Hillway's brochure, *M and the Whale* (1950), briefly discusses M's use of books about whales and whaling.

M. O. Percival's brief *A Reading of MD* (1950, 1967) rests its analysis on two principal interpretations. Ahab is likened to the Kierkegaardian sufferer who first experiences despair and ultimately becomes either demonic or religious, and Moby Dick is taken to represent a fusion of the opposites good and evil. Thus Ishmael, who allows for such a fusion, is saved, whereas Ahab is doomed by his commitment to demonism.

MD Centennial Essays, edited by Tyrus Hillway and L. S. Mansfield (1953), contains nine essays read at conferences held in 1951 in celebration of the centenary of the novel's publication. The contributors—H. A. Murray, Hillway, W. F. Bezanson, H. N. Smith, E. E. Leisy, H. W. Hetherington, Perry Miller, Randall Stewart, and W. L. Heflin—consider, in order, the psychological nature of Ahab's aggression, the theme of the relationship of man and the gods, the novel as a work of art, the image of society, the motif of fatalism, early reviews, M's relationship to Transcendentalism, his friendship with Hawthorne, his acquaintance with Nantucket. The most notable is Murray's "In Nomine Diaboli," which proposes that Ahab is a Lucifer figure and also represents the "Id," that Moby Dick represents both God and the "Superego," and that Ahab-M's attack is upon the agencies opposing "Eros" in nineteenth-century America.

Another German study of M's technique concentrates on *MD*: Hans Helmcke's *Die Funktion des Ich-Erzählers in HMs Roman "MD"* (1957). The first of its three parts deals with Ishmael's revelation of his personal character and his use of the first person singular, first plural, and second or third person. The second part relates the narrator to the work as a whole, notably to Ahab. The third part summarizes the use of the first-person narrator in the novels preceding *MD*. There is an introduction on the first-person narrator tradition in fiction and tables for *Typee, Mardi, WJ,* and *MD*.

Two pamphlets on *MD* appeared next. Gerhard Friedrich's *In Pursuit of MD: M's Image of Man* (1948), a Quaker study, proposes that man is represented in a series of paradoxes: Bildad and Peleg as fighting Quakers, Ahab as ungodly and godlike, Starbuck as a Quaker conscience which capitulates to Ahab, and Ishmael as detached but involved. John Borton's *HM: The Philosophical Implications of Literary Technique in MD* (1961) argues that Ishmael's point of view—both his picture of nature as ambiguous and his commitment to empirical fact—is reinforced by the implications of his being the narrator.

Janez Stanonik's *MD: The Myth and the Symbol: A Study in Folklore and Tradition* (Ljubljana, 1962) is a Yugoslavian study in four parts. The first discusses the accounts of legendary whales in the South Seas (including a French version first published in 1837, in which a Nantucket Negro kills a whale and claims the hand of a whaling captain's daughter); the next is a short survey of the whale in folklore and symbolic literature; the third treats M's use of popular traditions about whales (suggesting that Queequeg represents the Negro in the French version); the last proposes a mythological interpretation (in terms of a conflict of whiteness and blackness). There are notes, illustrations, and, in appendices, reprints of the French account and that of the sinking of the whale ship *Ann Alexander* by a whale shortly after the publication of *MD*.

Paul Brodtkorb, *Ishmael's White World: A Phenomenological Reading of MD* (1965), analyzes Ishmael in terms of his giving expression to the materiality of the elements, the disjunction of body and self, the tenuous relationship of self to the phenomenon of time. The argument is often abstruse, but the character projected—dominated by boredom, dread, and despair—is a convincing one.

Two studies of *IP* appeared in 1969. *M's IP: A Pilgrimage and Progress*, by Arnold Rampersad, touches on M's life during the years immediately before the composition of the novel, its source, and its serialization, and compares it with *Piers Plowman* and *Pilgrim's Progress*. Alexander Keyssar's *M's IP: Reflections on the American Dream* is a 50-page discussion of the novel as a story about the fact that the hopes of the common man are not realized in the world.

Two studies of M's tales complement each other. R. H. Fogle's *M's Shorter Tales* (1960) is a useful survey, giving on the whole conservative interpretations but referring in notes to others; there is a general introduction and separate chapters on "Bartleby," "Cock-a-Doodle-Doo!" "The Bell Tower," "The Piazza," "The Encantadas," and "Benito Cereno." Klaus Ensslen's *Ms Erzählungen: Stil- und strukturanalytische Untersuchungen* (1966), which includes *BB* in its discussion, attends particularly to the narrators, to rhetorical matters such as sentence rhythms and imagery, and to structure; it has fuller notes than Fogle's study.

"Bartleby" is the subject of the M Annual for 1965 (see below), *Bartleby the Scrivener*, edited by H. P. Vincent (1966). It contains ten papers, half of them read at the symposium at Oberlin College in November 1964, in conjunction with the production of the opera based on the story. Two (by composer Walter Aschaffenberg and librettist Jay Leyda) are about the opera, and two (by G. B.

Stone and John Haag) about the film of the story produced at the University of Washington in 1961–62. Murray's "Bartleby and I" is an imaginative colloquy between the attorney, the psychologist, the author, the scrivener, a biographer, two critics, a historian, climaxed by the psychologist's crediting M with the discovery of "the Bartleby complex." Maurice Friedman's "Bartleby and the Modern Exile" relates the story to Camus's *The Stranger* and Kafka's "The Judgment." A. W. Plumstead's "Bartleby: M's Venture into a New Genre" points out features in the story different from those in the longer fiction. Marjorie Dew's "The Attorney and the Scrivener: Quoth the Raven, 'Nevermore' " concludes that the narrator's realization of his responsibility for Bartleby is existential—he will "nevermore" be the same. In "Bartleby: The Christian Conscience" W. B. Stein sees the story as concerned with the moral relativism or pragmatic Christianity of the nineteenth century. M. L. D'Avanzo's "M's 'Bartleby' and Carlyle" compares the despair of Teufelsdröckh and the paralysis of Bartleby. Of especial value is the annotated bibliography by D. M. Fiene. The volume also contains a facsimile reproduction of the first printing of the story in *Putnam's*.

Bartleby (1969) by Susan Solomont and Ritchie Darling is a brief essay expliciting the story as an allegory of M's literary career.

2. Portions of Books

The number of critical studies of M in the form of substantial portions of books has increased, since his discovery as a major American author, from about half a dozen books annually during the first three decades to a dozen or more during the last two. More significant is the increasing variety of approaches to him represented by these books. They include not only histories of American literature and the American novel in particular, but accounts of American humor, American intellectual history, American mythology, symbolism, tragedy, and nineteenth-century western literature and thought. Most of the literary histories and books which touch on him slightly or conventionally are not noted in the following discussion.

Most of the notices of M in portions of books published during the first decade after Weaver's biography are chiefly of historical interest. Chief among them are H. S. Canby's *Definitions* (1922) and *Classic Americans* (1931), Carl Van Vechten's *Excavations* (1926), Percy Boynton's *More Contemporary Americans* (1927), V. L. Parrington's *MCAT* (1927), V. W. Brooks's *Emerson and Others* (1927), E. M. Forster's *Aspects of the Novel* (1927).

Some of the treatments of M in books published in the 1920's and 1930's are, however, as significant as those entirely devoted to him during this period.

The first of all these treatments, D. H. Lawrence's *Studies in Classic American Literature* (1923), is one of the most probing estimates (if a poetic one) with its declaration that Moby Dick is "the deepest blood-being of the white race . . . hunted by the maniacal fanatacism of our white mental consciousness" and that M himself "was determined Paradise existed. So he was always in Purgatory." Constance Rourke in *American Humor* (1931) was first to point out the important connection of M with the native humorous tradition. In the same year Vega Curl, in *Pasteboard Masks: Fact as Spiritual Symbol in the Novels of Hawthorne and M*, focussed attention on M's chief device and the American writer with whom he had most in common. See also Ivor Winters, *Maule's Curse* (1938).

In 1940 and 1941 appeared three books containing durable chapters on M. R. P. Blackmur's "The Craft of HM: A Putative Statement" in *The Expense of Greatness* (1940) is the chief presentation of the case that M failed to master the technique of the novel, having worked on the putative rather than the dramatic or representational level. R. H. Gabriel in *The Course of American Democratic Thought* (1940) discusses M as a critic of mid-nineteenth-century American ideals, who rejected particularly those of security and progress. A fourth of F. O. Matthiessen's *AmR* (1941) is devoted to M, surveying his literary career in the context of nineteenth-century American literature and politics and attending particularly to structure, language and Shakespearean influences in *MD*.

Chapters on M in two literary histories in the 1940's and 1950's deserve mention. That by Thorp in the *LHUS* (1948) is admirably thorough—in contrast to the few pages in the *CHAL* (1917–21); and that in Chase's *The American Novel and its Tradition* (1957) discusses M as exemplifying the American tradition of the novel as a kind of romance. See also Northrop Frye, *Anatomy of Criticism* (1957).

The 1950's saw several significant studies of M in parts of books. W. H. Auden in *The Enchafèd Flood, or the Romantic Iconography of the Sea* (1950) draws heavily on *MD* in his imaginative discussion of romantic images of the sea (as potential life) and the desert. In his *Symbolism and American Literature* (1953) C. N. Feidelson calls M and Emerson the two poles of the American symbolist movement, M being the more modern because of his complexity. M is also a focal figure in R. W. B. Lewis's *The American Adam* (1955), with its thesis that the major image of the American of the early nineteenth century was "a figure of heroic innocence and vast potentialities, poised at the start of a new history." Perry Miller's *The Raven and the Whale: The War of Words and Wits in the Era of Poe and M* (1956) touches on M as a New Yorker associated with editors Evart and George Duyckinck and Lewis Gaylord Clark. In Harry Levin's *The Power of Blackness: Hawthorne, Poe, M* (1958) M (author of the key phrase in the title) is credited with having first discerned this power in the American experience.

Portions of three books in the 1950's and 1960's discuss M in relation to tragedy: H. A. Myers in *Tragedy: A View of Life* (1956), R. B. Sewall in *The Vision of Tragedy* (1959), and M. R. Stern in "M's Tragic Imagination" in *Patterns of Commitment in American Literature* (1967). All concentrate on *MD*.

Half a dozen books in the 1960's partly dealing with M are of miscellaneous emphasis. M is cited in Leslie Fiedler's *Love and Death in the American Novel* (1960) in justification of the thesis that the American fictionist fails to deal with adult heterosexual love. D. G. Hoffman in *Form and Fable in American Fiction* (1960) deals with fabulous elements in *MD* and *CM*. In *The Limits of Metaphor: A Study of M, Conrad, and Faulkner* (1967) James Guetti analyzes the "languages" of *MD*. The concern of M, among several American novelists, with the relationship between reality and art forms is discussed by Joel Porte in *The Romance in America: Studies in Cooper, Poe, Hawthorne, M, and James* (1969). See also Leo Marx, *The Machine in the Garden* (1964); Loren Baritz, *City on a Hill* (1964).

One book in Italian and two in German in the 1960's contain chapters on M. That in Glauco Cambon's *La lotta con Proteo* (1963) emphasizes the complexities of M's thought and imagination. In *Shakespeare: Seine Welt—Unsere Welt* (1964) H.-J. Lang's essay "M und Shakespeare" proposes broad rather than specific Shakespearean influences. Klaus Lanzinger's *Die Epik im amerikanischen Roman: eine Studie zu James F. Cooper, HM, Frank Norris, und Thomas Wolfe* (1965) takes up *MD* only.

Finally, two books of 1968 consider M and another author. *M & Hawthorne in the Berkshires: A Symposium*, the M Annual for 1966 (see below), incorporates most of the papers read at a conference at Williamstown and Pittsfield, Mass., in September 1966. A brief Prelude is provided by H. P. Vincent, followed by eleven papers (two on Hawthorne only). L. S. Mansfield's "M and Hawthorne in the Berkshires" and Jeanne Howe's "M's Sensitive Years" (referring to his visit as a youth with his uncle in South Pittsfield) are biographical accounts. Morse Peckham, "Hawthorne and M as European Authors," relates them to the tradition of Romanticism. Maurita Willett, "The Letter A, Gules, and the Black Bubble," compares the endings of *The Scarlet Letter* and *MD*. F. D. Miller, "Another Chapter in the History of the Great White Whale," identifies a possible source of *MD*. E. S. Shneidman, "The Deaths of HM,"

points out the high incidence of death in M's fiction (with tables) and its implications about the author. Vincent's " 'And Still They Fall from the Masthead' "
focusses on White Jacket's fall from the yardarm.

Olson/M: A Study in Affinity by Ann Charters is more concerned with
Charles Olson than with M. It gives, however, a valuable account of Olson's
locating books once belonging to M, explicates *Call Me Ishmael*, and summarizes Olson's other writings about M (three reviews of books about him and
a poem).

3. Articles on Individual Works

The number of articles about M has increased during the last half-century
from about a dozen annually in the 1920's and 1930's to 20 in the 1940's to
30 in the 1950's to 40 in the early 1960's and nearly 80 by the end of that
decade. The substance of many has been incorporated in books (notably biographies, editions, books about individual novels, and Hetherington's study
of reviews). Those articles, those making generalized or widely conceded judgments, those considering M in small part, and book reviews are not noted in
the following discussion.[2]

a. *Typee, Omoo. Typee* and *Omoo* (hereafter in this section *T and O*)
have received little attention in articles. Earlier ones concentrate on autobiographical elements. B. C. Jones "American Frontier Humor in M's *T*" (*NYFQ*
59), cites tall tales, exaggeration, and rustic figures of speech. Two touch on
the image of Typee as Eden. Robert Stanton, "*T* and Milton: Paradise Well
Lost" (*MLN* 59), finds echoes of *Paradise Lost* in the description of the boy
and girl first seen in the valley and compares Tommo's entrance there to Satan's
into Eden. Richard Ruland, "M and the Fortunate Fall: Typee as Eden (*NCF*
68), distinguishes author from narrator, M believing that Typee was not a
paradise but an isolated part of the world, which Tommo (spokesman for the
popular reader) had to leave in order to preserve his identity. It is a fictional
chronicle rather than a well-formed novel, asserts Anderson, "M's South Sea
Romance" (*RG* 69). Two articles locate reviews: Tanselle "The First Review
of *T*" (*AL* 63); Richard Walser, "Another Early Review of *T*" (*AL* 65). See also
Hermann Augustin (*SchM* 67).

E. M. Eigner, "The Romantic Unity of *O*" (*PQ* 67), sees the novel unified
by the psychological development of the narrator, an alienated figure only
ostensibly regenerated. That the character of Jermin is based on Poe is suggested by Iola Haverstick, "A Note on Poe and *Pym* in M's *O*" (*PN* 69). R. M.

2. For more consideration of articles before 1956, see the original edition of *8AmA*.

Fletcher, "M's Use of Marquesan" (*AS* 64), dealing chiefly with *T* and *O*, notes that though M transcribed reasonably accurately, he often devised words for comic effect.

b. *Mardi.* *Mardi* (hereafter in this section *Ma*) is the subject of relatively few articles, sources and interpretation being the chief objects of inquiry. R. A. Davison, "M's *Ma* and John Skelton" (*ESQ* 66), discovers a parallel for Yillah's bird in "Philip Sparrow"; R. A. Rees, "M's Alma and The Book of Mormon" (*ESQ* 66), connects M's character with the two in Mormon scripture; and Mildred Travis, "Spenserian Analogues in *Ma* and *CM*" (*ESQ* 68), finds more in *Ma*. Allusions to Hawaiian places and persons are identified by A. G. Day, "Hawaiian Echoes in M's *Ma*" (*MLQ* 57); allusions to contemporary events by Koh Kasegawa, "Political Criticism in M's *Ma*" (*Thought Currents in Eng Lit* [Tokyo] 59). In "M's *Ma*: Bentley's Blunder?" (*PBSA* 68) J. F. Guido explains its failure in England by its appearance there in three volumes, the last two having less favorable reviews and fewer sales than the first. T. R. Ellis, "Another Broadside into *Ma*" (*AL* 69), locates an English burlesque.

Other articles treat plot and theme. Hillway, "Taji's Abdication in HM's *Ma*" (*AL* 44) and "Taji's Quest for Certainty" (*AL* 46), insists that he commits suicide. Nathalia Wright, "The Head and the Heart in M's *Ma*" (*PMLA* 51), proposes that Taji seeks an ideal man, with balanced head and heart. Kenneth Bernard, "M's *Ma* and the Second Loss of Paradise" (*LHR* 65), calls it the story also of the loss of America, originally but no longer a garden. The Samoa-Annatoo relationship is contrasted with that of Taji-Yillah-Hautia by Mildred Travis: "*Ma*: M's Allegory of Love" (*ESQ* 66). Barbara Blansett, " 'From Dark to Dark': *Ma* a Foreshadowing of *Pierre*" (*SoQ* 62), compares receptions, themes, female characters, and mountain imagery. Barbara Meldrum, "The Artist in M's *Ma*" (*SNNT* 69), finds that role as played by Taji and Babbalanja entails impersonality. The opening chapters are said to foreshadow *MD*, argues Klaus Lanzinger in "M's Beschreibung des Meeres in *Ma* im Hinblick auf *MD*" (*NS* 60), and Stuart Levine in "M's 'Voyage Thither,' " (*MQ* 62). According to Philip Graham, "The Riddle of M's *Ma*: A Reinterpretation" (*UTSE* 57), it is an allegory of man's development from prehistoric times.

c. *Redburn.* Like *Typee* and *Omoo*, *Redburn* (hereafter in this section *R*) and *WJ* early elicited articles on their autobiographical aspects. More recent ones about *R* concentrate on the title character. He is thought to mature by Heinz Kosok, " 'A sadder and a wiser boy': HMs *R* als *Novel of Initiation*" (*JA* 65), and "Redburn's Image of Childhood" (*ESQ* 65); but not by T. G. Lish,

"M's R: A Study in Dualism" (ELN 67), who thinks that in rejecting Bolton he fails to achieve brotherhood, and H. B. Franklin, "Redburn's Wicked End" (NCF 65), who blames him for Bolton's death. In opposition to both views, James Schroeter, "R and the Failure of Mythic Criticism" (AL 67), says he rejects aristocratic Bolton and plebeian Jackson, seeking an intermediate position. See also Robert Gale (ForumH 63).

M's view of evil at this time is examined by Gustaaf Van Cromphout, "HM's R considered in the Light of the Elder Henry James's The Nature of Evil" (RLV 63). The probable source of the description of Miguel's death is J. M. Good's The Book of Nature, notes George Perkins in "Death by Spontaneous Combustion in Marryat, M, Dickens, Zola, and Others" (Dickensian 64). Other works used are identified by J. C. Maxwell, "M Allusion to Pope" (AN&Q 64); and by H.-J. Lang, "Ms Dialog mit Captain Ringbolt" (JA 67), the latter referring to John Codman's Sailors' Life and Sailors' Yarns. See also Thorp (AL 38); Max Frank (KBAA 60).

d. White-Jacket. Most recent articles on WJ are about sources. Keith Huntress, "M's Use of a Source for WJ" (AL 45), P. S. Proctor, "A Source for the Flogging Incident in WJ" (AL 58) and "M's Best Authorities' " (NCF 60), and J. D. Seelye, " 'Spontaneous Impress of Truth': M's Jack Chase: A Source, an Analogue, a Conjecture" (NCF 66), identify accounts of naval life. The inspiration for Cuticle's cast is established by C. L. Regan, "M's Horned Woman" (ELN 67), as a sixteenth-century Welsh woman described in a pamphlet and alluded to in plays of the period. See also R. S. Ward (ESQ 61).

Symbolism in the novel was early pointed out by H. P. Vincent, "WJ: An Essay in Interpretation" (NEQ 49). Paul McCarthy in "Symbolic Elements in WJ" (MQ 66) calls the chief ones the Neversink, the sailor, the narrator; and in "The Use of Tom Brown in M's WJ" (ESQ 67) notes the occurrence of the name first for a dead, then for a living sailor, with implications that naval life destroys individuality. Priscilla Zirker, "Evidence of the Slavery Dilemma in WJ" (AQ 66), calls M's attitude ambivalent. WJ and Typee are compared (with emphasis on WJ) by Giovanni Gullace, "M natura umana e civiltà in Typee e in WJ" (RLMC 61). First to correct Matthiesson's misreading of a prominent passage was J. W. Nichol, "M's 'Soiled' Fish of the Sea" (AL 49).

e. Moby-Dick. Most of the early articles on MD concentrate on its meaning and the character of Ahab. H. A. Myers, "Captain Ahab's Discovery: The Tragic Meaning of MD" (NEQ 42), says he discovers the significance of his life in suffering. C. H. Cook, "Ahab's 'Intolerable Allegory' " (BUSE 55), explains his end by his allegorizing of Moby Dick. To Koh Kasegawa, " 'MD':

A Tragedy of Madness" (*Though Currents in Eng Lit* [Tokyo] 57), his madness is that of a political dictator. In "The Enigma of *MD*" (*Jour of Analyt Psych* [London] 58), James Kirsh identifies him as the ego in confrontation with the self (Moby Dick). Ahab errs, according to R. A. Watts, "The 'Seaward Peep': Ahab's Transgression" (*UR* 63), in attempting to explore the Absolute—in nineteenth century terms, the Oversoul. Thomas Woodson, "Ahab's Greatness: Prometheus as Narcissus" (*TLH* 66), calls him a Romantic and a Narcissistic hero in pursuing what he cannot grasp. He is compared to another legendary figure by Janet Dow, "Ahab: the Fisher King" (*ConnR* 69).

More recently Ishmael has received attention as the most important character. For R. M. Farnsworth, "Ishmael to the Royal Masthead" (*UR* 62), the story is Ishmael's, since he understands that attainable felicity resides in human relations rather than in the intellect. His salvation is ascribed by H. C. Brashers, "Ishmael's Tattoos" (*SR* 62), to his achievement of a balanced relation to the universe, through his figurative acquisition of Queequeg's tattoos. D. H. Hirsch, "The Dilemma of the Liberal Intellectual: M's Ishmael" (*TSLL* 63), concludes that Ishmael—and M—fused a Biblical world view with the liberalism of the Enlightenment through fraternal love. To T. W. Weissbuck and Bruce Stillians, "Ishmael the Ironist: The Anti-Salvation Theme in *MD*" (*ESQ* 63), however, he is unredeemed. His ability to see both dark and light is pointed out by Beongcheon Yu, "Ishmael's Equal Eye: The Source of Balance in *MD*" (*ELH* 65). Other explanations of his survival are made by C. F. Strauch, "Ishmael: Time and Personality in *MD*" (*SNNTS* 69), noting that he equates personality with the flux of time; G. H. Singleton, "Ishmael and the Covenant" (*Discourse* 69), suggesting that he was not one of the "covenanted" crew. See also Howard Vincent in *Themes and Directions in American Literature* (1969).

Several critics consider Ahab and Ishmael together. Two of the best comparisons are Alfred Kazin's in his Introduction to the Riverside Edition (1956) and Leon Howard's in *The American Novel* (1965). Both are victims of religious disillusion, according to Lawrance Thompson, "*MD*: One Way to Cut In" (*Carrell* 63), Ahab's expressed in acts, Ishmael's in words. John Halverson, "The Shadow in *MD*" (*AQ* 63), proposes that Ishmael and Ahab encounter Jungian unconscious "shadows" in Queequeg, Pip, and Fedallah, but only Ishmael is thereby saved. Their different ends are explained by S. W. Liebman, "The 'Body and Soul' Metaphor in *MD*" (*ESQ* 68), in that Ahab is associated with the soul only, Ishmael with soul and body. See also R. D. Rust (*ESQ* 63).

Other characters in the novel have been individually considered. Queequeg is the subject of Louis Leiter's "Queequeg's Coffin" (*NCF* 58), emphasizing the identification of Queequeg and Ishmael, and of Hennig Cohen's "M's Tomahawk Pipe: Artifact and Symbol" (*SNNTS* 69), proposing that Queequeg represents the farthest western reach of the American frontier. Perth is called a recreation of Hephaestus by John Satterfield, "Perth: an Organic Digression in *MD*" (*MLN* 59). The sympathetically drawn Bulkington is cited by S. A. Cowan, "In Praise of Self-Reliance: The Role of Bulkington in *MD*" (*AL* 67), as evidence that Emersonianism is not satirized in the novel. Moby Dick is the protagonist to Vincent Buckley, "The White Whale as Hero" (*CR* 66); the symbol of what men are living for to Kenji Noguchi, "An Essay on HM's *MD*: What is Moby Dick?" (*Bul of the Univ of Osaka Prefecture* 61); the evil power of Nature or the Not-me to Koh Kasegawa in "*MD* as a Symbolic Myth" (*SEL* 60); and the effete intellectual to C. M. Brown, "The White Whale" (*PR* 69). See also W. A. Evans (*SLitI* 69); M. P. Sullivan (*NCF* 65).

The multiple meanings of *MD* have often been noted. R. E. Watters, "The Meanings of the White Whale" (*UTQ* 51), points out many objects and subjects given diverse interpretations. John Parke, "Seven MDs" (*NEQ* 55), labels it adventure story, man-nature conflict, moral drama, picture of a neutral cosmos, argument that man must not seek power over nature, tragedy, assertion that evil cannot be eradicated. Five motifs are found by Rudolf Suhnel, "M's *MD*: versuch einer Deutung" (*NS* 56): Ishmael the wanderer, the story of the *Essex*, Polynesia, the ship as the world, the sea. Allen Austin, "The Three-Stranded Allegory of *MD*" (*CE* 65), identifies allegories based on a naturalistic philosophy and satires of Transcendentalism and Christianity. C. C. Walcutt, "The Soundings of *MD*" (*ArQ* 68), discovers six views of the universe: good, controlled by a benevolent god permitting evil, good and evil, evil, chaotic, orderly but godless.

More concentrated interpretations are those of R. V. Osbourn, "The White Whale and the Absolute" (*EIC* 56), taking a philosophical approach; H. C. Horsford, "The Design of the Argument in *MD*" (*MFS* 62), relating the theme to Hume's epistemology; Cándido Pérez Gállego, "*MD* como alegoría política" (*PSA* 67), analyzing it in Hobbesian terms; Thomas Werge, "*MD* and the Calvinist Tradition" (*SNNTS* 69), explaining Ahab's destruction by the theory that fallen man knows nothing except by revelation; M. J. Hoffman, "The Anti-Transcendentalism of *MD*" (*GaR* 69), calling *MD* "an almost totally ironic novel, perhaps a parody." Willam Glasser, "*MD*" (*SR* 69), feels that the action is influenced by fate, free will, and chance. Two early objections to a symbolic interpretation are still of interest: Montgomery Belgion, "Heterodoxy on *MD*?" (*SR* 47); E. E. Stoll, "Symbolism in *MD*" (*JHI* 51). See also

J. L. Aguirre (*Atlantico* 57); Ramiro Páez (*Atenea* 63); Jerome Ellison (*MQ* 67); H. B. Kulkarni (C. D. Narasimhaiah, ed., *Indian Response to American Literature*, 1969).

Many articles concentrate on portions of the novel as keys to its meaning. Four view the *Town-Ho's* story thus: Sherman Paul, "M's 'The Town-Ho's Story'" (*AL* 49), who calls it a portrayal of retributive justice (Radney corresponding to Ahab); Don Geiger, "M's Black God: Contrary Evidence in 'The Town-Ho's Story'" (*AL* 54), who compares Ahab to Steelkilt; Heinz Kosok, "Ishmael's Audience in 'The Town-Ho's Story'" (*N&Q* 67), who finds M commenting on his readers and his book; W. K. Spofford, "M's Ambiguities: A Re-evaluation of 'The Town-Ho's Story,'" (*AL* 69), who sees Steelkilt and Radney as ambiguous. S. W. D. Scott, "Some Implications of the Typhoon Scenes in *MD*" (*AL* 40), compares the movements of the *Pequod* to the conflict between Ahab and Starbuck. J. D. Young, "The Nine Games of the *Pequod*" (*AL* 54), notes that each deals with the problem of communication and its alternatives. In "The Function of the Cetological Chapters in *MD*" (*AL* 59), J. A. Ward argues that they speak metaphorically about all life and the problem of reality. The doubloon is called a symbol of double vision by Russell and Clare Goldfarb, "The Doubloon in *MD*," (*MQ* 61), and interpreted in terms of zodiacal images of balance by J. D. Seelye, "The Golden Navel: The Cabalism of Ahab's Doubloon" (*NCF* 60). S. C. Woodruff, "Stubb's Supper" (*ESQ* 66), calls it an exhibition of the vulturism of creation. Harold Aspiz, "Phrenologizing the Whale" (*NCF* 68), suggests that Ishmael's discourse on the inadequacy of Lavater and Gall to explain it emphasizes the delusive nature of Ahab's quest. Stubb's sermon is closer to M's view than Father Mapple's, according to Sanford Sternlicht, "Sermons in *MD*" (*BSUF* 69).

Several recent articles relate the novel to American history. Harry Slochower, "*MD*: The Myth of Democratic Expectancy" (*AQ* 50), calls it a continuation of and an expression of disillusion with that myth. Willie Weathers, "*MD* and the Nineteenth-Century Scene" (*TSLL* 60), finds echoes of the 1850 Anti-Slavery Convention among others. It is also related to the slavery controversy by C. H. Foster, "Something in Emblems: A Reinterpretation of *MD*" (*NEQ* 61). Philip Gleason, "*MD*: Meditation for Democracy" (*Person* 63), describes Ahab as a prototype of the post-Civil War entrepreneur, his mates and Ishmael as ineffectual opponents. Alan Heimert, "*MD* and American Political Symbolism" (*AQ* 63), identifies the *Pequod* with the Union and the doctrine of Manifest Destiny. That doctrine is also cited by José de Onis, "M y el mundo hispánico" (*CHA* 63), who connects the whiteness of the whale with the Spanish world. See also Drummond (*Sage* 66); M. R. Stern (*ESQ* 69).

Perhaps the largest number of articles are those dealing with sources. Most notable are the Bible and Shakespeare. L. N. Jeffrey provides "A Concordance to the Biblical Allusions in *MD*" (*BB* 56); D. G. Hoffman, "*MD*: Jonah's Whale or Job's?" (*SR* 60), takes a mythical point of view; C. H. Holman, "The Reconciliation of Ishmael: *MD* and the Book of Job" (*SAQ* 58), compares the two reconciliations. Other Biblical echoes are noted in T. C. F. Lowry (*Expl* 58), T. Y. Booth (*NCF* 63), and William Rosenfeld (*TSLL* 66). Edward Stone, "*MD* and Shakespeare, A Remonstrance" (*SQ* 56), finds Shakespearean influence in the earliest version; André le Vot, "Shakespeare et M: Le thème impérial dans *MD*" (*EA* 64), calls that theme (from *Macbeth*) one of human responsibilities; Julian Markels, "King Lear and *MD*: The Cultural Connection" (*MR* 68), sees the play reflecting the breakdown of a culture, the novel an anticipated cultural crisis. See also R. B. Sewall (*CompD* 67); C. D. Eby (*ELN* 67).

Other prominent authors to whom M was indebted include Bayle (Millicent Bell, "Pierre Bayle and *MD*" [*PMLA* 51], is a thorough study); Carlyle (M. L. D'Avanzo, " 'The Cassock' and Carlyle's 'Church-Clothes' " [*ESQ* 68], refers to *Sartor Resartus*; Alexander Welsh, "A M Debt to Carlyle" [*MLN* 58], refers to Chapter 69), Dante (H. H. Schless, "*MD* and Dante: A Critique and Time Scheme" [*BNYPL* 61], thinks the voyage, beginning at Christmas, ends at Easter), Emerson (E. J. Rose, "M, Emerson, and the Sphinx" [*NEQ* 63], compares Ahab's monologue on the whale's head to "The Sphinx"), Goethe (W. W. Betts, "*MD*: M's Faust" [*LHB* 59], finds the characterization of Ahab influenced by that of Faust), Hawthorne (Gerhard Friedrich, "A Note on Quakerism and *MD*: Hawthorne's 'The Gentle Boy' as a Possible Source" [*QH* 65]), Poe (J. J. McAleer, "Poe and Gothic Elements in *MD*" [*ESQ* 62], compares the descriptions of Ahab and the House of Usher; Jack Scherting, "The Bottle and the Coffin: Further Speculation on Poe and *MD*" [*PN* 68], suggests that M read "Ms. Found in a Bottle"). Owen Chase's *Shipwreck of the Whaleship Essex* was reprinted in 1962, with a transcription of M's notes in his copy.

Possible sources for several characters have been pointed out by David Jaffé, "Some Origins of *MD*: New Finds in an Old Source" (*AL* 57); "The Captain who Sat for the Portrait of Ahab" (*BUSE* 60), who finds influences on Queequeg and Ahab in Charles Wilkes' *Narrative of the U. S. Exploring Expedition . . . 1838–1842*; William Powers, "Bulkington as Henry Chatillon" (*WAL* 68), who thinks Bulkington modelled after the guide in Parkman's *Oregon Trail*; M. L. Ross, "Captain Truck and Captain Boomer" (*AL* 65), who notes that M's and Cooper's captains like to make introductions; and

Robert Shulman, "M's Thomas Fuller: An Outline for Starbuck and an Instance of the Creator as Critic" (*MLQ* 62), who refers to Fuller's *Holy and Profane State*.

Other proposed sources include theological works: Andrew Norton's *Evidences of the Genuineness of the Gospels*, according to Thomas Vargish, "Gnostic *Mythos* in *MD*" (*PMLA* 66); John Taylor's *Scripture Doctrine of Original Sin*, according to T. W. Herbert, "Calvinism and Cosmic Evil in *MD*" (*PMLA* 69); works on demonology and witchcraft: Helen Trimpi, "M's Use of Demonology and Witchcraft in MD" (*JHI* 69); contemporary burlesques and farces: R. B. Browne, "Popular Theater in *MD*" (*New Voices in American Studies*, 1966); contemporary fiction: Curtis Dahl, "Moby Dick's Cousin Behemoth" (*AL* 59), referring to Cornelius Mathews' *Behemoth*; C. D. Eby, Jr., "William Starbuck Mayo and HM" (*NEQ* 62), citing Mayo's *Kaloolah*; contemporary periodicals: M. A. Isani, "M and the 'Bloody Battle in Affghanistan' " (*AQ* 68). See also J. C. Maxwell, *N&Q* 67.

Other aspects of *MD* repeatedly studied include its composition, structure, style, point of view, and imagery. The fullest account of the composition is George Stewart's "The Two *MDs*" (*AL* 54), presenting the evidence that it was drastically revised. H. G. Eldridge, " 'Careful Disorder': The Structure of *MD*" (*AL* 67), divides it into six parts, based on the route of the *Pequod*. Dramatic devices are analyzed by Dan Vogel, "The Dramatic Chapters in MD" (*NCF* 58); Glauco Cambon, "Ishmael and the Problem of Formal Discontinuities in *MD*" (*MLN* 61); and T. R. Dale, "M and Aristotle: the Conclusion of *MD* as a Classical Tragedy" (*BUSE* 57). See also M. K. Travis (*ESQ* 67). Marcello Pagnini, "Struttura ideologica e struttura stillistica in *MD*" (*SA* 60), finds literal and symbolic ideologies matched by expository and poetic styles. Whatever is puzzling in the point of view, thinks W. B. Dillingham, "The Narrator of *MD*" (*ES* 68), is attributable to the narrator's state of mind as he recreates the events of his story. Vocabulary is examined by M. D. Clubb, "The Second Personal Pronoun in *MD*" (*AS* 60) ("you" in ordinary address, "thou" otherwise), and Gustav Kirchner, "Amerikanisches in Wortschatz, Wortbildung and Syntax von HMs *MD*," in *Mélanges Fernand Mossé* (1962). The imagery of fire is said by C. C. Walcutt, "The Fire Symbolism in *MD*" (*MLN* 44), to represent Ahab's acceptance of good and evil; by P. W. Miller, "Sun and Fire in M's *MD*" (*NCF* 58), to suggest rejection of a conventional deity. Otis Wheeler, "Humor in *MD*: Two Problems" (*AL* 57), explains inconsistencies by the existence of two manuscripts; Robert Shulman, "The Serious Function of M's Phallic Jones" (*AL* 61), points out that they satirize conventional values. See also Joseph Jones (*UTSE* 45); H. H. Kühnelt (*WBEP* 55). The significance of the *Pequod's* name is noted by L. G. Heller (*AS* 61), K. W. Cameron, *(ESQ* 62), and W. G. Braude (*Expl* 62). See also T. B. O'Daniel (*CLAJ* 58), Sister Mary Ellen (*MFS* 62), Allen Guttmann (*MLQ* 63), and Vito Amoruso *(SA* 67).

The reception of the novel is examined by L. R. Phelps, "*MD* in Germany" (*CL* 58); R. J. Newman, "An Early Berkshire Appraisal of *MD*" (*AQ* 57); and J. F. McDermott, "*The Spirit of the Times* Reviews *MD*" (*NEQ* 57). Glauco Cambon, "Le caccia ermeneutica a *MD*" (*SA* 62), summarizes the chief interpretations.

The influence on or estimate of *MD* by twentieth-century writers is noted by L. S. Roudiez, "Camus and *MD*" (*Sym* 61); D. P. Williams, "Hook and Ahab: Barrie's Strange Satire [in *Peter Pan*] on M" (*PMLA* 65); J. W. Beach, "Hart Crane [in "Voyages"] and *MD*" (*WR* 56); and Hans Bungert, "William Faulkner on *MD*: An Early Letter" (*SA* 63), in which he said *MD* was the novel he would most like to have written.

Two articles discuss the adaptation of the novel to film: M. R. Stern, "The Whale and the Minnow: *MD* and the Movies" (*CE* 56), and Hillway, "Hollywood Hunts the Whale" (*ColQ* 57).

f. *Pierre.* The chief approaches in articles to *Pierre* (hereafter in this section *P*) are interpretative, most taking biographical, psychological, and philosophical approaches. One of the earliest, E. L. G. Watson's "M's *P*" (*NEQ* 30), judges it most favorably as his "greatest book," the account of an altogether psychical experience. The autobiographical elements are emphasized by J. J. Mayoux in " 'P' or la 'saison en enfer' de M" (*LetN* 58); John Logan, in "Psychological Motifs in M's *P*" (*MinnR* 67); J. J. Gross in "The Face of Plinlimmon and the 'Failures' of the Fifties" (*ESQ* 62). To Mary Dichmann, "Absolutism in M's *P*" (*PMLA* 52), it is a statement of philosophical absolutism, to Valentina Poggi, "*P* il 'Kraken' di M" (*SA* 64), it is agnostic existentialism.

The most notable other interpretation is that of William Braswell, who argues that the work is satirical in "The Satirical Temper of M's *P*" (*AL* 36) and "M's Opinion of *P*" (*AL* 51). Pierre's character is analyzed by Hillway, who explains his defeat in moral terms in "Pierre the Fool of Virtue" (*AL* 49). F. C. Watkins, "M's Plotinus Plinlimmon and Pierre," in *Reality and Myth* (1964) finds him explained by the pamphlet; and Nicholas Canaday, "M's Pierre: At War with Social Convention" (*PLL* 69) refers to rebellious Enceladus. An early article, G. C. Homans's "The Dark Angel: The Tragedy of HM" (*NEQ* 32), discusses *Mardi, Moby-Dick*, and *P* as a trilogy, emphasizing the conclusiveness of the third novel. See also Saburo Yamaya (*Jour of Humanities* [Hosei Univ.] 57).

Several sources and literary parallels have been pointed out. They include *The Confessions of Jereboam O. Beauchamp*: G. R. Mower, "The Kentucky Tragedy: A Source for *P*" (*KFR* 68); Byron: J. J. Mogan, "*P* and *Manfred*: M's Study of the Byronic Hero" (*PLL* 65); the Cenci story: R. L. Carothers, "M's 'Cenci': A Portrait of *P*" (*BSUF* 69); Dante: G. Giovannini, "M's *P* and Dante's *Inferno*" (*PMLA* 49); Nathalia Wright, HM's *Inferno*" (*AL* 60); H. H. Schless, "Flaxman, Dante, and M's *P*" (*BNYPL* 60); Rita Collin, "*P*'s Metamorphosis of Dante's *Inferno*" (*AL* 68); Hawthorne: J. L. Kimmey, "Pierre and Robin: M's debt to Hawthorne" (*ESQ* 65), referring to "My Kinsman Major Molineux"; Marjorie McCorquodale, "M's Pierre as Hawthorne" (*UTSE* 54); Poe: Mildred Travis, "The Idea of Poe in *P*" (*ESQ* 68); Shakespeare: E. Yaggy, "Shakespeare and M's *P*" (*BPLQ* 54); Horace Walpole: E. J. Rose, " 'The Queenly Personality': Walpole, M, and Mother" (*L&P* 65), referring to *The Mysterious Mother*. The Hawthorne story is called a source also for *Redburn* by R. A. Davison in "Redburn, Pierre, and Robin: M's Debt to Hawthorne?" (*ESQ* 67). See also C. W. Bush (*JAmS* 67); G. Giovannini (*PMLA* 50); J. C. Mathews (*PMLA* 49); J. C. Maxwell (*N&Q* 65).

Technical aspects are the subject of other studies. Imagery connecting *P* with Buddhism is analyzed by Saburo Yamaya in "The Stone Image of M's *P*" (*SEL* 57); and R. K. Gupta discusses "Pasteboard Masks: A Study of Symbolism in *P*" (Sujit Mukhergee and D. V. K. Raghavacharyulu, eds., *Indian Essays in American Literature*, 1969). Gupta's "M's Use of Non-Novelistic Conventions in *P*" (*ESQ* 67) distinguishes those derived from the epic and the drama. Paul McCarthy, "M's Use of Painting in *P*" (*Discourse* 68), relates it to Pierre's changing sense of reality. The symbolic contrast of the country-city scenes is pointed out by Taizo Tanimoto, "Pierre the Shepherd: The Meaning of Saddle Meadows in M's *P*" (*DLit* 66). James Kissane, "Imagery, Myth, and M's *P*" (*AION-SG* 55), and Elémire Zolla, "Il linguaggio di *P*" (*SA* 57), are more general.

g. *Israel Potter*. *IP* has been only slightly considered in articles. The chief study of its relation to its principal source, Potter's narrative, is R. F. McCutcheon, "The Technique of M's *IP*" (*SAQ* 28). (See also the reprint of Potter, *The Life and Remarkable Adventures of Israel R. Potter*, 1962.) M's use of his London journal is examined in Raymona Hull, "London and M's *IP*" (*ESQ* 67). Others consider its theme: R. M. Farnsworth, "*IP*: Pathetic Comedy" (*BNYPL* 61); J. T. Frederick, "Symbol and Theme in M's *IP*" (*MFS* 62); and

Emilo Cecchi, "Two Notes on M" (*SR* 45); its treatment of American heroes: Kenny Jackson, "*IP*, M's 'Fourth of July Story' " (*CLAJ* 63); its structure and point of view: B. C. Bach, "M's *IP*: A Revelation of its Reputation and Meaning" (*Cithara* 67). A source for the account of the *Serapis-Bon Homme Richard* encounter is identified in a biography of Jones by Jack Russell, "*IP* and 'Song of Myself' " (*AL* 68), who suggests Whitman used *IP* for his account of the same encounter.

   h. *Stories.* Nearly all M's stories have received attention individually in articles. By far the greatest number have been devoted to "Benito Cereno" and "Bartleby the Scrivener" (hereafter "BC" and "B"). The two are compared by W. M. Gibson, "HM's 'B' and 'BC'," in *American Renaissance* (1963).

   The first began to attract attention earlier. A few articles note sources: H. H. Scudder, "M's *BC* and Captain Delano's Voyages" (*PMLA* 28), reprinting the original account, and W. T. Pilkington, "M's *BC*: Source and Technique" (*SSF* 65), referring to it; A. L. Vogelback, "Shakespeare and M's 'BC' " (*MLN* 52); Margaret Jackson, "M's Use of a Real Slave Mutiny in 'BC' " (*CLAJ* 60); G. R. Ridge and S. Davy, "A Bird and a Motto: Source for 'BC' " (*MissQ* 60), referring to "The Rime of the Ancient Mariner"; S L. Gross, "Mungo Park and Ledyard in M's *BC*" (*ELN* 65), referring to an article in *Putnam's.*

Most articles are divided between a moral-metaphysical interpretation (Babo being the embodiment of evil, Delano of unperceptive good will) and a socio-political one (the slaves corresponding chiefly to those in nineteenth-century America). In the first category are Rosalie Feltenstein, "M's 'BC' " (*AL* 47) (also discussing the chief source); S. T. Williams, " 'Follow Your Leader': M's 'BC' " (*VQR* 47), noting Catholic, Spanish, and American motifs; G. A. Cardwell, "M's Gray Story: Symbols and Meaning in 'BC' " (*BuR* 59); Max Putzel, "The Source and the Symbols of M's 'BC' " (*AL* 62); Barry Phillips, " 'The Good Captain': A Reading of 'BC' " (*TSLL* 62); D. D. Galloway, "HM's 'BC': An Anatomy" (*TSLL* 67), the last three emphasizing its ambiguities; R. M. Farnsworth, "Slavery and Innocence in 'BC' " (*ESQ* 66), suggesting that the Negroes represent the dark side of the white race. See also W. B. Stein (*Accent* 55); George Knox (*Person* 59); Robin Magowan (*CE* 62); Mary Rohrberger (*CE* 66).

   Articles with a socio-political approach fall into three main groups. Several see sympathy for the slaves: Joseph Schiffman, "Critical Problems in M's 'BC' " (*MLQ* 50); Warren D'Azevedo, "Revolt on the *San Dominick*" (*Phylon* 56); Allen Guttman, "The Enduring Innocence of Captain Amasa Delano" (*BUSE* 61); John Bernstein, " 'BC' and the Spanish Inquisition" (*NCF* 62), who finds a prediction of an uprising of all dark races; Robert Forrey "HM and the Negro Question" (*Mainstream* 62). A few recognize pro-slavery or ambivalent sentiments: Sidney Kaplan, "HM and the American National Sin: The Meaning of 'BC' " (*JNH* 56, 57); Kingsley Widmer, "The Perplexity of M: *BC*" (*SSF* 68); Margaret Vanderhaar, "A Re-Examination of 'BC' " (*AL* 68), who feels M opposed slavery but saw no end to the racial problem. Nicholas Canaday, "A New Reading of M's *BC*" (Waldo McNeir and L. B. Levy, eds., *Studies in American Literature*, 1960), discusses the relationship of authority and power which is implied. Others concentrate on Delano as a naïve American: E. F. Carlisle, "Captain Amasa Delano: M's American Fool" (*Criticism* 65); W. T. Pilkington, " 'BC' and the American National Character" (*Discourse* 65); Clinton Keeler, "M's Delano: Our Cheerful Axiologist" (*CLAJ* 66), calls him Emersonian. Two European views are also political: E. T. Galván," 'BC' o el mito de Europa" (*CHA* 52), identifies Cereno with Europe; Estuardo Núñez, "HM en El Peru" (*Panorama* 54), calls Delano an international ambassador. Ramiro Páez, "*BC*: La historia del motín del barco negrero en la bahía de Arauco" (*RdPac* 67), surveys metaphysical, sociological and psychological interpretations. The story is compared with Robert Lowell's play by Robert Ilson, " 'BC' from M to Lowell" (*Salmagundi* 67). See also Klaus Ensslen, *Kleine Beiträge zur amerikanischen Literaturgeschichte* (1960); F. W. Patterson (*AN&Q* 64); W. T. Pilkington (*TSLL* 66); R. J. Brophy (*ATQ* 69).

A few articles on "B" deal with sources or origins and technique: J. O. Conarroe, "M's B and Charles Lamb" (*SSF* 68), refers to the *Essays of Elia*; M. L. D'Avanzo, "M's 'B' and John Jacob Astor" (*NEQ* 68); R. L. Gale, "B— M's Father-in-Law" (*AION-SG* 62); Leedice Kissane, "Dangling Constructions in M's 'B' " (*AS* 61), notes they mark the narrator's changing attitude; J. L. Colwell and Gary Spitzer, " 'B' and 'The Raven': Parallels of the Irrational" (*GaR* 69). Most others concentrate on B or the narrator. Some of the earliest associate B with M or the isolated writer: Egbert Oliver, "A Second Look at 'B' " (*CE* 45), with Thoreau; Leo Marx, "M's Parable of the Walls" (*SR* 53) with M; John Gardner, " 'B': Art and Social Commitment" (*PQ* 64) with the artist manqúe; Frances Howard, "The Catalyst of Language: M's 'Symbol' " (*EJ* 68).

Later critics think the narrator more important. In 1962 Marvin Felheim in "Meaning and Structure in 'B' " (*CE*), Kingsley Widmer in "The Negative Affirmation: M's 'B' " (*MFS*), and Mordecai Marcus in "M's B as a Psychological Double," (*CE*), represented him thus. Others agree: Richard Abcarian in "The World of Love and the Spheres of Fright: M's 'B' " (*SSF* 64) sees the narrator accepting B's view of an indifferent universe; H. F. Smith in "M's

Master in Chancery and His Recalcitrant Clerk" (*AQ* 65) has Chancery representing the principle of ideality which B refutes; Norman Springer in "B and the Terror of Limitation" (*PMLA* 65) sees the narrator's perception of an incomprehensible creation as limited; and P. E Firchow in " 'B': Man and Metaphor" (*SSF* 68) finds B a dead letter sent the narrator. In a second analysis, "M's Radical Resistance: The Method and the Meaning of 'B' " (*SSNTS* 69), Widmer says it depicts the failure of Christian-rational America. It is called a story of loneliness, frustration, endurance, and the absurd by Augusto Guidi (*SA* 57); R. D. Spector (*NCF* 61); Frank Davidson (*ESQ* 62); Otto Reinert (Sigmund Skard and H. H. Wasser, eds., *Americana-Norvegica*, 1966); and Ray Browne (D. K. Wilgus, ed., *Folklore International*, 1967). L. B. Levy, "Hawthorne and the Idea of 'B' " (*ESQ* 67), relates it to the Agatha story. W. R. Patrick, "M's 'B' and the Doctrine of Necessity" (*AL* 69), explains B as compelled to will as he does.

Most of the articles on "The Encantadas" (hereafter "En") identify sources: Buford Jones, "Spenser and Shakespeare in 'En,' Sketch VI" (*ESQ* 64), and "M's Buccaneers and Crebillon's Sofa" (*ELN* 64); D. M. Eddy, "M's Response to Beaumont and Fletcher: A New Source for 'En' " (*AL* 68); C. N. Watson, "M's Agatha and Hunilla: A Literary Incarnation" (*ELN* 69); Reidar Ekner, " 'En' and 'BC'—On Sources and Imagination in M" (*Moderne Språk* 66), also touches on the parallels between Agatha and Hunilla. Imagery, themes, and point of view are studied by I. Newberry, " 'En': M's *Inferno*," (*AL* 66); D. S. Howington, "M's 'En': Imagery and Meaning" (*SLitI* 69); and H. D. Pearce, "The Narrator of 'Norfolk Isle and the Chola Widow' " (*SSF* 65). An influence on Conrad is suggested by G. J. Resink, "*Samburan Encantadas*" (*ES* 66).

Sexual symbolism in the second part of "The Paradise of Bachelors and The Tartarus of Maids" (hereafter 'P-T') is noted by E. H. Eby, "HM's 'Tartarus of Maids' " (*MLQ* 40); in both parts by Alvin Sandberg, "Erotic Patterns in 'P-T' " (*L&P* 68); and Beryl Rowland, "M's Bachelors and Maids: Interpretation through Symbol and Metaphor" (*AL* 69), according to both, the narrator being attracted by men, repelled by women. Other interpretations are those of W. R. Thompson, " 'P-T': A Reinterpretation" (*AQ* 57), which contrasts European leisure and American industrialism, and W. B Stein, "M's Eros" (*TSLL* 61), which discusses the degredation of Christian love. A source for the second story is noted by A. F. Beringause, "M and Chrétian de Troyes" (*AN&Q* 63).

"I and My Chimney" (hereafter "IMC") has had a variety of interpretations. It is autobiographical (referring particularly to M's mental examination in 1853) according to Sealts' "M's 'IMC' " (*AL* 41), and "M's Chimney, Re-

examined," in *Themes and Directions in American Literature* (1969); see also
W. G. Crowley (*ESQ* 69). S. C. Woodruff, "M and his Chimney" (*PMLA* 60),
argues that it represents time or history. It is a sexual symbol to D. T. Turner,
"Smoke from M's Chimney" (*CLAJ* 63), and E. H. Chatfield, "Levels of Meaning in M's 'IMC' " (*AI* 62); to W. J. Sowder, "M's 'IMC' " (*MissQ* 63), it is
the Negro in nineteenth-century America; to W B. Stein, "M's Chimney
Chivy" (*ESQ* 64), it is Christian faith.

Other stories have received less attention. "The Piazza" is called by W. B.
Stein, "M's Comedy of Faith" (*ELH* 60), a religious story; by D. T. Turner,
"A View of M's 'Piazza' " (*CLAJ* 63), an account of a transition from Romanticism to realism; by Helmbrecht Breinig, "The Destruction of Fairyland: M's
'Piazza' in the Tradition of the American Imagination" (*ELH* 68), a use of
fairyland as an imaginative realm; by Klaus Poenicke, "A View from the
Piazza: HM and the Legacy of the European Sublime" (*CLS* 67), a testing of
the theory by experience. "The Bell Tower" has been discussed as criticism of
technology by C. A. Fenton, " 'The Bell Tower': M and Technology (*AL* 51);
and H. H. Kühnelt, "The Bell-Tower: HM's Beitrag zur Robotliteratur" (*WBEP*
58). Marvin Fisher sees it as a fearful response to slavery, "M's 'Bell-Tower'; A
Double Thrust" (*AQ* 66); Valeria Verucci's " 'The Bell Tower' di HM" (*SA*
63) is a comprehensive analysis. See also H. B. Franklin in *American Science
Fiction of the Nineteenth Century* (1966).

"Cock-A-Doodle-Doo!" is said to be a satire on Thoreau by Egbert Oliver,
" 'Cock-A-Doodle-Doo!' and the Transcendental Hocus-Pocus" (*NEQ* 48),
and W. B. Stein, "M Roasts Thoreau's Cock" (*MLN* 59); and a reference to
Pauline Christianity, also by Stein, "M's Cock and the Bell of Saint Paul"
(*ESQ* 62); S P. Moss, "Cock-A-Doodle-Doo!' and Some Legends in M Scholar-
ship" (*AL* 68), refutes these views (and the view that M was hostile to Tran-
scendentalism). R. M. Tutt, " 'Jimmy Rose'—M's Displaced Noble" (*ESQ* 63),
calls him an aristocrat; Marvin Fisher, "M's 'Jimmy Rose': Truly Risen?" (*SSF*
66), a representative of Christianity in America. The Lightning-Rod Man is
Satan to E. W. Stockton, "A Commentary on M's 'The Lightning-Rod Man' "
(*PMASAL* 55); a Yankee peddler to Hershel Parker, "M's Salesman Story"
(*SSF* 64). E. O. Oliver, "HM's Lightning Rod Man," (*Philadelphia Forum,*
June 56), proposes he was drawn from Rev. John Todd, minister of the First
Church (Congregational) of Pittsfield, Mass.

"The Apple-Tree-Table" is connected with Thoreau's account of the episode
in Edward Stone, "M, Thoreau, and 'The Apple-Tree Table' " (*AL* 54); called
a story about a possible afterlife by M. O. Magaw, "Apolyptic Imagery in M's

"The Apple-Tree Table' " (*MQ* 67). W. R. Thompson, "M's 'The Fiddler': A Story in Dissolution" (*TSLL* 61), thinks the key imagery is death. R. D. Lynde, "M's Success in 'The Happy Failure': A Story of the River Hudson" (*CLAJ* 69), explicates it autobiographically and thematically.

Several stories are considered together by Reidar Ekner, " 'En' and 'BC' —On Sources and Imagination in M" (*Moderna Språk* 66); and Paul Deane, "HM: Four Views of American Commercial Society" (*RLV* 68), which points out criticism of it in "Jimmy Rose," and "The Fiddler."

As for the stories as a group, C. G. Hoffman, "The Shorter Fiction of HM" (*SAQ* 53), is an early high appraisal. Augusto Guidi, "Di alcuni racconti di M" (*AION-SG* 66), concentrating on four, also finds them artistically successful. Prevailing themes are discussed by Patricia Lacy, "The Agatha Theme in M's Stories" (*UTSE* 56); and Judith Slater, "The Domestic Adventurer in M's Tales" (*AL* 65). Leon Howard, "The Mystery of M's Short Stories" (Klaus Lanzinger, ed., *Americana-Austriaca*, 1966), suggests that they reflect his mental, literary, and sexual frustrations. See also B. C. Bach (*SLitI* 69).

i. *The Confidence-Man.* Articles on *CM* did not begin to appear until the 1940's. From the beginning sources and origins have attracted attention. J. J. Gross, "M's *CM*: The Problem of Source and Meaning" (*NM* 59), who thinks it depicts a Christfigure issuing an unreceived message, proposes as a source Joseph Glanvill's *Vanity of Dogmatizing*. The chief European literary connection is discussed by E. H. Rosenberry, "M's Ship of Fools" (*PMLA* 60). Pascal Reeves, " 'The Deaf Mute' Confidence Man: M's Imposter in Action" (*MLN* 60), records that in 1850 a professed deaf mute calling himself HM visited a North Carolinian having two deaf mute sons. Other American analogues are suggested by Paul Smith, "*CM* and the Literary World of New York" (*NCF* 61), citing opinions of Emerson expressed by the Duyckincks; H.-J. Lang, "Ein Ärgerteufel bei Hawthorne und M: Quellenunter-suchung zu *CM*" (*JA* 67), referring to "The Seven Vagabonds"; Johannes Dietrich, "The Original Confidence Man" (*AQ* 69), reporting the arrest of one in New York in 1849. Other influences are noted by J. H. Hartman, "*Volpone* as a Possible Source for M's *CM*," (*SUS* 65); F. E. Brouwer, "M's *CM* as Ship of Philosophers" (*SHR* 69), identifying several guises of the Confidence Man as Shaftesbury, Berkley, Butler, Schelling, and Paley.

Other articles discuss characters. The title character is defended by Philip Drew, "Appearance and Reality in M's *CM*" (*ELH* 64) (his actions are blameless); Ernest Tuveson, "The Creed of the Confidence-Man" (*ELH* 66) (though his optimism is delusive, men need it); Paul Brodtkorb, "*CM*: The Con-Man as Hero" (*SNNTS* 69) (since hypocrisy is widespread, the best attitude is a serenity like the Cosmopolitan's). He is compared to Moby Dick by M. O. Magaw, "*CM* and Christian Deity: M's Imagery of Ambiguity" (Rima Reck, ed., *Explorations of Literature*, 1966). To Lawrence Grauman, "Suggestions on the Future of *CM*" (*PLL* 65), he is an avatar of the Devil. Other Devil relationships are recognized by Parker, "The Metaphysics of Indian Hating" (*NCF* 63), who calls Moredock a Devil-hating Christian; and Paul McCarthy, "The 'Soldier of Fortune' in M's *CM*" (*ESQ* 63), who finds him a disciple of the Devil. See also Joseph Baim (*ATQ* 69); B. C. Bach (*Cithara* 69); Warner Berthoff (Hennig Cohen, ed., *Landmarks of American Writing*, 1969).

The structure has been repeatedly analyzed. It is said to be based on incomplete reversals: J. G. Cawelti, "Some Notes on the Structure of *CM*" (*AL* 57); repetitive activity: Edward Mitchell, "From Action to Essence: Some Notes on the Structure of M's *CM*" (*AL* 57); alternation of thesis and antithesis: Walter Dubler, "Theme and Structure in M's *CM*" (*AL* 61); and inconsistencies of life: D. R. Swanson, "The Structure of *CM*" (*CEA* 68). Merlin Bowen, "Tactics of Indirection in M's *CM*" (*SNNTS* 69), says they conceal the picture of an amoral God. Also touching on structure is Carolyn Karcher, "The Story of Charlemont: A Dramatization of M's Concepts of Fiction in *CM*: *His Masquerade*" (*NCF* 66).

Other articles are miscellaneous: Guido Botto, "L'ultimo romanzo di M" (*SA* 57), general and favorable; R. H. Orth, "An Early Review of *CM*" (*ESQ* 67); L. F. Seltzer, "Camus's Absurd and the World of M's *CM*" (*PMLA* 67). D. N. Summer, "The American West in M's *Mardi* and *CM*" (*RS* 68), emphasizes *CM*, believes that M moved from optimism to pessimism. J. D. Seelye, "Ungraspable Phantom: Reflections of Hawthorne in *Pierre* and *CM*" (*SNNTS* 69), also emphasizes *CM*.

j. *Poetry.* M's poetry has received attention only recently. The chief treatment is R. P. Warren's "M the Poet" (*KR* 46), and "M's Poems" (*SoR* 67), a longer, penetrating analysis, praising the anecdotal-dramatic poems most. Less comprehensive is R. H. Fogle, "M's Poetry" (*TSE* 62). Laurence Barrett, "The Differences in M's Poetry" (*PMLA* 55), discovers that the poetic symbolism differs from that in the fiction. W. B. Dillingham, " 'Neither Believer nor Infidel': Themes of M's Poetry" (*Person* 65), lists innate depravity, endless searching, loneliness, the folly of dogma. Classical values and subjects are considered by Jane Donahue, "M's Classicism: Law and Order in his Poetry" (*PLL* 69).

Battle-Pieces and Aspects of the War has been studied most often. General discussions are given by R H. Fogle, "M and the Civil War" (*TSE* 59), listing motifs in content, and others, including G. B. Montague (*UTSE* 56); H. E. Hand (*Jour of Human Relations* 63); Jack Lindeman (*ModA* 65, 66); R. O. Shaw (*LH* 66); and R. E. Hitt (*SLitI* 69). W. J. Kimball, "The M of *Battle-Pieces*: A Kindred Spirit" (*MQ* 69), suggests that M's attitudes to war and nationalism are pertinent today. Sources are identified by Hennig Cohen, "M and Webster's *The White Devil*" (*ESQ* 63); F. L Day, "M and Sherman March to the Sea" (*AN&Q* 64), a *Harper's* article; and L. B. Levy, "Hawthorne, M, and the Monitor" (*AL* 65), an *Atl* article by Hawthorne. Both poets are rated less than great by D. H. Hibler, "*Drum-Taps* and *Battle-Pieces*: M and Whitman on the Civil War" (*Person* 69).

Clarel has been studied for content and form by N. A. Ault, "The Sea Imagery in HM's *Clarel*" (*RSSCW* 59); R. H. Fogle, "M's *Clarel*: Doubt and Belief" (*TSE* 60); Elémire Zolla, "La struttura e le fonti di *Clarel*" (*SA* 64), emphasizing ideological structure. See also Claudio Gorlier (*Apprado* 67).

Timoleon is examined by Darrel Abel, " 'Laurel Twined with Thorn': the Theme of M's *Timoleon*" (*Person* 60), calling it isolation; and Robert Shulman, "M's 'Timoleon': From Plutarch to the Early Stages of *BB*" (*CL* 67), studying that source. According to Douglas Robillard, "Theme and Structure in M's *John Marr and Other Sailors*" (*ELN* 69), the theme is the artist's place in society, the structure dependent on the theme. Certain poems in this volume represent a search for psychic balance, according to W. B. Stein, "M's Poetry: Its Symbols of Individuation" (*L&P* 57). Both volumes and unpublished poems are considered by R. H Fogle, "The Themes of M's Later Poetry" (*TSE* 61), naming, among others, nostalgia, death, history, an indifferent nature. W. B. Stein, "Time, History and Religion: A Glimpse of M's Late Poetry" (*ArQ* 66), and L. H. Martin, "M and Christianity: The Late Poetry" (*MSE* 69), consider it hostile to Christianity.

"After the Pleasure Party," "The Admiral of the White," and "The Haglets" are discussed by W. B. Stein (*LHB* 60; *ELH* 58, 62). "Fragments from a Lost Gnostic Poem of the 12th Century" is the focus of J. B. Moore's "Ahab and Bartleby: Energy and Indolence" (*SSF* 64).

Late poetry and prose are considered in two articles by Sealts: "The Ghost of Major M" (*NEQ* 57), proposes M's uncle as a model for John Marr, Jimmy Rose, and Jack Gentian; "M's Burgundy Club Sketches" (*HLB* 68), thoroughly studies them.

k. *Billy Budd.* The aspect of *BB* (also BB) which has longest attracted attention in articles is Vere's insistence on Budd's execution, commonly discussed in terms of M's religious or philosophical attitude. One of the earliest, E. L. G

Watson, "M's Testament of Acceptance" (*NEQ* 33), first presents the case justifying Vere and concluding that M's attitude changed from rebellion in midlife to acceptance at the end. Others who generally agree include Charles Weir, "Malice Reconciled: A Note on M's *BB*" (*UTQ* 44); R. H. Fogle, "*BB*—Acceptance or Irony?" (*TSE* 58), and "*BB*: The Order of the Fall" (*NCF* 60), calling the reconciliation that of classical tragedy; and G. Giovannini, "The Hanging Scene in M's *BB*" (*MLN* 55), and J. S. Reist, Jr., "Surd Evil and Suffering Love" (*Universitas* 64), both emphasizing religious implications. L. T. Lemon, "*BB*: The Plot Against the Story" (*SSF* 64), feels the increasing emphasis on Vere shows M's sympathy for him. Wendell Glick, "Expediency and Absolute Morality in *BB*" (*PMLA* 53), and C. A. Reich, "The Tragedy of Justice in *BB*" (*YR* 67), argue that Vere is unable to save BB legally. To R. A. Duerkson, "The Deep Quandary in *BB*" (*NEQ* 68), it is society which is condemned. J. W. Rathbun, "*BB* and the Limits of Perception" (*NCF* 65), finds only the conclusion ironic. The pro-Vere view is basically adopted by E. H. Rosenberry, "The Problem of *BB*" (*PMLA* 65), but he proposes to reconcile differing views by recognizing an Aristotelian irony. See also Hidoo Okamoto (*SELit* 59); David Ketterer (*JAS* 69).

The first major indictment of Vere and argument that M's attitude was still rebellious is Joseph Schiffman, "M's Final State, Irony: A Re-examination of *BB* Criticism" (*AL* 50). Others who generally agree include Leonard Caspar, "The Case Against Captain Vere" (*Perspective* 52); H. M. Campbell, "The Hanging Scene in M's *BB*: A Reply to Mr. Giovannini" (*MLN* 55); Phil Withim, "*BB*: Testament of Resistance" (*MLQ* 59); Charles Mitchell, "M and the Spurious Truth of Legalism" (*CentR* 67), who refers to other works and calls Budd and Claggart aspects of Vere. Vere is blamed for aristocratic sympathies by R. B. Browne, "*BB*: Gospel of Democracy" (*NCF* 63) (who says he expresses Burkean sentiments at the trial); and Alice Chandler, "The Name Symbolism of Captain Vere" (*NCF* 67) (who notes its pejorative connotations in nineteenth-century fiction); and for prudential motives by Evelyn Schroth, "M's Judgment on Captain Vere" (*MQ* 69). See also Bernard Suits (*NCF* 63).

A third point of view is presented by Kenneth Ledbetter, "The Ambiguity of *BB*" (*TSLL* 62), and Paul Brodtkorb, "The Definitive *BB*: 'But aren't it all sham?'" (*PMLA* 67); the disunity of the work, which was never finished, causes divergence among critics. For a condemnation of every aspect of it, see Kingsley Widmer (*Novel* 68).

The character of Vere is further analyzed by others Two take up the reference to Montaigne: W. H. Kilbourne, "Montaigne and Captain Vere" (*AL* 62), emphasizes Montaigne's allegiance to the state; Robert Shulman, "Montaigne and the Technique and Tragedy of M's *BB*" (*CL* 64), emphasizes ironic differences between the two men. C. B. Ives, "*BB* and the Articles of War" (*AL* 62), points out that they did not dictate BB's execution and suggests that Vere's decision was self-punishment for his repression of the side of his nature represented by BB. His humanity is emphasized by J. C. Sherwood, "Vere as Collingwood: A Key to *BB*" (*AL* 64), which notes that both Nelson and Collingwood are admired in the story.

BB is given a Freudian interpretation by Robert Rogers, "The 'Ineludible Gripe' of *BB*" (*L&P* 64), who says his stammer betrays hostility toward King-God-parents. To Walter Sutton, "M and the Great God BB" (*PrS* 60), his name reflects a Buddhistic renunciation. His Biblical connections are explored by H. E. Hudson, "BB: Adam or Christ?" (*CraneR* 65). BB is called Rousseaustic, Claggart Hobbesian by J. B. Noone, Jr., "*BB*: Two Concepts of Nature" (*AL* 57).

The Dansker is variously interpreted. W. B. Stein, "The Motif of the Wise Old Man in *BB*" (*WHR* 60), declares both him and Vere guilty of sin against humanity. Hiromi Hofuji, "Another Aspect of *BB*" (*KAL* 67), emphasizes the non-Christian element, finds M unsympathetic toward him. To Cary Stokes, "The Dansker, M's Manifesto on Survival" (*EJ* 68), he is M's mouthpiece.

According to A. F. Gaskins, "Symbolic Nature of Claggart's Name" (*AN&Q* 67), it is derived from *clag*, meaning a sticky mass or stain or to stick or stick to.

Many articles deal with sources or origins. N. H. Pearson, "*BB*: 'The King's Yarn' " (*AQ* 51), emphasizes backgrounds (in M's and other works). W. J. Kimball, "Charles Sumner's Contribution to Chapter XVIII of *BB*" (*SAB* 67), refers to an article about the *Somers* mutiny in the *NAR*; see also Newton Arvin (*AL* 48). Other proposed sources include Jerrold: B. R. McElderry, Jr., "Three Earlier Treatments of the *BB* Theme" (*AL* 55), naming two plays; Richard and Tira Gollin, "Justice in an Earlier Treatment of the *BB* Theme" (*AL* 57); Godwin: R. A. Duerksen, "*Caleb Williams, Political Justice,* and *BB*" (*AL* 66), points out an incident of a young English farmer arraigned for murder; Marryat: N. F. Doubleday, "Jack Easy and BB" (*ELN* 64); Marvell: Michael Millgate, "M and Marvell: A Note on *BB*" (*ES* 68), explains implications in "Upon Appleton House"; Milton: R. L. Perry, "*BB*: M's *Paradise Lost*" (*MQ* 69); Schopenhauer: Olive Fite, "BB, Claggart, and Schopenhauer" (*NCF* 68), that is, Schopenhauer's exposition of the will to live; Vigny: P. W. London, "The Military Necessity: *BB* and Vigny (*CL* 62), refers to *Servitude et grandeur militaires*. Anne McNamara, "M's *BB*" (*Expl* 62), calls attention to classical allusions. Alice Chandler, "Captain Vere and the 'Tragedies of the Palace' " (*MFS* 67), identifies the reference to Peter the Great killing his son. See also K. W. Cameron, (*ESQ* 56); H.-J. Lang, in *Festschrift für Walther Fischer* (Heidelberg, 1959); George Monteiro (*ESQ* 63); R. L. Perry (*MQ* 69).

Various technical aspects have been examined. According to G. R. Wilson, "*BB* and M's Use of Dramatic Technique" (*SSF* 67), he refrained from exploiting the dramatic possibilities in order to increase an ambiguous effect. Joan Hall, "The Historical Chapters in *BB*" (*UR* 63), finds they help account for Vere's behavior. To R. W. Willett, "Nelson and Vere: Hero and Victim in *BB*, *Sailor*" (*PMLA* 67), the one is above, the other defeated by society. BB and Vere dominate certain parts, points out Paul McCarthy, "Character and Structure in *BB*" (*Discourse* 66). The imagery is given a comparative analysis by Vern Wagner, "*BB* as Moby Dick: an Alternate Reading," in *Studies in Honor of John Wilcox* (1958); and Sister Mary Ellen, "Parallels in Contrast: A Study of M's Imagery in *MD* and *BB*" (*SSF* 65). B. L. Reid, "Old M's Fable" (*MR* 68), thinks the stylization makes for a tone of fable, the characters being types. Vincent Freimarck, "Mainmast and Crucifix in *BB*" (*MLN* 57), notes that executions were customarily carried out from the foreyard, the implications of BB's from the mainmast being ironic. See also Leonard Nathanson (*Expl* 65).

The story is discussed in relation to other works by K. F. Knight, "M's Variations of the Theme of Failure: 'Bartleby' and *BB*" (*ArlQ* 69); and Robert Shattuck, "Two Inside Narratives: *BB* and *L'Étranger*" (*TSLL* 62). It is compared with the Coxe-Chapman dramatization by Arnold Goldsmith, "The 'Discovery Scene' in *BB*" (*MD* 61); and with Britten's opera by J. P. Renvoisé, "*BB*: Opéra de Benjamin Britten" (*EA* 65).

l. *Miscellaneous*. Perhaps the most important group of miscellaneous articles concerns M's reading. It included the ancients: William Braswell, "M's Use of Seneca" (*AL* 40); R. W. B. Lewis, "M on Homer" (*AL* 50); Sealts, "M's Neoplatonic Originals" (*MLN* 52); later philosophers and moralists: J. T. Frederick, "M's Early Acquaintance with Bayle" (*AL* 68); Aretta Stevens, "The Edition of Montaigne Read by M" (*PBSA* 68); Ruth Krift, " 'When Big Hearts Strike Together' " (*PLL* 69), refers to Sir Thomas Browne; European poets: Edward Fiess, "Byron's Dark Blue Ocean and M's Rolling Sea" (*ELN* 66); B. F. Head, "Camões and M" (*RCam* 64); J. C. Matthews, "M's Reading of Dante" (*FurmS* 58); his contemporaries: William Braswell, "M as a Critic of Emerson" (*AL* 37); W. E. Bezanson, "M's Reading of Arnold's Poetry" (*PMLA* 54); and R. F. Lucid, "The Influence of *Two Years Before the Mast* on HM" (*AL* 59). See also Hayford (*ELH* 44); J. D. Hart (*AL* 37). Miscellaneous works are identified by Cohen, "M's Copy of Thomas Duer Broughton's 'Popular Poetry of the Hindoos' " (*PBSA* 61); Sealts, "M and the Shakers," (*PBSUV* 49); Hillway, "Two Books in Young M's Library" (*BNYPL* 67). His reading of scientific works is reported by Elizabeth Foster, "M and Geology" (*AL* 45), and Hillway (*SAQ* 49, *AL* 49, *MLN* 50, *MLQ* 51).

Another important group of articles discusses M's technique as a novelist. Leon Howard's "M's Struggle with the Angel" (*MLQ* 40) is an illuminating general analysis. Nathalia Wright, "Form as Function in M" (*PMLA* 52), calls it organic. M. R. Stern, "Some Techniques of M's Perception" (*PMLA* 58), names repetition, contrast, multiple view, circular reflexion. Allen Hayman, "The Real and the Original: HM's Theory of Prose Fiction" (*MFS* 62), examines also his use of sources. Agnes Cannon, "M's Use of Sea Ballads and Songs" (*WF* 64), finds they contribute principally to realism and characterization. Symbolic images are pointed out by Richard Bridgman, "M's Roses" (*TSLL* 66), from *MD* to "Weeds and Wildings"; to Vicki Litman, "The Cottage and the Temple: M's Symbolic Use of Architecture" (*AQ* 69), the cottage signifies earthly possessions, the temple artistic perfection; and Arthur Sale, "The Glass Ship: A Recurrent Image in M" (*MLQ* 56), cites such enclosures as the Typee Valley, White Jacket's jacket, and Queequeg's coffin. J. W. Nichol, "M and the Midwest" (*PMLA* 51), traces his use of western scenes. Devices borrowed from drama are noted by N. B. Fagin, "HM and the Interior Monologue" (*AL* 35), and Fred Schroeder, " 'Enter Ahab, then All': Theatrical Elements in M's Fiction" (*DR* 66), discusses *MD*, "BC," and *BB*. Joan Hall, "M's Use of Interpolations" (*UR* 66), shows that the interpolations emphasize the main narrative line. See also H. S. Donow (*MLQ* 64).

M's language has received several illuminating analyses. J. M. Purcell, "M's Contributions to English" (*PMLA* 41), lists 180 words used in unauthoritative ways. C. M. Babcock studies M's vocabulary (*WF* 51, 52; *SFQ* 52, *Word Study* 53, *AS* 54). Though short, Leonard Lutwack's "M's Struggle with Style: the Plain, the Ornate, the Reflective" (*ForumH* 62) is valuable. Cohen, "Wordplay on Personal Names in the Writings of HM" (*TSL* 63), proves wordplay significant.

M's themes have attracted attention from the beginning. Among those repeatedly discussed are isolation: R. W. Watters, "M's 'Isolatoes' " (*PMLA* 45); Koh Kasegawa, "M's Image of Solitude," (*Ronshu* [Japan] 60); sociality: R. E. Watters, "M's 'Sociality' " (*AL* 45); Sealts, "M's 'Geniality' " (Max Schulz, ed., *Essays in American and English Literature Presented to Bruce Robert McElderry, Jr.*, 1967); existentialism: J. J. Boies, "Existential Nihilism and HM"

(*TWA* 61); Saada Ishag, "HM as an Existentialist: An Analysis of *Typee*, *Mardi*, *MD*, and *CM*" (*ESRS* 65); J. V. Hagopian, "M's L'homme revolté" (*ESQ* 65); B. C. Anderson, "The M-Kierkegaard Syndrome" (*Rendezvous* 69). Hillway, "HM's Major Themes" (Klaus Lanzinger, ed., *Americana-Austriaca*, 1966), lists reality *vs.* truth, man's professions *vs.* his acts, man's inability to control destiny, the need for a moral ideal. Others are identified by Elémire Zolla, "M y al abandono del zodíaco" (*PSA* 62); an endless search; J. A. Ward, "M and Failure" (*ESQ* 63); Sacvan Bercovitch, "M's Search for National Identity: Son and Father in *Redburn*, *Pierre*, and *BB*" (*CLAS* 67); Barbara Meldrum, "M on War" (*RS* 69), proposing his anti-war sentiment persisted but his hope for its realization diminished. M's treatment of the Negro is examined by C. I. Glicksberg, "M and the Negro Problem" (*Phylon* 50); Robert Forrey, "HM and the Negro Question" (*Mainstream* 62); and Eleanor Simpson, "M and the Negro: From *Typee* to 'BC' " (*AL* 69); his criticism of the church by J. J. Boies, "M's Quarrel with Anglicanism" (*ESQ* 63), and N. B. Houston, "Silent Apostles: M's Animus Against the Clergy" (*RS* 67). According to F. W. Turner, "M's Post-Meridian Fiction" (*MASJ* 69), "The Encantadas," "BC," *IP* and *CM*, explain the poor reception of *MD* and *Pierre* in terms of contemporary American culture. See also Theodore Gross (*ColQ* 69); G. A. Knox (*Ren* 46); J. C. Oates (*TSLL* 62); Luther Mansfield (S. J. Krause, ed., *Essays in Determinism in American Literature*, 1964); R. B. West (*PrS* 56).

Other articles relate M to other authors. Among his contemporaries Emerson and Hawthorne are most important, as suggested by Perry Miller, "M and Transcendentalism" (*VQR* 53); H.H. Hoeltje, "Hawthorne, M, and "Blackness' " (*AL* 65); S. L. Gross, "Hawthorne *versus* M" (*BuR* 67); and J. E. Miller, "Hawthorne and M: No! in Thunder" (*Quests Surd and Absurd*, 1969). He is also compared to Clemens: D. D. Anderson (*MTJ* 62); R. J. Callan (*Ren* 65); Camus: L. S. Roudiez (*FR* 58); Harry Tucker (*PMLA* 65); for rebuttal, see Tanselle (*PMLA* 66); Conrad: J. D. Green (*MFS* 62); Darwin: H. B. Franklin (*CentR* 67); Benjamin Lease (*Person* 68); Sade: Jean Greiner (*NRF* 67); Tennessee Williams: J. R. Hurt (*MD* 61).

M's reputation is the subject of H. H. Kühnelt, "The Reception of HM's Works in Germany and Austria," (*Innsbrucker Beiträge zur Kulturwissenschaft*, 1956); see also L. R. Phelps (*Sym* 59); Michael Zimmerman, "HM in the 1920's" (*BB* 66), with tables; J. T. Flanagan, "*The Spirit of the Times* Reviews M" (*JEGP* 65). Boris Gillenson, "M in Russia (for the 150th anniversary of his birth)" (*Soviet Lit* 69). A comprehensive analysis of his relation to his readers is made by William Charvat, "M and the Common Reader" (*SB* 59); see also

Robert Beum (*DR* 65). Conrad's aversion is noted by Frank MacShane, "Conrad on M" (*AL* 58), and Unamuno's admiration by M. G. Blanco, "Unamuno y el novelista norteamericano M" (*Insula* 65).

Criticism of peripheral writing is made by Luther Mansfield, "M's Comic Articles on Zachary Taylor" (*AL* 38); T. B. O'Daniel, "HM as a Writer of Journals" (*CLAJ* 61); and Augusto Guidi, "M e la statuaria classica" (*SR* 69), who refers chiefly to the 1857 journal. Textual corrections and problems are recognized by Hayford, "M's Usable or Visible Truth" (*MLN* 59), and Parker, "Species of 'Soiled Fish' " (*CEAAN* 68). The M supplement of *ESQ* (1962) contains 12 articles on methods of teaching his works. Cesare Pavese in *La letteratura americana e altri saggi*, (1953), and Agostino Lombardo (*SA* 57), are good general surveys. Pavese has been translated by Edwin Fussell as *American Literature: Essays and Opinions* (1970).

V. DISSERTATIONS AND PERIODICALS

Some 130 dissertations have been written on M (a few including him with other writers), from one in 1933 to a dozen a year in the late 1960's. Twenty-three have been published as books, and others (notably that by J. D. Seelye, 1966) are soon to be published. Relatively few are on individual works (though *Clarel* is the subject of half a dozen). There are five on *MD*, three on *Pierre*, two on *BB*, and three on *Mardi, MD*, and *Pierre*.

The aspects of M's writing which have been most often studied are style (including symbolism, imagery, point of view, structure), theme or thought (respecting such subjects as evil, existentialism, the individual in relation to society, nihilism, politics, progress, slavery, theology). Other students have examined his theories and use of art, contributions to magazines, reputation, interest in science, relation to Transcendentalism. Two consider the M revival and one compares the chief biographies.

Many of the early dissertations on portions of M's life contain valuable information which has been largely incorporated in books. Some of the most useful because the most factual deal with his reading: in ancient philosophy (Sealts, 1942) Shakespeare (Rosen, 1962; Long, 1966), Byron (Fuess, 1951), Carlyle (Greuberg, 1964; Braun, 1968). Two recent ones deserve special attention because of their documentary nature: Walker Cowen, "M's Marginalia" (1965), a complete transcription; and R. R. Ryan, "*Weeds and Wildings Chiefly With a Rose or Two* by HM: Reading Text and Genetic Text, Edited from the Manuscripts, with Introduction and Notes" (1967), much of which will be incorporated in the Northwestern-Newberry Edition.

The M Society News Letter, I–XV (1945–60), was issued under the auspices of the Society. It contains bibliographical and critical notes and a variety of valuable information relating to M and his writings.

Two M Annuals have been published, in the Kent Studies in English series in 1965 and 1966 (see above, *Bartleby the Scrivener* and *M & Hawthorne in the Berkshires*).

WALT WHITMAN[1]

Roger Asselineau

I. BIBLIOGRAPHIES

The first extensive bibliography of Walt Whitman (hereafter W or WW) was prepared by O. L. Triggs for Vol. X of the *Complete Writings of WW* (1902). It is still valuable for its listing of the earliest writing about W. The fullest bibliography was for a long time the one assembled by Emory Holloway and H. S. Saunders for Vol. II of the *CHAL* (1918). Supplementing the *CHAL* bibliography is G. W. Allen's *Twenty-Five Years of WW Bibliography, 1918–1942* (*BB Pamphlets*, No. 38, 1943). The same author's indispensable *WW Handbook* (1946) carries this bibliographical inventory two years further and discusses in detail all the important biographical and critical studies of book length and supplies briefer comment on other studies. It is complemented in its turn by the check-list compiled by E. A. Allen for the period 1945–1960 and published as an appendix to G. W. Allen's *WW as Man, Poet, and Legend* (1961), and by J. T. F. Tanner's *WW: A Supplementary Bibliography, 1961–1967* (1968). Every issue of the *WWR* contains a quarterly check-list of recent books, articles and reviews about W by William White, who will in time publish a full-scale bibliography of the writings of W, with an exhaustive check-list of biographical and critical works about him. He has already published "The WW Fellowship: An Account of Its Organization and a Check-List of Its Papers" (*PBSA* 57), "WW's Short Stories: Some Comments and a Bibliography" (*PBSA* 58) and "WW's Journalism: A Bibliography" (*WWR* 68).

The most extensive bibliography is that contained in *LHUS*, edited by R. E. Spiller *et al.* (1948) and its *Supplement*, edited by R. M. Ludwig (1959). Briefer selected and annotated bibliographies appear in Floyd Stovall, editor, *WW, Representative Selections* (AWS, 1934, 1961) and in the chapter compiled by

---

1. Professor Asselineau and the editor wish to acknowledge gratefully their debt to Willard Thorp, who wrote this chapter for the original edition of *8AmA*. Anyone who collates this edition with Professor Thorp's 1956 essay will find that this updated version is a genuine collaboration between Professors Asselineau and Thorp.

S. A. Corwin in *Hawthorne to Hemingway: An Annotated Bibliography from 1945 to 1963 About Nine American Authors*, edited by R. H. Woodward (1964). Collectors and librarians interested in the typographical minutiae of W first editions will find useful information in Frank Shay, *The Bibliography of WW* (1920) and in Carolyn Wells and A. F. Goldsmith, *A Concise Bibliography of the Works of WW, with a Supplement of Fifty Books About W* (1922; rev. ed., 1930, 1968).

A list of recordings and musical adaptations of *Leaves of Grass* (hereafter *LofG*) will be found in R. D. Faner, "W on Records" (*WWR* 62) and R. H. Woodward, "W on Records: Addenda" (*WWR* 62).

A complete bibliography of W bibliographies can be consulted: James F. T. Tanner, "WW Bibliographies: A Chronological Listing, 1902–1964" (*BB* 68).

II. MANUSCRIPT AND BOOK COLLECTIONS

After much selling and buying in the auction rooms the W manuscripts have finally been gathered in ten or so great collections, the majority of which are in public or university libraries. Almost all of this vast accumulation of materials derives ultimately from the literary property which W, by his will, gave to his three executors: Harned, Traubel, and Bucke.

The Library of Congress is the richest repository of W materials, which are distributed in some 29 individual collections (Thomas B. Harned, Carolyn Wells Houghton, Charles E. Feinberg, etc.). More than 1,000 items are listed in *WW: A Catalog Based Upon the Collections of the Library of Congress* (1955, 1967). Feinberg, one of the greatest W collectors, supplied an illuminating essay for this catalogue: "Notes on W Collections and Collectors." Part of his own collection, which has recently been acquired by the Library of Congress, is inventoried in F. E. Brewer, *WW: A Selection of the Manuscripts, Books, and Association Items Gathered by Charles E. Feinberg* (1955). The W Collection presented to Duke University in 1942 by Dr. and Mrs. J. C. Trent is fully described in E. F. Frey's *Catalogue of the W Collection in the Duke University Library* (1945). In the Lion Collection and the Henry W. and Albert A. Berg Collection the New York Public Library also possesses W materials of great value. The former collection has been described in detail by Paul Kabakian *et al.* in *WW: The Oscar Lion Collection* (1953) and some information about the latter can be found in L. M. Stark and J. D. Gordan, *WW's "LofG": A Centenary Exhibition from the Lion Collection and the Berg Collection of the New York Public Library* (1955). The W. D. Bayley Collection in the Library of Ohio Wesleyan University has been described by E. F. Amy (*Ohio Wesleyan Mag* 55) and the

Edward Naumburg, Jr., collection in the same library by its former owner in "A Collector Looks at W" (*PULC* 41). The Van Sinderen Collection of more than 600 items was acquired by Yale in 1940. (See S. T. Williams, "The Adrian Van Sinderen Collection of WW", *YULG* 41). The libraries of Brown University and the University of Pennsylvania possess important collections. The holdings of the former have been partly inventoried in *A List of Manuscripts, Books, Portraits, Broadsides, and Memorabilia . . . from the W Collection of Mrs. Frank Julian Sprague* (1939) and in "The W Collection" (*Univ of Penn Bul* 47). The materials at Brown have been described by C. B. Willard, "The Saunders Collection of Whitmania in the Brown University Library" (*BBr* 56). There exists no full description of the Clifton Waller Barrett W Collection now in the Library of the University of Virginia. It is only partly surveyed in Fredson Bowers's *W's Manuscripts* (1955), the *ABC* (56), and Herbert Cahoon's *Brief Account of the Clifton Waller Barrett Library* (1960). There is no description either of the important private collection of T. E. Hanley of Bradford, Pennsylvania, and of the late William S. Kennedy Collection now in the Rollins College Library. Information about smaller but quite interesting collections can be found in Dorothy Brown and Philip Durham, "WW Materials in the Huntington Library" (*HLQ* 55), Joseph Jones, "New Acquisitions" (*LCUT* 58), W. S. Yenawina, "The Hier WW Collection" (*Syracuse Univ Lib Assoc Bul* 60), G. K. Brown, "Modern Literary Manuscripts in the Morgan Library" (*PMLA* 52), and Archibald Sparke, *Collection of Whitmania in the Reference Library, Bolton* [England] (1931). A small collection of W manuscripts unexpectedly discovered in California and now kept in the library of the University of California at Berkeley is described in R. V. Grant, "The Livezey-W Manuscripts" (*WW Birthplace Bul* 61).

One sale catalogue should be mentioned: *Manuscripts, Autograph Letters, First Editions, and Portraits of WW* (1936), because the items in the R. M. Bucke Collection which it describes are now dispersed in several libraries.

III. EDITIONS

1. The Text.

Textual problems loom large in W scholarship because of the special nature of *LofG* and the haphazard manner in which W's prose works were published.

LofG is indeed a unique book of verse. It was the object of W's constant care throughout his poetical career from 1855 to his death in 1892. In the course of 37 years he brought out nine different editions. Each edition not only contained new poems, but the old ones had been corrected, cut, and enriched; sometimes both titles and punctuation had been changed and the arrangement of poems completely upset. So *LofG* is not one, but nine different books each with its own distinctive form and flavor, and the critic or student who wishes to know W's poetry thoroughly must not rest satisfied with the final 1892 edition even though W tried to impose it as the only "authorized" version. He must examine all the successive editions.

The easiest way of doing this is by using original editions. But they are not always available and some of them are even quite rare. Fortunately there are four excellent facsimile editions of the 1855 edition: the first one with an introduction by T. B. Mosher (1919), another with an introduction by C. J. Furness (1939), a third one reproducing both the 1855 *LofG* and some of the early reviews (1966), and the last one, a paper-back, with an introduction by Richard Bridgman (1968). Besides, Malcolm Cowley has reprinted the text of the 1855 edition (1959) with an introduction in which he claims that "in the first edition everything belongs together and everything helps to exhibit W at his best, W at his freshest and boldest in language." The text of the second edition has never been reprinted, but there exists a facsimile edition of the 1860 *LofG* with an introduction by R. H. Pearce (1961) who, contrary to Cowley, thinks that the third edition is W's greatest book, because the first two editions were mere diaries, whereas this one is an autobiography in the same sense as *Walden* and *Moby-Dick*. The growth of *LofG* from the second to the third edition has been studied with admirable thoroughness by Fredson Bowers in *W's Manuscripts: "LofG" 1860* (1955). Arthur Golden has analyzed with equal minuteness in a companion volume to a facsimile edition of *WW's Blue Book* (1968) the changes made by the poet in the copy of the 1860 edition which he kept in his desk in the Indian Bureau and which caused his dismissal by Secretary of the Interior James Harlan in 1865. The original text of *Drum-Taps* also has been reproduced in a facsimile edition with an introduction by F. D. Miller (1959) as well as *Memoranda During the War* and *Death of Abraham Lincoln* with an introduction by R. P. Basler (1962).

Some critics have studied W's rough drafts or early versions of specific poems. Emory Holloway has published one of the Ur-*Leaves* under the title of "Pictures" (*SWR* 25; sep. pub., 1927). H. W. Blodgett has published the text of a notebook containing rough drafts of the second edition, notably of "Sun-Down Poem" (later entitled "Crossing Brooklyn Ferry"): "Toward the Second Edition of *LofG*: An Unpublished W Notebook, 1855–56" (*WWR* 56; book form, 1959). *A Child's Reminiscence*, edited by T. O. Mabbott and R. G. Silver (1930) gives the first version of "Out of the Cradle" as published in the New York *Saturday Press* in 1859. An early version of "Hush'd be the Camps To-

Day" is printed in O. S. Coad's "A WW Manuscript" (*JRUL* 38). Manuscripts from the Barrett Collection are published and described in two articles by Fredson Bowers: "W's Manuscripts for the Original 'Calamus' Poems" (*SB* 53) and "The Manuscripts of WW's 'A Carol of Harvest for 1867' " (*MP* 54). Bowers also presented in *MP* (53) a diplomatic reprint of "The Manuscript of W's 'Passage to India.' "

The most convenient tool for studying the growth of *LofG*, however, would be a variorum edition. The literary executors, when they issued the *Complete Writings* (1902) realized this and on their invitation O. L. Triggs prepared for the third volume of this edition "Variorum Readings of *LofG*" which was reprinted with some revisions by Emory Holloway in his "Inclusive Edition," first published in 1924, but constantly reprinted since. Unfortunately the list of variorum readings compiled by Triggs was not complete or entirely accurate and contained only a small sampling of manuscript versions. It was a rather primitive and inadequate instrument. Scholars interested in *LofG* were very much in the same position as the architects of the Grand Academy of Lagado, who built houses from top to bottom, since they had to build their critical interpretations in the air and could not ground them on well-established texts and a full array of variant readings. This sorry situation will come to an end shortly after this essay appears, for a complete *Variorum Edition of LofG* in four volumes under the joint editorship of Harold Blodgett and Sculley Bradley, with the cooperation of Arthur Golden, is due to be issued in the fall of 1972. The poems will be arranged chronologically. It will give the 1881–1892 text, but will record all variants from both printed and unprinted sources.

The same editors already have published the "Comprehensive Reader's Edition" of *LofG* (1965, 1968) which gives the authentic text of the 1892 edition without any variants. Footnotes for each poem summarize the history of the text, clarify foreign or archaic expressions and identify unfamiliar allusions. Besides the 1892 *LofG*, the book contains passages excluded from *LofG* by W in the course of his revisions, uncollected and even unpublished poems, uncollected manuscript fragments, and all the prose prefaces and postfaces W wrote for *LofG*. The 1968 edition, which has a handier format than the 1965 one and is superior to it because a number of errors have been corrected, will undoubtedly supplant all previous editions of *LofG*.

In the absence of a variorum edition the growth of *LofG* through its successive editions was studied empirically in Allen's *WW Handbook* (1946), Frederick Schyberg's *WW* (1933; trans. 1951), and Roger Asselineau's *L'Evolution de WW* (1954; trans. 60–62). These books will be examined more closely in the section of this essay devoted to criticism.

In his lifetime W published only a small portion of his prose works in book form, the most complete collection being his *Complete Prose Works* (1892), but he was a much more voluminous author than his contemporaries thought. From his youth to his old age he constantly wrote articles, diaries, notebooks, work books, etc. for newspapers, magazines, and for himself; and he never destroyed anything; he even kept rough drafts or duplicates of even the most casual letters he wrote. So, when he died, his three literary executors had a considerable hoard to divide and considered it their duty to publish as much of this material as they could. R. M. Bucke published and edited under the title of *Calamus* the poet's letters to his young friend Peter Doyle (1897), *The Wound Dresser: A Series of Letters Written from the Hospitals in Washington during the War of Rebellion* (1898), and *Notes and Fragments* (1899). Harned, for his part, edited *Letters Written by WW to His Mother from 1866 to 1872* (1902). And in 1902 the three literary executors together issued *The Complete Writings* in 10 volumes which included, in addition to the works which W had published in his lifetime and the works previously published by Bucke and Harned, three memoirs by Harned ("WW and Oratory," "WW and Physique," "WW and His Second Boston Publishers"), an essay by Triggs on "The Growth of *LofG*," and a bibliography compiled by Triggs.

After 1902 the editing of W's uncollected writings went on. W. S. Kennedy edited *WW's Diary in Canada* (1904) and Horace Traubel W's notes on language under the title of *An American Primer* (1904, 1970). Scholars (and amateurs) diligently dug up editorials or sketches until then buried in newspaper files. Thus in 1920 Cleveland Rodgers and John Black edited *The Gathering of the Forces* in two volumes in which they collected W's contributions to the *Brooklyn Daily Eagle* in 1846 and 1847. Emory Holloway in *The Uncollected Poetry and Prose of WW* (2 vols., 1921, 1932) rescued from oblivion "a vast batch" of magazine publications which had not been included in the *Complete Prose* and a selection from his "countless newspaper stories, book reviews, editorials, criticisms of art, music, drama, etc." Holloway printed in particular for the first time extracts from W's notebooks, which are now (or were until some of them disappeared) in the Library of Congress. The value of this work is further enhanced by two long biographical and critical introductions and by a detailed subject-index.

When a journalist, W also tried his hand—not very successfully—at fiction. Five of his stories were exhumed and published by T. O. Mabbott: *The Half-Breed and Other Stories* (1927). His temperance novel, *Franklin Evans, or the Inebriate*, was republished separately in 1929 with an introduction by Holloway and again in 1967 as a paperback with an introduction by Jean Downey. As

Holloway points out, it is "crude foreshadowing of W's remarkable poetic auto-biography, to come thirteen years later."

The intrinsic value of the unpublished manuscripts collected by C. J. Furness in *WW's Workshop* (1928, 1964) is further increased by the illuminating critical notes supplied by the editor to clarify W's intentions and bring out his spiritual message. Under the title of *Faint Clews and Indirections* (1949) Clarence Gohdes and R. G. Silver have published a selection from the W papers in the Trent Collection. Of particular interest are W's notes on Rousseau and the *Nibelungenlied* and some early drafts of "Song of Myself."

When Holloway issued his *Uncollected Poetry and Prose of WW*, he had only limited access to the files of the Brooklyn *Daily Times*, for which W wrote editorials from 1857 to 1859. In 1932 with the collaboration of Vernolian Schwarz he presented an ample selection from these editorials: *I Sit and Look Out*. With the assistance of Ralph Adimari, he provided in 1936 still another selection of W's newspaper articles: *New York Dissected*. These pieces were written in 1855 and 1856 for *Life Illustrated*. The editors also reprinted a number of English and American reviews of the first edition of *LofG*, several of which were not known before. Finally in 1950 J. J. Rubin and C. A. Brown published *WW of the "New York Aurora."* The *Aurora* was the first New York daily of which W, then only twenty-one, was the editor. Though he was in charge of the *Aurora* for only two months in 1842, Rubin and Brown uncovered more than 180 articles and two poems written for it by W. An interesting travel piece which he wrote for the Philadelphia *Times* in 1879 is reprinted in Herbert Bergman's "WW on New Jersey" (*PNJHS* 48). Letters which he contributed to the *National Era* under the pseudonym of "Paumanok" were uncovered by R. G. Silver: "WW in 1850: Three Uncollected Articles" (*AL* 48). *WW's New York: From Manhattan to Montauk*, edited by H. M. Christman, (1963), is merely an unacknowledged reprint of the "Brooklyniana" which were first collected by Holloway in *Uncollected Poetry and Prose of WW* (1921).

Even some of W's minor prose pieces have been studied textually and/or critically by scholars. In 1947 Sculley Bradley and J. A. Stevenson published *WW's Backward Glances*, which reproduced in facsimile the manuscript of "A Backward Glance O'er Travel'd Roads" and throws an interesting light on W's methods of composition and his purpose in writing *LofG*. E. F. Grier edited, with a critical introduction, the text of *The Eighteenth Presidency* (1956), a political speech which W wrote for the presidential campaign of 1856, set up in type and circulated in proof, but never published. Furness and Catel discovered it independently. The former published it in his *WW Workshop* (1928) and the latter in pamphlet form (1928). Asselineau presents notes made by W while reading Taine's *History of English Literature* in "Un inédit de WW: Taine's *History of English Literature*" (*EA* 57) and "A Footnote to W's Essay on Taine" (*WWR* 58). He has analyzed the significance of these notes in "A Poet's Dilemma: WW's Attitude to Literary History and Literary Criticism" (*Literary History and Literary Criticism*, edited by Leon Edel, 1965).

This great wealth of publications unfortunately appeared in a very anarchistic manner without any plan or method. The quarry of W's prose was exploited unsystematically. Some sections of it were even left untouched. Not only were there regrettable omissions, but the results were quite uneven, each editor having his own textual policy and sometimes no policy at all. So it became increasingly clear that a new edition of the complete works was needed. This, as Allen has pointed out in "Editing the Writings of WW" (*A&S* 62–63), was a million-dollar project. Fortunately he convinced the New York University Press to carry it out. He assumed the general editorship himself together with Sculley Bradley and secured the collaboration of the leading W scholars. Thanks to their joint efforts the first volumes of *The Collected Writings of WW* began to appear in 1961. This title was preferred to the more pretentious one of *The Complete Writings*, because no edition can be absolutely complete, especially in the case of a writer like W whose papers and letters have been scattered to the four winds.

The complete series will comprise at least 19 volumes, eight of which have already been published. The *Comprehensive Reader's Edition* and the four volumes to come of the *Variorum Edition of "LofG"* have just been described. The five volumes of the *Correspondence* will be discussed in the next paragraph of this essay. Besides these, three volumes have appeared: *The Early Poems and the Fiction*, edited by T. L. Brasher, and *Prose Works 1892* (2 vols.), edited by Floyd Stovall. The three of them were issued almost simultaneously in 1963–64. *The Early Poems and the Fiction* include all the early poems prior to *LofG* which Holloway had collected in his *Uncollected Poetry and Prose*, the stories long out of print collected by T. O. Mabbott in *The Half-Breed and Other Stories*, and *Franklin Evans*. The poems and tales are arranged in chronological order within their categories. The texts and their variants have been transcribed from photographic or photostatic reproductions of the pieces as they appeared originally in either magazines or newspapers, so that this edition provides for the first time a complete and accurate text of W's fiction and early poetry. It throws light on his development during the 1840's and early 1850's before Walter Whitman was suddenly metamorphosed for eternity into the W we know. In *Prose Works 1892* Stovall has reprinted the text of W's last edition of his *Prose*

Works with no change except the correction of obvious printer's errors, but in the textual notes and in the appendix he has recorded every variant reading of every earlier printed text and even occasionally some important manuscript readings. Besides, Vol. II includes seven pieces which W omitted from his *Complete Prose Works*, notably "A Backward Glance O'er Travel'd Roads" and other prefaces.

The publication of *WW's Correspondence* presented serious problems and was especially needed since no complete edition of his letters had ever been attempted—though a number of them had been printed in two volumes of the *Complete Writings*, in the five volumes of *With WW in Camden*, in Charles Glicksberg's *WW and the Civil War*, and in *Faint Clews and Indirections*. There was also an excellent selection of letters in Holloway's *WW: Complete Poetry and Selected Prose and Letters* (1938), which printed many of these letters for the first time. Also, in 1949, Oscar Cargill edited Bucke's *The Wound Dresser* (1898), which consists in large part of W's letters to his mother during the Civil War, and T. B. Harned brought together in 1918 *The Letters of Anne Gilchrist and WW*. See also Grace Gilchrist, "Chats with WW" (*TBM* 1898). In 1936 A. F. Goldsmith issued *Letters Written by WW to His Mother, 1866–1872* with an introductory note by R. G. Silver, and in 1951 Horst Frenz edited *W and Rolleston: A Correspondence*. Batches of new W letters turned up frequently in the journals, but many still remained unpublished, and, as the published ones were scattered in the most inconvenient manner, the W scholar found himself greatly handicapped by the lack of a complete, coherent, and easily accessible documentation. To remedy this the general editors of *The Collected Writings* entrusted E. H. Miller with the task of publishing *WW's Correspondence*. Miller already had published in 1957, as a preliminary step, *WW's Correspondence: A Check-List* in order "to establish the location of all known letters and to smoke out letters unknown at that time." As a result some 300 new letters emerged from their hiding places, and the five volumes of *WW's Correspondence* (instead of the four originally planned) contain almost 2,800 letters. The task of collecting and editing all these materials was all the more slow and difficult, as new letters kept cropping up until the last volume was printed. So the publication of the *Correspondence* took nearly ten years. Vol. I, covering the years 1842–67, and Vol. II, the years 1868–75, both appeared in 1961; Vol. III for 1876–85 followed in 1964; Vol. IV for 1886–89 and Vol. V for 1890–92 were issued simultaneously in 1969. Not only was the text of the letters very carefully established, but the editor corrected erroneous dates or suggested plausible dates in difficult cases, identified recipients, and illuminated all historical or biographical allusions in remarkably precise footnotes. Moreover, whenever necessary, variants were given and showed how laborious the apparent spontaneity of W's epistolary style sometimes was.

The next volumes of *The Collected Writings* to appear will be *Notebooks, Diaries, and Prose Fragments* in two volumes, edited by Edward Grier and William White; *Journalistic Writings* in two volumes edited by Herbert Bergman and William White; and a *Bibliography* to be prepared by William White.

The publication of the Collected Writings will undoubtedly stimulate W scholarship and enable critics to carry their analyses further by providing them with a broader and firmer basis than ever was at the disposal of their predecessors.

2. Editions: Selected and Annotated

Since 1886, when *Poems of WW* was issued in England in the *Canterbury Poets Series*, many excellent editions of W's works have been printed for the use of students and the general reader. Only a small number of these volumes can be noted here. Floyd Stovall's *WW: Representative Selections* (1934; rev. ed., 1961) contains an introduction, an up-to-date selected bibliography and notes. Holloway's English edition of *LofG* (1947 and constantly repr.) is especially useful for its footnotes. The W volume in the Viking Portable Library, edited by Mark Van Doren (1945), offers selections from *LofG* and *Specimen Days* and prints the whole of *Democratic Vistas*. Cowley's *The Complete Poetry and Prose of WW* (2 vols., 1948, 1954), contains a provocative introduction which first appeared in four issues of the *NR* (46–47). A special feature of the Inner Sanctum Edition of *The Poetry and Prose of WW*, edited by Louis Untermeyer (1949), is its anthology of critical commentaries about W. A well-edited selection is Blodgett's *The Best of W* (1953) with an introduction and notes. *WW's Poems*, edited by Allen and C. T. Davis (1955, 1959), is the first volume of selections which provides ample introductions and precise notes to each of the poems chosen. There is also a long introduction on the nature of W's poetry. Another novelty: the 1855 poems are reprinted in their orginal version. *WW: Poet of American Democracy*, edited by Samuel Sillen (1955), is somewhat politically biased. *WW: Complete Poetry and Selected Prose*, edited by J. E. Miller, Jr. (1959), contains a long introduction and presents an interesting new feature: a "glossary of difficult terms." *LofG: Selections from a Great Poetic Work*, edited by Francis Griffith (1969), has a lively introduction and brief commentaries on the poems.

In England there has appeared a very competent selection, *WW: Selected Poems and Prose*, edited by A. N. Jeffares (1966), with a well-informed introduction and an up-to-date critical bibliography. In Eastern Germany, *WW: Poetry and Prose*, edited by the Czech Americanist Abe Čapek (1958), is an original sampling, especially of W's prose, but it tends to overemphasize the Bard of Democracy. In Japan W. T. Moore has published *W's Poems* (1956) ("Song of Myself" and "By Blue Ontario's Shore") with useful footnotes especially for foreign students and *"LofG" with Prose Essences* (1966), i.e. with prose summaries and notes. In 1968 Hans Reisiger's translation of *LofG, Grashalme*, was reprinted with an interesting postface by H.-J. Lang and similarly, in the following year, Kornei Chukovsky's Russian translation of *LofG* was reissued with important new critical comments by the two translators.

WW's Civil War, edited by the poet Walter Lowenfels (1960), is an anthology of published and unpublished texts by W on the Civil War. *The Poet and the President*, edited by William Coyle (1962), is an anthology of W's Lincoln poems and of critical comments on them. *Whitman, the Poet*, edited by J. C. Broderick (1962), is also an anthology of *LofG* and of critical essays about W.

The best anthologies of American Literature contain interesting introduction to W, notably by Allen in H. A. Pochmann and Allen, *Masters of American Literature* (1949, 1969); Sculley Bradley in Bradley, Beattie, and Long, *The American Tradition in American Literature* (1956); R. W. B Lewis in Perry Miller's *Major Writers of America* (1962), Asselineau in Charles Anderson's *American Literary Masters* (1965).

IV. BIOGRAPHY

Since W himself said of *LofG*: "who touches this, touches a man," it is vital to know something about the man, if one is to understand the book. His "life and recitative," these "jocund twain," as he called them, are very closely connected. So in his case biography is indispensable and the first critics of *LofG* were biographers. But they were faced with a formidable task, for despite all the lyrical exuberance of his poetry, W was in fact "secretive as an old hen" and left whole chunks of his life in the dark. On one point (his illegitimate children) he even deliberately lied. The singer of "the body electric" was particularly evasive about his sexual life.

The first account of W, a 46-page pamphlet by the fiery William D. O'Connor, *The Good Gray Poet: A Vindication* (1866; repr. in Bucke's *WW*, 1883) is, as the very title shows, a defense on the occasion of the poet's dismissal from his clerkship in the Department of the Interior rather than a biography proper. It contains the earliest versions of some of the episodes of the W legend and gives a first-hand description of the poet as he looked at that time. That W wrote part of O'Connor's pamphlet is asserted by Nathan Resnick in *WW and the Authorship of "The Good Gray Poet"* (1948), but this view is challenged by W. G. Milne in "W. D. O'Connor and the Authorship of *The Good Gray Poet"* (*AL* 53). It is likely that O'Connor did write the pamphlet himself, but W must have inspired it. Anyway with John Burroughs's *Notes on WW as Poet and Person* (1867) begins for good W's lifelong effort to present his autobiography through the words of others. He wrote parts of the book and used his editorial pencil on the rest. Convincing evidence of this is presented by H. P. Hier, Jr., in "The End of a Literary Mystery" (*AM* 24). The second edition (1871) contains "Supplementary Notes" consisting mostly of extracts from letters and newspaper accounts used by Burroughs to explain the genesis and peculiarities of *LofG*.

In 1883 Dr. Richard M. Bucke, a Canadian alienist, wrote the first comprehensive biography. Here again the poet supplied much of the materials, as is proved beyond a doubt by *W on W: The Maggin Manuscript of R. M. Bucke's "WW"*, edited by E. H. Miller (1969), and Harold Jaffe, "Bucke's 'WW': A Collaboration" (*WWR* 69). W was so much pleased with this idealized official portrait that he hoped no other study of his life would ever supplant it. In 1888 he asked Bucke "to let it stand as it is."

One of W's English admirers, J. A. Symonds, a student of Greek and Renaissance culture, published the first lucid and independent book on the poet: *WW: A Study* (1893, 1967, 1970). The biographical portion is derivative, but Symonds was the first critic to raise three important questions to which biographers thereafter would have to give attention. In the first place he deprecated the tone of eulogy which prevailed in the W circle in America and called for an objective evaluation of the poet—which he in some measure achieved in his study. He also tackled the important question raised by W's verse: was W the true bard of Democracy? And last but not least he was the first biographer to look deeply into the import of the poems about sex. To satisfy himself on the question of W's sex life he wrote to the poet a frank letter of inquiry to which he received the now famous reply: "Though unmarried I have had six children —two are dead—one living Southern grandchild, fine boy, writes to me occasionally—circumstances (connected with their fortune and benefit) have separated me from intimate relations."

The death of W inspired his literary executors to prepare a memorial volume, *In Re WW* (1893), which they intended to be regarded "in the light of the 'Annex' foreseen by WW" to Dr. Bucke's biography. This collection of 26 items, besides "Poems and Minor Pieces," is a strange pot-pourri: tributes by such devoted admirers as Symonds, Bucke, Burroughs, O'Connor, W. S. Kennedy, Robert Ingersoll, and Harned; translations from articles about W originally published in Germany, France, and Denmark; a gruesome report of the autopsy by Dr. Daniel Longaker. But the book contains some interesting things, in particular Traubel's "Notes from Conversations with George W. Whitman" and the accounts of W's funeral and of the last W birthday dinner in 1891.

In 1896 two friends of W published intimate accounts of their contacts with him: W. S. Kennedy, *Reminiscences of WW*, and Thomas Donaldson, *WW, The Man*. Though he admired W, Kennedy wrote more objectively of him than the other members of the Camden circle. Chiefly valuable are records of conversations with W and with friends who had known the poet. Donaldson's book adds much new information, particularly about the means by which W supported himself and was in part supported by his friends in his old age. In the same year, 1896, Burroughs published his second book on W, *W: A Study*. As the title indicates, it is more a work of criticism than of biography. (The biographical section occupies less than a third of the book.) The full story of the friendship of these two men is told in Clara Barrus's *W and Burroughs Comrades* (1931, 1968).

In 1905 the first scholarly biography was published: H. B. Binns's *Life of WW*. Binns was an Englishman, but he came to America in order to acquaint himself thoroughly with the places where W had lived. He cleared up many of the vague and contradictory statements made by early biographers and tried to date precisely the episodes of W's life. But Binns's error was his fanciful story of the "lady of the South" who "became the mother of [W's] child, perhaps in after years, of his children." This gratuitous invention was an attempt to reconcile the "evidence" about W's early sex life with the tenor of "Children of Adam."

Bliss Perry's *WW: His Life and Work*, which appeared the next year (1906; rev. 1908; repr. 1969), likewise seeks for the real facts. Where he lacked information Perry frankly says so instead of embroidering like Binns. Some of the value of his biography derives from materials put at Perry's disposal by John Burroughs, who had given up his plan of writing a complete life of W. Perry's work was rightly greeted by the reviewers as "calm" and "discriminating." It is one of the most lucid books about the poet.

In the main Edward Carpenter's *Days with WW, with Some Notes on his Life and Works* (1906) belongs with the work of the W idolaters. He even imitated W's free verse in *Towards Democracy* (1883). But Carpenter saw more deeply into W's nature than the other idolaters and thus concluded his chapter on "WW's Children"—with considerable boldness for 1906: "It is clear that throughout his life his intimacies with men were close and ardent; and it seems possible that these, in the later period, to some extent, supplied the deficiency on the other side." Carpenter saw that there were contradictions in W's life and work, contradictions which may have produced "a great tragic element in his nature." He supplemented this with *Some Friends of WW: A Study in Sex Psychology* (1906).

In 1906 there also appeared the first installment of Horace Traubel's *With WW in Camden*, which, as the work now stands in five volumes, constitutes one of the most curious episodes in the history of biographical writing. During the years 1888–92, Traubel visited W almost daily in Mickle Street at Camden. He listened reverently to W's rambling recollections, took notes unobtrusively, and received the letters and other documents which W dug out of the pile on the floor. W knew well enough that Traubel was planning to be his Boswell, for he charged him to "speak for me when I am dead." Traubel kept his promise—rather voluminously. The first volume of the series is 473 pages long; each of the others runs to over 500 pages. The second volume appeared in 1908, the third in 1914. (All were reprinted in 1961.) The fourth and fifth were published posthumously by Sculley Bradley in 1953 (repr. 1959) and 1964. If the rest of the manuscript is ever published, it will bring the story to the death of W. Though unorganized, this interminable biography has great value for the student of W. It is an inexhaustible repository of information and a fascinating record of W's keen judgments about politics and literature.

The first full length biography of W in French was Léon Bazalgette's *WW: L'homme et son oeuvre* (Paris, 1908), a bowdlerized translation of which appeared in 1920. This enthusiastic study is a throwback to the worshipful manner of Bucke and enlarges upon the New Orleans romance invented by Binns.

When the Macmillan Company of New York brought out its "American Extension" of the English Men of Letters Series, it included in 1909 a biography of W by G. R. Carpenter (repr. 1967). The poet was in respectable company with Emerson, Whittier, Prescott, and Bryant. Carpenter's neatly organized biography adds no new facts, but it explores with some success the impulses which brought *LofG* to birth. Seventeen years later (1926) W's biography appeared in the same series, as issued by the London house of Macmillan. The author, John Bailey, tried to sum up the case for W now that the hagiographers had departed.

Thirteen years of minute research went into the production of Emory Holloway's *W: An Interpretation in Narrative* (1926, 1969). When it appeared it was by all odds the most scholarly life of W, but Holloway is something less than candid in discussing the poet's sex life, and he clung to the New Orleans love affair. Besides, his book appeared when footnotes were unfashionable. There are none in his biography. However, his scholarship is sound and his citations in the text can be trusted. Holloway was a firm believer in W's heterosexuality and to prove his point undertook to find the traces of the illegitimate children of whose existence the poet had boasted in his letter to Symonds. Unfortunately his *Free and Lonesome Heart: The Secret of WW* (1960), in which he consigned the result of his research, has failed to convince anyone. *WW's Secret* (1955) by Ben Aronim is a mere fictitious extension of the New Orleans romance.

After Holloway's synthesis there appeared for nearly two decades only fragmentary studies or books primarily concerned with analyzing the poet's complex nature and its relation to his poetry rather than true biographies. Jean Catel's *WW: La naissance du poète* (Paris, 1929) attempted to account for the sudden efflorescence of *LofG* with the help of Freud. He threw out the legend of the healthy, hearty, virile young man and rejected the various New Orleans romances. To Catel there is no doubt that W was autoerotic and continued to be so until quite late in life. To console himself for his failure to make firm contact with the real world, W retreated into his imagination and created a compensating world of fantasy. Thus it was that the extraordinary 1855 volume was born.

The Danish scholar Frederick Schyberg published his *WW* in Copenhagen in 1933. This was translated by E. A. Allen in 1951 and appeared with an introduction by G. W. Allen. Making excellent use of the abundant information about W's personal life which was available by 1930, he penetrated deeper into WW's psyche than anyone before. Though he accepted Catel's thesis of the moody, unsatisfied youth who escaped into his joyful vision of democratic man and society, Schyberg's greatest contribution was his careful analysis of the successive editions of *LofG*. He followed W's revisions, suggesting what impulses prompted them. There was a chapter on "W in World Literature," revised and expanded for the translation, which, by placing W among the writers of his time, did much to dissipate the image of him as a unique phenomenon.

Among studies which are concerned with a single aspect or period of W's life, Esther Shepard's *WW's Pose* (1938) has a special merit. The book's thesis is that "the source of *LofG* is, in spite of W's protestations to the contrary, in the fragment of a book, the epilogue of a French novel, *The Countess of Rudolstadt* by George Sand." So to her W was a fraud and *LofG* a kind of forgery. This was going much too far. One critic called Shepard's repetitious study a "wrong" book devoted "not to finding something *about* W, but to trying to get something *on* him." Henri Roddier brought out the import of the influence of George Sand on W in a well-balanced article, "Pierre Leroux, George Sand et WW, ou l'éveil d'un poète" (*RLC* 57). As to Esther Shepard, undeterred by the poor reception of her book, she persisted in the deprecation of W and launched a new attack in 1953 in two articles: "An Inquiry into W's Method of Turning Prose into Poetry" and "Possible Sources of Some of W's Ideas and Symbols in 'Hermes Mercurius Trismegistus' and Other Works" (both in *MLQ*).

In the leftist 1930's Newton Arvin felt impelled to interpret W's life in the light of his social thinking. His *W* (1938, 1969) is a not wholly unsuccessful effort to align W with the socialist thought of the day and contains very lucid analyses of W's political thought.

More thesis-ridden is H. I. Fausset's *WW: Poet of Democracy* (1942, 1968). His main contention is that W was a split personality who was never able to achieve poise and unity either as prophet or poet. The ground-tone of his biography is depreciatory in spite of his sense of the importance of the poet.

On its appearance one reviewer called Haniel Long's *WW and the Springs of Courage* (1938) "an essay in personal biography and poetic public evangelism." It is another biographical study with a thesis, namely that W derived the courage to be himself from various personal and bookish contacts.

After all these partial studies there appeared again in 1943 a complete biography: H. S. Canby's *WW: An American*, which constitutes an excellent introduction for the general reader. This is not to suggest that the book is superficial. Canby's knowledge of W's America and his sympathetic understanding of W as man and artist are happily in conjunction here, but in the author's own words his work is not meant to be a "final book on W," but a personal interpretation, an attempt "to make intelligible W and his 'Leaves.' " It is a plausible and sensible interpretation of the poet's "inner life and of the mysterious creative process of poetry."

Two popularized biographies were widely read at the time of their publication: Edgar Lee Masters, *W* (1937) and Frances Winwar, *American Giant: WW and His Times* (1941). The numerous inaccuracies in the second of these were pointed out in a review by C. J. Furness (*AL* 42). Halfway between biography and fiction and not succeeding as either is Cameron Rogers's *The Magnificent Idler* (1926). A. E. Briggs's *WW: Thinker and Artist* (1952) is too subjective and cantankerous to be of much value. As to Grant Overton, *The Answerer* (1921), Elizabeth Corbett, *Walt: The Good Gray Poet Speaks for Himself* (1928), and John Erskine, *The Start of the Road* (1938), they are quite frankly novels based on W's life.

The 1950's were marked by the almost simultaneous appearance of two very elaborately documented biographies: Asselineau's *L'Evolution de WW asprès la première édition des "Feuilles d'herbe"* (Paris, 1954) and G. W. Allen's *The Solitary Singer, a Critical Biography of WW* (1955; rev. ed., 1967).

Asselineau's work runs to 567 pages. Following the pattern of the French thèse in treating first the man and then his work, it is actually two books in one and when it was translated (by the author with the co-operation of R. P. Adams and B. L. Cooper), it was published in two volumes as *The Evolution of WW*, Vol. I with the subtitle of *The Creation of a Personality* (1960), Vol. II with the subtitle of *The Creation of a Book* (1962). Though the author asserts that it was not his aim to write a new biography, the first volume *is* one, making full use of the accumulated knowledge about W. Asselineau's thesis is, in brief, as follows. Of W's many inner struggles the most difficult was against his homo-sexual desires. Without doubt it was his art which saved him by permitting him to express (literally) the troubled passions which haunted him. His poetry was a means of purification. It was not the song of the demi-god depicted by the hagiographers, but the sorrowful pouring forth of a sick soul which sought passionately to understand itself and recover its self-possession. *LofG* is in a way "Flowers of Evil." The story of W's development is not told from the inside as in a critical biography or focussed on one single theme; it is told from the outside, constructed piece by piece, carefully and lovingly and yet with detachment.

Allen's *The Solitary Singer* of the admirably apt title is certain to stand for a long time as the most detailed and reliable biography. In its 616 pages the author essayed "to trace consecutively the physical life of the man, the growth of his mind, and the development of his art out of his physical and mental experience." The extraordinary mass of details which Allen assembled and organized overbalances his account of the development of W's art, but the amount of new material he uncovered compensates for this deficiency. Some-what disappointing is his hesitancy to commit himself in discussing W's sexual life. His biography will long remain an indispensable source-book for W scholars. It contains the largest number of incontrovertible facts ever collected about the author of *LofG*.

Allen has also published a short biography of *WW* (1961) of less than 180 pages with more than 70 well-chosen illustrations and a bibliography. The German translation (1962) contains some special German bibliographical material. In *A Reader's Guide to WW* (1970), which is in a way a sequel to his *WW Handbook*, Allen has used a different method. As he says himself, "I have not attempted to give a condensed biography, but to indicate the more important biographical facts which help to explain the poems." This is a good definition of the present trend in W scholarship. The emphasis is more and more on the poems rather than on the man. Biography yields to criticism.

However some good biographies for the general public have recently been published: Adrien Stoutenbourg and L. N. Baker, *Listen America: A Life of WW* (1968) (specially meant for younger readers), and Barbara Marinacci, *O Wondrous Singer: An Introduction to WW* (1970). More specialized books have also appeared: Verne Dyson's interesting little book on the W country in Long Island, *Whitmanland* (1960), and *WW in Camden* (1952) by R. W. Wescott. The editor of W's *Early Poems and the Fiction*, T. L. Brasher, has written a well-documented study: *W as Editor of the "Brooklyn Eagle"* (1970). It is both a study of the two-year period when W edited the *Eagle* and a detailed critical analysis of the editorials which he wrote during that time, showing the genesis of the poet from the journalist and social commentator.

V. BIOGRAPHICAL MATERIALS

1. Books and Pamphlets

Several visitors to W printed recollections of their talks with him. One of the earliest of these is Sadakichi-Hartmann's *Conversations with WW* (1895). In 1898 an English physician, Dr. John Johnston, printed his *Diary of a Visit to WW and Some of his Friends in 1890*, which was re-issued in 1917 with the added recollections of another English visitor, J. W. Wallace: *Visits to WW in 1890–91 By Two Lancashire Friends*. There is valuable information about Emerson's influence on W, obtained from the poet himself, in J. T. Trowbridge's *My Own Story with Recollections of Noted Persons* (1903). Further material about W's last years will be found in H. S. Morris, *WW: A Brief Biography with Reminiscences* (1929). A delightful account of the impression made on the college student son of Robert Pearsall Smith, a wealthy Philadelphian, forms a chapter in Logan Pearsall Smith's *Unforgotten Years* (1939).

Some of W's friendships have been the subject of a special study. Elizabeth Gould's *Anne Gilchrist and WW* (1900) about the author of "An Englishwoman's Estimate of WW" (1870) is unfortunately too slight and reticent to be of much use. W. E. Walling's *W and Traubel* (1916) overestimates Traubel and says almost nothing about the friendship of the two men.

There are also a few useful studies of particular episodes and periods in W's life. In 1921 Elizabeth Keller, the professional nurse who attended W in his last illness, published *WW in Mickle Street*. (The main purpose of her book was to praise the devotion and self-sacrifice of W's housekeeper, Mrs. Mary Oates Davis and to accuse the poet of selfishness.) W's brief career as a teacher and his interest as an editor in the problems of education are treated in Florence Freedmans' *WW Looks at the Schools* (1950), which contains the editorials on school affairs which W wrote for the Brooklyn *Evening Star* in 1845–46.

The part played by Lincoln in W's life is inadequately and verbosely discussed in W. E. Barton's *Abraham Lincoln and WW* (1928), though the information about W's Lincoln lecture is useful. C. I. Glicksberg's compilation, *WW and the Civil War* (1933, 1963), was meant to controvert this book. Katherine Molinoff has published four informative monographs on obscure passages in W's life: *An Unpublished W Manuscript: The Record Book of the Smithtown Debating Society, 1837–1838* (1941); *Some Notes on W's Family* (1941): *W's Teaching at Smithtown 1837–38* (1942); and *WW at Southhold* (1966). The last of these pamphlets, however, seems to rest on rather shaky evidence.

2. Articles

The substance of most of the significant articles concerned with particular aspects or episodes of W's life has been absorbed into the full-scale biographies of Asselineau and Allen. Therefore only those articles will be mentioned here which are of special importance and are so detailed that these biographers could not make full use of them, or which have appeared later than their books.

A number of these articles are concerned with W's friends. In *AL* (59) C. Carroll Hollis has shown the importance of William Swinton's friendship in W's life. Swinton was a linguist who encouraged W's interest in words and lent him books about them. In her "Personal Recollections of WW" (*Atl* 07) Ellen (O'Connor) Calder, wife of W's friend and champion, provided important first-hand information about the poet's Washington years. The story of W's friendship and eventual break with O'Connor has been carefully explored by Florence Freedman, "New Light on an Old Quarrel: WW and W. D. O'Connor" (*WWR* 65). Among the many accounts of W's last years, W. R. Thayer's "Personal Recollections of WW" (*Scribner's* 19) is of special interest because Thayer, a proper Bostonian, questioned W closely and argued with him. Brief but shrewd observations about W and his disciples will be found in William White's "WW and Sir William Osler" (*AL* 39). (Osler was one of the physicians who attended W in the 1880's. He was a detached observer.) Information on the Camden Circle will also be found in Henry Chupak, "WW and the Camden Circle" (*PNJHS* 55) and on W and his doctors in H. B. Barnshaw, "WW's Physicians in Camden" (*Trans of the Coll of Physicians of Phila* 64), and C. E. Feinberg, "WW and His Doctors" (*Archives of Internal Med* 64). On his old age, one may also consult B. A. Thompson, "Edward Wilkins: Male Nurse to WW" (*WWR* 69) and W. J. Speers, "WW's Camden Days" (*Phila Enquirer Mag* 70).

W wrote for Bryant's *Evening Post* in the 1850's and possibly into the Civil War period. What is known of the Bryant-W friendship is told by C. I.

Glicksberg in "W and Bryant" (*Fantasy* 35). The complicated relationship between Emerson and W is explored in three excellent articles: J. B. Moore, "The Master of W" (*SP* 26); Clarence Gohdes, "W and Emerson" (*SR* 29); and Carlos Baker, "The Road to Concord: Another Milestone in the W-Emerson Friendship" (*PULC* 46). J. T. Trowbridge's efforts to enhance W's artistic reputation in New England and the personal relationship between the two men is fully treated in three articles by R. A. Coleman: "Trowbridge and W" (*PMLA* 48); "Further Reminiscences of WW" (*MLN* 48); and "Trowbridge and O'Connor: Unpublished Correspondence with Special Reference to WW" (*AL* 51).

Another series of articles examines W's contributions to newspapers and magazines. Emory Holloway's "More Light on W" (*AM* 24) discusses W's editorial experiences when he was with the Brooklyn *Evening Star*, which he mentioned only briefly in his *W* in 1926. Esther Shepard in "WW's Whereabouts in the Winter of 1842–43" (*AL* 57) concludes that he may have written for the New York *Sun* while employed on *The Plebeian*, and Holloway in "More Temperance Tales by W" (*AL* 56) reveals that W wrote another temperance story, "The Mariner," part of which at least appeared in the New York *Washingtonian and Organ* in 1843. Portia Baker's "WW and the *Atl*" (*AL* 34) examines W's relationship with the members of the *Atl* circle and the reasons for the small attention the magazine gave him. There is a companion article by the same author: "WW's Relationships with Some New York Magazines" (*AL* 35). The first of these two articles is to some extent supplemented by Jean Rivière, "Howells and W After 1881" (*WWR* 66). In his "WW, the *Galaxy* and *Democratic Vistas*" (*AL* 51) E. F. Grier has brought to light information about W's connection with an important New York monthly. The article follows in particular the genesis and development of *Democratic Vistas* through articles which appeared in the *Galaxy*.

A number of articles which help to clarify particular episodes in W's life also deserve mention here. In "A W Collector Destroys a W Myth" (*PBSA* 58) Feinberg definitely proves that in the 1850's W made his living as a building contractor rather than as a carpenter, as he later wanted people to believe. William White has given an excellent account of the controversial number of copies of *LofG* printed in 1855, "The First *LofG*: How many copies?" (*PBSA* 63). In 1856 or 1857 W contracted a small debt to James Parton, the husband of Fanny Fern whose *Fern Leaves from Fanny's Portfolio* (1853) may have had some influence on the title and binding of the first edition of *LofG*. The poet's detractors, during his life and after his death, asserted that he never paid it. New information about this affair, which partially clears his name, is supplied by O. S. Coad's "W vs. Parton" (*JRUL* 40), and additional information about W's life during this period will be found in J. F. McDermott, "W and the Partons: Glimpses from the Diary of Thomas Butler Gunn, 1856–1860" (*AL* 57). Using manuscripts in the Library of Congress, C. I. Glicksberg tried to clear up a hitherto obscure period in W's life in his "WW in 1862" (*AL* 34). In this same year W received a letter from an "Ellen Eyre" which possibly implies that they had sexual relations. Allen in *The Solitary Singer*, however, makes little of this episode, though Holloway in "W Pursued" (*AL* 55) suggested that the name conceals the identity of Ada Clare, an actress, or of Mrs. Juliette A. Beach of Albion, N. Y., one of W's female pursuers. In "WW's Dark Lady" (*UKCR* 43) Frances Winwar had made a similar hypothesis based on the fanciful interpretation of a passage in Ellen Calder's article which the *Atl* had suppressed "for reasons of delicacy." Asselineau, on the contrary, in "WW, Child of Adam, Three Unpublished Letters to W" (*MLQ* 49) lights up certain aspects of W's (potential) homosexuality during the Civil War. Between 1865 and 1873 W held several Federal clerkships; very precise information about these was assembled in an important article by Dixon Wecter, "WW as Civil Servant" (*PMLA* 43). In the summer of 1876 W began to stay for long periods at the Stafford farm on Timber Creek, near Kirkwood, N. J. These visits are described in Sculley Bradley's "WW on Timber Creek" (*AL* 33). Peter Van Egmond studies W as a lecturer in his old age in "WW on the Platform" (*SSJ* 67).

Three articles of a more general biographical interest remain to be mentioned. That untiring literary detective Holloway gathered together some of the evidence of the poet's anonymous puffery in "W as His Own Press Agent" (*AM* 29). Edward Hungerford's "WW and his Chart of Bumps" (*AL* 31) demonstrates the extraordinary consequences in W's life and art which derived from that important day in July 1849 when he had his bumps read by Lorenzo Fowler and received the flattering "Phrenological Notes on WW," which he had bound into copies of the 1855 *LofG*. Hungerford, however, went a little too far when he claimed that this extremely favorable reading of his "chart of bumps" first gave W the ambition to be a poet. W's fondness for the theater as a young man and his *obiter dicta* about actors and their styles have been studied by Floyd Stovall in "WW and the Dramatic Stage in New York" (*SP* 53).

Curiously enough, W's sexual life has been the subject of very few articles. Only two deserve to be mentioned: Gustav Bychowski's "WW: A Study in Sublimation" (*Psychoanalysis and the Soc Sci* 51) is a searching and candid examination of W's sex life, though, like most psychoanalytical interpretations of the life of a writer, it tends to use the poet's verses as if they were spoken from the analyst's couch. S. E. Whicher in "W's Awakening to Death: Toward a Biographical reading of 'Out of the Cradle Endlessly Rocking' " (SIR 61; repr. in The Presence of WW, edited by R. W. B. Lewis, and in E. H. Miller's A Century of W Criticism) sees this poem as the culmination of an "emotional crisis stemming from some sort of homosexual 'love affair,' " thus running the risk of being accused of biographical fallacy.

In concluding this section attention should be called to Harvey O'Higgins's "Alias WW" (HM 29; repr. as book, 1929, 1930). This attack on W as a mediocre journalist, a borrower of the styles of other authors, a writer of anonymous blurbs of his own work, a narcissist who posed as a "fine brute" of a man is important only because it is typical of the way in which many who have disliked W the man have written about his life. An effective answer to O'Higgins and all such detractors was made by F. I. Carpenter in his "WW's 'Eidólon' " (CE 42), which demonstrates why W's "pose" (it would rather now-adays be called "mask" or "persona") was necessary to him as a person and a poet. Asselineau has also pointed out that this accusation of insincerity is meaningless since, as Valéry says: "Every work of art is a fake," and W for his part has created himself while creating his book. His life is an illustration of Oscar Wilde's paradox that nature imitates art. He addresses us "Out from behind [the] mask" of his poetry, but his mask stuck to his face and he could not remove it any more. As he himself once declared to the policeman who ordered him to remove his false face, thinking he was wearing a false beard: "Do we not all wear 'false faces'?"

VI. CRITICISM

Leaving W's "life," we now come to his "recitative." The mass of writing about W which may be termed critical (some of it very loosely) is enormous. The reasons why this great cairn has been piled up are not in the least obscure. W has always attracted antagonists eager to show that he is a shallow thinker and a second-rate poet. But his defenders have been more numerous than his detractors. Year by year they have added stones to the cairn of criticism and commentary: W as Hegelian, W as Transcendentalist, W as the Prophet of Personalism or Democracy or World Government, W as the Most Genuinely American of American Poets, W as the Christ of Our Age. Because W lived to be seventy-three, wrote much editorial prose in his youth, much poetry in his middle years, and talked unceasingly to his disciples in his Camden days, the scholiast with LofG and With WW in Camden before him could turn out an endless series of papers. Much of this sort of criticism is trivial. The reader must therefore be warned that this section will be long in spite of the fact that a stout effort has been made to eliminate items which are of little interest or by now out of date.

1. General Studies: Books and Articles

Only a very few book-length critical studies stand out in the mass of earlier writing about W. O. L. Triggs's *Browning and W: A Study in Democracy* (1893) has the virtues of a period piece. It attempts to show how the contributions of science, philosophy, and ethical truth, informed by the spirit of Romanticism, merge in the poetry of both Browning and W and make their work a part of "modern prophetical literature." John Burroughs's final words on his poet friend, *W: A Study* (1896), is still of use because, although some of his interpretations are mere paraphrases of the poet's own romantic theories, he also read W correctly as the emancipator of those who hoped for "the triumph of democracy and of science," believed in "realism and positivism" and were possessed of "the religious hunger that flees the churches." Basil de Selincourt's *WW: A Critical Study* (1914, 1968) was the first study of W to concentrate on the criticism of his works, as the title indicates. Though many of de Selincourt's conclusions are vitiated by his Romantic view of W (he serenely accepts the New Orleans "lady of gentle birth" and the six illegitimate children), his comments on the constructive principles, unity, style and music of *LofG* were remarkable for the time. He very shrewdly observed W's "actual personality by the side of the assumed personality of the hero of *LofG*," but almost completely ignored "Song of Myself."

Several of the biographies described in the preceding sections are, of course, concerned with understanding and evaluating W's poetry and prose. Chief among these are the studies by Perry (1906), G. R. Carpenter (1909, 1967), Catel (1929), Schyberg (1933, 1951), Arvin (1938), Fausset (1942, 1968) and Canby (1943). But there were also important chapters devoted to W in books on more general subjects. Important in its time because of its length and fairness, and the prestige of the writer was E. C. Stedman's section on W in his *Poets of America* (1885). W. S. Kennedy's "Drift and Cumulus" in *Reminiscences of WW* (1896) can be taken as an official pronouncement of the Camden disciples. George Santayana's "The Poetry of Barbarism" (in *Interpretations of Poetry and Religion*, 1900)—the Barbarians are WW and Browning—has probably evoked more defenses of W than any other essay by a detractor. Santayana's style drives his barbs deep: W, he says, "has approached common life without bringing in his mind any higher standard by which to criticize it; he has seen it, not in contrast with an ideal, but as the expression of forces more indeterminate and elementary than itself; and the vulgar, in this cosmic setting, has appeared to him sublime." He failed to see that "the ideal and the real are dynamically continuous," as William James put it. P. E. More's essay (*Shelburne Essays*, 4th ser., 1906) is more sympathetic than one might expect from a New Humanist, especially so in its discussion of W's experience of war and death. Surprisingly modern in its understanding of the complexities which a critic of W faces is Stuart Sherman's essay in *Americans* (1922). (It contains, incidentally, an excellent refutation of Santayana.) The W essay in D. H. Lawrence's *Studies in Classic American Literature* (1923) contains some brilliant insights mixed with some wrongheaded prejudices. In particular, Lawrence criticizes W for wanting to merge with everything, but does not realize that this "efflux" was neutralized by a compensating "influx," W's refusal to surrender his own precious "identity." As one would expect, W was for V. L. Parrington "a great figure, the greatest assuredly in our literature" ("The Afterglow of the Enlightenment—WW", in *MCAT* (1930). In spite of his obsession with political and economic problems, he fully sympathized with W and found comfort in his abiding faith in democracy "in a time of huge infidelities" after World War I. Another sympathetic general study, written in his happiest impressionistic vein, is contained in four chapters of V. W. Brooks's *The Times of Melville and W* (1947). Canby's W chapter in *LHUS* is admirably concise and comprehensive. However, one of the most acute studies of W in English is the long fourth book of F. O. Matthiessen's *AmR* (1941). As the title of the main chapter indicates ("Only a language experiment"), Matthiessen's primary aim was to get at the secret of W's penetration and force as a poet, and he did so very searchingly, but, though he also studied the poet's "Vision and Attitude" and his "Landscapes projected masculine, full-sized and golden," he had a tendency to concentrate on the manner to the detriment of the matter and on the aesthetic theories to the detriment of the poet's practice, forgetting that W had also defined *LofG* "as an attempt, from first to last, to put *a Person*, a human being (myself in the latter half of the Nineteenth Century, in America), freely, fully and truly on record."

This one-sidedness has been avoided by Asselineau in his book-length study, *The Evolution of WW: The Creation of a Book* (1962), which is divided into two parts: "The Main Themes of *LofG*" and "The Progress of [W's] Art," and attempts to cover every conceivable aspect of W's thought and style systematically, though sometimes too quickly as in the chapter on Prosody. This is not a static survey, however, for the author follows the same chronological method as in his biography and constantly compares and confronts the various editions of *LofG*, a method which brings out the underlying consistency of W's major themes. On the other hand he never forgets the man behind the book, just as in his biography he keeps reminding the reader that W created his personality and his poetry at the same time. In particular, in the chapter entitled "Sex Life—'The Love that dare not speak its name,' " he describes the impact on *LofG* of W's latent but undeniable homosexuality. Asselineau shows the deep roots of the poet's religious metaphysics and fundamental aesthetics in W's mysticism and in what he calls "the poetry of the body." He analyzes the inner tensions of W's politics in chapters entitled: " 'These States' —Egocentrism and Patriotism", "Democracy—'Myself' and Man 'En-Masse' " and "Democracy and Racialism—Slavery". As to the progress of W's art, it is studied from the threefold point of view of style, language and prosody. This book was enthusiastically received by W scholars as soon as it appeared in French in 1954. Yet, as Seymour Betsky has pointed out, "Whose WW? French Scholar and American Critics" (*ES* 66), it tends to overintellectualize W's poetry and to emphasize his ideas to the detriment of what took place in the lower layers of his mind. It breaks the mysterious nebula of his Self into clear, hard-cut fragments. It clarifies the poet's meaning, but ignores some of his obscurities. It distills the essence of *LofG*, but to some extent fails to study the secret alchemy of W's transmutation of dross into the (impure) gold of his poetry.

It is this exploration of W's Protean Self and mysterious methods that a number of critics have undertaken since the middle 1950's, stressing the unconscious rather than the conscious. The year 1955 saw the publication of three studies which are mainly evaluative in character. The symposium edited by Milton Hindus, *"LofG" One Hundred Years After* (repr. 1960) contains essays by W. C. Williams, Richard Chase, Leslie Fiedler, Kenneth Burke, David Daiches and J. M. Murry. All these essays (with the exception of Chase's, which is biographical and discusses at length the New Orleans episode) reassess W's achievement from the vantage point of the centennial year of *LofG*. Their general drift may be summed up in words of one of the contributors: WW "is a poet whom we must begin now to rescue from parody as well as apotheosis." Of course, W. C. Williams is above all interested in the practitioner of free verse whom he wants to enlist in his service against T. S. Eliot. Leslie Fiedler studies the various "Images of WW" (most of them distortions) which have gained currency since the first appearance of *LofG*. (He has included this essay in a book of his own, *An End to Innocence*, 1955). David Daiches analyzes the combination of epic and lyric strains in *LofG*. Kenneth Burke is concerned with the transmutation of political philosophy into poetry in "When

Lilacs Last . . . ," and John Middleton Murry concentrates (without falling into clichés) on W as poet-prophet of democracy. Three lectures delivered at the Library of Congress in the centennial year have been printed as *WW: Man, Poet, Philosopher* (1955; repr. 1969). The lecturers who addressed themselves to these topics were, respectively, Allen, Mark Van Doren, and David Daiches. Chase's *WW Reconsidered* (1955) follows a chronological pattern, but only the first chapter is primarily biographical; the rest of the book is a critical examination of *LofG*. Chase's most original contribution is his description of "Song of Myself" as "a profound and lovely comic drama" in which he finds uninhibited American vitality and the language of the tall tale. (On this point, however, he was merely following Constance Rourke who had developed some of the same views in *American Humor*, 1931). This is a rather aberrant interpretation, for, if the comic implies exuberance, the converse is not always true, exuberance does not necessarily lead to the comic and Chase completely distorts W's poem by paying exclusive attention to its tone and ignoring its contents. The comic must not be confused with the cosmic. The book thus contains a number of stimulating but debatable opinions. The UMPAW in which Chase summed up his views on W in 1961 is much better balanced than his longer study.

In the year of the centennial of the first *LofG* there also appeared R. P. Adams's "W: A Brief Revaluation" (*TSE*), which consists of an interesting parallel with Emerson, a good analysis of W's theory of literature, and interesting remarks on the imagery and rhythm of his poetry.

Beginning with *A Critical Guide to "LofG"* (1957), J. E. Miller, Jr., has devoted three books to W. His first and most important one is a piece of New Criticism in which he examines the poems in the final edition, avoiding as much as he can—though not too systematically—biography and textual criticism. His study consists of two parts. The first one is a series of structural analyses of "Song of Myself" and "Calamus." The second one is an attempt to bring out "a comprehensive structure for the whole of *LofG*." Miller reads "Song of Myself" as an "inverted mystical experience." The inversion is debatable, but the rest of the interpretation is sound. The contents of the poem are fully analyzed. Miller, who refuses to see in "Calamus" an expression of homosexual love, tends to exaggerate the unity and consistency of spiritual love W put in it. As to the structural order which he finds in the whole of *LofG*, it is "the articulation of the prototype of the New World," a reading which definitely overstresses the poet's nationalism. So the book is not an entirely reliable "guide." *WW* (1962), Miller's second book, is meant for the beginner rather than the specialist. It explicates in detail and clearly the best known poems and contains an interesting study of the recurring images in *LofG*: the grass, the sea, the bird. In *W's 'Song of Myself': Origin, Growth, Meaning* (1964), his third book, also intended for the student, Miller invites exploration. He supplies the reader with the basic materials for a penetration in depth of the poem: 1855, 1892, and early notebook versions of "Song of Myself," which reveal W in the process of creation. He also quotes six critics each with a different view of the poem: Carl Strauch, Randall Jarrell, Chase, R. H. Pearce, Cowley and himself. *Start with the Sun: Studies in Cosmic Poetry* (1961) was written in collaboration by Miller, Karl Shapiro, and Bernice Slote. It is a neo-Romantic manifesto, and *LofG* is used as a strategic base from which to launch an attack on T. S. Eliot, as if there were a difference in kind and not merely in degree between the two poets. This is completely wrong, as Sydney Musgrove has shown in *T. S. Eliot and WW* (1952). Miller himself came to realize it and wrote an essay entitled "W and Eliot: The Poetry of Mysticism" in which he puts side by side "Song of Myself" and "Four Quartets," two forms of what he calls "dramatized mysticism." He published this piece together with "WW: The Quest for Identity" and "WW: The Quest for the Spirit" in a collection entitled *Quests Surd and Absurd* (1967).

R. W. B. Lewis's *The Presence of WW* (1962) is meant to testify to the vital presence of W in the twentieth century and consists of two series of essays by diverse hands read at the English Institute. The first one is centered on "Out of the Cradle Endlessly Rocking." S. E. Whicher interprets it biographically as a poem of tragic acceptance, Paul Fussell, Jr., psychologically and artistically as the reconciliation of contending opposites, Chase as a romance and a relative failure as compared to "Song of Myself" and "The Sleepers," and Pearce, on the contrary, as a culmination in W's greatest book, the 1860 *LofG*. The second series of essays explores the range of W's influence through a parallel between W and Dylan Thomas by J. W. Miller, Jr., a study of W as working for the prose tradition which extends through Pound to W. C. Williams by Samuel Hynes, and an analysis of "the delicate strength of *LofG*" and its impact on some Spanish poets by J. A. Wright. The book, like *LofG* itself, is thus made up of "stimulating disagreements," as the editor points out.

Taking the opposite course to Chase's interpretation of "Song of Myself" as a "comic drama of the self," V. K. Chari, a Sanskrit scholar, shows in *W in the Light of Vegdantic Mysticism* (1964, paperback, 1969) a surprising number of parallelisms between *LofG* and Vedantic mystical literature. Comparison here is not used to detect influences but "as a critical instrument to define and illustrate W's most basic ideas." For Chari the ecstasy recorded in section five of "Song of Myself" is a real one described "in retrospect," which eventually

led W to the discovery of his "mystical identity," "the real I or Me or You."
Rediscovering by himself the processes of Vegdantic mysticism, W attained
"cosmic consciousness" and hoped ultimately to merge with the formless Absolute, "the sea of God" in "Passage to India." Chari, however, tends to exaggerate the monism of W, who never succeeded in completely fusing "body"
and "soul" and to minimize the influence of German idealism in *LofG*. Another
Indian scholar, O. K. Nambiar, similarly explores the Yoga context of *LofG*
in *WW and Yoga* (1966), but his approach is more pragmatic and less philosophical. He interprets W as "primarily a religious genius who delivered a
message of special importance to us and our day." He believes not only in the
genuineness of the ecstasy recorded in section five of "Song of Myself," but
also in W's animal magnetism—which he thinks accounts for the poet's emphasis on "touch." The parallels between *LofG* and oriental thought had already
struck Thoreau, Edward Carpenter, and some orientalists in W's lifetime. It is
no wonder therefore that a third Indian scholar, T. R. Rajasekharaiah, thinks
he has found *The Roots of W's Grass* (1970) in books and articles on India
which the poet read in the 1850's in the New York libraries (particularly the
Astor). His claim, however, that they were "the Eastern Sources of WW's
Poetry" is exaggerated. He has only found one factor among many in the
genesis of *LofG*. The similarities he points out are quite enlightening anyhow.

The most important contribution to W scholarship in recent years, however, is rather E. H. Miller's *WW's Poetry—A Psychological Journey* (1968;
paperback, 1969). This is a global study of the man and his poetry—since the
two are indistinguishable and W's poetry is essentially autobiographical. With
the help of psychoanalysis the author maps out W's spiritual itinerary from
"There Was a Child Went Forth" to "Passage to India," and, to begin with,
diagnoses the cause of the poet's abnormality: his "perfect" mother did not
love him as much as he wanted and preferred his eldest brother. W thus becomes a new Narcissus absorbed in the contemplation of himself and the world
(which amounts to the same thing) and groping through incoherent visions
for the lost paradise of his infancy and his mother's womb and bosom, a man-
child, father-mother, condemned to hermaphroditism, but swollen with desires
which he boldly sings for lack of a better outlet. This searching interpretation
of the facts of W's life enables Miller to decode the major poems of *LofG* with
a precision and subtlety never equalled before. He shows the underlying unity
and consistency of the imagery even when it seems most incoherent, and, by
revealing some of the secret roots of W's poetry, accounts for its quasi-visceral
appeal. The great merit of the author, besides, is that his lucidity as a (psycho)-
analyst is allied with a keen artistic sensibility. He does not treat W's poems as

if they were mere documents written by a mentally diseased person; he never forgets that they are works of art and he makes the reader feel their beauty. It is a fascinating book. Yet it has its limitations. It brings to light the hidden roots of the poems, but often ignores the leaves. W is described to us holding a leaf of grass and lying on a bank by a wood as on a psychoanalyst's couch. In this position he makes a rather obscure confession which Miller clarifies for us. But what about the leaf of grass? Miller forgets about it, though all the time W has been trying to answer the child's question: "What is the grass?" In short, all the religious mysticism and transcendentalism of *LofG* has evaporated. We are shown only that part of W which is below the belt. It is no doubt important to bring out what W has not been willing—or able—to say, but it is no less vital to analyze what he has actually said—and this is hardly done at all in this book, for all its acuteness, and perhaps because of it.

Other useful books are those which G. W. Allen has written to supplement his *WW Handbook*. His *WW as Man, Poet, and Legend* (1961) not only contains some essays he had already published elsewhere, but also an interesting study, "Mutations in W's Art," in which he shows that, contrary to Cowley's opinion, each edition of *LofG* has its merit, and none is really inferior to the first one; a survey of "Translations of W Since World War II"; and in the section devoted to "The Legend" a remarkable chapter on "W's Image in the Twentieth Century," which discusses the various interpretations of *LofG* in the preceding 60 years and emphasizes the enormous change in critical attitude toward W since the beginning of the century: he is now considered as worthy of serious and sympathetic critical attention as Yeats or Eliot. A very useful check-list of "W Publications 1945–1960" by E. A. Allen is given in the appendix. This book is complemented by *A Reader's Guide to WW* (1970), in which the chapter "Root-Center" is a sequel to "W's Image in the Twentieth Century" in the former volume. "The Foreground" and "Perennial Leaves" are quintessential surveys of W's life and poetry respectively. "Man or Beast?" and "Form and Structure" contain stimulating views on the personality of the poet and his art. The essays in these two books are models of impartial and open criticism. Together with the *WW Handbook* they constitute an excellent synthesis of all existing W scholarship. Allen did not collect in this last volume an essay on "The Two Poets of *LofG*" (i.e. the materialistic Sancho Panza and the mystical Don Quixote) which he contributed to *Patterns of Commitment in American Literature* (1967), edited by Marston LaFrance. To commemorate the excellent work done by Allen in the field of W scholarship over a period of 30 years as biographer, critic, and editor, E. H. Miller edited in 1970 *The Artistic Legacy of WW: A Tribute to Gay Wilson Allen* in which Red Rorem, who has set several of W's poems to music, discusses his relationship to the poet in "Words without Song," Max Kozloff studies "WW and American Art," and Miller himself more particularly examines "The Radical Vision of W and Pollock." Robert Duncan for his part defines the impact of *LofG* on his own poetry and Allen discusses "The Iconography of WW," i.e. the images of this most Narcissistic poet which a number of painters and photographers offered to the public both in his lifetime and later.

Some critics have tried to define certain aspects of W by comparison with other writers. In *The Greatness of Man: An Essay on Dostoyevsky and W* (1961) Perry Westbrook studies the two authors as religious prophets concerned with the spiritual dilemmas of men, and in *W and Nietzsche: A Comparative Study of Their Thought* (1964) C. N. Stavrou draws up a list of echoes of W's thought in Nietzsche, but actually there are more contrasts than similarities between the two authors.

Two brief general introductions to W have also been written besides Chase's: one in French by a poet, Alain Bosquet (*W*, 1959), another by an Australian academic critic and poet, Geoffrey Dutton (*WW*, 1961, 1966). Both are less compilations than original and perceptive works of criticism.

The language barrier unfortunately will prevent most scholars from reading M. O. Mendelson's *Zhizn' i tvorchestvo Uitmena* (*Life and Works of W*, 1965), written in Russian, which describes W above all as the poet of the people and the champion of all the oppressed, and Shunsuke Kamei's *Myth and Reality* (1967) written in Japanese. The latter, however, contains an eight-page summary of the author's thesis in English. It explores the gap between the image of W as a vociferous prophet of democracy and the tormented poet that he actually was.

In an essay published in *American Classics Reconsidered* (1958), edited by H. C. Gardiner, S.J., Ernest Sandeen studies W from a Roman Catholic point of view under the title of "WW: Ego in Eden," "a pagan Eden, complete with the phallic serpent." David Daiches in *The Young Rebel in American Literature* (1959), edited by Carl Bode, regards "WW as Innovator" above all and N. A. Jeffares in *The Great Experiment in American Literature* (1961), also edited by Carl Bode, similarly concentrates on "W: The Barbaric Yawp." On the contrary, Pearce in *The Continuity of American Poetry* (1961) shows in his chapter on "The Long View: An American Epic" that the epic aspirations of W are related to a constant theme in American poetry, the relation between the self and the world. In a later essay, "W and Our Hope for Poetry" (D. C. Allen and H. T. Rowell, eds., *The Poetic Tradition*, 1968), starting from a poem by Robert Duncan, Pearce interprets *LofG* as an attempt to react against the dehumanization which gathered speed in the United States after the Civil War with the growing industrialization. In his own way W thus discovered and commented on what Marx called "alienation." C. T. Davis gives his own version of continuity in American literature and W's insertion in it in "WW and the Problem of an American Tradition" (*CLAJ* 61). Tony Tanner in *The Reign of Wonder* (1965) examines the development of wonder and naïveté in American literature under the impact of Romanticism and studies "WW's Ecstatic First Step" in this context. H. H. Waggoner devotes an excellent chapter to W, "Signing for Body and Soul," in his *American Poets from the Puritans to the Present* (1968) and salutes him in conclusion as "the archetypal American poet and the greatest we have had."

Some of the most interesting articles about W in the last two decades concentrate on the elucidation of the major poems, like John Lovell, Jr.'s "Appreciating W: 'Passage to India' " (*MLQ* 60), L. K. Davidson's "W's 'Song of Myself': An Analysis" (*Litera* 60; *DA* 60), and M. S. Reynolds's "WW's Early Prose and 'The Sleepers' " (*AL* 69). The problem of W's identity has also frequently attracted the attention of critics of late years. It has been examined by E. F. Carlisle, "WW: The Drama of Identity" (*Criticism* 68), from an existentialist point of view; by S. A. Black, "W and the Failure of Mysticism: Identity and Identification" (*WWR* 69); by P. Y. Coleman, "WW's Ambiguities of 'I' " (*PLL* 69); by Klaus Poenicke, " 'The Test of Death and Night': Pose und bewältigte Wirklichkeit in Ws *LofG*" (Dieter Riesner and Helmut Gneuss, eds., *Festschrift für Walter Hübner*, Berlin, 1964). Denis Donoghue in his chapter on W in *Connoisseurs of Chaos* (1965) discusses the same problem in terms of Wallace Stevens's poetry, as if *LofG* were W's "notes towards a supreme fiction," the supreme fiction that is Man. For him W fuses being and becoming. Asselineau follows the physical as well as spiritual itinerary of W in "WW: From Paumanok to More than America" (*PLL* 69). He describes— more lyrically than critically—the constantly increasing idealism of W's democratic views (in *LofG*) as he passed from the rural America of his youth to the urban and industrial America of his middle and old age.

The best articles or contributions to W criticism have been collected in several anthologies: Leo Marx emphasizes *The Americanness of WW* (1960), Pearce W's art and the integrity of *LofG* in *W* (1962), and J. C. Broderick the technique, prosody, style, and language of the poet in *W: the Poet* (1962). William Coyle concentrates on the Lincoln poems in *The Poet and the President* (1962). The most complete and best balanced of these anthologies is probably *WW* (1969), edited by Francis Murphy. By presenting the articles in chronological order in *A Century of W Criticism* (1969) E. H. Miller shows the changing trends in literary taste and intellectual concern over the past 100 years in America and abroad. *Studies in WW's "LofG"* (1954), edited by H. R. Warfel, is merely a collection of papers written by a group of German students.

2. Fundamental Ideas: Religion, Philosophy, Science, Society

A number of critics have been particularly attracted by the religious philosophy implicit in *LofG* and have attempted to define it—sometimes with an excess of zeal and precision. W has thus been described variously as a mystic, a pantheist, a panpsychist, a personalist (his own term). His friend, Dr. Bucke, the Canadian psychiatrist, was so much impressed by his particular kind of mystical insight that he wrote a book about it, *Cosmic Consciousness: A Study in the Evolution of the Human Mind* (1901, often repr.). Here W appears in the company of Buddha, Jesus, St. Paul, and less eminent possessors of this mysterious faculty. Charles Cestre examined the relation between W's mysticism and his poetical powers in "WW: Le mystique, le lyrique" (*RAA* 30). W as monist and pantheist is discussed in Maynard Shipley's "Democracy and Religion" (*Open Court* 19). In "The Quaker Influence on WW" (*AL* 70) Lawrence Templin explains "how W went beyond Quakerism, recognizing both his differences and his likenesses to the followers of the Inner Light." O. F. Pucciani's "WW and the Nineteenth Century" (*Arts and Action: Twice a Year Press*, 1948) emphasizes the part played by W in the movement away from traditional Christianity caused by the new historical relativism. W described his whole programme and the faith required for its fulfillment in an essay entitled "Personalism" which he wrote for the *Galaxy* in 1868 and later incorporated in *Democratic Vistas*. Bronson Alcott took up the concept of personalism and introduced it into American philosophy. (See Allen's *WW Handbook* for an excellent discussion of this movement.) How W's concept accords with the latter-day development of this philosophy is indicated by William Maxwell: "Some Personalist Elements in the Poetry of W" (*Person* 31).

The studies which have been made of various facets of W's philosophy are more rewarding than those which deal with his religion as a whole. Maximilian Beck's "WW's Intuition of Reality" (*Ethics* 42) emphasizes "his infinite delight in pure real existence" and thus shows how he anticipated Bergson. Somewhat similar conclusions were reached by H. A. Myers in his excellent article, "W's Consistency" (*AL* 36).

The specific problem of W's Hegelianism has been discussed by two scholars: M. C. Boatright, "W and Hegel" (*UTSE* 29) and O. W. Parsons, "W the Non-Hegelian" (*PMLA* 43). The second article is in large part a refutation of the first one, but it is not totally convincing. There are also two studies of the

similarities, but more particularly the differences between W's Transcendentalism and that of the Concord group: Norman Foerster, "W and the Cult of Confusion" (*NAR* 21) and Leon Howard, "For a Critique of WW's Transcendentalism" (*MLN* 32). The chapter on W in F. W. Conner's *Cosmic Optimism, A
Study of the Interpretation of Evolution by American Poets from Emerson to
Robinson* (1949) is mainly concerned with the "high-water mark of 'cosmic
optimism,' " which was reached in W's writings; but the chapter also contains
an excellent review of W's interest in other contemporary philosophies, chiefly
those emanating from Germany. This aspect of W's philosophy is also discussed by H. M. Jones in the chapter entitled "The Cosmic Optimism of WW"
in his book on Belief and Disbelief in American Literature (1967). The related
problem of evil has been searchingly explored in several essays: S. J. Kahn,
"The American Backgrounds of W's Sense of Evil" (*ScH* 55) and "W's Black
Lucifer" (*PMLA* 56); Charles Hughes, "Impact of Evil on the Poetry of WW"
(*WWR* 69); Lester Goodson, "W and the Problem of Evil" (*WWR* 70). On the
other hand the interrelationship of sex and death in *LofG* has been analyzed by
Clark Griffith in "Sex and Death: The Significance of W's Calamus Themes"
(*PQ* 60).

E. W. Taylor in an "Analysis and Comparison of the 1855 and 1891 Versions of W's 'To Think of Time' " (*WWR*, 1967) illustrates the growing intel-
lectualization of the poet's metaphysics. Using a non-theological method of approach, Georges Poulet has studied time in *LofG* in *Le Point de Départ* (1964)
and so has Allen in "WW's Inner Space" (*PLL* 69). R. D. McGhee analyzes various "Concepts of Time in W's Poetry" (*WWR* 69) but fails to detect the impact
of German Transcendentalism on *LofG*.

Some critics have rather been concerned with W's ethics and have stressed
his stoicism and healthy-mindedness, for instance C. E. Pulos in "W and Epictetus: The Stoical Element in *LofG*" (*JEGP* 56), S. J. Kahn in "W's Stoicism"
(*ScH* 62), and Stuart Holroyd in *Emergence from Chaos* (1957).

As for W's interest in natural phenomena and his knowledge and use of scientific ideas, it will be sufficient to mention Joseph Beaver's *WW: Poet of Science* (1951). It takes cognizance of earlier studies by A. L. Cooke, "W's Indebtedness to the Scientific Thought of His Day" (*UTSE* 36), Clarence Dugdale,
"W's Knowledge of Astronomy" (*ibid.*), and Newton Arvin's *W* (1938), but it
goes beyond them in the amount of evidence cited. After proving that W had
intelligently assimilated a number of popular books on astronomy and other
sciences, Beaver conclusively demonstrates the poet's interest in the phenomena of the physical universe and the accuracy of his observations and scientific allusions. The impact of the theory of evolution on *LofG* has been more

particularly studied in two articles: J. F. T. Tanner, "The Lamarckian Theory of Progress in *LofG*" (*WWR* 63), and E. J. Pfeifer, "The Theory of Evolution and W's 'Passage to India' " (*ESQ* 66).

W is known the world over as the poet of democracy and many a writer desirous to champion the democratic society has sought to enlist him in support of his cause. Yet few articles of importance have been written about his social thought or his political views. The older essays on these subjects are too naive or rhetorical to be of much value. (For example, see Edward Dowden, "The Poetry of Democracy: WW" in *Studies in Literature*, 1878, and F. B. Gummere, "W and Taine" in *Democracy and Poetry*, 1911.) C. J. Furness's "WW's Politics" (*AM* 29) has a promising title but the article does little more than show, by examining a sheaf of manuscript notes, that W studied the Constitution in order to enlighten himself on the legal aspects of the slavery question. Though H. A. Myers's "W's Conception of Spiritual Democracy, 1855–1856" (*AL* 34) concentrates on a very brief period in W's life, it emphasizes a facet of his political thought which is of capital importance in *LofG*. In "WW and the American Tradition" (*VQR* 55) Floyd Stovall has studied to good effect the relation of W's thought to the basic concepts of the free individual, the moral law, and progress. A. L. Cooke's "W's Background in the Industrial Movement of His Time" (*UTSE* 35), though slight, assembles some useful information. G. R. Roy in "WW, George Sand and Certain French Socialists" (*RLC* 55) and Henri Roddier in "Pierre Leroux, George Sand et WW, ou l'éveil d'un poète" (*RLC* 57) have shown how certain French socialistic theories reached W through George Sand's novels. But not even the leftist critics have said much of value about W's democratic poetry. Samuel Sillen's anthology, *WW: Poet of American Democracy* (1944, 1955) arranges the poems conveniently to stress particular social themes, but the introduction is loose and rambling. Of more interest, because of its orthodox Marxist approach and Russian origin, is the translation of D. S. Mirsky's "WW: Poet of American Democracy" (*Dialectics*, Critics Group, 1937). L. M. Clark's *WW's Concept of the American Common Man* (1955) is a painstaking and useful compilation of almost every published statement by W about the Common Man, but by wresting the quotations from their journalistic and historical contexts the author distorts and denatures the poet's thought to the extent of turning him into a racist contemptuous of Indians and Negroes alike. The realism of the journalist is made to obliterate the idealism of the Bard. It must be admitted, however, that there was a dichotomy between the journalist and the poet, and Oscar Cargill lucidly explores it in "WW and Civil Rights" (Max Schulz, ed., *Essays in American and English Literature Presented to Bruce McElderry, Jr.*, 1967). This lack of consistency has also been studied by

T. F. Andrews in "WW and Slavery: A Reconsideration of One Aspect of His Concept of the American Common Man" (*CLAJ* 66). Paschal Reeves discusses another of W's waverings in "The Silhouette of the State in *Democratic Vistas*: Hegelian or Whitmanian?" (*Person* 62). Though succinct, Leo Marx's "Democratic Vistas: Notes for a discussion of W and the Problems of Democratic (Mass?) Culture in America" (*ESQ* 61) contains some seminal ideas.

Other critics have been more interested in analyzing the relationship between poetry and politics in *LofG*, in particular Abraham Chapman in "Democracy as a Poetic Principle in *LofG*" (*WSL* 66) and R. G. Hanson in "W as Social Theorist: Worker in Poetics and Politics" (*WWR* 70). R. B. Hooph emphasizes the importance of W's democratic inspiration in the 1860 edition of *LofG* in " 'Chants Democratic and Native American': A Neglected Sequence in the Growth of *LofG*" (*AL* 70), but shows that in later editions W dropped the theme. After failing to convince his contemporaries to adopt his vision of the republic of the common man, he irrevocably turned inward.

In *Frontier: American Literature and the American West* (1965), in which he takes the opposite view to Frederick J. Turner and claims that the West was a mere dream which never came true, Edwin Fussell devotes the whole last chapter ("WW's *LofG*") to showing that W in 1855–60 "had achieved the poetry of the West, savage poetry, at precisely the moment when the West disappeared" and was therefore condemned to be a "retrospective poet" during the rest of his career, but he tends to exaggerate the importance of "the Western matter" in *LofG* and arbitrarily to establish a cause and effect relationship between the decline of the West and the decline of W as a poet after what he calls "the culmination" of his career in 1860.

The fact remains that the best analyses of W's social thought are still to be found in three books already mentioned: Arvin's *W* (1938), Allen's *WW Handbook* (1946), and Asselineau's *The Evolution of WW: The Creation of a Book* (1962). Two more articles, however, deserve mention because they contain interesting evaluations of W's strictures on American society: Emory Holloway's "W as a Critic of America" (*SP* 23) and M. E. Curti's "WW, Critic of America" (*SR* 28).

3. Literary Technique

In these days of increasing secularization readers and critics are less and less concerned with W's metaphysics. Under the influence of new criticism and structuralism they are more and more interested in the form and structure of *LofG* rather than in its contents. W himself once said, "I sometimes think the Leaves is only a language experiment." He is now being taken at his word.

Critics prefer to discuss him as a poet rather than as a prophet. Some of the most important recent W studies have concentrated on his literary techniques and his growth as an artist.

His earlier admirers often felt that they had to apologize for his lack of artistry. Gradually it has become apparent that he was in the company of those nineteenth-century poets who attempted to remove the restrictions of the traditional metrical forms. Eventually it was discovered that he had indeed been one of the most powerful leaders in this movement. His friend W. S. Kennedy made a beginning in two sections of his *Fight of a Book for the World* (1926): "The Growth of *LofG* as a Work of Art" and "Elucidations and Analyses of Difficult Poems in *LofG*." He also provided a useful tool in this volume, "Index of Dates Covering All the Poems of All the Editions of *LofG*." Killis Campbell's "The Evolution of W as Artist" (*AL* 34) carried further the work begun by Kennedy. The most important studies of W's artistic growth have been based on comparisons of versions of the poems as they were revised from edition to edition. O. L. Triggs made the first (and quite superficial) investigation of this sort in 1902, "The Growth of *LofG*" (*Complete Writings*, Vol. X). This method of studying W was later used with excellent results in three books: Allen, *WW Handbook* (1946), Frederick Schyberg, *WW* (1951), Asselineau, *The Evolution of WW: The Creation of a Book* (1962).

Several useful studies have been made of the organizing principles to be discerned in *LofG*. Though the article is brief, there are interesting ideas in I. C. Story's "The Structural Patterns of *LofG*" (*Pacific Univ Bul* 42). Richard Bridgman tries to discover the meaning of W's private number system in the various editions of *LofG* from 1856 to 1881 in "W Calendar Leaves" (*CE* 64). Examining the "Main Drifts in W's Poetry" (*AL* 32), Floyd Stovall found out that W employed three different organizing themes at different stages of his poetical career (love of freedom, love of death, spirituality). Though the article strains to make its point, there is some merit in Ferner Nuhn's "*LofG* Viewed as an Epic" (*ArQ* 51). Allen discusses one of the recurrent organizing themes of W's poetry in "WW's 'Long Journey' Motif" (*JEGP* 39). W's use of Hegelian dialectic in shaping poetry (particularly in "Chanting the Square Deific" and "Out of the Cradle . . .") is explored by A. H. Marks in "W's Triadic Imagery" (*AL* 51). S. K. Coffman, Jr., has chosen two specific examples to show the form of W's apparently formless catalogues in " 'Crossing Brooklyn Ferry': A Note on the Catalogue Technique in W's Poetry" (*MP* 54) and in "Form and Meaning in W's 'Passage to India' " (*PMLA* 55). His analyses bring to light underlying "patterns of images." R. R. Griffin reaches the same conclusions in "Notes on Structural Devices in W's Poetry" (*TSL* 61) and "The Interconnectedness of

'Our Old Feuillage' " (*WWR* 62). V. V. Chatman III also detects "Figures of Repetition in W's 'Song of Myself' " (*BNYPL* 65). The challenge offered by this poem has been taken up by several critics, notably J. N. Nagle in "Towards a Theory of Structure in 'Song of Myself' " (*WWR* 69), and Griffith Dudding in "The Function of Imagery in 'Song of Myself' " (*WWR* 67). The views of critics on this poem from Santayana to J. E. Miller, Jr., are discussed by Ronald Beck in "The Structure of 'Song of Myself' and the Critics" (*WWR* 69). Patterns of imagery have been found in other poems too: B. J. Leggett, "The Structure of W's 'On Journeys Through the States' " (*WWR* 68), A. H. Rosenfeld, "The Eagle and the Axe: A Study of W's 'Song of the Broad-Axe' " (*AI* 68), Sr. M. P. Slattery, "Patterns of Imagery in W's 'There Was a Child Went Forth' " (*WWR* 69), E. E. Sullivan, Jr., "Thematic Unfolding in W's 'Drum-Taps' " (*ESQ* 63), and J. W. Gargano, "Technique in 'Crossing Brooklyn Ferry' " (*JEGP* 63). The complexities of W's catalogue technique are discussed in general terms in Mattie Swayne's "W's Catalogue Rhetoric" (*UTSE* 41) and in Lawrence Buell's "Transcendentalist Rhetoric: Vision vs. Form" (*AL* 68). Buell compares W's catalogues to Emerson's paragraphs. According to him, both writers make the same demands on the reader. They invite him to participate and complete.

In an attempt to account for the peculiarities of *LofG* some critics have compared W's poetry with other arts: Alice Ahlers with the cinema in "Cinematographic Technique in *LofG*" (*WWR* 66) and Robert Faner more appropriately with music in *WW and Opera* (1951). Faner lists the operas W attended, quotes from his journalistic articles about singers, culls out his allusions to musical forms and instruments, and then attempts to assess in detail the influence of operatic style on W's poetry. But he occasionally runs into difficulty by trying to prove too much. W actually knew next to nothing about the technical aspects of music and Faner's endeavors to discover W using the sonata ("whether he was closely aware of the details of form or not"!) do not succeed. Nor is his chapter on "Melody" pertinent. Yet other critics have rashly followed his lead, notably M. C. Patterson in " 'Lilacs': A Sonata" (*WWR* 68) and C. S. Lenhart in "WW and Music in *LofG*" (*Musical Influences on American Poetry*, 1956). S. J. Krause in "W, Music and 'Proud Music of the Storm' " (*PMLA* 57) is on firmer ground since in this particular instance W obviously wanted to emulate music.

In 1896 W. S. Kennedy attempted to explain W's technical effects in "The Style of *LofG*" (in *Reminiscences of WW*), but he did not command the critical vocabulary adequate to his task. In 1929–30 there appeared three excellent studies which led the way to further explorations of W's techniques. Jean Catel's *Rythme et langage dans la 1ère édition des "LofG"* (Paris, 1930) examines first the transition in W's writing from the rhetoric of his early prose, published and unpublished, to the rhetorical verse of the 1855 edition. The second half of this monograph deals with particular features of his poetical style, from vocabulary to the rhythmical grouping of lines. Lois Ware's "Poetic Conventions in *LofG*" (*SP* 29) shows that W was not as wildly radical in technique as his early defamers declared, and in 1929 A. N. Wiley studied the "Reiterative Devices in *LofG*" (*AL*). These devices are epanaphora or initial repetition and epinalepsis or repetition within the line. For his part, R. P. Adams in "W's 'Lilacs' and the Tradition of Pastoral Elegy" (*PMLA* 57) points out that "When Lilacs Last in the Dooryard Bloom'd" is no "barbaric yawp" but a traditional elegy in new dress.

Concentrating on "Song of Myself," K. A. Preuschen analyzes the characteristics of the new lyrical style invented by W in "Zur Entstehung der neuen Lyrik in Amerika" (*JA* 63). W's new symbolistic technique, his use of "indirection," as he called it, is studied by T. J. Rountree in "WW's Indirect Expression and Its Application to 'Song of Myself' " (*PMLA* 58), E. H. Eby in "WW's Indirections" (*WWR* 66), and S. J. Kahn in "W's Allegorical Lyricism" (*SecH* 66). Two Italian critics have written perceptive essays on the subject: Glauco Cambon, "La parola come emanazione: Note marginali sullo stile di W" (*SA* 59) and Sergio Perosa, "Il linguaggio de W" in Mario Praz *et al.*, *Il simbolismo nella letteratura nord-americana* (Firenze, 1965).

W's use of language has been admirably studied in depth by Matthiessen in the chapter of his *AmR* (1941) entitled "Only a Language Experiment" and more statically by Asselineau in the chapter on "Language: Innovations and Traditions" in the second volume of his *Evolution of WW* (1962), which is only an inadequate survey of a vast subject. The study of W's language, however, has not yet been done thoroughly—though a small number of articles have broken ground: Rebecca Coy's "A Study of W's Diction" (*UTSE* 36) and four papers by Louise Pound: "WW and the Classics" (*SWR* 25), "WW and Italian Music" (*AM* 25), "WW's Neologisms" (*ibid.*), and "WW and the French Language" (*AS* 26). (The second and fourth of these papers have been collected in her *Selected Writings*, 1949.) Martin Christadler has carefully analyzed W's theories of language and his application of them to his poetry in "WW: Sprachtheorie und Dichtung" (*JA* 68). The French element in W's vocabulary has also been studied by K. H. Francis, "WW's French" (*MLR* 56), and his love of the vernacular both by C. Carroll Hollis in "W and the American Idiom" (*QJS* 57) and Leo Marx in "The Vernacular Tradition in American Literature" (*NS* 58). Some curious information about his interest in words is supplied by Hollis in two articles: "Names in *LofG*" (*Names* 57) and "W's Word-Games" (*WWR* 58). The publication of E. H. Eby's *A Concordance of WW's "LofG,"* and *Selected Prose Writings* (1949–54) should have stimulated research, but no thorough stylistic study of *LofG* or W's prose has been undertaken yet, except on a limited subject by a Finnish linguist, Niilo Peltola in *The Compound Epithet and Its Use in American Poetry from Bradstreet through W* (1956). In his chapter on W he points out that "a great number of W's compound epithets bespeak his strong pictorial, visual power, his tendency to see objects in a static and synchronic way" and that about nine per cent are alliterative in spite of his claim that he had discarded the conventional tricks of poetic diction (a rather irrelevant objection). He concludes, however, and quite rightly, that W "contributed to the freeing of the poetic diction of American verse from conventional, ornamental, non-functional compound epithets." Peltola does not seem to have used Eby's *Concordance*, which unfortunately will now have to be re-done. It is based on the text of *The Complete Writings* (1902), which *The Collected Writings* in course of publication will render obsolete.

As to W's prosody, strangely enough, long before American scholars began their investigation of it, it was the subject of a remarkable treatise published in Italy, Pasquale Jannacone's *La poesia di WW e l'evoluzione delle forme ritmiche* (1898). Jannacone's fine ear for rhythm and his extensive knowledge of metrics enabled him to analyze W's verse accurately and perceptively. His little book should be better known than it is. It is a pity it has never been translated into English. Allen has written two very useful chapters on W's prosody, one in his *American Prosody* (1935) and the other in his *WW Handbook* (1946). He is concerned above all with the devices the poet used (parallelism, the "envelope," phonetic recurrence, initial, medial, and final reiteration, etc.) in order to give rhythmical shape to his meters. The conclusion reached by Bradley in his "The Fundamental Metrical Principle in W's Poetry" (*AL* 39) can be summed up in his own words: "His revolution centered on three things: a new emphasis, to the point of organic use, upon ancient repetitive devices . . . ; the construction of stanzas and larger units on the basis of rhythmic balance and parallelism; his conscious rejection of syllabic meter in favor of that more ancient and native English meter based on the rhythmic 'period' between the stresses." W's prosody has also been examined briefly by R. E. Cory ("The Prosody of WW," *NDQ* 60) and by Harvey Gross in *Sound and Form in Modern Poetry: A Study of Prosody from Thomas Hardy to Robert Lowell* (1964). James McNally has concentrated on "Varieties of Alliterations in W" (*WWR* 67). Georgiana Pollak interprets W's prosody in terms of music in "The Relationship of Music to *LofG*" (*CE* 54) and concludes that W "simply perceived his rhythmic needs worked out in the speech rhythms of the recitative and transferred some of its devices to his poetry." For Roger Mitchell in "A Prosody for W?" (*PMLA* 69), "WW's poetry is constructed of groups rather than stresses, though stresses are used to measure the size of groups . . . Whether measured in groups/line or stresses/line, his most consistent rhythmic form is the parabola. His use of it occasionally shows a formality and intricacy which are never attributed to him." For a modern poet's insight into W's art one should read Randall Jarrell's shrewd and sympathetic "Some Lines from W" (*Poetry and the Age*, 1953).

W has thus been more and more studied as a conscious and conscientious artist and in the last decade two books about his artistry and aesthetics have been published. C. R. Metzger's *Thoreau and W: A Study of their Esthetics* (1961), however, is disappointing. It contains a wealth of quotations from Thoreau and W illustrating the interrelationship of their aesthetics and their Transcendentalist philosophy, but the emphasis is laid on *Democratic Vistas. LofG* is hardly quoted at all. W the poet never has his say, though the center of his aesthetics is not to be found in his prose but everywhere in his poems. Besides, the poetry of the body is systematically ignored; only the poetry of the soul is considered worth examining by the author, who, to make things worse, insists on describing both W and Thoreau as Protestant communicants. H. J. Waskow in *W: Explorations in Form* (1966) concentrates on form but does not arbitrarily separate it from its vital roots in W's thought and personality, which he studies in the first part of his book under the title of "W's Habit of Mind." He insists on the constant triplicity or "bipolar unity" of W, "who in his response to almost any problem is committed simultaneously to each polar position and to the polar positions unified." The second part of the book narrows down to structure. The major poems of *LofG* are sorted out into four main categories: 1) those which have direction and tend to didacticism, 2) those which have no direction and tend to imagism, 3) those which have direction and take the shape of narratives, 4) those which are meant to be indirect, like "Song of Myself" and "The Sleepers," which Waskow, after Allen and C. T. Davis, calls "monodramas." The book contains a series of "explications de texte" which brilliantly light up the major poems, but this method has its drawbacks like any method when applied too systematically: the contents of the poems tend to be underestimated and the biographical implications of "Calamus," for instance, ignored in favor of New Critical ambiguities. In spite of this shortcoming, this is a masterly study of *LofG* which succeeds remarkably in clarifying W's poetry.

W himself has in turn described *LofG* as the expression of a personality (and *ipso facto* of a *Weltanschauung*), as a "language experiment" and an "image-making work." This survey of W criticism reveals a growing tendency on the part of critics to concentrate on the second aspect of his poetry. They dissect his art with a bold and adroit scalpel and explore his form. There remains, however, to study his imagery, to follow the subterranean itineraries of his images before they blossom up in the poems. This has hardly been attempted at all until now, except by the Japanese critic Haruo Shimizu in an untranslated *Study of W's Imagery* (1957), which he summed up in the June 1959 issue of the *WWR*.

4. Whitman as Critic

W's critical writing has not been much studied, and yet it would be a very rewarding subject, for W was an extremely keen critic with brilliant intuitions and a sure grasp of essentials. Norman Foerster touched upon it in his chapter on "Whitman" in *American Criticism* (1928). One should also consult M. O. Johnson's "WW as a Critic of Literature" (*Univ of Nebr Stud* 38) and a brief article on "Literary Criticism in *Specimen Days*" by James Bristol (*WWR* 66). Asselineau has studied W's theory of criticism in "A Poet's Dilemma: WW's Attitude to Literary History and Literary Criticism" (Leon Edel, ed., *Literary History and Literary Criticism*, 1964).

5. Explications of Specific Poems

A fairly large number of useful explications of particular W poems have appeared, and some of them deserve to be mentioned: G. L. Sixbey, " 'Chanting the Square Deific': A Study in W's Religion" (*AL* 37); Leo Spitzer, " 'Explication de texte' Applied to W's 'Out of the Cradle Endlessly Rocking' " (*EHL* 49; repr. in his *Essays on English and American Literature*, 1962); C. F. Strauch, "The Structure of WW's 'Song of Myself' " (*EJ* 38); John Lovell, Jr., "Appreciating W: 'Passage to India' " (*MLQ* 60). Harold Aspiz reveals the phrenological substructure of "There Was a Child . . ." in "Educating the Kosmos: 'There Was a Child Went Forth' " (*AQ* 66) and of "Unfolded out of the Folds" in "Unfolding the Folds" (*WWR* 66). Analyses of difficult passages in W's poems appear frequently in the *Explicator* and have been later reassembled in *Explicator Cyclopedia* (1966) or in the *WWR*. About the mystery of the 28 bathers in section 11 of "Song of Myself," see O. K. Nambiar, "W's Twenty-Eight Bathers," in Sujit Mukherjee and D. V. K. Raghavacharyulu, eds., *Indian Essays in American Literature* (Bombay, 1969).

6. Parodies

Parody is a form of criticism. The compilation made by H. S. Saunders, *Parodies on WW* (1923), proves that he is one of the most parodied poets in English. It also proves that several excellent wits (Quiller-Couch, Carolyn

Wells, Ezra Pound, Christopher Morley, G. K. Chesterton, etc.) have had their fun with his catalogues and his apostrophes to lowly persons, places, and things. *The Antic Muse* (1955), edited by R. P. Falk, reprints some of these parodies and adds "A Classic Waits for Me" by E. B. White.

7. Sources and Influences

Though W was self-taught and a desultory reader, he read widely and in many different fields. Since he often kept extensive notes or pasted up articles which struck his fancy, scholars have been able to identify many of the works which influenced him. In "Notes on W's Reading" (*AL* 54) Stovall tracked down the sources of 112 items printed by Bucke in *Notes and Fragments* (1899). A less systematic study is David Goodale's "Some of WW's Borrowings" (*AL* 28).

Studies of the influence of English writers on W are chiefly concerned with Shakespeare and Carlyle. The first extensive investigation of Shakespeare's influence was R. C. Harrison's "WW and Shakespeare" (*PMLA* 29), followed by C. J. Furness's "WW's Estimate of Shakespeare" (*Harvard Stud and Notes in Philol and Lit* 32). These two authors claimed that W's early repudiation of Shakespeare's "feudalism" prevented him for a time from appreciating Shakespeare's poetry. But Stovall in his "W, Shakespeare and Democracy" (*JEGP* 52) corrects these views and concludes that W was aware, before he wrote *LofG*, of Shakespeare's unrivaled greatness as a poet. In another article, "W's Knowledge of Shakespeare" (*SP* 52), Stovall demonstrates that much of W's early knowledge of Shakespeare was derived from performances of the plays he attended and from J. P. Collier's biography. Three articles deal with W's reactions to Carlyle's ideas: Gregory Paine, "The Literary Relations of W and Carlyle with Especial Reference to Their Contrasting Views on Democracy" (*SP* 39); F. M. Smith, "W's Poet-Prophet and Carlyle's Hero" (*PMLA* 40), and "W's Debt to Carlyle's *Sartor Resartus*" (*MLQ* 42). Paine contends that though W made a vigorous reply to Carlyle's "Shooting Niagara, and After?" in his "Democracy" (later included in *Democratic Vistas*) in the end he believed that Carlyle's fears were to some extent justified. Smith holds to the view that Carlyle may have had a seminal influence on the gestation of *LofG*.

Asselineau detects an influence of Wordsworth's aesthetics (rather than of his poetical practice) on *LofG* in "W et Wordsworth: étude d'une influence indirecte" (*RLC* 55). Shelley's influence is not convincingly established in two articles published in the *WWR* (68): R. A. Duerksen's "Markings by W in His Copy of Shelley's *Works*" and M. K. Sanders's "Shelley's Promethean Shadow on *LofG*." But C. B. Willard has shown that on two occasions W was indebted to Tennyson: "W and Tennyson's 'Ulysses' " (*WWR* 56).

W's indebtedness to German thinkers and writers has been much debated. Richard Riethmuller surveyed the subject generally (and rather superficially) in "WW and the Germans," *German American Annals* (1906). More substantial is R. P. Falk, "WW and German Thought" (*JEGP* 41). W. B. Fulghum, Jr., produces good evidence in "W's Debt to Joseph Gostwick" (*AL* 41) that W was indebted to Gostwick's popular handbook, *German Literature* (1854), for information about the German philosophers—and about the *Nibelungenlied* too, according to W. A. Little ("WW and the *Nibelungenlied*," *PMLA* 65). Sr. Mary Eleanor discusses another possible intermediary in "Hedge's *Prose Writers of Germany* as a Source of W's Knowledge of German Philosophy" (*MLN* 46).

Some well-documented articles which assess other writers or works influential in W's career may be briefly mentioned: Allen, "Biblical Echoes in WW's Works" (*AL* 34); F. I. Carpenter, "The Vogue of Ossian in America" (*AL* 31); Allen, "WW and Jules Michelet" (*EA* 37), which shows that "To the Man-of-War Bird" is the paraphrase of a prose passage in *The Bird*; A. B. Benson, "WW's Interest in Swedish Writers" (*JEGP* 32). The influence of Poe's "Raven" on "Out of the Cradle Endlessly Rocking" has been pointed out in three articles: N. J. Davison (*PN* 68), Milton Hindus (*WWR* 57), and above all, J. M. DeFalco (*ibid.* 70).

VII. FAME AND INFLUENCE

Even before his death W was becoming famous as a figure in world literature. He had been translated, not always adequately, into German, French, Danish, Dutch, Italian, and Russian. His English admirers were proud that they had taken him up at a time when his compatriots were still trying to ignore him. W was vain of his growing reputation abroad and did everything he could to enlarge it. He and his Camden disciples kept every review of his work which came from Europe or other parts of the world. In 1926 W. S. Kennedy drew on this storehouse of criticism for his triumphant *The Fight of a Book for the World*. Each new generation of writers has found something new to admire in *LofG*. By turns he has appealed to symbolists and unanimists (Jules Romains), to democrats, to members of the "intermediate sex" (Edward Carpenter's phrase), to Vedantists, to revolutionists all over the world, to nationalists, and internationalists. Meanwhile translations into new languages have appeared—Spanish, Polish, Finnish, Jugoslavian, Roumanian, Czech, Portuguese, Hebrew,

Japanese, Chinese, Urdu, Bengali, and other Indian languages. The wings of W's soul were indeed plumed for far flights, and it has made its "passage to more than India."

Though the subject of W's fame and influence is a vast one, it has been excellently surveyed in Allen's *WW Handbook* (1946) and in Schyberg's long chapter on "W in World Literature" (*WW*, 1951). There is also a general article on the subject by Maurice Herra [i.e., Asselineau] "Feuilles d'herbe in Europe et en Amérique Latine" (*Europe* 55). Besides, in 1955, Allen edited *WW Abroad*, which contains samples of foreign criticism and selected bibliographies completing and updating those given in the *WW Handbook*. The countries represented are Germany, France, Norway, Denmark, Sweden, Russia, Italy, Spanish America, Israel, Japan, and India. The most interesting texts are Giovanni Papini's and Cesare Pavese's appreciations of *LofG*, the lyrical essay by Unamuno on the magic of W's language, and the comments on W and democracy by the Brazilian critic, Gilberto Freyre. Unfortunately no revised edition of this book and no other book of the same kind have appeared since, except for a long and well-documented study in Japanese, which has not been translated yet and is thus inaccessible to most W scholars: Shunsuke Kamei, *WW in Modern Literature: A Comparative Study of Japanese and Western Appreciations* (1970). However many articles and even books on W's critical reception in various countries have been published and it is possible for anyone interested in the subject of W's influence to make his own synthesis or selection.

Harold Blodgett's *WW in England* (1934) was written nearly forty years ago, but is not badly out of date since the wave of enthusiasm for W in England began to recede in the first years of this century. Douglas Grant's pamphlet on *WW and His English Admirers* (1962) covers only the nineteenth century. W. D. Templeman in "Hopkins and W: Evidence of Influence and Echoes" (*PQ* 54) actually cannot prove that there was an influence of W on the English poet. Sydney Musgrove in *T. S. Eliot and WW* (1952) sometimes also gives the impression of trying to prove too much but points out the recurrence in Eliot's poetry of rhythmical patterns common in W and succeeds in showing that there are conscious or unconscious reminiscences of some of W's poems in T. S. Eliot's poetry. Herbert Howarth has written an interesting essay on "W and the Irish Writers" (*CL* 60). W's influence in Australasia has been investigated by A. L. McLeod in *WW in Australia and New Zealand* (1964), J. T. F. Tanner in "W's Reception 'Down Under'" (*WWR* 65), and Joseph Jones in "Emerson and W 'Down Under'" (*ESQ* 66). In South Africa General J. C. Smuts was quite interested in W's mysticism and the *Selections from the Smuts Papers* (1966) contain extracts from an early book on the American poet, which was the starting-point of his philosophical treatise, *Holism and Evolution* (1926). In India the influence of W's lyricism and his "vers-libre" technique has been felt even by poets writing in their native languages (Pashto, for instance) and by Tagore both in his English and Bengalee poems: See Robert Gilkey, "Tagore and W" (*Quest* 62).

Several studies deal with the fame of W in Germany: O. E. Lessing, "WW and his German Critics" (*JEGP* 10); G. D. Clark, "WW in Germany" (*TR* 21); Anna Jacobson, "WW in Germany since 1914" (*GR* 26); and Harry Law-Robertson, "WW in Deutschland" (*Giessener Beitrage zur deutschen Philol* 35). Law-Robertson's dissertation contains a full list of German translations of *LofG* and of critical estimates of them. E. A. McCormick's *Die sprachliche Eigenart von WWs "LofG" in deutschen Übertragung* (1953) compares the various German translations of *LofG*. W's influence on German poets is studied by D. W. Schumann in "Observations on Enumerative Style in Modern German Poetry" (*PMLA* 44). H. Pongs concentrates on W's influence on Stefan George (*CL* 52; repr. in *WW Abroad*).

W's impact was particularly strong in France. Fernand Baldensperger's "WW and France" (*Columbia Univ Quar* 19) contains an interesting account of "le whitmanisme" of the 1910's. S. A. Rhode's "The Influence of WW on André Gide" shows conclusively that W transformed Gide's life and career. Unfortunately the article says little about the revolt Gide led against Bazalgette's idealized translation of *LofG* and his *Le Poème-Evangile de WW* (1921), which is the most extraordinary piece of hagiography in all the W literature. The same subject is studied by Martin Kanes (the author of a very thorough unpublished dissertation for the University of Paris on W's influence in France) in "W, Gide and Bazalgette" (*CL* 62). P. M. Jones's "W and Verhaeren" (*Aberystwyth Stud* 14) finds no influence of the American poet on "the visionary of Belgium," but points out striking parallels. Jones's studies of W's influence in France have culminated in two judicious chapters of his *The Background of Modern French Poetry* (1951): "W and the Symbolists" and "W and the Origins of the *Vers Libre*." Pierre Brunel refuses to acknowledge W's influence on Paul Claudel in "L'image de l'orchestre et la tentation symphonique chez WW et P. Claudel" (*RLM* 66).

In spite of entirely different literary traditions W's influence has been felt in Italy too, as Rea McCain shows in "WW in Italy" (*Italica* 43) and, above all, Mariolina Meliadò in an excellent descriptive bibliography ("La Fortuna di WW in Italia," *SA* 61) and Glauco Cambon in "WW in Italia" (*aut aut* 57).

LofG reached Spain rather late. No Castilian translation of it appeared until 1912, but its influence was quite strong in South America. Writing in 1938, J. E.

Englekirk averred in "Notes on W in Spanish America" that since the turn of the century W has been "one of the leading spiritual forces in young Spanish America." In a copious book, *WW en Hispanoamérica* (1954), Fernando Alegría supplies a wealth of information about the impact of *LofG* in Latin America. He shows how W's life and works became better and better known, he analyzes the poet's philosophical ideas and attitude to sex, he describes his influence on modernist and post-modernist poets, and finally compares the merits of the various Spanish translations of *LofG*. A supplement to this book appeared in the *WWR* in 1966: H. C. Woodbridge, "Additional Bibliography in Spanish." Fernando Alegría has devoted a special essay to the influence of W on José Martí, the Cuban poet: "El W de José Martí" (*Humanismo* 54), and Manuel Blanco has described his influence on Unamuno: "WW y Unamuno" (*Cultura Universitaria* 55; *Atlantico* 56). The most lucid admirer of W in South America is the Argentinian poet-critic Jorge Borges. His attitude to W is analyzed by D. T. Jaén in "Borges y W" (*Hispania* 67). In *Homage to WW* (1969), D. T. Jaén has collected and translated a number of poems by Spanish and South American writers, notably Borges, Rubén Darío, Lorca, and Pablo Neruda.

The relationship between W and the Protean Portuguese poet Fernando Pessoa, who wrote a beautiful "Salutation to WW" under the "heteronym" of Alvaro de Campos, is studied by Rainer Hess in *APK* (64).

Information about W's influence in Roumania will be found in G. I. Rand, "WW in Rumania" (*ESQ* 66). Allen has studied "WW's Reputation in Scandinavia" (*PBSA* 46). This essay can be supplemented by Frederic Fleisher's "WW's Swedish Reception" (*WWR* 57) and Lars Åhnebrink's "WW and Sweden" (*WWR* 60).

For W's reception in Czarist Russia one must rely on Albert Parry's very amusing, but not well documented "WW in Russia" (*AM* 34). In the early years of the Soviet regime W was extravagantly admired and imitated by the revolutionary poets, in particular by Maiakovski. The best account of W's reputation in Soviet Russia is still the essay contributed to *WW Abroad* (1955) by Stephen Stepanchev. Kornei Chukovsky's translation of *LofG* has gone through many editions, and his role in the diffusion of W's poetry in Russia has been described by J. C. Fiske in "Kornei Chukovsky: Interpreter of W" (*KFLQ* 54).

Joseph Remenyi's "WW in Hungarian Literature" (*AL* 44), though disappointingly brief, is indicative of W's ever-widening influence.

The critical reception of *LofG* in Japan is studied not only in Shunsuke Kamei's recent book, which has already been mentioned, *WW in Modern Literature* (1970), but also in several articles, notably in one by the same author, fortunately written in English: "W in Japan" (*RG* 69). Two earlier articles are still worth consulting: Sabura Ota, "WW and Japanese Literature" (*Asia and the Humanities* 59) and Noriko Nabeshima, "WW in Japan" (*SEL* 65).

As to the reputation of WW in the United States, it is the subject of *W's American Fame: The Growth of His Reputation in America after 1892* (1950) by C. B. Willard. Willard reviews the work of most of the biographers, the journalistic and academic critics, and the creative writers. The story of W's influence on Richard Hovey and others is told by C. T. Kindilien in a chapter of his book on *American Poetry in the Eighteen Nineties* (1956): "W and the Vagabondians." The vagaries of Ezra Pound's attitude to W are analyzed in C. B. Williard's "E. Pound's Appraisal of WW" (*MLN* 57) and "E. Pound and the W Message" (*RLC* 57). The influence of W on Pound is assessed—rather negatively—by Herbert Bergman in "E. Pound and WW" (*AL* 55). J. E. Breslin has studied "W and the Early Development of W. C. Williams" (*PMLA* 67) and V. K. Chari, "W and the Beat Poets" (*ESQ* 65). To celebrate the centennial of *LofG* in 1955 a group of American poets wrote poems in his honor (in particular Charles Olson, Louis Zukovsky, Langston Hughes, Richard Eberhart, W. C. Williams). These poems were collected under the title of *WW: A Centennial Celebration* (1954), a special issue of the *Beloit Poetry Journal*.

Even a writer of fiction like Jack London bears the stamp of W's influence, as Arthur Barrett shows in *Jack London and WW* (1969). This influence is still more obvious in the case of William James; see J. T. F. Tanner, "WW and William James" (*Calamus*, 70). Henry Miller has described himself the impact which *LofG* made upon him in *The Books in My Life* (1951) and returned to the subject in *Stand Still Like the Humming-Bird* (1962).

Thus W's fame and influence have been described and explored by many scholars, but much still remains to be done in this field. Besides, many of the studies which have been mentioned need updating.

VIII. SPECIALIZED PERIODICALS

Ever since 1890 (two years before the poet's death) there have been periodicals exclusively devoted to W worship or W scholarship. 1) *The Conservator* (1890–1919), edited by Horace Traubel, appeared monthly in principle, published some interesting articles, but the focus shifted gradually from W to Traubel himself. The Library of Congress keeps the typescript of the complete index compiled by H. S. Saunders. 2) *The WW Fellowship Papers* (1894–1919) appeared irregularly and contained only occasionally contributions of lasting interest. William White has given a check-list of them in "The WW Fellowship

. . ." (*PBSA* 57). 3) *The WW Foundation Bulletin* (1948–1955) appeared annually and contained a bibliography. 4) *The WW Birthplace Bulletin* (1957–1961), a quarterly edited by Verne Dyson, dealt chiefly with W's Long Island years. 5) The *WW Newsletter*, a quarterly founded by Allen in 1955 and edited by William White, changed its name to *WW Review* in 1959. It publishes scholarly articles and an exhaustive quarterly check-list of recent publications on W compiled by White. 6) *Calamus* (1969–), founded and edited by W. T. Moore, is intended for a broader public of W enthusiasts.

MARK TWAIN[1]

Harry Hayden Clark

I. BIBLIOGRAPHY

Merle Johnson's *A Bibliography of the Works of Mark Twain* (hereafter MT or T), *Samuel Langhorne Clemens: A List of First Editions in Book Form and of First Printings in Periodicals and Occasional Publications of his Various Literary Activities* in the much revised 1935 edition was standard for its date. But this must now be supplemented by "MT's Juvenilia" (*AL* 30); Ivan Benson's *MT's Western Years* (1938), which includes "Periodical Bibliography: Bibliography of the Writings of MT in the Newspapers and Magazines of Nevada and California, 1861–1866"; E. M. Branch's "A Chronological Bibliography of the Writings of Samuel Clemens to June 8, 1867" (*AL* 46); Lewis Leary's *AAL* (1954, 1970); *LHUS* (1948; sup. 1959). See also the *Twainian* for October 1939, December 1940, and February and June 1943. Edward Wagenknecht's revision for the third edition of his *MT: The Man and his Work* (1935, 1961, 1967) includes a "commentary" on scholarship covering the five-year period from 1960–65, with remarks which are often suggestive and useful. *MFS* (1968) carried in its special T issue "Criticism of MT: A Selected Checklist," pp. 93–139, compiled by Maurice Beebe and John Feaster. For a bibliography documenting T's reputation, see Roger Asselineau's list (discussed below under "Influence of MT").

Jacob Blanck's many-volumed *BAL* (1955 ff.) now includes T's own work (listed under Clemens), and the whole of the 24th volume in the new Iowa-California edition of T's *Works* is to be devoted to a bibliography by W. B. Todd. It is possible that in connection with their joint editorial work John Gerber and Frederick Anderson may issue a bibliography emphasizing unpublished papers and fragments of MSS. *8AmA*, edited by Floyd Stovall (1956), has in its 1963 re-issue a bibliographical appendix by J. C. Mathews, covering selected

1. Professor Clark died while this book was in press. The editor is grateful to Professor Howard G. Baetzhold of Butler University for reading, correcting, and making additions to this essay.

items for the 1956–62 period. *ALS*, edited by James Woodress (1965–69); J. A. Robbins (1970–), has had, since its inception in 1965 under the auspices of the MLA, a long critical section on T by John Gerber, to whose acute appraisals reference here will occasionally be made. One may keep abreast of current T scholarship by consulting the annual *MLA International Bibliography*, as well as the quarterly listings in *AL*.

There are many important MS collections, the largest of which is the papers of the T estate at the University of California at Berkeley. For an early description of this material, when Bernard De Voto was literary executor, see his article, "The MT papers" (*SR* 38). C. J. Armstrong ("MT's Early Writings Discovered," *MHR* 30) describes the Hannibal Papers presented to the State Historical Society at Columbia, Missouri. *YULG* (43) describes the Frear Collection at Yale. The University of California has the Moffett Collection described in the *NYT* (54). The Berg Collection of the New York Public Library has an important collection of T manuscripts, and the William Dean Howells Papers at Harvard include T's letters to Howells. The University of Virginia, the Buffalo Public Library, the Huntington Library, and the Princeton Library also have valuable T collections, as does the Library of Congress.

II. EDITIONS AND TEXTS

The most complete and definitive edition is *The Writings of MT*, edited by A. B. Paine (37 vols., 1922–25). There are also the Author's National Edition of *The Writings of MT* (22 vols., 1899–1900); the Underwood Edition of *The Writings of MT* (25 vols., 1901–07); and *MT's Works* (23 vols., 1933). Much of T's writing is to be found outside these collections. *MT's Speeches* (1910) and a more inclusive edition of 1923, the important *Notebook* (1935), and the *Autobiography* (2 vols., 1924) were all edited by A. B. Paine, along with the *Letters, Arranged with Comment* (2 vols., 1917). *MT in Eruption*, edited by Bernard De Voto (1940), may be regarded as a third volume of the *Autobiography*, to be used with caution in the light of DeLancey Ferguson's findings in "The Uncollected Portion of MT's Autobiography" (*AL* 36). In 1959 Charles Neider published *The Autobiography of MT*, in which he arranged the contents of Paine's and De Voto's volumes (though not all of them) chronologically. He also added a few heretofore unpublished passages. For the complete *Autobiography*, however, we shall have to await the volumes edited by Frederick Anderson for the Iowa-California edition. Dixon Wecter edited *MT in Three Moods* (1948), *MT to Mrs. Fairbanks* (1949), and *The Love Letters of MT* (1949), three collections of basic material. Lewis Leary edited MT's *Letters to Mary [B. Rogers, 1900–10]* (1961). S. C. Webster's *MT: Business Man* (1946) includes letters as well as biography.

Ivan Benson's *MT's Western Years* (1938) includes "Selected MT Western Items," and E. M. Branch's *Literary Apprenticeship of MT* (1950) includes "Selections from MT's Apprenticeship Writings, 1852–67." See also *MT of the [Virginia City] "Enterprise": Newspaper Articles & Other Documents, 1862–1864*, and *MT: San Francisco Correspondent—Selections from His Letters to "The Territorial Enterprise," 1865–1866*, both edited by H. N. Smith with the assistance of Frederick Anderson (1957), and *Clemens of the "Call,"* edited by E. M. Branch (1970).

A good bit of additional early journalism also has been recovered from its original source and reprinted: B. R. McElderry, Jr., has edited *Contributions to the "Galaxy," 1868–1871* (1961); F. R. Rogers brought out *The Pattern for MT's "Roughing It": Letters from Nevada by Samuel and Orion Clemens, 1861–1862* (1961); D. M. McKeithan issued *Traveling with the Innocents Abroad: MT's Original Reports from Europe & the Holy Land* (1958). Also now available are Henry Duskis, editor, *The Forgotten Writings of MT* (1963), which contains T's contributions—many of them of doubtful authenticity—to the Buffalo *Express* (1869–71), and Bernard Taper, editor, *MT's San Francisco* 1963), which includes selections from T's 1863–66 newspaper writings. Two other collections of previously unprinted material are De Voto's edition of *Letters from the Earth*, which Clara Clemens refused in 1939 to have published and which appeared only in 1962, with a preface by H. N. Smith, and a curious but interesting volume by A. L. Scott, *On the Poetry of MT* (1966), which contains 65 of the 120 poems T is known to have written.

Also especially noteworthy is W. F. Frear's *MT and Hawaii* (1947), a complete assembly of all T's writing on that subject, with elaborate commentary. See also the following not in the collected editions: *The Curious Republic of Gondour* (1919); *Sketches of the Sixties*, by Bret Harte and MT, edited by John Howell (1927); *Adventures of Thomas Jefferson Snodgrass*, edited by Charles Honce (1928)[2]; *The Washoe Giant in San Francisco*, edited by Franklin Walker (1938); *Letters from the Sandwich Islands*, edited by G. E. Dane (1937, 1938); *Letters from Honolulu*, edited by Thomas Nickerson (1939); *MT's Travels with Mr. Brown*, edited by Franklin Walker and G. E. Dane (1940); *Republican Let-*

2. *The Letters of Quintus Curtius Snodgrass* (ed., E. E. Leisy, 1946) will be found on library shelves with T material, but they recently have been proven not to be by T. See C. S. Brinegar, "MT and the Quintus Curtius Snodgrass Letters" (*JASA* 63), and Allan Bates, "The Quintus Curtius Snodgrass Letters: A Clarification of the MT Canon" (*AL* 64).

ters (1941) and *Washington in 1868* (1943), both edited by Cyril Clemens (see *AL* 43 for corrections); *MT's Letters in the Muscatine Journal*, edited by E. M. Branch (1942); Walter Blair's "MT, New York Correspondent" (*AL* 39); E. E. Leisy, "MT and Isaiah Sellers" (*AL* 42); *MT's Letters to Will Bowen*, edited by Theodore Hornberger (1941); C. B. Taylor's *MT's Margins on Thackeray's "Swift"* (1935); *Report from Paradise*, edited by Dixon Wecter (1952), containing two opening chapters of *Captain Stormfield's Visit* and "Letter from the Recording Angel"; H. W. Fischer, *Abroad with MT and Eugene Field* (1922), to be used with caution, as the text is based partly on Fischer's memory; "Fenimore Cooper's Further Literary Offences," edited by De Voto (*NEQ* 46); G. H. Brownell: "Two Hitherto Unknown T Tales" (*Twainian* 46), "Seven New T Tales Discovered by Chance" (*Twainian* 43), "Where and When Were These T Tales First Printed?" (*Twainian* 44), the first, second, and third of "American Travel Letters Series Two," reprinted from the *Alta California* (*Twainian* 47, 49), and "MT's Letters in the San Francisco *Call*" (*Twainian* 49, 52). Many of F. W. Lorch's valuable studies listed in Leary's *AAL* include citations from newspapers of T's original lectures, as do two doctoral dissertations: S. T. Donner's "The Speaking and Reading of MT" (Northwestern, 1946), and J. C. Ervin's "MT: Speechmaker" (Mo., 1950). Lorch has climaxed his long interest in T as public speaker with a detailed and valuable study, *The Trouble Begins at Eight: MT's Lecture Tours* (1968), which is complementary to but does not supplant Paul Fatout's very readable volume, *MT on the Lecture Circuit* (1960, 1969). Both volumes use the MT Papers and cite many newspaper reports of lectures.

There are several facsimile editions that should be noted: Hamlin Hill and Walter Blair edited *The Art of Huckleberry Finn: Text, Sources, Criticism* (1962); Hill alone brought out *A Connecticut Yankee: A Facsimile of the First Edition* (1963); Frederick Anderson edited *Pudd'nhead Wilson: A Facsimile of the First Edition* (1968) with introduction, notes on the text and a bibliography. Also noteworthy here is F. R. Rogers's edition of *Simon Wheeler, Detective* (1964), which prints the text of the MS with T's working notes, and Anderson's edition of *"Ah Sin": A Dramatic Work by MT and Bret Harte* (1961).

The big news at this time is of course the massive new editions under way. In 1960 the *MT-Howells Letters . . . 1872–1910* in two carefully footnoted volumes appeared under the impeccable editorship of H. N. Smith and W. M. Gibson, with the assistance of Frederick Anderson, who has been since 1962 literary editor of the Berkeley T collection. In 1967 a one-volume *Selected MT-Howells Letters*, edited by Anderson, Gibson, and Smith, appeared with two recently discovered Howells letters not in the earlier two-volume edition. These volumes show, among other things, how often T relied on Howells's judgment in matters of taste and suggestions for revision.

The MT Papers, in about fifteen volumes under Anderson's direction, will include writings which for the most part have been unpublished. Six volumes have appeared so far: *MT's "Which Was the Dream?" and Other Symbolic Writings of the Later Years*, edited by J. S. Tuckey (1967); *MT's Letters to his Publishers, 1867–1894*, edited by Hamlin Hill (1967); *MT's Satires and Burlesques*, edited by F. R. Rogers (1968); *MT's Correspondence with Henry Huttleston Rogers, 1893–1909*, edited by Lewis Leary (1969); *MT's Hannibal, Huck and Tom*, edited by Walter Blair (1969); and *MT's Mysterious Stranger Manuscripts*, edited by W. M. Gibson (1969). Anderson is editing the forthcoming T *Notebooks*; Richard Bridgman will edit a volume or two of miscellaneous literary material; Tuckey will edit another volume of later writings, including the "Eddypus" MSS; and about five volumes of T's correspondence will be issued eventually, edited by Anderson and Hill.

The Iowa-California edition of the *Works of MT* will appear in 24 volumes, the first three scheduled for 1971 or 1972: *Innocents Abroad, Roughing It,* and the *Philosophical Works*. The next three will probably be *Tom Sawyer, Pudd'nhead Wilson* and *Prince and the Pauper*. Thereafter the volumes should continue to appear at the rate of three a year until the edition is complete. The work is under the direction of an editorial board consisting of John Gerber, chairman; Paul Baender, secretary; Walter Blair, W. M. Gibson, and W. B. Todd. Frederick Anderson is series editor for both the *Works of MT* and the *MT Papers*. A grant from the Office of Education has helped cover the cost of the editorial work, and the University of Iowa and the University of California presses are dividing the cost of production.

Volumes and editors are as follows, and where indicated by initials after a title the works concerned will be hereafter referred to by the abbreviated form: 1. *Innocents Abroad (IA)*, Leon Dickinson; 2. *Roughing It (RI)*, F. R. Rogers; 3. *A Tramp Abroad*, A. E. Stone, Jr.; 4. *Life on the Mississippi (LM)*, Allan Bates; 5. *Following the Equator*, Gladys Bellamy; 6. *Shorter Travel Pieces*, Hennig Cohen and Robert Regan; 7. *The Gilded Age (GA)*, Hamlin Hill; 8. *Tom Sawyer (TS), Tom Sawyer Abroad, Tom Sawyer Detective*, John Gerber; 9. *Prince and the Pauper (P&P)*, Roger Salomon; 10. *Huckleberry Finn (HF)*, Walter Blair; 11. *Connecticut Yankee (CY)*, J. D. Williams; 12. *Pudd'nhead Wilson (PW)*, Arlin Turner; 13. *Joan of Arc (JA)*, A. E. Stone, Jr.; 14. *Early Short Fiction*, E. M. Branch; 15. *Middle Short Fiction*, Howard Baetzhold; 16. *Late Short Fiction*, Howard Baetzhold; 17. *Literary Essays*, J. S. Tuckey; 18. *Religious and Philosophical Essays*, Paul Baender; 19–20. *Political-*

Social Essays, Louis Budd; 21. *Speeches*, Paul Fatout; 22–23. *Autobiography*, Frederick Anderson; 24. *Bibliography*, W. B. Todd.

III. BIOGRAPHIES

The first fairly important biography was by Archibald Henderson (London, 1911). This presented T as a fellow Southern gentleman. T's friend and literary executor, A. B. Paine, published *MT, A Biography: The Personal and Literary Life of Samuel Langhorne Clemens* (3 vols., 1912). Emphasis is placed on what is colorful, vivid and entertaining, and on those aspects of T which show his integrity and fineness. In this biography, designed for the general reader, later experts have found many minor errors or lapses, but the work is still indispensable.

V. W. Brooks's *The Ordeal of MT* (1920, rev. 1933), as he himself later admitted, was written to prove a thesis. T is presented as a potential artist and satirist who was "thwarted" by being obliged to conform to a commercial industrial America and its prudish Victorian taboos as these operated through his mother and his wife, and through Mrs. Fairbanks, Howells, the Rev. J. H. Twichell, and money-getters such as H. H. Rogers and Andrew Carnegie. What especially enraged re-revisionists such as Bernard De Voto was Brooks's notion that T's Western frontier was "a desert of human sand!—the barrenest spot in all Christendom, surely, for the seed of genius to fall in." Perhaps not enough credit has been given Brooks for his sympathetic analysis of the good effects on T's art of two experiences associated with the frontier—the craftsmanship of piloting and the craftsmanship of oral storytelling gained from Negroes and Westerners. Moreover, in riding his thesis, Brooks assembled considerable evidence about T's despair and his tragic sense which helped to show that he was more than a funny man. Brooks makes a sharp distinction between humor and satire, and accuses T of lacking courage to satirize spokesmen of the order which had befriended him. Brooks's view of Mrs. Clemens as censor has been corrected by DeLancey Ferguson in "The Case for MT's Wife" (*UTQ* 39), by James Cox in *MT: The Fate of Humor* (1966), and by others. Brooks tends to neglect literary influences and the influence of science. Brooks's indictment and the rebuttals have been ably summarized by E. H. Long, "T's Ordeal in Retrospect" (*SWR* 63). Lewis Leary edited a multitude of essays focused on this issue in *MT's Wound* (1962).

Whatever Brooks's faults, his book has been a catalyst. De Voto subtitled his *MT's America* (1932) "An Essay in the Correction of Ideas" and aimed it directly at Brooks's theory that the frontier thwarted T. His counter-thesis is that "MT was a frontier humorist. His literary intelligence was shaped by the life of the frontier and found expression in the themes and forms developed by the humor of the frontier." De Voto analyzes in detail and with great gusto the writings and techniques of A. B. Longstreet, G. W. Harris, J. G. Baldwin, T. B. Thorpe, Dan DeQuille, and others with whose work T was familiar. (His view that "the minds of T and Artemus Ward, their methods, and their effects are antipathetic" has been sensibly questioned by Walter Blair in his generally eulogistic review in *AL* 33.) It should be noted that De Voto emphasizes the ruthlessness as well as the good aspects of the frontier. His criticisms of frontier elements in T's work are usually shrewd and stimulating, but he tends to be unduly harsh toward non-frontier work such as the "chaotic" *CY*, and *JA*, which he regards as "Mediocre or worse." Those desiring a balanced view would do well to supplement De Voto's excellent study of frontier influences with Kenneth Andrews's scholarly and yet warmly sympathetic *Nook Farm: MT's Hartford Circle* (1950), which deals with the influence of the East during his 20 years (1871–91) with friends such as the C. D. Warners, Harriet Beecher Stowe, the Hookers, and Twichell (spokesman of Horace Bushnell's meliorism).

Edward Wagenknecht's main thesis in *MT: The Man and His Work* (1935; rev. 1961, 1967) is that the man and his work are one. When he does express conclusions, they are generally sensible, and he favors interpretations sympathetic toward T, although he thinks his wife's influence was "negative rather than positive." He assembles most of the relevant evidence regarding his political, literary, and religious attitudes, without trying to explain them. Robert Spiller, in his review of Wagenknecht's book (*AL* 36), finds it mediatory rather than judicial as regards controversial issues. He thinks that "of a critical analysis surely we have a right to something more comprehensive in understanding and judgment." Yet Spiller concludes that partly because of Wagenknecht's fairness in citing opposing evidence his book is "among the most useful that we have on the subject" for introductory purposes, since it shows what the main problems are if it does not try to solve them. Wagenknecht mainly accepts the frontier thesis of De Voto, and accepts M. M. Brashear's primary findings (*MT: Son of Missouri*, 1934) about eighteenth-century literary influences.

The best full-length biography is DeLancey Ferguson's *MT: Man and Legend* (1943), which corrects errors in the legend and emphasizes T's "career as a writing man" and "the forces which made him a writer." Ferguson necessarily presents a less colorful and vivacious personality than does Paine because he passes "over lightly, or ignore[s], his [T's] multifarious nonliterary doings." Within his limits, Ferguson's biography is rich in sturdy common sense and salty judgments. He offers valuable material on revisions in *IA* and *HF*. Walter Blair's discriminating review (*AL* 44) finds much to praise but deplores the neglect of revisions of other work such as *RI* and the slighting of details regarding T's earlier career. (On the latter, Ferguson can be profitably supplemented by Ivan Benson, Dixon Wecter, Edgar Branch, and H. N. Smith.) Ferguson provides much more criticism of individual stories than does Paine, but the analyses are necessarily brief.

Dixon Wecter's untimely death prevented the completion of his proposed multivolume biography of T, and only *Sam Clemens of Hannibal* (1952) has since been published by his executors. Chapters XIII ("Instruments of Culture") and IX ("The Precious Dream of Death") stress the Hannibal element in the development of T's mind and personality; the first notes the cultural advantages of life in Hannibal, while the latter dwells on the violence to be seen in the frontier town, such as the shooting of the town drunk and T's watching through a keyhole the post-mortem done on his father. Wecter sometimes assigns greater importance to Hannibal experiences than seems warranted, but the book (based on exhaustive coverage of Hannibal newspapers and local history) fills a real need.

Justin Kaplan's *Mr. Clemens and MT* (1966) is a widely distributed, popular biography that won a Pulitzer Prize, but as a scholarly study it has limitations. Baender in *PQ* (68) deals with the book judiciously. He is grateful for a semi-comprehensive biography to follow A. B. Paine's, but he elaborates the following faults: Kaplan begins when T is over 30 years of age, thus dodging the whole vital problem of formative factors. (Even if the reader uses Dixon Wecter's *Samuel Clemens of Hannibal*, there will still be a dozen years of his life, including the important years as pilot, not yet covered in depth.) Baender thinks that Kaplan does not emphasize sufficiently T's involvement with political and social ideas, matters which Kaplan tends to explain away by assumed inner psychological needs or a "temperamental solipsism." Kaplan tends to assume a "contemptuous" stance regarding T, partly because he was a parvenu given to fear of humiliation and envy. (As a whole the book does tend, as Sydney Krause thought in his review in *NEQ*, to make a reader think of T as a wretched man with a still more wretched character—note especially his treatment of Bret Harte and Webster.) While Blair's review in *AL* claims that Kaplan often manipulates evidence in the interest of sexual suggestiveness, Baender shows that Kaplan ignores strong evidence when he has T deny that women in his day were aware of any urgent sexuality. Kaplan over-emphasizes T's "confusion of motives." His work has many "factual inaccuracies" and despite numerous notes there are many unidentified quotations or allusions. He over-emphasizes T's rootlessness and the book shows a lack of perspective. (The episodes involving Grant and his *Memoirs*, as well as T's passion for money are given disproportionate attention.) And there are many dubious interpretations, such as that which claims that the ending of *CY* involves a wholesale attack on a technological civilization as opposed to a pastoral one, and that at the end of the book T has "come home to Hannibal."

Thoroughly knowledgeable through editing T's massive correspondence with H. H. Rogers, who was instrumental in getting T out of bankruptcy, Lewis Leary (*Carrell* 68) concludes that "Clemens, in a very real, very human sense, exchanged moral for financial bankruptcy," feeling under obligations (unlike his socialist friend Howells) to remain silent about the rapacity of the business tycoons such as Rogers, Rockefeller, and Andrew Carnegie. Hamlin Hill (*SoR* 68) concludes that any exhaustive future biographer will have to present T as in his later years "motivated almost entirely by fear—fear of failure . . . fear of offending, fear . . . of being laughed at." In *Susy and MT*, edited by E. C. Salsbury (1965), the views in dialogue-form without much authorial intrusion may arouse skepticism as regards the juxtaposition, but the editor has used hundreds of letters both by family and by friends. If the impression of a tranquil idyl may not be quite correct in the light of the perspective of the total record, the book may serve as a counter-balance to current attempts to present T as completely wretched in the period before Susy died in 1896.

Studies of T's growing despair will be more fully considered later in relation to his ideas, but a few predominantly biographical explanations may be mentioned here. In "The Devil and Samuel Clemens" (*VQR* 47) C. O. Parsons makes a psychological examination of T's mind through his writings in order to show that he suffered from a guilt complex because of various childhood experiences, such as jealousy of his brother Henry. This, Parsons thinks, led him to condemn the moral sense or conscience. Much is made of T's occasional condemnation of God and his sympathetic portrayal of the devil.

Brooks attributed T's despair mainly to the suppression of his natural individuality and satirical genius in the midst of an industrial and Victorian environment. Andrews (*Nook Farm*) emphasizes T's maladjustment, his later yearning for the River simplicities of his youth, and especially his dismay at a civilization which succumbed to money-lust and the "California sudden riches disease."

W. M. Gibson has meticulously edited three versions of *MT's* "*Mysterious Stranger*" [hereafter *MS*] *Manuscripts* (1969) with 139 pages of notes, cancellations, and emendations. Gibson shows that Paine and Duneka in their 1916 published version "deleted nearly a quarter of the text" of the first (1897–1900) draft, mainly invented the astrologer, and "skillfully grafted on the now famous last chapter [involving evil as a dream] written for the third version." Though Gibson feels that perhaps "a writer or editor who is more sympathetic to T's divided mind and creative dilemma in his late life may in the future, produce a better version," Paul Carter in his review (*AL* 70) thinks such a version unlikely. Clearly, T wrote but did not himself append this dream ending to the present version. On the other hand, Paine had been willed the power to use his editorial judgment, and T had already used the dream or nightmare ending for the conclusion of *CY*, thus softening its tragedy. Anyway, Gibson has been scrupulously honest in showing the reader precisely what the tangled situation actually is. J. S. Tuckey ("MT's Later Dialogue: The 'Me' and the Machine," *AL* 70), partly following Blair, shows that T "had not been completely converted by his own eloquence" about determinism and despair earlier; and that, in relation to *MS* and *What is Man?* actually "he had not one but two philosophies" involving an alternating sympathy now for pessimistic despair and now for an optimistic acceptance of the mystery of life and of evil as a dream, the issue being "unresolved," and complete despair "not confirmed." And, of course, his long obsession with the determinism of environment and heredity in relation to the whole scientific trend of the age must be taken into account, as suggested in H. H. Waggoner's "Science in the Thought of MT" (*AL* 37). De Voto's essay on "The Symbols of Despair" (in *MT at Work*, 1942) based on a study of all the manuscripts culminating in *MS*, argues that blaming himself for the increasing disasters led him to the verge of insanity and that he "saved himself in the end, and came back from the edge of insanity" by formulating a determinism which absolved him of personal blame. But De Voto's essay has been completely supplanted by J. S. Tuckey's *MT and Little Satan*, which proves De Voto's analysis of the chronology of the MSS of *MS* to be entirely erroneous (see under *MS*), and hence his conclusion is not valid. In "MT's Despair: An Explanation in Terms of His Humanity" (*SAQ* 35), R. D. Altick attributed T's later despair to arrested development. According to Altick, T had been prepared in his youth to think of success in terms of being rich "at the expense of the development of his idealistic-intellectual-artistic side." When old age came he was unprepared for it.

An important study, covering a key period of T's life (1869–1879), the publication of his early works, and the influence of subscription publishing on those works, is presented in Hamlin Hill's *MT and Elisha Bliss* (1964). A useful introductory work and a helpful tool for the scholar is E. H. Long's *MT Handbook* (1957). Its six sections, each with annotated bibliography, discuss (1) development of T biography, (2) influences of Hannibal and the West, (3) T as "man of letters," (4) growth of T's mind and art, (5) T's political, social, religious, and philosophical ideas, and (6) evaluation of T's literary stature in the United States, England, France, Germany, Scandinavia, and Russia.

Several other peripheral items for T biography should be noted: L. A. Strong's *Joseph Hopkins Twichell: MT's Friend and Pastor* (1966); Rachel Varble's *Jane Clemens: The Story of MT's Mother* (1964); and Dorothy Quick's *Enchantment: A Little Girl's Friendship with MT* (1960). Anyone interested in photographs of T should look at Milton Meltzer's *MT Himself: A Pictorial Biography* (1960).

There are also two studies of T as a traveler: Dewey Ganzel, *MT Abroad: The Cruise of the "Quaker City"* (1968), and A. L. Scott, *MT at Large* (1969), both of which will be treated later.

III. CRITICISM

1. Influences and Sources

Brooks's disparagement of the frontier occasioned much defense of its influence on T, and since 1930, when F. J. Meine brought out his racy *Tall Tales of the Southwest*, T has been variously approached through the writings of such figures as A. B. Longstreet, W. T. Thompson, Sol Smith, J. J. Hooper, J. G. Baldwin, J. M. Field, G. W. Harris, T. B. Thorpe, and H. C. Jones. De Voto's *MT's America* especially emphasized T's *general* kinship with the spirit of these men, but attacked the quest for specific parallels and sources. Walter Blair in *Native American Humor* (1937, 1960) not only interpreted T's humor as the culmination or "summary" of a long indigenous tradition, but provided full bibliographical guidance and pointed out several convincing parallels such as that between Shillaber's Mrs. Partington and Tom Sawyer's Aunt Polly. Blair discusses narrative method, techniques, the use of frames and settings, characterization, the shadings of the vernacular, and even "the picaresque method."

Kenneth Lynn's *MT and Southwestern Humor* (1959) should perhaps be mentioned here, if only to comment on the rather misleading title. The book does not really analyze the influence on T of the earlier writers. Rather, it divides into two parts. As John Gerber noted (*AL* 61), the first half is concerned chiefly with discussing Southwestern humor as "an agency of political thought," and the second with showing T's humor as "a manifestation of psychological disturbance," with slim connection between the two halves. Though the first part presents some fresh information, the book does not add much to the understanding of T the man or the writer.

T's reading and indebtedness to the European literary tradition has received needed attention. Useful guidance will be found in Harold Aspiz's unpublished doctoral dissertation ("MT's Reading" UCLA, 1950), directed by Wecter; but a great deal has been published on this important topic. (Blair's *MT and HF* [1960], and O. H. Moore's "MT and *Don Quixote*," which deal with this subject, will be discussed under *HF* below.) M. M. Brashear's *MT: Son of Missouri* (1934, 1964) combines much sympathetically presented cultural data on Hannibal and the very important matter of T's debt to eighteenth-century writers such as Swift, Smollett, Goldsmith, Voltaire, and especially Thomas Paine. Another pertinent study is E. H. Hemminghaus' "MT's German Provenience" (*MLQ* 54), which "is not intended . . . to trace the influence of German writers upon MT," but only to determine the "extent of his reading and acquaintance-ship with German writers."

Correcting De Voto's statement that John Phoenix (G. H. Derby) "suggested nothing whatever to MT," G. C. Bellamy proves conclusively in "MT's Indebtedness to John Phoenix" (*AL* 41) his indebtedness for five items, including the Whittier birthday speech. D. M. McKeithan, "MT's Letters of Thomas Jefferson Snodgrass" (*PQ* 53), shows these letters "probably owe more to W. T. Thompson's *Major Jones's Sketches of Travel* (1847) than to any single item." R. H. Wilson's "Malory in *CY*" has been well studied (*UTSE* 48). H. G. Baetzhold, *MT and John Bull: The British Connection* (1970), discusses among other matters (see "General Critiques") the influence of British authors on T's works and thought. In the chronological narrative there appear importantly Arnold, Carlyle, Darwin, FitzGerald (*Omar Khayyam*), W. S. Gilbert, Kipling, Malory, Pepys, Scott, George Standring (a radical whose *People's History of the English Aristocracy*, 1887, influenced *CY*), and Mrs. Humphry Ward. Of particular importance is the tracing of the influence of W. E. H. Lecky's *History of European Morals* throughout T's works. In addition, three lengthy "postscripts" provide a closely packed survey of T's readings in and reactions to many other British writers, including Browning, Dickens (see also J. H. Gardner's "MT and Dickens," *PMLA* 70), Goldsmith (whose "Citizen of the World" shared with *Don Quixote* the honor of being T's "beau ideal"), Shakespeare, Jane Austen, J. M. Barrie, Robert Burns, Coleridge, Defoe, Dowden on Shelley, George Eliot, Leigh Hunt, Macaulay, Milton, Swift, Tennyson, and Wordsworth. Sydney Krause, *MT as Critic*, which will be discussed under "Literary, Aesthetic Ideas," includes excellent surveys on T's reactions to Cooper, Scott, Goldsmith, Howells, Macaulay, E. W. Howe, Bret Harte, Zola, and the playwright Adolph Wilbrandt. Margaret Duckett, *MT and Bret Harte* (1964), probes the way in which T, after acknowledging Harte's help in polishing and improving his style while he was in San Francisco working on *IA*, later quarreled with Harte and treated him spitefully. "MT's Comments on Bret Harte's Stories" (*AL* 54) by Bradford Booth, shows T's mixed feelings toward Harte's stories. One reason may have been that T's publishing house, headed by Webster, lost money on Harte's novel *Gabriel Conroy*, which T himself helped to have accepted.

Harold Aspiz, "Lecky's Influence on MT" (*Sci & Soc* 62), includes the interesting point (illustrated in *CY*) that while Lecky may have led T to share his glorification of a technological civilization and the idea of progress, Lecky had himself acknowledged that if technology were adopted too early, the forces of throne and altar might be successful in causing the populace to "retrogress" back to feudalism.

G. A. Cardwell's admirable *Twins of Genius* (1953) prints the interchange of letters between T and Cable—18 by T and 20 by Cable—from 1881 to 1906, and centers attention on their four-months' lecture tour in 1884–85. Cardwell shows that Cable, whose *Dr. Sevier* had just been published and whose article defending Negro rights appeared during the tour, often received more newspaper praise than T did, and that earlier, when writing *HF*, T had a very high opinion of Cable's liberal Southern views. Hence Cardwell suggests that if *HF* excels T's earlier work in its insight into the Southern code and traditional way of life, this enrichment may have come from the general spirit of Cable. For "Cable was the only prominent southern writer of the time who had effected a fusion at all similar, the only one of T's friends who could easily have helped T to precipitate and order his ideas about the South." A more recent examination of the T-Cable relationship is Arlin Turner's *MT and George W. Cable: The Record of a Literary Friendship* (1960). Turner also has written a well-balanced article, "MT and the South: An Affair of Love and Anger" (*SoR* 68), in which he presents the effects of the region on T.

Bradford Booth, "MT's Comments on Holmes's *Autocrat*" (*AL* 50), concludes that it is "by no means impossible that a growing admiration for the Autocrat's urbane high comedy and for his infinite subtlety had its effect on MT's development." T always spoke of Holmes with "mingled reverence and affection"; both were in revolt against Calvinism, and both wrote of Jonathan Edwards as "insane." Ferguson too (*MT: Man and Legend*) thinks that as early as 1861 in the Snodgrass letters Brown's "source" is obviously the young fellow John in *The Autocrat*.

T's indebtedness to folklore has been studied in Constance Rourke's *American Humor* (1931), B. J. Whiting's "Guyuscutus, Royal Nonesuch and Other Hoaxes" (*SFQ* 44), and V. R. West's *Folklore in the Works of MT* (1930). These studies now have been superseded by R. W. Frantz, Jr., "The Role of

Folklore in *HF*" (*AL* 56), which is especially thorough and discriminating, and by D. G. Hoffman, *Form and Fable in American Fiction* (1961).

Journalism as an influence has been treated by Ivan Benson in *MT's Western Years* (1938); by A. L. Vogelback in "MT: Newspaper Contributor" (*AL* 48); by E. M. Branch in *Literary Apprenticeship of MT* (1950) and *Clemens of the "Call"* (1970); by H. N. Smith in his important book, *MT of the "Enterprise"* (1957); by Paul Fatout in *MT in Virginia City* (1964); by J. Q. Reed in "MT: West Coast Journalist" (*MQ* 60); by C. M. Pickett in "MT as Journalist and Literary Man: A Contrast" (*JQ* 61). The last item compares the *Alta California* letters and their revision in *IA*, as does D. M. McKeithan in his introduction to the original newspaper texts in *Traveling with the Innocents Abroad* (1958). Of course journalism crops up frequently in the *MT-Howells Letters* as the common background of the two men. See also B. R. McElderry's introduction to *Contributions to the "Galaxy"* (1961).

2. Religious-Ethical Ideas

While there is in print no comprehensive scholarly book on T's religious ideas, some help will be found in Wagenknecht's relevant chapters in his 1967 edition, and fresh data will be found in T's *Letters from the Earth*, especially "The Great Dark" edited by De Veto (1962), and Charles Neider's edition of five dictations of 1906, which T called "Reflections on Religion" (*HudR* 63); and in Caroline Harnsberger, *MT: Family Man* (1961), which includes marginalia from books by R. K. Jones. Many have speculated on T's debt to his ancestral Calvinism, and E. H. Long, *MT Handbook* (1957), has called his later deterministic views Calvinism without God. Brashear thinks Tom Paine's deism influenced T's religious ideas, along with his reading of other eighteenth-century writers such as Hume and Voltaire. A. E. Jones in "MT and Freemasonry" (*AL* 54) states that in T's works there are more than 100 allusions to Freemasonry, and he quotes passages from T and from Albert Pike's authoritative work on Freemasonry, indicating that the two men agreed that creeds are of human origin, that their diversity is to be explained merely by environmental differences, and that the "great unvarying laws" of nature should make man humble. Andrews (*Nook Farm*) thinks T's revolt against his native Calvinism was surely aided during the Hartford years by the pervasive teachings of Horace Bushnell, which emphasized a natural goodness such as is reflected in Colonel Sellers, Huck, and Jim. But this meliorism may have seemed eventually to T not to square with the facts of life. Tom Paine may have influenced his hostility toward a politically established church and his strong anti-medievalism.

Among other studies relating to T's religious-ethical views are the following: M. C. Babcock, "MT: A Heretic in Heaven" (*ETC* 61) and "MT's Religious Creed" (*SCQ* 66); A. E. Jones, "Heterodox Thought in MT's Hannibal" (*AHQ* 51), and "MT and the Determinism of *What Is Man?*" (*AL* 57), based on a dissertation which is especially enlightening about T's religious development; H. M. Jones on T's pessimism in his *Belief and Disbelief in American Literature* (1967); J. F. McDermott, "MT and the Bible" (*PLL* 68); Allison Ensor, *MT and the Bible* (1969), to be read along with Louis Budd's "MT and Joseph the Patriarch" (*AQ* 64); S. E. Gross, "MT on the Serenity of Unbelief: An Unpublished Letter to C. W. Stoddard" (*HLQ* 59); Paul Carter, "MT: Moralist in Disguise" (*UCSLL* 57); Sherwood Cummings, "*What is Man?*: The Scientific Sources," in *Essays on Determinism in American Literature* (S. J. Krause, ed., 1964); A. A. Durocher, "MT and the Roman Catholic Church" (*JCMVASA* 60); C. O. Parsons, "The Background of *MS*" (*AL* 60) and "The Devil and MT" (*VQR* 47); Tony Tanner, "The Lost America—The Despair of Henry Adams and MT" (*ModA* 61); H. W. Morgan, "MT: The Optimist as Pessimist" in his *American Writers in Rebellion* (1965); Milton Rickels, "Samuel Clemens and the Conscience of Comedy" (*SoR* 68); Janet Smith's introduction to her edition of *MT and the Damned Human Race* (1962); A. E. Stone, *The Innocent Eye* (1961), and "MT's Joan of Arc: The Child as Goddess" (*AL* 59); Colin Wilson, "Madach's *Tragedy of Man* and MT's *MS*" in his *Eagle and Earwig* (London, 1965); Chester Davis, "MT's Religious Belief as Indicated by the Notations in his Books" (*Twainian* 55), an article which includes marginalia on Lecky against whom T revolted—T claimed that environment deformed man's conscience.

Although Gerber remarks that W. C. Spengemann's *MT and the Backwoods Angel: The Matter of Innocence in . . . Clemens* (1966) includes too many things in its all-embracing definition, it is good to have a book-length treatment of this central issue. Over 20 pages are devoted to *HF*, although *PW* is much slighted. Spengemann arrives at his (debatable?) conclusion: "Clemens' original conception that evil and good are not absolutely irreconcilable, does not seem to change substantially between *IA* and *MS*" (p. 133), by emphasizing T's early passage about the need to make a typical lecture like a plank with assorted holes in it, i.e., with an underlying seriousness to be punctuated by humor in places. G. C. Bellamy in *MT as a Literary Artist* (1950) distinguishes four "bases" of T's mind—moralism, involving free-willed responsibility; determinism; pessimism; and what she calls "patheticism," or a peculiar sympathy with individuals. She emphasizes the logical inconsistency of moralism and determinism.

3. Political and Social Attitudes

Louis Budd's *MT: Social Philosopher* (1962) is our best survey of T's political-social views, not only as revealed in *GA* and *CY*, which dealt with current political doings, but also as revealed in writings less well known. Budd is able to show that T was more consistently conservative than is generally supposed—slanting his writing toward the general Republican point of view until he turned mugwump in supporting Grover Cleveland. His satiric attacks on the opposition were much more frequent than is generally supposed. The main difference between Budd's interpretation and Philip Foner's in *MT: Social Critic* (1958) is that Budd concludes that T's social criticism fell mostly within "the allowable range of dissent and did not mean to interfere with business as usual," while Foner emphasized what T called his Sansculotte side. Foner thinks T questioned the validity of the Free Enterprise system. If he tends to be less judicious than Budd in balancing evidence, Foner's writing makes lively reading because it makes the most of T's incandescent rage against such matters as medieval cruelties toward the underprivileged.

Further consideration of T's social and political thought may be found in Walter Blair's brilliant article, "The French Revolution and *HF*" (*MP* 57), which deals with T's reading on the Revolution in Taine, Carlyle, Dickens, and others. (For influence of the French Revolution on *CY*, and for many other considerations of T's political-social ideas, see Baetzhold's *MT and John Bull*.) From the early days T was a good deal of a moralist and humanitarian who used some of his humor for the satiric correction of political corruption. His chapters of *GA* grew in part out of his experience as secretary to a Western senator in Washington and his alert observations there of the actual workings of the democratic process. On the other hand, Brooks (*Ordeal of MT*) charged that T did not dare satirize actual individuals and abuses, but A. L. Vogelback in "MT and the Tammany Ring" (*PMLA* 55) discovered T's "Revised Catechism" in the New York *Tribune* (27 Sept. 1871), which named names and by its deadly satire in a Biblical frame helped to bring members of the ring to justice. W. F. Taylor's chapter on T in *The Economic Novel in America* (1942) is judicious in treating *GA* as exposing the "forms of business and political piracy." He shows that even if T slighted problems raised by the machine and industrialism, *CY* united praise of the machine with a Paine-like passion for social justice. (T's unpublished essay, "Knights of Labor," defended labor's right to organize.)

Another important influence on T's social thought is treated well in Paul Carter's "The Influence of W. D. Howells upon MT's Social Satire" (*UCSLL*

53). Carter shows that far from being the stultifying influence Brooks imagined, Howells as a political liberal ardently encouraged satire in *P&P* and *CY* and urged T on to more slashing attacks on imperialism. W. M. Gibson in "MT and Howells: Anti-Imperialists" (*NEQ* 47) reviews the years 1898–1902, from the Boer War to General Funston's capture of Aguinaldo. While Howells wrote against imperialism "more steadily," T did so with "more fire." Because the general public was mainly for imperialism, T courted popular displeasure and loss of sales by his position. (See also Paul Carter's brief "MT and War," *Twainian* 42.) A. L. Scott's "MT: Critic of Conquest" (*DR* 55) cites the constant reprintings of his work as a refutation of current Russian charges that the United States is trying to silence voices opposing imperialism. Scott argues that "In China and Cuba, in Hawaii and the Congo, everywhere MT demanded that the little man be given a square deal. . . . MT has done more than any other writer towards making the concept of liberty a part of the American heritage."

Yet on the subject of the Civil War T was uncommitted. Gerber in "MT's 'Private Campaign'" (*CWH* 55) throws light on T's apparent indifference toward the War, as does F. W. Lorch's "MT and the 'Campaign that Failed'" (*AL* 41). G. H. Orians' "Walter Scott, MT, and the Civil War" (*SAQ* 41) also illuminates T's attitude while showing that he characteristically exaggerated Scott's vogue and influence in bringing on the War. D. M. McKeithan provides on this topic "More about MT's War with the English Critics" (*MLN* 48).

T's social thought and its American or European origin has generated much discussion. To V. L. Parrington in his spirited but one-sided essay in *MCAT*, the humorist represents "everything European fallen away," yet Parrington emphasizes T's passionate democracy as a "product of the [European or French revolutionary] Enlightenment as it passed into the psychology of western Americans," retaining "the militant idealism of Jeffersonian times" and the "nature philosophy." Parrington skillfully connects *P&P*, the "picaresque" *HF*, *CY*, and *JA* in their common attack on evil as bred by throne and altar, irrationality, and a credulous conformity to "unrighteous customs and laws of caste." F. R. Leavis, on the other hand, in "The Americanness of American Literature" (*Com* 52) protests against what he thinks is the widespread idea that T was divorced from the European tradition and was merely a "frontier story-teller." Leavis argues (and few American critics would disagree today) that only a "mature, subtle, and sophisticated" intellect could have produced *HF* and *PW*, and he thinks that the central theme of *HF* is "the complexity of ethical evaluation in any society that has a complex tradition." T, while indebted to the frontier, has "kept a vigorous hold on his heritage of civilization."

T was a frequent observer of events and trends in the Old World. Having crossed the ocean more than 30 times, he came to have decided opinions about international affairs. One of the best brief studies of this subject is A. L. Scott's "MT Looks at Europe" (*SAQ* 53), which eventually became *MT at Large* (1969), an edition with careful notes of T's opinions, not only from his three travel books, letters, and essays, but also from the great MS collection at Berkeley. While T never arrived at an over-all theory of "design," his instincts led him to an idea of liberty and to a championship of those in bondage as the core of his internationalism. C. A. Brown's review (*Thought* 69) concluded that while history has proved T right about many of his opinions, "it began to strike him that such abuses were exhibitions of the flaws of human nature in general," making T as he grew older less defiantly and exclusively American, and more humble and responsive to Europe, as well as more outspoken about the limitations of the "damned human race." This collection of T's opinions about many nations serves to document Roger Salomon's view of T in *T and the Image of History* (treated below).

As might be expected of a post-Civil War writer, science and Darwinism made their impact on his social and political thought. On the question of T's attitude towards science or technology, one should see Hamlin Hill's "MT's Brace of Brief Satirical Lectures on Science" (*NEQ* 61) and Hyatt Waggoner's "Science in the Thought of MT" (*AL* 37). These should be supplemented by articles by Sherwood Cummings listed in the Beebe-Feaster bibliography. Social Darwinism is prominent in *The American Claimant* (hereafter *AC*) and is considered by C. L. Grimm, "*AC*: Reclamation of a Farce" (*AQ* 67); also Philip Williams in "MT and Social Darwinism" (*ESELL* 66) and Baender in "Alias MacFarlane: A Revision of MT Biography (*AL* 66). Baender argues that this character to whom T attributed many ideas associated with the evolutionists should be considered merely a fictitious spokesman for some of T's later ideas associating pessimism with science.

A few other relevant studies will be cited later under the heading of individual works such as *CY*. Andrews's *Nook Farm* contains much that illuminates T's political and social views in relation to those of his Hartford friends and to his turn from the Republican Party in 1884 when he came out for Cleveland. Howells said that while T eventually "justified the labor unions as the sole present help of the weak against the strong," it was impossible to convert him to socialism.

4. Literary, Aesthetic Ideas

Recent scholarship has made it emphatically clear that despite his lack of formal education T was a reasonably well read and a highly calculating, self-conscious literary artist, devoted to craftsmanship. "To me," he said, "the most important feature of my life is its literary feature." As in the case of Whitman, T's proper recognition was retarded by the failure of many critics to understand what he aimed at in his craft and by inept attempts to measure him by standards from which he revolted. In addition to a multitude of passages in his several volumes of letters and *Autobiography* and episodes sandwiched into his fiction (such as the satire on the "sensation" novel in *RI*), his literary commentary includes such essays as "Fenimore Cooper's Literary Offences," "How to Tell a Story," "In Defence of Harriet Shelley," and "Is Shakespeare Dead?" It will be remembered that his piloting developed peculiar powers of precise observation and memory, making him impatient with the vagueness of Scott and Cooper. And his pragmatic oral testing of his stories on actual live audiences night after night on his tours, watching the faces of his listeners and revising repeatedly, resulted in a "natural" style which modern writers such as Hemingway have admired.

Three useful articles have been devoted to T's literary theory since Brander Matthews's "MT and the Art of Writing" (*HM* 20). S. B. Liljegren in "The Revolt against Romanticism in American Literature as Evidenced in the Work of S. L. Clemens" (*SN* 45) surveyed T's attacks on Scott and Cooper, and his satires on the earlier terror novel and ballads such as "Peter Bell" and "The Wreck of the Hesperus." G. W. Feinstein discusses ably "MT's Idea of Story Structure" (*AL* 46) emphasizing the spontaneous flow of narrative, organicism, departure from the three unities, the art of the paragraph and the sentence, the illuminating incident, and the idea of form as the externalization of the writer's own individualized thinking. E. H. Goold's "MT on the Writing of Fiction" (*AL* 54) surveys such topics as his dependence on experience and observation; factuality and probability; authentic characterization; realistic dialogue; his allegedly weak plot construction; his idea that situation and incident should develop organically from the over-all plot and contribute to the logical development; his idea that there can be no complete originality; his idea of propriety. "He practiced and advocated the decorous Mid-Victorian realism of a Howells or a Thackeray rather than the stronger, naturalistic variety of Thomas Hardy or George Moore."

Another scholar who has studied T's principles and practices of writing is R. A. Wiggins, whose "MT and the Drama" (*AL* 53) supersedes earlier studies of this topic by Brander Matthews and Rodman Gilder. Wiggins effectively indicates T's considerable indebtedness to the drama in his lavish use of dialogue (about 80 per cent in his best books), "his structural emphasis upon scene," settings which often read like stage directions, attention to costuming, dramatic scenes, and the use of the "visual-kinetic style" in rendering certain episodes. He claims that T seldom rendered a character "in the round," but emphasized one dramatic trait. Wiggins followed up this study with *MT: Jackleg Novelist* (1964), in which he examined T's fictional practice as improvisation. Taking his cue from T's reference to himself as "jackleg," Wiggins argues that T deliberately depended on "the unconscious" to inspire his pen and that the results, while often brilliant, sometimes did not succeed in wresting meaning from his experience. For discussions of style in T, see Richard Poirier, *A World Elsewhere: The Place of Style in American Literature* (1966), and Richard Bridgman, *The Colloquial Style in America* (1966).

Of major importance is S. J. Krause, "T's Method and Theory of Composition" (*MP* 59). After mentioning "glaring discrepancies" in T's various comments and his occasional suggestions that he could not be a serious artist for long, Krause takes up his extensive and careful revisions in *PW, P&P, RI, TS* and *HF*, revisions which boil down to a considerable "artistic consciousness" roughly in accord with his rules of romantic fiction, which preface his essay on Cooper and which are implied in his criticism of Walter Scott. While T's general view that he was merely the amanuensis of his imagination has much in common with the romantic view of the imagination as divorced from purely rational controls, in practice an important aspect of T's automatic writing is that his sense of organization and unique form of a given work emerged only *after* he had absorbed himself in a story and totally identified himself with the persona of his characters, a process involving an empathy conducive to the most self-conscious craftsmanship in revision. T's iterated plea for naturalness is deceptive, because in perfecting the diction of the vernacular, he labored long and patiently at revisions. This was especially true in *HF*, as Blair has shown in *MT* and *HF* and H. N. Smith in *MT: The Development of a Writer* (see below under "*HF*" and "General Critiques").

Krause's *MT as Critic* (1957) is also significant. Of its three parts—T's Early Criticism: The Critic as Muggins; T's Later Criticism: The Critic as Grumbler; and T's Appreciative Criticism: From History into Life—the third is the most valuable. The first two establish T's critical poses somewhat too patly, for though the "muggins" (the fool) is perhaps more characteristic of the early works, the pose occurs after *A Tramp Abroad*; and the grumbler appears in both the early and the later works. Moreover, much of T's "grumbling" was not a *pose*. In Part III, however, the treatment of T's criticisms of Macaulay, Howells, Howe, Zola, and Wilbrandt leave little to be desired, and show that T was a far more astute literary critic than he has generally been considered.

5. Language and the Vernacular

Most of the critics of T have noted the distinctively oral quality of his style. He told Howells, "I amend dialect stuff by talking and talking it till it sounds right" (Ferguson, p. 175). "You write as a man *talks*," he advised an amateur in 1884, "and very few can reach that height of excellence." See also T's "Concerning the American Language" (1882).

The chief studies of T's language are the following: R. L. Ramsay and F. G. Emberson, "A MT Lexicon" (*UMS* 38); F. G. Emberson, "MT's Vocabulary: A General Survey" (*UMS* 35); Katherine Buxbaum, "MT and American Dialect" (*AS* 27); C. J. Lowell, "The Background of MT's Vocabulary" (*AS* 47); J. N. Tidwell, "MT's Representation of Negro Speech" (*AS* 42), which concludes: "MT was both sincere and competent in his representation of the dialect of Nigger Jim. He revealed the salient low colloquial, Southern, and negro features of Jim's speech, not by a thoroughly 'consistent' spelling of every word, but by what is better, an accurate one." H. L. Mencken (*American Language*, 1930) says MT "deliberately engrafted" the American West's "greater liberty and more fluent idiom upon the stem of English, and so lent the dignity of his high achievement to a dialect that was as unmistakably American as the point of view underlying it." Thus he added great range and variety to "Boston" or "Oxford" English, a fact which enabled him to give sharp individuality to his fictional characters.

6. General Critiques

E. M. Branch, *The Literary Apprenticeship of MT* (1950), makes the most detailed analysis we have, chronologically arranged, of T's writings up to 1867. In addition, his book includes an incisive analysis of the thematic structure of *HF* intended to prove that T's thinking was essentially continuous from his Nevada and California journalism to his later moralism, reformism, and pessimism. Differing from De Voto, Branch says, "The difference between MT's social and philosophic thinking in 1866 and in 1900 is a difference not in values and sympathies but in experience and insight."

G. C. Bellamy's *MT as a Literary Artist* (1950) has been highly praised by most scholars, and G. F. Whicher (*NYTBR* 50) said that she had "set the appropriate keystone on the arch of MT criticism." Her two major contributions (after balanced analysis of Brooks and De Voto) are, first, her demonstration that T was a conscious literary craftsman and painstaking artist; and second, her analysis of the conflict in his mind between free-willed and responsible moralism and a paralyzing determinism. The first is supported with "convincing proof," according to Blair in his review (*AL* 51), but he thinks that the second may overemphasize T's admittedly weak philosophical thought at the expense of more literary criteria. Some may "feel that she has been so preoccupied with the thought in the works that she has not satisfactorily considered their form" in terms of the overall structure of the individual books. Blair also suggests the need for more attention to T's ideas of craftsmanship.

As the work of one of our most experienced critics, H. S. Canby's *Turn West, Turn East* (1951), comparing and contrasting T and Henry James in such a way as to throw the distinctive work of each into sharp relief, is readable and thought-provoking.

Some comprehensive essays on T in histories of fiction deserve mention. Alexander Cowie in *The Rise of the American Novel* (1948) devotes more than fifty pages to T, supporting his careful concern with all sides of given issues by more than 200 precise notes. In addition to analyses of the major books, Cowie has excellent summaries of T's opinions concerning political-social, religious-ethical, and literary questions. Cowie's critical judgments are rich in insight and his writing is spirited and readable.

Dixon Wecter's 22-page essay in *LHUS* (1948) draws on his knowledge of the T papers, of which he was custodian. Wecter notes the cruelties and evils T saw in his boyhood and chronicled in *HF*, but he concludes that "on the whole happiness outweighed grief." Especially instructive for those who struggle to bring unity out of T's work is Wecter's finding contradiction or "dualism which self-observation would have shown running like a paradox through his nature: gullible and skeptical by turns, realistic and sentimental, a satirist who gave hostages to the established order, a frontiersman who bowed his neck obediently to Victorian mores [and visited Europe about 30 times], and an idealist who loved the trappings of pomp and wealth. Incessantly he contradicted himself on a variety of subjects. His was not a single-track mind, but a whole switchyard." Unlike some recent interpreters of *IA*, Wecter sees it as helping "to belittle our romantic allegiance to Europe, feeding our emergent nationalism." His unrivaled investigations of T's early years convinced Wecter that "fear of sex . . . seems to lie at the root of MT's nature . . . leaving woman not an object of desire but of reverential chivalry." This essay is on the whole one of the very best informed and illuminating essays we have.

Of major importance is Roger Salomon's *T and the Image of History* (1961). Salomon thinks that up to the mid-portion of *CY·* (1889) T followed the "Whig Hypothesis" of historians such as Macaulay in adopting the theory of the gradual progress of civilization. The increasing influence of science he associated with modern medicine and humanitarianism (as opposed to "superstition" and feudalism); technology, however, could become the tool of men who lust for power, the tool of material prosperity and of the development of a new kind of hierarchy of social classes; see Salomon's chapter three, "The Mad Philosopher: Twain as Prophet of Doom." Hank Morgan allowed his crusade for technological reform to sour into a contempt for the populace (whom he professed to save) as mere "muck," a populace which reverted to loving their chains associated with monarchy and the medieval (politically established) church. Unlike Budd (*MT: Social Philosopher*), Salomon sees Morgan's downfall as "The Fall of Prometheus" and T's main escape as being toward "The Cosmic Woman: Joan of Arc" (chapter eight), or toward "Escape from History," as Salomon entitled his initial essay on *JA* (*PQ* 61), or an "Escape as Nihilism: *MS*" (chapter nine). Salomon argues that in his view of history T was not following any Spencerian doctrine of evolution (p. 25), but simply a bird's eye view of the sharp contrast (from the humanitarian standpoint) of the Middle Ages and the mid-nineteenth century. In his interpretation of *MS* Salomon does not have the new findings of John Tuckey and W. M. Gibson, which partially outmode his view. H. F. May, reviewing Salomon's book (*AHR* 62), accepts his very broad tracking of T's "downward path from progressivism to despair," but regards the *explanations* for T's changing emotional reactions as "less satisfactory." It is not always easy to tell, writes May, "whether Salomon is ascribing T's inner conflicts to personal traits, historical events, or to a general ambiguity on American culture. From a historian's point of view, there are too many casual references to Whig historians [such as Herbert Butterfield], existentialism, and even the eighteenth century (or whatever earlier date one arbitrarily chooses from which to trace the origins of our modern and scientific world-order). Points are made too often by analogy with other writers or citation of recent criticism and not enough by close examination either of T's reading or his milieu." Budd and Baetzhold in their consideration of *CY* pay more attention to the possible influence of George Standring, Henry C. Lea on the Church, George Kennan, as well as Matthew Arnold's slurs on Grant's style, American "funny men" and the "lack of reverence" in American newspapers (which T defended in *AC*). Nevertheless, Salomon's masterful presentation of a topic of broad human interest is thought-provoking and rich in insights beyond his special thesis.

James Cox's frequently illuminating *MT: The Fate of Humor* (1966) takes an *a priori* approach and is much concerned with the genres of humor and satire. T's fate and genius, he writes, was to project "the world as entertainment" by invading the "citadel of seriousness" and converting it to pleasure and laughter. Humor and nothing else—not satire—was the essence of T's imagination, believes Cox, whose analyses of T's forms of humor yield "fresh evaluations and clearly tend to raise his stature as innovator and as artist" (Edgar Branch, *AL* 67). This work dissects T's humor and isolates such feelings as anger, indignation, shame, and guilt—all discharged into T's writing. There, transformed by imaginative play, they yielded "a gain of pleasure," but "as far as he tried to be serious he inevitably failed." Branch believes that Cox's "brilliant concentration on the forms of humor leads him . . . to slight other literary elements in his analyses." He also takes exception to Cox's view that Huck's courageous "act of positive virtue" (helping free Jim while believing he will go to hell) negates his true self and for that reason necessarily consigns him to the role—including the shoddy morality—of Tom Sawyer. "I suspect that Freud's conception of humor, which Mr. Cox uses with creative ingenuity, misleads him here and that it is, in fact, inadequate to the complexity of humor in Clemens' masterpiece." Sidney Krause (*NEQ* 67) agrees with Branch: "Many readers . . . will feel that this [Huck's negation of self] is less the fate of T's departure from humor than of Cox's theory of humor, which can neither accommodate a departure from these dimensions nor coexist with it." Such an imprisonment in theory also is partly responsible for his treating *CY* as a disaster and for his conclusion, contrary to A. E. Stone's *Innocent Eye* (1961), that *JA*, first serialized without T's name as author, is so bad one could wish it were a parody.

Among the passages that T marked in his copy of Thackeray's essay on Swift (C. B. Taylor, *MT's Margins on Thackeray's "Swift,"* p. 31) is this definition of the function of humor, which shows that T approved of mixing satire and humor: "The humorous writer professes to awaken and direct your love, your pity, your kindness—your scorn for untruth, pretension, imposture [thus the humorist is also partly a satirist-reformer]—your tenderness for the weak, the poor, the unhappy. . . . He comments on all the ordinary actions and passions of life almost. He takes upon himself to be the week-day preacher."

Cox might be more convincing if he had proceeded inductively and placed less emphasis on setting up somewhat arbitrary dogmas of rhetoric. Thus we are told that "the satiric Morgan [in *CY*] can never really be effective, because the narrow range of his burlesque style cannot tolerate enough analytic intelligence or wit to discharge his growing indignation" (p. 204). Cox is confident that "Hank's style, like Huck's, will tell us everything [including the conflict of ideas?] about the book" (p. 213). It seems to be assumed that as abstract entities satire and burlesque are mutually exclusive, that satire must include an effort to reform with reference to some ethical or other standard, and that burlesque is limited to travesty or caricature without any element of reform.

Another provocative book is Pascal Covici's *MT's Humor* (1962), which adds to the evidence that T's literary craftsmanship was not merely that of a "divine amateur." Covici analyses the uses to which T put the humor in his works, beginning with materials derived from the Old Southwest and the "poker-face" tradition, through various uses of parody and burlesque, to interesting discussions of the ending of *HF* as a hoax on the reader and, finally, of *MS* as a revelation of how society, and then the universe itself, "become gigantic hoaxes, imposing themselves on credulous man only so long as he will accept them at face value." As Budd has said (*AL* 63), Covici is better on T's artistry than on his ideas and would be on firmer ground "if he had taken the position that he is talking about what T's works mean to us now rather than what they meant to their author."

F. R. Rogers' *MT's Burlesque Patterns* (1960) is a close study of the ways in which T, from his earliest San Francisco writings (including burlesques of travels) and especially his letters from Hawaii, developed distinctive burlesque patterns through *HF*. Kenneth Lynn in his somewhat critical review (*AL* 61) concludes that Rogers "convincingly demonstrates that in its early stages *HF* was intended by T to be a burlesque detective story not unlike . . . Simon Wheeler" (1877). But Lynn adds that Rogers's "contention that T superimposed the theme of Huck's struggle with his conscience (about helping Jim escape from slavery) at a very late stage in the composition . . . does not . . . compel belief." Lynn deplores the lack of a full analysis of *CY*, and he regards as a "major flaw" the fact that Rogers does not seem to grasp the principle that creation is an "act of transformation" transcending the sum of the parts of which the creation is composed. A. L. Scott (*Chicago Tribune*) thinks that Rogers has "a sound thesis," especially in his stress of the fact that, far from being a "Divine amateur," T worked by trial and error to try to find for his various MSS (many of which Rogers examined in their unpublished state) "the proper form." Henry Pochmann (*AL* 67) praises Rogers's edition of *MT's Satires and Burlesques* (1967) as part of the MT Papers but remarks that "there is as yet no agreement with Mr. Rogers that burlesque was the chief vehicle by which T learned the craft of authorship."

Among books which aim to treat T with reasonable comprehensiveness, *MT: The Development of a Writer* (1962) by H. N. Smith is the most original, the most acute, the most provocative, and the most sophisticated. Smith, formerly custodian of the Berkeley collection of unpublished Twainiana, provides penetrating analyses of nine major works from the standpoint of T's quest for a unified point of view as managed best in *HF*. The emphasis, strictly literary, is concerned with T's "two ways of viewing the world" (from the standpoints of the vernacular and of gentility). But, as Mark Schorer does in "Technique as Discovery" (*HudR* 48), Smith sees an organic relation between technique (such as the quest of a point of view) and meaning or ideas. Smith's freshness and brilliance are illustrated best in his perceptive chapter on *HF*, entitled "A Sound Heart and a Deformed Conscience," the latter (tormenting Huck for helping a slave escape) having been deformed by a social environment defending the righteousness of slavery. While acknowledging Smith's merits, Odell Shepard (*Nation* 63) thought that the book slighted "the profound influence upon T's writing of his experience as a lecturer." In addition, Granville Hicks (*SatR* 62) thought that Smith treated T's final phase of pessimism too summarily.

Smith has appealed in an almost bewitching way to those who like to be modish and sophisticated and who are enamored of the current doctrine that the analysis of literary technique reveals attitudes and ideas. Among the humorists and especially in the West Smith in his preface assumes that:

> . . . vernacular values were at odds with the values cherished by accredited spokesmen for American society. The vernacular perspective was potentially subversive: conservative critics accused the humorists not only of coarseness but of irreverence. This state of affairs placed formidable obstacles in the way of MT, who presented the paradox of a humorist seeking recognition as a serious writer. His efforts to find an alternative to the prevailing cult of gentility and to define his own role in society appear in his work as a series of difficulties in the management of narrative viewpoint. His degree of success in solving all three problems can be traced in his progress toward the creation of a consistent fictional persona to serve as the protagonist of first-person narratives. Thus [assuming the organic theory] his technical innovations might be described with equal accuracy as an ethical, a sociological, or a literary undertaking.

In other words, Smith centers on the deep tension between two conflicting sets of values, those he calls "vernacular" based on what the average man actually sees and experiences, and those he labels stereotypes associated with gentility or ideality "parading fanciful associations [cf. Kames, Blair, and Archibald Alison] in place of the actual scene" which illustrates "the divorce between literature and first hand experience that was the fatal weakness of the traditional culture" (p. 26). Despite Wordsworth's endeavor (as a follower of Hartley's associationism) to sanctify images of lowly life for poetry, Smith thinks that associationists such as Kames had originally held that "those who depend for food upon bodily labor, are usually devoid of taste," and thus spokesmen of ideality tended to be politically and socially conservative. If offhand this approach to attitudes and ideas seems indirect, one must admit that Smith is remarkably adroit and persuasive, with a finely attuned ear for verbal nuances which deviate on one side toward sentimentality, or what Huck calls the "soul-butter" of the King pretending to be the "diseased" Wilk's British brother, and on the other side toward the stereotyped language reflecting The Establishment. In his comment in *ALS* for 1963 Gerber finds Smith's book "especially il-luminating," but that its approach in terms of language "tends to oversimplify T's moral and artistic dilemmas," although the thesis is "a useful instrument for separating the meretricious from the meritorious."

Smith's *MT's Fable of Progress: Political and Economic Ideas in CY* (1964) modifies his view in *The Development*, here treating Hank Morgan not as a vernacular but a capitalist persona who eventually, after posing as a reformer of feudalism which oppressed the populace, eventually came to denounce the populace as "muck." T was in this book (in so far as he merely attacked feudal-ism) in accord with the later Howells and C. D. Warner; he made his hero initially an entrepreneur rather than spokesman of gentility; and T failed to develop fully his hero as a potential Prometheus. Gerber (*ALS* for 1964), while recognizing Smith's "probing" book as our "most detailed statement" about *CY*, concludes that it "raises more questions than it answers." Gerber questions whether the book does show that T "turned his back on the genteel perspective in writing this novel." Finally Gerber wonders whether, especially in the ending, the "book is really deliberate and profound and systematic enough to deserve being called a philosophic fable which sets forth a theory of capital-ism, and an interpretation of the historical process that has brought it into being.' "

Robert Regan's *Unpromising Heroes: MT and his Characters* (1966) is one of the most appealing broad-guaged general interpretations. While its Freudian thesis involves the rivalry of the younger brother with his father or his representative, Regan diversifies his illustrations, taking them from most of T's major characters, and is especially interesting on *CY*, *PW*, and *AC*. Gibson finds Regan often "fresh and persuasive" (*AL* 67); his thesis is but-tressed by folk tradition and analogues in General Grant and Anson Burlin-game, and on the whole the book is rich in "practical criticism."

A. E. Stone's *The Innocent Eye: Childhood in MT's Imagination* (1961) is peculiarly gracious in both style and interpretation. It provides revealing contrasts and comparisons between T's changing views of the way the child's imagination works and the views of a large number of other American authors who have depicted children from Hawthorne through Henry James and Henry

Adams. It treats the whole range of T's child characters but is particularly interesting on *JA*. The fictive persona, Sieur Louis, tells the story of Joan from the
dual standpoint of a young associate and an old man occasionally disillusioned.
The persona offers three different explanations for Joan's unique power: he
mentions but does not accept the notion that she was "the Catholic Christian's
special gift from heaven; he presents Michelet's view (partly refuted) that she
drew her power from the lowly people of France; and he advances his personal
and unique contribution that she derived her powers from nature (symbolized
by her Fairy Tree) "anterior to reason and to human institutions" but based
on an inborn "intuition which could not err." Stone shows that this interpretation during T's bankruptcy "clearly fitted his own spiritual condition, which
was in many respects identical in its perilously balanced pessimism and nostalgia with that of his spokesman. That he could represent Joan simultaneously
as Christian, democrat, and nature goddess, and yet not exclusively any one
of these, argues a spiritual ambivalence, a tension among skepticism, determinism, and faith, which was, by 1896, far from being resolved." In his review
(*AL* 62) Blair concludes that Stone's comments on *JA* "are far and away the best
that have appeared," and he finds the comments on *HF* from the angle of adolescence "particularly enlightening." He especially praises Stone for bringing
together "all the unpublished fragments related to his topic."

   Baetzhold's *MT and John Bull* (1970), already mentioned under "Sources
and Influences," is the product of some fifteen years work. Massively documented and carefully taking all conflicting attitudes into account, it charts
the course of T's relations with Britain from the staunch approval of the 1870's
to the stormy quarrel that culminated in *CY*, and thence to reconciliation and the
renewed admiration of his later years. In describing the effects of that relationship on T's thought and works, it also traces the development of his political, social, and philosophical ideas, particularly as they were influenced by
British writers. Besides showing specific influences on T's writings, it considers
his personal relationships with a number of contemporary British authors.

   Anthologies of divergent interpretations of T have continued to multiply,
and many of these are useful in making out-of-the-way selections inexpensively
accessible. Among such collections are: Lewis Leary, editor, *A Casebook on
MT's Wound* (1962), with selections centering on the controversy between the
followers of Brooks and De Voto; Claude Simpson, editor, *Twentieth Century
Interpretations of "HF"* (1968), with a good introduction and well-balanced selections; A.L. Scott, editor, *T: Selected Criticism* (1955); B. A. Marks, editor,
MT's "HF" (1959), with selections by critics such as R. P. Adams, Baldanza, Cox,

and Leo Marx; H. N. Smith, editor, *MT: A Collection of Critical Essays* (1963), with an authoritative introduction on changing emphases from T's day to ours; Sculley Bradley *et al.*, editors,"*HF*": *An Annotated Text, Backgrounds and Sources, Essays in Criticism* (1962); Richard Lettis *et al.*, editors, "*HF*" *and its Critics* (1962); Kenneth Lynn, editor, "*HF*": *Text, Sources and Criticism* (1961); Guy Cardwell, editor, *Discussions of MT* (1962), with an introduction which concludes that T's reputation is not yet a closed issue; Justin Kaplan, editor, *MT: a Profile* (1967), with selections from Howells to Kaplan himself, and an introduction emphasizing the lack of unity in T's own personality; J. S. Tuckey, editor, *MT's "MS" and the Critics* (1968), which draws on the editor's intimate knowledge of the MT Papers. In addition *AQ* (1964) put out a special T issue containing 12 articles by such T experts as Krause, Budd, Salomon, and Hill, and *MFS* (1968) issued a special T number with another nine articles.

7. Studies of *Huckleberry Finn*

DeLancey Ferguson in "Huck Finn Aborning" (*Colophon* 38) and in his biography of T finds that out of over 900 changes in the MS now at the Buffalo Public Library—changes which show how self-conscious T's craftsmanship was —only about 30 were made by his wife. De Voto in *MT at Work* (1942) thinks this is quite a number, and he points out that only three-quarters of the MS is available, and hence there may have been other changes. Howells also read the proof sheets, much to T's satisfaction. Scott (*AL* 55) has shown that Gilder published four parts (about a fourth of the whole) in the *Century*, making considerable alterations with the author's hearty approval. The book was published in England prior to the American edition. Jacob Blanck "In Re *HF*" (*New Colophon* 50) has provided other bibliographical details. In his valuable account of "The Publication and Reception of *HF* (*AL* 39) A. L. Vogelback finds that it was reviewed immediately only in the *Century* (May 1885, by T. S. Perry, favorably), but there was a good deal of sporadic newspaper comment about the book's being "vulgar," "coarse," and "inelegant," comment reflecting the genteel tradition. (Blair in *MT and "HF"* notes several other early reviews.) The publicity given the book by its being banned by the Concord Library and by T's reading from it on his lecture tours helped to sell about 40,000 copies within a few months of publication. Howells praised it only privately, but Joel Chandler Harris defended it as "wholesome" (*Critic* 1885) and wrote T that he regarded it as "the most original contribution that has yet been made to American literature."

Like most multifaceted masterpieces, *HF* can be profitably viewed from many different angles. Wecter and others have illustrated the way in which in some of the more memorable scenes and characters T drew on his memories of Hannibal and his boyhood. Andrews (*Nook Farm*) and others have argued that the book owed much to T's "equilibrium in the middle eighties"; he was happy in his family life and successful as the author of *P&P* (1882), and his leisurely revisiting of familiar haunts to finish *LM* (1883) had tempered his detachment with a mellow nostalgia associated with scenes of his boyhood.

Those interested in the maintenance of a unified point of view have followed Henry James's friend, T. S. Perry, in his praise of the "autobiographical form." Every scene is "given, not described. . . . What is inimitable, however, is the reflection of the whole series of adventures in the mind of the . . . hero," the 14-year-old boy who provides the tone and limits of the story, as well as the language and the rich illusion of reality.

Gerber has done masterfully discriminating work devoted to the thesis that T needed a persona to energize his creative imagination and to channel it. Injustice would be done to the detailed complexity of his closely reasoned technical work by trying to summarize it too briefly. If *HF* (with the exception of Sherburn's speech) has consistency in point of view, *CY* falls short partly because

in three consecutive paragraphs the Yankee narrator sounds like a Malory ("he lightly took his spear and gat him hence"), a sentimental novelist ("Thet could remember him as he was in the freshness and strength of his young manhood, when he kissed his child and delivered it to his mother's hands and went away into the long oblivion"), an American rustic ("when you can say that of a man, he has struck bottom, I reckon"), and an essayist gifted with erratic literary elegance (". . . all gentle cant and philosophizing to the contrary notwithstanding, no people in the world ever did achieve freedom by goody-goody talk and moral suasion"). Taken as a whole, the writing in *CY*, despite its basic colloquialism, is just about as patchwork a production as the ill-defined point of view should lead us to expect ("The Relation between Point of View and Style in . . . MT," H. C. Martin, ed., *Style in Prose Fiction: EIE*, 1958).

Gerber's "MT's Use of the Comic Pose" (*PMLA* 62) develops three points: some of the more common comic poses of superiority in T, a description of some of the more common comic poses of inferiority, and certain general reflections upon T's use of the comic pose to explain his "humor's variety, continuousness, and economy." What is refreshing here is the objectivity and detachment, illustrated in a willingness to concede that good as T was in *IA*, "it cannot be said that he substantially exploited its [the comic pose's] finest aesthetic possibilities," and in his earlier work he "rarely used it to give a work tonal and structural unity."

Then there is the question of joyousness versus evil in *HF*. Critics such as

Canby and Cowie feel that "delight" and an appealing escape "from the pangs of adulthood" predominate, following T. S. Perry, who stressed a "total absence of morbidness." But Brooks thinks the "moral" of the book is "that all civilization is inevitably a hateful error, something that stands in the way of life and thwarts it as the civilization of the Gilded Age had thwarted MT." This is repeated in Brooks's *New England: Indian Summer*. J. M. Cox's study of Huck's "Sad Initiation" will be taken up shortly in another connection, but it emphasizes "two images, rebirth and death." V. S. Pritchett (*NSN* 41) has also stressed the theme of "cruelty," citing some eight instances. On the whole, however, it would seem that this emphasis on evil and death does not take into account the perspective of the book as a whole and Huck's boyish ability to see both good and evil and accept them, as emphasized by Andrews in *Nook Farm*. Huck "cried a little" when Buck was shot in the feud, but he "takes rascality for granted" and continues on his journey essentially "unaffected by the violence he sees." De Voto (*MT at Work*, 1942) recognizes the evils Huck encounters but protests against symbolic interpretation and reading into the story of "metaphysical abstractions," such as the Fall of Man.

In contrast to Brooks's view is the view of Parrington, Branch, Bellamy, and others, who emphasize the freeing of Jim from slavery and the satiric attack on inhumane institutions. Parrington relates Huck to T's reformer's crusade in his other books against "unrighteous customs and laws of caste" and (following A. B. Paine) he makes Huck center on a conflict of "ethics" climaxed in having "to decide, forever, betwixt two things" involving Jim's status. Branch thinks it centers on the quest for freedom and the conflict between "two providences" which offer standards of right conduct: "Miss Watson's to behave and conform in selfish safety for fear of 'the bad place'; the Widow's to give unselfish aid to others. The alternatives are self-centered, conventional morality and humanitarian idealism," the latter of which Huck (assuming free will) chooses.

Parts of the story certainly supports the thesis involving brotherhood. Lionel Trilling's introduction of 1952, for example, emphasizes the earlier passage where Huck tries condescendingly to tease Jim (who had grieved over Huck as lost) by leading him to think the storm was a dream, followed by Huck's repentantly coming to "humble myself to a nigger." When Jim realized that the debris caused by the storm proved Huck was making fun of him, he says (symbolically), "Dat truck dah is *trash*; en trash is what people is dat puts dirt on de head er dey fren's en makes 'em ashamed." However, while all this is surely an important and appealing element in the novel, this interpretation would tend to imply that Jim is the central character on whose escape everything is focused. Are there not several episodes of importance to which Jim has no relation—such as the Boggs-Sherburn story, the Shepherdson-Grangerford feud, and the Wilks story? Does this centering on Jim take into account the totality of the book? Trilling's introduction, however, which came before T. S. Eliot's but develops his idea about the River being a God, is highly suggestive and charming as a whole, if more fanciful than scholarly. Like Eliot, Trilling finds "a certain formal aptness" in the disputed last nine chapters of the book. He regards Huck as "the least carefree of boys."

HF is also seen as social history. De Voto, whose long and thoughtful studies command respect, concludes (*MT's America*); "The completeness of the society must be insisted upon. . . . The portraiture which begins among the dregs with old man Finn ends with the Grangerfords. Between these strata has come every level of the South." Ferguson and Andrews also take this view.

Other critics find the clue to the form of *HF* in its relation to the picaresque tradition, especially as that is represented by Smollett's translation of *Don Quixote*. In 1907, while T was still alive, F. W. Chandler in *The Literature of Roguery* (II, 488) argued that

Huck . . . is a rogue with limitations. Although ready in lies, deceits, and disguises, and a petty thief, he is sound at heart [as T himself insisted, *Autobiography*, II, 174]. He scruples at helping to steal a "nigger"; he cannot bring himself to join with professional rogues in a swindle of moment; [safeguarding Mary Jane's money from the king and duke] he protects the weak, and is loyal to his friends. To the Don Quixote of the imaginative Tom Sawyer, he plays a delightful Sancho.

This brief generalization was elaborately documented by O. H. Moore's "MT and Don Quixote" (*PMLA* 22), which finds some parallels also in *IA* and in *CY* as a satire on chivalric medievalism. As early as 1860 T called Goldsmith's *Citizen of the World* and *Don Quixote* "my *beau ideals* of fine writing" (*Letters*, I, 45). In Chapter XLVI of *LM* T contrasts Scott's "chivalry silliness" and "the good work done by Cervantes," who "swept the world's admiration for the medieval chivalry-silliness out of existence." Incidentally, Moore's case has been much strengthened by Franklin Walker and G. E. Dane (*MT's Travels with Mr. Brown*, 1940) in which they find Cervantes's technique used in 1866 and 1867. Moore concludes that

especially in *HF*, T parallels closely the masterpiece of Cervantes. He alters the character of Tom Sawyer so that, like Don Quixote, he is an omnivorous reader of romance, and desires to act out the roles of his favorite heroes. He alters also the character of Huckleberry Finn, transforming him from a very imaginative character to a prosaic Sancho Panza, a foil to the brilliant Tom Sawyer.

Of greater importance than any parallelism of details is the possibility that Cervantes provided T with sanction for expressing the two conflicting sides of his nature, the romantic and the realistic. Note also that this picaresque interpretation illuminates T's irony, his satire aimed at caste rituals such as the feud, and his sympathetic humanitarianism. (Parrington called *HF* "the one great picaresque tale of the frontier" involving "rebellion against sham.")

There is of course no question that T's materials are richly indigenous and based on his own earthy observations; the point is that these were poured into the picaresque mold. The theory accords with T's belief that narrative should be free, with "no law," and it makes sense of his warning that we should not seek in his book a plot (of the Aristotelian cause-and-effect kind). And the theory helps to explain T's responsiveness to both beauty and ugliness as well as his apparent contradictions: his frontier realism and his occasional Victorian sentiment. In short, provided one does not claim any slavish imitation but interprets the picaresque tradition broadly, the theory of T's following it offers an approach to *HF* which would transcend by including most of the essentials in the other interpretations. This is especially true as regards the much-disputed question of whether the conclusion is a major flaw or part of a reasonable design by a self-conscious artist.

Defense of the disputed ending of *HF* has come from those who stress, as does J. M. Cox in "Remarks on the Sad Initiation of Huckleberry Finn" (*SR* 54), the idea that *HF* is really the story of a boy supposed dead who seeks identification. Cox concludes that regardless of stylistic flaws, the final chapters are structurally "vital and necessary." In acknowledging he is "born again" and in his great vitality, Huck (according to Cox) "transcends the empty rituals of Tom Sawyer's universe and achieves mythic significance." Jim is "the conscience of the novel, the spiritual yardstick by which all men are measured." Lauriat Lane's "Why *HF* is a Great World Novel" (*CE* 55) not only deals with the "total dramatic and moral irony," the passage from youth into maturity, and the epic representation of "all levels of society from the lowest to the highest," but stresses the rebirth-identification theme which is clinched "only" in the final chapters "when [Huck] is finally forced to assume this real self in the eyes of the world." Lane does not find Huck's final desire to escape further "sivilizing" inconsistent (as do some others) with the thesis that Huck has gone through a "maturing experience." Both Cox and Lane are richly suggestive on a "mythic" level, as are Eliot and Trilling.

H. E. Gerber in "MT's *HF*" (*Expl* 54) divides the book into five sections in terms of the alternation of land and river scenes, finding the climax in Chapter XXXI. Frank Baldanza in "The Structure of *HF*" (*AL* 55) dismisses Cox's kind of symbol as well as emphasis on Jim's liberation and on the picaresque, and centers on "rhythmic stitchings" or the "principle of repetition and variation," of which he specifies a dozen instances, such as Tom's talk of Jim's keeping a rattlesnake in the Phelpses' cabin and Jim's being bitten by one on Jackson's Island. These are interesting, but their meaning or significance is not very clear. Contrary to most recent critics, Baldanza says that "if we hold to any aesthetic standards at all, we hardly have the right to make extravagant claims for a book which we must admit in the same breath is negligible as a work of art." He does, however, bring his study to a final focus on the passage dealing with Huck's rebirth or identification, although Tom is likened to "Doubting Thomas"— "an oblique recall of the previous references to Moses and Solomon and the biblical kings."

Leo Marx in "Mr. Eliot, Mr. Trilling, and *HF*" (*ASch* 53) makes the best attempt to refute defenses of the ending, which Marx thinks a "failure." His weightiest argument is that Jim, who has hitherto grown in dignity, is now made to demean himself and to play a passive role to Tom's shenanigans; thus "the flimsy devices of plot, the discordant farcical tone, and the disintegration of the major characters all betray the failure of the ending." On the whole the "frame" structure and the ending remain fascinating topics for debate.

Blair's *MT and "HF"* (1960) is to be recommended as the most detailed and incisive study that we have of what helped to shape this book that (up to 1960) sold over ten million copies. Blair, after studying T MSS in some nine library collections from New York to California with attention to different types of paper and various colored ink, establishes the complicated course of composition and shows that T's revisiting the river in 1882 was not so vital an influence on the novel as earlier critics had thought. Blair is very illuminating on the complex manner in which T zigzagged along, letting the MS alone for long periods, and inserting key chapters in work long considered finished. Blair emphasizes Sherburn's saying (as the book temporarily departs from Huck's adolescent point of view) that Sherburn knows "the average man of the world is a coward" (p. 337). Since Blair has done so much work on the frontier and on T's early environment in the West, it is striking to find him saying in his Preface, "But I believe that even more important than T's remembered experiences were ways he manipulated and augmented them when he transmuted them into fiction."

Blair apparently has turned from speculation about the frontier in general to a concern with T's precise reading, especially as it related to W. E. H. Lecky and to commentators on the French Revolution such as Carlyle. T may have followed Lecky in the first part of *CY* where he attributes progress to the rise of technology and industrialism, but he certainly reflects in other parts his reaction against Lecky's strong belief in the values of reliance on an intuitive conscience as opposed to passive acceptance of determinism. T just before writing *HF* had read in Hartford a paper, "What Is Happiness?" in which (as Blair says) he "championed determinism and selfish motivation," and in general Blair concludes that "In bellicose marginalia [on Lecky's books] in notebooks, in works published and unpublished, T worked steadily to build up a strong case against Lecky" (p. viii). Thus this reaction was a strong influence in leading T to talk repeatedly about man in general tending to have a kind heart but a conscience deformed by training, by which he meant the determinism of environment and of heredity.

Blair does not devote much space to discussing what he calls (p. 354) "the inferior escape chapters at the end." He notes that in the final revision of the MS in Chapter XLIII T "canceled [an]earlier passage [which] shows the author overcoming an impulse to include broad comedy and having the doctor instead give a straightforward account, free from jests." This emphasizes Jim's nobility when (in Chapter XL) "at great personal risk [Jim] abandons his escape until a doctor attends Tom's wound." Huck pays Jim "a compliment astounding for a poor white: 'I knowed he was white inside.'" But Blair says that the final chapters "would do for silly romances about prison escapes what Cervantes had done for silly romances in his day. More important, he [T] would juxtapose with a serious narrative about a flight to achieve freedom which develops certain themes, a burlesque narrative touching upon similar topics" (p. 349). Blair mentions T. S. Eliot's defense of the escape chapters (see Eliot's 1950 Introduction) and O. H. Moore's article (see above), but he concludes that scholars "approving the terminal chapters admit they 'fall off.' And I have seen no convincing argument that they are not overlong" (p. 348). Blair says that in the escape chapters T's "chief crimes are against characterization: Jim, whom the reader and Huck have come to love and admire, becomes a victim of meaningless torture, a cartoon. Huck, who has fought against codes of civilization, follows one of the silliest of them" (p. 350). But Blair notes that in the burlesque involving escape, the "end jousts at an impressive number of writers about prison life and escapes—Baron Trenck, Casanova, Cellini, Henry IV, Dumas, Carlyle, Dickens (notably *A Tale of Two Cities*), as well as more obscure writers such as X. B. Saintine and Baring-Gould. . . . Chapters, endlessly it seems, show Tom complicating things to follow bookish authorities while Huck offers commonsensible protests" (p. 350). After all his fine detail and cogent logic Blair concludes, regarding the final chapters, that having written furiously for weeks, "perhaps even the ebullient T was tired to the point of reckless improvisation" and "horsing around" (p. 350). "Perhaps." But T after the original draft did keep the MS for "more than seven months" for elaborate revision (p. 351).

Apart from Blair's argument, one might mention that if, as some interpreters claim, HF is centered on reformist satire of southern institutions such as slavery and the feud, and Huck's journey is a "sad initiation" into life's obstacles from which he is supposed to learn, then having Huck merely light out for the territory and refrain from coming home to put his lessons into practice tends to make the whole reformist theme seem futile. Or one may, of course, view the concluding escape chapters as completing the "frame" begun in the first three chapters (at the end of which Cervantes is glorified by Tom), and thus interpret the ending as a coherent reformist attack on the romantic or sentimental, which T heartily disliked. On another matter, Hamlin Hill tried to get around arguments about whether or not the raft scene (originally written for HF but used in LM) should be included by saying one should accept the chapter because T wrote it. Why not use a similar logic in the case of the ending of HF?

H. N. Smith's 1958 introduction to HF in the Riverside Edition centers on alienation from society, on the use of a naive point of view of a 14–15 year old boy, and on the vernacular. Smith uses Blair's data about the complex zigzag course of composition during seven or eight years, but "contradicts" the much publicized view that Huck has become disgusted with current (1840?) southern acceptance of slavery which was supposed to have motivated his escape to the territory and the view that Huck through his initiation "has matured." Actually Smith thinks of the novel as "not realistic but symbolic in structure" and the last ten chapters involving the "Evasion" as Huck's reversion to "Tom's fantasy-world." Smith emphasizes the fact that T's "depiction of Huck's inner life suggests a contrast between the thought and feeling that to some degree parallels the [bipolar] contrast between the Shore [cf. Grangerford-Sheperdson feud and the attempt of Duke and Dauphin to rob the Wilks family] and the River" representing freedom from convention and natural goodness of heart. Smith stresses the fact, however, that this natural goodness is dramatized in Huck, the mask-persona, and is not the actual belief of T himself, whose views of "average" human rapacity and cowardice are expressed by Sherburn, who is an "exception" to the persona. Huck of the final chapters is "diminished" and "inferior" to the Huck who in the middle section "humbled himself" to the slave. The novel represents the way "a sound heart & deformed conscience came into collision & conscience [formed by the southern environment] suffers defeat." The vernacular "shadings" consistently used are seen as "new," as is Smith's own elaboration of the structural principle of "bipolarity."

This very condensed introduction is thought-provoking, especially in its admission of Huck's inability to admit that slavery is wrong and that "primitivism . . . is implicit" in the book, as well as anti-intellectualism and regard for "the accumulated experience of the past."

R. P. Adams's introduction to *HF* in C. R. Anderson's anthology, *American Literary Masters* (1965), essentially the same as his "Unity and Coherence of *HF*" (*TSE* 56) and widely reprinted in anthologies of criticism, is carefully and thoughtfully considered and should be read beside Smith's 1958 introduction, for Adams differs on some key points. He stresses three instances where Huck makes decisions to aid in the escape of Jim, whom he considers "the noblest character . . . a slave." He believes "the chief crisis in Huck's development is a moral decision concerning that slave and involving Huck's whole attitude, feeling, and judgment about the aristocratic American society that fostered and depended on slavery." Huck can do right (as we view the question today) only by doing wrong according to the southern code in vogue in Huck's actual environment. Adams makes an important point in connecting T's dislike of current sentimentality ("soul butter") with his dislike of Walter Scott as spokesman for sentimentality associated with the defense of chivalry, throne, and altar. Adams does not do as much as Smith does with the management of point of view, but he places more emphasis on death and rebirth, withdrawal and return. On the other hand, Adams stresses Huck's development through his initiation into life's successive experiences without considering very fully the question of the implication of Huck's apparent lack of maturing. Instead of merely escaping to the territory, he might have returned to civilization in a constructive effort to try to help society put into practice the important lessons his initiation is supposed to have taught him. Anyway, Adams and Smith together provoke keen discussion.

L. B. Levy in "Society and Conscience in *HF*" (*NCF* 64) concludes that in considering Huck's decision not to return Jim to slavery other scholars have treated the problem in a more schematic way than the book itself justifies. Sydney Krause in "Huck's First Moral Crisis" (*MQ* 65) argues that the reader should keep in mind how much Huck still has to learn at the point where the steamboat hits the raft, a point at which T laid the MS aside. J. R. Boggan in "That Slap, Huck. Did It Hurt?" (*ELN* 64) argues that Huck's decision to go to hell has not been adequately prepared for. M. J. Hoffman in "Huck's Ironic Circle" (*GaR* 69) believes that the disputed opening and closing exist and need no one's justification, "For T has created an elaborate ironic structure that demands we be taken in by our initial perceptions of Huckleberry Finn. It is important that we be deceived so that what happens to Huck later on will shock us into seeing that the problems posed in the book are unresolvable either in fiction or in life." The defense of the last ten chapters, or Tom's plan for "The Evasion," has been discussed in a series of articles (to be found in Beebe-Feaster's list) under Clarence Brown, R. B. Browne, Bruce Carstensen, A. E. Dyson (especially worth reading), Chadwick Hansen, Carson Gibb, C. C. Loomis, T. A. Gullason, John Hill, B. A. Spacks, and A. E. Stone.

8. Studies of Other Individual Works

a. *Innocents Abroad.* L. T. Dickinson's essays are model studies: "Marketing a Best-Seller: MT's *IA*" (*PBSA* 47) and "MT's Revisions in Writing *IA*" (*AL* 47). The latter demonstrates skillfully how T's 50-odd letters to the *Alta California* were revised in the interest of clarity, decorum, toning down of irreverence, turning the "merely ludicrous into something rather subtly and richly humorous." C. E. Shain's "The Journal of the *Quaker City* Captain" (*NEQ* 55) presents fresh evidence that T exceeded a humorist's license in exaggerating the sanctimoniousness of Captain Duncan (with whom he later quarreled publicly) and in criticizing the directors of the cruise and the gossipy passengers.

Dewey Ganzel's *MT Abroad: The Cruise of the "Quaker City"* (1958) is the most comprehensive account of the voyage which resulted in *IA*. Drawing on T's published and unpublished writings, newspapers, the journals and correspondence of other passengers, and the captain's log, as well as on the work of Leon Dickinson, Ganzel presents a study that John Gerber has judged "essential for an informed reading of *IA*" (*ALS* for 1968). Despite some weaknesses, notable among them an underestimation of the influence of Mary Mason Fairbanks, the book is valuable both for its insights into T's creative methods and for its revelation of exactly what is fact and what is fiction in *IA*.

b. *The Gilded Age.* B. M. French's *MT and "GA"* (1965) covers every conceivable aspect of this book (1873) on which T collaborated with C. D. Warner. It includes a discussion of the extant MS, 60 pages of notes, and citations of over 50 contemporary reviews. Somewhat pedestrian in presentation, French shows the "original conception of *GA* to have been a burlesque of the popular sentimental and sensational novel" of the period. Hamlin Hill (*AL* 66), though praising the book, is "not convinced that this intention was sustained as far into the novel as Laura's death [based on a current criminal, Laura Fair], which French reads as 'part of the burlesque of contemporary fiction.'" His final chapter centers on the book's satire of contemporary economic and speculative society (illustrated by the actual Senator Samuel Pomeroy as Dilworthy) and on T's ambivalent attitude toward the Gilded Age. There was a deep contradiction in T's own personality, which was torn between the materialistic dream of success and wrath at economic corruption. In the collaboration French finds that while E. E. Leisy's article (*AL* 37) is in broad outlines still valuable, the extant MS shows that "mutual interpolations . . . were frequent and caused a greater interweaving of the collaborators' work than would appear from the basic division" and that T's ideas were frequently "absorbed into the portions written by Warner" (p. 68). If Laura, Clay, Colonel Sellers, and Senator Dilworthy are essentially T's contribution, Warner is mainly responsible for Sterling, Brierly, the Bolton family, Squire Montague and his daughter Alice, the promoter Bigler, and Colonel Selby. But the collaboration was so interwoven that the book as a whole may be taken to represent the views of either man. (Warner in later novels such as *That Fortune* [1899] and *A Little Journey into the World* [1889] was just about as critical as T of the speculative trend of the later nineteenth century.)

c. *Tom Sawyer.*   *TS* should be approached in De Voto's 1939 edition with its valuable prologue on "The Boy's Manuscript" written in 1870 or 1871 and here printed for the first time. De Voto treats the relation between the book and T's boyhood friend Will Bowen and others, after whom he probably patterned his characters. Blair's "On the Structure of *TS*" (*MP* 39) concludes that *TS* represented a "fictional working-out of the author's antipathy to the conventional plot structure of juvenile tales," of the goody-goody boys' books then popular and already derided by books by J. J. Hooper, Max Adeler, and T. B. Aldrich. Blair shows that there are four "lines of action" in the plot: "the story of Tom and Becky, the story of Tom and Muff Potter, the Jackson's Island episode, and the series of happenings (which might be called the Injun Joe story) leading to the discovery of the treasure." Of the 35 chapters Blair finds only four which are not concerned with these four lines of action.

Hamlin Hill in "The Composition and the Structure of *TS*" (*AL* 61), analyzing the original MS of *TS* at Georgetown University, seeks to refute those who have found Blair's arguments unconvincing. Though he begins by presenting examples which might support T's own suggestions that the book was a sort of "ragbag" of memories, thrown together out of recollection and association, he goes on to show how other materials in the MS support the "maturation" theory. Among them he cites the marginal suggestion that Tom take a whipping for Becky, T's decision not to have Tom go off on a journey, and the idea of keeping the piece of bark with the scrawled message where Aunt Polly will later discover it. Hill concludes that though the various episodes and anecdotes mentioned in the margins came to T "chaotically and without formal significance," his "selectivity and rearrangement of the material provided him with the structure he envisioned, roughly, in his early outline of the book."

Lewis Leary, "Tom, Huck: Innocence on Trial" (*VQR* 54), argues that adventure (symbolized by Tom) at least as much as common sense (Huck) leads to the wiping out of evil as far as the boys are concerned. This very stimulating article, rich in insight, includes analysis of the intricate time-scheme as well as the structure of these two boys' books; contrary to the usual view, Leary argues briefly that Tom grows and develops more than does Huck. Since at the end Huck still wishes to escape from being "sivilized," it is argued that he doesn't essentially change at all. But "Tom's solution [in the conclusion of *HF*] is in the direction of Henry James's solution, of James Branch Cabell's, even of Ernest Hemingway's. It is escape through avoidance of what one wishes to avoid by creation of values of one's own which transcend reality because they seem finally more real than reality. . . . Recognize the illusion, but cherish it."

A useful paperback edition of *TS*, which contains text, notes, and five background and critical articles was edited by R. D. Spector (1967).

d. *Life on the Mississippi.* A. L. Scott in "MT Revises *Old Times on the Mississippi*" (*JEGP* 55) points out some 45 changes but says "several dozen might have been made by a conscientious proof reader." As a result of long study of T, Scott adds that except for the revision of *IA*, already studied by Dickinson, "MT's approach towards editing his own printed works was casual, perfunctory, and bored."

e. *The Prince and the Pauper.* L. T. Dickinson's "The Source of *P&P*" (*MLN* 49) has been corrected as regards the debt to Charlotte M. Yonge's *Prince and the Page* and supplemented in a number of respects by Baetzhold (see above), but Dickinson provides valuable matter on historical works which T followed "quite closely."

f. *A Connecticut Yankee.* J. B. Hoben's excellent pioneer investigation, "MT's CY: A Genetic Study" (*AL* 46), which argued that Matthew Arnold's slurs on American civilization, our humorists, and General Grant's grammar "evoked the spirit which transformed an unpromising sentimental romance into a promising satire," has now been superseded in a number of particulars by Baetzhold's "The Course of Composition of *CY*: A Reinterpretation" (*AL* 61). Baetzhold's article—expanded and somewhat modified in *MT and John Bull*—besides correcting the dates of composition of various portions of *CY* shows that Arnold was only one of a number of influences on the shift from burlesque "contrast" to more serious satire of monarchy, aristocracy, and the Established Church. Also to be noted is F. W. Lorch's "Hawaiian Feudalism and MT's *CY*" (*AL* 58).

After suggesting certain changes in the MS of *CY*, the supposedly timid and "genteel" E. C. Stedman (*Life and Letters*, II, 370–372) noted his hearty approval of the book, and even feared that the public would overlook the book's concern with abuses still evident in 1889. Blair suggests (*Horse Sense in American Humor*, 1942) that *CY* attacks (1) current spoils system appointments (in the fable about military exams) which Cleveland opposed, (2) the River and Harbor Bill (in the fable of King Arthur's appropriation for the "king's evil"), and (3) the high tariff which Cleveland had flayed in 1887 (in the discussion by the Boss and Marco concerning free trade). Baetzhold in *MT and John Bull* shows the relationships of some of these episodes, and of many other matters, to contemporary concerns in England. Robert Wilson's study of T's use of Malory has been cited ("Influences and Sources"), as has Olin Moore's consideration (see under *HF*) of the influence of *Don Quixote*. (Also see T's Chapter XII and Sister M. T. Roades, "Don Quixote and *CY*," *MTQ* 38.)

Baetzhold's judicious balancing of interpretations is evident in his conclusion that "because of the numerous confusions in *CY*, the question of Clemens' ultimate intention will probably remain a matter of critical controversy," depending upon the particular inferences drawn from T's contrasts of medieval feudalism and modernity, his indications (partly from Lecky) that a technological-rational education will root out "superstition" and insure eventual progress; and his notebook entry in the summer of 1888, while he was writing *CY* that "the thing in man [of all ages including the present] that makes him cruel to a slave is in him permanently and will not be rooted out for a million years." Baetzhold's view is that T had not so much "subconsciously lost faith in the possibilities of technological progress," but that he had become at least partially convinced that man's innate inhumanity—reflected in "superstition, ignorance, subservience to custom"—was an insurmountable obstacle to any drastic and enduring "progress."

Opposed to De Voto and those who stress the indigenous and mythic, the very conservative Stuart Sherman (*CHAL*) concluded that *CY* "represents MT more completely than any other single book. . . . It displays every variety of his style from the mock-heroic and shirt-sleeve journalese of the Yankee's familiar vein to the careful euphonies of his descriptions of English landscape and the Dantean mordancy of the chapter 'In the Queen's Dungeons.' It exhibits his humor in moods from the grimmest to the gayest. . . . [He is here] the representative of democratic America, preaching the gospel of common-sense and practical improvement and liberty and equality and free thought inherited from Franklin, Paine, Jefferson, and Ingersoll. . . . CY is his *Don Quixote*, a sincere book, full of lifelong convictions earnestly held, a book charged with a rude iconoclastic humour, intended like the work of Cervantes to hasten the end of an obsolescent civilization," whose evils he traced to "monarchy, aristocracy, and an established church."

Dissatisfied with his own earlier interpretation of CY, in which he tried to consider Morgan as a vernacular hero, H. N. Smith tries in *MT's Fable of Progress* (1964) to reconsider Morgan as a capitalist, a spokesman of "Political and Economic Ideas" of 1889, in relation to the Genteel Tradition and to the turn "From Burlesque to Nightmare." (Smith introduces interesting comparisons between T's CY and Howells's *A Hazard of New Fortunes and* C. D. Warner's *A Little Journey*.) Although much is made of T's nostalgia for the pastoralism of his native Hannibal, Smith thinks that Morgan eventually comes to regard the populace he is trying to elevate by technology as only "muck"; the populace is enslaved to environment and heredity and returns to a love of their "chains," a feudalistic state and church. Smith's conclusion (p. 107) is that

> MT's proclamation of this doctrine [that men will revert to unreason equated by T with Original Sin] through a protagonist with whom he is now fully identified reveals an absolute despair. . . . At some point in the composition [during which he wavered in high hopes of his Paige typesetting machine, which does not drive him bankrupt until a short time later] of this fable he had passed the great divide of his career as a writer. . . . When he found it impossible to show how the values represented by his vernacular protagonist could survive in an industrial society, he lost his faith in the value system of that society. Henceforth he worked as a writer in a kind of spiritual vacuum. His imagination was virtually paralyzed.

Smith does well in reminding us that the Yankee's whole fable about the sixth century is a dream or nightmare.

g. *Pudd'nhead Wilson.* In discussing PW, Smith in *MT: The Development of a Writer* uses the passage from CY on man being the deterministic by-product of both environment and heredity as a device for analyzing PW. In accord with his over-all thesis, Smith emphasizes the fact that "In PW the disintegration of the vernacular persona has proceeded further [than in CY]," the vernacular being conceived as an index to faith in the essential goodness of the populace. "Roxy tries to conceal the truth that her son [Tom Driscoll] is a slave [or has 1/32d negro blood], whereas Wilson's function is to reveal it. The grim social reality reasserted through his agency [as a lawyer depending on finger-print identification] has no place for the vernacular that Wilson represents." Smith associates PW's non-vernacularism with the fact (as T wrote his wife) that "I have never thought of Pudd'nhead as a *character*, but only as a piece of machinery—a button or a crank or a lever, with a useful function to perform in a machine, but no dignity above that." He represents analytical intelligence as opposed to organic wholeness such as Huck had. Smith thinks the "problem of tone" or point of view is difficult or ambivalent, since in the context of T's other works one has a "suspicion that he intends to caricature Judge Driscoll's pride of ancestry" with the acceptance of duelling, while "the reader is expected to feel contempt for Tom because he is too cowardly to challenge the Count."

Smith thinks there is significance that T "deleted from the final version" his earlier passage to the effect that "slavery was to blame, not innate nature. It placed the slave below the brute, without the white man's realizing it." Since T wrote PW in a desperate attempt at a "fresh" plot (involving finger-printing, a plot which "would sell," just after his bankruptcy), one wonders whether such passages were deleted to avoid alienating southern readers, or whether T could have cultivated some degree of ambivalence about matters such as heredity so as to make the book widely debated and widely read? Smith notes that "Tom's most atrocious act, his betrayal of [his mother] Roxy by selling her down the river after she has helped him pay his debts . . . comes after he is aware that he is a Negro and himself legally a slave." But Smith tends to soft-pedal these aspects of the book as "not an expression of aristocratic arrogance but of the unmotivated melodramatic villany that T ascribes to Tom along with the sociologically determined traits."

Assuming that slaves were to southerners one form of property, G. M. Spangler ("*PW*: A Parable of Property," *AL* 70) provides a competent analysis of the structure and themes of the book as a whole, and concludes,

Biographically related to T's own financial distress and historically to an America dominated by robber barons, the book, far from being incoherent or inconsistent, is remarkable among T's works for its unity, a unity which derives from its pervasive concern with the theme of property. . . .

Anne Wigger, "The Composition of MT's *PW*: Chronology and Development" (*MP* 57); D. M. McKeithan, "The Morgan Manuscript of *PW*" (*UESALL* 61); and "*PW*: 'A Literary Caesarian Operation'" by R. A. Wiggins (*CE* 63) all illuminate the development of this manuscript.

Frederick Anderson's 30-page introduction to a reprint of the first edition of *PW* (1968) is especially useful for its full annotated bibliography, its elaborate citing of contemporary British and American reviews, and its citing of the main changes in revisions (paralleling the studies cited above by McKeithan and Wigger). Anderson views the book as very hostile to slavery, but he tends to avoid the question of racism. M. D. Coburn in " 'Training is Everything': PW" (ML 70) is in accord with James Cox on PW as representing the end of the American dream for T. Coburn, after studying PW from the standpoint of Wilson's seeking social acceptance for 20 years, says the outcome of the story signals "the end of T's hope in man." He also calls T's vision satiric rather than ironic, and he sees the book as "rejecting absolutely the possibility of social or individual self-regeneration. . . . The book is a bitter attack on the country he [T] wished to regard as a land of rugged individualists."

Since 1955 several illuminating studies of PW have appeared F. R. Leavis ("MT's Neglected Classic: The Moral Astringency of PW," Com 56) elaborates his 1955 introduction to the book. He is concerned with an aesthetic reading which stresses multiple irony and discusses PW's relation to HF and to the folk-mind (following De Voto), PW's departure from naivety and its belonging "frankly to sophisticated literary tradition," T's emphasis on the town as having some degree of beauty and order, and T's respect for the traits of the gentleman (except for the dueller's code of honor). Leavis claims that irony apart "the distinctively satiric plays no great part" in PW, and he imagines that "T unmistakably admires Judge Driscoll and Pembroke Howard" (a point which Cox attacks). He thinks "that Wilson, the poised and preeminently civilized moral center of the drama," whose views we take to be very close to T's, is not, all the same, "to be identified with him." But his main point is that the book being "a classic of the use of popular modes—of the sensational and the melodramatic—for the purpose of significant art," PW in its overall attitude "is remote from cynicism or pessimism." It conveys neither "contempt for human nature nor a rejection of civilization." At the end, Roxy "demonstrates the wholly common humanity of the 'nigger' and the white."

If one has misgivings about Leslie Fiedler's suggestion of homosexuality in "Come Back to the Raft Ag'in, Huck Honey" (PR 48), Fiedler's study of PW in "As Free as Any Cretur'" (NR 55) shows much insight in discerning that here T turns from his hope that evil could be remedied by changing outward institutions of state and church (as in the first part of CY) to his later view that evil is somehow ingrained in man's very nature. "Perhaps the supreme achievement of this book," says Fiedler, "is to have rendered such indignities [as Roxy's saying 'it's the nigger in you'] not in terms of melodrama or as a parochial 'special problem' but as a local instance of some universal guilt and doom. . . . The false Tom . . . embodies also its 'dark necessity'—and must lie, steal, kill and boast until in his hubris he reveals himself as the slave we all secretly are." Fiedler stresses the book's "tragic inevitability" and finds it "superior" to *HF* because, "morally, it is one of the most honest books in our literature." R. E. Spiller (*Cycle of American Literature*, 1955) says *PW* shows the beginning of T's later extreme pessimism: "Basically it is an acceptance of the new position suggested by the science of Darwin and his followers that had apparently deprived mankind once and for all of his free will to act in a mechanically predetermined universe." Thus *PW* takes on important new significance as a kind of watershed in T's development.

h. *Joan of Arc.* Since T said he originally began *JA* as "a companion to *P&P*," Parrington in accord with his political-social interest linked these books illuminatingly with *CY* as hostile to a "mean property consciousness" and to "bishops and kings," as contrasted with the faith that "peasants are people." On the other hand, Mentor Williams in "MT's Joan of Arc" (*MAQR* 48) subordinates the castigation of "church bigots" and the King to the phychological problem of why T regarded *JA* as "the best" of all his books, took "seven times the pleasure" in writing it he did in the others, and devoted more than four years to its preparation. Williams's answer is that his glorification of Joan fulfilled a deep spiritual and emotional need at a time when a sense of futility and his business failure, which was a result of misplaced confidence in the Machine, robbed him of hope. In Joan he found "by far the most extraordinary person the human race has ever produced," a find which (as Canby and Wagenknecht agree) greatly helped to temper his pessimism. "Joan was the measure of man's potentialities," Williams concludes. E. H. Long in "Sut Lovingood and MT's *JA*" (*MLN* 49) finds that T modeled the scene in which the bull stung by bees disrupts a funeral procession on a tall tale by G. W. Harris. See also Bronia Sielewicz in "Joan and MT" (Edward Wagenknecht, ed., *Joan of Arc: An Anthology of History and Literature*, 1948), and M. A. Wyman, "A Note on MT" (*CE* 46). Most critics agree that what distinguishes *JA* from its historical sources is not only T's invention of humorous characters and episodes, especially in the early chapters, but the fact that (as in *HF*) the whole story is unified in point of view, being presented through the eyes of a devoted "page and secretary," the Sieur Louis de Conte. (See also A. E. Stone's masterful study, cited earlier.)

i. *"The Man that Corrupted Hadleyburg."* This story has been the center of controversy since Brooks called it the first instance of T's completely outspoken exposure of supposedly incorruptible people, in deference to whom he previously had been publicly silent. Bellamy has argued that it merely climaxes a long and growing conflict between his "Moralism and Determinism," which accounts for the fact that "There is no continuity of motivation, no steadiness of emotional effect, no philosophical unity to the story." On the other hand, Everett Carter (*Howells and the Age of Realism*, 1954) argues interestingly that "on the scale of increasing sympathy, we generally find that the same ordinary, common people he celebrated in *HF*, like Jack Halliday who led the townspeople of Hadleyburg in their scoffing of the Incorruptibles, ranked high, while the pretentious, self-righteous 'pillars of society' were very low." G. A. Cardwell in "MT's Hadleyburg" (*OSAHQ* 51) shows that T probably had in mind no one town such as Oberlin. The history of the composition of "The Morgan Manuscript of 'The Man That Corrupted Hadleyburg,' " has been illuminatingly studied by D. M. McKeithan (*TSLL* 61). Differing with Bellamy's interpretation of this story, C. S. Burhans, Jr., in "The Sober Affirmations of MT's Hadleyburg" (*AL* 62) argues persuasively that the story essentially belongs to a long "positive tradition."

j. *The Mysterious Stranger* (also see under "Biography"). J. S. Tuckey's *MT and Little Satan* (1963) is an especially significant work in that it paves the way for a reinterpretation of *MS* and of other writings of T's later years. As already mentioned, this careful study completely refutes De Voto's dating of the MSS and his contention that the Eseldorf version of the story marked T's return to artistic health "from the edge of insanity." Tuckey establishes the following chronological stages among the related MSS: (1) a "pre-Eseldorf" version, set in America, written probably in October 1897; (2) the Eseldorf story, set in Austria, written during three periods between November 1897, and August 1900; (3) the Hannibal version, set in Hannibal, written in November and December, 1898; and (4) the "Print Shop" version, laid in Austria, written during five periods between November 1902, and September 1908. Gibson's introduction to The "*MS*" *Manuscripts* credits Tuckey with having provided the foundation for that edition.

9. Influence of Mark Twain

Clarence Gohdes points out that the enormous European sale of T's books was aided by his various visits around the globe, which "occasioned newspaper publicity astonishing in quantity and fervor." Malcolm Cowley ("American Books Abroad," *LHUS*) finds that "In the Kaiser's Germany, MT had been by far the most popular American author; there were exactly 100 translations of his various works between 1890 and 1913." The Russians bought 3,100,100 copies of his books, the demand for T being second only to that for Jack London. Hence T provided Europe with its most widely circulated image of the American and of our ideals, and he must have done a great deal to condition European attitudes towards the United States. Russian interest in T may be charted from Clarence Gohdes, editor, *Russian Studies of American Literature* (comp. V. A. Libman; trans. R. V. Allen, 1969). There have been at least two studies of T in Russian. One curiosity is M. O. Mendelson's *MT* (Moscow, 1939), a typical Soviet interpretation of nearly 300 pages, twisting T's later pessimism into proof of the unsatisfying character of American civilization: "Disappointed in bourgeois society, T transferred his disillusionment to the entire human race." The other study is A. Starcev's *MT i Amerika* (Moscow, 1963). For other items which enlighten us about recent Russian views of T, see R. D. Lakin's "MT and the Cold War" (*MQ* 61); Mendelson's "MT's Unpublished Literary Heritage" (*Soviet Rev* 61); and Charles Neider's *MT and the Russians: An Exchange of Views* (1960). Incidentally, by insisting that Clara Clemens Samossoud was hiding some evidence damaging to the United States in refusing to let the University of California open the T Papers to qualified scholars, the Russians were inadvertently instrumental in persuading T's daughter to make the papers available and to allow their publication.

The Italians also have been much interested in T, and a survey by Carla Consiglio, "La fortuna di MT in Italia" (*SA* 58), showed that translation of T in Italy began as early as 1891 with *P&P*, and critical studies first appeared in 1913. Most of T's works are available in Italian translation, and there is a full length study in print: *MT* by Piero Mirizzi (Rome, 1965).

Elsewhere in Europe and the rest of the world T enjoys great vogue. Those interested in charting this international popularity and the critical reaction to him may do so by consulting Roger Asselineau's *The Literary Reputation of MT from 1910 to 1950: A Critical Essay and A Bibliography* (Paris, 1954), the latter running to 1,333 items and including articles from Europe and Latin America.

Besides T's international vogue as an American spokesman, his writing has had a great impact on subsequent generations of artists. Though his ideas, as H. N. Smith thinks, tended to be naive and thin in his later period, he exerted a great influence through his style and craftsmanship:

American literature of the twentieth century owes a substantial debt to the author of *HF*. Writers as different from one another as Sherwood Anderson and Ernest Hemingway have acknowledged the influence of this book on their prose, and in addition one has to take into account the development of the humorous mode by writers like E. B. White, James Thurber, S. J. Perelman, and A. J. Liebling. These evidences demonstrate an important continuity in literary technique and attitude. Where the followers of Whitman have too often moved toward the loose oratory of Thomas Wolfe or Carl Sandburg, the influence of MT has encouraged discipline and craftsmanship.

Paradoxically enough, the rank rabble party of Jacksonism turns out to have set in motion an austere cult of style that has given to American literature an esthetic tradition as pure and rigorous as that of the Symbolists themselves ("Origins of a Native American Literary Tradition" in Margaret Denny and W. H. Gilman, eds., *The American Writer and The European Tradition*, 1950).

In the first chapter of *The Green Hills of Africa* (1935) Hemingway, who was later to win the Nobel Prize, said: "All modern American literature comes from one book by MT called *HF* . . . it's the best book we've had. All American writing comes from that. There was nothing before. There has been nothing as good since." Philip Young's *Hemingway* develops his subject's debt to T fully, in fact almost too extravagantly. But T's influence on present-day literature is surely as pervasive as that of any of our nineteenth-century writers.

HENRY JAMES
Robert L. Gale

I. BIBLIOGRAPHY

Henry James (hereafter called J or HJ) wrote 22 novels, 112 short stories (plus a chapter in a round-robin novel called *The Whole Family*), 15 plays, seven books of criticism and in addition numerous critical pieces not collected in his lifetime, two biographies, seven books of travel writing, a few small incidental books, many miscellaneous items, nine notebooks (now published in one volume), and more than ten thousand letters. If everything he ever wrote were assembled into one massive edition, it would come to 65 or more big volumes totaling at least ten million words. He is the most prolific American writer of undisputed eminence, and it follows that criticism of him has been significant, varied, and extensive.

The student of J has the advantage of starting with a definitive bibliography, Leon Edel and D. H. Laurence, *A Bibliography of HJ* (1957, rev. ed. 1961). It supersedes F. A. King's partial, chronological list of J's writings in *The Novels of HJ* by E. L. Cary (1905, 1964), as well as the fuller and more accurate list by LeRoy Phillips in 1906, revised as *A Bibliography of the Writings of HJ* (1930, 1968), and other now-outmoded partial lists.

The Edel-Laurence bibliography, a model of devoted, meticulous scholarship, is divided into original works, contributions to books, published letters, contributions to periodicals, translations by others of J's writings, and miscellanea. A glance at this 427-page bibliography should convince anyone of J's incredible fecundity. The bibliography lists and describes 75 book-length works, often in more than one volume each, published in J's lifetime, and 29 books—sometimes only new combinations of old material—issued after his death through 1960. In addition, Edel and Laurence list 43 contributions by J to books by or partly about others, and 582 periodical items.

The most useful list of books and articles about J is the compilation by Maurice Beebe and W. T. Stafford in a Special Number of *MFS* (66). This selected checklist is divided into two parts: (1) "books and monographs dealing primarily with J, certain essays which seem . . . especially important, and any general study of J containing at least one extended discussion of a single work of fiction" and (2) a list which locates almost every novel or story in the standard collected editions; tells where J comments on it, in his prefaces, letters, or notebooks; cites editions containing editorial apparatus; cross-refers to general studies listed in the first section; and identifies discussions not previously listed.

Beebe and Stafford acknowledge their indebtedness to the following previous bibliographies: L. N. Richardson, editor, *HJ: Representative Selections* (AWS, 1941, rev. ed. 1966); E. C. Hamilton, "Bibliographical and Critical Studies of HJ, 1941–1948" (*AL* 49); V. R. Dunbar, "Addenda . . ." to the preceding work (*AL* 50); and Lewis Leary, *AAL* (1954, 1970).

A handy though selective bibliography on J is contained in *LHUS* (1948) and its supplement (1959). A thorough list of published writings about J's personality is contained in Simon Nowell-Smith's *Legend of the Master* (1948). Of great value is R. N. Foley's *Criticism in American Periodicals of the Works of HJ from 1866 to 1916* (1944). J. W. Beach includes a remarkable 100-page bibliographical essay on criticism of J from 1918 to the early 1950's in the 1954 revision of his pioneering *Method of HJ* (1918). An excellent recent selective bibliography is contained in the revised edition of C. P. Kelley's *Early Development of HJ* (1930, 1965). A very useful recent general bibliography is Hugh Holman's *The American Novel through HJ* (1966), which has an intelligently selective and divided listing for J.

The most satisfactory recent listings are in the bibliographies and reviews of current scholarship in *PMLA, AL, TCL, AQ, SSF, Abstracts of Eng Stud, Amer Lit Abstracts, Essay and Gen Lit Index*, and the formidable *Internationale Bibliographie der Zeitschriftenliteratur aus allen Gebeiten des Wissens*. Of great value is *ALS*, edited by James Woodress (1965–69) and by J. A. Robbins (1970–   ). B. R. McElderry, Jr., wrote the early J chapters, and Stafford has written the more recent ones. Mention should be made of Woodress's *DAL* (1968), which lists 179 doctoral dissertations wholly or partly on J—more than for any other American writer. For titles and abstracts of over 30 more recent dissertations, see *DA*.

II. EDITIONS

The most beautiful selected edition of J's fiction is the New York Edition, published by Scribner's in 24 volumes, planned and edited by J, plus two supplementary and posthumous volumes (1907–17). The 67 novels and short stories in this edition were thoroughly revised by the author, especially the earlier ones. The edition therefore contains in many cases texts basically different both in style and in other details affecting interpretations of character and incident. This edition also contains J's celebrated critical prefaces, 18 in number. R. P. Blackmur reprinted, with an illuminating introduction, J's prefaces as *The Art of the Novel* (1934). All of the selections in the New York Edition, including the prefaces, and in addition all other novels and short stories published by J during his lifetime (with minor exceptions) were reprinted in London by Macmillan in 35 volumes, edited by Percy Lubbock (1921–23). Scribner's recently reissued the New York Edition (1961–65). But neither the New York Edition nor the London Edition is complete, since both lack the essays and plays. Furthermore, J often revised his novels and short stories, particularly the earlier ones, between serial and first book publication. Recently Edel edited *The Complete Tales of HJ* (1961–64), which is the first complete edition of J's 112 short stories. *The Bodley Head HJ* (1967–   ) consists to date of eight volumes, all novels and in no particular order. So the short fiction is readily available; but there is as yet no complete edition of the novels, most of which, however, are available in paperback reprints, often well edited. A variorum edition of the texts of J's fiction, long and short, would be of immense value but would be astronomically expensive.

A definitive edition of the plays and notes toward plays is provided in *The Complete Plays of HJ*, edited by Edel (1949); of the dramatic criticism in *The Scenic Art, Notes on Acting and the Drama, 1872–1901*, edited by Allan Wade (1948); of the art criticism in *The Painter's Eye*, edited by J. L. Sweeney (1956); and some of J's newspaper essays in *HJ: Parisian Sketches: Letters to the "New York Tribune" 1875–1876*, edited by Edel and I. D. Lind (1957). The narrative version of J's play *The Other House* was republished, with an introduction, by Edel (1947). There is no complete edition of J's critical essays nor of his travel essays. Partial collections of critical essays include *Notes and Reviews of HJ*, edited by Pierre de Chaignon la Rose (1921, 1968), and *Literary Reviews of HJ*, edited by Albert Mordell (1957). Several other selections of criticism by J are available in paperback. The best selection of J's extensive and varied travel writings is M. D. Zabel's edition, *The Art of Travel: Scenes and Journeys in America, England, France and Italy from the Travel Writings of HJ* (1958, 1970), which also contains a bibliography.

The story of J's notebooks is interesting. Nine of them, covering the period from November 1878, to May 1911, turned up in the Harvard University Library. Planned as early as 1873 as a depository for J's ideas and materials for fiction, these notebooks are mainly valuable as a source for studying the creative processes of the novelist with reference to particular works and for the light they shed on general problems of his life and on his development as an artist. They were edited by F. O. Matthiessen and K. B. Murdock, with an introductory essay, as *The Notebooks of HJ* (1947, 1953), with all of the authority of painstaking scholarship and perhaps too much critical commentary.

The best edition of J's autobiographical volumes—*A Small Boy and Others* (1913), *Notes of a Son and Brother* (1914), and *The Middle Years* (1917), a posthumous fragment—is that of F. W. Dupee and is called *HJ: Autobiography* (1956).

Lubbock's pioneering selected edition of *The Letters of HJ* (1920) has extensive biographical commentary. Of the several thousand letters at his disposal then, Lubbock printed only about 400, which tend to emphasize the later rather than the formative stages of J's long career. In addition to the letters in the Lubbock selection, McElderry (*BB* 52) reports that he found over 700 letters dispersed in more than 100 sources and then describes the contents of almost 100 volumes or articles containing letters from J. More recent letter finds have been made: see *CLQ* (43, 53); C. J. Weber and Burdett Gardner (*PMLA* 53, 54); and Edel and L. H. Powers (*BNYPL* 58—repr. in book form as part of *Howells and J: A Double Billing* . . . , ed. by W. M. Gibson, 1958). George Monteiro prints 45 letters by J in *HJ and John Hay: The Record of a Friendship* (1965). Minor discoveries of letters have also been recently made, and some of them are mentioned below.

Edel edited *Selected Letters of HJ* (1955) and is now at work on a multivolume edition of J's letters, with one volume to contain letters to William James and another for letters to William Dean Howells.

III. MANUSCRIPTS

Manuscripts and papers of J are widely scattered, but all of the materials retained by the family have been deposited in the Houghton Library at Harvard University, which is now the official repository. This priceless trove was first decribed by R. B. Perry (*HULN* 42) and for the most part contains letters and manuscripts by Henry James, Sr., William James, and J. The manuscript papers comprise 13 boxes of letters to and eight boxes of letters from various correspondents, 13 boxes of manuscripts (mainly dramatic—see Edel, ed.. *Complete Plays of HJ*, and Edel, *HLB* 49), and the manuscript of the revision of *The American*. Since the date of Perry's descriptive essay, Harvard has added other manuscript, typescript, and proof material (see Edel and Laurence, *Bibliography of HJ*). The most important recent acquisitions are as follows: manuscripts of *Confidence*, "En Provence," "The Jolly Corner" (hereafter called

"Corner"), *The Princess Casamassima* (hereafter *Princess*), the revision of *The Portrait of a Lady* (hereafter *Portrait*), a previously unpublished essay called "Very Modern Rome" (*HLB* 54), and minor essays and early reviews; typescripts of *The Sense of the Past* (hereafter *Past*), *The Ivory Tower* (hereafter *Tower*), the autobiographical fragment *The Middle Years*, and minor pieces; and the originals of more than 500 letters to various persons, and several hundred transcripts of letters (including six boxes of those assembled by Lubbock for his edition). Harvard also has a large number of books from J's personal library, many of which contain annotations or presentation inscriptions.

Second in importance to Harvard's holdings are those in the Collection of American Literature, Yale University Library, which has both manuscripts and letters. Manuscripts include handwritten corrections to the page-proofs of "The American Volunteer Motor-Ambulance Corps in France"; "New England: An Autumn Impression," partly in typescript and the rest in manuscript (plus corrected and revised galleys); and manuscript fragments of *The Europeans*, "A Bundle of Letters," and "The Pension Beaurepas." Yale has the typescript of "The Present Literary Situation in France," and in addition it has a copy of *The Tragic Muse* (hereafter *Muse*) with revisions possibly in J's hand. Yale's J letters total about 800, including many to J. B. Pinker, Edith Wharton, and W. E. Norris.

In the Library of Congress, the J Collection consists primarily of notes, clippings, and cards about J and his work, but also includes 22 letters by J. The most extensive holdings of J manuscripts at the Library of Congress are the numerous letters from him in the papers of others there, including L. C. Moulton, Moreton Frewen, Whitelaw Reid, B. H. Ticknor, Owen Wister, John Hay, J. M. Howells, Manton Marble, J. R. Young, Henry White, H. C. Andersen, J. L. M. Curry, Edmund Gosse, Joseph and Elizabeth Pennell, and L. P. Smith. The Bevan Autograph Collection also has J material.

Several university libraries have notable collections. In the Brotherton Collection, University of Leeds Library, are almost 300 J letters, mostly to Gosse. Also at Leeds, in the Clement K. Shorter Collection, are 19 additional letters. The Colby College Library has 155 letters by HJ to various persons, including Annie Fields, R. W. Gilder, Gosse, W. D. Howells, and T. S. Perry and his wife; the library also has a copy of one youthful poem by J. At the University of Rochester Library are eight J letters, some rather short. In the Bunting Papers and the Herrick Papers, University of Chicago, are six J letters. In the Library of the University of California at Los Angeles are five J letters, mostly brief.

Holdings in non-academic offices are numerous. The Department of Manuscripts, British Museum, has dozens of letters from J, mostly to M. B. B. Edwards, Gosse, and Shorter, in the Ashley Collection, which also contains a tribute by J to James Payn (*Illust London News*, 9 Apr 1898); the British Museum also has the large, recently acquired collection of J letters to Messrs. Macmillan, 1878–1914 (for a few samples, see *Letters to Macmillan*, ed. by Simon Nowell-Smith, 1967). The Scribner archives house typescripts of "Flickerbridge," "The Great Good Place," and a published copy of "A Light Man" graced by J's handwritten corrections. Other J material in manuscript and typescript may be found in the Huntington Library, the Morgan Library, the Berg Collection at the New York Public Library, the Gluck Collection at the Buffalo Public Library, the Century Association in New York, and in private hands (see Edel and Laurence, *Bibliography of HJ*, and the bibliography in H. M. Hyde's *HJ at Home*, 1969).

IV. BIOGRAPHY

Biographical material having to do with J may be divided into records of his ancestors and relatives, major studies of J himself, treatments of J and his friends, and studies of minor aspects of his life.

1. Forebears and Relatives

Part of the biographical study of J worth only brief consideration here is scholarship dealing with his forebears and immediate relatives. Genealogical study begins with "William James of Albany, New York, and His Descendants," by Katharine Hastings (*NY Genealog and Biog Rec* 24) and with a chart of the family issued by the Colby College Library in 1943. The first serious attempt to follow family traits through several generations was C. H. Grattan's *The Three Jameses: A Family of Minds* (1932, 1962). This book contains the first study of the Irish immigrant grandfather William James and his Swedenborgian philosopher-son Henry James, Sr. The accounts of the more famous William and HJ in the third generation are full enough to allow dominant family characteristics and ideas to form into a pattern of similarities and mutations with important psychological implications.

Meanwhile, the definitive *Thought and Character of William James* by R. B. Perry (1935) fills out the portrait presented by the philosopher's *Letters*, edited by his son Henry James (1920), of the novelist brother, to whom there was a subtle and profound psychological tie. With the edition by A. R. Burr of the journals of the invalid sister—*Alice James: Her Brothers, Her Journals* (1934, re-ed. by Edel, 1964)—further information about the mother and the lesser-known brothers, Garth Wilkinson James and Robertson James, was also made available. In 1947 Matthiessen published *The James Family: Including Selec-*

tions from the Writings of Henry James, Senior, William, Henry, and Alice James. This is a detailed study of the influence of the liberated religious faith and the skepticism of the elder James on his two sons, who disappointed their father's hopes for a new age of religion by applying his discovered freedoms to secular problems, when they applied them at all. More a source book than a finished biographical study, it remains a substantial authority on the family as a whole. Matthiessen's theory is that William and HJ are arrayed on opposite sides of their father's antithesis between doing and being, and so afford a study in contrast within a frame of identity. It is of incidental interest to note here that Quentin Anderson in *The American HJ* (1957) posits the theory that J avoided spiritual expatriation by inheriting from his father an elaborate psychological, philosophical, and theological body of thought which enabled him to construct his major-phase trilogy—*The Ambassadors, The Wings of the Dove* (hereafter *Dove*), *The Golden Bowl* (hereafter *Bowl*)—as a complicated Swedenborgian allegory. (Anderson's work will be considered in detail below.)

2. Major Biographical Studies

The biographical study of J himself was long delayed because of his own reticence, the fear in some early would-be biographers that there was little to be said about a life outwardly so uneventful, the paradoxical magnitude of such a task, and the initial unavailability of manuscript material. But at last a massive biography by Edel in five volumes is nearly complete: *HJ: The Untried Years, 1843–1870* (1953); *HJ: The Conquest of London, 1870–1881* (1962); *HJ: The Middle Years, 1882–1895* (1962); and *HJ: The Treacherous Years, 1895–1901* (1969). The fifth volume will be *HJ: The Master, 1902–1916.* Edel's aim is to relate J's inner life to his works. Employing a psychoanalytical approach, Edel sometimes goes out on a limb, for which reason reviewers and other readers are sharply divided into opposing camps. Regardless of one's persuasion, however, it is true that since Edel not only has unlimited access to unpublished family papers but also thoroughly knows all of J's works, his biography is indispensable. Perhaps the chief weaknesses in it are that it is on occasion oddly Freudian, it consciously avoids "gossip and anecdotage"—which some readers of biography have valid reason to value—it steadfastly refuses to build upon insights published by other critics of J's writings, and its abbreviated documentation is hard to follow. All Jamesian scholars, however, are indebted to Edel for his creative and smoothly readable combination of biographical information and critical acumen.

Pre-Edel biographical studies of J all build solidly on the autobiographical volumes—*A Small Boy and Others, Notes of a Son and Brother,* and *The Mid-*

dle Years—which the novelist dictated in his last years and left incomplete at his death. They are an old man's memoirs, highly subjective, written in J's famous major-phase style, and depending on few documents and notes other than some letters from his father and his cousin Minny Temple; but they have a special quality of self-revelation which a more formal record could never achieve. Written ostensibly to provide material for the biography of his brother William, they tell far more about J's own place in the family than they do of William's, and a careful reading enables one to reconstruct from these notes the quality of the author's juvenile personality. His own remarks that his autobiographical work is "vitiated perhaps by the effort to comprehend more than it contains" suggests the kind of revelation they provide. C. P. Kelley in her *Early Development of HJ* shows how useful these reminiscences are even while she is objecting that J did not really wish to get back to the mood of his early years because he wrongly thought the literary production of his early phase "hideous."

Of great importance to an understanding of the evolution of J's inner life are the 18 critical prefaces, noted above. They tell how J got many of the ideas —"wind-blown germs"—which resulted in some of his finest works of fiction, how he let his imagination play with these ideas, some of his creative and editorial problems, various kinds of aesthetic success, and the like. Blackmur has erroneously labeled these critical essays "the most sustained and . . . the most eloquent and original piece of literary criticism in existence" (*Art of Novel*), but it is true that they are highly illuminating. Another source of light for those who wish to see how J the creative artist operated is his *Notebooks,* noted above. More intimately than do the public prefaces, the *Notebooks* reveal J privately worrying over his ideas, teasing them into shape, adjuring himself to take care to avoid this pitfall or that, trying out samples of his writing on his own ear, and often commending himself on certain esoteric successes.

Lubbock's introductions to successive sections of his edition of J's *Letters* comprise a kind of running biography, of charm and value, dealing with J's middle and later years. The last, incomplete volume of his *Autobiography* opens with February 1869; and the first letter which Lubbock prints is one from J in London to his sister Alice, dated 10 March 1869.

The death of J in 1916 occurred at a time in American literary history when critics were in the mood to emphasize psychological and sociological factors in the lives of major writers. This predilection resulted in certain biographical treatments of J now properly regarded as more important for what they say about American cultural history than about J the man. Critics like Rebecca West, V. W. Brooks, and V. L. Parrington began to stress the connections between American literature and American life, which for them meant narrowly placing the individual in the political and social development of the nation. Thus the novelist of the international theme or of the remote American past became the author without a country or an age of his own, the expatriate who never achieved a profound new loyalty. Anticipating Brooks, West in her short, provocative *HJ* (1916, 1968) provides more a critique of the fiction than a biography but follows a strictly biographical pattern. She relates J's works closely to his early experiences and to the reaction of an American consciousness to European culture. As she does so, she develops the paradox that, because he had the complex fate to be both an American and a product of international culture, "he felt at home only in exile." Her appreciative discussion of J's principal novels and short stories is therefore tinged with scorn for lack of passion in a novelist of manners of a mannerless American-international set.

The theory of frustration due to environment was soon given its fullest expression, by Brooks in *The Pilgrimage of HJ* (1925). This book presents a portrait of the sophisticated American artist, alienated from his own society on the one hand, because of its lack of culture, and from the society of a more cultured European world on the other, because of his alien birth. Brooks's study is important in the history of Jamesian biographical criticism because it so memorably overstates the paradox of the artist without a country that it reveals the fallacy as well as the core of truth in its simplistic formula.

Later biographical critics who maintained essentially the same theory of frustration were less doctrinaire and more subtle, beginning with Ferner Nuhn's *The Wind Blew from the East: A Study in the Orientation of American Culture* (1942), and continuing with R. C. LeClair's *Three American Travelers in England: James Russell Lowell, Henry Adams, HJ* (1945), Jean Simon's *Le roman Américain aux XXᵉ siècle* (1949), and especially H. S. Canby's *Turn West, Turn East: Mark Twain and HJ* (1951, 1965). Canby's Plutarchian study builds on the same critic's previous essays (*HW* 16, *SatR* 48) and his thin study of J in *Definitions: Essays in Contemporary Criticism* (1922). At the same time, however, it fortunately reflects the changing critical currents of succeeding eras as it leaves doctrine behind while preserving an essentially social frame of reference for personality. Constance Rourke also illustrates this same healthy critical change in her *American Humor* (1931), and so does Brooks himself when he treats J later and more sympathetically in his charming *New England: Indian Summer* (1940).

A solid, early critic of J who may have helped Brooks mend his ways was Pelham Edgar, who directly answered Brooks (*QQ* 32) and who earlier in *HJ, Man and Author* (1917, 1964) had argued that J the artist soon exhausted his

American materials and that his move to Europe was therefore good both for his social personality and for his art. Edgar quickly established this critical approach in biographical terms, then grouped J's works according to setting, themes, and genres, and finally discussed everything critically. This book was workmanlike and appreciative, but it is notable today mainly for its forward-looking biographical insights and also for being one of the first extended studies to emphasize J's later novels.

Partly because of Edgar, present-day biographical commentators on J see their subject as a legitimately American artist. The opening of the James family papers dispelled some of the air of mystery hovering about the novelist, although mysteries still exist. Modern psychology has helped to explain some of the problems of J's personality, even though present-day analysts would be the first to insist that his psyche has by no means been definitively probed. Perhaps the best single work to illustrate the healthy shift in modern aesthetic perspective is F. W. Dupee's unpretentious but durable *HJ* (1951, rev. 1956 and 1965). Taking for granted the inner chronicle which J himself defines as the highest form of experience, Dupee legitimately ignores the tiresome subject of alienation, seemingly paradoxical but really irrelevant, and presents a straightforward record of the known facts, which he presents in more detail than does any other biographer before Edel.

Another fine study is McElderry's *HJ* (1965), which may lack the sophistication of Dupee's study and the detail of Edel's, but which is recommended as a virtually perfect introduction to J. It displays a commendable balance of biographical and critical information, is well written, and is notable for its authority and temperate theorizing. A very competent partial biographical study is LeClair's *Young HJ* (1955), painstakingly detailed but unfortunately overshadowed by Edel's first volume (1953), which treats the identical period. Two early articles by Edel (*UTQ* 33, 41) show a growing interest in the biographical problems. Edel was influenced, as most students of J have been, by the trend toward psychoanalysis epitomized in Edmund Wilson's seminal study of Jamesian ambiguity (*H&H*, 34; rev. in *The Triple Thinkers*, 1938, rev. 1948). Edel has also made use of a curiously doctrinaire study by Saul Rosenzweig (*C&P* 43; *PR* 44), which starts with a supposedly well-developed "Oedipus situation" in J, posits a psychological castration theory emphasizing frustration and traumatic escape into fantasy and then into ghost stories, and suggests that J could resolve his neurosis only when he identified himself with social action late in life. This dangerous theory was accepted and interpreted literally by many critics and biographers who seemed to favor it over Brooks's theory of alienation. Edel endeavors to discredit Rosenzweig's theory by adducing evidence of the same sort that Rosenzweig uses to support it. Edel and others accept the theory of psychological rather than physical injury and proceed to a convincing consideration of J's relationships with his immediate family and Minny Temple as the basis of his creative personality.

3. James and His Friends

One of the most delightful books of its kind is *The Legend of the Master* (1948), a compilation by Nowell-Smith of more than a hundred anecdotes told about J by friends and acquaintances. The book is prefaced by an essay which traces legends about J, both accurate and apocryphal, to their sometimes conflicting sources. The compiler then reprints items about J's appearance, his talk, social occasions involving J, his plays, his friends, his work habits, Lamb House, his efforts in World War I, and his death. Nowell-Smith's book is both scholarly and fun.

In a book whose main purpose is to reprint Howells's articles and reviews about J, Albert Mordell in introductions to his three chronological subdivisions discusses the personal and professional friendship of the two men. The book is called *The Discovery of a Genius: William Dean Howells and HJ* (1961), for which S. E. Bowman has provided an extensive introduction.

G. S. Hellman (*Century* 26) and, more recently, J. A. Smith, in *HJ and Robert Louis Stevenson* (1948), have told the story of a significant friendship. E. K. Brown does the same thing for J and Joseph Conrad (*YR* 46). Conrad wrote an appreciation of J in *Notes on Life and Letters* (1921). Ford Madox Hueffer (Ford) recalled impressions of J in *HJ: A Critical Study* (1913, 1964) and again in *Return to Yesterday* (1932) and also *Portrait from Life* (1937). Edith Wharton paid tribute to J in *A Backward Glance* (1934). Millicent Bell in *Edith Wharton and HJ* (1965) discusses not only the friendship of the two expatriate novelists but also J's supposed influence upon Wharton's works. A serious misunderstanding ended a lifelong friendship between J and H. G. Wells when J's 1914 essay on "The Younger Generation [of Novelists]" provoked Wells's satiric *Boon* (1915), in which J was resolved, as J himself later phrased it, into "an unmitigated mistake." The episode forms the climax of a work edited by Edel and G. N. Ray, *HJ and H. G. Wells* (1958). Stafford discusses the James family's friendship with Emerson (*PMLA* 53). Michael Swan treats J's relationship with Andersen (*LonM* 55; *Harper's Baz* 55). The most recent book-length discussion of a literary friendship involving J is Monteiro's *HJ and John Hay* (1965), a rich little book in which the editor expertly places the two men in their times, details their friendship, summarizes their opinions of each other, reprints Hay's notice introducing J as New York *Tribune* correspondent and Hay's review of "Daisy Miller" (hereafter "Daisy") and *Portrait*, and then presents the J-Hay correspondence—all with admirable notes.

More casual and not always reverent briefer records of meetings with J include those of Sydney Brooks (*HW* 04), Witter Bynner (*Critic* 05; *SatR* 43), Robert Herrick (*YR* 23), Muriel Draper (*HM* 29), Hamlin Garland (*Roadside Meetings*, 1931; see also McElderry, *AL* 52), Compton Mackenzie (*Life and Letters Today*, 1943), and Paul Bourget (*CambJ* 50). Alice Boughton tells of taking photographs of J (*H&H* 34); and O. H. Dunbar (*Critic* 05) and W. C. France (*Bookman* 05) discuss J as a lecturer (see also M. P. Harris, *AL* 51).

4. Minor Aspects

Relatively minor aspects of J's life are revealed in many incidental essays. See J. W. White's interpretation of J's attitude toward Germany, England, and the United States in the early years of World War I (*Lond Spect* 15); for a more favorable view, see John Russell (*NewS* 43). Very minor biographical sources include the anonymous article on J and the English Association (*Scrutiny* 46) and E. S. Roscoe on J and the Reform Club (*Bookman* 25). Geoffrey Keynes's brief *HJ at Cambridge* (1967) is of sentimental interest only.

The most revealing of all personal reminiscences are the accounts by the secretary-typist who took his old-age dictation. Theodora Bosanquet published articles (*Fortnightly* 17; *Liv Age* 17; *Bookman* 17; *YR* 20) which she expanded into *HJ at Work* (1924, 1970), and by revealing his method, stirred up a controversy as to whether or not the involutions of his later style were the result of this surrender to the machine. Edel published (*Atl* 68) the "deathbed" dictation about Napoleon by J, then in delirium, to Miss Bosanquet. This material, incidentally, was the occasion of a ridiculous exchange of letters in the *TLS* between Edel and H. M. Hyde (2, 9, 23, 30 May, 13 June 68).

Also of interest is Hyde's *HJ at Home*, which builds on the same author's *Story of Lamb House, Rye: The Home of HJ* (1966). It gives the full account of J's various residences—in Mayfair and Kensington, down in Rye (especially at Lamb House), and finally in Chelsea—of his visitors and visiting habits, and finally of his activities during the first years of World War I. Other treatments of J and his residence at Rye are Louise Boit's recollections of J as her landlord there (*Atl* 46) and Simon Fleet's essay on J at Rye (*ModA* 66).

Essays of the 1950's largely biographical in nature include those by I. D. Lind, "The Inadequate Vulgarity of HJ" (*PMLA* 51); A. R. Ferguson, "The Triple Quest of HJ: Fame, Art, and Fortune" (*AL* 56); Michael Millgate, "The Novelist and the Businessman" (*SA* 59), and Stafford, "William James as Critic of his Brother Henry" (*Person* 59). Biographical essays of the 1960's are relatively few in number. Material on J's travels was published by Umberto Mariani (*SA* 60; *NCF* 64), Donald Emerson (*TWA* 63), and Alberta Fabris (*SA* 63). M. F. Deakin contrasts J's real and fictive quests (*BuR* 66). J. C. Major writes about J, Daudet, and Oxford (*N&Q* 66).

V. CRITICISM

There seems to be no ideal way to outline a discussion of criticism about a major author. One may divide the criticism into early and late, long and short, general and specific; or one may consider criticism of different types of writing by the author. But any approach is apt to be somewhat repetitious and also to let certain important critical works slip through. Since I must, however, adopt one approach and then follow it, I have decided to discuss J criticism according to this pattern: (1) book-length criticism (before 1950; from 1950 to the present—minor studies, major studies, books on individual books), (2) chapters or parts of books, and (3) articles (before 1916, 1916–1933, 1934–1949, the 1950's, and the 1960's).

1. Books

The J boom is one of the most astounding literary phenonema of our time. Incredibly enough, it shows no sign of slackening, even though it started in the mid-1930's. For proof of its persistence, one need only note that before 1930, 11 book-length studies exclusively devoted to J were published; in the 1930's, six more appeared; in the 1940's, another six; in the 1950's, 15; and from 1960 to early 1970, no less than 53. These figures do not include books juxtaposing J and a comparable writer, for example Canby's *Turn West, Turn East* or Bruce Lowery's *Marcel Proust et HJ: une confrontation* (Paris, 1964); or books treating J along with several other figures, such as W. C. Brownell's *American Prose Masters* (1909, 1963), A. J. A. Waldock's *J, Joyce, and Others* (1937), or R. W. Stallman's *The Houses That J Built and Other Literary Studies* (1961). Nor do these figures take into account either study guides to individual works (of which there are more than a dozen, some of them very good) or books reprinting essays about J by several critics.[1] For no other American author, with the possible recent exception of William Faulkner, can such a skyrocketing critical trend be cited.

1. See F. W. Dupee, ed., *The Question of HJ* (1945); Naomi Lebowitz, ed., *Discussions of HJ* (1962); Leon Edel, ed. *Twentieth Century Views of HJ* (1963); W. T. Stafford, ed., *Perspectives on J's "Portrait"* (1967); Peter Buitenhuis, ed., *Twentieth Century Interpretations of "Portrait"* (1968); Roger Gard, ed., *HJ: The Critical Heritage* (1968); Tony Tanner, ed., *HJ: Modern Comments* (1968, 1970); and A. E. Stone, Jr., ed., *Twentieth Century Interpretations of "The Ambassadors"* (1969).

Books on J are of several sorts. Some, like Bosanquet's *HJ at Work*, V. W. Brooks's *Pilgrimage of HJ*, and Edel's multi-volume study, are strictly biographical or psychographical. Others offer full-scale critiques of J's works and may be exemplified by E. L. Cary's *Novels of HJ*, the first effort of any length on the subject, or J. W. Beach's *Method of HJ*, which is still richly rewarding. Still others treat restricted thematic or technical aspects; two examples are J. A. Ward's *Imagination of Disaster: Evil in the Fiction of HJ* (1961)and Sr. M. C. Sharp's *Confidante in HJ: Evolution and Moral Value of a Fictive Character* (1963). Still others consider a restricted number of works or even only a single work, for instance, Walter Isle's *Experiments in Form: HJ's Novels, 1896–1901* (1968) or J. F. Blackall's *Jamesian Ambiguity and "The Sacred Fount"* (1965). Few book-length studies have been devoted to any phase of J's non-fictional writings; notable exceptions include Morris Roberts's *HJ's Criticism* (1929, 1965), Edel's *Les années dramatiques* (1931) and *Prefaces of HJ* (1931).

a. *Books before 1950.* The first book on J, E. L. Cary's *Novels of HJ* (1905), exhibits more good sense than depth. It is moderately analytical and very appreciative, recognizes J's skill at portraiture, reveals his moral concerns, and excellently evaluates his heroines. Next came Hueffer (Ford), whose *HJ, a Critical Study* is a mannered, subjective recollection and appreciation, displaying charm but also superficiality. The next author of a significant book on J was West, whose article on reading J in wartime (*NR* 15) led to her stimulating monograph, *HJ*. This work helped to inaugurate a new era in Jamesian criticism. West quarrels with J's allegedly pallid view of Europe, ridicules his treatment of women and of passion, and sees his early work as adversely affected by Hawthorne and his last novels as showing the signs of age. Still she manages to convey a vivid sense of the quality of his genius—especially as revealed in a few 1888–95 stories.

The study of J's techniques became the special province of Beach, whose *The Method of HJ* begins with J's assumption that writing fiction is an art and may be complex and precise; discusses J's methods under Idea, Picture, Revelation, Suspense, Point of View, Dialogue, Eliminations, Tone, Romance, and Ethics; and blocks out J's career in six chronological stages. "It is the chief distinction of James," says this pioneering critic, "that he was the first to write novels in English with a full and fine sense of the principles of composition." All subsequent criticism of J is indebted directly or indirectly to Beach.

Besides its value as biography Pelham Edgar's *HJ, Man and Author* is important critically. Edgar began to turn his attention to stylistic matters in an essay on J's method (*Proc & Trans Royal Soc Canada* 19). In an essay on J's art (*Nat Rev* 24), Edgar analyzed the novelist's method of control. In a third essay (*DR* 25), he anticipated his book by analyzing J's major-phase novels. In his book, Edgar comprehensively studies the novelist's whole corpus, wisely refusing to choose between early and late works but instead proving that differences are only aspects of one genius.

Edmund Wilson reviewed Edgar's book (*NR* 27) and called for "a thorough exploration of his [J's] fiction to find out what is actually in it—that is, precisely what is supposed to happen in each of his novels and stories and precisely what inferences we are supposed to draw." The challenge was usually better answered in short articles through the 1930's and 1940's, as we shall see below, than in the book-length studies published then. Most of the profound books on J follow and owe much to Matthiessen's *HJ: The Major Phase* (1944) but become abundant only in the 1950's and later. Meanwhile, back in the 1920's, a few other books appeared. Bosanquet's *HJ at Work*, already mentioned, is illuminating. At Strasbourg, M. R. Garnier completed a careful, enthusiastic study, *HJ et la France* (1927), which reveals the depth of J's knowledge of France and things French, and is the first of several specialized studies of J and specific countries which he knew and loved. Finally, the first study of any aspect of J's non-fictional writings appeared also in the 1920's, Morris Roberts's *HJ's Criticism* (1929), which maintains both a careful objectivity and a consistent theory about J as a critic, as it follows him from early reviews and *French Poets and Novelists* through *Partial Portraits* to the prefaces (which are slighted) and *Notes on Novelists*. Roberts shows how the critical mind is reflected in the fiction, and deals fairly with the limitations and paradoxes of J's personality and art.

Throughout the 1930's and the 1940's, article-length criticism was generally superior to books. The three best books in the 1930's came early, Kelley's *Early Development of HJ* (1930), Edel's *Les années dramatiques* (Paris, 1931), and *Prefaces of HJ* (Paris, 1931). Kelley thoroughly analyzes all of J's reviews, essays, and tales which she could then identify from 1864 to 1881. She discusses the influence of French writers, especially Balzac, on young J; points out the aid Howells offered him; and is especially painstaking in her consideration of the veneration in which J held Turgenev and George Eliot. The solidity and permanent value of Kelley's pioneering study are demonstrated by L. N. Richardson in his charming introduction to its revised edition (1965). Edel's books are good in their own right but have been incorporated in his multitudinous later publications, chiefly his work on the drama in his definitive and carefully annotated *The Plays of HJ* (1949). Edel's study of the prefaces is much less significant; and it has remained for later critics, beginning with Blackmur, to work in greater detail on them.

Other books in the 1930's are less important. One is Elizabeth Robin's *Theatre and Friendship: Some HJ Letters, with a Commentary* (1932, 1969), which first illuminates the subject of J's rather slight friendship with the distinguished actress and others of her circle. Robins gives the impression of more intimacy with the novelist than J's letters, as printed, substantiate. These are merely lively with good-natured badinage. Further, the best letters in this book are addressed not to Robins but to their mutual friend, Mrs. Hugh Bell. E. M. Snell's *Modern Fables of HJ* (1935) is of limited worth, and one wonders why it was ever expensively reprinted (1967). The remaining book appearing in the 1930's is Patricia Diffené's *HJ: Versuch einer Würdigung seiner Eigenart* (1939), a Marburg dissertation on aspects of J's unique style.

As the Depression limited critical publications in the 1930's, so did World War II in the early 1940's. Even so Matthiessen produced *HJ: The Major Phase* (1944), one of the two first-rate critical books of the decade, and also edited *HJ: Stories of Writers and Artists* (1944) and *The American Novels and Stories of HJ* (1947), both of which have good introductions. *HJ: The Major Phase* is a frontal attack on the elder critics of both the genteel school and the Brooks-Parrington persuasion. Matthiessen quotes and uses Wharton's comment that for J "every great novel must first of all be based on a profound sense of moral values and then constructed with a classic unity and economy of means"; the critic goes on to conclude that traditional misconceptions have resulted from attempts to separate content from form as well as from the mistaken assumption that J's devotion to art was an alienation from life. With this point, which is central to *The Major Phase*, modern Jamesian criticism takes its real start. Matthiessen sets a high standard by superbly explicating his thesis with evidence from four of J's final novels. He places his emphasis on the sense of life to be gained from a thorough analysis of a single character in the setting of problems determining that character. Thus he sees these novels on the three levels of ethical import, personality, and style—just as J himself saw them. In an appendix, Matthiessen examines J's 1908 revision of *Portrait*. This fine essay remains one of the best on the exceedingly difficult problem of J's revisions.

The only other book on J published in the 1940's which still holds up is Elizabeth Stevenson's brief *The Crooked Corridor: A Study of HJ* (1949). Stevenson regards as the main theme in J's work the collision of the individual and society. She provides apt illustrations by considering Roderick Hudson, Hyacinth Robinson, and Milly Theale, and concludes by examining J's attitudes and craftsmanship. One weakness in her work may be that it makes too little direct use of previous criticism, especially by Beach and Matthiessen.

Other book-length studies published in the 1940's are less substantial, although each has its merits. Foley's *Criticism in American Periodicals of the Works of HJ from 1866 to 1916* has obvious uses; and Osborn Andreas's unpretentious little book, *HJ and the Expanding Horizon: A Study of the Meaning and Style of J's Fiction* (1948), surveys all but ten of J's novels and tales and categorizes their main themes into ten groups. One weakness of the study stems from the author's erroneous assumption that each piece of fiction has only one theme. The strength of Andreas's work lies in its genuine introductory value. The first three chapters are by far the best.

The first book on J by an Italian critic was published in 1948: Paolo Milano's *HJ, o il proscritto volontario*. Milano treats J's literary exploitation of the international theme, with the European "estetica e araldica, incrostata di sottigliezza e di tradizione," and the American "fisiologica e morale, corazzata di muscoli e di integrità." Of several works presenting this contrast, Milano finds *Portrait* the most successful. He is discontented with *Princess*, prefers *The Bostonians*, and is dissatisfied with *Muse*. After digressing to consider J's poetics and his prefaces, Milano turns to the great works of the novelist's "seconda maniera," praising *What Maisie Knew* (hereafter *Maisie*) for its treatment of the child and *Dove* as J's best novel. But his finest work, Milano thinks, is J's short fiction, treated here according to theme. Milano regards "The Beast in the Jungle" (hereafter "Beast") as containing "in noce" all of J's motives.

b. *Books from 1950 to the Present.* In the two decades from 1950 on, sixty-eight books exclusively devoted to J have appeared. At least a dozen of them are of enormous value.

i) Minor Studies. Swan wrote two little booklets on J in the early 1950's: *HJ* (1950) and *HJ* (1952). The first is an introductory essay on representative novels of J's three main periods: *Roderick Hudson* (hereafter *Hudson*), *Portrait*, and *Bowl*. The second is in three parts: J's life related to his work, an analysis of the fiction according to thematic groups, and J's attitudes as revealed in his fiction. The middle section expertly handles *Princess*, but the little book has several errors (uncorrected in the 2nd ed., 1967). Nilita Vientós Gastón's brief *Introducción a HJ* (1956) is composed of a series of short chapters: on "El hombre J"; his concept of the novel; *Ambassadors* as exemplary since it involves a hero of sensibility; such heiresses as Daisy Miller, Catherine Sloper, Isabel Archer, Milly Theale, and Maggie Verver; portraits of artists and writers in several of J's works, mostly short stories; and a comparison of J's theories of the novel with those of Ortega y Gasset in *Ideas sobre la novela*. C. G. Hoffmann tackles a rich and suggestive topic in his *Short Novels of HJ* (1957); the result, though too brief, elucidates not only J's development of the nouvelle but also the relationship of his nouvelles to the other fiction in his canon. Georges Markow-Totevy's *HJ*, with a preface by André Maurois (1958, trans. 1969), is the first extended study of J in French but, like Vientós Gastón's similar monograph in Spanish, is somewhat elementary. Markow-Totevy begins with a brief biography and then discusses in successive chapters J's international theme, his depiction of contemporary manners, freedom and restraint in his characters, their "enthusiasm for life," "love without passion" (perhaps the best section in the book), stories about artists, the sense of the past, and the supernatural. The critic closes by summarizing J's art and then valuably defining his place today.

Edel's *HJ* (1960) is virtually perfect of its kind, but it is only a 37-page pamphlet. Edel outlines the main facts of J's life and literary production; but space is so limited that he must polish off *Confidence*, *Washington Square* (hereafter *Square*), and *The Europeans* in one paragraph. Helen Horne's *Basic Ideas of J's Aesthetics as Expressed in the Short Stories Concerning Artists and Writers* (1960) is a relentlessly documented dissertation which surveys relevant criticism, interprets J's short stories about art and artists, considers "relevant ideas," and concludes that J's aesthetic theory is expressed in his fiction. D. W. Jefferson's *HJ* (1960) is brief but penetrating and is initially thematic in approach: passionate pilgrims, the American girl, and English themes. In addition, it discusses J's *Autobiography*, the evolution of his method, his major phase, and his critics. The little book has the limited range of Swan's work but is more rewarding. Robert Marks's *J's Later Novels: An Interpretation* (1960) is a small and curious study of an enormous subject, most of which was better treated by Matthiessen in his *Major Phase*. Marks develops the thesis that *The Awkward Age* (hereafter *Age*), *Dove*, *Ambassadors*, *Bowl*, and *Tower* are all like "The Turn of the Screw" (hereafter "Turn Screw"), in which "everything is regulated and exhibited in double and . . . we so get the rich real and the rich romantic at a stroke, and its appeal to the imagination is thereby doubled." Each of the main chapters has a summary of the "romance" and then an exposition of the "real" story. The result, when successful, reveals depths in J's irony and attempts the sort of criticism which J. A. Clair does more skillfully in *The Ironic Dimension in the Fiction of HJ* (1965), discussed below. Marks's work is vitiated by a muddy, pseudo-Jamesian style. Darrel Abel's *Simplified Approach to J* (1964), part of his three-volume guide called *American Literature* (1963), is more than a study guide because interwoven with plot summaries of most of the novels are solid, down-to-earth insights of great use to the begin-

ning student. The short stories are skimpily treated, and what passes for a bibliography is almost totally useless. Edgardo Cozarinsky's *El laberinto de la
aparienca* (Buenos Aires, 1964) is in two parts: (1) "El espectador en el laberinto," discussing the role of the narrator of *The Sacred Fount* (hereafter
Fount), and comparing J's ambiguities with those of Proust and Hawthorne;
(2) "Los instrumentos del novelista," tracing the symbolic imagination in "la
traducion norteamericana," with emphasis on Cooper, Hawthorne, J's prefaces,
his *Hawthorne,* and his major-phase novels. R. F. Franklin in *An Index to HJ's
Prefaces to the New York Edition* (1966) offers a helpful name, title, and concept index to the prefaces. David Galloway's very short monograph, *HJ: "The
Portrait of a Lady"* (1967) aims to clarify and evaluate the novel. The author
treats briefly and cogently the probable genesis of *Portrait* in life and literature;
its heroine's psychology, consciousness, illusions, fears, and sense of freedom
and duty; the other Americans in the novel who go abroad; its organic imagery
(sex, house, art, military, animal, flower, religion, water, and light), and its
"sense of representational form." J. W. Heimer's *The Lesson of New England:
HJ and His Native Region* (1967) briefly sees New England as a touchstone for
J's thinking, in spite of his family's obvious rootlessness. Heimer shows that J
accepted New England until 1875, seemingly condemned the region as puritan
and reformatory thereafter until 1903, but at last became reconciled to it.
Stressed most are *Europeans, Bostonians,* and *The American Scene* (hereafter
Scene). Also in 1967, Keynes published his brief *HJ in Cambridge,* noted above.
Hugh Fox's *HJ, A Critical Introduction* (1968) is an extremely elementary and
superficial review in chronological order of the plots and ideas of most of J's
fiction and plays. R. R. Kossmann's *HJ, Dramatist* (1969) is a careful academic
study of a subject which is both unpromising and critically exhausted. Finally,
Powers's *The Merrill Guide to HJ* (1969) is a terribly brief introduction and,
like Edel's pamphlet, under 40 pages. Powers smoothly reviews the major novels, slights or ignores most of the stories, and stresses the importance of the allegory beneath J's "thick and real-looking surface."

ii) Major Studies. Of the 50-odd significant books published since 1950
the following have already been sufficiently discussed: Edel's biography, Le-
Clair's *Young HJ,* Dupee's *HJ,* McElderry's *HJ,* and Hyde's *Story of Lamb
House* and *HJ at Home.* What remains is most impressive in variety, ingenuity,
and devotion to the Master.

The best possible introduction to the long fiction is Oscar Cargill's *Novels
of HJ* (1961). First he considers the novels (1871–81), from *Watch and Ward*
(hereafter *Watch*) through *Portrait*: in this fruitful decade J portrayed char-

acter with increasing sharpness and skill. Next Cargill discusses four novels in which J experimented with French naturalistic techniques, perhaps most successfully in *Princess*, then traces the effect of J's dramatic ventures on his subsequent fiction, most notably *Age*, takes up the 1902–04 trilogy and includes some of the finest discussions of those novels since Matthiessen. Finally, he treats the novels after *Bowl*, including *The Outcry* and J's chapter in *Whole Family*—both often neglected.

James Kraft, in *The Early Tales of HJ* (1969), does skillfully for J's first 37 short stories (1864–79) what Cargill does for all of J's novels. Kraft probes the foundation of J's fiction, analyzes its evolution, discusses his "important concept of morality" among lovers and artists, and describes frivolous and cultured American women, and materialistic American males. He demonstrates that by the time of *Portrait* J was ready to present his distinctive international theme and his ethically relativistic characters.

S. G. Putt's *HJ: A Reader's Guide* (1966), a bulky, physically ugly book, is a systematic commentary on all of the fiction and is organized chronologically and thematically, in a confusing way. For example, the first chapter, though entitled "Apprenticeship in America," considers *Watch*, legitimately enough, but then leaps forward through time to *Square* and "Corner." Other sections concern the pro-European pilgrim from America, schizoids, later transatlantic tales, public-private tensions, art stories, marriage tales, ghost stories, the unfinished novels, and J's four best novels. Putt is most urbane as he leads the ordinary reader around certain recent critical excesses and through J's own verbal extravagances to the novelist's discriminating quality, social insight, and essential Americanness.

Somewhat better is another general introduction, D. W. Jefferson's *HJ and the Modern Reader* (1964), which begins bravely with the twin assumptions that J is great and is readable. Jefferson suggests two approaches to his subject, by way of tone and moral content, contrasts J's Americans and his Englishmen, and concludes with an analysis of his art, especially as revealed in certain short stories and the three major-phase novels.

The next two titles, Maxwell Geismar's *HJ and the Jacobites* (1963; called in England *HJ and His Cult*) and Powers's *HJ: An Introduction and Interpretation* (1970), are vastly different. Geismar's attack on J and his critical defenders is far and away the most vicious since Brooks's *The Pilgrimage of HJ*, to whom Geismar dutifully dedicates his effort. On the other hand, Powers has written a splendid little apologia for J the Master.

Geismar denies major stature to J, claiming that the novelist lacks range, awareness of sexual passion, and knowledge of commercial and financial matters, that he has an atrocious style and regards females as nicest when they are prenubile and wealthy, writes always from his limited point of view regardless of what the critics say, and is only trickily dramatic as a consequence of his *années dramatiques*. These assumptions cast a grim shadow over the long book, which takes the alternately spellbound and outraged reader chronologically through J's various writings—most of the fiction, of course, but also *Hawthorne, Guy Domville, Autobiography*, and much other non-fiction, though of the travel books only *Scene* in detail. We are in the presence here of an incisive but erratic and hopelessly prejudiced critic who can see virtually nothing of merit in the Old Pretender. For one so determined to find fault with J's prose style, Geismar often overwrites badly, punctuates with unique imprecision, and habitually substitutes vituperative and shock phrasing for steady, logical refutation of his hated Jacobites. Philip Rahv seems justified when he observes that "Never in the history of American criticism . . . has an American writer of stature been subjected . . . to such ruthless abuse. . . . Mr. Geismar strikes me as not at all functioning in this book as a literary critic . . . but as a Left-wing sociologist *manqué*. . . . But even worse . : . is the irresponsible, amateur and punitive Freudianism which Mr. Geismar employs so copiously in his attempt to discredit James" (*Book Week* 63).

By contrast, Powers's rather short book is one of the finest general introductions to J in a small compass. It opens with a discussion of the treatment of self-reliance and responsibility in J's works, and then challenges the reader to admire J precisely because he is oblique, like life, and complex, like all significant pleasures. A biographical chapter, which relies on J's letters and *Notebooks*, shows the interrelationship of his life and works, and has the virtues of accuracy and graceful composition. The main body concerns the fiction, first themes, then techniques. Finally, Powers argues that all his life J believed and demonstrated that fiction is a fine art the aim of which is to represent life faithfully.

Books on specific subjects have been numerous. Some deal with themes, others with techniques, still others with special theses. Evidence adduced in these studies may come eclectically from anything by J or may be restricted to one generic or chronological phase of his work. In quality these books range widely. A given work may approach J partly by theme, partly through techniques, and partly in terms of a thesis. But for the sake of simplifying meaningfully, I should like to categorize.

Seven books deal with themes or topics running through all or most of J's works. They are E. T. Bowden's *Themes of HJ: A System of Observation through the Visual Arts* (1956, 1969), Christof Wegelin's *Image of Europe in*

HJ (1958), J. A. Ward's *Imagination of Disaster: Evil in the Fiction of HJ* (1961), Jörg Hasler's *Switzerland in the Life and Work of HJ* (1966), Cristina Giorcelli's *HJ e l'Italia* (1968), Alberta Fabris's *HJ e la Francia* (1969), and Muriel Shine's *Fictional Children of HJ* (1969).

Bowden's purpose in *The Themes of HJ* is to help ordinary readers and scholars to understand the works by approaching them through the visual arts. His first chapter relentlessly establishes J's personal relationship with those arts, mainly painting. Bowden shows how J contrasts Europe and Europeans on the one hand, and the United States and Americans on the other, by revealing differences in their visual arts, not only painting but also architecture and to a slight extent sculpture. Especially pleasant are the explications of house symbolism and the treatment of art imagery in characterization. Bowden points out that J in his middle years seemingly tired of the international theme and therefore turned to fiction dramatizing moral decision-making; again visual arts elucidate the subject. The major-phase novels are shown to be experimental and thematically conjunctive. This study might have been improved by a prose style less humorlessly academic, by the use of evidence from more of the short stories, here ignored in favor mainly of six novels—*Hudson, American, Portrait, Spoils, Dove,* and *Bowl*—relied on too heavily, by making use of previous Jamesian criticism (which is rarely cited except in disfavor), and by a regular index. And perhaps a better title: the book is not really about J's themes.

Wegelin's distinguished *Image of Europe in HJ* handles the international theme, shows J's relationship to previously held American attitudes toward Europe and things European, and traces the organic evolution of his treatment of international situations which inspired some of his best fiction. Wegelin moves from a consideration of the international theme—best and most typical in J when centered on self-reliant, independent young American girls in England, France, and Italy—to major-phase contrasts between Americans and Europeans for the purpose of implicitly philosophizing on social and spiritual morality itself. Wegelin has a late chapter called "The Expatriate as American," which is especially good, and a high point is his treatment of the short story "An International Episode," with its corrosive pride and prejudice on both sides of the Atlantic.

Related to Europe in the eyes of many readers of J is the theme of evil, the subject of Ward's *Imagination of Disaster*. This and his later *Search for Form* attempt together to explain J's popularity today. Ward writes in the conclusion of his earlier study that "A greater religious seriousness . . . and a disillusionment with political and scientific solutions to human anxiety are at least as influential in the James revival as modern criticism's high regard for fictional technique." *The Imagination of Disaster* has to do with J's substance; *The Search for Form*, with his structural techniques. Ward suggests that J regards as evil any force, external or internal, which hinders the individual either in his efforts to move toward moral and spiritual completion, or in his growth toward desired intellectual, emotional, and aesthetic betterment. While not everyone will accept this subjective definition, all the same Ward valuably elucidates the ambiguous theme as it shifts through about 50 of J's novels and short stories. The most abundant evidence comes from *Ambassadors*, *American*, *Age*, *Bowl*, *Portrait*, "Turn Screw," and *Dove*, in all of which meddling and deception are at their peak and in most of which the dramatic movement is away from American legalistic Puritanism and rigid innocence. Ward suggests that in the Boston of *Bostonians* vestigial remains of impractical Puritanism produce frustration, stuffiness, commercialism, and vulgarity; but he shies away from the lesbianism latent in the novel, just as he generally avoids sexual aberrations elsewhere in J.

In *Switzerland in the Life and Work of HJ*, Hasler applies the methods used by Garnier in *HJ et la France*. He demonstrates J's knowledge and love of Switzerland, then investigates J's artistic use of his Swiss memories, both cosmopolitan and romantically rural. The high point is his long treatment of J's early story "At Isella," which involves an American's descent from Switzerland into Italy and parallels J's own 1869 travels. Hasler's attempt to document his dangerous assumption that the narrator of the story should be identified with J results in some confusing parallel quotations but also some daring insights into J's occasional habit of equating American touristic love of Switzerland with "second-hand sensibility" and a kind of puritan rigidity. Hasler bravely adds that the more independent Americans in J's fiction are fonder of Italy. The rest of this study summarizes J's response to specific Swiss locales and his minor use of Switzerland in other fiction. Remorselessly thorough, Hasler even footnotes his footnotes.

Giorcelli's *HJ e l'Italia* demonstrates that Italy offers the novelist a beautiful natural spectacle, a gallery of art, sophisticated literature, and a complex old civilization. Of all this material J made moral and artistic use; but he ignored Italian politics, Catholicism, and Italian literary society. In her huge *HJ e la Francia*, Fabris writes of J's knowledge of France and things French, the Jamesian "narratore e la visione romantica della Francia," his awareness of French dramatic techniques, the use of French civilization in *Ambassadors*, and his American females in France.

Shine's *Fictional Children of HJ* is perhaps prophetic of the specialized type of study that we may expect in the immediate future. It sets the subject against a background of attitudes toward children in world literature and shows that J's early critical comments about such children are more significant than his use of children in his own early tales. Beginning with "Master Eustace" and Daisy Miller's brother, however, Jamesian small fry become unique characters. Shine points out that as children Isabel Archer needed more discipline and Catherine Sloper more love. The critic excellently treats the plights of "spoiled" children and then takes up sacrificed children such as Dolcino in "The Author of Beltraffio." J's best-known fictive children appeared between 1890 and 1900, a period during which the novelist harked back with poignancy and fear to memories of his own childhood. Shine regards Morgan Moreen of "The Pupil" and Miles of "Turn Screw" as the most skillfully delineated juveniles from that period, before and after which J was concerned with the sheltered *jeune fille*. Maisie is accorded a whole chapter, as is Nanda of *Age*; there is a chapter on adolescence and the maturing process, during which young people move from " 'unseeing' to 'seeing,' from 'unknowing' to 'knowing,' and from passivity to active engagement . . ." This is a splendid study of an important element in J, and is done with charm, firmness, and admirable academic honesty.

Fifteen books deal with aspects of J's artistic techniques—craft in general, form, elements of drama, aspects of the comic spirit, the function of minor character types, imagery, and irony.

In *The Expense of Vision: Essays on the Craft of HJ* (1964), L. B. Holland shows the evolution of J's analytic, constructive, dramatic, and vicarious imagination through seven fictional works: *Portrait*, *Spoils*, "The Aspern Papers" (hereafter "Aspern"), *Fount*, *Dove*, *Ambassadors*, and *Bowl*. At the outset, he asserts vaguely that "J's was not an art which began with a literary symbolic form and then built poems or novels around them. Yet his works *are* symbolic constructs of a more ambitious order whose motive lies deeper than the strictly literary aims which implement them." Holland thinks that J was determined "to forge or shape a changing world, to create a society, to take his place in a community-in-the-making by joining the process of making it." Unfortunately too often Holland relies on long plot summaries and does not prove his thesis.

Another book on craft is K. B. Vaid's *Technique in the Tales of HJ* (1964). "The Author's Deputy" (Part I) contains analyses of ten stories told from the first-person point of view; "The Author Himself" (Part II) considers a dozen tales told by what Vaid wrongly regards as omniscient narrators. He thinks the first type of story comic and the teller reliable but undeveloped; the second type tragic and the teller subjected to "rigorous artistic discipline." Vaid habitually derogates previous J criticism, peremptorily rejecting Edmund

Wilson's interpretation of "Turn Screw" and taking a simplistic position instead. Yet he is helpful when he concentrates on analysis and explication and expertly handles "The Figure in the Carpet," "Madame de Mauves" (hereafter "Mauves"), "Pupil," "Fordham Castle," and "Great Good Place."

Three books on aspects of form in J were published in the late 1960's. The best is Ward's *Search for Form: Studies in the Structure of J's Fiction* (1967), a closely reasoned argument that (1) J paradoxically but with admirable resultant tensions builds his best work "both from the outside in" (that is, scientifically or neoclassically) and also "from the inside out" (that is, organically or romantically), and that (2) the form of his best fiction is "determined by logical and spatial conceptions of relationship rather than chronological ones." The book contains critical analyses of seven separate works. The chapter on *Watch* is the most sustained critical exploration to date of that unpromising novel. "Mauves" is critically praised for its structure, symmetry, character relationships, tensions, narrative development, and settings. To *Europeans* Ward applies his scientific-organic yardstick, measuring J's use of traditional comic elements, which are accompanied by an organic unfolding of the clash between responsibility and opportunism. A fine discussion deals with *Princess*, which is both naturalistic and Victorian, with imagistic, scenic, and thematic strains unified by Hyacinth Robinson's consciousness as the young man moves from illusion to betrayal. Ward demonstrates that in *Maisie* J's "preconceived form [that of a three-act play] achieves its relevance and vitality as the novel undergoes its major 'development'—the exhibition of Maisie's growth of mind." Excellent also is Ward's handling of the structural complexities of *Dove*, including "the parallel between Milly and Kate, the theme and technique of indirection, the underlying rhythm, the scenes that synthetically depict the whole," as well as prefiguring action, developmental plotting, spirals of conspiracy, transfers of the locations of consciousness, procrastination and aggressiveness in the mild characters, periodic removals of Milly and Densher and Kate from the scene, and Densher's transfer of allegiance. Finally Ward considers the structure of *Bowl*, which he demonstrates to be not only "a palimpsest—a great and delicately unified novel in its own right, but also a repository of many of the older forms and experiments." Noteworthy throughout this major study are Ward's subtly modulated academic style, his tact in using the thoughts of many previous critics and delicately adjusting them to his purposes, and his comprehensive method.

Walter Isle's *Experiments in Form: HJ's Novels, 1896–1901* (1968), discusses the lessons J learned by writing plays in the early 1890's, as reflected in his next five novels—*Other House, Spoils, Maisie, Age,* and *Fount.* Isle points out that these works are shorter than the ponderous novels of J's 1880's, and are also more concentrated, static, elaborate technically, concerned with point of view, ambiguous, dramatic, replete with dialogue, and preoccupied with individual confusion. *Other House* may be weak in characterization and construction, but in scene and dialogue it interestingly resembles effects by Ibsen and Chekhov, and it points toward later technical concerns. *Spoils* is basically a dramatization of its heroine's loss of connections with life but concomitantly the preservation of her spiritual freedom—all of which is reflected in the novel's tight structure. *Maisie* dramatizes, by means of balanced opposites of theme, character, and plot, an adolescent's discovery of her identity. The closed form of *Age*, J's most scenic novel, matches the self-revealing society it depicts, both through comedy having overtones of Restoration wit and also through tragedy revealing Nanda's alienation. The strikingly experimental *Fount* combines simplicity of external action with complexity of narrative technique and has the suspense of good drama. Though full of random insights, Isle's book is somewhat disappointing: its opening chapters promise more than the rest delivers, and what is said is sometimes obvious.

Sallie Sears in *The Negative Imagination: Form and Perspective in the Novels of HJ* (1968) is more penetrating than Isle but less impressive than Ward. Her thesis is that "J characteristically polarized the structures of his imaginative world, establishing them as oppositions, as extremes that could not meet, as equally desirable yet mutually exclusive possibilities for life." His characters dislike compromise and "define happiness as having everything, all alternatives, all possibilities." They reject limitations and yet live in delimiting social ambiances, and when hero and villain alike seek to change immutable reality, the result is a slow stripping away of illusions and the revelation of "a house of pain and death . . . , a nonworld." J's wholeness lies in his artistic form, with "each piece of his designs seem[ing] to fit diabolically with every other to lead to the inevitable woe." Hence the title, of which Sears says, "I have called this vision 'negative' rather than 'tragic' in part because J could not assert positive values with any degree of success or conviction." Treated in detail as proofs of this thesis are *Europeans*, *Maisie*, *Dove*, and *Bowl*. Especially notable is Sears's fine use of J's prefaces.

Next to be considered are three comparatively short books dealing with aspects of drama in J's fiction: F. C. Crews's *The Tragedy of Manners: Moral Drama in the Later Novels of HJ* (1957); L. B. Levy's *Versions of Melodrama: A Study of the Fiction and Drama of HJ, 1865–1897* (1957); and Joseph Wiesenfarth's *HJ and the Dramatic Analogy: A Study of the Major Novels of the Middle Period* (1963).

Crews's study, only an extended explicative essay, contends that J in his consciously ambiguous major-phase fiction deliberately avoids baldly endorsing any single point of view but instead presents characters in dramatic opposition to each other while in the process of redefining themselves. Ambivalent traits and behavior patterns in Isabel Archer and Hyacinth Robinson are discussed for the support they offer to this interesting and valid thesis. Crews is especially discriminating in his remarks on *Bowl*.

Levy's *Versions of Melodrama* is a modest monograph which attempts to elucidate the moral qualities of J's fiction and plays from 1865 to 1897 by isolating and analyzing their melodramatic elements. Levy places J in the melodramatic tradition, and considers naturalistic and subjective melodrama in some of J's works, the melodrama of imagined disaster, J's theatrical melodramas, and finally melodrama as a novelistic technique. This booklet is of limited value, for the obvious reasons that melodrama is ingrained in all of J's imaginative writings and is forever shading off into either the comic or the tragic—and of course into realism and satire as well.

Wiesenfarth's *HJ and the Dramatic Analogy*, the best of the trio, suggests that J prized in novels the following dramatic qualities: intensity (tightness of structure, reader involvement, character conflict), objectivity (dialogue, absence of authorial commentary), and economy (concentration of representation, emphasis). J employed the following dramatic elements: language (the imagistic, metaphoric, symbolic matrix), action (Aristotelian *praxis*, the varied pattern of doing and experiencing, direction and march of subject), scene (objectification of inward and outward aspects of action by movement, setting, and gesture), picture (non-dialogue structural blocks, balanced and composed whole —to represent, summarize, provide for personal sensibility, prepare for scene), and center (someone's consciousness, unity of aesthetic treatment and composition). Wiesenfarth devotes separate chapters to a consideration of intensity in *Spoils*, economy in *Maisie*, and objectivity in *Age*. Finally, he considers *Fount* in the light of his critical theory, developed and applied earlier. His book, which deals with the dramatic and not merely the theatrical in J's fiction, is profound, lucid, and thorough.

Two books deal with aspects of the comic in J: Richard Poirier's *The Comic Sense of HJ: A Study of the Early Novels* (1960) and E. D. Leyburn's *Strange Alloy: The Relation of Comedy to Tragedy in the Fiction of HJ*, with a foreword by W. T. Stafford (1968).

Poirier's *Comic Sense*, a serious, valuable study, treats J as a novelist of profound ideas who was constantly tempted to abridge the proper freedom of his characters to illustrate those ideas but who rose above the temptation partly through comedy. Poirier rightly insists that it should be fun to read J, particularly before he developed his major-phase "air of muffled majesty toward which he makes us anxiously solicitous." J enjoyed writing and aimed to be an exciting entertainer. Poirier, to illustrate his thesis—"Reverence for the mobility and drama of life is the particular province of Henry James; it is literally the heart of his comedy"—considers *Hudson, American, Europeans,* and *Portrait,* and also *Confidence* and *Square* less fully. Poirier's readings of the early novels are for the most part the finest yet presented. Poirier reiterates his dictum that comic sparks are generated from the clash in J's fiction between "the most freely suggestive dramatic rendering of action" and "the use of characters who exemplify certain predetermined categories of human experience"; but this welcome repetition never prevents the critic from including the richest possible digressions into his subject's life and intellectual milieu. *The Comic Sense* is indispensable to an understanding of the early J.

One might think that Leyburn's *Strange Alloy*, which analyzes J's mixture of the comic and the tragic, began as a corrective to Ward's *Imagination of Disaster* and Poirier's *Comic Sense*. Such is not the case, however; Ward is aware of lightness in the late works of J, and Poirier is aware of the tragic in the early J. In addition, Leyburn, concerned with representative fiction written throughout J's career, writes of fiction not stressed in either Ward or Poirier. Her title comes from the preface to *Maisie*: "No themes are so human as those that reflect for us, out of the confusion of life, the close connexion of bliss and bale, of the things that help with the things that hurt, so dangling before us for ever that bright hard medal, of so strange an alloy, one face of which is somebody's right and ease and the other somebody's pain and wrong." As Leyburn says, the image suggests "the presence and alternation of good and bad," also a "fusing and intermingling"; further, J "regards his human mixture sometimes comically, sometimes tragically, and sometimes with an irony so complex as to seem comic and tragic at once, as if he were showing both sides of the medal at the same time." Leyburn surveys, among other things, J's earliest tales and *Watch*; assays the alloy in *Hudson, American,* "Daisy Miller" (hereafter "Daisy"), *Square,* and *Portrait*; considers international tragedy and comedy (in "Pension Beaurepas," *The Reverberator,* and *Bowl*); and discusses fools who cause suffering (in *Spoils, Muse,* and other works).

The two books dealing with the functions of two minor character types in J's fiction are M. C. Sharp's *Confidante in HJ: Evolution and Moral Value of a Fictive Type* (1963) and Ora Segal's *Lucid Reflector: The Observer in HJ's Fiction* (1969). Sharp's study is an unpretentious but genuinely sophisticated and knowledgeable exploration of the technical functions of the confidante in J's fiction. The author discusses minor confidantes like Mrs. Prest from "Aspern" and May Bartram from "Beast," and major ones like Madame Merle (who in some senses does not qualify), Fleda Vetch, Mrs. Wix, Maria Gostrey, Susan Stringham, and Fanny Assingham. Finally, Sharp places J's confidantes "in a wider perspective, in order to make an assessment of the implications of J's fondness for this technique in relation to his total moral sense." This charming book ranges over most of J's best fiction, both showing that early confidantes foreshadow later ones and also reminding us of lesser ones when it discusses major confidantes.

In *The Lucid Reflector*, Segal traces the evolution of the observer in more than a dozen important novels and stories, with special attention to "Mauves," *Portrait*, "Lady Barbarina," "Aspern," "The Liar," *Bowl*, and a few tales of literary life. She notes the observer's shift from subsidiary to central position and defines J's typical observer: "He is not omniscient, and his moral and epistemological perspectives are necessarily limited. This enables J to show his two main authorial activities—narration and interpretation—in the making, that is, to present them as complicated, groping processes of observation and evaluation. Narration thus ceases to be the expression of authoritative omniscience. Instead, the story generally progresses by means of a series of encounters between the observer and the protagonist, in the course of which the former gradually achieves a comprehensive view of the case." Segal's index is especially valuable through its inclusion of many abstract technical concepts.

Two book-length studies have been devoted to J's use of imagery: Alexander Holder-Barell's *Development of Imagery and Its Functional Significance in HJ's Novels* (1959, 1966) and R. L. Gale's *Caught Image: Figurative Language in the Fiction of HJ* (1964).

Holder-Barell considers similes, metaphors, and symbols in six representative novels: *Hudson, Portrait, Spoils, Ambassadors, Dove,* and *Bowl*; the study is divided into four main parts: expanding images, characterizing images, images concretizing abstractions, and constructive images. He discusses among other symbols those of European corruption, wealth, and good and evil. He wrongly disparages the categorizing approach to imagery and yet uses it intermittently, has little to say about J's revisions, and gives insufficient credit to earlier critics.

B. R. McElderry *(Person* 65) describes Gale's *Caught Image:* "Of importance for all students of imagery is a perceptive review of previous studies of imagery (in the 'Foreword'). Excluding dead metaphors . . . Gale has tabulated 16,902 images in the 135 novels and stories by J. . . . Admitting some defects in Caroline Spurgeon's method of classifying images by subject, Gale nevertheless follows it. It is not surprising that the major categories in J are nature comparisons with water, flowers, and animals; and 'man images' drawn from war, art, and religion. . . . Gale's illustrations are well selected, his definitions clear, and his claims modest. He demonstrates that the statistical method, sensibly used, can yield fresh insights. Gale concludes that for J, 'the natural world, when unimproved by art or religion, is fraught less with sweet pleasure than with sudden violence.' Oddly, a number of sexual images betray an awkward naïveté which in isolated phrases might pass unnoticed. The mythical dualism of J's imagery gives pattern to his habitual exaggeration, sometimes serious, sometimes playful. What might have been a pedestrian study has been developed into a useful and stimulating book."

J. A. Clair in *The Ironic Dimension in the Fiction of HJ* (1965) offers the only book-length study to date of J's irony. Clair's daring little book is a study of unreliable centers of revelation, operative irony resulting from the combination of narrative representation and scenic presentation, dramatic *clous*, ambiguous and therefore sometimes comic dialogue, the juxtaposition of liars and dupes, and the mistaking of antagonists for confidantes. Clair treats seven works: "Four Meetings," "Corner," "Turn Screw," *Bowl*, *Spoils*, "The Chaperon," and "A London Life." Perhaps the best treatment is that of "London Life," in which loose Selina Berrington, failing to persuade her sister Laura Wing to become her ally, is viewed as setting out to compromise the prim girl so that she will not dare to testify against her in the divorce court. Clair regards Fleda Vetch as forlorn, perspicacious, and selfishly motivated; Maggie Verver, as selfishly forcing Charlotte Stant Verver and Prince Amerigo to conspire, against their will, to save both Maggie and her father; and Alice Staverton, as a liar who hires the "ghost." The other readings seem less successful; but Clair leads the reader astutely, anticipates objections, is tolerant of opposition, does not ignore evidence, and writes logically.

Less interesting are most of the six books published since 1950 having general theses. They vary in worth from H. T. McCarthy's difficult little study called *HJ: The Creative Process* (1958, 1968) to Dorothea Krook's superb *Ordeal of Consciousness in HJ* (1962). In between are Quentin Anderson's controversial *American HJ* (1957), W. F. Wright's eclectic book called *The Madness of Art: A Study of HJ* (1962), Edward Stone's collection of essays, *The Battle and the Books: Some Aspects of HJ* (1964), and Naomi Lebowitz's wide-ranging *Imagination of Loving: HJ's Legacy to the Novel* (1965).

One of the most controversial, sporadically illuminating, and exasperating books ever published on J is Anderson's *American HJ*, which contends that the novelist son transported to Europe his Irish Swedenborgian father's moral sense and mysticism, and once there wove both into his most significant fiction, especially his major-phase trilogy, of which Anderson, reading the late novels as elaborate allegory by "our domestic Dante," writes: "*Ambassadors* has for its subject the failure of the law, and its correspondent 'church' is New England's, here standing for the elder J's 'Jewish' church. *Dove* treats the redemption of an individual [Merton Densher] by an exemplary savior, Milly Theale; the correspondent church is 'Christian.' *Bowl*'s subject is the regeneration of mankind, and its correspondent church is that of the new Jerusalem announced by Swedenborg." Anderson has apt remarks to make about the elder James and his writings, and occasionally provides important insights into some of J's shorter fiction, and into parts of J's portrait, house, and bowl symbols. But his main thesis seems untenable, and his critical arrogance is enormous.

In *HJ: The Creative Process*, McCarthy presents a systematic study of J's aesthetic theory and how it evolved. He discusses the novelist's concern with "the relation of art to experience," aesthetic perceptions, the function of "feeling in the creative process," both "dramatic form" in and also organic form of fiction, J's theory as related to his practice, his "concept of prose as an aesthetic medium," and finally his awareness of a writer's responsibility "to his work and to society." The book is brief and abstract and is now overshadowed by Ward's more profound *Search for Form*.

One of the best studies ever to focus on J is Krook's *Ordeal of Consciousness*. Like all profound books on J, it limits its range—in this case to *Portrait, Muse, Age, Fount, Dove, Bowl*, and the short stories collected in *The Better Sort* (1903) and *The Finer Grain* (1910). Krook's aim is to elucidate representative works "connected by the theme of 'being and seeing,'" and to explore and define "consciousness in J's particular meaning of the term." Her choice of works was determined by their representativeness and difficulty. Extensive plot summaries and quotations make the book valuable to the general reader, while a penetrating and discriminating intelligence, a love for J, and a graceful style are virtues which Jamesian specialists should particularly admire. In her opening chapter, Krook identifies salient English, European, and American traits in J's gallery of characters; explains that J typically depicts the rich because he is interested in the moral aspects of power in a society including exciting, almost Shakespearian persons of various kinds of superiority; and then shows that characters in J's fictive social milieu typify the "tragic condition of man" in general, because "it is in this infinitely encumbered and encrusted condition of life that the fundamental human passions can be exhibited in a way more beautiful than they could in any other. For . . . it is in this condition that both the noble and the destructive passions show with an 'ideal' intensity, complexity and completeness such as could not be attained under the condition of primitive simplicity that the Wordsworthian ideal postulates."

The chapter on *Portrait* is a study guide, in the best sense, culminating in a long explication of crucial Chapter 42 of the novel. The treatment of *Muse* is disappointing, but competently presents contrasts between the political aspects of the Dormer family and Nick's and Miriam Rooth's representative and related artistic lives. Krook reads "Turn Screw" as "a moral fable which powerfully dramatises certain fundamental facts of our spiritual existence—chiefly, the reality of evil . . . , the reality of good, and the possibility of redemption ('salvation') for the victim of the evil by the power of human love." *Age* is treated partly for the light "its moral preoccupations and its dramatic method" shed on later works. Irony, ambiguity, and epistemological considerations in *Fount* are discussed. Then follows what Oscar Cargill (*AL* 63) regards as the best part. He feels that her essay on *Dove* "is certainly one of the finest studies of this novel," analyzing as it does "the tragedy of the alienation of Kate Croy and Merton Densher." Cargill also admires the long discussion of *Bowl* and singles out for special praise Krook's analysis of the relationship between J's later stories and novels.

W. F. Wright's *Madness of Art* begins with a splendid first chapter which summarizes J's view of life as a welter of impressions, relics from the past, and present-day sensitive and mannered social creatures, all to be transmuted into edited, balanced, living art by the ministrant's imagination, taste, and craft. Wright treats three significant Jamesian themes: the forces of darkness (commercialism, evil in society, ugliness in life, demonic forces within the individual); the dark-dispelling counter force, called here "Sensitivity of feeling and imagination" (appreciation, vicarious adventure, sympathy); and then "the ultimate theme: the quest for reality" (wonder, the mystery of evil, the sense of the past, the need to infer, identity crises). He ends by discussing J's fusion of theme and art—his "weaving of silver threads and tapping on golden nails." The book has too much summary but innumerable fine insights, and on the whole is rich, mellow, and resonant.

The Battle and the Books by Stone divides into two quite separate parts: a subjective survey of J's reputation, prompted in part by Geismar's ill-tempered *HJ and the Jacobites*, and a loosely, mechanically unified collection of essays on some of J's works. The better part is the first, which addresses itself to J's limitations, summarizes "the extreme reactions to J from the time of his death until yesterday," and slowly advances upon Geismar to demolish his erroneous assertions. The other half includes essays on the fragility and merits of the plot of *Watch*, J's borrowings (from Hawthorne, Victor Cherbuliez, and William Black), the functional aspects of names and other foreshadowing devices in J's fiction, fairy-tale motifs in his work, and his influence on James Thurber and John Balderston. Appendices on J and Hawthorne further attest to the piecemeal but profoundly illuminating nature of Stone's work.

Lebowitz's *Imagination of Loving: HJ's Legacy to the Novel* also has two separate parts. The first is an extended essay showing J's belief that "real life, like the novel's life, demands relationship, and relationship demands commitment, and commitment demands painful exile from the first Eden before entrance into the second." Lebowitz concentrates on *Portrait*, *Fount*, *Dove*, *Ambassadors*, and *Bowl* (her favorite novel), works which best reveal "the amount and nature of 'felt life' in the novelist . . . and the direction of his moral imagination." J's most fully conscious characters are made to "explore their relationship, [and thus] they can make moral judgments based on the contrast between honest and full communion and the communion that is built on secrecy, on information without love, or on the influence of unchanging objects and pictures." The narrator of *Fount* is a novelist "enjoying the game of sharing composition with his more conscious characters," and the book itself is "a critical blueprint for a future novel." The short second part of Lebowitz's work is about J's legacy to later novelists, especially Saul Bellow. Suggestive comparisons are presented involving J on the one hand and on the other Jane Austen, Balzac, George Eliot, Flaubert, Hawthorne, D. H. Lawrence, Maupassant, and Zola. This work is too casually allusive and at times unjustifiably certain of its generalizations, but it is refreshing to find a recent book concentrating on J's meanings rather than on yet another aspect of his technique.

One more book on J published in the 1960's deserves brief mention: Gale's *Plots and Characters in the Fiction of HJ* (1965), a useful reference work in which the plots of all of the fictional works, alphabetically arranged, are summarized, named characters are listed following each summary, and all 1,630 characters are identified in a continuous alphabetical sequence.

iii) Books on Individual Books. There have been three books on J's "Turn Screw," and a separate book each on *Portrait*, *Princess*, *Fount*, and *Ambassadors*, not to mention skillful critical editions of "Daisy," *Confidence*, *Square*, "Turn Screw," and *Ambassadors*, and book-length collections of previously written critical essays on *Portrait* and *Ambassadors*.

"Turn Screw" is J's most provocative and controversial piece of fiction. Not quite forty thousand words in length, it has occasioned over ten times that much critical wordage, much of it excellent. The first "book" on it was Gerald Willen's *Casebook on HJ's "The Turn of the Screw"* (1960, rev. ed. 1969), which prints the 1898 text, pertinent material by J, 15 critical essays on it, a bibliography, and some exercises. Muriel West has written an impressionistic account, *A Stormy Night with "The Turn of the Screw"* (1964), which is a mild spoof, a bit silly and overpriced but acute. West wonders about various literary influences and discusses the Gothic novel, its nineteenth-century continuators, Austen, and some Freudian aspects. T. M. Cranfill and R. L. Clark, Jr., in *An Anatomy of "The Turn of the Screw"* (1965) weigh the relative merits of interpretations by apparitionists and non-apparitionists, review the plot and the characters of the story, and vote in favor of the non-apparitionists. Oddly, the book moves with some of the suspense of the tale itself. The 16-page bibliography is made usefully evaluative by an elaborate system of abbreviations indicating main points of the critics. Robert Kimbrough's edition of "Turn Screw" (1966) contains the 1908 text, background and source material, pertinent comments by J, reprints of early critical reactions (through 1923), 11 major essays (including previously unpublished ones by Martina Slaughter, S. P. Rosenbaum, and J. J. Enck), and a brief bibliography. Eli Siegel's *J and the Children: A Consideration of HJ's "The Turn of the Screw"* (1968) is highly subjective, being selections from transcripts of 24 recorded "talks." In his main argument, Siegel attempts socratically to show that Wilson's reading of "Turn Screw" is evasive and to suggest that the children—corrupted by Peter Quint and Miss Jessel while those adults were alive—corrupt their ghosts. Siegel's method is to quote from the text, to comment—often whimsically— and to query with a naïveté which is sometimes apparent and occasionally real. At his best he is electrifying and forces us to validate literature by looking anew at life, but now and then he offends his readers by assuming that they are simple and that he can hypnotize them with pseudo-profundities and quirky talk.

W. H. Tilley's *Background of "The Princess Casamassima"* (1961) is a succinct monograph which discusses problems J faced in making "his version of conspiracy [by European revolutionists] seem credible to the public," his interest in the social revolution of the 1870's and 1880's, his reading of the London *Times*, his borrowings from literature dealing with revolutionists and journalistic accounts of real-life revolutionists, and the significance of J's novel.

In 1962 Herbert Ruhm edited J's *Confidence* for the first time from the manuscript. He provides editorial notes, gives J's interlinear and footnote emendations, compares first serial and first American edition texts, indicates doubtful readings, considers other textual matters, includes the pertinent entry about *Confidence* from the *Notebooks*, reprints nine contemporary reviews, and appends a long bibliography. Ruhm also published textual variants in his edition of *Lady Barberina and Other Tales* (1961).

W. T. Stafford in *J's "Daisy Miller": The Story, The Play, The Critics* (1963) reprints the 1878 short story, the 1882 dramatic version, and 26 pieces of criticism.

S. P. Rosenbaum has prepared a superb critical edition of *Ambassadors* (1964), which prints J's preface, the 1909 text, and a list of variants from it appearing in the *NAR* serial edition, the first American edition (1903) and the first English edition (also 1903). Rosenbaum includes his own essay on J's revisionary process. In addition are entries from J's *Notebooks*, his long statement of intent, and comments on the novel in letters to friends. Comparatively skimpy is the section reprinting critical commentary by others. A second book devoted to *Ambassadors* is *Erzähler-, Figuren- und Leserperspektive in HJ's Roman "The Ambassadors"* by Frieder Busch (1967). This study is in five parts: on narrator perspective, the perspective of the "wahrnemenden Figur," the "Zeitdimension" of perspective, reader perspective, and finally various aspects of J's works in general.

Fount, the most curious novel J ever wrote, is also the subject of a book-length study: J. F. Blackall's *Jamesian Ambiguity and "The Sacred Fount"* (1965). It is worth the attention of Jamesians, for its review and bibliography of the extensive criticism of the novel now available, but the book has limited usefulness. An explication of the narrator's perhaps innocent little comparison of himself to "the exclusive king with his Wagner opera" is, according to R. A. Ranald (*NCF* 66), "In some ways, the most interesting and the freshest material"; but other readers may find it tedious. After all, the pertinent passage in the novel is only nine words within dashes in one long sentence, and Blackall's protracted expatiation on it bears some resemblances to the regrettable card-house building by the narrator.

Of the books devoted to *Portrait*, Galloway's study has been described above. Another book is Stafford's *Perspectives on J's "The Portrait of a Lady"* (1967). The editor describes the contents when he writes as follows in his penetrating introduction: "From the author himself, from the early reviews of the novel, and from the literary historians and critics who have given it their attention unfolds this history of how one great example of the nineteenth-century creative imagination became a part of the literary consciousness of the Western world." The main body of this organic symposium includes essays by 14 fine critics. A bibliography of almost 100 items follows.

Gerald Willen also has edited *Square* (1970), providing an authoritative text (that of 1881), selected criticism, and a brief bibliography.

Other editions of works by J sometimes reprint critical commentary. A good example is Dupee's edition of *Ambassadors* (1960). Other editions have especially fine introductions, for example, the one in Lionel Trilling's *Princess* (1948; intro. repr. in *Liberal Imagination*, 1950).

2. Chapters or Parts of Books

It is impractical to try to discuss all of the books in which J looms as a considerable part. In some, for example, Bell's *Edith Wharton and HJ* or Canby's *Turn West, Turn East*, J accounts for at least half of the space available. In others, for example, David Lodge's *Language of Fiction* (1967), J is a significant but in no sense an overriding feature. The titles of still other books, for example, Louis Auchincloss's *Reflections of a Jacobite* (1961), sound as though they might throw real light on our subject but are disappointing. In addition, several *Festschriften* contain essays on J; a few of them are considered below in my discussion of recent "articles."

In the absence of more space, I must restrict myself to brief mention of several of the dozens of books which consider J along with other writers. F. L. Pattee, pioneer professor of American literature, treats J in *A History of American Literature since 1870* (1915) and in *The Development of the American Short Story* (1923). Lubbock in his *Craft of Fiction* (1921) uses J's fiction, particularly *Ambassadors,* to illustrate "the art of dramatizing the picture of somebody's experience." A. H. Quinn in *American Fiction* (1936) finds J limited in range of experience and too "international" to reflect American life accurately. Bernard Smith in *Forces in American Criticism* (1939) starts by discussing the trend toward realism as something more than a method but loses his way when he tries to impose a doctrinal value judgment on his findings.

Four important books consider J among other writers. In *Maule's Curse* (1938), Yvor Winters offers a controversial study of the discrepancy between an inherited moral sense and the moral relativity of the American experience. He finds this discrepancy illustrated in J's separation of ethical choice from a natural frame of moral ideas and his treatment of it as an element of character and of plot only. Most later critics are in considerable disagreeement with Winters. F. O. Matthiessen's *AmR* (1941) is in several ways a transitional study, bridging the gap between older aims and methods on the one hand and those of the New Criticism on the other. Discussing Hawthorne's term "romance" as distinct from the novel in the context in which J himself would have placed it, Matthiessen theorizes that J at the outset reflected Hawthorne's method of romance, then renounced Hawthorne when J turned from romance to realism, but returned to Hawthorne's material in the later novels—improving on his methods through awareness of his limitations. In his symbolism, J perfected the allegory in which Hawthorne failed and thus provided a link to T. S. Eliot. In *The Great Tradition* (1948, 1964), F. R. Leavis includes an examination of the influence of George Eliot's *Daniel Deronda* on *Portrait*. Downgrading *Ambassadors*, among other major-phase novels, Leavis prefers J's earlier work and, as does Matthiessen, notes Hawthorne's influence on it. In *The Complex Fate* (1952), Marius Bewley follows the lead of Leavis, who provides an introduction and two interpolations. Bewley begins with a consideration of Hawthorne, J, and the American novel, compares *The Blithedale Romance* with *Bostonians* and *The Marble Faun* with *Dove*. Among other items, Bewley includes somewhat verbose essays on appearance and reality in J, commentaries on *Maisie* and "Turn Screw," and discussions of J and his brother William.

Other books consider J and other authors. Stephen Spender in *The Destructive Element* (1935, 1938, 1953) sees J in the early novels as a modern writer seeking a moral subject but confronted by the decadence of modern society. The artist's remaining choice is to make an art of life and a life of art, which J did by drawing on early experience but using it only symbolically to impose a clearer and more acceptable meaning on life. A. J. A. Waldock in *J, Joyce, and Others* (1937) is valuable on style, particularly when discussing *Bowl*. LeClair offers interesting comparisons in *Three American Travelers in England: James Russell Lowell, Henry Adams, and HJ* (1945). E. T. Bowden regards Isabel Archer as a "mighty individual" in *The Dungeon of the Heart: Human Isolation and the American Novel* (1961). R. W. Stallman's *Houses That J Built and Other Literary Studies* (1961) suffers from disunity. It collects previously printed essays on house symbolism and other matters in *Portrait*, the time theme in *Ambassadors*, and its text; only a fifth of the book concerns J. A fine recent comparative study is Alan Holder's *Three Voyagers in Search of Europe* (1966), which focuses on the gains and losses of expatriation, and on cultural and critical detachment.

3. Critical Articles

The number of critical articles on J is appallingly great. Perceptive ones written before his death in 1916 are few, but since then there have been more that 1,200, many of which are as valuable as the best books on the subject. They include essays on both general and specific subjects, and also short studies of particular works.

a. *Articles before 1916.* The early changes in J's reputation are detailed in Foley's *Criticism in American Periodicals of the Works of J from 1866 to*

1916, noted above; in D. M. Murray's 1948 dissertation, "The Critical Reputation of HJ in English Periodicals, 1879–1916" (pub. in part [1882–1890], *AL* 52); and in Roger Gard's *HJ: The Critical Heritage* (1968), a huge collection of almost 200 critical comments on J from 1866 through 1920. The most significant reviews of J's works during his lifetime are in *Nation, Critic, Dial, Atl, HM, Scribner's,* and *NAR*; and the most influential early general critical summaries were written by Howells (*Atl* 1875; *Century* 1882; *NAR* 03—see Mordell, ed., *Discovery of a Genius*), Horace Scudder (*Atl* 1882, 86, 90, 93), Oliver Elton (*Modern Studies* 07), Morton Fullerton (*QR* 09), and Rebecca West (*NR* 15, noted above).

Howells deserves special praise for urging the public in 1875 to read J, for commending him in 1882 as a realist, and for lauding in 1903 his depiction of feminine characters. Scudder understood the artistry behind *Portrait, Bostonians, Muse,* and certain short stories. Elton elucidated J's ghost stories and *Dove*. Fullerton praised the late novels. On the other hand, lesser critics decried J's alleged obscurity, deplored his major-phase style, and accused the novelist of substituting art for life, and of being an ethical relativist.

b. *Articles between 1916 and 1933.* J's renunciation of his American citizenship in favor of British citizenship shortly before his death was a paradoxical act, since it meant that the novelist was turning from his native land just as it was preparing to honor its literary geniuses, and he was identifying himself with a foreign tradition in which he must always seem slightly alien. One factor influencing 1916–34 Jamesian criticism was the discovery by historians that the United States had its own literary history and that an indigenous movement was in progress. Simultaneously, humanistic research in general was becoming more exacting; so J's works began to be scrutinized in relation to his life. Oddly, more paradoxes emerged: the more J and his writings were understood, the less reason there seemed for revering the nearly completed New York Edition. Internationalism, which had seemed a limitation, now deepened into what seemed to be an expression of alienation; for J blended neither into nationalistic currents nor into the naturalistic movement.

All the same, in 1916, when J died, both British and American critics mainly wrote appreciative commemorations. *NAR* reprinted Howells's essay on J's later work (*NAR* 03) and Conrad's appreciation (*NAR* 03), together with a laudatory impression by Edith Wyatt. *Dial* printed an appraisal by E. E. Hale. *Atl* published Helen and Wilson Follett's reverent summation. E. P. Dargan wrote of J's "two cities"—Cosmopolis and Ars Longa (*NR* 16). In England, Lubbock, then at work collecting J's letters, published a profound review of J (*QR* 16), which stresses his sense for life, cosmopolitanism, distinction between describing life and dramatizing it, and war years.

Soon, however, such backward-looking encomiums began to be countered and J was viewed once more as alienated and frustrated. In a humorous little attack, Philip Guedalla cleverly—if inaccurately—divided J into James the First, James the Second, and the Old Pretender (*NewS* 19). In 1923, V. W. Brooks published three socio-psychological articles (*Dial*) as trial flights for his *Pilgrimage of HJ*, already discussed. Dorothy Bethurum wisely affirmed J's moral consciousness (*SR* 23), and soon thereafter Edna Kenton, among others, took Brooks to task (*Bookman* 25). But late in the 1920's and on into the 1930's several critics continued to rebuke J for his alleged indifference to politics: Grattan (*Nation* 32) and Robert Cantwell (*NR* 34) are representative of this group. William Troy deserves special mention for his early revelation of modern qualities in J's best work (*Bookman* 31).

At about the same time, academic journals began to publish scholarly essays of a specialized nature. These include Hélène Harvitt's and R. D. Havens's separate essays on the revisions of *Hudson* (*PMLA* 24, 25); E. J. Goodspeed's suggestion of a model—Julia Newberry—for Daisy Miller (*Atl* 34); and Kenton's brilliant early note on J's *années dramatiques* as the transitional period between J as pictorialist and J as dramatic novelist (*TArts* 28). Lubbock's edition of the *Letters* not only occasioned some perceptive reviews but also stimulated biographical and technical re-examinations of J and his works. A slightly earlier influence was T. S. Eliot, who wrote two notes at Ezra Pound's request for a special J number of *Little Review* (18). Eliot's bold overstatements, for example, that J "had a mind so fine that no idea could violate it" and that "There are advantages, indeed, in coming from a large, flat country which no one wants to visit," helped swing criticism of J from a romantic to a neoclassical orientation. Further, Eliot inspired reassessments of the Hawthorne element in J. Pound's own notes, four in number and all appearing in the same special issue (reprinted in his *Instigations*, 1920), stressed the content of J's thought but still complemented Eliot's in their enthusiasm for J's achievement, a dramatization of personal tyrannies, and hence an expression of concern about conflicting forces in modern life.

Less important were several other short essays and reviews in journals. The first special J number was that of the *Egoist* (18). In addition, Roberta Cornelius (*SR* 19) wrote about the novelist's methodology as discussed in his prefaces; Wilfred Randell (*Fortnightly* 21) defended J's understanding of and love for people outside his class; and Kenton (*Arts* 24) partly anticipated Wilson's Freudian reading of "Turn Screw." By the time of the J revival, beginning about 1934, the influence of Beach, Lubbock, and Edgar was dominant, and that of V. W. Brooks rightly recessive.

c. *Articles between 1934 and 1949.* The J boom may be said to have begun about 1934 with an upsurge of interest in all aspects of his writing and thought. J seemed more alive than many writers active and productive in the 1930's, both because enough time had by then passed to clarify obscurities and dispel objections, and because critics were beginning to see the limitations of movements and tempers toward which J had never been sympathetic—gentility, idealism, literal realism, nationalism, and naturalism, for several examples. The new critics who analyzed the work of art as such and used discoveries of modern psychologists as part of their method began to regard J as a pioneer in the theory and the practice of fiction. Numerous essays appearing in journals supplemented book-length criticism by such pioneers as Beach, Edel, Edgar, Kelley, and Roberts.

Contributing enormously to the revival was the J commemorative issue of *H&H* (34). The editor, Lincoln Kirstein, proposed that J could serve as "an admirable point of departure for an inquest into the present condition of our literature" and reported that the contributors to the J number formed "a younger generation who, as yet, had not expressed their gratitude to the great novelist." Older scholars and academicians were conspicuous by their absence, but those present included many who would become leaders in Jamesian study through the 1940s. They included Lawrence Leighton, Stephen Spender, Newton Arvin, Edna Kenton, Marianne Moore, John Wheelwright, and Francis Fergusson. R. P. Blackmur first printed here what became his preface to J's prefaces, and Edmund Wilson's reading of "Turn Screw" opened vistas of criticism.

By the time of the next commemorative issue (*KR* 43), edited by R. P. Warren in the centennial year, most of the modern approaches to J had been established. This symposium had important articles by Fergusson, Jacques Barzun, Sweeney, and Matthiessen. Austin Warren's essay is perhaps the finest comment of its length on the poetic imagery of the major-phase novels.

Of almost 40 other articles appearing between 1934 and 1943, only a few are significant today. W. H. Auden's poem "At the Grave of HJ" (*PR* 41) is a unique call. Influence and comparison studies include those by the following: W. C. D. Pacey (on the influence of French writers on J, *AL* 41), Harold Cooper (on J's review naming Trollope as author of an anonymously published novel, *MLN* 43), Daniel Lerner (on Turgenev's influence on J, *SEER* 41), and Weber (on dissimilarities in J and Hardy, *MTQ* 43). On J and drama: E. L. Forbes (*NEQ* 38). On J's pathetically trapped observers: L. C. Knights (*SoR*

39). On J's contradictions and his archetypal heroines: Rahv (*NR* 43, *PR* 43). On J and morality: Spender (*London Merc* 34) and Randall Stewart (*UR* 43). On J, myth, and symbolism: Troy (*NR* 43). Articles on specific works: Blackmur (on *Fount*, *KR* 42), N. B. Fagan ("Turn Screw," *MLN* 41), and R. L. Wolff ("Turn Screw," *AL* 41). Nostalgic essays: Witter Bynner (*SatR* 43), L. P. Smith (*Atl* 43), Hugh Walpole (*Horizon* 40), and Wharton (*LHJ* 34).

The last years of the 1940's are notable for many fine articles. The following are among the best, excluding the few already mentioned and those later incorporated into books discussed above. On J's letters: M. D. Howe (*YR* 49) and John LaFarge (*NEQ* 49). Essays comparing J to other writers: Viola Dunbar (*Hudson* and Dumas, *fils*, *MLN* 48), Edouard Roditi (J and Wilde, *UR* 48), Francis Steegmuller (J and Maupassant, *Cornhill* 48), and George Hemphill (Hemingway and J, *KR* 49). Articles on specific works: on the revision of *American* (R. A. Gettmann, *AL* 45); "Daisy" (E. F. Hoxie, *NEQ* 45; Dunbar, *PQ* 48); J's criticism (Laurence Barrett, *AL* 49); J's plays (Edel, *UTQ* 49; Henry Popkin, *TArts* 49); *Fount* (C. J. Raeth, *ELH* 49); and "Turn Screw" (R. B. Heilman, *MLN* 47, *UR* 48; Waldock, *MLN* 47; Oliver Evans, *PR* 49; G. A. Reed, *AL* 49; and F. X. Roellinger, Jr., *AL* 49). Essays of a more general nature: Malcolm Cowley (J before 1895 and after, *NR* 45), Katherine Hoskins (J and the future of the novel, *SR* 46), R. W. Short (J's sentence structure, *AL* 46), A. R. Tintner (the meaning of art objects in J's fiction, *PMLA* 46), Roberts (foreshortening, *RES* 46, and J's final phase, *YR* 47), Clinton Oliver (social criticism in J, *AR* 47), Beach (J's *Notebooks*, *Furioso* 48), and Heidi Specker (shifts in criticism of J, *ES* 48).

d. *Articles in the 1950's.* Throughout the 1950's more than 30 articles a year, on the average, were published on J. Of this extensive output, which matched the great increase in the production of books, only a fraction is of permanent value. And many of the best essays, not considered here, went into book-length studies published later by their respective authors.

Articles concerning J's novels accounted for the largest single category, with *American*, *Portrait*, *Ambassadors*, *Dove*, and *Bowl* inspiring the most activity.

American: Joan Bennett discusses the artistry of its fable, conflicts, humor, and scenic structure (*ChiR* 56). F. C. Watkins considers Christopher Newman's "final instinct" during the burning of the murder evidence (*NCF* 57). J. A. Clair controversially eyes Mrs. Bread as Claire de Cintré's mother (*PMLA* 59—see also F. V. Bernard, *N&Q* 66). J. W. Gargano studies the novel's "sometimes . . . labored" foreshadowing (*MLN* 59). J. R. Moore points out chronological and other "inconsistencies" (*NCF* 59).

Portrait: H. G. Flynn and H. C. Key oddly treat "gestation" (*CE* 59); for replies, see J. E. Wallace and J. C. Broderick, and then Key (all in *CE* 60). Powers analyzes unity in and the denouement of the novel (*NCF* 59). W. B. Stein discusses Isabel as a sexually frigid "Victorian Griselda" and brings in pertinent comments from *The Education of Henry Adams* (*WHR* 59). Ernest Sandeen expertly compares Isabel and Milly Theale (*PMLA* 54).

Ambassadors: R. E. Young points out a printing error (*AL* 50), to which note Edel objects (*AL* 51); see Young's reply and then Edel's (both in *AL* 52)—the exchange is unnecessarily heated. W. M. Gibson charmingly discusses metaphorical patterns in the plot (*NEQ* 51). Patricia Evans touches on "the match image" (*MLN* 55). Stein explicates the central "golden nail" metaphor (*CE* 56). Edel discusses time in the novel (*MLN* 58), in reply to Stallman (*MLN* 57), who replies (*MLN* 61). J. E. Tilford, Jr., expertly analyzes deviations from Strether's point of view (*MFS* 58—see also J. Davis, *KN* 65).

Dove: D. C. Muecke ingeniously diagrams Milly's flight and Kate Croy's and Merton Densher's altered paths as well (*NCF* 54). Jean Kimball treats revelatory abyss imagery (*NCF* 56). J. J. Firebaugh regards idealistic Densher as "solipsistic modern man" (*UTSE* 58). C. R. Crow superbly handles the novel's intricate style (*EIE* 58). (See also Giorgio Melchiori under "Daisy" below.)

Bowl: Myron Ochshorn touches on Edenic symbolism, in a review (*NMQ* 52). Firebaugh discusses the pragmatic, anti-absolutist Ververs (*EIC* 54), to which comments E. N. Perrin and C. B. Cox separately object (*EIC* 55). Fergusson observes that the story does not become allegorical at the expense of verisimilitude (*SR* 55). Caroline Gordon strenuously develops the thesis that businessman Adam Verver is "our national hero" (*SR* 55). Paola Bompard writes brilliantly of evil, structure, symbolism, and psychological struggle (*SA* 56). Kimball sees Charlotte as J's final "lady" with the drama of her struggle giving focus to the novel (*AL* 57). J. R. Theobald criticizes motivation (*TCL* 57). J. L. Spencer analyzes central symbolism (*MFS* 58). Enck applauds the wholeness of effect through imagery in the novel (*TWA* 58).

As for some of the other novels, C. R. Anderson regards Basil Ransom of *Bostonians* as a well-portrayed Southerner (*AL* 55), while W. R. Martin notes the novel's fairy-tale structure (*ESA* 59). *Spoils* inspired P. F. Quinn to write of Fleda as an ethical absolutist (*SR* 54); Winthrop Tilley, on soap-opera elements in it (*WHR* 56); and Broderick, on the novel as moral and aesthetic parable (*NCF* 59). Firebaugh discusses craftsmanship and pragmatism in *Age* (*VQR* 51), while H. K. Girling analyzes the function of the words "wonder" and "beauty" (and their variations) therein (*EIC* 58). Three essays on *Maisie* are by W. S. Worden, who compares entries in the *Notebooks* with the final version of the novel (*PMLA* 53); Adele Brebner, who suggests teaching *Maisie* as a work of pathos and humor (*CE* 56); and H. W. Wilson, who discusses the corruption of sensitive Maisie's innocence (*CE* 56—but see also Edward Wasiolek, *CE* 60). As for *Princess*, M. S. Wilkins sees the name Casamicciola as a possible source of the name Casamassima (*NCF* 57); and Firebaugh brilliantly reads the novel as Schopenhauerian (*NCF* 58). J's other novels seemed less inspiring in the 1950's. However, for free will in *Hudson*, see Dunbar (*MLN* 52); "unconscious motivation" in *Confidence*, Levy (*AL* 56); the triumph of art in *Muse*, Powers (*PMLA* 58), and the character of Gabriel Nash in the same novel, Powers (*NCF* 59); and the *donnée* of *Reverberator*, George Knox (*EIHC* 59).

Of the few dozen essays in the 1950's on individual stories, more concern "Turn Screw" than any other tale. See the bibliographies of Willen's *Casebook* and Cranfill and Clark's *Anatomy* for details of the following inharmonious group: Hoffmann (*UR* 53), Carvel Collins (*Expl* 55), Levy (*CE* 56), Firebaugh (*MFS* 57), H. C. Goddard (*NCF* 57), John Lydenberg (*NCF* 57), John Silver (*AL* 57), G. N. Dove (*TSL* 58), D. M. Davis (*GSE* 59), Ignace Feuerlicht (*JEGP* 59), and A. E. Jones (*PMLA* 59). "Pupil" was suddenly subjected to many interpretations: see Terence Martin and J. V. Hagopian (separately in *MFS* 59), Seymour Lainoff (*NCF* 59), and especially Stein (*ArQ* 59). "Daisy" inspired reassessments by T. P. Coffin (*WF* 58), E. L. Volpe (*BPLQ* 58), and especially Peter Buitenhuis (*AQ* 59); in addition, Giorgio Melchiori expertly traces Eugenio from "Daisy" to *Dove* (*SA* 56). For J's chapter "The Married Son" in the round-robin novel *Whole Family*, see McElderry (*PS* 50) and E. F. Walbridge (*PBSA* 58).

The subject of J's revisions continued to intrigue critics in the 1950's. To tackle the entire question would of course require a corporation of patient scholars, with extensive equipment and funds. But the following represents fine work: Dunbar on "Daisy" (*MLN* 50); A. F. Gegenheimer on "A Passionate Pilgrim" (*AL* 51); McElderry on *Watch* (*MLN* 52); S. M. Humphreys (*N&Q* 54) and Edel (*N&Q* 55) on *Ambassadors*; Isadore Traschen (*AL* 54, *NEQ* 56), M. F. Schulz (*AL* 55), and Watkins (*NCF* 57, noted above) on *American*; and S. J. Krause on *Portrait* (*AL* 58—see his first footnote for bibliographical details, and see also Stein, *WHR* 59, noted above).

Source studies, identification of models for some of J's characters, and articles comparing J and other authors abounded in the 1950's. The most notable include the following: Edel (J and Balzac, *NEQ* 51), E. G. Fay (J and Balzac, *FR* 51), Lerner and Cargill (J and Greek literature, *PMLA* 51), Herbert Edwards (J and Ibsen, *AL* 52), Miriam Allott (*Dove* and Bronzino, *MLN* 53; *Bowl* and

George Eliot, *N&Q* 53; "A Landscape Painter" and Tennyson, *N&Q* 55; and *Dove* and Ruskin, *N&Q* 56), Alwyn Berland (J and Forster, *CambJ* 53), J. R. Lucke ("Beast" and Hawthorne, *NEQ* 53), H. L. Rypins (Sir James Mackenzie as model for Sir Luke Strett in *Dove*, *AL* 53), McElderry (J and Gertrude Atherton, *CLQ* 54), A. K. Baxter (J and Hawthorne, *NCF* 55), Q. D. Leavis (J, Dickens, and George Eliot, *HudR* 55), R. J. Niess ("The Madonna of the Future" and Zola, *RLC* 56), Camilla Zauli-Naldi (J and Trollope, *SA* 57), Bowman (*Portrait* and Turgenev, *EA* 58), Cargill (J and Howells, *AL* 58—see also his helpful bibliographical footnote), Edwin Fussell (J and Hawthorne, *AQ* 58), R. F. Gleckner ("Mauves" and Hawthorne, *MLN* 58), John Kinnaird (J and Whitman, *PR* 58), Stafford ("The Birthplace" and Shakespeare, *PMLA* 58), Nathalia Wright (J and the Greenough family, *AQ* 58), Feuerlicht ("Turn Screw" and Goethe, *JEGP* 59, noted above), J. H. Frantz ("Brooksmith" as source for "In the Cage," *MLN* 59), James Hafley (J and Poe, *ArQ* 59), R. W. Kretsch (J and Balzac, *NCF* 59), and Bebe Spanos (Princess Christina and Princess Casamassima, *PQ* 59—see also Monteiro, *PQ* 62).

Dozens of essays appeared in the 1950's on J's techniques and on subjects of a general nature. Space forbids inclusion of much detail. However, among several other topics, scholars dealt with J and critical aspects (Short, *PMLA* 50; Blackmur, *Accent* 51; Edel, *NEQ* 51; and René Wellek, *AL* 58), philosophy and religion (Graham Greene, *Dieu Vivant* 51; J. H. Raleigh, *PMLA* 51; G. H. Bantock, *CambJ* 53; Firebaugh, *JAAC* 53; M. A. Goldberg, *WHR* 57; R. M. Slabey, *AL* 58; W. H. Gass, *Accent* 58; A. L. Goldsmith, *NCF* 58; and Fox, *ArQ* 59), sex and family aspects (J. W. Schroeder, *AL* 51; and Volpe, *MLN* 56, *NCF* 58), money and taste (B. A. Booth, *NCF* 53; and Barbara Melchiori, *SA* 57), imagery and symbolism (Allott, *EIC* 53; Louise Dauner, *UR* 52; Short, *PMLA* 53; and Priscilla Gibson, *PMLA* 54), innocence and renunciation (Lotus Snow *UTQ* 53; Beebe, *SAQ* 54; and Berland, *KM* 58), politics and society (C. R. Anderson, *SAQ* 55; Irving Howe, *WR* 54; and Ward, *ArQ* 59), rhetorical aspects (Carlo Izzo, *SA* 56; Knox, *CE* 56; and Jean Deurbergue, *Criticism* [Paris] 56), and travel and racial elements (G. H. Blanke, *NS* 56; Levy, *Com* 58; Gale, *NCF* 59; and Gerhard Baumgaertel, *Sym* 59).

In the 1950's, the difficult and still challenging problem of J's possible influence on later authors was considered (J. J. Robinson, on Budd Schulberg, *MLN* 52; Bell, on Wharton, *MLN* 57, *PMLA* 59 [see also Bell's *Edith Wharton and HJ*, noted above]; G. M. Bielenstein, on Rosa Praed, *Meanjin* 57; and Leyburn, on Wharton, *MFS* 59). J's *Scene* was discussed (A. W. Stevens, *TCL* 55; and Wright Morris, *TQ* 58), as were J's critical essays (McElderry, *RS* 57), and his plays (Popkin, *NEQ* 51; and McElderry, *ArQ* 52). Bibliographical and related matters were considered (Dunbar, *AL* 50; J. R. Russell, *URLB* 56; Laurence, *PBSA* 58; and an anonymous critic, *CLQ* 58). New J letters were discovered and published (for example, see Russell, *URLB* 56, noted above; Henry Brewster, *Botteghe Oscure* 57; Edel and Powers, *BNYPL* 58, noted above; and Rosenbaum, *AL* 59); for details on all letter finds through 1960, see Edel and Laurence, *Bibliography of HJ*.

Three journals in the 1950's devoted whole issues to J: *MFS* (57), *NCF* (57), and *ArQ* (59).

e. *Articles in the 1960's*. In the 1960's an astounding explosion of articles on J occurred. As in the 1950's, this output matched the tremendous increase in the books. Of the 60 or so essays appearing each year through the 1960's, many seem unlikely to have permanent value; moreover, several, also unmentioned below, were incorporated unchanged or improved into books already identified. The survivors may be divided and briefly discussed as follows.

Of the articles on individual novels, most were concentrated on *American*, *Portrait*, *Bostonians*, *Princess*, *Spoils*, *Maisie*, *Age*, *Fount*, and *Ambassadors*. Unpredictably, *Dove* and *Bowl* were comparatively neglected.

American: Sigmund Hoftun criticizes the point of view for shifting from observer to author to hero (*Edda* 61). Edmund Creeth efficiently relates Murillo's Madonna to religious Claire, and the young Marquise de Bellegarde's red dress to violence (*N&Q* 62). Knox sees the novel as fable (*Anglia* 65). G. A. Cook briefly treats names in the novel (*CEA* 66). F. R. Horowitz attempts to deal with controversial time elements (*CLAJ* 66). E. R. Zietlow regards the novel as flawed because Newman with inconsistent immorality burns the murder evidence (*CLAJ* 66). Agostino Lombardo relates *American* to the myth of Othello (Vittorio Gabrieli, ed., *Friendship's Garland: Essays Presented to Mario Praz on His Seventieth Birthday*, 1966). Hisashi Noda traces Mrs. Tristram's function in Newman's education (*KAL* 67).

Portrait: M. E. Grenander, B. J. Rahn, and Francine Valvo explain the novel's intricate time scheme (*AL* 60). Marion Montgomery finds a flaw in "James's ultimate failure to let structure as well as subject, character, and setting evolve" (*UR* 60). L. J. Moss briefly discusses transitional devices (*CEA* 60). V. F. Blehl contrasts freedom and commitment (*Person* 61—see also Michael Wilding, *Balcony* 65). Toshiro Watanabe studies Isabel (*Eibungakukai-Kaiho* 63). T. F. Smith discusses the novel's ending (*4Q* 64). P. O. Williams explicates Gilbert Osmond's candlestick-and-snuffers image (*Expl* 64). P. S. Chauhan (*Lit Criterion* 65) and J. H. Friend (*NCF* 65) analyze the novel's felicitous design and structure. John Rodenbeck explicates the recurrent "bolted door" image (*MFS* 65). Tony Tanner comments on Isabel's many fears, induced by her "failure of vision" (*CritQ* 65). Manfred Mackenzie reads the novel as "ironic melodrama" (*MFS* 66). Lucy Schneider labels the story a "one-kiss novel" and elaborates (*CLAJ* 66). C. R. Anderson discusses person, place, and thing in it (Clarence Gohdes, ed., *Essays on American Literature in Honor of Jay B. Hubbell*, 1967). J. M. Newton discusses Isabel's spiritual "disease" and J's wrong-headedness in not noticing it (*CQ* 67), but V. H. Strandberg sees Isabel as angel and Madonna (*UR* 68). Charles Feidelson discusses J's degree of development at the time of *Portrait* and the direction of his work thereafter (*Ventures* 68). J. T. Frederick analyzes imagery in the novel's crucial Chapter 42 (*ArQ* 69). Marjorie Perloff intriguingly reads the novel as an ironic fairy tale, with Isabel a Cinderella who turns into the wicked stepmother (*NCF* 69). Seymour Kleinberg considers the novel's sexual ambivalence (*MarkR* 69). Rebecca Patterson forces certain resemblances between fully portrayed Isabel and merely sketched Madame de Mauves (*MQ* 60). Stephen Reid contrasts spoken and implied pledges in both *Portrait* and *Spoils* (*MFS* 66).

Bostonians: William McMurray briefly discusses "pragmatic realism" and the dangers of "absolutist forms in our activity" (*NCF* 62). R. E. Long identifies feminist Dr. Mary Walker as a possible source for Dr. Mary Prance (*NCF* 64). A. A. Hamblen discusses the feminists of the 1870's (and their opponents) as providers of background for the witty novel (*GaR* 66). D. B. Green analyzes its cluster of witchcraft images (*PLL* 67). C. R. Goldfarb treats its names (*IEY* 68). Gerald Haslam considers what he calls "Olive Chancellor's painful victory" (*RS* 68). Alfred Habegger surveys criticism of *Bostonians* and analyzes the novel's lack of unity "in its narrative technique" but not in its two-pronged subject—the feminine movement and American sexuality (*NCF* 69). Graham Burns offers a superb general review, stressing Olive Chancellor's "obsessional" psychology (*CR* 69). J. L. Kimmey reveals the indirect influence of *Bostonians* on *Princess* (*TSLL* 68).

Princess: J. M. Luecke regards Hyacinth as possessed of a "fallible consciousness" and as acting on "false assumptions" (*MP* 63). Monteiro skillfully traces the career of the Princess as that of an "heiress in defeat" (*ES* 64). D. G. Halliburton views the novel as "the story of a quest . . . directed toward ostensibly secular goals" (*MFS* 65). Walter Dubler describes the hero as "a divided mind" and his story as a deterministic document (*MFS* 66). Kimmey analyzes the hero's "bewilderment" as a function of irony and paradox (*NCF* 67). M. E. Hartsock astutely shows the novel's relevance to problems of violence now (*SNNTS* 69).

Spoils: A. H. Roper discusses its altruistic heroine and its battle, storm, and flight metaphors (*AL* 60). Gargano considers complexities behind Fleda's "single brave act" (*SR* 61). Goldsmith discusses the novel's maltese cross (*Ren* 64). R. C. McLean regards Fleda as "a thoroughly unreliable interpreter of her experience" and Owen Gereth as willing to profess love of her to get the spoils back to Poynton (*AL* 64). E. K. Iszak traces the novel's compositional evolution, stressing the *Notebooks* (*TSLL* 65). T. G. Hunt treats the "technique of showing a developing and growing consciousness" (*Discourse* 66). P. L. Greene considers point of view (*NCF* 67). Stein traces Fleda's poignant, absurd, self-deceiving behavior (*MFS* 68—see also D. J. Schneider, *ConnR* 69). A. W. Bellringer began in 1966 to discuss J's unintended involvement in the therefore flawed *Spoils* (*EIC* 66), to which John Lucas published a rejoinder, saying that J remained intentionally uninvolved (*EIC* 66); Bellringer fired a second salvo, this one on J's intentions (*EIC* 67), to which Lucas again replied (*EIC* 68). The whole controversy reveals insights but also has its ludicrous side. Nina Baym traces J's changing conception of Fleda (*PMLA* 69). Hartsock offers a detailed reading of the novel as comedy (*ES* 69). Snow treats furniture imagery in it and in *Bowl* (*ELH* 63).

Maisie: Gargano writes on the evolution of a moral sense in the novel (*NCF* 61). J. A. Hynes sees Maisie as a pragmatic middle-of-the-roader (*ELH* 65). J. C. McCloskey views the novel as a study of corrupted childhood and adolescence as Maisie gradually learns to imitate her parents (*AL* 65). H. R. Wolf sees Maisie as a Rankian heroine (*AI* 66). Hamblen discusses the power of "absolute raw sex" in *Maisie* (*MQ* 68). Martha Banta analyzes its combination of "comic tone and 'horrors'" (*NEQ* 69).

Age began to inspire greater numbers of scholars in the 1960's. They discuss age contrasts of its characters (Séamus Cooney, *MLN* 60); Vanderbank's refusal to propose (Gerald Levin, *UR* 61); appearance, reality, and the device of implication (Silvarra Colognesi, *SA* 63); the dramatic quality of the novel's scenes (Eben Bass, *PMLA* 64); refinement (N. K. Rao, *LCrit* 65); the theme of the duty of man to explore his consciousness honestly (Hartsock, *CritQ* 67); the theme of personal and social salvation (Gargano, *TSLL* 67); *Age* and its accurate reflection of the English scene of its time (Elizabeth Owen, *VS* 67); and J's conception of society in *Age* (W. F. Hall, *NCF* 68). (See also J. B. Kaye, *NCF* 63, under *Ambassadors* below.)

Fount and its intricacies engaged many critics in the early 1960's. For a baker's dozen of articles see Blackall's book (discussed above), the publication of which, let us hope, signals a moratorium for at least a decade on drafts from the depleted *Fount*. (But see C. T. Samuels on its illuminating ambivalence in *Novel* 68; also J. B. Kaye, *NCF* 63, under *Ambassadors* below.)

Ambassadors: M. K. Michael discusses uses of the word "wonderful" (*MLN* 60). Ian Watt indefatigably analyzes the novel's first paragraph (*EIC* 60). H. R. Coursen, Jr., adumbrates the Cleopatra allusion which helps to characterize Madame de Vionnet (*NEQ* 61). R. E. Garis sees Strether as changed by his sight of Chad Newsome and Madame de Vionnet in the country, and J's style as changing in sympathy (*MFS* 62). J. Q. Reed analyzes the "Four stages in the creation of *The Ambassadors*" (*MQ* 62). Austin Warren considers Strether's New England conscience (*MinnR* 62—but see also Raymond Thorberg, *N&Q* 69). M. L. Williamson cleverly discusses Madame de Vionnet's timely lapse into French (*N&Q* 62). Tsugio Aoki considers Strether's imagination (*SELit* 63). R. N. Hudspeth treats innocence and maturation (*TSLL* 64). Epifanio San Juan, Jr., considers the gradual increase in Strether's awareness (*MQ* 64). Hartsock comprehensively views Strether as a moral man (*MLQ* 65 —see also T. J. Bontly, *WSL* 69). U. C. Knoepflmacher provocatively compares the novel and Shakespeare's *Antony and Cleopatra* (*NCF* 65). H. L. Terrie, Jr., notes J's depiction of the city of Chester (*ES* 65). Tanner sees central significance in "Strether's stance on the balcony" (*CritQ* 66). L. M. Cecil briefly probes Chad's allegedly "virtuous attachment" (*AQ* 67). Fränze Friese sees a "Muster" in the novel's "Teppich" (*TuK* 66). D. J. Schneider extensively treats ironic imagery and symbolism (*Criticism* 67). D. J. Dooley follows E. M. Forster's lead (see his *Aspects of the Novel*, 1927) and neatly treats the hourglass pattern of *Ambassadors* (*NEQ* 68). J. N. Wise considers its "tidal" movement (*ArlQ* 69). Ward regards Strether's transformation in Europe as a typical "Jamesian [religious] conversion" (*SoR* 69). Brian Lee sees *Ambassadors*, *Dove*, and *Bowl* as a unit showing "J's dependence, not on his father's unique Swedenborgian system, but on the native intellectual climate of which they both [father and son] partook" (*RMS* 62). Viola Hopkins shows how J changed Gloriani, who first appeared in *Hudson*, when he presented the sculptor again in *Ambassadors* and "The Velvet Glove" (*NCF* 63). J. B. Kaye sees Strether's triumph as the resolution of conflicts dramatized earlier by HJ—in *Age* and *Fount*—between consideration and predatoriness (*NCF* 63). McLean relates *Ambassadors* to "Mauves" (*MLQ* 67). Michael Shriber compares J's "representation of cognition" in "Daisy" and *Ambassadors* (*Lang&S* 69).

Although *Ambassadors* received generous attention in the 1960's, the other novels in the major-phase trilogy were somewhat neglected. Leo Bersani analyzes the narrator as center in *Dove* (*MFS* 60). H. H. Clark sees Milly's story as a drama in which her "anti-materialistic idealism" triumphs over the cruel social Darwinism of those about the girl (*TWA* 63). Konomu Itagaki considers "indirection" in the novel (*SELit* 65). Q. G. Kraft writes of life-death tensions

(*Criticism* 65). Stephen Koch sees Milly as a "transcendent" register of truth (*MFS* 66). Gustaaf Van Cromphout handles non-international, universal aspects (*MinnR* 66). John Hagan cleverly considers height symbolism in relation to Milly's spiritual changes (*CLAJ* 67). Bell reviews the plot with possessiveness and money in mind (*MR* 69). As for *Bowl*, Gale explicates its Io image (*Expl* 60). R. T. Todasco treats the relation of imagery to theme (*TSLL* 62). Owen scrutinizes "the given appearance" of its so-called bad heroine Charlotte (*EIC* 63). Alan Rose comments on its "spatial form" (*MFS* 66). C. G. Mercer discusses Adam Verver as "Yankee businessman" (*NCF* 67). Margaret Trieschmann sees the Prince's "Roman venality" and Maggie's initial "wilful ignorance of human suffering" as sources of evil (*IEY* 67). Snow's essay, noted above in connection with *Spoils*, considers furniture imagery in *Bowl* as well (*ELH* 63).

Most of J's other novels were relatively neglected in the journals of the 1960's. *Europeans* was studied by Deborah Austin (*JGE* 62), Buitenhuis (*UTQ* 62), Bass (*Expl* 64), and H. Vandermoere (*ES* 69). *Muse* was treated by W. F. Hall (*NCF* 66), E. H. Lockridge (*MFS* 66), and Snow (*MFS* 66—she also considers *Hudson* here). The posthumous novels also came in for some consideration: for *Past*, see D. W. Beams (*Criticism* 63) and Sergio Perosa (*SA* 66); for *Tower*, see Buitenhuis (*UTQ* 64) and Putt (*English* 66). As for the other novels: for *Watch*, see Levy (*ArlQ* 68); for *Hudson*, see Michi Takahashi (*ESBAL* 63), J. Kraft (*TQ* 68), and John Scherting (*ArQ* 69); for *Confidence*, see Hamblen (*UR* 69); and for *Square*, see Glauco Cambon (*NCF* 61) and Haruhiko Nakazato (*Kamereon* 62).

Articles published in the 1960's and concerned with individual short stories show a slight decline in volume, with the constant exception of "Turn Screw." The best of about 40 essays on it include those by D. P. Costello on structure (*MLN* 60); A. E. Stone on "original sin in the minds of the very young" (*SUB* 61); Cargill on Freud's case of Miss Lucy R. and on J's sister Alice (*PMLA* 63); Cranfill and Clark on caste (*TSLL* 63); C. B. Ives on the ghosts (*NCF* 63); Nirmal Mukherji on ambiguous evil (*CalR* 63); Slabey on Douglas's beginning to read the manuscript on the day of the Feast of the Holy Innocents (*NS* 63), and on "several ambiguous pronouns" and "the governess's unusually acute vision" (*CLAJ* 65); Mark Spilka on the governess as a prurient example of Victorian hothouse purity and domesticity (*L&P* 63—but see also Arthur Efron, *Paunch* 64); Knox on incubi and succubi (*WF* 63); H.-J. Lang on the Gothic tradition of Poe and Hawthorne behind the story (*JA* 64); Vittoria Sanna on several "considerazioni" in it (*AION-SG* 63); L. D. Rubin, Jr., on its ambivalences (*MFS* 64); Eric Solomon on the thorough villainy of Mrs. Grose (*UR* 64); Muriel West on Miles's death (*PMLA* 64); Hildegard Domaniecki on the words "turn" and "straight" (*JA* 65), and on education's thumb-screws (*TuK* 66); Nobushige Tadokoro (*KAL* 65) and also A. W. Thompson (*REL* 65) on hallucination; Stanley Trachtenberg on Douglas as Miles grown up (*MFS* 65); John Fraser on "the peculiarly *American* nature" of the governess (*MQ* 66); C. K. Aldrich on Mrs. Grose's hate-inspired encouragement of the governess (*MFS* 67); Gerhard Irle on the effects of hallucination on community illusion (*SG* 67); E. D. Aswell on distortions (*NCF* 68); P. N. Siegel on Miss Jessel as a mirror image of the governess (*L&P* 68); and Juliet McMaster on the governess's habit of standing where the ghosts have stood (*SSF* 69).

After "Turn Screw," the short stories treated most frequently and best in articles in the 1960's are "The Real Thing," "Aspern," "Figure in Carpet," "Corner," "Author of Beltraffio," "Daisy," "Birthplace," "In the Cage," and "Mauves."

"Real Thing": Earle Labor considers three levels of meaning (*CE* 62); Kenneth Bernard notes the artist-narrator's emerging compassion (*BYUS* 62); Gale sees satirical allusions to the *Black and White* magazine (*SSF* 63); Harold Kehler reads "Churm" as East End London patois for "charm" (*Expl* 67); David Toor comments on narrative irony (*UR* 67); Lavonne Mueller describes "the phenomenal self" in it (*ForumH* 68); and Powers considers the ethics of the artist in it and "The Liar" (*TSLL* 61).

Hitherto neglected aspects of "Aspern" are irony (Jacob Korg, *CE* 62—see also R. S. Phillips, *CE* 62; and Samuel Hux, *BSUF* 69); the felt life (Hartsock, *SSF* 67); poetic justice (McLean, *PLL* 67); "modal counterpoint" (J. M. Mellard, *PLL* 68); and the goodness of the narrator (A. S. Brylowski, *CentR* 69).

New interpretations, sometimes rather brief, of "Figure in Carpet" are offered by Mark Kanzer (*AI* 60), Powers (*AL* 61), Lainoff (*BUSE* 61), Ann Gossman (*Descant* 62), Levy (*AL* 62), and G. A. Finch (*TCL* 68).

For "Corner," see W. A. Freedman on its Platonic, Biblical, Dantesque universality (*TSLL* 62); F. C. Thompson on the "eerily luminous submarine metaphor" (*Expl* 63); Earl Rovit on its ghosts (*TSL* 65); and Courtney Johnson on its being "a story of self-discovery" (*AI* 67).

"Author of Beltraffio" tardily interested article-writers: see D. H. Reiman on its unconsciously self-exposing narrator (*TSLL* 62—but see also James Scoggins, *TSLL* 63); and V. H. Winner on its imperfectly fused aesthetics and morality (*PMLA* 68).

"Daisy": Gargano on innocence (*SAQ* 60); Tadokoro on structure (*FRLS* 63); Carol Ohmann on J's altered intention (*AL* 64); J. H. Randall III on the genteel reader (*AQ* 65); R. P. Draper on Winterbourne's "uncertainty and moral confusion" (*SSF* 69); and D. E. Houghton on illness (*L&P* 69). (See also Shriber, *Lang&S* 69, noted above.)

"Birthplace": George Arms discusses its religious imagery (*TSL* 63); J. V. Holleran sees Morris Gedge as fallen and conscience-stricken (*PLL* 66); and M. L. Ross contends that J provides "narrative tension" by first shocking and then flattering the reader (*SSF* 66).

"In the Cage," once labeled "a forgotten story" by A. C. Friend (*SAQ* 54), was praised for its imagery by Blackall (*UTQ* 62), for its attempt to dramatize the problems of knowing by Wilhelm Füger (*NS* 62), and for its characterization by Aswell (*TSLL* 67).

"Mauves" has a lovely heroine, according to Patterson (*MQ* 60, noted above), and a confused, disappointed observer, according to Charles Kaplan (*Expl* 61) and McLean (*RS* 65).

Brief mention should be made here of sound articles on "Four Meetings" by R. J. Griffin (*UR* 62), L. M. Jones (*Expl* 62), and Lothar Hönnighausen (*GRM* 67—which also treats "Velvet Glove"); on "Great Good Place" by Harry Silverstein (*NEQ* 62) and M. E. Herx (*CE* 63); and on "The Tree of Knowledge" by S. I. Bellman (*SSF* 64) and T. J. Truss, Jr. (*UMSE* 65).

Many other stories, in some cases perhaps properly neglected, occasioned only a single article or note through the 1960's. For "Abasement of the Northmores," see Gale (*PMLA* 63); "The Beldonald Holbein," Thorberg (*SHR* 68); "The Bench of Desolation," Segal (*NCF* 65); "Brooksmith," Eddy Dow (*Expl* 69); "Crapy Cornelia," S. B. Purdy (*Style* 67); "De Grey, a Romance," John Tytel (*MarkR* 69); "International Episode," Howell Daniels (*BAASB* 60); "Landscape Painter," Melchiori (*SA* 64); "Liar," Segal (*RES* 65); "The Lesson of the Master," C. R. Smith (*SSF* 69); "A Light Man," C. K. Fish (*ELN* 65); "The Marriages," Dale and Cheris Kramer (*UR* 66); "The Middle Years," Gale (*Expl* 63); "Maud-Evelyn," M. L. D'Avanzo (*IEY* 68); "Mrs. Medwin," Bernard (*Discourse* 63); "The Next Time," Gale (*Expl* 62); "Pandora," Gale (*SSF* 64); "A Passionate Pilgrim," Nakazato (*St Paul's Rev* 62); and "A Round of Visits," Purdy (*SSF* 69). E. F. Jost treats existential love in "Beast" (*Eng Rec* 66); Johnson discusses paradoxes in the relationship between Marcher and May (*SSF* 69).

A few more critics addressed themselves in the 1960's to the problem of the revision of individual works of fiction. Grenander considers *Hudson* and *Princess* (*PMLA* 60); Vincent Tartella (*NCF* 60), Shitsuyu Iwase (*Queries* 62), and Maqbool Aziz (*EIC* 68), "Four Meetings"; M. B. Durkin, *Reverberator* (*AL* 61); Stafford, *American* (*NCF* 63); Brian Birch, *Ambassadors* (*Library* 65);

Cranfill and Clark, "Turn Screw" (*NCF* 65); Fish, "The Story of a Master-piece" (*MP* 65); Izsak (*TSLL* 65, noted above) and Rosenbaum (*SB* 66), *Spoils*; Fish, *Watch* (*NCF* 67); Charles Vandersee, "Pandora" (*SB* 68); D. J. Bazzanella, *Portrait* (*AL* 69); Sacvan Bercovitch, *Hudson* (*NCF* 69); and H. F. Smith and Michael Peinovich, *Bostonians* (*BNYPL* 69). The final word, however, on the enormous topic of J's revisions in general has yet to be written.

Non-fictional works were the subject of several articles in the 1960's. The dramatic version of "Daisy" is treated by M. J. Mendelsohn (*MD* 64); Kimball King considers theory and practice in the plays in general (*MD* 67). *Scene* is discussed in detail by Fabris (*SA* 60), more briefly by Irving Howe (*NR* 67) and Alan Trachtenberg (*MR* 67). J's critical theory is the subject of three enlightening essays by Emerson (*CE* 60, *TWA* 62, 63). More specific criticism by J, that of his prefaces, occasioned articles by Gale (*ForumH* 61, *RLV* 64) and Stafford (*AL* 63). William Hoffa discusses J's *Autobiography* as a "final preface" (*SR* 69). As for J's letters, see Edel (*TLS*, 17 June 65), F. L. Standley (*VN* 65), B. H. McClary (*ELN* 66), and Jean Bruneau (*RLC* 68).

Article-length studies of alleged sources and influence, and of analogues to aspects of J's writings proliferated bewilderingly in the 1960's. General studies include those of Wegelin on the international novel (*PMLA* 62); Berland, who beautifully places J in "the aesthetic tradition" (*JHI* 62); Melchiori, who writes about J and the fine arts (*SA* 64); Margaret Lane, who philosophizes on ghost stories, particularly "Turn Screw" (*CM* 67); Raleigh, on *Princess* and several other "city" novels (*VS* 68); and Robert Schulman, on J and "the modern comedy of knowledge" (*Criticism* 68). More specific studies relate J and the following: Henry Adams—Tanner (*TriQ* 68). Arnold—Edward Engleberg, on *Hudson* (*Criticism* 68). Augier—Habegger, on "The Siege of London" (*MFS* 69). Austen— Irène Simon (*ES* 62) and Wiesenfarth (*4Q* 65). James Baldwin—Charles Newman (*YR* 66). Balzac—Gargano, on *Ambassadors* (*MLN* 60); P. G. Adams (*RLC* 61); Ivo Vidan, on *Princess* (*SRAZ* 66); and Maurita Willett, on *American* (*RLC* 67). Baudelaire—Gargano (*MLN* 60). Beerbohm —John Felstiner (*KR* 67). Walter Besant—John Goode (David Howard *et al.*, eds., *Tradition and Tolerance in Nineteenth-Century Fiction, 1967*). Benjamin Britten—Marcel Schneider, on *Tower* (*NRF* 65). Browning—Melchiori (*Friendship's Garland*, 1966). Cather—Hagime Okita (*Albion* 61). Cherbuliez—J. L. Tribble, on *Portrait* (*AL* 68); and M. F. Deakin, on "Daisy" (*CLS* 69). Chekhov—Claude Roy (*NRF* 62). Agatha Christie—Hamblen, on *Dove* (*Discourse* 69). Colette—Marvin Mudrick, on *Ambassadors* (*HudR* 62). Conrad—Walter O'Grady, on *Ambassadors* (*MFS* 65); Vidan, on *Princess* (*SRAZ* 66, noted above); Watt (Maynard Mack and Ian Gregor, eds., *Imagined*

Worlds, 1968). Stephen Crane—T. A. Gullason (*Person* 61). Thomas Crawford—Gale, on *Hudson* (*AQ* 61), on *Portrait* (*SA* 65). Dreiser—Buitenhuis (*UTQ* 64, noted above). Dumas, *fils*—C. E. Maguire, on *American* (*MD* 67); Habegger, on "Siege of London" (*MFS* 69). Dürrenmatt—Heilman, on "Turn Screw" (*CL* 61). George Eliot—R. L. Selig, on *Bostonians* (*NCF* 61); Lainoff, on "Figure in Carpet" (*VN* 62); George Levine, on *Portrait* (*ELH* 63); and Biancamaria Pisapia (*SA* 67). T. S. Eliot—Holder (*PMLA* 63). Emerson—Rovit (*ASch* 64). Faulkner—Cleanth Brooks, on *American* (*Shen* 64). F. Scott Fitzgerald—Brooks (*ibid.*); Kermit Vanderbilt, on *American* (*MR* 65); J. N. Riddell (*MFS* 66); R. O. Stephens and James Ellis (*ELN* 67); Barry Gross, on *American* (*PMASAL* 68); and J. S. Hill, on *Ambassadors* (*FN* 68). Flaubert—Marjorie Ryan, on *Ambassadors* (*N&Q* 61). Ford—R. W. Lid (*PrS* 61). Forster—Ryan, on *Ambassadors* (*N&Q* 61, noted above; and V. A. Shahane (*Osmania JES* 61). Gide—R. H. Abel, on *Portrait* and *Dove* (*MQ* 68). Hardy—O'Grady (*MFS* 65, noted above) and C. J. Weber (*HLB* 68). Hawthorne—E. H. Rosenberry, on "Liar" (*MLN* 61); Gale, on *Fount* (*SA* 62); Monteiro, on "Beast" (*TSLL* 62—see also Jane Gottschalk, *WSL* 67); R. W. B. Lewis (R. H. Pearce, ed., *Hawthorne Centenary Essays*, 64); Long, on *Bostonians* (*NCF* 64), and on *Ambassadors* (*NEQ* 69); Q. Kraft, on *Hudson* (*ELH* 69); C. T. Samuels, on "Turn Screw" (*ASch* 68); and Jay Bochner, on *Portrait* (*TSLL* 69). Hemingway—Stephens and Ellis (*ELN* 67, noted above). Alexander Herzen—Taylor Stoehr, on *Princess* (*SoRA* 68). Howells—D. H. Hirsch, on "Daisy" (*ELN* 63); C. M. Kirk (*CE* 63); R. B. Salomon (*AQ* 64); Patricia Kane (*MinnR* 67); and Long, on *Ambassadors* (*NEQ* 69, noted above). Joyce—Stephen Reid, on "Beast" (*AI* 63); Virgil Hutton, on *Ambassadors* (*EWR* 66); and Wilding, on *Portrait* (*ES* 69). Keats—S. L. Mooney, on *Bowl* (*MLQ* 61). Kipling—E. L. Gilbert (*KJ* 64). Madame de La Fayette—B. C. Rountree, on "Mauves" (*SSF* 64); and J. K. Simon, on "Mauves" (*CLS* 66); Sinclair Lewis—D. R. Brown (*SLNews* 69). Lubbock—Robert Liddell (*KR* 67). Andrew Lytle—Jack De Bellis, on "Turn Screw" (*Crit* 66). Malamud—Bellman (*CEJ* 65). Maupassant—T. M. Stegnitz, on "Paste" (*AL* 64). Mérimée—Philip Grover (*PP* 68). Pascal—Andreach, on "The Ghostly Rental" (*CLS* 67). Pound—Holder (*AL* 63). Proust—Lowery (*RdP* 64). "The Revolt of the Daughters" (an 1894 series in a British magazine) —H. L. Hill, Jr. (*N&Q* 61). Henri Rivière—Thorberg, on *Portrait* (*SAB* 69). Sainte-Beuve—Kamerbeek, on *Ambassadors* (*RLC* 62); and Grover (*PP* 68, noted above). "Saintine" (J. X. Boniface)—Frantz, on "In the Cage" (*N&Q* 60). George Sand—Deakin, on "Daisy" (*CLS* 69, noted above); and D. A. Leeming (*RLC* 69). J. S. Sargent—Richard Gilman (*AH* 61). Shakespeare—Melchiori (*ShN* 67). Shaw—D. L. Schwartz, Jr. (*ShawR* 67). Madame de Staël—Deakin, on "Daisy" (*CLS* 69, noted above). Stendhal—J. R. Dove, on *Princess* (W. F. McNair, ed., *Studies in Comparative Literature*, 1962). Stevenson—Girling (*WascanaR* 68). Howard Sturgis—Elmer Borklund (*MP* 61). Taine—Grover (*PP* 68, noted above). Tarkington—Hamblen, on "Daisy" (*Cresset* 67). Tennyson—Melchiori (*Arte e storia: Studi in onore di Leonello Vincenti*, 1965, and *REL* 65). Tolstoy—Wasiolek (*MFS* 61). Robert Towers—Bellman (*CEJ* 65, noted above). Rodolphe Töpffer—R. K. Martin (*RomN* 69). Trollope—B. G. Kenney, on *Portrait* (*VN* 64). Turgenev—Hamilton, on *Princess* (*SAQ* 62); Vidan (G. R. Hibbard, ed., *Renaissance and Modern Essays Presented to Vivian de Sola Pinto . . .*, 1966); and Deakin, on "Daisy" (*CLS* 69, noted above). Mark Twain—Cambon, on *Maisie* (*SA* 60); Herbert Feinstein, on "Turn Screw" (*AI* 60); Tanner (*NCF* 61); Richard VanDerBeets, on *American* (*WHR* 63); Salomon (*AQ* 64, noted above); and Banta, on *American* (*MFS* 69). Wharton—Sanna (*SA* 64); Hamblen (*UR* 65); Bell (*LonM* 66); J. W. Tuttleton (*MASJ* 66); and Wegelin (*SoR* 69). James Whistler—Gilman (*AH* 61, noted above). Whitman—William White (*RES* 69). Virginia Woolf— J. O. Smith (*TCL* 64). Zola—Powers (*UTQ* 60).

Essays on aspects of J's techniques include considerations of imagery and symbolism (Holder, *ES* 60; Melchiori, in Mario Praz, *et al.*, *Il Simbolismo nella letteratura Nord-Americana . . .*, 1965, and *CritQ* 65); diction (Emerson, *TWA* 60; John Paterson, *AL* 60; Hisayoshi Watanabe, *AL* 62; D. D. Walker, *WHR* 63; and Purdy, *AS* 67, *PQ* 69, and *WSL* 69); visual arts (Hopkins, *PMLA* 61, and *Criticism* 67); form and structure (F. J. Hoffman, *VQR* 61; Terrie, *NCF* 61; Allott, *REL* 62; Hideo Higuchi, *Shuryu* 62; Manfred Mackenzie, *PQ* 62; L. E. Scanlon, *ForumH* 63; and Bersani, *PR* 69); J's *données* (C. F. Burgess, *L&P* 63); and J's use of names (Richard Gerber, *Anglia* 63; and Gale, *Names* 66).

Many splendid essays published in the 1960's were devoted to general aspects and topics. The explosiveness of criticism on J is such that these articles sometimes do not fit tidily into categories, but there were essays dealing with consciousness, imagination, creativity, artistic perceptions, and aesthetics: Irene Samuel (*BNYPL* 65), Goode (*NLR* 66), Rosenbaum (*Criticism* 66), H. M. Munford (*TuK* 66), Amei Ortmann (*TuK* 66), Richard Wilson (*ES* 66), Ross Labrie (*AL* 68), and W. R. McDonald (*TSLL* 69). Freedom, morality, society, and tragedy: Dove (*TSLL* 60), Powers (*UTQ* 62), Q. Kraft (*CE* 65), L. W. Wagner (*SDR* 65), Wiesenfarth (*4Q* 66), Frederick Willey (*SoR* 66), R. J. Reilly (*AL* 67), and Van Cromphout (*ES* 68). Perversion, femininity, marriage, and fatherhood: Sharp (*UTQ* 66), Munro Beattie (Marston LaFrance, ed., *Patterns of Commitment in American Literature*, 1967), Hartsock (*MLQ* 68), and R. M. Meldrum (*RS* 69). Evil, disease, Gothicism, ghosts, shame, and death: J. L. Roberts (*ArQ* 61), Banta (*NEQ* 64, and *YR* 67), Hamblen (*DR* 64), Elémire Zolla (*Elsinore* 66), Thorberg (*DR* 67), and M. Mackenzie (*SoRA* 68). Nationalism and place: Lucas (*SA* 65), Jonah Raskin (*AQ* 65), Berland (*WascanaR* 66), G. G. Struble (François Jost, ed., *Proceedings of the . . . International Comparative Literature Association, 1966*), Edel (*UTQ* 67), and Cushing Strout (*SA* 67).

Writers of other significant articles published in the busy 1960's include the following: Mark Kanzer, on J's belief that art is more real than life (*AI* 60—see also M. A. Mays, *AL* 68); Murray, on J in composition courses (*CE* 63); Akio Onishi, on the unity of three neglected international tales (*Bungaku Ronshu* 63); Bass, on the unity of the stories J first published in *The Yellow Book* (*SSF* 64); Aswell, on J and artistic collaboration (*Criticism* 66); Javier Coy, on recent criticism of J (*FMod* 65); Gwen Matheson, on J's depiction of artists and ladies (*DR* 68); J. V. Antush, on money (*ArQ* 69); and R. K. Martin, on J's reading at Harvard in the 1860's (*AL* 69).

Bibliographical essays on J waned somewhat in the 1960's. They do, however, include the following significant ones: Edel (*HLB* 60), J. C. Maxwell (*EIC* 61), and Watt (*EIC* 61), all on the text of *Ambassadors*; Monteiro, on the missing manuscript of *Muse* (*AN&Q* 63); Birch, on sundry bibliographical and textual matters, mainly concerning *Ambassadors* and *Bowl* (*Library* 65, noted above); Hershel Parker, on a textual error in *American* (*AL* 65); G. M. Gliddon, on the lack of J editions (*TLS*, 24 Feb. 66—but see reply 3 Mar. 66); and E. R. Hagemann, on satires, parodies, jokes, gossip, cartoons, verses, playlets, anecdotes, and reviews leveled at J in *Life*, 1883–1916 (*PBSA* 68).

NOTES ON CONTRIBUTORS

ROGER ASSELINEAU was born in 1915 at Orléans, France, and educated at the Sorbonne (licence, agrégation, doctorat ès lettres). He taught English and American literature at the universities of Clermont-Ferrand and Lyon before being appointed professor of American literature at the Sorbonne in 1960. He has also taught American literature at the State University of New York at Albany and the University of California at Davis. He is the author of *The Literary Reputation of Mark Twain, 1900–1950* (1954); *Réalisme, Rêve et Expressionnisme dans "Winesburg, Ohio"* (1957); *The Evolution of Walt Whitman*, 2 volumes (1960–62); *Robert Frost* (in French) (1964); and the University of Minnesota pamphlet *Poe* (1970). He has edited *Configuration Critique de Sherwood Anderson* (1963), *The Literary Reputation of Hemingway in Europe* (1965), *and L'Oeuvre Romanesque Complète d'Ernest Hemingway*, 2 volumes (1966–69). He has also translated *Leaves of Grass* into French (1956) and is currently working on a new edition of this translation.

WALTER BLAIR was born in Spokane, Washington, in 1900. He holds a Ph.B. degree from Yale University and a Ph.D. from the University of Chicago. He taught briefly at the University of Minnesota and then for many years at the University of Chicago, where he chaired the English department from 1951 to 1960 and became an emeritus professor in 1968. He has been visiting professor at the Universities of Arkansas, Texas, and Wisconsin, the State University of New York at Albany, Cornell, Harvard, and Stanford universities, and Goethe University in Frankfort. He has published several articles about nineteenth-century New England authors; but his chief interests, American humor and Mark Twain, were represented in a number of articles and books beginning with *Native American Humor* (1937, revised edition 1960), continuing with *Mark Twain and Huck Finn* (1960), and including most recently *Mark Twain's Hannibal, Huck & Tom* (1969). He is on editorial boards supervising the Mark Twain Papers Series and Mark Twain's Collected Works.

HARRY HAYDEN CLARK, who was born in New Milford, Connecticut, in 1901, died on June 6, 1971, after a short illness. He took his bachelor's degree at Trinity College in 1923 and his master's from Harvard the following year. He held fellowships from the Guggenheim Foundation, the Rockefeller Fund, and the Library of Congress, and was awarded an LL.D. degree by Bowling Green State University in 1951. He taught at Yale University and Middlebury College, but after 1928 was a member of the faculty of the University of Wisconsin at Madison. In his long and distinguished career as scholar and teacher Professor Clark directed 104 dissertations. He was general editor of the American Writers Series (23 volumes) and edited *James Russell Lowell* (AWS, 1947), *Thomas Paine* (AWS, 1944), *Transitions in American*

Literary History (1954), and *Major American Poets* (1936). He was a frequent contributor to periodicals and served on the editorial board of *American Literature*.

ROBERT L. GALE was born in Des Moines, Iowa, in 1919. He was educated at Dartmouth College (B.A., 1942) and at Columbia University (M.A., 1947; Ph.D., 1952). He has taught at Columbia University, the Universities of Delaware, and Mississippi, and (as Fulbright lecturer) at the Istituto Universitario Orientale in Naples, Italy. Since 1959 he has been at the University of Pittsburgh (where he is now Professor of and Director of Graduate Studies in English). He is the author of *The Caught Image: Figurative Language in the Fiction of Henry James* (1964); *Thomas Crawford: American Sculptor* (1964); *Richard Henry Dana, Jr.* (1969); and *Francis Parkman* (forthcoming). He is writing a *Plots and Characters* series; to date, volumes have been published on *Henry James* (1965), *Nathaniel Hawthorne* (1968), *Herman Melville* (1969), and *Edgar Allan Poe* (1970), and one on *Mark Twain* is forthcoming. He is a contributor to *American Literary Scholarship* and is currently writing a book-length study of William Bartram.

JAY BROADUS HUBBELL was born in Virginia in 1885 and is a graduate of the University of Richmond. He has an M.A. from Harvard and a Ph.D. from Columbia. He taught at Southern Methodist University from 1915 to 1927 and at Duke University from 1927 until his retirement in 1954. He is the author of many articles and of several books, two of which are *The South in American Literature, 1607–1900* (1954) and *South and Southwest: Literary Essays and Reminiscences* (1965). His anthology, *American Life in Literature*, was reprinted three times for the United States Armed Forces Institute. The Duke University Press soon will publish his next book, *Who Are the Major American Writers? A Study of the Changing Literary Canon*. He was Chairman of the Editorial Board of *American Literature* from 1929 to 1954. In 1964 the American Literature Section of the Modern Language Association created the Jay B. Hubbell Medallion "In honor of the distinguished contribution of Professor Jay B. Hubbell to the history of the literature of the United States. . . ."

FLOYD STOVALL was born in Texas July 7, 1896, and educated in the public schools and at the University of Texas, where he received his B.A., M.A., and Ph.D. degrees. He taught for several years at the University of Texas and then at North Texas State College. Later he went to the University of North Carolina in 1949 and to the University of Virginia as Edgar Allan Poe Professor of English in 1955. He retired in 1967. Although his first book was on Shelley, his publications have been chiefly in American literature, including the following: *American Idealism* (1943); an edition of Poe's poems, with variant readings and textual notes (1965); an edition of Whitman's major prose works (1962–63); and a critical work, *Edgar Poe the Poet* (1969). Professor Stovall also was the original editor of *Eight American Authors* (1956) and has served on the editorial board of *American Literature*.

LEWIS LEARY was born in Blauvelt, New York, in 1906. He took his bachelor's degree from the University of Vermont and his A.M. and Ph.D. degrees from Columbia University. After teaching at the American University in Beirut and the University of Miami, he was a member of the faculty of Duke University for eight years and of Columbia University for seventeen (seven as chairman of his department) until he took up his present position at the University of North Carolina in 1969. Among the books he has written are *That Rascal Freneau* (1941) and *The Literary Career of Nathaniel Tucker* (1951); among those he has edited are *Mark Twain's Letters to Mary* (1961); *Articles on American Literature, 1900–1950* (1954); and *Articles on American Literature, 1959–1967* (1970). He has served on the editorial board of *American Literature*, has contributed frequently to periodicals, and is the author of several of the University of Minnesota Pamphlets on American Writers.

JAMES WOODRESS was born in Webster Groves, Missouri, in 1916, and educated at Amherst College (A.B., 1938), New York University (A.M., 1943), and Duke University (Ph.D., 1950). After a period in journalism with the United Press and in the army in World War II, he taught at Grinnell College, Butler University, and San Fernando Valley State College before joining the English faculty at the University of California at Davis, where he now is Chairman. His books include *Howells and Italy* (1952); *Booth Tarkington: Gentleman from Indiana* (1955); *A Yankee's Odyssey: The Life of Joel Barlow* (1958); and *Willa Cather: Her Life and Art* (1970). He was editor of *American Literary Scholarship* (1965–69) and has held fellowships from the Guggenheim and Ford foundations and Fulbright appointments in France and Italy.

NATHALIA WRIGHT was born in Athens, Georgia, in 1917 and holds her B.A. degree from Maryville College and her M.A. and Ph.D. degrees from Yale University. She is presently Professor of English at the University of Tennessee. She has written *Melville's Use of the Bible* (1949); *Horatio Greenough, The First American Sculptor* (1963); and *American Novelists in Italy* (1965). As one of the editors of *The Complete Works of Washington Irving* she brought out *Journals and Notebooks, Vol. I, 1803–1806* (1969). She has held fellowships from the Guggenheim Foundation and the American Association of University Women.

INDEX

In the Norton Library

LITERATURE